7-19 41

THE PERVERSION OF
KNOWLEDGE

THE PERVERSION OF
KNOWLEDGE

THE TRUE STORY OF SOVIET SCIENCE

Vadim J. Birstein

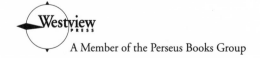

A Member of the Perseus Books Group

Copyright © 2001 by Westview Press, A Member of the Perseus Books Group

Westview Press books are available at special discounts for bulk purchases in the United States by corporations, institutions, and other organizations. For more information, please contact the Special Markets Department at The Perseus Books Group, 11 Cambridge Center, Cambridge MA 02142, or call (617) 252-5298.

Published in 2001 in the United States of America by Westview Press, 5500 Central Avenue, Boulder, Colorado 80301–2877, and in the United Kingdom by Westview Press, 12 Hid's Copse Road, Cumnor Hill, Oxford OX2 9JJ

Find us on the World Wide Web at www.westviewpress.com

A CIP catalog record for this book is available from the Library of Congress.
ISBN 0-8133-3907-3

The paper used in this publication meets the requirements of the American National Standard for Permanence of Paper for Printed Library Materials Z39.48–1984.

10   9   8   7   6   5   4   3   2   1

DEC 17 2001

To Kathryn

There is only one hope . . . it is absolute openness and the absence of any secrecy in science. Only thus can we hope that the scientists who succeed will be those who do not confuse exceptional human beings with experimental animals.

—B. Müller-Hill, *Murderous Science*

Everything can be taken from a man but one thing, the last of the human freedoms—to choose one's attitude in any given set of circumstances, to choose one's own way.

—V. Frankl, *Man's Search for Meaning*

CONTENTS

LIST OF
ILLUSTRATIONS

LIST OF ACRONYMS
AND ABBREVIATIONS

Dalstroi	Main Directorate for Building in the Far East
EKO	Economical Department
FAPSI	Federal Government Communications and Information Agency
FSB	Federal Security Service
GEU	Main Economic Directorate
Gidroproekt	Directorate for Projecting, Planning, and Research
GKO	State Committee of Defense
Glavgidrostroi	Main Directorate of Camps for Hydrotechnical Construction
Glavlit	Main Directorate on the Literature and Publishing Houses
Glavmikrobioprom	Main Administration of the Microbiological Industry
Glavpromstroi, or GULPS	Main Directorate of Camps for Industrial Construction
Glavsortupr	Main Directorate of Seed Varieties
Goelro	State Energy Committee
Gosizdat	State Publishing Company
GosNIIOKhT	State Scientific Research Institute of Organic Chemistry and Technology
Gosplan	State Planning Committee
GPU	State Political Directorate
GTU	Main Directorate of Transportation
GUGB	Main Directorate of State Security
GUILGMP	Main Directorate of Camps of the Mining-Metallurgic Industry
IEB	Institute of Experimental Biology
IEM	Gamaleya Institute of Epidemiology and Microbiology

IMEMO	Institute for World Economy and International Relations
INO	Foreign Department
IVAN	Institute for Oriental Studies
JAC	Jewish Anti-Fascist Committee
KEPS	Commission for the Study of Natural-Productive Forces
KGB	Committee of State Security
KI	Committee on Information
KTPH	Kazan Psychiatric Prison Hospital
KUBU	Commission to Improve Living Conditions of Scientists
MGB	USSR Ministry of State Security
Minmedbioprom	Ministry of the Medical and Microbiological Industries
MOIP	Moscow Society of Naturalists
Narkompros	Commissariat of Education
Narkomzdrav	Commissariat of Health
Narkomzem	Commissariat of Agriculture
NEP	New Economic Policy
NKVD	People's Commissariat of the Interior
NTO	Scientific Technology Section of the VSNKh
NTS	Popular Labor Alliance of Russian Solidarists
OAU	VCheKa Administrative-Organizational Department
OGPU	United State Political Directorate
OMNI	Society of Moscow Scientific Institute
OO	Special Department
OOT	Department of Operational Equipment
OSO	MGB Special Board
OSS	Office of Strategic Services
OTU	Operational-Technical Directorate
OVD	Department for Investigation of Especially Important Cases
PBO	Petrograd Armed Organization
Politotdel	Political Department
RFYaTs-VNIITF	Russian Federation Nuclear Center
RNP	Russian National Party
ROVS	White Russian Military Union
RSFSR	Russian Federation
SMERSH	Military Counterintelligence
SO	Secret Department

SOD	Council of Men in Public Life
SOE	Special Operation Executive
SOU	Secret-Operational Directorate
Sovinformburo	Soviet Information Agency
Sovmin	Council of Ministers
Sovnarkom	Council of People's Commissars
StB	Czechoslovak Security Service
SVR	Foreign Intelligence Service
TKP	Labor Peasant Party
TseKUBU	Central Commission to Improve Living Conditions of Scientists
TsNIIST	Central Scientific Investigation Institute for Special Technology
VARNITSO	All-Union Association of Workers of Science and Technique to Assist the Socialist Construction
VASKhNIL	All-Union Academy of Agricultural Sciences, or Agricultural Academy
VCheKa	All-Russian Extraordinary Commission
VIEM	All-Union Institute of Experimental Medicine
VIR	All-Union Institute of Plant Breeding
VNII Genetika	All-Union Research Institute of Genetics and Selection of Microorganisms
VNII-1	All-Union Research Institute One for Gold and Rare Metals
VNIRO	All-Union Scientific Research Institute of Fisheries and Oceanography
VRK	Military-Revolutionary Committee
VSNKh	Supreme Council of National Economy
VTsIK	All-Russian Central Executive Committee
VTsSPS	All-Russian Council of Trade Unions

FOREWORD

Drawing upon the many new sources that have appeared since the Soviet Union was dissolved, including materials from the KGB archives, Dr. Birstein offers a detailed and fascinating account of how the so-called poison laboratory was established under the auspices of the Soviet secret police, the NKVD (People's Commissariat of the Interior). Headed from the 1930s to the 1950s by a biochemist and physician named Grigory Mairanovsky, this laboratory served as the base for inhumane and cruel medical experiments on unsuspecting prisoners who had been condemned to death by the notorious Soviet judicial system. The usual procedure was for those conducting the experiments to lure the victim into complacency by feigning a straightforward medical examination and then, under the guise of a legitimate medication, injecting poison into the victim. The resulting deaths, observed through secret peepholes with detachment by the physicians, were often excruciatingly painful and agonizing.

Those participating in these terrible experiments on humans justified their actions by considering them in the context of a larger war against the enemies of the Soviet people. These poisons were part of their arsenal of weapons in this war, and they were operating on the orders of the highest Soviet authorities. But, as Dr. Birstein demonstrates, the perpetrators of these experiments were in fact sadistic criminals with no regard for human life. Furthermore, the scientists and doctors involved in these biomedical projects sacrificed the integrity of the entire Soviet scientific community by making scientific research a tool of the totalitarian state.

—*Dr. Amy Knight*
Adjunct Research Professor,
Institute of European and Russian Studies,
Carleton University, Ottawa, Canada

ACKNOWLEDGMENTS

I AM VERY GRATEFUL to my colleagues from the human rights organization Memorial (Moscow, Russia), Arsenii Roginsky, Nikita Petrov, Nikita Okhotin, and Gennady Kuzovkin, for their help in finding archival materials and their notes to the manuscript. Dr. Amy Knight (Institute of European and Russian Studies, Carleton University, Ottawa, Canada) and Susanne Berger (Washington, DC) patiently read the manuscript and made valuable comments. Dr. Milton Leitenberg (Center for International and Security Studies, University of Maryland) also suggested changes that improved the text immensely. Dr. Vil Mirzayanov (Princeton, NJ) provided me with the information on Soviet plans to use ricin as a chemical weapon. Dr. Maria Keipert (Politisches Archiv des Auswartigen Amt, Bonn, Germany) sent me information regarding the former German diplomats kept after World War II in Soviet captivity. Dr. Raissa Berg (Paris, France) helped me to understand many events of the 1930s–1940s. Dr. James Atz (American Museum of Natural History, NY) kindly allowed me to work with his collection of copies of papers on the Trofim Lysenko affair. Professor Erhard Geissler (Max Delbrück Center for Molecular Medicine, Berlin-Buch, Germany) sent me copies of some valuable archival materials and of his own works, despite his illness at that time. Ms. Catherine Fitzpatrick (New York) kindly provided me with a copy of her translation of the manuscript by Vladimir Bobryonev and Valery Ryazentsev. Dr. Anthony Rimmington (Center for Russian and East European Studies, University of Birmingham, Birminghan, U.K.) and Dr. Mark Wheelis (Division of Biological Sciences, University of California, Davis, CA) provided me with copies of their published and unpublished papers on biological weapons. Sergei Gitman (Moscow) gave me his photo of Vladimir Prison. Professor Daniel Wikler (Department of History of Medicine, University of Wisconsin, Madison, WI) invited me to give talks on the NKVD-MGB experiments on humans at the conferences Human Genome Research in an Independent World:

International Aspects of Social and Ethical Issues in Human Genome Research (Bethesda, MD, June 2–4, 1991), and at the Third Congress of Bioethics (San Francisco, November 22–24, 1996). Mr. Tug Yourgrau, vice president of Powderhouse Productions, Inc. (Somerville, MA) invited me to participate in the TV report "Poisons—Discovery Magazine" (1997).

INTRODUCTION

THIS BOOK IS ABOUT the state control of science in the Soviet Union. Since I am a geneticist, my primary focus is on the fields I know best: biology and medicine. Several books have been published recently in English and Russian on the issue, but they cover only limited time periods.[1] Moreover, they do not describe in detail the origins of the control and the leading role of the Soviet security services in establishing such control.

The Soviet regime was not the first to intervene in the work of the Russian Academy of Sciences and universities. The first incident occurred in the mid-eighteenth century. In 1747, Ribeiro Sanchez, a Jewish Portuguese doctor who had worked in Russia since 1731, was elected honorary academician of the St. Petersburg Academy of Sciences (established by Peter the Great in 1725) and received a pension from the academy.[2] In 1732, Empress Elizabeth, the daughter of Peter the Great, ordered that Sanchez be deprived of his title and pension—the empress had issued a law prohibiting any Jew from living in the Russian Empire. Ironically, in 1762 the new Russian empress, Catherine the Great, ordered that Dr. Sanchez's membership in the academy be restored. He had saved her life many years before, when she was fifteen. In later years, liberal university professors and teachers were under constant secret scrutiny by the Special Department of the Tsarist Police Department.[3] However, a unique situation developed in the twentieth-century Soviet Union. Control grew with the development of a particular tool of control—the Soviet political secret service, or VCheKa (All-Russian Extraordinary Commission)—and continued during all its transformations into the current FSB (Federal Security Service) and SVR (Foreign Intelligence Service) (see Tables I.1 and I.2).

The Soviet Union's efforts to control science were part of its larger effort to control the "intelligentsia"—not an easy Russian term to define.[4] In general, it is used to describe educated middle-class intellectuals. But traditionally in Russia, members of the intelligentsia were considered to have high ethical standards and a moral obligation and commitment to popular enlightenment and education. From the earliest days of their power, the Bolsheviks treated the old intelligentsia as bourgeoisie, a class they thought

1

Table I.1 Main Changes in the NKVD/KGB Structure, 1917 – Present[i]

No.	Office (Full Russian Name)	Name in English	Russian Acronym	Years of Existence	Main Areas of Responsibility
1.	Narodnyi Komissariat Vnutrennikh Del RSFSR	People's Commissariat of the Interior of the Russian Federation (RSFSR)	NKVD (of the RSFSR)	1917 – 30	Police function, organization of prisoners' work
2.	Vserossiiskaya Chrezvychainaya Komissiya pri Soviete Narodnykh Komissarov	All-Russian Emergency Comission under the Council of Soviet Commissars	VCheKa	1917 – 22	Actions against counterrevolution and sabotage
3.	Gosudarstvennoe Politicheskoe Upravlenie pri NKVD RSFSR	State Political Directorate under the NKVD of the RSFSR	GPU	1922	Actions against counterrevolution, sabotage, spies, and smuggling; control of the state borders
4.	Ob'edinennoe Gosudarstvennoe Politicheskoe Upravlenie pri Soviete Narodnykh Komissarov	United State Political Directorate under the Council of Soviet Commissars	OGPU	1922 – 34	Control of the local GPU offices and of special departments in the army
5.	Narodnyi Komissariat Vnutrennikh Del SSSR (included Glavnoe Upravlenie Gosudarstvennoi Bezopasnosti)	The USSR People's Commissariat of the Interior (a merged body of the OGPU and the Russian Federation NKVD; included Main State Security Directorate)	NKVD (included GUGB)	July 1934 – February 1941	*GUGB*: counterintelligence, intelligence, actions against political parties, anti-Soviet elements, and terrorists; control of special investigation prisons; *GULAG*: control of prisoners in prisons and labor camps; guarding state borders; *OSO*: special trials;[ii] etc.
6.	Narodnyi Komissariat Vnutrennikh Del SSSR	The USSR People's Commissariat of the Interior	NKVD	February 1941 – July 1941	Police; control of prisons, labor camps, concentration camps for POWs and of numerous directorates of slave labor camps in all branches of state economy, including *Dalstroi*; creation of special operational techniques; fire-fighting directorate; etc.
7.	Narodnyi Komissariat Gosudarstvennoi Bezopasnosti SSSR (former GUGB)	The USSR State Security People's Commissariat (former GUGB)	NKGB	February 1941 – July 1941	Foreign intelligence, counterintelligence, investigation of political cases, usage of operational techniques, etc.

No.	Office (Full Russian Name)	Name in English	Russian Acronym	Years of Existence	Main Areas of Responsibility
8.	Narodnyi Komissariat Vnutrennikh Del SSSR (NKVD merged with NKGB)	The USSR People's Commissariat of the Interior	NKVD	July 1941 – April 1943	Foreign intelligence; counterintelligence; political surveillance; investigation of political cases; control of prisons, POW camps, GULAG, other labor camps in different branches of the economy; interior troops; creation of special operational techniques; control of state archives; etc.
9.	Narodnyi Komissariat Vnutrennikh Del SSSR	The USSR People's Commissariat of the Interior	NKVD	April 1943 – March 1946	Control of the GULAG and other labor camps in different branches of the economy; interior troops and border guards; etc.
9.	Narodnyi Komissariat Gosudarstvennoi Bezopasnosti SSSR	The USSR State Security People's Commissariat	NKGB	April 1943 – March 1946	Intelligence; counterintelligence; terrorist actions on the territories occupied by Germans; usage of the operational techniques; censorship; control of the state archives; etc.
10.	Ministerstvo Gosudarstvennoi Bezopasnosti SSSR (former NKGB)	The USSR Ministry of State Security	MGB	March 1946 – March 1953	Intelligence; counterintelligence; military counterintelligence; usage of the operational techniques; censorship; investigation of political cases; creation of operational technique; usage of operational techniques; atomic espionage; OSO (special trials), etc.
11.	Ministerstvo Vnutrennikh Del SSSR (former NKVD)	The USSR Ministry of the Interior	MVD	March 1946 – March 1953	Control of labor camps in all branches of economy; GULAG; OSO; different special troops (including the Border Guards and the Interior); etc.
12.	Ministerstvo Vnutrennikh Del SSSR USSR (MGB merged with MVD)	The USSR Ministry of the Interior	MVD	March 1953 – March 1954	All functions of the former MGB and MVD

(continues)

Table I.1 (continued)

No.	Office (Full Russian Name)	Name in English	Russian Acronym	Years of Existence	Main Areas of Responsibility
13.	Komitet Gosudarstvennoi Bezopasnosti pri Soviete Ministrov SSSR	Committee of State Security (under the USSR Council of Ministers)	KGB	March 1954 – December 1991	Foreign intelligence; counterintelligence; military counterintelligence; fight against anti-Soviet elements; operational and technical department; Border Guards; etc.
14.	Ministerstvo Vnutrennikh Del SSSR	The USSR Ministry of the Interior	MVD	March 1954 – August 1991	Control of prisons and labor camps; police; interior troops; etc.
15.	Tsentral'naya Sluzba Razvedki, later Sluzhba Vneshnei Razvedki (former Pervoe Glavnoe Upravlenie KGB)	Central Intelligence Service, later Foreign Intelligence Service (former First KGB Main Directorate)	TsSR, later SVR	December 1991 – present	Foreign intelligence
16.	Mezhrespublikanskaya Sluzhba Bezopasnosti	Interrepublican Security Service	MSB	November – December 1991	Main KGB and MVD functions without foreign intelligence
17.	Ministerstvo Bezopasnosti i Vnutrennikh Del	Ministry of Security and Internal Affairs	MBVD	December 1991 – January 1992	The same
18.	Agenstvo Federal'noi Bezopasnosti	Federal Security Agency	AFB	January 1992	The same
19.	Ministerstvo Bezopasnosti, then Federal'naya Sluzhba Kontrrazvedki, then Federal'naya Sluzhba Bezopasnosti	Ministry of Security, then Federal Security Agency, then Federal Security Service	MB, then FSK, then FSB	1992 – present	Counterintelligence, military counterintelligence, transportation security, anti-terrorism actions, surveillance
20.	Federal'noe Agenstvo Pravitel'stvennoi Svyazi i Informatsii (former 8th KGB Main Directorate, the 16th KGB Directorate, and Communication Troops)	Federal Agency for Government Communication and Information	FAPSI	December 1991 – present	Control of government telephone lines, high-frequency communication systems, cryptography services

No.	Office (Full Russian Name)	Name in English	Russian Acronym	Years of Existence	Main Areas of Responsibility
21.	Glavnoe Upravlenie Okhrany (former 9th KGB Main Directorate)	Main Guard Directorate	GUO	December 1991 – present	No legally defined function; accountable to the President. Includes Presidential Regiment and the Alfa Group (an elite special former 7th KGB Main Directorate commandos)
22.	Federal'naya Pogranichnaya Sluzhba (former KGB Border Guards Main Directorate)	Federal Border Service	FPS	1992 – present	Guarding Russia's land frontiers and the perimeter of the Russian Federation coastal waters
23.	Ministerstvo Vnytrennikh Del	Ministry of Internal Affairs	MVD	1991 – present	Interior troops; police; fire-fighters department, etc.

i Data from Kokurin and Petrov, *Lubyanka*, pp. 7-102; Waller, J. M., *Secret Empire: The KGB in Russia Today* (Boulder, CO): Westview Press, 1994), pp. 118-141, and Knight, A., *Spies Without Cloaks: The KGB's Successors* (Princeton, NJ: Princeton University Press, 1996), pp. 30-37; Mlechin, L., *Predsedateli KGB: Rassekrechennye sud'by* [The KGB Chairmen: Declassified Biographies] (Moscow: Tsentrpoligraf, 1999a), pp. 648-649 (in Russian).

ii The Special Council (OSO), an out-of-judicial tribunal, was established under the NKVD in 1934. At first the OSO was in charge of the decisions on the administrative exile of persons "dangerous for the society," the imprisonment in labor camps up to 5 years, and the expulsion of foreign citizens from the USSR (p. 274 in Chebrikov, Victor M., G. F. Grigorenko, N. A. Dushin, and F. D. Bobkov (eds.) *Istoriya sovetskikh organov gosudarstvennoi bezopasnosti. Uchebnik. "Sovershenno sekretno"* [History of the Soviet Security Service. A Textbook. "Top Secret"] (Vysshaya Shkola KGB: Moscow, 1977), 600 pp. (in Russian). Available at http://www.fas.harvard.edu/~hpcws/documents.htm. The Commissar/Minister of Internal Affairs (or State Security) chaired the OSO, and his deputies were the Council members. In 1937, the 5-year limit was increased to 10 years. In the mid–1940s–early 1950s, the OSO applied sentences of 20 and 25 years, and in 1953, for lifetime imprisonment. The OSO existed under the MVD until 1950. From 1946 till March 1953 there was the OSO under the MGB, and from March 1953 till September 1953 the OSO was under the MVD. It was disbanded on September 1, 1953 (Rossi, Jacques, *The Gulag Handbook* [Paragon House: New York, 1989], pp. 271-272; Kokurin and Petrov, *Lubyanka*, pp. 130-131).

Table I.2 List of the VCheKa/KGB Chairmen, 1917 – Present

Name of the Chairman[1]	Security Service[2]	Years
1. Dzerzhinsky, Feliks Edmundovich	VCheKa/GPU/ OGPU	1917 (Dec.)–1926 (July)
2. Menzhinsky*, Vyacheslav Rudolfovich	OGPU	1926 (July)–1934 (May)
3. Yagoda*, Genrikh Grigoryevich	NKVD	1934 (July)–1936 (Sept.)
4. Yezhov*, Nikolai Ivanovich	NKVD	1936 (Sept.)–1938 (Nov.)
5. Beria*, Lavrentii Pavlovich	NKVD	1938 (Nov.)–1945 (Dec.)
6. Merkulov*, Vsevolod Nikolaevich	NKGB	1941 (Feb.–July)
7. Merkulov*, Vsevolod Nikolaevich	NKGB/MGB	1943 (April)–1946 (May)
8. Kruglov*, Sergei Nikiforovich	NKVD	1945 (Dec.)–1946 (March)
9. Abakumov*, Viktor Semyonovich	MGB	1946 (May)–1951 (July)
10. Kruglov*, Sergei Nikiforovich	MVD	1946 (March)–1953 (March)
11. Ogol'tsov*, Sergei Ivanovich	Acting, MGB	1951 (Aug.–Dec.)
12. Ignatiev*, Semyon Denisovich	MGB	1951 (Dec.)–1953 (March)
13. Beria*, Lavrentii Pavlovich	MVD	1953 (March–June)
14. Kruglov*, Sergei Nikiforovich	MVD	1953 (June)–1956 (Jan.)
14. Serov*, Ivan Aleksandrovich	KGB	1954 (March)–1958 (Dec.)
15. Shelepin, Aleksandr Nikolaevich	KGB	1958 (Dec.)–1961 (Nov.)
16. Semichastny, VladimirYefimovich	KGB	1961 (Nov.)–1967 (May)
17. Andropov*, Yurii Vladimirovich	KGB	1967 (May)–1982 (May)
18. Fyodorchuk, Vitalii Vasilyevich	KGB	1982 (May–Dec.)
19. Chebrikov, Viktor Mikhailovich	KGB	1982 (Dec.)–1988 (Oct.)
20. Kryuchkov*, Vladimir Aleksandrovich	KGB	1988 (Oct.)–1991 (August)
21. Shebarshin, Leonid Vladimirovich	Acting, KGB	1991 (August 22)
22. Bakatin*, Vadim Viktorovich	KGB/MSB	1991 (August–December)
23. Primakov*, Yevgenii Maximovich	TsSR/SVR	1991–1996 (Jan.)
24. Barannikov, Viktor Pavlovich	MBVD	1991 (Dec.)–1992 (Jan.)
25. Ivanenko, Viktor Valentinovich	AFB	1992 (Jan., one week)
26. Barannikov, Viktor Pavlovich	AFB/MB	1992 (Jan.)–1993 (Sept.)
27. Golushko*, Nikolai Mikhailovich	MB/FSK	1993 (Dec.)–1994 (Febr.)
28. Stepashin*, Sergei Vadimiovich[3]	FSK/FSB	1994 (Febr.)–1995 (June)
29. Barsukov, Mikhail Ivanovich	FSB	1995 (July)–1996 (June)
30. Kovalev, Nikolai Dmitrievich	FSB	1996 (July)–1998 (July)
31. Putin*, Vladimir Vladimirovich[4]	FSB	1998 (July)–1999 (August)
32. Patrushev, Nikolai Platonovich	FSB	1999 (August)–present
33. Trubnikov*, Vyacheslav Ivanovich	SVR	1996 (Jan.)–2000 (May)
34. Sergei Lebedev Ivanovich[5]	SVR	2000 (May)–present

[1] Names mentioned in the text are marked with an asterisk (*).
[2] Full titles of agencies are given in Table I.I.
[3] In 1997–May 1999, Sergei Stepashin was the Interior (MVD) Minister. From May 12, 1999, until August 9, 1999, he was Prime Minister. Vladimir Rushailo succeeded Stepashin as MVD Minister.
[4] On August August 9, 1999, President Yeltsin appointed Putin Acting Prime Minister. On December 31, 1999, President Yeltsin resigned and transferred his power to Prime Minister Putin as Acting President. In March 2000 Putin was elected Russian President.
[5] Anonymous, "Putin introduces new spymaster," BBC News, May 23 (2000).

should gradually disappear, to be replaced by newly educated industrial workers (the proletariat) and poor peasants. According to Bolshevik doctrine, Communist society should consist of just two classes: the proletariat and peasants. The newly created proletarian intelligentsia should form a layer between these two classes and serve them. For a while, during the Civil War (1918–1921) and the years of the New Economic Policy (NEP) declared by Vladimir Lenin, the regime to some extent tolerated the old "bourgeois" intelligentsia, which included scientists. The NEP included denationalization of small businesses and legalization of private trade—that is, some capitalist economic forms were allowed to coexist with the socialist forms. The NEP was proclaimed on March 15, 1921, at the Tenth Communist Party Congress, and it officially ended in December 1929 (it ended de facto in April 1928).[5] With the demise of the NEP, any tolerance toward the old intelligentsia evaporated.

In writing this book, I have used many formerly secret documents not published until the 1990s. Unfortunately, the originals of most of them are still unavailable and are kept in the secret files of the FSB/SVR archives. All these documents are in Russian, frequently written in a special metaphoric language used by NKVD/KGB officers. Only since 1997 have three fundamental reference books been published in Russian that have allowed me to put the events in Soviet science into historical context. These three texts cover three crucial areas: the history of the Soviet security services,[6] the prison and labor camp system,[7] and biographies of the main officials during the first two decades of the Soviet secret service.[8]

My book also deals extensively with the pernicious effects of Lysenkoism, a body of dialectic Marxist beliefs almost magical in nature, created by Trofim Lysenko, a largely uneducated agronomist.[9] Between the late 1920s and the 1950s, every biologist in the Soviet Union had to decide whether to accept Trofim Lysenko's pseudobiology, which had been approved by the Communist Party and Stalin himself, or whether to follow the dictates of his or her own professional knowledge and ethics. Uneducated Soviet leaders appreciated Lysenko's denial of the existence of genes as the basis of inheritance (and the chromosomes where the genes are located) and species as the basis of evolution. It was much easier for them to understand Lysenko's simplified anthropomorphic ideas that individuals within a species "help" each other (i.e., that there is no competition within the same species) and inherit changes from environmental conditions than to deal with the complicated knowledge of "bourgeois" geneticists and evolutionists who were products of the hated intelligentsia.

Analysis of the rise of Lysenko also highlights the resilience and great courage of many scientists who maintained moral and ethical norms against all odds. As in Nazi Germany, scientists in the Soviet Union faced a moral dilemma: Should they follow the demands of the ruling regime and participate in unethical, sometimes criminal research, or should they follow their own consciences and refuse to participate? In the latter case, the decision could cost a scientist his or her professional career, freedom, and even life itself, and could endanger family and friends, as well. However, the regime succeeded in producing some scientists who did not hesitate to fulfill and support any demand of the Party and its secret police. The material presented in Chapters 2 and 3 illustrates this point.

Only recently has it become known that in the Soviet Union, as in Nazi Germany, humans were used for biomedical experiments—scientists who worked for the security service tested the action of poisons on human subjects. I first became aware of these experiments in 1990, while working as a volunteer researcher for the Moscow human rights organization Memorial.[10] My specialty was foreign prisoners in the Gulag.[11] That same year, as a Memorial representative, I was included as a member of the International Commission on the Fate and Whereabouts of Raoul Wallenberg, which was organized with the support of the Soviet Interior Ministry under Vadim Bakatin.[12]

Memorial created an archive of materials on the history of political repression in the Soviet Union and on the victims of that repression. Some documents in this archive concern Grigory Mairanovsky, a Muscovite, biochemist, and doctor who was the head of Laboratory No. 1 within the Soviet state security system from the 1930s through the 1950s (see Table I.1 for the chronological lineage of the security system: VCheKa; GPU [State Political Directorate]; OGPU [United State Political Directorate]; NKVD; MGB [USSR Ministry of State Security] and KGB [Committee of State Security]). The existence of this laboratory was a closely held Soviet state secret. Memorial's historians and journalists published some information about this laboratory between 1990 and 1993 in the *Moscow News*[13] and other newspapers.[14] Also, State Prosecutor Vladimir Bobryonev and military journalist Valery Ryazentsev included documents on Mairanovsky and his NKVD-MGB supervisors from the still-closed KGB archives in the manuscript of their book *The Ghosts of Varsonofyevsky Lane: Laboratory of Death—How the Soviet Secret Police Experimented on People and Poisoned Their Enemies,* which was translated into English in 1996 but not published at that time.[15] It has since been published in a shortened form in German.[16] In addition, Bobryonev used the main events and real archival documents for his roman à clef, *"Doctor Death,"* or the Ghosts of Varsonofyevsky Lane, published in Russian.[17]

In the case of Nazi Germany, literature on the involvement of bioscientists and doctors in experiments on humans is abundant.[18] For instance, Benno Müller-Hill has analyzed this topic in detail in various articles[19] and in his book *Murderous Science*.[20] Until 1990, it was not widely known that at the same time the countries of the Axis, Nazi Germany, and Japan[21] were conducting horrifying experiments on humans in concentration camps, the same testing was going on in the Allied camp, in the Soviet Union. The London murder of the Bulgarian dissident and writer Georgi Markov by means of a small poisoned bullet in October 1978[22] was possible only because of the long history of NKVD-MGB-KGB poison research. Many details of these medical experiments are still secret.

During my research, I was saddened to read about experiments conducted by American doctors for the Central Intelligence Agency (the CIA, created in 1947) in the late 1940s–1950s.[23] Of course, these experiments cannot be compared with those conducted by the Nazi doctors or Mairanovsky, but subjecting patients without their knowledge or consent to drug testing, electroshock treatment, and so on was a terrible breach of human rights.[24] Two former members of the U.S. intelligence service, Victor Marchetti and John Marks, published a book about the whole issue, using knowledge they had obtained while working for the CIA and State Department Intelligence and Research Bureau.[25] CIA officials were predictably outraged. The CIA director at the time, William Colby, wrote in his memoirs:

> The outlines of their [Marchetti and Marks's] book indicated that they intended to reveal and criticize a number of CIA's activities, including those that CIA had undertaken with foreigners . . . Marchetti, Marks and their publisher . . . published the book with blank spaces showing the items we [the CIA] had initially identified as classified but then had withdrawn our objections. And they made a great publicity campaign out of our [the CIA's] "censorship," which certainly added to the book's sale.[26]

Despite the pressure from CIA officials, John Marks continued to collect material on unlawful experiments and finally published his analysis in *The Search for the "Manchurian Candidate."*[27] He revealed therein the terrifying American experiments during the Cold War using radioactive substances on volunteer convicts and servicemen, as well as on cancer patients, performed in connection with the Manhattan Project development of the A-bomb and H-bomb.[28] The details were released through the work of the Advisory Committee on Human Radiation Experiments in 1994–1995. The committee was chaired by the bioethicist Ruth Faden, the daughter of Holocaust survivors.

Even more shocking for me was the recently released information about secret experiments of British military scientists from the 1940s to the 1960s. According to the press, more than 3,100 humans (volunteer military personnel) were exposed to the most dreadful nerve gases—sarin, tabun, and soman[29]—at the Chemical and Biological Defence Establishment in Porton Down, Wiltshire.[30] In a particularly large experiment conducted on 396 men in 1953, in which scientists sought to estimate how much nerve gas would kill a man through layers of clothing or on bare skin, a twenty-year-old airman named Ronald Maddison died. In 1999, the British police started to investigate this old case. It is alarming that a new gas chamber for tests of the next generation of nerve agents was built and opened at Porton Down in 1995, with a projected life of twenty years.[31] Additionally, at least 100 air, sea, and land tests of germ-warfare-like substances were carried out in three regions of England in the 1960s–1970s.[32]

I have presented material about Mairanovsky's activities at two international meetings on bioethics.[33] However, this volume is the result of much wider research. It shows that Mairanovsky's experiments were possible only because of the security services' involvement in Soviet science. The security service (commonly known as the KGB) was not separate from the Communist Party in the way that the CIA is from the American Congress. Quite to the contrary, it was proudly named "the Sword and Shield of the Party" and used a sword and a shield as its insignia. In many respects, a Soviet scientist's career depended on Communist Party membership and a good relationship with the KGB. Secret service control was conducted at many levels. It began with demands to be "politically correct" in one's support of Communist ideology and often involved coercion to inform on fellow scientists. The Academy of Sciences had, and still has, special secret departments headed by high-ranking state security officers. In addition, the secret service assigned acting and retired officers to work as scientists at the universities and research institutes. Sergei Muromtsev, Mairanovsky's colleague in MGB secret experiments on humans, is a good example of the merger of MGB activity with Lysenkoism. As I will describe in Chapter 2, Muromtsev was one of Lysenko's most enthusiastic supporters.

Unexpectedly, in recently declassified and published documents,[34] the name of Mairanovsky's superior, Pavel Sudoplatov, one of the most ruthless NKVD/MGB executioners, appeared not only with Mairanovsky's but also in connection with the case against the famous geneticist Nikolai Vavilov, who was arrested by the NKVD in 1940. Sudoplatov was called in at the end of his case, in 1942, when Vavilov was dying of dystrophy in prison after having been tortured during the long NKVD "investigation." It remains unknown what the NKVD wanted to use the geneticist for.

I am personally convinced that Mairanovsky served as an inspiration to Stalin for the "killer-doctor" image he successfully exploited in the famous Doctors' Plot case—a part of Stalin's sophisticated plan to depose powerful members of the inner circle of the Politburo[35] by employing anti-Semitic hysteria. The official anti-Semitic campaign against the "Cosmopolitans," the term used to refer to Jews in the Soviet mass media at the time, started in 1947 and intensified after the MGB-staged murder of a famous actor and head of the Jewish Anti-Fascist Committee, Solomon Mikhoels, in January 1948.[36] It culminated in 1951–1952 with the MGB-created Doctors' Plot case, which was personally directed by Stalin.

However, the war against the Jews (as an ethnic group, not as a religion) started even earlier. During the 1939 secret Soviet-Nazi peace negotiations, Stalin told Nazi foreign minister Joachim Ribbentrop that the Soviet government was not interested in saving Polish Jews and that the Soviet leaders were just waiting until there were enough non-Jewish intellectuals so they could end the overwhelming presence of Jews in the Soviet administration. In 1943, a Plenum of the Central Committee issued a decree saying that the Russian nation (in an ethnic sense) was the leader in the USSR and that saving Jews from Nazi extermination was not a priority in the war. Following this decree, secret orders were issued to remove officers of Jewish descent from leading positions in the army and to list minimal numbers of Jews for military awards.[37]

Also, this was not the first time Stalin used the "killer-doctor" image. Several famous doctors had been accused of killing high Party officials during Nikolai Bukharin's trial in 1938. But that trial did not have an openly anti-Semitic character, although several of its major defendants were Jews. In 1951–1952, the situation was different. Taking into account Hitler's successful extermination of European Jews, Stalin considered sending the Soviet Jews into exile and to special labor camps. Given the anti-Semitic hysteria that was growing in the country, he could easily use this stratagem to replace those in his closest political circle who had acquired too much power.

In 1951, Minister Viktor Abakumov, Mairanovsky's and Sudoplatov's superior in the MGB, became one of the first victims of this campaign. Although he was not a Jew, Abakumov was accused of creating a Jewish plot within the MGB. On November 18, 1950, Yakov Etinger, a Kremlin Hospital doctor, was the first arrested.[38] Others were arrested later. All of them were accused of being part of the Jewish "Doctors' Plot." Allegedly, they planned to kill high Party officials during medical treatments. Not all of the arrested doctors were Jews, but it hardly mattered.

As epigraphs in the sections exposing Mairanovsky's experiments, I give examples of comparable situations in Nazi Germany, including documents from the Nuremberg Doctors' trial. The similarity of these events is striking.

Overall, it is clear that many in the Soviet scientific elite were involved in state crimes. Many in the academic establishment knew about Mairanovsky's dreadful experiments and approved them, awarding him with scientific degrees and titles. Some of these people were internationally recognized as prominent scientists. Mairanovsky's work was also connected with the development of biological and chemical weapons: He used components of these substances for his tests on humans.

Like Mairanovsky's experiments, Soviet biological and chemical warfare military programs were under the control of the military, the Academy of Sciences, and the security service. Until recently, a special Inter-Agency Council coordinated efforts of the Ministries of Health, Agriculture, and Defense, the chemical industry, the KGB, and the Academy of Sciences in the development of biological weapons.[39] Some leaders of the chemical and biological weapons programs had high military rank, in addition to bearing the title of academician. Unfortunately, even today the Western scientific community does not seem to understand how deeply science in the Soviet Union (and still currently in Russia) was controlled by the security service.[40] This former Soviet scientific elite has managed to hold onto its status and privileges even now, amid the economic turmoil of the new Russia. Loren Graham, one of the main historians of Soviet and Russian science, recently wrote:

> The scientists in the Soviet Union who controlled the Academy of Sciences lost most of their financial advantages after the country collapsed [in 1991], but they fought most strenuously to retain their nonmonetary perquisites and influences, especially their roles as the administrators and leaders of the science establishment. As a result, Russia is today the only major country in the world in which several hundred leading, and often quite senior, scientists, chosen by themselves, are in charge of the fundamental science establishment, directing its laboratories and institutes. They fiercely defend that privilege even at a time when they cannot pay the researchers who work in those laboratories and institutes.[41]

I started my training in biology while Lysenko was still in power, and I remember Lysenkoist "professors"—usually Communist Party functionaries who falsified the results of their experiments or received their degrees for work completed by others. Some of these pseudoscientists were NKVD/ MGB/KGB informers or officers. I also know the other side of this story. I knew personally those geneticists and evolutionists who did not make compromises with their consciences. Some of them spent many years in Soviet labor camps because of their anti-Lysenkoist positions. And I cannot forget the fate of the thousands of other scientists who became victims of the Soviet totalitarian regime, those who perished in Soviet labor camps, were shot to death, or died during OGPU/NKVD/MGB/KGB "interrogations" from the 1920s through the 1950s.

I have tried to present the material in this book as a personal issue. I would like each reader to ask: What would I do in such a situation? Would I accept the conditions of the regime, be loyal to it, and possibly become an informer if it would help my professional career? Or would I even go to work within the system of secret services, which would mean a good salary and a powerful position? Would I use convicts under death sentence for experiments? Or, as a scientist, would I review the results of such experiments? Would I maintain humanistic and moral values and even fight for them in a situation in which my activities would condemn not only myself but my family and friends as well?

1

SCIENCE UNDER SIEGE

To give a list of all Soviet scientists who were repressed by the secret police would be not only impossible but tedious.
—L. R. Graham, *What Have We Learned
About Science and Technology from the
Russian Experience?*

AFTER THEIR SUCCESSFUL 1917 coup d'état, the Bolsheviks made control of scientists and other Russian intelligentsia one of their first priorities. Their primary concern was members of the intelligentsia who had participated in the Provisional Government, which existed between the February Revolution and the Bolshevik takeover in November. During this brief nine-month period, the Academy of Sciences, universities, and other scientific institutions became independent from state control for the first and last time in their history. The Bolsheviks were well aware that these professionals were capable of quickly understanding the naked desire for power behind their grand promises.

In 1928, a corresponding member of the academy (elected in 1927), the noted metallurgist Vladimir Grum-Grzhimailo (1864–1928) wrote a particularly prescient note to the Presidium of the Scientific Technical Directorate of the Council of People's Commissars (Sovnarkom):

> Marx's theory is a backward hypothesis, which has already lost ground. It was created when muscular [physical] labor flourished and when almost zero technical and industrial knowledge was available. Now everything is changing, and I am absolutely convinced that in 50 years there will be no proletariat. The ideal of engineers is . . . a plant without workers. This will provide people with such abundance of life resources that there will be no need for the class struggle. Capitalism is very successful in introducing this future culture . . . But in fact the power in Russia is in the hands of

Bolsheviks . . . [They] want to experiment with the creation of a Socialist state. The price for this will be extremely high . . . [1]

Naturally, after this letter the election of Grum-Grzhimailo to full membership in the academy was blocked.[2] Fortunately, Grum-Grzhimailo died
soon after he wrote this note and escaped the attention of the OGPU forever.

On December 21, 1934, seventeen years after the Bolshevik Revolution,
the famous eighty-five-year-old physiologist and academician Ivan Pavlov
(1849–1936), wrote a letter to the Sovnarkom:[3]

> To the USSR Council of People's Commissars:
> . . . You believe in vain in the all-world revolution . . . You disperse
> not revolution, but fascism with great success throughout the world
> . . . Fascism did not exist before your revolution . . . You are terror
> and violence . . . How many times did your newspapers write: "The
> hour [of the world revolution] has come"? The result was that new
> fascism appeared in different places. Yes, because of your indirect in-
> fluence fascism will take over step-by-step the whole civilized
> world, except its mighty Anglo-Saxon part (England, and, probably,
> the United States), [which] has already introduced the core of so-
> cialism—that labor is the main duty and real dignity of a human be-
> ing, and it is the basis of relationships between people that provides
> each person with the opportunity to live. They will *reach* this ideal
> [socialism] *preserving* all their precious cultural achievements, which
> cost many sacrifices and much time . . .
> We have been and are living now in the atmosphere of continu-
> ing terror and violence . . .
> Am I alone in thinking and feeling this way?
> Have pity on the Motherland and us.
>
> Academician Ivan Pavlov
> Leningrad, December 21, 1934.

It is amazing how profoundly Pavlov understood the role the Bolshevik
regime played in world politics. But Pavlov was alone in his revolt. Because
he was the only living Russian Nobel Prize winner, he enjoyed a unique
position in Soviet scientific society. His institute had received state support
on the personal order of Vladimir Lenin since the takeover. Despite this, at
the beginning of the 1930s, the OGPU had five volumes of "operational
materials" from informants on Academician Pavlov.[4]

The Sovnarkom chairman, Vyacheslav Molotov, to whom I will return several times in this book, answered the academician on January 2, 1935:[5]

> I would like to tell you my frank opinion that your political views are completely baseless and unpersuasive. For instance, your examples of "civilized states" such as England and the United States . . . I can only express my surprise that you tried to make categorical conclusions on principal political questions in a scientific area which you, apparently, have no knowledge of. I can only add that the political leaders of the USSR would never allow themselves to use such ardor [Molotov used the very ironic and insulting Russian word *retivost*] in questions of physiology, the field in which your scientific authority is without question.
>
> With this, I will allow myself to stop answering your letter.
>
> Chairman of the USSR SNK V. Molotov
>
> I have sent copies of your letter and my answer to President of the Academy of Sciences A. P. Karpinsky.

But Molotov was disingenuous to say that those in political power would never allow themselves to interfere in questions of physiology. At the time Pavlov wrote his appeal, science and scientists had already been thoroughly infiltrated by the Bolsheviks, and the Party constantly intervened in science and scientific matters. By sending copies of Pavlov's letter and his own answer to President Karpinsky, Molotov evidently expected Karpinsky to restrain Academician Pavlov.

Of course, from the perspective of Bolshevik ideology, the old intelligentsia only had to be tolerated until it could be replaced by newly trained scientists from the ranks of the proletariat. These newcomers would be totally obligated to the system and thus completely compliant. The Bolsheviks used poisonous propaganda to turn the masses against the old intelligentsia, accusing them of being "bourgeoisie," a concept hard to understand today since the word, which means a middle-class person concerned with materialist gain and conventional morality, describes the majority of people in contemporary developed countries. However, in the 1920s and 1930s in Russia, it resonated for the majority of Russians, who had never had an opportunity to own anything of real value. The "bourgeoisie," according to Bolshevik ideology, was by nature the main enemy of the working people and should be exterminated. This idea was put in action from the very beginning of the Bolshevik regime—in 1917 and 1918, Russian cities witnessed the massacre of hundreds of educated people by revolutionary sailors and soldiers on the streets.

THE ACADEMY OF SCIENCES: BEGINNINGS

In contrast to Western Europe and the United States, the Academy of Sciences was created in Russia before any of the universities were established. The St. Petersburg (Imperial) Academy was created by Peter the Great in 1725. On December 27, 1725, the first meeting of the St. Petersburg Academy of Sciences and Arts took place, but Peter the Great died before he approved the academy's governing statutes. Peter's daughter, Empress Elizabeth, finally approved them on June 24, 1747. On September 30, 1783, on the order of Catherine the Great, a second Imperial Russian Academy was established in St. Petersburg. Functions of the academies were overlapping, with the St. Petersburg Academy in charge of natural and humanitarian sciences and the Imperial Russian Academy in charge only of humanitarian sciences. On October 19, 1841, Tsar Nicholas I ordered the two to merge into one—the Imperial St. Petersburg Academy. The Russian Academy became its Russian Language and Literature Division. The statutes of the St. Petersburg Academy were approved by Nicholas I in 1836 and were in force until 1927.[6] The first Russian university opened in Moscow in 1755. In 1917, before the February Revolution, there were forty-four full members of the academy, and the academy had authority over five laboratories, seven museums, the Russian Archaeological Institute in Constantinople (now Istanbul), the Pulkovo Astronomic Observatory, with two departments near St. Petersburg, the Main Physical Observatory of the Meteorology Service, and twenty-one scientific commissions.[7]

Members of the academy enjoyed very high status in Russian society. Academicians received the title of *tainyi sovetnik* (privy councillor), which was equivalent to the rank of general in the army. In 1727, the eleven founding members introduced three categories of membership: adjunct or assistant academician for junior scholars with potential; ordinary (or full) member; and extraordinary academician. In 1759, the additional title of corresponding member was added for members who lived outside St. Petersburg. There were also foreign and honorary members. In 1917, there were forty-four academicians and a staff of 176 members.[8] Historians and linguists were most numerous (twenty-four members), followed by biologists (seven), geologists (four), mathematicians (four), and chemists (three). There was also a physicist, an astrophysicist, a meteorologist, and an economist.[9] The majority of academicians were university professors and continued their university careers after their election to the academy.[10]

In 1917, before the revolution, the academy included many internationally known scientists. The majority were specialists on history and linguistics, but there were also prominent natural scientists. The physiologist Ivan Pavlov was the most famous. In 1904, he was awarded the Nobel Prize for his study of nervous mechanisms controlling the digestive glands. His surgical experiments created a new scientific discipline—physiology. Pavlov's book *Lectures on the Work of the Digestive Glands*, published in Russian in 1897, was immediately translated into German, French, and English.[11] As one of his devoted students, Professor Boris Babkin, wrote, "[A]fter 1898—the date when the German translation of Pavlov's book appeared—every physiologist and every clinician based his study of the normal and abnormal physiology of the alimentary canal on Pavlov's *Lectures*."[12]

Some other biologists were also famous. The work of Academician Vladimir Zalensky (1847–1918; known as Salensky in German publications) was the first to describe the early embryogenesis of invertebrates and low vertebrates, including sturgeons.[13] The botanist and academician Vladimir Palladin (1859–1922), a devoted supporter of Darwinian evolutionary theory, was one of the first scientists to study plant respiration. In contrast, two other botanists and academicians, Andrei Famintsyn (1835–1918) and Ivan Borodin (1847–1930), were known for their opposition to Darwin's theory.[14]

Academicians-chemists, physicists, and mathematicians also achieved international recognition. Aleksei Kurnakov (1860–1941) was a distinguished physical chemist who studied alloys. Pavel Valden (1863–1957; or Paul Walden) was an organic chemist who emigrated after the revolution to Germany and from 1919 headed the Chemical Institute of Rostock University. Vladimir Ipatieff (1857–1952) was a unique specialist on catalytic reactions at high temperatures and studied the nature of the separation of metals under hydrogenation pressure. Later, he played an important role in the creation of the Soviet chemical warfare industry, as will be discussed presently. However, in 1930, he refused to return to the Soviet Union and eventually moved to the United States.[15] Aleksei Krylov (1863–1945) was called "an encyclopedist of naval arts and sciences: he was a mathematician, a shipbuilding engineer and theoretician, an artillery expert, and a historian of science."[16] Academician Aleksei Lyapunov (1857–1918) was known for his works on probability theory.[17] Academician Pyotr Lazarev (1878–1942), a physicist and biophysicist (he worked mainly in molecular physics and photochemistry) developed a theory of oceanic currents and the change in the earth's climate over geological periods.[18]

But this does not mean that the academy always elected the most qualified Russian scientists. In 1880, the most distinguished chemist of the time, the author of the Periodic Law of atomic weights, Dmitrii Mendeleev

(1834–1907), was not elected to the academy.[19] In 1893, the academy voted against the full membership of another scientist, mathematical crystallographer Yevgenii Fedorov. His theoretical models of the structure of crystals were confirmed later by X-ray studies. In 1901, Fedorov was elected as an "adjunct" member, but in 1905 he resigned from the academy because, as he stated at that time, the academy was a hindrance to modern organization of scientific work.[20] Furthermore, before the February Revolution, the academy did not accept scientists of Jewish origin.

After the outbreak of World War I, the role of the academy as coordinator of scientific research became extremely important. In spring 1915, the General Assembly of the Academy unanimously decided to create the Commission for the Study of Natural-Productive Forces (KEPS), to be headed by Academician Vladimir Vernadsky (1863–1934), a mineralogist, crystallographer and geochemist, one of the most independent-minded Russian, and later Soviet, academicians.[21] The special War Chemical Committee chaired by Academician Ipatieff was another example. The committee had five branches: explosives, poison gases, incendiaries and flame throwers, gas masks, and acids. Academicians Aleksei Kurnakov and Pavel Valden took part in its work as permanent members.[22]

According to the academy statutes adopted in 1836, which stayed in effect until 1917, the president of the academy was selected from the elite of Russian society and then appointed by the tsar.[23] The last appointed president, Great Prince Konstantin Romanov (a member of Tsar Nicholas II's family), died on June 11, 1915.[24] After the February Revolution of 1917, the Provisional Government approved changes in the governing statutes proposed by the academicians regarding the election of their president. On May 15, 1917, for the first time in the history of the Imperial Academy of Sciences,[25] the academicians voted for their president. Aleksandr Karpinsky, a prominent geologist, was elected unanimously (twenty-seven academicians attended this meeting). The botanist Ivan Borodin was appointed acting vice president.[26] On July 11, 1917, at Meeting No. 39 of the Provisional Government, the Imperial Academy was renamed the Russian Academy.

During the final years of the tsarist regime, the academy did not support the conservative politics of the government, seeing all too clearly the incompetence of the government, especially in the areas of science, technology, and the economy. P. Vannovsky, minister of people's education, was in charge of supervising the day-to-day affairs of the academy, with his decisions being approved by the tsar. When politically sensitive matters were involved, Nicholas II simply ordered Vannovsky to ignore the academicians' opinion. The most scandalous situation occurred after the election of the famous writer and opponent to the regime, Maxim Gorky (his real name was

Aleksei Peshkov) as honorary academician. On February 25, 1902, Nicholas II ordered that this "mistake" be corrected and on March 11, 1902, the official magazine *Pravitel'stvennyi Vestnik* [Governmental Bulletin] published a note that the academy had canceled the election of Gorky. The minister did not even bother to inform the academy of this publication.[27] Only on March 29, 1917, after the February Revolution, did the official *Vestnik Vremennogo Pravitelstva* [Bulletin of the Provisional Government] announce: "The Literature Branch [of the academy] has confirmed the writer A. M. Peshkov's (M. Gorky) Honorary Academician membership."[28] The article was signed by the permanent secretary of the Academy of Sciences, Ordinary Academician Sergei Oldenburg. Later, the Orientalist Oldenburg (1863–1934) played one of the key roles during the Sovietization of the academy, trying to save the remnants of the academy's independence.[29]

The academy supported the Provisional Government completely, but, unfortunately, it was weak and indecisive. On July 21, the government was reshuffled, and Aleksandr Kerensky, minister of war and navy, became its chairman. Permanent Secretary Oldenburg was appointed minister of people's education, and the geochemist academician Vernadsky became deputy minister. He continued to serve as deputy minister after Oldenburg's resignation on August 31.[30]

Most academicians regarded the Bolshevik takeover on November 7, 1917, as a national catastrophe.[31] Discussions about the political situation in the country were held at two emergency meetings, on November 18 and 21, 1917. At the second meeting, a strong anti–Bolshevik resolution was adopted. Only the chairman of the chemical committee, Lieutenant General Vladimir Ipatieff, was against the resolution.

But Academician Vernadsky went further, participating in an attempt to continue the work of the Provisional Government underground, after most of its members had been arrested.[32] On November 19, the Bolshevik newspaper *Pravda* [The Truth] published an order of the Military-Revolutionary Committee (VRK)[33] to arrest members of the underground government. Vernadsky was on the list. The VRK was established by the Bolshevik-dominated Petrograd (named Leningrad after 1924) Soviet on October 12, 1917, and was the engine of the Bolshevik takeover. From October 29, 1917, on, it affiliated itself with the All-Russian Central Executive Committee (VTsIK), the beginnings of the Soviet government. Usually the VRK is considered the predecessor of the first Soviet secret service, the All-Russian Extraordinary Commission, or VCheKa. Three days later, the academy voted to send Vernadsky "to the Southern part of the country because of his bad health . . . " The same day, he was able to leave Petrograd for the Ukraine and his life was saved.[34] In the Ukraine, Vernadsky managed to escape the terrors of the Bolshevik/White Russian Civil War and in March 1921, returned to Moscow. He was detained soon after, in July 1921.[35]

At the last emergency academy meeting, on December 22, 1917, it became evident that the new regime would not subsidize the academy if it did not recognize the authority of the Sovnarkom. In January 1918, President Karpinsky began negotiations with the commissar of education, Anatolii Lunacharsky. Financial support for academicians and the future goals of the academy under the new government were discussed. The Commissariat of Education (Narkompros) wanted the academy to turn immediately to the problems of industry. Finally, a kind of compromise was achieved—the academy received financial support, and a special commission developed a plan for the study of natural resources and the creation of physical chemistry and applied chemistry institutes.

Despite the Bolsheviks' promises of financial support, the economic situation for the academy became desperate in 1918, the first year of the Civil War. From 1918 to 1919, nine Petrograd academicians died from hunger or dystrophy. Among them were botanist Andrei Famintsyn and zoologist and embryologist Vladimir Zalensky. Zoologist Dmitrii Anuchin (1843–1923) and botanist and plant physiologist Vladimir Palladin died soon after. Only botanist Ivan Borodin, zoologist Nikolai Nasonov (1855–1939), and Ivan Pavlov lived to witness the replacement of the old academy members with new Soviet academicians and the transition of the academy into a huge structure of research institutes under Communist Party control.

In 1919, things got a little better. Academician Ipatieff recalled:

> At length in 1919 the members of the Academy of Sciences were given a monthly ration of forty pounds of bread, two pounds of buckwheat, two pounds of sugar, and one pound of some kind of vegetable oil or butter. Only Academy members were so treated. A month or so later the government gave all registered scientists monthly rations, a "scientist" being defined as one who had published scientific articles . . . The scientists were divided into groups, and for two years each group came for its rations on days announced in advance. The more well-to-do scientists carried away their rations on sleds in the winter and in little carts in the summer; others used their backs. These rations undoubtedly saved the lives of many talented men . . . [36]

Due to Lenin's special decree dated January 24, 1921, the famous academician Ivan Pavlov and his colleagues were able to continue their physiological research during the Civil War.[37] The decree ordered establishment of "a special committee" to be chaired by Maxim Gorky, who would be given "the broad powers to direct this committee to create as soon as possible the most favorable conditions for safeguarding the scientific work of Academician Pavlov and his collaborates."[38]

Also, the special Commission to Improve Living Conditions of Scientists (KUBU), chaired by Honorary Academician Gorky, was organized in December 1919.[39] In November 1921, it became the Central Commission, or the TseKUBU. Ipatieff gives details:

> Later, the scientists were divided into five groups, the fifth including only the few who had international reputations, the classifying being done by the so-called KUBU. Financial assistance was based on the same classification . . . Being in the fifth group, I received seventy "gold" rubles [$35] a month, while the monthly pay of the first group was about ten "gold" rubles [$5] . . . Besides this, special buildings were reserved for scientists at various health resorts and the KUBU decided which scientists were to go to them.[40]

Moreover, the government supported Vernadsky's reports about the necessity of research institutes within the academy and the plan he developed for these institutes in 1916–1917.[41] In 1918, the Physical Chemistry Institute and the Institute for the Study of Platinum and Other Valuable Metals were the first newly organized research centers. In 1920, ten new members were elected to the academy.[42] Among them was the young physicist Abram Ioffe, the first Jew to become an academician. In 1921, Vernadsky established three institutes—Medical Biology, Physical Technology, and Radium—in Petrograd.[43] By 1922, fundamental research was the domain of the academy, while applied, industrial, and technical research became concentrated in the institutes and laboratories of a separate institution, the newly created (1918) Scientific Technology Section of the VSNKh (NTO).[44] By 1925, there were sixty-two institutions within the academy, including six research institutes, two independent laboratories, eight museums, thirty-five commissions and committees, and so forth.[45]

However, the new regime would not accept Vernadsky's guiding principle that science should be subsidized but not controlled by the government. In 1917, he wrote:

> The organization of scientific work should be granted to a free creative scientific society of Russian scientists, which cannot and must not be regulated by the state. Bureaucratic rules are not for science. Government support of scientific work, and not government organization of science should be the goal.[46]

The same academicians repeated to the Sovnarkom in 1918:

Only science and scientists should have the right and obligation to discover and develop the best forms of organization of scientific work within the country and of its interrelationships with government, which would result in a free growth of the former and support provided by the latter.[47]

This was definitely contrary to the Bolsheviks' idea of the role of science in their new communism. The new term, "Communist science," appeared in the mass media:

One should consider Communist science to be only another form of collective work, and not magic acts in inaccessible temples, which lead to [a creation of] a sinecure, the development of a class psychology of priests, and to conscious or conscientious charlatanism.[48]

THE TACTICAL CENTER CASE

During investigation, do not try to find materials and proofs that the accused [person] had acted or campaigned against the Soviets. The first question[s] you should ask him, must be: to which class does he belong, what is his [social] origin, level of education, or profession. These questions should determine the fate of the accused. This is the essence of the Red Terror.

—Martyn Latsis, member of the VCheKa Collegium,
in the magazine *Krasnyi Terror [Red Terror]*[49]

On December 20, 1917, the VCheKa was established under the Soviet Council of Commissars.[50] Its goal was "to combat counterrevolution and sabotage." Felix Dzerzhinsky (1877–1926), a Polish nobleman by origin and a fanatic Bolshevik, was appointed its chairman.[51] Dzerzhinsky, a founder of the Social Democratic Parties of Lithuania and Poland, was elected a member of the Bolshevik Central Committee in 1906. Ironically, he gave a speech criticizing Stalin at a joint meeting of the Central Committee and the Central Control Commission, and his vociferous disagreements with Stalin during the years 1925–1926 caused him to have a heart attack that led to his death in 1926.

In January 1919, the Special Department was created to combat counterrevolution and espionage in the Red Army. In February 1919, a special Secret Department (SO) was formed to combat counterrevolutionaries within the

The original (from December 1920) VCheKa-KGB building at Lubyanka (Dzerzhinsky) Square (before rebuilding), 1926. (Postcard from Rashit Yangirov Archive [Moscow])

middle class (the "petit bourgeoisie"), the intelligentsia, and among priests.[52] Later, in January 1921, it became a part of the Secret Operational Directorate (SOU). Then, in September 1919, the Economical Department (EKO) was formed to combat counterrevolutionary acts and sabotage in industry. Finally, in December 1920, the Foreign Department (INO), in charge of foreign intelligence, was created as a division of the Secret Department. The SOU and EKO and their successors became the main secret security structures that developed control over Soviet science. The INO and its successors harbored secret scientific institutions that will be described in Chapter 2. In 1922, the VCheKa was renamed the State Political Directorate (GPU).

According to the materials from the archive of a former OGPU/NKVD agent named Pavlovsky, the VCheKa/GPU financed its existence with bribes and smuggling and from confiscations during searches and arrests. This blatant criminality created a climate of corruption that has permeated the security service from its birth up to the present day. Special commissions for combating smuggling and bribery were used not only for their stated purpose but also to establish "green lines" for smuggled goods and bribes. Each secret agent was allowed to smuggle up to 200 gold rubles' worth of goods into the country. In 1921, the VCheKa Administrative-Organizational Department (OAU) was put in charge of coordinating all financial activity (among other duties). This department supervised cinemas, restaurants, and show business in Moscow and Petrograd and ran its own chain of shops, which sold the belongings of arrested or executed persons. It also had branches abroad, such as a Soviet cinema in Berlin.[53]

At the beginning of 1920, the plenipotentiary of the VCheKa Special Department (OO),[54] Yakov Agranov,[55] fabricated the first political show trial against the allegedly anti-Soviet Tactical Center group. Even though the task of the OO was to combat counterrevolution and spies in the Red Army, this show trial involved many scientists. In January 1920, the OO was headed by Dzerzhinsky himself, with Ivan Pavlunovsky (1888–1937) as deputy head. There were four "plenipotentiaries" within it, Vyacheslav Menzhinsky, Artur Artuzov (1891–1937), Karl Lander (1883–1937), and Yakov Agranov. The future NKVD commissar Genrikh Yagoda was in charge of administration; V. Gerson was the OO secretary.

During the preparation of the Tactical Center trial, principles and methods used in many future cases were developed. In February 1920, the VCheKa arrested a group of alleged counterrevolutionaries, two of whom, Professors Nikolai Vinogradsky and Sergei Kotlyarevsky, soon began to cooperate with Agranov's team of investigators. They gave detailed testimonies against their imprisoned colleagues and even acted as stool pigeons.[56] From August 16 through 20, 1920, the Supreme Revolutionary Tribunal, chaired by VCheKa deputy chairman Ivan Ksenofontov, heard the Tactical Center case in the hall of the Polytechnic Museum. The first Soviet general prosecutor, Nikolai Krylenko,[57] claimed in his opening remarks: "During this court session we will deal with the trial of history against the activity of Russian intelligentsia."[58]

According to Krylenko and the official VCheKa version,[59] the Tactical Center was a secret political organization that had been established in February 1919 and consisted of three clandestine groups: the Council of Men in Public Life (SOD), headed by Dmitrii Shchepkin and Sergei Leontiev; the National Center, headed by Nikolai Shchepkin and Sergei Trubetskoi; and the Union for the Regeneration of Russia, led by a historian, Sergei Melgunov. All the leaders had been professors and prominent politicians before the Bolshevik coup. Supposedly, the National Center was an underground military organization planning a military coup in Moscow. In fact, the VCheKa had only intercepted one letter from two liberal politicians, Myakotin and Fedotov, to one of the White movement leaders, General Anton Denikin, appealing for him to change his "policy in the agrarian, Jewish [i.e., to stop Jewish pogroms administered by the soldiers of

Denikin's army] and national questions."[60] The Petrograd branch of the National Center was also accused of contacts with the British spy Paul Dukes, a former assistant conductor of the Mariinsky (now Kirov) Theater who worked for British intelligence in Russia in 1918–1919. According to the VCheKa version, Dukes helped to finance the National Center's groups in Moscow and Petrograd.[61] Nothing of this sort is mentioned in Duke's memoirs.

Before the trial, the VCheKa Special Department arrested 1,000 alleged members of the Tactical Center and investigated the case. The newspapers published a list of sixty-seven executed members of the National Center, including two of its leaders, Nikolai Shchepkin and the Moscow school-teacher (gymnasium) Aleksandr Alfyorov, and Alfyorov's wife, Aleksandra, also a teacher. Before being shot, Aleksandra Alfyorova managed to smuggle a letter written in prison to her pupils:[62]

> Dear girls!
> My fate has been decided. I have the last request to you: continue to study as well as you did when I was alive. The Motherland will need your knowledge, never forget this. I wish you well and to have an honest and interesting life.
>
> A. Alfyorova.

The Revolutionary Tribunal pronounced the Tactical Center guilty of plotting the overthrow of the Soviet state with a view to establish a military dictatorship under Admiral Aleksandr Kolchak, the former Arctic explorer who was leading the White forces in Siberia.[63] However, Prosecutor Krylenko did not produce any proof that the center in fact existed. There was no program or membership lists, nor any coordinated plan of action. He demanded the death sentence for twenty-four defendants, including the geneticist Nikolai Koltsov, whose trial notes are discussed in Chapter 4. Leontiev, Dmitrii Shchepkin, Trubetskoi, and Melgunov were sentenced to death, for contact with the British spy Dukes, among other things.

Aleksandra Tolstaya, the youngest of the writer Leo Tolstoy's daughters, who was also among the arrested, showed amazing self-composure during the trial and managed to get the best of Krylenko on at least one occasion, which she vividly described in her memoir:

> "Citizen Tolstoi," Krylenko asked me, "what was your role in the Tactical Center?"
> "My role," I answered in a loud voice, "my role consisted in heating the samovar for the members of the Tactical Center."

"And serving tea?"
"Yes, and serving tea."
"That was the only part you had in the business?"
"Yes."[64]

The audience laughed and the prosecutor was ruffled. Tolstaya was imprisoned for a few months in a Moscow monastery that had been turned into a concentration camp; she later emigrated to the United States, where she organized the Tolstoy Fund to help Russian immigrants.

To punish some of the defendants, Krylenko invented what became later known as "*sharashki,*" special institutions where imprisoned professionals worked according to their specialty: "Steiman, because of his profound legal knowledge, as well as Stempkovsky, because of his same knowledge in agriculture, should be put in a camp for two years, where they should be used as professionals according to the Regulations in the concentration camps."[65] However, Krylenko suggested releasing the prominent economist Nikolai Kondratiev. Later, in 1930, Kondratiev was arrested as an alleged leader of the other OGPU-invented Labor Peasant Party and sentenced in 1932 to eight years' imprisonment. On September 17, 1938, he was resentenced to death and was shot immediately after the trial.[66]

But in 1920 the grip of the Bolsheviks was not yet complete. Tolstaya recalled that on the last day of the trial, after Krylenko demanded the death sentence for five of the defendants, Leon Trotsky, then commissar of defense, suddenly appeared at the trial and spoke in favor of one of these defendants.[67] It became known that on Lenin's personal intervention, to whom many prominent and influential people appealed, the case against the center was closed.[68] For the five defendants, the death sentence was instantly commuted to ten years' imprisonment. The others were sentenced to various terms, and some were pardoned. Later, many of the defendants emigrated or were exiled abroad.

AN APPEAL WITHOUT AN ANSWER

My Lord, it has become so hard for any decent person to live in your Socialist Paradise.

—Academician Ivan Pavlov, letter to one of
the Bolshevik leaders, Nikolai Bukharin[69]

After the end of the Tactical Center affair in 1921, Yakov Agranov fabricated a second case, claiming a "counterrevolution plot" by the nonexistent Petrograd Armed Organization (PBO). This became known as the Tagantsev case.[70] A VCheKa Presidium report, "On the plot against the Soviet Authorities discovered in Petrograd," dated August 29, 1921, was published in the daily *Petrogradskya Pravda* [Petrograd's Truth] on September 1, 1921.[71] The report included a list of sixty-one participants in the plot and their alleged plan to stage an armed uprising against the Bolsheviks.[72] According to the report, the PBO was in contact with the British, Polish, and Finnish intelligence services. Also, the PBO supposedly planned to kill some of the Bolshevik leaders. The case was under the personal control of Dzerzhinsky and Lenin.[73]

However, at the time of the report's publication, these people had already been shot without a trial. The list included many scientists: geographer Vladimir Tagantsev (1889–1921), chemist Mikhail Tikhvinsky (1868–1921), economist Nikolai Lazarevsky (1868–1921), geologist Viktor Kozlovsky (1883–1921), engineer Grigorii Maksimov (1889–1921), and Nikolai Gumilev (1886–1921), one of the best Russian poets and the former husband of another famous poet, Anna Akhmatova. Others were sailors, former officers, students, white-collar workers, housewives, and nurses. There were representatives of all classes, from peasant to aristocracy, and of all ages, from nineteen to sixty. Copies of the list were posted everywhere in Petrograd.

In fact, there was no PBO "plot." More than 200 persons were arrested by the VCheKa that summer of 1921.[74] Agranov used Vladimir Tagantsev, who was among the arrested, to create the case. Professor Tagantsev was secretary of the Academy Sapropelic Society (sapropel is the substance on the bottom of lakes). A special Academy Sapropelic Station was located at the former Tagantsev family country estate. There Tagantsev was arrested with his wife, and their children were put in an orphanage.[75] In vain, Tagantsev's father, the famous criminologist, academician, and former senator, Nikolai Tagantsev (1889–1923), and Mrs. Anna Kad'yan[76] appealed to Vladimir Lenin asking for the release of Vladimir Tagantsev.[77] Both knew Lenin and his parents personally. But Lenin trusted Dzerzhinsky more than his own friends. On June 19, Lenin received Dzerzhinsky's description of Vladimir Tagantsev:

> Tagantsev Vl[adimir]. Nik[olaevich]. . . . is an active member of the right-ist terrorist organization "The Union for the Revival of Russia" which is connected with and organizes sailors from [the fortress] Kronstadt who live now in Finland. As an experiment, it blew up the monument to Volodarsky. He is an uncompromising and dangerous enemy of the Soviet regime. The case is very extensive and will not be finished soon.[78]

Moisei Volodarsky (1891–1918, a pseudonym of Goldstein), chairman of the Petrograd Committee, was assassinated by the Left Socialist revolutionary Sergeev in June 1918.[79] Knowing that Vladimir Tagantsev had already been shot, Lenin answered Mrs. Kad'yan: "The accusations against him are so serious and the evidence so convincing that it is impossible to release him now."[80]

Although the details of the case are still unknown, it is apparent that Tagantsev in fact was in contact with Russian immigrants in Finland, especially the survivors of the Kronstadt uprising against the Bolsheviks in March 1921.[81] Kronstadt was a strategic island fortress and naval base in the Gulf of Finland about twenty miles west of Petrograd. Its garrison played an active and important role in the Bolshevik Revolution in 1917 and later in the Civil War. But in March 1921, the sailors of the fortress rose up against the regime with the slogan "Soviets Without Communists."[82] They demanded the restoration of political freedom, the release of arrested Socialists, and elections. They had a deep hatred for the VCheKa: "The power of the police and the gendarme monarchy passed into the hands of the Communist usurpers, who, instead of giving the people freedom, instilled in them the constant fear of falling into the torture chambers of the Cheka, which in their horrors far exceed the gendarme administration of the tsarist regime," wrote the rebels' newspaper.[83] On March 16, about 50,000 Red Army troops and volunteers under the command of General Mikhail Tukhachevsky crossed the open ice and attacked the fortress, which was defended by 15,000 sailors and soldiers. After two days of fierce fighting, the fortress was in Bolshevik hands again. The captured Kronstadters filled the jails and dungeons of Petrograd. "Months later they were still being shot in small batches, a senseless and criminal agony," witnessed a contemporary.[84] Later, on June 11, 1937, Deputy Commissar of Defense Marshal Tukhachevsky and a group of the highest-level Red Army commanders were charged with treason. The next day, they were tried in a closed military court and shot.[85]

The Petrograd office of the VCheKa had its informants among the immigrants, who lived in the barracks of the fortress Ino. This fortress had been given to Finland in 1918 (now it is the town of Privetinskoe, near St. Petersburg). The informants became aware of Tagantsev's and several of his friends' contacts with the immigrants.[86] At first Tagantsev refused to answer Agranov's questions. After he had spent forty-five days in terrible conditions, Agranov offered him a compromise: If Tagantsev disclosed all members of his organization, he would guarantee fair treatment and judgment of all arrested. If Tagantsev refused, all persons, whether guilty or innocent, would be shot. After three hours of hesitation, Tagantsev accepted the proposal, and on July 28, 1921, the agreement was put in writing. Tagantsev promised to give detailed testimony about the PBO and its members "to lighten the fate of the members of our process." Agranov promised a fair open trial and no death penalty for any arrested person.

The events that followed showed that the agreement was simply a Chekist trick. Agranov immediately received Commissar Dzerzhinsky's approval to finish the Tagantsev case.[87] After Tagantsev's following two-day interrogation, additional mass arrests began in Petrograd on July 31.

The Russian Physical Chemistry Society tried to save the arrested chemists Mikhail Tikhvinsky, Aleksandr Gorbov, and Boris Byzov. In a letter to Lenin, the society characterized the arrested chemists as "outstanding specialists in the most important branches of chemistry and chemical technology."[88] They asked for "an urgent interrogation and the release of the arrested." Only Byzov was helped by the letter. He escaped death but was condemned to two years' forced labor. Lenin was extremely irritated by the letter. On September 3, 1921 (i.e., after Tikhvinsky had already been shot), he wrote a note on the letter: "To Comrade Gorbunov [Lenin's secretary and later permanent secretary of the Academy of Sciences]: Send an inquiry to the VCheKa. Tikhvinsky was not arrested 'accidentally': Chemistry and the counterrevolution do not exclude each other."[89] After the personal intercession of Maxim Gorky, Gorbov was also released. As a result of an appeal by the geologist and paleontologist Nikolai Yakovlev to Lenin, the three geologists V. Yavorsky, N. Pogrebov, and P. Butov were released.[90]

All the others were shot between August 24 and 29 near Ivanovskaya Station, not far from Petrograd. The description of the execution given in an official publication in 1922 reminds one of the work of the Nazi Einsatzgruppen:

> The arrested were brought during the night before daybreak. They were forced to dig a pit. When the pit was half-done, [the Chekists] ordered the arrested to take off their clothes. The arrested started to scream for help. A group of the doomed was pushed into the pit and [the Chekists] began shooting. The rest of the arrested were forced to step down on the top of corpses and were killed the same way. After this the pit, in which still living wounded victims groaned, was covered with earth.[91]

The VCheKa's action was undertaken to terrify the Russian population, especially the intelligentsia. But the result was the opposite. According to Academician Vernadsky, the published list of names of the victims "had a shocking effect and produced not a feeling of fear, but of hatred and contempt" against the Bolshevik regime.[92] Academy president Aleksandr Karpinsky, who had a reputation for loyalty to the Bolsheviks, sent Lenin a bitter letter in which he openly protested against the regime. He never again confronted the authorities so strongly as in the letter dated November 21, 1921:

> Dear Vladimir Il'ich:
>
> . . . I . . . can see how these events [arrests and executions] provoked a deep moral indignation because of their unjustified cruelty which was so poorly motivated and is harmful to our country and real international interests. The execution of scientists, . . . for instance, Prof. Lazarevsky or Prof. Tikhvinsky, who, according to the opinion of his colleagues, was not involved in any political activity, caused an irretrievable blow not only to his relatives, but to his numerous former and current pupils. Therefore, it creates inevitably hatred to the current regime, under which a group of persons not controlled by the highest state authorities can decide the fate of many citizens, extremely important for the state, without any elementary guarantees of justice. The majority of people understand that the only goal of the events was to terrify [citizens]. But you, with your life experience, know that such kind of a terror does not lead to this goal. On the contrary, giving a [human] life no value, it [the terror] can result in such events which will shake our already wretched, suffering country again and again.
>
> The whole world sees you as the Head of the modern Russian State, and you know better than I which measures should be taken to protect your name and the state from new threatening troubles.
>
> Yours sincerely respectful and completely devoted,
Academician A. Karpinsky,
President of the Russian Academy of Sciences.[93]

Lenin did not answer the letter. The original has Lenin's note: "To Comrade Gorbunov: Put this into the archive."[94] The terror continued. More people were arrested, mainly accused of being connected with the British and French secret services.[95] In autumn 1921, twenty-five more people were shot as members of the PBO "plot."[96] On December 21, 1921, the Sovnarkom issued a special Resolution on Political Control in which the GPU was put in charge of secretly registering all former noblemen, industrialists, merchants, priests, and potentially anti-Soviet representatives of the intelligentsia.[97]

After the Tagantsev case, at the beginning of 1922, Lenin concluded that it was necessary to send to exile "the writers and professors who are helping the counterrevolution."[98] The deportation was under the control of the

Special Bureau in Charge of Administrative Exile of Anti-Soviet Elements and Intelligentsia. Created in November 1922 within the Secret Operational Directorate of the GPU, it existed for approximately four months[99] and was headed by the specialist on intelligentsia, Yakov Agranov. Georgii Prokofiev, whose name we will encounter again in the Vavilov case (Chapter 4), was appointed deputy chairman of this bureau. A special Commission of the Politburo, headed by Dzerzhinsky's deputy Iosif Unshlikht, approved lists of names created by the VCheKa.

In July–August 1922, the GPU prepared the first list of names for the Politburo meetings. At first the lists of names were scrutinized by the special Commission of the Bolshevik (Communist) Party Central Committee.[100] On August 18, 1922, Unshlikht reported personally to Lenin:

> According to your order, I'm sending you the lists of names of the intelligentsia in Moscow, Peter [i.e., Petrograd], and the Ukraine, approved by the Politburo. The operation was conducted in Moscow and Peter from the 16th to 17th, and in the Ukraine, from the 17th to 18th, respectively. Today the Moscow public was informed about the deportation abroad and **they were notified in advance** that the unauthorized return to the RSFSR [Russian Federation] would be punished by being shot to death . . . I'll send you the information about the deportation daily. (Bold in original)[101]

On August 31, 1922, the lists were published in *Pravda* under the title "The First Notification in Advance."[102] The short article pronounced: "On the decision of the State Political Directorate (GPU), the most active counterrevolutionary elements among professors, doctors, agronomists, and writers were sent to exile to the northern regions. A part of them have been deported abroad." In November 1922, the deportation of more than 300 scientists, philosophers, and writers from Russia started. Among them there were historian Sergei Melgunov, condemned at the Tactical Center trial, and the famous philosopher Semyon Frank, an uncle of the biophysicist Gleb Frank, whom we will meet in the following chapters. Many of those expelled were sent abroad against their will.[103]

CLASS SELECTION

After Tagantsev's case, the academy was left to rest in peace for a while. The new regime was more concerned with the situation at the universities. The political activity of students had been a constant problem of the tsarist regime. Now the Bolsheviks were facing the same problem. They needed professors loyal to the regime in order to create a new type of intelligentsia through the education of students from the worker and peasant classes only.

Historically, universities in Russia had been organized later than the academy: The first was Moscow University, established in 1755; in 1914, there were ten universities in Russia. Like the academy, they were imperial institutions, which meant that they were managed by the Ministry of Education, and appointments of the administration were approved by the tsar. This was changed after the Revolution of 1905. As a result of the revolution, on October 17, 1905, Tsar Nicholas II signed the imperial manifesto proclaiming Russia to be a constitutional monarchy. At a special conference, the new minister of education, Count Ivan Tolstoi, together with a group of university professors, reformed the University Statute and higher education on the whole.[104] Now rectors were to be elected by the faculty councils (although the elected rectors would still be confirmed by the tsar). Also, police and troops could not enter the grounds of the universities without informing the rectors.

But in February 1911, after the police stormed Moscow University, everything changed. The newly appointed minister of education, Lev Kasso, dismissed the rector, his assistant, and his deputy. One-third of the professors and junior faculty members (131 in all, including 44 percent of the professors and lecturers in natural sciences) resigned immediately.[105] Academician Vernadsky and future academicians Pyotr Lazarev and Aleksandr Vinogradov were among them. Many of those who resigned went to private schools and research institutions. Nikolai Koltsov, for instance, became a professor at Shanyavsky University, formerly known as Moscow City People's University, which had been organized and funded by the Polish count and successful industrialist General Alfons Shanyavsky. The university accepted sixteen-year-old males and females of any religion and without any restriction or previous diploma. The right-wing nationalist newspapers called it "Jewish University" or "a network of Polish sedition in Moscow, the heart of Russia." The university had two main departments: the Scientific-Popular Department, which was a high school, and the Department of Natural Sciences, History, and Philosophy, which provided university education. Besides that, there were several separate courses: for preschool education, library work, home education, and cooperation. In 1912, there were 3,600 students.[106]

Koltsov began teaching there in 1906. In 1917, he married a former Shanyavsky University student, Maria Sadovnikova.[107] I will describe the tragic end of the both in Chapter 4. Koltsov also taught at the Advanced Courses for Women (also known as Moscow Women's University). He opened research laboratories in both institutions. Both universities were independent and existed on private donations and students' admission fees. Koltsov and many other professors were invited back to Moscow University in March 1917, after the Provisional Government granted universities independent status. In addition, Koltsov became the director of the Institute of Experimental Biology, also created through private donations and opened after the February Revolution. This institute and the Physical Institute (later the Institute of Biological Physics and then Institute of Physics and Biophysics), which was opened in January 1917 under the directorship of Academician Pyotr Lazarev, were organized by the Society of Moscow Scientific Institute (OMNI). OMNI was established in 1912 as an independent privately funded institution and was not controlled by the government. However, after November 1917, all private institutions, including universities and institutes, were nationalized by the Bolshevik regime.

The Bolsheviks were determined to bring independent-minded professors such as Koltsov under control even more than the academicians in Petrograd (Koltsov was a corresponding member of the academy because he lived in Moscow). In 1919, Lenin formulated the official Party policy toward scientists and intellectuals: "The intellectual forces of the workers and peasants are growing and gaining strength in the struggle to overthrow the bourgeoisie and its henchmen, the intellectual lackeys of capital, who imagine they are the brains of the nation. Actually, they are not brains, but shit."[108]

Besides arrests and show trials, another method began to be used to control science and the universities: Members of the Bolshevik Party, frequently of low professional level, were assigned in high numbers to the universities and colleges with the idea that they would replace the old professors. In 1921, Academician Vernadsky wrote about this situation to his son, Georgii (known as George in the United States), who emigrated in 1920, first going to Prague and then, in 1927, to the United States:

Everything is spoiled and getting worse, but no one can do anything about it. Recently there was a Congress of [University] Rectors, Deans and Workers of the High School. As usual, it was a false [meeting]. . . . The number of bureaucrats, Communists, and . . . "red" Professors is almost twice as high as those who had been elected. Everywhere the minority and majority are broken up along this line . . . The new project is insane and without a future: bureaucrats and Communists are introduced into the faculties and councils, and they do not have even any right at the offices of the Commissariat! . . . There were student riots in Moscow because of this. They were quickly suppressed: the leaders were beaten up at the CheKa, then all students were dismissed and shortly after that sent to their homes, and everybody became calm.[109]

At the beginning of 1922, Lenin became seriously ill (he had progressive syphilis) and started to work from the hospital in Gorki, a small town near Moscow (after Lenin's death, renamed Gorki Leninskie), later the location of Trofim Lysenko's headquarters and his "experimental" station. In April 1922, Stalin replaced Lenin as general secretary of the Bolshevik Party. Despite Lenin's illness, he continued to organize the control of science and the intelligentsia. Now it was also the turn of professional scientific meetings, unions, and publications.

In May–July 1922, on the basis of notes written by Commissar of Health Nikolai Semashko, the Politburo discussed the possibility of organizing the first Doctors' Plot case. Lenin sent Semashko's notes to Stalin with a request to show them *strictly secretly* (Lenin's words!) to Dzerzhinsky and the Politburo members.[110] Semashko was very concerned about the system of regional doctors, which had existed in Russia since the late nineteenth century, viewing it as a threat to centralization. This issue was discussed at the All-Russian Congress of Doctors in May 1922, whose members voted in favor of the local systems, considering that much more progressive than the central system proposed by Semashko. However, the Politburo did not take action against the doctors at this time.

In his letter to Dzerzhinsky regarding measures against the intelligentsia (dated May 19, 1922), Lenin was especially irritated by economists:

... The third issue of the Petrograd journal *Economist*, published by the 11th branch of the Russian Technical Society, has on its cover a list of names of the [editorial] board . . . All of them are evident counterrevolutionaries, helpers to Entente [i.e., Western Allies],[111] its servants and spies, who corrupt our students. It is necessary to organize measures against them, to capture these "military spies" constantly, and to deport them abroad systematically.[112]

Lenin hated economists and economy as a science because he was determined to replace the traditional economy, based primarily on the works of Adam Smith, with the Marxist centralized planned economy, which, as we know now, failed completely after seventy years of Communist power. Even before the Bolshevik Revolution, Lenin used humiliating terms for the economists: "On the whole, professors-economists are only scientific shop-assistants of the class of capitalists, and professors of philosophy are scientific shop-assistants of the theologies."[113]

As a result of Lenin's requests to Dzerzhinsky, in June 1922 the Politburo adopted the following recently declassified resolution introducing strong GPU/OGPU censorship of all intellectual activity in the Soviet Union:

Draft Resolution

To guarantee the order in VU [High School, i.e., universities and colleges] institutions, it is necessary to establish a commission consisting of representatives of the Glavprofobr [Main Directorate of Professional Education] and the GPU (Yakovleva[114] and Unshlikht) to work on the following questions:

> filtration of students for the next academic year;
> establishing of strong restrictions for acceptance of students of non-proletarian origin;
> establishing of political loyalty certificates for students that are not sent by professional Party organizations and are paying fees for education.

The same Commission should introduce rules for meetings and unions of students and professors, which should restrict the autonomous status of the VUZ (i.e., the university or college).

No Meeting or All-Russian Congress of specialists (medical doctors, agronomists, engineers, lawyers, etc.) should be allowed without GPU authorization . . .

Beginning from June 10, the GPU should register once again all scientific, religious, academic, and other societies and unions through the Narkomvnudel [Commissariat of Inner Affairs or NKVD].[115] New societies cannot be created without the appropriate registration by the GPU. All unregistered societies must be considered illegal and immediately disbanded.

The VTsSPS [All-Russian Council of Trade Unions] should not allow the creation and/or function of any union of specialists besides professional unions, and the existent sections within unions should be reorganized with the involvement of the GPU. The VTsSPS can issue permits for the creation of new sections of specialists only after receiving GPU permission.

The VTsSPS Presidium should give the GPU a [legal] right to use administrative exile for three years and the deportation abroad for all persons whose presence in the territory of the Soviet Republic is dangerous for revolutionary order.

Together with the GPU, the Politotdel [Political Department] of the Gosizdat [State Publishing Company] should check all periodicals published by private societies, sections of specialists within Trade Unions, and by different Narkomats (Narkomzem [Commissariat of Agriculture], Narkompros [Commissariat of Education], etc.) The publications which do not correspond to the line of Soviet politics must be closed (the *Journal of Pirogov Society* [the Society of Medical Doctors], etc.).[116]

This draft was based on a report to Dzerzhinsky by Yakov Agranov, dated June 1, 1922.[117] The draft was accepted at the Politburo meeting on June 8, 1922.[118] A special GPU commission began to control the acceptance of students by the universities and colleges.[119] A social-class-based selection of students had already been introduced by the Sovnarkom decree signed by Lenin and published on August 6, 1918.[120] The decree instructed the Commissariat of Education (Narkompros) that priority should be given to students from the proletariat and poor peasantry, who were to be assured of receiving stipends. The OGPU restricted the number of students with "non-proletarian" backgrounds (children from the intelligentsia class). For acceptance, students had to have a special certificate of their political loyalty to the regime provided by the GPU.[121] Additionally, any student organization had to be approved by the administration of the institution and registered at the local NKVD.[122] The famous academician Ivan Pavlov was among the very few scientists who protested against the restrictive admission policies.[123]

*I remember my mother's own stories about how the selection worked in 1927–1928. She applied for admission to the medical departments of two Moscow universities of the time. At the first she was rejected after the first exam on "political science," which, in fact, was a kind of interrogation about her background, family, and political opinions by Party functionaries. She was not accepted because of her "bourgeois" background: My grandfather, Georgii Luppo, was an agricultural scientist who organized and directed a small museum at the Moscow Society of Agriculture. So my mother went dressed up as a peasant girl to the same "exam" at the second institute and pretended that she had just arrived from a distant provincial place. This time she was accepted.**

The resolution introduced the censorship of all professional scientific journals and books, and the GPU took charge of enforcing this censorship. That same June, the Main Directorate on the Literature and Publishing Houses (Glavlit) was created. Its duty was "a preliminary study of all works prepared for publication or distribution, manuscripts or printed materials, periodicals and non-periodical materials, photos, drawings, maps, etc."[124] Later on, the selling of used books and published materials was also taken under control. Lists of forbidden publications were sent periodically to every bookstore, and any used book could not be sold without the special stamp of a GPU/NKVD/MGB/KGB inspector.[125] This system existed until the end of the 1980s.

---

*Italicized inserts throughout the book are Vadim Birstein's reflections.

With direction from Lenin, on September 5, 1922, Dzerzhinsky wrote his deputy, Unshlikht, the following instruction:

> The information [on the intelligentsia] should be collected by all our [the GPU] departments and transferred to the Department on Intelligentsia. An investigation file should be established on each intellectual, and each group and subgroup [of intelligentsia] should be investigated in all capacities by the competent comrades among whom our Department [on Intelligentsia] will distribute the study of these groups. . . . You should remember that the goal of our Department should be not only sending them to exile, but also . . . demoralizing [the intelligentsia] and promoting those persons who are ready to support the Soviet government without any reservation.[126]

This instruction is key to understanding many events that followed in the history of Soviet science, some of which I will discuss in other chapters. Apparently, this instruction was also the first step in the creation of the special Secret Political Department within the Main Directorate of State Security (GUGB) in the NKVD, and after many reorganizations, in 1949 it became the Fifth MGB Directorate and ended up as the notorious Fifth KGB Directorate, the office that in the 1970s–1980s was in charge of combating Soviet dissidents such as Academician Andrei Sakharov, physicist Yurii Orlov, biologist Sergei Kovalev, and many other scientists.[127]

THE LAST STRAW

In February 1923, Lenin's health completely deteriorated. According to the memoirs of Vyacheslav Molotov, a Bolshevik colleague of Lenin and then Stalin, Lenin "asked Stalin to bring him some poison. Stalin didn't bring it, even though he had promised. He said later that Lenin probably bore a grudge towards him because of this. 'Even if you insist, I cannot do it,' Stalin said. The problem was discussed at the Politburo."[128] Molotov did not deny the possibility that later, in 1953, Stalin was poisoned. To the question of an interviewer, "Was Stalin poisoned?" Molotov answered: "Possibly. But who is there to prove it now?"[129] Poisons definitely played a serious role in Soviet history. The most mysterious of all poisoning cases will be discussed in Chapter 2.

In March 1923, a stroke immobilized Lenin, and in January 1924, he died. The attitude of the Party leaders toward scientists and intellectuals became even worse. Stalin, the new Bolshevik and Soviet leader, did not tolerate any independent thinking. On the surface, the signs were encouraging. In 1925, there were forty-two full members, 268 corresponding members (103 Soviet and 165 foreign), and 924 researchers and technicians within the academy system.[130] But by 1930, state control of the Academy of Sciences was largely complete.[131] On June 18, 1927, the Council of People's Commissars approved the new Academy Statute, doubling the number of academic positions from forty-three to eighty-five (which allowed the Party to restrict the influence of scientists within the academy), and introduced new rules for the voting system.[132] On April 19, 1928, *Pravda* announced forty-two positions for the next elections. On July 21, 1928, the daily paper *Izvestiya* published a list of 205 candidates created by the Central Committee and the academy.[133]

The Politburo created a special commission to supervise the election. All regional Party organizations received the Central Committee "Top Secret" instruction "On a secret intervention in the campaign on the Academy of Sciences election" with two lists of names: List No. 1 with names of those candidates who should be supported by Party members and List No. 2 with those who should not be elected.[134] The first list contained the names of ten Party functionaries, plus thirty-two well-known scientists such as Nikolai Vavilov, Dmitrii Pryanishnikov, and Nikolai Zelinsky (all three are discussed in Chapter 4). The second list contained the names of those whom the highest Party authorities did not recommend, such as Nikolai Koltsov, Leon Orbeli, and Lev (or Leo) Berg.

The results of voting in the Academy Physical, Mathematical, and Humanitarian Divisions on December 5 and 12, 1928, were depressing. Candidates from List No. 1 were elected without regard to whether they were scientists or Party functionaries. Academician Ivan Pavlov, who never accepted Bolshevik control, once again tried to protest in his letter to the Sovnarkom on December 19, 1928: "We, representatives of science, are now regarded as incompetent in our own area and we are ordered to elect as Academy members people, whom we, with clear conscience, can't regard as scientists. Without exaggeration one can say that the old intelligentsia is partly exterminated, and partly becomes corrupt."[135]

However, there was a hint of a revolt in the results of voting: Four candidates from List No. 2 (microbiologist Georgii Nadson, historian Matvei Lyubavsky, philologist Mikhail M. Pokrovsky, and Sinologist Vasilii Alekseev) were also elected. Later, two of these academicians were arrested: Lyubavsky in 1930, and Nadson in 1937. Nadson, former director of the Academy Institute of Microbiology, was condemned to death on April 14, 1939, as a "member of a counter-revolutionary organization" and was shot the next day.[136] But the voting of the academy general meeting on January 12, 1929, was in fact an open revolt—academicians did not approve the election of three Communist candidates from List No. 1: philosopher Abram Deborin (1881–1963), historian Nikolai Lukin (1885–1940), and a historian of literature, Vladimir Friche (1870–1929). Academicians did not dare to vote against Bolshevik leader Nikolai Bukharin, but they did not approve Bukharin's cousin Lukin, a poorly known scientist.

Academy President Karpinsky was afraid of the Party's retaliation. He ordered an urgent meeting of the Presidium. Ivan Pavlov, Ivan Borodin, and some others tried in vain at the next extraordinary academy general meeting on January 17, 1929, to persuade that the reelection procedure would be a violation of the Academy Statute.[137] Twenty-eight of forty-one academicians present voted for the reelection.

On February 17, 1929, the next academy general meeting repeated the reelection of the three candidates. Only fifty-four of seventy-nine academicians were present.[138] The majority of those absent claimed to be ill. The newly elected "Party" academicians were included in the electorate. All three Communist candidates were elected. Soon after that, an Old Bolshevik, Gleb Krzhizhanovsky, was appointed vice president of the academy.[139] This was the end. The academy had been destroyed. At the time, the government level of the academy was supervised by the Central Executive Scientific Committee. The next year (1930), Anatolii Lunacharsky, the chairman of this committee and one of the main Bolshevik critics of the old academy, was elected an academy member.[140] In 1931, a new body named the Commission to Assist Scientists was created under the Council of Commissars, to be presided over by one of the main Bolshevik functionaries, Valerian Kuibyshev.[141] It included the same Lunacharsky; a Marxist historian and the new permanent secretary of the academy, Vyacheslav Volgin;[142] Academician Aleksei Bach, a Bolshevik supporter; and two real academicians, the physicist Ioffe and the geneticist Nikolai Vavilov.[143] To make control of the academy even easier, in 1934 the Academy Presidium and its main institutions were transferred from Leningrad to Moscow.

CLEANSING

After the election in February 1929, the academy consisted of 82 full and 263 corresponding members, and the number of scientists and technicians working in its institutions reached 1,000.[144] For the first time in the history of the academy, ten high-ranking Party functionaries, including Nikolai Bukharin, were elected full members of the academy as a result of intense government pressure.[145] The next year, Bukharin became a member of the Academy Presidium, and in 1932, he was appointed director of the Academy Institute of the History of Natural Sciences and Technology.[146] This institute had been created in 1921 as the Commission on the History of Science (later "of Knowledge"), with Academician Vernadsky as its chair. On October 3, 1930, Bukharin was elected the new chair. On February 28, 1932, after Bukharin made a request to the Presidium, the academy general meeting decided to turn the commission into an institute.

The biochemist Aleksei Bach, who directed the Institute of Biochemistry, also became an academician. He had spent thirty-two years abroad, returning to Russia after the Bolshevik coup and becoming an enthusiastic supporter of the new regime. From 1927, he headed the All-Union Association of Workers of Science and Technique to Assist the Socialist Construction (VARNITSO), which played the crucial role in the Sovietization of Russian Science and the academy.[147] VARNITSO was created in Moscow in response to the independent position of the Academy of Sciences, which at the time was still located in Leningrad. Besides Bach, Boris Zbarsky, Aleksandr Oparin, and Andrei Vyshinsky (all discussed in this book) were the main organizers of VARNITSO and its work. In 1928, Bach was a public prosecutor in the Shakhty (Mines) case in Moscow, the first show trial since 1922. This trial against fifty-three representatives of the technical intelligentsia described as wreckers, spies, and saboteurs ended the NEP period and ushered in a series of "wreckers' trials."[148] Eleven of the accused were sentenced to death. An American journalist, Eugene Lyons, witnessed the trial and described its horrifying details. The OGPU used every opportunity to destroy the defendants. Even a son of one of the accused demanded death for his father. A letter from the twelve- or thirteen-year-old Kyrill, published in that morning's *Pravda*, was read into the record: "I denounce my father [Andrei Kolodoob] as a whole-hearted traitor and an enemy of the working class. I demand for him the severest penalty. I reject him and the name he bears. Hereafter, I shall no longer call myself Kolodoob but Shakhtin."[149]

In addition, the new Academy Statute of 1929 introduced a new powerful loyalty test to the regime: Paragraph 19, which declared that a member of the academy "could be deprived his Academic title for acts of sabotage against the USSR," was included.[150] The wise academician Vernadsky clearly saw what would happen next. In a secret letter to his son George dated July 16, 1929, Vernadsky wrote:

> The [Communist] Party is a world of intrigues and arbitrariness. And on the Party's orders a decent person acts indecently, justified by the [Party] discipline. . . . Every appointment of a Communist means that a Communist group and a Communist outside organ become extremely influential . . . A greedy and hungry Communist crowd finds a new way to make a

profit: to take positions [in science]. Secret information on political and ideological disloyalty are sent [to the supervisors] . . . and a cleansing starts.

. . . Until now the Academy of Sciences was not touched by this process. Now it comes . . . [151]

At the end of June 1929, a special state commission chaired by a member of the Control Commission of the Bolshevik Party Central Committee, Yurii Figatner (1889–1937), started work on "cleansing" the staff of the Academy of Sciences of its "class enemies." The commission included a scientist, P. Nikiforov (director of the Seismology Institute), a representative of guards at the buildings of the academy, three workers from the main Leningrad factories, two other persons, and two OGPU representatives.[152] The commission cleansed 781 employees from the academy, mostly specialists in humanitarian sciences, based on their noble or bourgeois origin. It became clear a couple of months later that for most of these people, losing their job was only the first step toward their arrest by the OGPU.

In October 1929, the chairman of the OGPU Special Commission on Cleansing, one of the most ruthless Chekists, Yakov Peters, and another member of the presidium of the same commission, Yakov Agranov, the intelligentsia specialist, arrived in Leningrad to help the Figatner Commission.[153] On November 5, the Politburo established a new investigation commission consisting of Figatner, the Russian chief prosecutor Nikolai Krylenko, Peters, and Agranov.[154] This commission found many documents, including the Acts of Abdications of Nicholas II and his brother Mikhail, stored at the Academy Library, which, according to the commission, should have been in the State Central Archive instead. The commission used the existence of these purely historical documents to fabricate a "monarchist plot." Arrests of academy members and former academy employees started. In sum, 115 historians were arrested in Leningrad and Moscow, including four outstanding academicians, Sergei Platonov (1860–1933), Eugenii Tarle (1875–1955), Nikolai Likhachev, and Matvei Lyubavsky (1860–1936), as members of the nonexistent "All-People's Union of Struggle for the Restoration of Free Russia." The arrests were sanctioned by the Politburo.[155] Of these academicians, Likhachev was not only an outstanding specialist in Russian history and art history but also a collector of artwork and books. He gave his collection of icons to the Russian Museum in Leningrad and his collection of manuscripts and antique books to the Academy of Sciences. The last collection became the basis of the Academy Institute of Books, Documents, and Writing.

The Academy of Sciences did not wait for the end of the OGPU investigation. In vain, then president Vladimir Karpinsky, eighty-two years old, tried to persuade his colleagues at the academy general meeting on February 2, 1931, that "there should be freedom of opinions [within the Academy] and of opportunities to express them publicly."[156] The frightened academicians and newly elected Party elite academicians voted unanimously to expel Platonov, Tarle, Likhachev, and Lyubavsky from the academy.

According to the OGPU Academicians case, since 1927 Academician Platonov allegedly headed a plot of monarchists who planned a foreign intervention to restore the monarchy in Russia. Supposedly, Platonov would have been appointed prime minister and Academician Tarle foreign minister in the new monarchist Russian government. During the investigation, Platonov was kept in a separate room.[157] An OGPU interrogator, Andrei Mosevich, forced him to write false testimony.[158] Also, Platonov was interrogated by the deputy head, Sergei Zhupakhin, and the head, Mikhail Stepanov, of OGPU's Secret Department of the Leningrad Branch. The investigators had a highly professional scientific consultant—the just elected (among other Party functionaries) academician Mikhail N. Pokrovsky. He cooperated with the OGPU on the instruction of OGPU Chairman Menzhinsky.[159]

On February 10, 1931, the OGPU three-member court (troika) convicted thirty alleged plotters to five to ten years of hard labor in labor camps. This state security three-member court existed from 1918 until July 10, 1934, when it was replaced by the Special Board of the MGB (OSO) under the NKVD.[160] On May 10, 1931, forty more arrested people were condemned to ten years of hard labor in the dreaded Solovki Camp, and six members of the "plot" were condemned to death and shot. Finally, on August 8, 1931, the OGPU Collegium convicted twenty scientists to five years' labor in Pechora labor camps and fifteen other scientists, including Platonov, Tarle, Likhachev, and Lyubavsky, to five years of exile in different provincial towns. Platonov died in 1933 while he was in exile in Samara. Lyubavsky died in exile in Ufa, Bashkiria, in 1936. Tarle was much luckier: He was released in 1932 after the intervention of the Soviet minister of culture and Academician Anatolii Lunacharsky.[161] He returned to Leningrad and continued his successful career. Like Tarle, Likhachev returned to Leningrad, where he died in 1936.

Party authorities were content with the OGPU results. The chairman of the Politburo's Commission on Assistance to the Work of the Academy of Sciences (in fact, "assistance" meant Party control),[162] Avel Yenukidze wrote: "We achieved our goal. Messieurs Academicians [Yenukidze ironically used the word "Messieurs" to show that academicians were not "comrades"] have understood that they cannot make fools of us. Now they will be released [from imprisonment] step by step, but we will not allow them to conduct anti-Soviet action any more." What Yenukidze could not predict was that in a few years, in 1937–1940, he, Figatner, and all the OGPU/KGB functionaries who took part in the organization of the Academicians case (Peters, Agranov, Zhupakhin, and Stepanov), would be arrested by the NKVD to be shot or to die in imprisonment.

After 1930, expulsion from the academy became a routine procedure. In 1938, Karpinsky's successor as president, the botanist Vladimir Komarov reviewed a list of twenty-one members selected for expulsion at the academy general meeting. After a number of rhetorical questions—"Does anybody want to say something?" "Does anybody want an explanation?" and "Is everything clear?"—Komarov stated: "Let me conclude that the General Meeting joins the opinion of the Presidium [of the academy] and confirms the expulsion of these persons."[163] The paragraph allowing the expulsion of an academy member because of his "unpatriotic" or "anti-Soviet" behavior was kept in all later versions of the statutes of the Soviet Academy.[164] People like Dmitrii Pryanishnikov, Pyotr Kapitsa, and Andrei Sakharov, who publicly raised their voices in defense of their arrested colleagues, were rare among the majority of compliant scientists who followed Party orders in exchange for their elite position in Soviet society.

THE PARTY KNOWS BETTER

However, the selection of students and scientists according to class origin and loyalty tests was not enough for the regime and its leader, Josef Stalin. Once in power, Stalin decided that he and the Party would decide which scientific theory was correct. The most odious example is the Lysenko affair, which started in 1927. Lysenko's rise to power has been well documented, especially in recently published monographs for which authors had access to newly released archival materials.[165] Here I will discuss in general Lysenko's ideas and some events that will clarify the mechanisms the Party set in play to control science.

For some reason, biology was the scientific discipline most vulnerable to Party interference. Perhaps this was because, as Party functionaries seem to have thought, biology did not appear to require as much training or specialized skill as physics. Supposedly, it was enough to have read Friedrich Engels's *Dialectics of Nature* and to follow Marx and Engels's acceptance of Darwin's theory of natural selection to understand the problems of biology. In any case, Marxist philosophers such as Mark Mitin, who specialized in criticizing the "bourgeois" philosophy,[166] and Isaak Prezent, who became Lysenko's chief ideologist, or even Stalin himself, who had no biology background, had no problem with participating in "discussions" on genetics and evolution with professionals.[167] Although some similar "discussions" were organized in chemistry and physics in the late 1940s, they were stopped because of the military value of these sciences and their importance for the A-bomb and H-bomb projects.

Lysenkoism, a body of "dialectic Marxist" beliefs almost magical in nature, was created by Trofim Lysenko, a largely uneducated agronomist.[168] Soviet leaders appreciated Lysenko's denial of the existence of genes as the basis of inheritance (and chromosomes where the genes are located) and of species as the basis of evolution. It was much easier for them to understand Lysenko's simplified anthropomorphic ideas that individuals within a species "help" each other (i.e., there is no competition within the same species) and inherit changes from environmental conditions than it was for them to deal with the complicated knowledge of "bourgeois" geneticists and evolutionists.

I was very surprised to see the interpretation of Lysenkoism's roots in the recent book *What Have We Learned About Science and Technology from the Russian Experience?* by the well-known historian of Soviet science Loren R. Graham.[169] According to Graham, the end of Lysenkoism in 1964–1965 ushered in the acceptance of Western-style genetics. This is simply not true. A profound understanding of genetics and evolution existed in Russian biology before Lysenko came to power in the middle of the 1930s and, possibly, even before American biologists recognized the importance of genetics. In Chapter 4, I will describe briefly the fate of the brilliant Russian biologist Nikolai Koltsov, one of the creators of modern evolutionary theory and genetics. His influence on Russian biology in the 1920s to the early 1930s was profound.[170] Also, it is a simplification to mention Lysenko's peasant background as his main advantage in comparison with other biologists.[171] Many anti-Lysenkoist geneticists of the 1930s had a peasant or other low-class background (for instance, Professors Georgii Karpechenko and Mikhail Lobashov, Academician Anton Zhebrak, whom I will mention below).

The phenomenon of Lysenko should be considered not in scientific but in political and sociological terms, with an understanding of Soviet reality in the late 1920s to early 1930s, when Stalin's ideological goal was to create a community of scientists that could be easily manipulated by Soviet leaders. Of the Western biologists, the Russian-born American geneticist Theodosius Dobzhansky (who emigrated to the United States in 1927) understood this better than others.[172] Young Lysenko became known not as an author of scientific publications but as the hero in a long article published in 1927 in the main Communist newspaper *Pravda*.[173]

For ideological reasons, the author of the article, Vitalii Fyodorovich, highlighted Lysenko's peasant background as the basis of his success in science.

By the time of Lysenko's first "discovery" in the late 1920s, the process of the vernalization of plants, which refers to the influence of temperature on the transition from one physiological phase to another, was already a well-established fact. Apparently, Lysenko was not aware of this because he simply did not read scientific literature. The success of vernalization, or, in Lysenko's terminology, "yarovization," was also announced in *Pravda* and other Communist Party newspapers.[174] Standard scientific methods were not followed in any of Lysenko's "experiments," and he considered the statistical analysis of data to be "harmful" for biology. No doubt Lysenko's refusal to use standard scientific methods had a more practical purpose—it made the disproving of his results impossible since he never clearly explained his methods. Step by step, Lysenko's "Marxist-Michurinist genetics" replaced the "bourgeois Weismannist-Morganist-Mendelist theory" of inheritance in the Soviet Union.

Ivan Michurin (1855–1935) was a breeder of apple trees and, in fact, had nothing to do with Lysenko's "Michurinist genetics."[175] However, Lysenko applied the terms "Michurinist genetics" or "Michurinist doctrine" to his own pseudotheories. This term had positive meaning in the Soviet ideological language. Lysenko and his followers applied negative labels to the real geneticists who were their enemies: "the Weismannists, Morganists, and/or Mendelists." By the end of the 1940s, these terms had become almost synonymous with the ideological slur "enemies of the people." The labels stressed the "bourgeois" roots of the real genetics: The German biologist August Weismann (1834–1914) was one of the founders of genetics; the American geneticist and Nobel Prize winner (1933) Thomas H. Morgan (1866–1945) established the chromosome theory of heredity; and the Austrian botanist Gregor Mendel (1843–1884) described the basic laws of inheritance in mathematical terms. The discoveries of these scientists were exactly what the Lysenkoists desperately tried to deny.

In 1945, the famous British evolutionist Julian Huxley and Professor Eric Ashby attended a Lysenko lecture in Moscow and were shocked by what they heard. Lysenko presented his "theory" of fertilization: The best oocyte chooses the best spermatozoon, and everything occurs as a "love-based marriage" during which one cell "eats" another. The inheritance in the first generation depends on the cell that "ate" the other one. When somebody asked Lysenko how to describe the segregation of characters in the second generation (which is the basic law in Mendelian genetics), Lysenko answered: "This is belching." Eleonora Manevich, who translated Lysenko's speech to Huxley and Ashby, recalled that both of them shuddered at the description of sex cells "eating" each other. Huxley hid his discomfort by fussing with his glasses.[176] Later, he paraphrased Lysenko's answer in his book on Soviet genetics: "Segregation is Nature's belching; unassimilated hereditary material is belched out."[177]

Lysenko's understanding of speciation and evolution was more confusing nonsense. His "creative Darwinism" included the following statements:

> Nobody knows what a species is, and everything written in books is not true.

> Environmental conditions are the leading factor of life, and the living form of substances is a result and a derivative [of them], but this does not mean that the living form is the same as the non-living. The mutton meat is formed of hay and grass. The living form is a result of the non-living form . . . the living form appears from non-living form through the living form. The body of a live sheep (i.e. the sheep which is still running) is formed from the mutton meat, but not from grass.[178]

> A species is a species, a qualitatively distinct state of living form of substance.[179]

Please note that these are not poor translations from Russian. In Russian, these statements sound as absurd as they do in English.

Also, according to Lysenko, there is no intraspecies competition, that is, there is no class struggle between members of the same species. On the contrary, all members of the same species "help" each other: "There is not, and cannot be, a class society in any plant or animal species. Therefore, there is not, and cannot be, here class struggle, though it might be called, in biology, intraspecies competition."[180] "In nature the life of any individual is subjected to the interests of its species."[181] "All intraspecies relationships among individuals . . . are directed toward the securing of the existence and thriving of a species and this means, towards the increasing of the number of individuals in a species."[182]

Even more disturbing was his belief that one species could somehow transform itself into another. "The transformation of one species into another occurs at a single leap . . . By means of 'retraining' . . . after two, three, or four years of autumn planting [*Triticus*] *durum* [i.e., hard wheat] turns into [*T.*] *vulgare* [soft wheat], i.e., hard, 28-chromosome wheat turns into various forms of soft, 42-chromosome wheat."[183] Lysenko also believed that wheat can be transformed into rye. According to him, sometimes in wheat plants "small grains of rye plant emerge," and these "small grains" grow into rye grains. Lysenko also explained how a species of bird can turn into another. The molecular biologist and geneticist Valery Soyfer recalled:

In several lectures and speeches, he [Lysenko] announced that warblers had given birth to cuckoos! I heard him say this myself in a lecture at Moscow State University in the spring of 1955. He described how the lazy cuckoo placed its eggs in the nest of a warbler, and the warbler is then compelled by the "law of life of a biological species" to pay for letting the cuckoo take advantage of it by feeding on caterpillars, and as a result of the change in diet, it hatches cuckoos instead of warblers.[184]

The geneticist Dobzhansky, mentioned earlier, compared Lysenko's transformation of *Triticus durum* into *T. vulgare* with the birth of a lion by a domestic cat, and the transformation of wheat into rye with the transformation of a dog into a fox, or vice versa.[185]

In 1934, at the Seventeenth Bolshevik (Communist) Party Congress, Lysenko received the highest recognition of the Party. The commissar of agriculture, Yakov Yakovlev, praised Lysenko in his speech:

Such people as agronomist Lysenko, a practical worker whose vernalization of plants has opened a new chapter in agricultural science, who is now heeded by the entire agricultural world, not only here [in the Soviet Union], but abroad as well . . . These are the people . . . who will be the backbone of the real Bolshevik apparatus, the creation of which is demanded by the Party, by Comrade Stalin.[186]

That same year, Lysenko was elected to the Ukrainian Academy of Sciences and became research supervisor of the Ukrainian Institute of Plant Breeding and Genetics. He was appointed director of this institute two years later. Stalin was so moved by Lysenko's speech at the Second All-Union Congress of Kolkhoz Shockworkers in the Kremlin in February 1935 that he jumped up, clapping, and shouted: "Bravo, Comrade Lysenko, bravo!"[187] Of course, after this the whole hall broke out in applause. Lysenko knew what to say. He proclaimed that only the kolkhoz system of agriculture introduced by Stalin in 1929 was "the one and only scientific guiding principle, which Comrade Stalin teaches us daily."[188]

Lysenko's cynicism and pragmatism become clear in his mention of the kolkhoz system. On November 7, 1928, in the *Pravda* article "A Year of Great Change," Stalin ordered the creation of kolkhozes (collective farms) to replace traditional small, separate farms. Two simultaneous processes were organized: the creation of kolkhozes and the liquidation of the kulaks, who were the most enterprising, educated, and independent-minded peasants. Millions of kulaks and members of their families were sent to the labor camps or exiled to Siberia and Central Asia.[189] In addition, a five-year economic plan was introduced by the government. "Shockworkers" *(udarni-ki)* was the name given to those who claimed that they would fulfill the five-year plan in four years.

Lysenko's absurdity dominated Soviet biology from the mid-1930s until the late 1960s. There were three significant events during the Lysenko period: Stalin's personal championing of Lysenko in February 1935, the election of Lysenko to the Academy of Sciences in 1939 (instead of the brilliant geneticist and evolutionist Nikolai Koltsov), and the August 1948 session of the All-Union Academy of Agricultural Sciences, or Agricultural Academy (VASKhNIL), during which Lysenkoism was accepted as a party line. At the 1939 academy meeting, Lysenko was not alone in becoming a member. Stalin and other party functionaries were "elected" to the academy as "honorary members." Stalin himself was behind the August 1948 session of the Agricultural Academy, which disrupted the development of genetics and evolutionary theory in the Soviet Union for almost thirty years. Stalin looked through the draft of the speech written by Lysenko for the session and made numerous editorial changes beforehand.[190]

Julian Huxley was among those few Western biologists who understood that Lysenkoism was not a science but rather a party ideology: "A political party has imposed its own dogmatic view of what must be correct and incorrect, and so violated the essential spirit of science."[191] Another biologist, Robert Cook, even compared Lysenkoism to religious faith: "Lysenkoism . . . is the only scientific discipline in existence today whose validity depends, not on experiment, but on certification as to purity and truth, in content and concept, by government fiat."[192]

After Lysenko came to power, the career, freedom, and sometimes even the life of a biologist in the Soviet Union depended on his or her decision to accept or reject Lysenkoism.

Some American historians of biology did not understand the profound role of Communist ideology (which included Lysenko's "Michurinist biology") in the professional work of Soviet scientists. For instance, Mark Adams wrote: "I would argue, then, that ideology has played a less significant role than we have tended to assume."[193] Although Adams visited Moscow several times and collected incredibly valuable materials, including priceless interviews with old geneticists, he never worked as a Soviet employee and evidently never understood the whole picture.

Unfortunately, real geneticists at first did not understand the danger Lysenko posed. Academician Nikolai Vavilov, at the time president of the Agricultural Academy, did nothing initially to stop the rising star of "People's Academician" Lysenko. And this had lethal consequences for him (Chapter 4).

Incredibly, very few contemporaries understood the ideological similarity between Stalin's regime and the Nazis in the 1930s. The Russian émigré and satirical poet Aminand Shpolyansky, who wrote under the pseudonym "Don-Aminado," was a rare example:

> In terms of world dimension
> The power of ideas is undefeated:
> There is no change of trains
> Between Narym and Dachau.[194]

Narym was a group of famous Soviet labor camps in the Krasnoyarsk Region in Siberia.[195] Also, to some extent, there is a parallel between Lysenko and the Nazi doctors who experimented on humans. Several of them, like Lysenko, believed in the inheritance of acquired characteristics. Lysenko declared that through "training" at particular temperatures, plants can change their inheritance or even become new species; or that a change in diet can result in the transformation of one animal species into another. The Nazi doctors went even further. One of the most sordid SS doctors in Auschwitz, the University of Münster anatomy professor Johann Paul Kremer, believed in the inheritance of traumatically acquired deformities.[196]

In 1939, Lysenko became a full academician. He had already been president of the Agricultural Academy. He received Stalin's personal attention and represented the Party line in biology. In 1940, his archenemy Nikolai Vavilov was arrested by the NKVD (not without Lysenko's help) and then perished. However, World War II postponed Lysenko's final triumph, which occurred in August 1948. I will describe all these events in Chapter 4.

THE DOCTORS' PLOT CASE, THE ALLILUEVA CASE, AND THE JAC CASE

After World War II, in 1947, Stalin began one of his last campaigns against the intelligentsia, especially those of Jewish origin ("Cosmopolitans without the Motherland" as they were called in the mass media), which ended in 1952–1953 with the arrests of high-ranking physicians, members of the so-called Doctors' Plot, which allegedly aimed to murder Soviet leaders, including Stalin. It is necessary to explain that in the Soviet Union, as in Nazi Germany, Jewish identity meant not religion but ethnic origin (or "race" in Nazi terminology). This critical point has created a lot of misunderstanding in the American public of events during the Holocaust in Europe and of Russian anti-Semitism in general. The Nazi laws against the Jews were racial, not religious.[197] In Nazi Germany, half Jews who had a Jewish father and a non-Jewish German mother (*Mischling* of the first degree) were treated as full-blooded Jews.[198] In the same manner, half Jews with a Jewish family name (father's name) were treated as full-blooded Jews in the Soviet Union. Moreover, the personnel department in any institution usually wanted to know the names of not only parents but also of grandparents of employees.

However, the arrest of Jewish doctors had a long history. The first time "doctor-killers" were discussed was at the trial of the "anti-Soviet organization of the Ukrainian bourgeois nationalists" in Kharkov in March–August 1930. One of the accused supposedly said: "We expressed desires that doctors, using their positions and providing the outstanding Communist patients with a poison or an inoculation of a bacterial culture, would help them to die."[199] The next step was in 1938: As I will describe in Chapter 2, the doctors Dmitrii Pletnev, Lev Levin, and Ignatii Kazakov were accused at the Bukharin trial of killing prominent Soviet writers and party leaders. Levin and Kazakov were shot just after the end of the trial, and Pletnev was shot in 1941.

It appears that the sentencing of Levin and Pletnev was Stalin's personal revenge. In 1932, both refused to sign a false death certificate for Nadezhda Allilueva, Stalin's second wife, who allegedly committed suicide with a gun. However, members of her family and others who knew Nadezhda Allilueva were convinced that Stalin had shot his wife himself, because the bullet entry wound was at the back of Nadezhda's head.[200] The Kremlin Hospital's doctors were ordered to certify her death from appendicitis. Levin and Pletnev refused.[201]

But this was not the end of Nadezhda Allilueva's story and the implication of Stalin's estranged family members and their friends as part of the effort to cleanse society of unsavory elements. The Allilueva case was just beginning. In 1937, Nadezhda's brother, Pavel Alliluev, political commissar of the armed forces, was first put under NKVD surveillance and then dismissed from his post.[202] He "mysteriously" died on December 2, 1938, from poisoning. Stalin kept Nadezhda Allilueva's "History of Illness" and Pavel Alliluev's postmortem report in his private archive at his apartment in the Kremlin.[203]

Before that, on January 20, 1938, Stanislav Redens, the husband of Nadezhda's sister Anna Allilueva, received a new appointment: He became the NKVD commissar of the Kazakh Republic.[204] In fact, this was a form of exile. Before that Redens had worked with NKVD Commissar Genrikh Yagoda and then was one of the deputies of the next commissar, Nikolai Yezhov. In December, 1938, he was recalled to Moscow, and three weeks after Pavel Alliluev's death, on December 22, 1938, was arrested. In vain,

Stalin's sister-in-law Anna tried to see Stalin and persuade him to take pity on Redens: Stalin refused to see her.[205] On January 21, 1940, Redens was condemned to death and was shot in 1941.

At the end of 1937, Stalin dealt with the family of his first wife, Yekaterina Svanidze. Her brother, Aleksandr Svanidze (who was commissar of finance in Georgia), his wife Maria, and their small son (Stalin's nephew) were arrested.[206] Maria's diary was passed to Stalin, and he kept it in his personal archive together with the Alliluevs' documents: The diary contained too many secrets about Stalin's relatives and Stalin himself.[207] Aleksandr Svanidze was shot to death in a labor camp on August 20, 1941, and his wife was shot on March 3, 1942.[208] Their son, Jony Svanidze, was released from a labor camp, where he had spent seventeen years, after Stalin's death.

Finally, the arrest of Anna and Yevgeniya Allilueva (Yevgeniya was Pavel Alliluev's widow) and their friends in December 1947 (Allilueva case) was a "prelude" to the anti-Semitic cases of 1947–1953, which ended up as the Doctors' Plot case. Anna and Yevgeniya were sentenced in 1948 to ten years' imprisonment for espionage and were released in 1954, after Stalin's death.[209] Stalin explained to his daughter Svetlana that "they knew too much and they talked too much. And it helped our enemies."[210] Both spent more than six years in solitary confinement in Vladimir Prison, the main Soviet prison for the most important political convicts (Chapter 3). For reasons of secrecy, some of the prisoners were deprived of their names and kept there under numbers assigned to them after the trials. The arrested high-ranking members of the Soviet nomenklatura were given numbers even during the investigation. Thus, after his arrest in 1938, former NKVD commissar Yezhov was put in the hospital of Sukhanovo Prison as Patient No. 1,[211] and later on, arrested MGB minister Abakumov was kept as No. 15.[212] The same system of numbers instead of names for victims of show trials condemned to imprisonment was introduced by the Soviet MGB "advisers" in Hungary and, possibly, in all of Eastern Europe.[213] After conviction, Yevgeniya Allilueva was kept in Vladimir Prison as No. 22, and Anna, as No. 23 (Documents 1 and 2, Appendix II).

According to prisoner cards in Vladimir Prison (many of which are recorded in Appendix II as numbered documents), the accusations and terms for Yevgeniya and Anna Allilueva in 1948 differed (Documents 1 and 2, Appendix II). Yevgenia was accused of various violations of the dreaded Article 58 of the Russian Criminal Code: treason against the Motherland (Article 58-1a), anti-Soviet propaganda (Article 58-10, pt. 1), and membership in an anti-Soviet organization (Article 58-11); she received ten years' imprisonment. Anna was condemned initially to five years' imprisonment. During this period, the transfer of these prisoners through different cells of

The main yard of Vladimir Prison, the main Soviet prison for important political prisoners from the 1940s to the 1980s. (Photo by Sergei Gitman [Moscow], 1998)

Vladimir Prison was definitely coordinated and frequently happened on the same day (see numbers of corpuses and cells in Documents 1 and 2). However, on December 27, 1952, Anna Allilueva was retried and convicted of five more years for alleged anti-Soviet propaganda (Article 58-10, pt. 2) and membership in an anti-Soviet organization (Article 58-11). Both Alliluevs were released soon after Stalin's death, in late April 1953. When Anna returned to Moscow in 1954, she was mentally ill and suffered from auditory hallucinations.[214] Yevgeniya could not talk for a while. "All the muscles of her mouth had been idle for such a long time while she was in solitary with no one to talk with," recalled her son.[215]

Yevgeniya's second husband, Nikolai Molochnikov, a scientist and a Jew, was also arrested and condemned as a traitor (Article 19-58-1a), anti-Soviet propagandist (58-10, pt. 1), and member of an anti-Soviet organization (58-11) to twenty-five years' imprisonment (Documents 3 and 4, Appendix II).[216] According to Ariadna Balashova, a friend of Yevgeniya who was also arrested, Molochnikov was mercilessly beaten during interrogations.[217] Later he was kept in Vladimir Prison as Number 21 (Document 3, Appendix II). During interrogations, Yevgeniya Allilueva realized that Molochnikov was an NKVD/MGB agent who had for years supplied information on the Alliluev family.[218] After release from prison (the case was abolished on March 20, 1954), Yevgeniya divorced Molochnikov. However, both Anna and Yevgeniya returned from Vladimir with great faith in Stalin. In the meantime, all the events concerning the relatives of Stalin's wives had occurred with his personal involvement, and the whole case was started on his personal order.[219]

On January 6, 1948, Yevgeniya's daughter, Kira Allilueva, an actress at the Moscow Malyi Theater (her stage name was Politkovskaya), was also arrested. She was accused of "providing information about the family's private life to persons working in the American embassy" and convicted to five years of exile in Ivanovo Region, not far from Moscow.[220]

On the top of all this, Iosif Moroz (or Moroz-Morozov), father of Grigory Moroz, Svetlana Stalina's Jewish husband at the time, was also arrested, tried, and condemned as a traitor and member of an anti-Soviet organization (Articles 58-10, pt. 2, and 58-11) to fifteen years' imprisonment (Document 5, Appendix II). Before that, after his son had married Svetlana Stalina, Iosif Moroz became a guest at the Barvikha Governmental Sanatorium.[221] Although he did not have a scientific degree, he used to introduce himself as a professor and an Old Bolshevik. He became acquainted with Molotov's wife, Polina Zhemchuzhina, Academician Lina Stern (director of the Academy Institute of Physiology), and others. In 1945, Stern hired Moroz as her deputy director in charge of the Administrative and Household Equipment Section of the institute. These connections of Moroz with the highest Jewish elite in Soviet society were later used by the MGB for anti-Semite cases.

Moroz spent five years in Vladimir Prison. It is possible that he, like the other members of Stalin's family, was kept under a number (it is not known which prisoners had Nos. 16–20 in Vladimir Prison at that time). In April 1953, Moroz was transferred to Moscow on the personal order of the first deputy head of the MVD, Bogdan Kobulov (Document 5, Appendix II) and, evidently, released soon after that. This order had apparently been given in connection with the secret Presidium (Politburo) decision dated April 3, 1953, to stop the Doctors' Plot case and rehabilitate the arrested.[222]

It is interesting that December 4, 1951, is the last date of the transfer of all Stalin's imprisoned relatives from one cell to another (Documents 1–5, Appendix II). Definitely, something occurred after that date. Yevgeniya Allilueva's friend Ariadna Balashova recalled that Anna Allilueva was moved to Moscow before Stalin's birthday on December 21. It was expected that she and other relatives would be pardoned by him. Nothing of the sort happened.

Lidiya Shatunovskaya, a graduate student of the State Institute of Theater Arts, and her husband, the well-known physicist Lev Tumerman, were among the friends of Yevgeniya Allilueva arrested in December 1947 (Documents 6 and 7, Appendix II). Shatunovskaya was an adopted daughter of Petr Krasikov, an Old Bolshevik, member of the Central Executive Committee, and deputy chairman of the Supreme Court. Her first husband was a high-ranking Soviet administrator. Later, Shatunovskaya described in detail how the Allilueva case quickly became purely anti-Semitic, especially after the murder of the actor and head of the Soviet Jewish Anti-Fascist Committee (JAC) Solomon Mikhoels on January 13, 1948, by MGB agents. The JAC was a Jewish organization created in 1942 by Soviet authorities that coordinated the anti-Fascist activity of Soviet Jews and successfully disseminated in the United States information about the Nazi atrocities against the Jews on the territories occupied by the Nazis.[223] On the personal order of Stalin, Abakumov organized the killing of Mikhoels and an MGB agent, Vladimir Golubov-Potapov, in Minsk, the capital of Belorussia. The operation was under personal supervision of first deputy MGB minister Sergei Ogol'tsov, Belorussian MGB minister Lavrentii Tsanava (one of the main henchmen of Lavrentii Beria, the main organizer of the Soviet state security system), and head of one of the departments within the Second (Counterintelligence) Department, Fyodor Shubnyakov.[224]

"We will exterminate all Jews in prisons and camps," Vladimir Komarov, one of the most brutal MGB investigators, told Shatunovskaya during interrogations in 1948.[225] Being "tall, stout, with round shoulders and a short neck,"[226] Komarov "specialized" in beatings and torturing prisoners during interrogations. In the late 1940s–early 1950s, there were two special rooms for torture in Lubyanka Prison: Room No. 31 (known as the one used for "preliminary torture") and Room No. 4, where Komarov "worked."[227] But the main tortures were in Lefortovo Prison. "My most terrifying memoirs are about the nights when I was forced to sit on a stool in an investigation cell next to Komarov's office," Shatunovskaya recalled. "All night long I heard blows by a [rubber] truncheon and shrieks, shrieks . . . From time to time Komarov rushed into the room, his eyes were red, grasped me from the stool, shook me and roared: "Do you hear? We will treat you the same way!"[228]

Komarov was absolutely cynical and extremely sadistic, but rather clever.[229] However, this high-ranking MGB officer could hardly write. Later, during his own interrogation (Komarov was arrested in 1951 after the arrest of MGB minister Abakumov), Komarov testified:

Abakumov frequently told me that . . . I could not write at all. Honestly, I'd like to confess he was right, since writing testimonies of the arrested persons was a weak point [in our work] because all of us [i.e., MGB investigators] were semiliterate.[230]

Komarov reported the results of the "interrogations" of Shatunovskaya to Stalin directly, and Stalin gave instructions on how to torture the victim. Komarov yelled at Shatunovskaya: "This is Party and State politics! . . . We will destroy the so-called Jewish culture, and all of you, the Zionists, will be exterminated. All of you!" During the late 1940s–early 1950s, anti-Semitism was used by Soviet MGB interrogators not only in Moscow but also in the countries of Eastern Europe. In Prague, another notorious MGB investigator, Mikhail Likhachev (like Komarov, Likhachev was deputy head of the MGB Department for Investigation of Especially Important Cases [OVD]), who was in charge of organizing the infamous Slansky show trial, told one of the arrested high-ranking Communists, Eugen Loebl, during the interrogation in 1949: "You are not a Communist, and you are not a Czechoslovak. You are a dirty Jew, that's what you are. Israel is your only real fatherland, and you have sold out Socialism to your bosses, the Zionist, imperialist leaders of world Jewry. Let me tell you: the time is approaching fast when we'll have to exterminate all your kind."[231]

Both Shatunovskaya and her husband were later put in Vladimir Prison (Documents 6 and 7, Appendix II). They were released after Stalin's death, but Tumerman had scars for the rest of his life from the terrible torture he received during Komarov's interrogations. From her ordeal as a prisoner, Shatunovskaya had a damaged spinal column and arm and leg joints, as well as a weak heart and bad sight. During his imprisonment, another physicist published the results of Tumerman's scientific studies under his own name. After his release, Tumerman worked at the Institute of Molecular Biology until he and his family emigrated to Israel.[232]

Rebecca Levina (1899–1964), an aged economist and corresponding member of the Academy of Sciences, was also arrested in 1948 in connection with the Allilueva case.[233] Before that, in December 1947, her coworker, also an economist (and senior scientist) Isaak Goldstein (1892–1953) had been arrested together with his wife (without a prosecutor's sanction). Unfortunately for him, in the 1920s he had worked with Yevgeniya Allilueva at the Soviet Commercial Office in Berlin. Now he became a key person in the Allilueva case and fell into the hands of Abakumov and his professional torturers.

During the first interrogations, Levina insisted that she was innocent. The investigators, Colonels Georgii Sorokin and Mikhail Likhachev, used sleep deprivation and lengthy "standing" interrogations that usually ended when Levina fainted, fell down, and was then cruelly beaten. The investigators broke the old lady's front teeth. They struck her body with a rubber baton on the buttocks, legs, back, and genitals. After this, Levina finally "confessed."

On May 29, 1948, all of the eleven or twelve members of the Allilueva case were sentenced by a special MGB council (the OSO) to ten to twenty-five years' imprisonment. Two friends of Yevgeniya Allilueva, a married couple named Zaitsev, were convicted as "American spies" to twenty-five years' imprisonment.[234] Before his arrest, Vitalii Zaitsev, a lawyer and employee of the Foreign Ministry, worked at the American Embassy in Moscow. This was enough to consider him a spy. Maryana Zaitseva's mother, Tatyana Fradkina, received "only" ten years.[235] All three of them were put in Vladimir Prison, where they were kept in solitary confinement. Fradkina died on January 7, 1951. Levina got ten years in Vladimir (Document 8, Appendix II). Goldstein was tried by the OSO separately, on October 29, 1949, and condemned to twenty-five years' imprisonment as a spy; as with the others, he was put in Vladimir Prison (Document 9, Appendix II). He died there on October 30, 1953, after Stalin's death, while waiting for a reevaluation of his case.

As for Svetlana Stalina's Jewish husband Grigory Moroz, Stalin simply told Svetlana: "You cannot be Morozov's wife any more. Today he must leave [our apartment in] the Kremlin . . . I know you love him and do not want him to be chained to a prison wheelbarrow [in a mine]."[236] Soon, on Stalin's order, Svetlana married Yurii Zhdanov without divorcing Moroz. Yurii was a son of one of the main Party leaders of the time, Andrei Zhdanov. As I will describe in Chapter 4, in 1948 Yurii Zhdanov played an important role in the Lysenko affair.

In 1953, Levina was transferred from Vladimir Prison to a mental prison hospital in Kazan widely known for its especially harsh regime (later, in the 1960s–1970s, many dissidents were put into this "hospital"). In 1939, NKVD commissar Beria ordered the transfer of Kazan Psychiatric Hospital under NKVD control. On July 13, 1945, NKVD deputy commissar Vasilii Chernyshov issued special regulations for the NKVD doctors and prisoners of the NKVD Kazan Psychiatric Prison Hospital (KTPH). In the 1940s–1950s, convicts were sent to the KTPH for enforced treatment following the decision of a court (criminal cases) or the OSO (political cases).[237] After "treatment" at Kazan Hospital, Levina was released, by that time completely insane.

While Levina was in jail, her husband, professor of pathologic physiology Lev Levin, was persecuted as a Jew. Her son Mikhail (1921–1992), who later became a well-known radio physicist, was arrested even earlier, in 1944.[238] He was a close friend of Academician Sakharov from their university years, and Sakharov mentioned Mikhail Levin in his memoirs with warm feeling: "Only one physicist in all of the USSR came to see me (and twice) in [exile in] Gorky without official permission—my former university classmate, Misha Levin."[239] In 1944, Levin, together with a group of friends, was charged with an attempt on Stalin's life. All of them lived in the center of

The Interior (NKVD) Commissar Lavrentii Beria at a meeting, 1938 (right figure, wearing pince-nez). In the late 1930s to the early 1940s, Laboratory No. 1 was subordinated directly to Beria. (Photo from the Russian State Archive of Cinema and Photo Documents [Moscow])

Moscow in apartment buildings on Arbat Street, right on the auto route Stalin and his guards used to go back and forth from Stalin's dacha in the Moscow suburbs (where Stalin lived) to the Kremlin. During interrogations, Mikhail Levin managed to persuade the NKGB investigators that the accusation was complete nonsense. The attempt was physically impossible: The windows of all the rooms where the accused lived faced closed yards and not Arbat Street, and, therefore, it was not possible to shoot from the windows at passing cars. Naturally, the arrested were not released but sentenced to imprisonment in labor camps. Mikhail Levin spent a year in an institute for imprisoned scientists, the so-called *sharashka*. Although he was released from prison in 1945, Levin was forced to live in Gorky, the future location of Academician Sakharov's exile in the 1980s. Only in 1956 was Levin allowed to return to Moscow, where he started to work at the Academy Radiotechnical Institute.

I was lucky to have been acquainted with Dr. Levin. In the summer of 1980, we rented houses not far from each other at a resort town called Narva in Estonia, where we spent a month with our children. Dr. Levin's encyclopedic knowledge of European and Russian history was amazing. Also, he was a poet.

In 1949, the famous physiologist and academician Lina Stern was arrested in connection with the anti-Semitic "Jewish Anti-Fascist Committee case."[240] In 1925, Stern moved from Switzerland, where she was a professor at Geneva University, to the USSR.[241] From 1925 until her arrest, she was a professor at the Second Moscow Medical Institute and director (from 1929) of the Institute of Physiology. She was the only woman to be a member of both Soviet academies, the Academy of Sciences and the Academy of Medical Sciences. The actor Mikhoels chaired the JAC, and Dr. Stern was a member of this committee.

The JAC case was initiated by reports of MGB minister Abakumov to the Central Committee and Council of Ministers in January and March 1948 about the "testimonies" of Isaak Goldstein and another arrested Jewish prisoner, Zakhar Grinberg, who was a senior scientist at the Academy Institute of World Literature. Dr. Grinberg, a friend of Goldstein, was the closest aide of Solomon Mikhoels in the JAC on matters concerning the Jewish scientific intelligentsia.[242] In his reports, Abakumov claimed that the "testimonies" of Goldstein and Grinberg showed that the JAC was involved in the movement toward Jewish nationalism. These false "testimonies" were signed by Goldstein after torture.[243] Later, on October 2, 1953, Goldstein wrote from Vladimir Prison: "In total, I was beaten eight times . . . Exhausted by these day-and-night interrogations, terrorized by tortures, swearing, and threats, I fell into a deep despair and total moral miasma, and started to incriminate myself and others in very serious crimes."[244]

Abakumov personally visited Lefortovo Prison to witness the "confession" of Goldstein. The final version of the "confession" was prepared by the deputy head of Abakumov's secretariat, Colonel Yakov Broverman, and sent to Stalin. It said that Mikhoels, supposedly on behalf of his American friends, ordered Goldstein to get close to Svetlana Stalina through her Jewish husband, Grigory Moroz.[245]

Finally, in the official MGB document to the Politburo "On the Jewish Anti-Fascist Committee," dated March 26, 1948, the MGB (i.e., Abakumov) accused the JAC of anti-Soviet nationalistic activity and contacts with the American secret services. On November 20, 1948, the Politburo approved a document in which the MGB was ordered to dissolve the JAC. At the end of 1948, the arrests of JAC members started.[246] Stalin appointed a Politburo member, Georgii Malenkov to supervise the JAC case.

Even family members of Soviet leaders were not safe from arrest and investigation. As "honorary academician" and the second in command in the Soviet Union, Vyacheslav Molotov recalled in his memoirs, in 1948 at a Politburo meeting Stalin ordered Molotov to divorce his wife, Polina Zhemchuzhina (1897–1970), a candidate member of the Central Committee. "At the end of 1948 we were divorced. But in 1949, in February [in fact, on January 21] she was arrested," recalled Molotov.[247] Zhemchuzhina was accused of long-standing connection with the Jewish nationalists: She was a Jewess by origin and was considered to be a part of a Jewish plot within the JAC case.

Before her arrest, Zhemchuzhina was expelled from the Party at a Central Committee meeting. At first Molotov abstained, but after several days, on January 20, 1949, he wrote a top-secret note addressed to Stalin: "I hereby declare that after thinking the matter over I now vote in favor of the Central Committee's decision . . . Furthermore, I acknowledge that I was gravely at fault in not restraining in time a person near to me from taking false steps and from dealings with such anti-Soviet nationalists as Mikhoels."[248]

The note did not prevent the punishment of Molotov for his hesitation and abstention: He was dismissed from his post of foreign minister and another "honorary academician," General Prosecutor Andrei Vyshinsky, replaced him.

Besides torture, Zhemchuzhina's investigation involved another sordid tactic. Two male prisoners were forced to "testify" that they had participated in "group sex" with the elderly Bolshevik woman.[249] Finally, Zhemchuzhina was tried by the OSO, condemned to five-year exile, and sent to the distant Kustanai Region in Kazakhstan as "Prisoner No. 12."

Concerning the accusations against Lina Stern, besides her membership in the JAC, there was one more "incriminating" fact about her participation in the "Jewish plot." She was connected with the Allilueva case through Iosif Moroz, the father of Stalin's son-in-law, Grigory, who had already been convicted for alleged Jewish nationalistic "anti-Soviet propaganda." In 1945, Lina Stern had employed Moroz as her deputy director at the Institute of Physiology. At the time of the arrest, Stern was seventy-two years old. At the interrogation, when MGB minister Abakumov roared at her, "You old whore!" she replied: "So that's the way a minister speaks to an Academician."[250]

In late March 1950, the investigation of the JAC case was completed. Grinberg died in prison before that, on December 22, 1949 (officially of a heart attack). The Military Collegium of the USSR Supreme Court heard the case for two months, starting on May 8, 1952. All defendants were accused of nationalistic and espionage activity for the United States. In the courtroom, four prisoners, including Stern, recanted the statements they made during interrogations and denied their guilt.[251] On July 18, 1952, the court convicted fifteen members of the JAC, thirteen men and two women, all of them being famous Jewish writers, poets, actors, translators, and so on, to death. The chair of the collegium, Justice Lieutenant General V. Cheptsov, tried in vain to appeal to Chief Prosecutor General Safonov and then to Georgii Malenkov, insisting on the necessity of returning the case for further investigation.[252] He also sent Solomon Lozovsky's (the main defendant) statement after sentencing with the denial of guilt to Stalin (Lozovsky was an Old Bolshevik, whom Stalin had known personally for many years). No new instructions followed from the Politburo, and the convicts were executed on August 12, 1952. Among them was Boris Shimeliovich (1892–1952), chief doctor of the Botkin Central Clinical Hospital in Moscow. His arrest and conviction was a prelude to the Doctors' Plot case.

Lina Stern was lucky: She received three and a half years' imprisonment and five years of exile to the town of Jambul in Central Asia (Kazakhstan), from which she returned after Stalin's death.[253] It was quite unusual that she had not been expelled from the academy, and because of that, soon she was appointed head of a laboratory at the Academy Institute of Biophysics.

The relatives of the executed were arrested and exiled to Kazakhstan. They were not told that their loved ones were already dead.[254] On the whole, about 110 people were arrested and persecuted in 1948–1952 in connection with the JAC case.[255] During all these years, there was a massive propaganda campaign in the Soviet press against "Cosmopolitans without a Motherland" (as the Jews were called). Step by step, professionals of Jewish origin were cleansed from their jobs.[256]

However, the JAC case sealed the career of Minister Abakumov. As I have already mentioned, on July 12, 1951, Abakumov was arrested. He was accused of "treason against the Motherland committed by a military person" (Article 58-1b of the Russian Criminal Code).[257] Also arrested were the main creators of the JAC case and many other political cases of the late 1940s: head of the OVD Department, Major General Aleksandr Leonov and his deputies, Komarov, Likhachev, and Schwartzman, as well as the head of Abakumov's secretariat, Ivan Chernov and his deputy Broverman. The list of accusations against Abakumov was prepared by the new head of the OVD Department, Mikhail Ryumin (see Chapter 2). Ryumin's main accusation was that Abakumov prohibited him, Ryumin, from interrogating the arrested professor Yakov Etinger about an alleged plot to murder a candidate of the Politburo, Aleksei Shcherbakov, and the intentional placement of Etinger in severe conditions in Lefortovo Prison, where Etinger died without revealing information about the "Jewish plot" of medical doctors.

Dr. Yakov Etinger (1887–1951), professor of the Second Moscow Medical Institute, was arrested on November 18, 1950. He had been singled out before that by MGB investigators. Etinger regularly visited the JAC, where he had read international Jewish periodicals. During an interrogation in 1949, he had been mentioned as one of the leaders of Jewish nationalists in Soviet medicine by the arrested JAC secretary, a Jewish poet named Isaak Fefer: "His [Etinger's] nationalistic views were entirely shared by the Academician B. I. Zbarsky, Professor of the Second Moscow Medical Institute A. B. Topchan, Director of the Clinic of Remedial Nutrition M. I. Pevzner, senior general practitioner of the Soviet Army M. S. Vovsi . . . "[258] In fact, Abram Topchan had numerous positions: chief doctor of the Moscow Gradskaya (City) Hospital, director of the Clinic of Urology, and from 1937, rector of the Second Moscow Medical Institute.[259] As for the last person, Miron Vovsi (1897–1960), he was not only a member of the Medical Academy, chief therapist of the Soviet army, a consultant-therapist of the Kremlin Medical Directorate, and the editor in chief of the journal *Klinicheskaya Meditsina* (Clinical Medicine) but also a cousin of Solomon Mikhoels, who had already been assassinated.[260]

This was the first list of individuals later considered by Ryumin as members of the "Doctors' Plot." Also, the MGB taped "anti-Soviet" conversations of Dr. Etinger with his son and Professor Zbarsky. During interrogations, Etinger was incriminated with "slanderous inventions" about Shcherbakov and a Politburo member, Malenkov. Etinger's wife, Rebekka Viktorova, who was also a doctor (arrested on June 16, 1951), and his stepson (arrested on October 17, 1950) were forced to testify against him. However, Etinger denied all accusations and refused to "confess." On January 5, 1951, he was transferred to Lefortovo Prison, where he was put in a wet cell where cold air was pumped in. After four months of such "treatment," on March 2, 1951, Etinger died. As usual, the prison's death certificate stated that death was caused by a "heart attack."[261]

On March 1, 1952, Rebekka Viktorova was sentenced by the OSO to ten years' imprisonment for "anti-Soviet propaganda" (Article 58-10, pt. I).[262] At first she was put in MVD Prison No. 3 in Novocherkassk, whence she was transferred to Vladimir Prison on February 14, 1953.

Etinger's case allowed Ryumin to finalize a list of sixteen high-ranking doctors of Jewish origin who were allegedly "Jewish nationalists who expressed their discontent with Soviet power and slandered the national policy of the Communist (Bolshevik) Party and the Soviet State." Of course, the list included the above-mentioned Zbarsky, Topchan, Pevzner, Vovsi, and many others. These doctors were doomed, and Ryumin got his chance to play against his superior, Minister Abakumov.

At the same time, based on the false testimony of one of Abakumov's men, Lev Schwartzman (he was arrested on July 13, 1951), the investigation of the "Jewish plot within the MGB" started. Before his arrest, Schwartzman usually worked with Komarov writing falsified transcripts of the interrogated prisoner, whom Komarov forced to sign under torture.[263] As I will describe in Chapter 2, beginning in September 1951, practically all MGB colonels and generals of Jewish extraction were arrested, and officers of the lower ranks were expelled from the MGB. A real MGB doctor-killer, Grigory Mairanovsky, and one of his supervisors, Naum Eitingon, were among the arrested, and a case against "the Jewish Doctor-poisoner" Mairanovsky was under investigation.

During that same September in 1951, Etinger's son was brought back from a Far Eastern labor camp to Lefortovo Prison in Moscow and forced to testify about the existence of the "Doctors' Plot."[264] The rest was a technical problem for Ryumin. The development of events was under Stalin's personal control. In January 1952, he threatened the new MGB minister, Ignatiev, that if he did not "uncover the terrorists, the American agents among the doctors, he would follow Abakumov."[265] Stalin also ordered the arrest of Dr. R. Ryzhikov, deputy director of the Barvikha Governmental Sanatorium, to uncover the "criminal plans" of Dr. Vladimir Vinogradov, senior general practitioner of the Kremlin Medical Directorate. Further, during the interrogations, Likhachev, a former deputy head of the OVD Department, gave testimony in support of Ryumin's version that Abakumov had patronized the plot of Kremlin's Jewish doctors. In September 1952, Minister Ignatiev showed Stalin a statement written by Ryumin stating that investigation materials showed that with a great degree of certainty, Jewish doctors had killed Shcherbakov and Zhdanov. After this, the MGB received Stalin's sanction for arrests of doctors.[266]

From October through December 1952, high-ranking medical professors (many from the Kremlin Hospital) were arrested. On January 13, 1953, fifteen of them were accused in the press of conspiracy. Members of this "Doctors' Plot" supposedly prescribed harmful treatments that had caused the death of such Party leaders as Politburo member Andrei Zhdanov and many generals. Ten of the accused were Jews. The government statement said:

> It has been established that all these killer-doctors, these monsters in human form, tramping the holy banner of science and desecrating the honor

of the man of science, were hired agents of foreign intelligence services. Most of the participants in the terrorist group (M. S. Vovsi, B. B. Kogan, A. I. Feldman, A. M. Grinstein, Ya. G. Etinger, and others) had ties with the international Jewish bourgeois nationalist organization Joint, established by American intelligence services for the alleged purpose of providing material aid to Jews in other countries. The true purpose of this organization is to conduct extensive terrorist and other subversive activities in many countries, including the Soviet Union, under the guidance of American intelligence services. The arrested Vovsi told investigators that he had received instructions "to exterminate the leading cadres of the USSR" from the USA through the Joint organization, via Dr. Shimeliovich [i.e., through the JAC] . . . Other participants in the terrorist group (V. N. Vinogradov, M. B. Kogan, P. I. Yegorov) proved to be longtime agents of the British intelligence service. The investigation will be completed in the near future.[267]

Of these doctors, Boris Kogan (1896–1967) was a professor at the First Moscow Medical Institute and a consultant at the Barvikha Sanatorium of the Central Committee. Dr. Feldman (1880–1960) was a professor-otolaryngologist who headed a department at the Moscow Regional Scientific Research Clinical Institute. From 1936–1952, he was also a consultant at the Kremlin Medical Directorate.[268] Professor-therapist P. Yegorov (1899–?) headed the Kremlin Medical Directorate. All those mentioned in this text, except Vinogradov and Yegorov, were Jews.

Ryumin's team included even Stalin in the list of the supposed future victims of doctor-killers. During new interrogations, Vovsi and Kogan were forced to sign "testimonies" that in July 1952, they agreed to direct killings of Stalin, Beria, and Malenkov.[269] As documents in the former KGB archives demonstrate, the handcuffed and beaten Dr. Vovsi, after the threats by Ryumin and his team that "[w]e'll quarter you, hang you, impale you," "confessed" that he received orders from the "bosses overseas," that is, American Zionists.[270] After the same treatment and Ryumin's threat to torture him with two torches at the same time, Professor Yegorov admitted that he had "disabled" the secretary of the French Communist Party, Maurice Thorez, and had "killed" Georgi Dimitrov, the leader of the Bulgarian Communists, as well as Andrei Zhdanov and Aleksei Shcherbakov, and had damaged the health of many other Soviet and foreign Communist leaders.[271] The minutes of all interrogations were sent directly to Stalin.

In January–February 1953, a new wave of arrests followed. On the whole, thirty-seven were arrested between the end of 1952 and the beginning of

1953 in connection with the Doctors' Plot case.[272] Of those, twenty-eight were doctors, and the others were members of their families. Natalia Rapoport, the daughter of Yakov Rapoport, one of the arrested doctors, recently recalled: "As I found out later, every night [my parents] were waiting for being arrested and visited their rare friends [who had not been arrested yet]. They gave them some money and warm clothes for me. In case of my mother's arrest someone [of these friends] would send me to her to a labor camp . . . "[273]

In early 1953, my family lived in a big apartment building in the downtown area of Moscow. Like most Soviet families, we had a room in a "communal apartment." My grandmother and uncle lived in the next room. Five other families occupied the remaining five rooms of the apartment. At the end of 1952, my grandmother, who was a doctor and a Jew, lost her job. Many other high-ranking doctors lived in our huge apartment building. During that spring, almost each night somebody was arrested. Each night my parents waited for the MGB's knock at our door. The MGB could arrest my father, a biologist and an anti-Lysenkoist, or my grandmother, a doctor. My parents discussed in whispers something that I could not understand at the time: what to do in case of possible deportation.

Many years later I found out the meaning of their night whispers. According to Stalin's plan, after the Doctors' trial and execution of the accused Kremlin doctors, all Jews would be deported from the cities to special labor camps. Stalin's scenario consisted of five "acts."[274] First, sentencing doctors after their full confession. Second, execution by public hanging. Third, Jewish pogroms through the country. Fourth, an appeal by Jewish celebrities to Stalin asking for protection from pogroms and for permission to leave the big cities. Fifth, mass deportation of Jews "at their own request" to Siberian camps.

According to Nikita Khrushchev, the whole scenario was discussed at a meeting of the Central Committee Presidium (i.e., Politburo) in February 1953.[275] Stalin's resolution on the deportation of Soviet Jews to a special separate zone within the USSR was not passed. Stalin fainted and fell to the floor. This was the first indication of his serious health condition. He died two weeks after the meeting.

In the morning, at school, I heard the laughing of my classmates. One of them was a son of our building's superintendent. According to the MGB rules, a superintendent had to attend the arrest of an inhabitant of his (or her) building. Our superintendent's son told my classmates funny stories about the previous night's arrests. Laughing, he used to say to me: "This night one more of your fellows was taken! My mom (the superintendent was a woman) said that it was so funny!" It was not clear if he meant one more Jew, a doctor, or simply an educated person. It was dangerous to belong to the intelligentsia at that time. I can still hear the laughter of my classmates when I recall those days.

Ryumin interrogated doctors personally and supervised their torture. Even his appearance was "horrifying . . . He was very short, and his small-sized, like children's, galoshes stood in the same office. My heart dropped every time when he looked at me," victim Ariadna Balashova later recalled. Additionally, Ryumin created a commission of three medical professors from the Kremlin Hospital (M. A. Sokolov, V. F. Chervakov, and S. A. Gilyarovsky) and deputy head of the MGB Central Clinic (N. N. Kupysheva) that conducted a special investigation of the medical treatment of Zhdanov and other alleged victims of "killer-doctors."[276] The pattern of Vinogradov, Shereshevsky and other doctors' betrayal of Professor Pletnev in 1938, when they testified against Pletnev as official experts (see Chapter 2), was repeated. This time Vinogradov and Shereshevsky themselves were the object of the "investigation" by the MGB-selected commission of "experts."

Despite all efforts, the efficiency of Ryumin's investigation of doctors and the Jews who were former MGB officers was apparently low. Later Ryumin testified:

In September 1952 [MGB Minister] Ignatiev reproached me . . . that our information on the investigation cases looked very weak comparatively with that Abakumov had used to send to the Authorities [i.e., Stalin and the Politburo] . . . Ignatiev stressed many times that if we did not succeed in obtaining the necessary testimonies from the doctors-Jews, both of us would be dismissed and possibly arrested.[277]

However, on November 14, 1952, only Ryumin was dismissed, and Ignatiev was placed personally in charge of the Doctors' Plot case. After sophisticated torture techniques were applied, each one of the doctors confessed to all the fabrications suggested by their interrogators. One can clearly see Professor Pletnev's model of 1938 (Chapter 2) in the Doctors' Plot case. One of the arrested, Professor Vladimir Vasilenko, signed the following "testimony" on November 15, 1952:

The trial on Pletnev's case . . . revealed for me the technique of killing patients by administrating incorrect treatments. From the materials of the case I understood . . . that the doctor could not only damage his patient's health, but also lead the patient to death by cunning methods. I thought about this many times during the years that followed, remembering Pletnev, whom I

personally knew. In July 1948, when I visited the ill Zhdanov [a member of
the Politburo] at his bedside, I unwittingly remembered again Pletnev and
his killings . . . And I decided to kill Zhdanov A. A.[278]

In January 1953, a group of MGB operatives brought "Prisoner No. 12"
Zhemchuzhina from Kazakhstan back to Lubyanka in Moscow. Through
February 1953, she was interrogated every day in connection with the
Doctors' Plot. As Larissa Vasilieva, who had access to Zhemchuzhina's investigation file at the KGB/FSB Archive, writes, "in her files are excerpts from
the interrogations of Doctors Vinogradov, Kogan, Vovsi, who all confirmed
that she was a Jewish nationalist."[279] The last document in the file dated
March 23 is unique; it contains the following phrase: "It is now established
that the statements by Kogan and Vovsi in the case against Zhemchuzhina
were extorted through brutality and beatings."[280] On March 2, interrogations suddenly stopped: Stalin was dying. He died on March 5, 1953, and the
nightmare of the Doctors' Plot case was terminated.

Molotov was restored as foreign minister immediately after Stalin's death,
on March 5, 1953. On March 9, the day of Stalin's funeral and Molotov's
birthday, Khrushchev and Malenkov asked Molotov what he wanted for his
birthday. He wanted his wife back. The next day Zhemchuzhina was summoned to see Beria and her husband. She fainted in Beria's office when she
was told that Stalin had died. Zhemchuzhina was released, and her case was
closed on March 23. Like Allilueva, despite her experience she remained a
staunch Stalinist.[281] So did her husband.[282]

Incidentally, Molotov was not the only Politburo member whose wife was
arrested. The wife of Mikhail Kalinin (1875–1946), Ekaterina, was arrested
much earlier, on October 25, 1938.[283] Kalinin was one of Lenin's first adherents. In 1919, he was elected to the Central Committee, and from 1926 until
his death, he was a Politburo member. From 1938–1946, Kalinin chaired the
Presidium of the Supreme Soviet, meaning that he was formal head of the
Soviet government. But in fact, he was a "decorative" figure and had no
power. During the investigation, which was conducted under the personal
supervision of Beria and Bogdan Kobulov, Ekaterina Kalinina was tortured
in Lefortovo Prison. On April 22, 1939, Kalinina was condemned to fifteen-
year imprisonment in a labor camp as a "Trotskyist." Only on December 14,
1946, did a special decree of the Presidium of the Supreme Soviet order her
release. The decree was signed by the secretary of the Presidium, and not by
Kalinin. For eight more years, Ekaterina Kalinina struggled for official rehabilitation. Finally, she received a document stating that "there was no evidence against her anti-Soviet activities" and that "Kalinina's arrest was an act
of retribution by Beria and Kobulov."

On April 1, 1953, Beria, the new head of state security (now named the MVD),[284] approved the draft resolution of the Presidium (i.e., the Politburo) to release the arrested doctors, and on April 3, 1953, the Presidium adopted this resolution.[285] Many of the arrested were released immediately, but several others remained imprisoned for one more year. They were released in February 1954, following the order of the new MVD minister, Sergei Kruglov. On April 27, 1954, Dr. Etinger's wife was moved from Vladimir Prison to Moscow and released.[286] Although Dr. Vovsi was released after Stalin's death, he still became a victim of the executioners: He died soon of osteosarcoma, which formed in those places of his body that had been beaten the most extensively during interrogations.

Ryumin was arrested on March 17, 1953. The death of Dr. Etinger became a special point of discussion at the Presidium meetings as one of the main accusations against Ryumin during the investigation of his activity.[287] In 1952, Ryumin included the case of Etinger in the list of accusations against Abakumov, and Abakumov was interrogated by Prosecutor Mogichev regarding Etinger's alleged anti-Soviet activity.[288] Now Beria personally supervised the investigation of Ryumin. On March 28, 1953, he told Ryumin: "You will never see me again and I'll never see you again. We will exterminate you."[289] In early July 1954, half a year after the execution of Beria and his cronies and five months before the execution of Abakumov, Ryumin was sentenced to death by the Military Collegium of the USSR Supreme Court. He was shot on July 22, 1954.[290] Schwartzman was tried in 1956 separately from Beria's and Abakumov's other men and condemned to death.[291]

MEMORIES

In the 1950s–1980s, the control of science by the KGB was overwhelming. However, the details of their control over daily life in scientific institutes is not widely known. When I joined the scientific community in the 1960s, I was aware that each institution had a so-called First (or Special) Department with a retired KGB officer as head, in charge of maintaining secrecy and political control.[292] A good example is Sergei Ogol'tsov, who in 1951 for two months became the MGB acting minister. Later he was expelled from the Communist Party and fired from the KGB, but until his retirement, Ogol'tsov was deputy director of security (another name for a head of the First Department) at the top-secret Scientific Research Institute No. 1.[293] Fyodor Popov, a professional MGB/KGB officer who headed the counter-intelligence division that supervised Academician Andrei Sakharov in the 1950s, wrote about the goals of the First Department: "The First (secret)

Department is a structural secret subdivision of an institution or organization whose task is to prepare, register, and give secret documents to those involved [in the secret work] and to control the movement and treatment of these documents."[294]

Possibly, this was the official instruction. But in fact, no manuscript of any scientific paper could be sent to press without a cover document signed by the head of the First Department. These officers had no knowledge or understanding of the scientific matters they guarded. The retired KGB officer Popov even now is convinced that only "some of the theoretical statements of Lysenko were not supported experimentally and did not find industrial application."[295]

In addition, every scientist knew that there were so-called curators of every scientific institution at the KGB headquarters in charge of "supervising" the life of the institutions. I am aware of the mention of KGB "curators" in only one book by a Russian scientist, in the very true and honest memoirs of Professor Aleksandrov.[296] I was one of those who had an opportunity to verify that "curators" exist (usually only a few persons in the administration of the institution knew about these curators). In 1984, my contract with the Academy of Sciences' Koltsov Institute of Developmental Biology in Moscow where I had been working was not renewed. At the First Department of my institute, which was located in an office behind an iron door, the retired KGB officer who worked there told me that "there was an order from the organs" (e.g., the KGB). I was not surprised, since almost all my friends were dissidents or refuseniks. Also, I was involved with Amnesty International, an organization that Soviet officials and the KGB considered "anti-Soviet." Some of my friends were serving terms in labor camps as political prisoners, and I helped their families when I could (which was dangerous during those years).

The "order from the organs" in the metaphoric language of Soviet secret service meant that I would be unemployed and without any opportunity to continue my scientific career (and eventually might be arrested for leading a "parasitic lifestyle," i.e., for having no job). My first scientific book on the genetics of amphibians, which I had already submitted in manuscript form to the printing house of the Moscow State University, was stopped and never published. The manuscript simply disappeared without a trace. My editor told me in a whisper: "They (i.e., the KGB officers) came to the head of the publishing house and demanded your manuscript." In these circumstances, the possibility that my second book would be published was very low, since the documents that were necessary for publishing, according to Soviet rules, had mysteriously disappeared from the file attached to the manuscript. The only weapon I had was to write letters about my unem-

ployment and the problems with my manuscripts to all imaginable branches of power in the former Soviet Union: the KGB, the Central Committee
of the Communist Party, the Academy Presidium, and so on. It is a long
story, and here I want to mention only my experience with the KGB and
the Academy Presidium.

A few days after I had sent my letter to the KGB, I received a phone call.
A polite voice asked me to come to the KGB Office in Charge of Moscow
and the Moscow Region. There, I was greeted by an officer who said that
he was the curator of my institute, and, therefore, my curator. (According to
the current Russian press, the FSB "curators" are still in existence. Their language, when they try to recruit informers, remains the same: "You have to
understand us.")[297] He knew my problems in detail and assured me that the
KGB could not have given any order about my employment. He told me
that although he was in charge of only my institute, he knew that as a
geneticist I would find a job at the Academy Institute of General Genetics.

I followed his recommendation. The first person whom I accidentally ran
across at the Institute of Genetics was the same KGB curator! He was carrying documents from the scientific secretary of the institute to a special
room of the "First Department" behind an iron door. It was evident that he
was determined to look through the documents. He was not happy to see
me because I reminded him that he had told me that he was in charge of
only one institute. Also I was curious about what he was doing with the
documents. I did not get a job in that institute, or in others.

After this, I tried to meet the vice president of the Soviet Academy of
Sciences, Academician Yurii Ovchinnikov, who headed the Academy
Biology and Chemistry Divisions and who had already sent me a letter. I
received it from the Central Committee of the Communist Party, because
Academician Ovchinnikov was also a member of the Central Committee.
The letter claimed that I would receive a job at any institute of the acade-
my if the director of the institute would send a special inquiry for me to
Ovchinnikov himself. The rules of this game were obvious: The KGB cura-
tors of all institutes had already been informed of my existence, and no
director would write such an inquiry. After many phone calls to
Ovchinnikov's secretary, she told me that Yurii Anatol'evich was too busy to
see me and that he had asked her to arrange my appointment with Dr.
Vladimir Sokolov, secretary academician of the Academy Biology Branch.
Biologists who knew details of Academician Sokolov's career referred to
him as "the volleyball player." The Biology Department of Moscow State
University accepted him as a student because he was a talented sportsman.
Later he married a daughter of a Politburo member, and this "family con-
nection" guaranteed him a career at the academy. Ovchinnikov's secretary

told me that the meeting would take place at the Biology Department of Moscow State University.

I arrived at the Biology Department, where I had been a student twenty years before and where my father, a professor of zoology, had worked almost all his life. The speech of Academician Sokolov, who was secretary academician until his death in 1998, as well as the director of the huge Academy Institute of Evolutionary Morphology and Ecology of Animals and the chairman of the Department of Vertebrate Zoology at the Moscow University,[298] was very short. He told me: "Your last name is Birstein [which meant, 'You are a Jew,' because Russian names would sound like Sokolov, Ivanov, Petrov, and so forth]. That is why you must find a job as a merchant."

It was not surprising that Academician Sokolov remembered my last name. In the 1960s, my father was invited to an international congress in England. After a long process of clearance by the Party and KGB officials, he was allowed to go to a zoological congress. He had already boarded the plane to England when suddenly he was called on the radio and asked to exit the plane. While he stood in front of the plane, trying to figure out what had happened, he saw young, handsome Sokolov taking his place on the plane. Evidently, for Party officials, Sokolov, a well-connected party functionary, was more important as a representative of Soviet science than a professional in the field, a nonmember of the Party with a Jewish name.

There was no sense in my continuing the conversation with Sokolov. Academician Sokolov followed Communist Party and KGB orders (do not forget that all appointments at the academy, as well as the results of elections within the academy, were approved by the Central Committee of the Communist Party, and, therefore, by the KGB). I contacted the regional, City of Moscow, and Central Committee Communist Party departments in charge of science, as well as the Russian Federation and Soviet Council deputies.[299] My Russian Federation deputy was president of the Soviet Pedagogical Academy, and the Soviet deputy was rector of Moscow State University. Everybody listened to me attentively. I told them: "The Soviet Constitution guarantees employment to every Soviet citizen according to his or her level of education and degrees. I am an unemployed geneticist, a Candidate of Biological Sciences. I am an example that this guarantee is not fulfilled." All officials replied that they could not help me find any position at Moscow research institutes, at Moscow University, or even at an elementary or secondary school. It seemed that neither the Party nor the Soviet authorities were able to solve my problem.

Finally, I was invited to meet Vladimir Sverchkov, the head of the Academy First Department. When I arrived at the Academy Presidium, two KGB men, typically dressed in plainclothes, were waiting for me and showed me to their boss's office. Outside the office was a poster with photos of the Academy First Department members. I learned from the poster that I was escorted by two KGB colonels, and their boss had the rank of a KGB general. Inside the office, a very impressive looking man with gray hair and good manners tried for forty minutes to persuade me that his department and the KGB had nothing to do with my unemployment and problems of publishing scientific books. His point was simple: within the academy, I had never had access to or worked with secret materials. It was true, my work was not secret and, therefore, I could not release any state secret. Evidently, another KGB department, not the First, was in charge of my problems and the fate of my manuscripts.

From time to time, I received phone calls that possibly came from the other KGB department. A polite voice (not the curator's) invited or, to be precise, ordered me to come to the KGB Office in Charge of Moscow and the Moscow Region. I strongly rejected meetings with the KGB men offered in "safe apartments" or hotels. Each time, different KGB officers met me in the long corridors of one of the Lubyanka buildings. Usually there were two officers: the "bad" one, who threatened me during the meeting, and the "good" one, who pretended to be sympathetic to my problems. They insisted in calling these meetings *besedy,* or "talks," rather than "interrogations," while they named many of my friends during these "talks" and tried to get information from me about them. I knew that this form of meeting gave them an opportunity to record our conversations without my knowledge (according to the law, during interrogations, the interrogator should inform the interrogated person about any recording), and I was very cautious with my answers. The "bad" officer used to mention details of my life that the KGB could only know only if my apartment had been bugged. This was a common KGB tactic: The "organs" know everything.

The end of every "talk" was the same. After having talked to me about my job problems, the officers repeated the following: "You must understand us. You are a talented scientist (our experts evaluated your papers) and you should work at the Academy of Sciences. It is so unfortunate that you are unemployed. If you understand us, you will work at any Moscow Academy institute of your choice. If you don't, you know what happened to some of your friends: They have been arrested." All these meetings of course were designed to get me to collaborate in some way with the KGB in exchange for the opportunity to continue my professional work. My goal was to show them that because of my moral principles, I would not collaborate with them under any circumstances. I responded to their hints by "playing dumb," pretending not to understand what the officers were offering me. I asked them to tell me plainly what they meant by the phrase "You must understand us." My tactic, to force the KGB officer to say something straight, which they never do, worked well. The officers got angry, ordered me to leave the KGB building, and left me alone for a while.

This was not the first time in my life when I consciously refused to work under Soviet structures I considered immoral. Before my graduation in 1966, representatives of the Defense Ministry visited Moscow University and talked to every student who might be useful to the biological warfare institutes. During our years at the university, all of us were trained as specialists in biological warfare and automatically received the rank of junior lieutenant of the medical service and, in principle, could be forced to work at a military institute. The officers who visited the university promised a lot—a high salary and a quick career in military biological science. At that time, sophisticated methods of genetic engineering had just been discovered, and the military desperately needed high-level molecular biologists for the development of new programs on biological warfare.

It was easy to reject the offer of the military. But the next step was more difficult. After my graduation, I was assigned to work at one of the newly created Main Administration of the Microbiological Industry (Glavmikrobioprom) institutes, the VNII Syntez Belka, that is, the Institute of Protein Synthesis. In the Soviet university system, after graduation students must sign a contract with their future place of work, not according to the interests of the student but according to the demands of scientific institutions and schools that particular year. Supposedly, this was the price for the free university education. But there were some tricks that allowed students to escape this signing and get hired by an institution where they wanted to work.

When I visited the VNII Syntez Belka for the first time, it became clear to me that it was connected with secret work, probably with the development of some biological weapon. It was heavily guarded by plainclothes KGB men. The head of the Personnel Department, who appeared to be a retired KGB officer, submitted my documents for the special clearance needed to be employed at that institute (it was not clear if I would be accepted at all because of my Jewish name). To work at a secret institute on a military project was the last thing I wanted in my life. But I was lucky. The checking took a long time, during which I passed exams for a graduate student position *(aspirantura)*. I started to work at the Radiobiology Department of the Kurchatov Institute of Atomic Energy on my Candidate (Ph.D.) dissertation on classic genetics of the fruit fly *Drosophila,* which had nothing in common with military projects.

The Radiobiology Department was created within the Kurchatov Institute in 1958. At first it included only two laboratories, Microorganisms Genetics and Selection, headed by Sos Alikhanyan (I will describe his career in Chapter 4), and the Biochemical Laboratory, headed by a well-known molecular biologist and geneticist, Roman Khesin (1922–1986). At the beginning of the 1960s, seven more DNA and genetics laboratories were established within the department. I was accepted at Dr. Khesin's laboratory, at the time the only laboratory in the USSR that worked on the biochemical genetics of eukaryotes. Much later, on January 1, 1978, the Biology Department was renamed the Institute of Molecular Genetics and transferred from the Ministry of Medium Engineering (i.e., the Atomic Ministry), under which Kurchatov Institute existed, to the system of the Academy of Sciences.

In the 1970s, VNII Syntez Belka became one of the basic institutes working on biological weapons.[300] Later, in 1985, the Glavmikrobioprom was merged with the USSR Ministry of Medical Industry into the Ministry of the Medical and Microbiological Industries (Minmedbioprom).[301] The former head of Glavmikrobioprom, Valery Bykov, was appointed to head the new ministry. He was also appointed chairman of the Inter-Agency Scientific and Technical Council, which coordinated the Biopreparat program on new types of biological weapons.[302]

Concerning both of these jobs, I could reject the work that I considered immoral only because I was a Muscovite and had Moscow's *propiska* (police permission to live in Moscow, a system that still exists despite being declared unconstitutional in the early 1990s). I could be finicky and wait until a position in academic science came through. Other talented scientists mentioned in this book, for example, Drs. Vil Mirzayanov and Ken Alibek, did not have the same privilege. They were born in small towns far from Moscow. Working on chemical and biological weapons was their only chance to have a serious professional career and gain the *propiska* required to live in Moscow.

In 1985, I appealed to my former "boss" Khesin, who became a corresponding member of the academy, for help regarding my job after I had been interrogated by the KGB counterintelligence (Second Main Directorate) concerning Khesin's closest friend, David Goldfarb. Dr. Goldfarb was the father of my old friend Alex, who had emigrated first to Israel and then to the United States. Dr. Golfarb was also trying to emigrate to Israel but was not allowed to go by the Soviet officials and, therefore, was a long-term "refusenik."[303] I visited Dr. Goldfarb from time to time simply as his son's friend. During my interrogation, the KGB counterintelligence officers became furious. They did not get any information from me about Dr. Goldfarb and his friends (and I honestly did not know anything regarding their questions), but I managed to get information from them: that the KGB had been trying to create a political case against a "plot" of Jewish scientists who allegedly tried to smuggle scientific secrets to Israel and the United States. After this interrogation, my professional future looked very grim. Khesin, with whom I had an uneasy relationship but who had the reputation of being courageous both as a scientist and a person,[304] was at the peak of his career at this time. He was very upset to hear about Dr. Goldfarb's problems with the KGB. However, he told me that he could not take me into his lab or provide me with any other support. He evidently did not want to or could not afford to have a problem with the "organs" after providing me with help.

In 1986, I escaped the further interest of the KGB by moving from Moscow to the northern part of Russia, above the Arctic Circle. I signed a three-year contract with the academy's small Murmansk Marine Biology Institute, located in the Dalnie Zelentsy inlet about 300 miles from Murmansk on the Kola Peninsula (later, after I left it, the institute was transferred to Murmansk). This was the same institute where two anti-Lysenkoists, Yurii Polyansky and Mikhail Kamshilov, found jobs after they had been expelled from their institutes after the August 1948 session of the Agricultural Academy, or VASKhNIL.[305] However, during my time in Murmansk, the professional level of most of the scientists working at that institute was very low. The head of the laboratory in which I was placed (and the Party secretary of the institute), a histologist by training, immediately told me after my arrival that he did not know what terms such as "genes" and "chromosomes" meant. The director of the institute was a Party appointee who had succeeded in defending his doctoral dissertation at Moscow University only after a special request of the Murmansk Regional Party Committee to the Moscow University Party Committee (in the 1990s, he became an academician). However, this director was not aware of my problems with the KGB. Work above the Arctic Circle gave me a legal opportunity to retain my Moscow *propiska* and to later return to Moscow without a problem. After I left for Murmansk, my wife, who had stayed in Moscow, suddenly started to receive phone calls from the Moscow City police, who desperately requested information about my whereabouts. Of course, very soon the local KGB curator of the Murmansk Institute found out exactly where I was.

While I worked above the Arctic Circle, I managed to publish my second scientific book on genetics *(Cytogenetic and Molecular Aspects of Vertebrate Evolution)* at the Academy Publishing House, Nauka.[306] There was a separate struggle with the KGB concerning publishing this book. I had several special meetings with KGB officers at their headquarters regarding the documents necessary for publishing it, which had been confiscated by a KGB agent. Finally, the intervention of Academician Aleksandr Yanshin, who was vice president of the academy (in the Earth Sciences Division) and president of the Moscow Society of Naturalists and who supported my book, saved the situation and the book was finally published in 1987. I defended it at my institute in Moscow as a Doctor of Biological Sciences thesis. The book was also given an award by the Moscow Society of Naturalists.

In three years, I was back in Moscow, and after 1990, I was able to work at the Koltsov Institute of Developmental Biology. Despite all the talk about perestroika and glasnost in the press (Mikhail Gorbachev's new Party line of openness and partial freedom of the mass media), nothing had changed in terms of KGB control of the academy institutes in Moscow. The same officer worked at the First Department of the institute, and to attend a conference or work abroad, a scientist still needed permission from the same "mysterious" organs, alias the KGB.

I saw the institute's First Department officer for the last time when I visited Moscow in 1997. I had been working in the United States for six years already and had been listed at my institute in Moscow all that time as being on leave of absence. The officer told me: "It's really unfortunate that the Institute's best guys like you are working abroad now." It seemed that he had completely forgotten that several years before, his organization—the KGB—almost turned me into a political prisoner with his help. In 2000, he was still at the institute.

In 1990, after my return to Moscow, I joined the Moscow human rights group Memorial, which is dedicated to the memory of the victims of the Soviet regime. Memorial collects documentary materials and helps survivors of Stalin's camps. I was interested in the history of the control of science, especially biology, and in the fate of foreign prisoners in the Gulag. Soon I realized that there was an early unknown area of Soviet-controlled science—like in Nazi Germany, a special secret laboratory that used human subjects for biomedical experiments. The fact that some members of the scientific elite not only knew about these experiments but supported them was especially shocking.

PSYCHOLOGICAL UNDERPINNINGS

No doubt the interventions of the Party and secret services in scientific issues, including the rise of Lysenko, had an ideological and psychological origin. Stalin and the other Party leaders had no formal education or training (Bukharin was an unusual exception from this rule). No doubt on some level this made them feel insecure, especially around educated scientists. This goes a long way toward explaining their desire to dominate and control scientists, even when the destruction of these talented people severely damaged the fortunes of the Soviet Union (for example, declining crop yields because of the Lysenko nonsense).

The personal attitude of Stalin to scientists was very cynical. In the early 1930s, the dictator said to Academician Axel Berg, a well-known radio-physicist and specialist in the theory of information: "Scientists work well only when some of their colleagues are imprisoned."[307] Security commissar Lavrentii Beria's rudeness toward scientists after he had been appointed head of the Special Committee (the Soviet atomic project) in 1945[308] was well known. The outstanding physicist, Academician Pyotr Kapitsa, refused to work under Beria's supervision (which was almost suicidal). He wrote to Stalin stating his reasons: "Comrades Beria, Malenkov, and Voznesensky behave as superhumans at the Special Committee. Especially Comrade Beria."[309] After this communication was received, Kapitsa was dismissed from the committee, and in 1946, he was deprived of all his positions and put under house arrest until Stalin's death.[310] Stalin personally ordered Beria not to arrest Kapitsa. At a meeting in the Kremlin, Stalin told Beria: "I'll dismiss him [Kapitsa] if you like, but *you* mustn't touch him."[311] According to some sources, later, in 1953, Beria planned an assassination of Kapitsa, evidently as an act of revenge.[312]

Kapitsa was the only prominent Soviet physicist who refused to participate in the A-bomb project under the supervision of Beria and other Party functionaries. He consciously decided to follow Pavlov's example of resistance. Pavlov told him: ". . . Only I am saying here aloud what I am thinking about, and when I die, you should do the same because this is so necessary for our Motherland."[313] And Kapitsa answered: "I will not be afraid to say what I am really thinking." It is not surprising, however, that other scientists who were not so prominent did not resist. They knew exactly what would happen to them if they did not succeed in their work. Beria kept in his desk a list of names of all scientists with notes on what kind of punishment, from the death penalty to a certain number of years of imprisonment in labor camps, each scientist would receive if the bomb project was not completed on time.[314] Later, in 1980–1981, Kapitsa actively defended Sakharov. He wrote two strong letters to KGB chairman Yurii Andropov demanding the return of Sakharov from exile in Gorky.[315]

Academician Kapitsa was right. Like Nazi leaders, the Soviet Communist and NKVD-MGB elite fancied themselves to be superhuman. According to the writer Kirill Stolyarov, the following testimony of MGB colonel Savitsky is in Beria's MGB investigation file:

Once in Germany B[ogdan] Kobulov [at the time deputy head of the So-viet Military Administration] said in the presence of my wife and Adjutant Mikitenko that people and their descendants are divided by inheritance into the "chosen" and "unchosen." The "chosen" should be leaders and have key positions in society, and the "unchosen" are only fit to work. When I tried to object to this, Kobulov screamed: "Do not speak drivel, you don't understand anything!"[316]

For the entire time I dealt with the security service officers within the academy, at Moscow University, and especially in the Lubyanka headquarters, I perceived the same attitude: The officers of all ranks tried to show me that they were special and in some way superior to others. The "unchosen" were expected simply to obey the orders from the "chosen" and accept their understanding of life and values, which definitely were opposite to mine. In the current Russian political situation, such officers have become leaders of the government and economy. The control of science has merely shifted: Control according to the ideological Party line has morphed into control through financial support. It is too early to expect that in this climate, moral and ethical issues of science such as choosing whether to participate in the development of new types of biological or chemical weapons (despite all international agreements) will become a serious matter.

According to the writer Leonid Mlechin, Academician Yevgenii Varga (1879–1964), who directed the Academy Institute of World Economy and World Politics from 1927 to 1947 and in the 1920s–1940s was the main economist within the Comintern,[317] had a very low opinion of the secret services. In 1947, he stated: "A decent person won't work as an interrogator or at the secret police. Only the scum of society works there and, naturally, such elements do not follow the issue but they are interested in their own careers. They are suspicious of everyone they observe. They put suspects in prisons until such an atmosphere is created [in the society] when everyone suspects everybody."[318] No wonder that Academician Varga did not enjoy Stalin's favor. In 1948, he was condemned for his professional economic views and in 1949, the institute he directed was closed down.[319]

It becomes clear from reading the reports of independent journalists in Chechnya in 2001 that the methods and mentality of FSB officers have remained unchanged to the present day. Without any hesitation, twenty-year-old FSB lieutenants attach electrodes to the hands of a sixty-year-old Chechen woman and increase the current step by step because she does not "dance" enthusiastically; that is, in their opinion, her convulsions are not strong enough.[320] Her only "guilt" is that she is a Chechen civilian who has been kidnapped by the Russian military for ransom. Someday these young officers will return to Moscow and other Russian cities. They have acquired good practical knowledge of how to control people.

2

DEADLY SCIENCE

We do not have and cannot have old foundations of moral and "humanism," invented by the bourgeoisie . . . We are allowed to do anything . . .

—The Red Sword, the newspaper
of the VCheKa troops[1]

For thirty years, from the early 1920s until the death of Stalin, biochemists, chemists, and toxicologists working for the security services researched deadly chemicals used in executions and assassinations and conducted deadly poison tests on humans. This was in addition to and allied with military research on biological and chemical weapons. The most disturbing aspect of this research was that this group was not isolated from regular scientific circles. A group of well-known scientists, professors, and academicians knew about these experiments and approved them.

In this chapter, I have used some documents from the 1953 investigation files of the Beria and Grigory Mairanovsky cases published by military prosecutor Vladimir Bobryonev and journalist Valery Ryazentsev, who had special access to the files. These documents were published in Russian in Bobryonev's roman à clef *"Doktor Smert," ili Varsonofievskie prizraki* ("Doctor Death," or the Ghosts of Varsonofyevsky Lane), which I will cite as *"Doktor Smert."* In this book, Mairanovsky becomes "Mogilevsky" and his laboratory is named Laboratory "X," but the real names of most of the other people are retained. Transcripts of the 1953 interrogations are cited with the real dates and names of the interrogators, but the questions and answers are not preceded by speakers' names. However, excerpts from the transcripts with the speakers indicated, as well as Maironvsky's letters, are given in the English translation of the main part of the unpublished version of this book by Bobryonev and Ryazentsev, entitled *The Ghosts of Varsonofyevsky Lane: Laboratory of Death—How The Soviet Secret Police Experimented on People and*

Poisoned Their Enemies. To avoid misinterpretation, I have used the English translation of the documents cited in this version.[2]

I also provide information in this chapter about two more people who worked closely with Mairanovsky: Pavel Sudoplatov and Naum Eitingon. Sudoplatov, one of the most ruthless people in Stalin's NKVD/MGB, began working at the GPU in 1921. In the 1930s, he worked at the OGPU/NKVD Foreign Department and was in charge of organizing political assassinations, including the murder of Leon Trotsky in 1940. During World War II, he headed the NKVD/NKGB Fourth Department, which was in charge of sabotage and terrorist activity behind enemy lines. In 1945, he was promoted to lieutenant general, and in 1946, he was appointed head of the MGB DR Service (sabotage and terror). From 1950–1953, Sudoplatov headed Bureau No. 1, in charge of terrorist activity abroad.

Naum Eitingon (alias "Colonel Naum Kotov" during the Spanish Civil War, "Comrade Pablo," "Pierre," "Leont'ev," "Rabinovich," "Sakhov," "Valery," and "Lyova"), Sudoplatov's longtime deputy, joined the CheKa Foreign Department in 1921.[3] He spoke many languages fluently and throughout the 1930s worked all over Western Europe and the United States. He was in charge of terrorist acts in Paris and organized the kidnappings of White generals Aleksandr Kutepov and Yevgenii Miller, as well as the killing of Trotsky's son, Lev Sedov. In 1939, he was appointed deputy head of the NKVD Second Department under Sudoplatov. In 1940, Eitingon worked with Sudoplatov on the Trotsky assassination. In the United States, the activity of Sudoplatov's Bureau No. 1 and Eitingon's role in the assassination of Trotsky were described by the defector and former MGB/KGB officer Peter Deriabin in testimony before a Senate committee in March 1965.[4] A recently published 1939 NKVD document described a detailed plan to assassinate Trotsky (referred to as "a Duck") and included the code names of the main participants, including Sudoplatov and Eitingon.[5] An unpublished secret decree of the Presidium of the USSR Highest Council mentioned awarding the following persons for their execution of the organization of Trotsky's murder: Caridad Mercader (mother of Ramon, the killer), Naum Eitingon, Lev Vasilevsky (NKVD *rezident,* i.e., an undercover Foreign Intelligence chief, who served as first secretary of the Soviet Embassy under the alias "Tarasov"), Pavel Sudoplatov, Iosif Grigulevich, and Pavel Pastelnyak (acting *rezident* in 1940).[6] Later, under Eitingon's supervision from Moscow, Vasilevsky-Tarasov tried to organize an escape of the killer Ramon Mercader from a Mexican prison.[7] From 1946 to 1950, the team of Sudoplatov, Eitingon, and Maironovsky carried out executions of victims on the order of Stalin and Politburo members. I will present the details of these assassinations below.

In 1994, the publication of Sudoplatov's memoirs, *Special Tasks: The Memoirs of an Unwanted Witness,* written with one of his sons, Anatolii, and two American historians,[8] caused a furor in both American and Russian historical and scientific communities. The book presents a mixture of real information and false statements. Misinformation that the leading American and European physicists J. Robert Oppenheimer, Enrico Fermi, Leo Szilard, and Niels Bohr acted as Soviet spies by transferring secrets to the Soviets was criticized by both American and Russian physicists and historians,[9] as well as by Russian and U.S. government officials,[10] and former secret service colleagues. For instance, Zoya Zarubina, a former MGB officer who worked as a translator at Sudoplatov's "S" Department in charge of the Atomic Bomb Papers, refuted Sudoplatov's claims about Oppenheimer.[11] The historian David Holloway responded: "Sudoplatov's motives [to make money or to magnify the role of the KGB] may be understandable, but his American coauthors are very much to blame for not making the effort to check out his serious, but unsustained, charges [against the American and European physicists]."[12]

Sudoplatov does provide some real information on the role of Eitingon and Mairanovsky in numerous killings,[13] but many details about Mairanovsky's work and Sudoplatov's characterization of him as a high-level scientist are fictitious.[14] I can add to this that the memoirs of Sudoplatov's former cell mates in Vladimir Prison do not support his version of events regarding the period after his arrest.[15] Their descriptions of Sudoplatov's simulation of a psychiatric illness contradict the details given in the book. The last version of Sudoplatov's memoirs, *Special Operations: Lubyanka and the Kremlin, the 1930s–1950s* published only in 1998 in Russian, contains a more truthful version of these events.[16] Also, the recently released documents show that the MVD doctors took part in the falsification of Sudoplatov's disease.[17] Sudoplatov's transfer from Moscow's Butyrka Prison to the MVD Leningrad Psychiatric Prison Hospital during the investigation of Beria's case saved Sudoplatov's life. Otherwise, there was a high probability that he would have been condemned to death along with Beria, Merkulov, and their close associates.

There is a further problem with Sudoplatov's book. In 1990, my colleague in an investigation of the Raoul Wallenberg case, the Moscow journalist Vladimir Abarinov, called Sudoplatov and asked him what he knew about Wallenberg. Sudoplatov answered that he had never heard the name Wallenberg before. Surprisingly, a whole chapter about Raoul Wallenberg appeared in his memoirs four years later, in 1994.[18] For all these reasons, in this chapter I will use Sudoplatov's memoirs only if they agree with other sources.

THE FIRST SECRET LABORATORIES

There is no exact information about the early history of poison laboratories within the Soviet secret services. The data are scarce and secondary, basically scattered in memoirs. Sudoplatov claimed the first laboratory was established in 1921 under the name "Special Office" and that Professor Ignatii Kazakov headed it.[19] Possibly, when Lenin asked Stalin to give him poison, he meant this "office" as the source. Later, at Bukharin's show trial in 1938, Professor Kazakov was among three doctors accused of being "killers"; however, no connection with the OGPU laboratory was ever mentioned. Bobryonev and Ryzentsev wrote that Professor Boris Zbarsky, a biochemist (at the time deputy director of the Institute of Biochemistry), was a consultant for the narcotics experiments done at this lab.[20] This coincides with a note in a book by Sudoplatov's son Andrei stating that scientific research at the laboratory "was conducted by specialists from the Institute of Biochemistry headed by Academician Bach."[21] Zbarsky's son, Professor Iliya Zbarsky, also recalled that in the 1920s his father had a close relationship with Dzerzhinsky and then, after Dzerzhinsky's death in 1926, "maintained excellent relationships with his deputy, Genrikh Yagoda."[22] He remembered that in 1927 Yagoda gave Boris Zbarsky a box with explosives for analysis. Later, Zbarsky headed a small laboratory in charge of the mummification and maintenance of Vladimir Lenin's body.[23] However, Academician Ipatieff, who knew Zbarsky personally very well, wrote in his memoirs:

> Actually, he [Zbarsky] had merely been present at the embalming, which was done by Professor [Vladimir] Vorobiev. . . A biochemist by profession, a Socialist-Revolutionist in political beliefs, a lively individual and a good conversationalist, a braggart, and an expert at worming favors from officials, Zbarsky was many things but not a serious scientist.[24]

As described in Chapter 1, in 1952–1953, Zbarsky fell out of Stalin's favor and during the anti-Semitic purges was one of the accused "doctor-killers."

In 1926, under Dzerzhinsky's successor, Vyacheslav Menzhinsky (OGPU chairman, 1926–1934), a secret group was created to conduct terrorist acts abroad. It had its own laboratory of chemical and biological poisons.[25] The team was called simply "Yasha's Group" after the name of its head, Yakov Serebryansky. Serebryansky was convicted before the Revolution in 1909 as one of the killers of the Minsk prison commandant. From 1923, he worked in Palestine as an OGPU agent, and in 1925, he moved to France and then Belgium.[26] According to Sudoplatov, Yasha's Group "had established its networks in the 1920s in France, Germany, and Scandinavia. It chose its members from people of the Comintern underground who were not involved in any open propaganda activities and who had kept their membership in national Communist parties secret."[27]

In 1930, Serebryansky organized the kidnapping of General Aleksandr Kutepov, head of the White Russian Military Union (ROVS) in Paris.[28] On Sunday, January 26, 1930, Kutepov was abducted from a street in a fashionable area of Paris. However, the chloroform used by the kidnappers was too much for Kutepov's ailing heart. He died several days later aboard a Soviet steamer while being taken to the Soviet Union. For Kutepov's kidnapping, Serebryansky was awarded the Order of the Red Banner.[29]

In the 1930s, a "special operations" group under Serebryansky's supervision also operated in the United States.[30] Eventually, the group "grew into an elite service, more than 200-strong, dedicated to hunting down 'enemies of the people' on both sides of the Atlantic."[31] Possibly, through this network the NKVD agents stole a booklet in 1935 from an American laboratory with a secret formula for a powerful bactericide, which was later used in the USSR under the name the "Zbarsky bactericide."[32]

Seven years later, Serebryansky's group seems to have perfected its drugging technique. On September 22, 1937, members of his group successfully drugged and kidnapped the White Russian general Yevgenii Miller, who had succeeded Kutepov as head of ROVS.[33] Miller was abducted on a Paris street, drugged, and put in a trunk that was loaded onto a Soviet freighter in Le Havre. Miller survived the trip to Moscow, where he was interrogated at NKVD headquarters, and finally shot.

In 1937 and until Serebryansky's arrest on November 10, 1938, Yasha's Group was a separate unit under the NKVD commissar.[34] In 1938, accusations were leveled against Serebryansky that a laboratory that was part of his group produced poisons and contagious microbes not to kill enemies, but leaders of the country.[35] He was condemned to death on July 7, 1941, but on the intervention of Sudoplatov (at the time, head of Special Group on terrorism under NKVD commissar Beria), Serebryansky was amnestied and released on September 8, 1941. Later Yasha's Group was reorganized into a Special Group (Department "DR") of the NKVD/NKGB, headed by Sudoplatov.

According to investigative journalist Arkady Vaksberg,[36] the direct predecessor of Mairanovsky's lab was a poison research laboratory organized within the Soviet security service in the early 1930s under the supervision of NKVD chief Genrikh Yagoda. Yagoda is usually mentioned as a pharmacist or a chemist by training.[37] Actually, he had worked as an apprentice at a small jewelry or printing studio. From 1923, Yagoda was Dzerzhinsky's second deputy (Menzhinsky was first deputy); in 1929, he became Menzhinsky's first deputy, and in 1934, after Menzhinsky's death, he was appointed NKVD commissar (1934–1936).[38] In fact, since 1929 Yagoda really had acted as head of the OGPU/NKVD because of Menzhinsky's poor health.[39] Apparently, Yagoda's laboratory was a continuation of the "Special Office." Although information about this laboratory is sketchy, the lab was discussed during the infamous Bukharin show trial of 1938 as the basis of the accusation against Yagoda.[40]

At the Bukharin trial that took place in Moscow from March 2 to 12, 1938, Yagoda was convicted of organizing the murders of several important people during fake medical treatments. The list of alleged victims included the writer Maxim Gorky and his son; Yagoda's predecessor Vyacheslav Menzhinsky; and vice chairman of the USSR Council of People's Commissars Valerian Kuibyshev.[41] Yagoda was also accused of creating a secret laboratory, of developing poisons, and of attempting to poison his successor, Nikolai Yezhov. It is interesting to note how the show trial mixed true accusations—Yagoda did run a secret laboratory that developed poisons, with the full knowledge and approval of Stalin, of course—with falsehoods: Yagoda did not try to poison Yezhov. On March 8, 1938, State General Prosecutor Andrei Vyshinsky (who succeeded Krylenko) interrogated Yagoda's assistant, Pavel Bulanov:

Vyshinsky: Tell us, please, was Yagoda interested in poisons generally?
Bulanov: Exceptionally.
Vyshinsky: How was his special interest in poisons expressed?
Bulanov: He acquired this interest approximately in 1934 . . . I know, for example, that he formed a very close acquaintanceship with a number of chemists and gave direct instructions to build, or rather to arrange, a chemical laboratory.
Vyshinsky: What for?
Bulanov: It was always emphasized that it must be under the control of Yagoda, as he had in his arsenal a sufficient number of poisons as means for definite ends.
Vyshinsky: What ends?
Bulanov: For counterrevolutionary ends, for purposes of assassination. I know that he employed a number of people on this work. The setting up of this laboratory was an actual fact . . . Yagoda warned me that this matter was so important that the people mentioned must be allowed unlimited funds and that no accounts were to be demanded.[42]

Of course, this was a show trial and the accused persons had no other choice than to follow the scenario prepared under the guidance of

Vyshinsky, approved by Stalin and, evidently, the Politburo. But it is interesting that Bulanov's answers included real details of the secret laboratory's work, its direct subordination to the state security commissar, and its clandestine nature.

Yagoda's alleged plan to assassinate Yezhov was quite unrealistic, but it was designed to impress the show trial's audience. Bulanov testified:

> When he [Yagoda] was removed from his post as People's Commissar of Internal Affairs, he directly set about laying poison in the office and those rooms which adjoined the office in the building of the People's Commissariat of Internal Affairs which Nikolai Ivanovich Yezhov was to occupy. He instructed me personally to prepare a poison, namely, to take mercury and to dissolve it in acid. . . . I recall that he cautioned me against sulfuric acid, against burns, odor and more of the same kind . . . I carried out these instructions of Yagoda and made the solution. The spraying of the office which Yezhov was to occupy and the adjoining rooms, the rugs, carpets and curtains was done by [an NKVD officer] Savolainen in the presence of Yagoda and myself. This was on September 29 [1936]. Yagoda told me that this spraying must be done five, six, or seven times, which was done. Two or three times I prepared large flasks of this solution and gave them to Savolainen. He did the spraying with a spray. I recall that it was a large metallic cylinder with a large bulb . . . It was kept in Yagoda's dressing room; it was a foreign-made spray . . . [43]

Many victims from Bukharin's show trial were later rehabilitated. According to Russian law, a special procedure can "rehabilitate" a person condemned to imprisonment or to death for political crimes under the dreaded Article 58 of Stalin's Criminal Code. At present, usually close relatives of the former political prisoner submit a request to the General Prosecutor's Office to initiate the process of rehabilitation. In 1988, the Russian General Prosecutor's Office, during the rehabilitation process of victims of the Bukharin trial, issued an official statement regarding this incident:

> The terrorist act against N. I. Yezhov (mercury poisoning) was falsified by Yezhov himself and a former Head of the NKVD Counterintelligence Department, [Nikolai] Nikolaev . . . Nikolaev consulted with the Head of the RKKA [Red Army] Chemical Academy Anovitsky on methods of mercury poisoning. After this he rubbed mercury into the upholstery of the furniture at Yezhov's office and then provided [a sample of it] for analysis. NKVD officer Savolainen, who had had access to Yezhov's office,

"confessed" after systematic beatings [during interrogations] to preparing the poisoning of Yezhov by mercury. After Savolainen's arrest a jar with mercury was placed secretly in the hallway of the building where he lived. This jar was "discovered" later and was filed as material evidence in the case.[44]

This story sheds some light on how the NKVD/MGB provided "evidence" for show trials. But, as I will describe below, the spraying of toxic chemicals was in fact used by the NKVD/MGB/KGB for assassinations.

During the trial, three doctors were accused of carrying out Yagoda's orders and killing prominent writers and party leaders: the prominent cardiologist Dr. Dmitrii Pletnev (professor of the Institute of Functional Diagnostics), Dr. Lev Levin (a consultant at the Kremlin Hospital), and Ignatii Kazakov (director of the Scientific Research Institute of Metabolism and Endocrinology).[45] Two more doctors were also arrested in connection with the Bukharin case: A. I. Vinogradov of the NKVD medical section, and the head of the Kremlin Hospital, Khodorovsky. During the trial, Dr. Vinogradov was accused (together with Dr. Levin) of giving the wrong medical treatment to Gorky's son, Maxim, on the order of Yagoda.[46] However, both Vinogradov and Khodorovsky "mysteriously" died during the investigation before the trial.[47]

This was the second trial of Professor Pletnev. An NKVD provocation preceded Professor Pletnev's arrest. On June 8, 1937, the main USSR daily *Pravda* published an unsigned article entitled "Professor—Rapist, Sadist." It described that three years earlier while examining a woman called "B." in the article, Pletnev supposedly bit her on the breast. As a result, B. developed chronic mastitis and became disabled. The article caused a flow of angry letters, including some from medical colleagues such as Vladimir Zelenin, Boris Kogan, Yefim Gelstein, and Miron Vovsi.[48] The behavior of Vladimir Vinogradov was even more disgusting. One of Pletnev's best pupils, he agreed to act as an expert witness and confirm the indictment against Pletnev, during the latter's investigation.[49] After Pletnev's arrest, Vinogradov became Stalin's personal physician. The expert commission consisted of prominent professors: D. Burmin (known as a professional rival of Pletnev), N. Shereshevsky, V. Vinogradov, D. Rossiisky, and V. Zipalov.[50] Later, in 1952–1953, Zelenin, Kogan, Gelstein, Vovsi, Vinogradov, and Shereshevsky became victims of the "Doctors' Plot," and a new commission consisting of doctor-experts confirmed their alleged "criminal intentions" to kill Soviet leaders.

At first Pletnev was tried in a closed session of the Moscow City Court because he refused to plead guilty. On July 18, 1937, the court pronounced a two-year suspended sentence.[51] However, this was not enough for General Prosecutor Vyshinsky, who personally disliked the famous and independent doctor. Their conflict had started in 1925, when Vyshinsky was appointed rector of Moscow University. Vyshinsky immediately fired old professors on the basis of their "bourgeois origin," and Pletnev opposed these actions in his clinic.[52] On March 12, 1938, Vyshinsky accused Pletnev in an article in *Pravda*: "The history and the chronicle of the criminal killings tell us that during the last decades poisonings by professional killers almost disappeared. These poisoners were replaced by doctors." However, as I have described in the previous chapter, the reason for the arrest of Drs. Pletnev and Levin in connection with Bukharin's trial might have been deeper: In 1932 they refused to sign a false death certificate for Nadezhda Allilueva, Stalin's second wife.

The subject of poisons played a poignant role in the Bukharin trial. Bukharin agreed to participate in the show trial on the condition that he be given poison after the trial. He wrote to Stalin: ". . . Let me urge you by all that is dear to you to let me, instead of being shot, take poison in my cell (give me morphine, so I can go to sleep and never wake up again). Take pity on me, let me spend my last minutes in my own way . . . "[53] He repeated the same request in a letter to the investigator Lazar Kogan[54] during the trial: "Remember about the c-u-p. You promised it to me and I hope that you will NOT cheat me . . . I believe that you will fulfill my request. I ask you not to profoundly distress and disappoint me . . . "[55]

The figure of Nikolai Bukharin has always intrigued me. He was an extremely educated person. He wrote serious studies on economy and philosophy and on the history of culture. He was a good writer and did excellent, practically professional drawings and paintings. According to the memoirs of Bukharin's widow Anna Larina, in 1935–1936, three of his paintings were exhibited at the most famous and prestigious museum of Russian art, the Tretyakov Gallery in Moscow.[56] He was also a good naturalist. My father told me that when he was a boy, from time to time my grandparents took him and my uncle to a country house (a "dacha" in Russian) in the suburbs of Moscow that belonged to the Commission for Improving the Living Conditions of Scientists, the TseKUBU. My grandfather Avadii Birstein was a rather famous Moscow doctor. He graduated from the Medical Department of Moscow University in 1890, which was quite an accomplishment since according to laws of the Russian Empire, Jews could apply only to the medical and juridical departments of universities and amount to about 6 percent of all students at these departments. In 1914, my grandfather, at the time the author of several original surgical methods, was invited to the newly opened Institute of Traumatology in Moscow. There, he was elected chief surgeon by the staff of doctors. After the revolution, my grandfather received help from the TseKUBU, in recognition of his service.

On Sundays, some of the Bolshevik leaders, especially Bukharin, visited this dacha. Bukharin took my eight-year-old father for long entomological excursions, which my father remembered all his life. Today, some of Bukharin's drawings of insects have been published, and I think that he could easily have been a professional zoologist. At the same time, despite all his intelligence and education, Bukharin was a stanch Bolshevik who sincerely believed in the existence of only one, socialist approach to organization of the economy and society.[57]

Once I asked my grandmother what she and my grandfather, who died in 1922, had in common with the Bolsheviks who visited the dacha. I felt she could have nothing in common with them. Two of her brothers were active in Russian politics at the beginning of the twentieth century, even becoming members of the State Duma: Grigory (Girsh) Bruck represented the Zionist Party, and Pavel Bruck was a member of the liberal party of Constitutional Democrats. Both later emigrated, to Palestine and Paris, respectively. In 1907, she volunteered to assist the Jewish emigration movement. As a doctor, she accompanied and supervised a huge group of Jewish emigrants that arrived in New York on the ship Moskwa. *I still keep her pass to Ellis Island, issued to "Dr. Sophie J. Bruck, representing Jewish Colonization Society" on October 3, 1907. To my question about the Bolsheviks, my grandmother answered exactly as Countess Alexandra Tolstoy did at the Tactical Center trial: "I heated a samovar for them."*

Emotionally, it is difficult to read the memoirs of those who witnessed the trial. "The admission of three of the doctors—Levin, Pletnev and Kazakov—were especially convincing," Professor Iliya Zbarsky recalled. He continued:

They confessed that on the orders of People's Commissar for the Interior Yagoda . . . they had treated the writer Maxim Gorky, and his son Maxim Peshkov, in such a way as to accelerate their death. They had done the same in cases . . . of many other . . . figures. Their testimony went into detail about how they administered poison to their patients. These statements made such an impression on me that I became convinced the accused men were guilty. Most of them begged that their lives be spared. Some, like Yagoda . . . went down on their knees and tearfully implored "beloved Comrade Stalin" to pardon them. It was rumored later that Stalin had been present at the trial, peering through a spy-hole in the wall and thoroughly enjoying the spectacle.[58]

Yagoda, Bulanov, Bukharin, and sixteen other trial defendants were condemned to death.[59] Of course, Stalin did not keep his word. Apparently, he was outraged: in the last speech, Bukharin denied not only his own guilt, but the reason of the whole trial. "After only a few minutes his moral and intellectual superiority over his accusers was plain," recalled Zbarsky.[60] Two doctors, Levin and Kazakov, were shot right after the trial's conclusion.[61] Yagoda was shot two days afterward, on March 15, 1938.[62] Bukharin was shot last, on the same day.

Yagoda's wife was also arrested and shot, and his parents were arrested and died in labor camps.[63] All of Yagoda's closest assistants were arrested one by one and shot. Yagoda was not rehabilitated in the 1980s–1990s. It is interesting that Vyacheslav Molotov, the long-term chairman of the USSR Council of Commissars (1930–1946) and subsequently of the Council of Ministers (1946–1949), a Politburo member and the second most important person in the Soviet Union after Stalin, believed the poisoning accusations were true even forty years after Yagoda's death.[64]

Only in the late 1990s did members of Memorial (Moscow) discover the location of the burial site of Bukharin, Bulanov, Kazakov, Levin, some other victims of this show trial, and Yagoda's wife and sister, at a special NKVD execution site in the suburbs of Moscow near the village of Kommunarka, on the property of Yagoda's former dacha.[65] This mass grave contains the bodies of approximately 4,500 men and women executed by NKVD assassins from 1937 to 1941. According to archival documents, on the whole 32,000 of the arrested Muscovites were shot by the NKVD during this period (29,200 of them in 1937–1938) in Lubyanka Prison and at two suburban sites, near the villages of Kommunarka and Butovo.[66] Some of the bodies were cremated at the former Donskoi Monastery in Moscow, and ashes were buried near the crematorium in this monastery.

Dr. Pletnev's fate was different: The sixty-six-year-old professor was sentenced to twenty-five years' imprisonment "with the confiscation of all his personal property."[67] The confiscation of his property was a very pragmatic point: He had a good collection of art that he had started to purchase before the Bolshevik Revolution. Pletnev was put into Vladimir Prison. In his appeal to the Soviet leaders, he described the interrogations during the preparation of the Bukharin trial:

All charges made against me were a falsification. My "confession" was forced out of me by violence and deception . . . When I did not give way the investigation literally said: "If the leadership suppose you to be guilty then even if you were 100 percent innocent, you would be guilty . . . " Appalling bad language was used against me, and the threat of the death penalty. I was dragged by my collar, choked and tortured with sleepiness: over a period of five weeks I slept for only 2–3 of every 24 hours. They threatened to tear out my throat and with it my confession; they threatened to beat me with rubber truncheons . . . All of which reduced me to a paralysis of half of my body. I am numbed by the cold-blooded lying of those pygmies and worms that are carrying on their subversive work. Show that the truth is as possible to establish in the Union [USSR] as in other civilized countries . . . May the truth shine forth![68]

His words were heeded by the Soviet leaders: On September 8, 1941, Pletnev was resentenced to death. He was shot three days later in the city of Orel's prison, where the inhabitants of Vladimir Prison had been moved at the beginning of the war.[69]

It is hard to believe, but Joseph E. Davies, the American ambassador to Moscow in 1936–1938 and a close friend of the American president Franklin D. Roosevelt, considered the victims of the Bukharin trail to have been members of a true anti-Soviet plot. Mr. Davies attended some of the court sessions and described the trial in his extremely popular book *Mission to Moscow*, published in 1941.[70] The book sold 700,000 copies and was translated into thirteen languages.[71] Davies knew Dr. Pletnev and some of the other defendants personally. However, he wrote in his diary: "The 'last words' of Pletnev, [Arkadii] Rosengoltz [former commissar for foreign trade], and other defendants were harrowing in their interest and tragedy . . . The defendants in this trial, including some of these men, according to their statements wanted war!"[72] In the official telegram to Secretary of State Cordell Hull dated March 17, 1938, Davies concluded: ". . . It is my opinion so far [as] the political defendants are concerned [that] sufficient crimes under Soviet law, among those charged in the indictment, were established by the proof and beyond a reasonable doubt to justify the verdict of guilty of treason and the adjudication of the punishment provided by Soviet criminal status."[73]

With the involvement of the White House, Davies signed a contract with Warner Brothers for a film based on his book.[74] This propaganda movie under the same name *Mission to Moscow* was directed by the famous Hungarian-born Michael Curtiz and was finished in 1943. Curtiz's previous film *Casablanca* is known as one of the best American movies. The script of *Mission* was written by another Hollywood luminary, screenwriter and producer Howard W. Koch, the author of the script for *Casablanca*. During the filming, Davies kept Roosevelt informed on *Mission's* progress.[75] After the release, *Mission* was named "Hollywood's most controversial film ever."[76] John Dewey, who had headed the American commission of inquiry into the Moscow trials, called this movie "the first instance in our country of totalitarian propaganda—a propaganda which falsifies history through distortion, omission or pure invention of facts."[77]

The movie was so favorable for the Soviet Union and its leaders that in 1947 it was cited by the House Un-American Activities Committee.[78] Davies stubbornly defended it. Finally, Koch was labeled a "Communist" and blacklisted by the committee for a decade.[79]

In 2001, *Mission to Moscow* was shown on the American Movie Classics TV channel as part of a Curtiz retrospective. I was stunned by Davies's and Koch's presentation of the victims of the Bukharin trial as conscious "enemies of the Soviet people" and of Prosecutor Vyshinsky, Stalin, and Molotov as real fighters against these traitors. The movie went far beyond Davies's book. Definitely, the two Americans had been completely fooled by the carefully staged performance in Moscow. The producer of the movie, Robert Buckner, later said: "It is now common historical knowledge, of course, that Stalin brainwashed him [Davies] completely."[80] Koch, who died in February 2001, was confident even in the 1990s that he had been right. In an interview with Griffin Fariello, he said: "It's the thing I value the most in my life—that I was able to stand for something that needed to be said."[81]

In 1937–1938, after the fall of Yagoda, a period of purges of Politburo members and of the old guard NKVD began under the guidance of the new NKVD commissar, Nikolai Yezhov. Apparently, the methods of "Yasha's Group" were in use even at Lubyanka headquarters and the Kremlin. On February 17, 1938, the chief of the NKVD Foreign Department, Abram Slutsky, was found "slumped awkwardly across an armchair with an empty tea glass at his side [at the office of Yezhov's deputy, Mikhail Frinovsky]. Frinovsky confidentially announced that a doctor had already ascertained that Slutsky had died of a heart attack. Several NKVD officers who knew from experience the symptoms of cyanide poisoning observed the telltale blue spots on the face of their late Foreign Department chief."[82]

Later, on February 3, 1940, during his own trial, Yezhov testified: "As far as Slutsky is concerned, I had instructions from the directing organs [i.e., the Politburo]—don't arrest Slutsky, get rid of him some other way . . . Otherwise our own agents abroad would have run for safety. So Slutsky was poisoned."[83] Recently, the Russian historians Nikita Petrov and Konstantin Skorkin were able to identify Slutsky's assassins. Slutsky was poisoned by the deputy head of the GUGB Twelfth Department, Mikhail Alekhin, and Deputy Commissar Leonid Zakovsky. The GUGB Twelfth Department was established within the NKVD on August 7, 1937, and for a short time, until January 17, 1938, was headed by Semen Zhukovsky. This is the first precise information about the poisons laboratory within the secret service.

Apparently, Alekhin was a specialist in poisons and poisoning (he had some professional education and attended the Military Academy for three years), and Zakovsky supervised the operation. Since Frinovsky was not surprised by Slutsky's sudden death in his office, it seems he was also involved in the plot. After Slutsky's death, his deputy, Sergei Shpigelglass, took over the NKVD Foreign Department as acting head.

Slutsky's fate was not unique in 1938–1939. As already described, in late 1938, Pavel Alliluev also died of "a heart attack" in the Kremlin Hospital. However, his postmortem report said: "When he was admitted [to the Clinic], he was unconscious, cyanotic, and apparently dying."[84]

Lenin's widow, Nadezhda Krupskaya, was practically cut off from political life in the 1930s. But apparently she was still a potential threat to Stalin's power: She might say something against Stalin at the Eighteenth Congress of the Bolshevik Party, scheduled for March 1939. She conveniently died on February 27, 1939, just before the Congress. The symptoms were the same as Pavel Alliluev's. Her death certificate issued at the Kremlin Hospital pronounced: "The illness began with severe pains throughout the abdomen, accompanied by repeated vomiting, a very fast pulse, and cyanosis of the nose and the extremities . . . Cardiac arrest set in and Comrade Krupskaya died."[85] Cyanide had become fashionable.

Yezhov's terror was unleashed not only within the country but also abroad. Poisons were widely used by special "mobile groups" in different European countries and the United States that traced and liquidated NKVD agents who refused to follow orders to return to Moscow (which usually meant a death sentence) or those who tried to defect to the West.[86] In summer 1937, Shpigelglass personally headed a "mobile group" in Paris determined to kill a defector, a former Soviet agent named Ignace Poretsky (alias "Reiss").[87] At first the plan was to poison him with chocolates laced with strychnine. But finally he was shot. Although the killers escaped, the Swiss police, which investigated the case, found a suitcase left by one of the assassins with a detailed plan of the Mexican home of Leon Trotsky, Stalin's most hated enemy.

The strange death of Lev Sedov, the son of Leon Trotsky, in Paris on February 16, 1938, was probably caused by poisoning with an unknown drug. The official historians of the current Foreign Intelligence Service (SVR) claim that there are no documents in the NKVD/KGB/SVR files supporting this possibility. Nonetheless, they found Yakov Serebryansky's report, dated 1937, which says that Serebryansky and his group received an order from Moscow to kidnap Sedov and bring him to Moscow.[88] In the middle of 1937, everything was ready to move Sedov out of France secretly by a boat or a private plane (Serebryansky's terrorist group bought both), but according to this official SVR version, Sedov's sudden death after a surgical operation put an end to the plan.

Vasilii Mitrokhin, a long-term worker at the KGB archives who defected to England in 1992, agrees that the contemporary SVR files contain no proof that the NKVD was responsible for Sedov's death. However, he concludes: "What remains in doubt is whether Sedov was murdered by the NKVD in February 1938 or whether he died of natural causes before he could be assassinated."[89] Sedov had never realized that his most trusted friend and colleague in Paris, whom he knew as "Étienne" Zborowski (his real name was Mark Zborowski; alias "Maks," "Mak," "Tulip," and "Kant") was, in fact, an NKVD agent who was in contact with Serebryansky's group.[90] The fact that Zborowski persuaded Sedov to go not to a French hospital but to a Russian private clinic and refused to reveal its address to Sedov's French colleagues still makes Sedov's death suspicious.

The rise of the new commissar, Lavrentii Beria, began before Yezhov's end. On August 22, 1938, first secretary of the Georgian Communist Party Beria was appointed first deputy NKVD commissar.[91] Two weeks later, on September 8, Yezhov's first deputy, Frinovsky, was dismissed, then arrested and shot. On September 29, 1938, Beria was appointed head of the GUGB, and his former colleague from the Central Committee of the Georgian Communist Party Vsevolod Merkulov became Beria's deputy. The same day,

Lavrentii Beria, a Politburo member and head of the Soviet atomic project. Photo taken in 1946 at a demonstration of airplanes at the Tushino Airport (Moscow). (Photo from Memorial's Archive [Moscow])

Security (NKGB) Commissar Vsevolod Merkulov (1945). Merkulov was second in charge of Laboratory No. 1. (Photo from the Russian State Archive of Cinema and Photo Documents [Moscow])

yet a new structure of the NKVD was announced and a reorganization started.

Yezhov's short but bloodthirsty reign (in 1937, 936,750 Soviet citizens were arrested for committing "counterrevolutionary crimes" and 353,074 were shot; in 1938, 638,509 were arrested for political crimes and 328,618 were shot)[92] ended on November 24, 1938, when Stalin signed a Politburo resolution dismissing him. On November 25, Beria was appointed commissar, and Merkulov, the first deputy commissar and head of the GUGB. Yezhov was accused of "political unreliability" and arrested on April 10, 1939. On February 4, 1940, after a one-day trial, Yezhov was condemned to death for "treason against the Motherland, wrecking, spying, preparation of terrorist acts, and organization of assassinations of persons he did not like." Nothing was said, of course, about the fact that the terrorist acts and assassinations had been ordered by the Politburo and Stalin. Yezhov was shot in the basement of the Military Tribunal building on Nikol'sky Street in front of the Kremlin.[93] In June 1998, the Military Collegium of the Russian Supreme Court refused to rehabilitate Yezhov.[94]

THE LABORATORY OF DEATH: A SHORT HISTORY

September 1938 became a period of drastic changes in the NKVD structure, including the subordination of research laboratories. Beria and Merkulov brought from Georgia a team of Communist Party and local NKVD functionaries who became key persons in the NKVD/NKGB/MGB structure until Stalin's death in 1953. Shpigelglass was replaced by Vladimir Dekanozov, a former deputy chairman of the Georgia Council of People's Commissars with a reputation as "the hangman of Baku" because of the death sentences he had handed out in the Caucasus in the 1920s.[95] Besides the Foreign Department (now named the GUGB NKVD Fifth Department), Dekanozov simultaneously headed the GUGB Third (Counterintelligence) Department and became deputy NKVD commissar.

The changes in the GUGB Twelfth Department (which included the predecessor of Mairanovsky's lab) started even earlier. On June 9, 1938, the GUGB Twelfth Department was renamed the Second Special Department (Operational Equipment) and Mikhail Alekhin was appointed its acting head.[96] However, on September 13, soon after Frinovsky's dismissal, Alekhin was arrested. In a year he was condemned as a "German spy" and shot. Yevgenii Lapshin was appointed acting head of the Second Department and Arkady Osinkin, his deputy.[97] The same month, Valentin Kravchenko, who later, in 1942, supervised Mairanovsky's laboratory, joined this department as an engineer. That same September, Mairanovsky started his cooperation with the NKVD. Possibly, the poisons laboratory within "Yasha's Group" was merged with the Second Department after Serabryansky's arrest on October 11, 1938.

On February 20, 1939, this Second Special Department was divided in two, with the new Second Special Department headed by Lapshin (621 persons), and the Fourth Special Department headed by Mikhail Filimonov (61 persons).[98] The toxicological laboratory, known as Laboratory No. 1 or "The Kamera" (the word *kamera* in Russian has a sinister meaning—a cell in a prison or a chamber for torture) and now headed by Mairanovsky, was included in Filimonov's department (Table 2.1). There were two laboratories

**Table 2.1 Changes in Subordination of
Special Secret Laboratory No. 1 in 1939–1978[1]**

Date of Change	Commissariat/Ministry		Directorate and Head	Department and Head	Laboratory and Head
	Name	Commissar			
Feb. 20, 1939	NKVD	L. Beria, 1st Deputy V. Merkulov		4th Special Dept. (Laboratories), M. Filimonov, 61 staff members	Laboratory No. 1, G. Mairanovsky
Feb. 26, 1941	NKGB (NKVD was divided into NKVD and NKGB)	V. Merkulov, Deputy B. Kobulov	1st Directorate	8th Department, M. Filimonov	Laboratory No. 1, G. Mairanovsky
July 31, 1941	NKVD (NKVD merged with NKGB)	L. Beria, 1st Deputy V. Merkulov	4th Special Department, V. Kravchenko	10th Division (Laboratories), M. Filimonov	Laboratory No. 1, G. Mairanovsky
Jan. 18, 1942	NKVD (NKVD merged with NKGB)	L. Beria, 1st Deputy V. Merkulov	4th Directorate, P. Sudolatov (Deputy N. Eitingon)	4th Department, M. Filimonov	Laboratory No. 1, G. Mairanovsky
June 1, 1942	NKVD (NKVD merged with NKGB)	L. Beria, 1st Deputy V. Merkulov	4th Directorate, P. Sudolatov (Deputy N. Eitingon)	5th Department, M. Filimonov	Laboratory No. 1, G. Mairanovsky
May 14, 1943	NKGB (NKVD divided into NKVD and NKGB)	V. Merkulov, 1st Deputy B. Kobulov	4th Directorate, P. Sudoplatov (Deputy N. Eitingon)	5th Department, M. Filimonov	Laboratory No. 1, G. Mairanovsky
Aug. 20, 1946	MGB	V. Abakumov, 1st Deputy S. Ogol'tsov	(4th Directorate dissolved)	Department of Operational Equipment (OOT), F. Zhelezov	Laboratory, G. Mairanovsky (Senior Engineer)
Mar. 14, 1953	MVD	L. Beria, 1st Deputies S. Kruglov, B.Kobulov, I. Serov		5th Special Dept.	Laboratory No. 12, V. Naumov
Mar. 18, 1954	KGB	S. Kruglov, 1st Deputy K. Lunev		5th Special Dept.	Laboratory No. 12, V. Naumov
July 2, 1959	KGB	A. Shelepin	Directorate of Operational Equipment		Laboratory No. 12, V. Naumov (?)
1978	KGB	Yu. Andropov	Operational-Technical Directorate (OTU)		Central Investigation Institute for Special Technology

[1] Data from Kokurin and Petrov, *Lubyanka*, pp. 22–25, 55, 60, 73, 128; Petrov and Skorkin, *Kto rukovodil NKVD*, pp. 380 and 421. Also see the text.

The corner of Bol'shaya Lubyanka Street and Varsonofyevsky Lane.
Laboratory No. 1 was located in the yard of this building.
(Photo by Vadim Birstein [New York], 1997)

(called divisions, later departments), under the supervision of Mairanovsky and Sergei Muromtsev within Laboratory No. 1.[99]

The head of the newly created Fourth Special Department, Mikhail Petrovich Filimonov, was a chemist, and it seems that he had a Candidate of Science scientific degree. At least, he was a graduate student at the Moscow Institute of Precise Chemical Technologies.[100] He joined the NKVD in December 1938. At first, Filimonov was deputy head of the Eleventh Division of the GUGB Fifth (Foreign Intelligence) Department.

The reorganization was finalized on March 9, 1939.[101] From this time and until mid-1946, Filimonov's department, including Mairanovsky's laboratory, was located in a nice-looking building behind the main NKVD headquarters, known as Lubyanka, on the corner of Bol'shaya Lubyanka Street and Varsonofyevsky Lane. The previous location of the experimental laboratory had been in two different NKVD buildings: in Kuchino, a town outside Moscow, and on Fourth Meshchanskaya Street, then in a distant part of Moscow not far from Butyrka Prison.[102] The official address of the new building, No. 11 Varsonofyevsky Lane, had a bad reputation among Muscovites. The basement of the inner part of this building, with an entrance from the yard, was known since the 1920s as "the execution garage," where special VCheKa executioners shot victims condemned to death. This building still exists; however, the entrance into the yard is blocked.[103]

In 1939, another part of the building, also with an entrance from the yard, was given to Filimonov's department. Vasilii Blokhin, who was both the commandant of Lubyanka Prison and the chief executioner, became a close collaborator of Mairanovsky's: Blokhin was in charge of providing prisoners for experiments. One can imagine that this work did not bother Blokhin much, since he executed innumerable NKVD victims. Here is a description of his work: "He [Blokhin] put on a special uniform: a brown leather apron, a leather cap, a pair of long leather gloves . . . A person was ordered to enter a soundproof room and was shot [by Blokhin] in the head from behind . . . "[104]

That same March in 1939, Stalin personally, in the presence of Beria, ordered Sudoplatov to develop an efficient plan to kill Trotsky.[105] Eitingon, who had just returned from Spain, where he was an NKVD *rezident*, joined the operation and later became the main organizer of Trotsky's murder in Mexico. The details of the operation were discussed with the new head (formerly deputy head) of the GUGB Fifth (Foreign Intelligence) Department, Pavel Fitin. Chemicals from Filimonov's secret NKVD toxicological laboratory were considered among possible tools for use in Trotsky's assassination. Stalin approved the plan in early August 1939.[106] The plan included the following possible means of assassination: "Poisoning of food [or] water; an explosion in the house; an explosion of the car using T.N.T.; smothering; an attack with a knife; a hit on the head; firing a gun. An armed group attack is also possible."[107] Poisoning was considered to be the easiest method.

In the end, Trotsky was attacked by a member of Eitingon's team (Eitingon's alias for the operation was "Tom"), the Spanish Communist Ramon Mercader, with an ice pick.[108] The day after the assassination attempt, on August 21, 1941, Trotsky died in a hospital.[109] In May 1944, the Mexican Federal Court condemned the killer Ramon Mercader (under his alias name "Jacques Mornard") to twenty years' imprisonment. After his release in May 1960, Mercader went to Moscow, where he was immediately secretly awarded the highest Soviet order, the Hero of the Soviet Union. In 1974, Mercader left Moscow for Cuba, where he died in 1978.

Filimonov was the supervisor of the experimental laboratories from 1939 during all the reorganizations (see Table 2.1). On January 18, 1942, as a result of the new reorganization, the NKVD Fourth Department was promoted to a directorate and combined with the NKVD Second Department, with Sudoplatov as its head.[110] Eitingon became Sudoplatov's deputy on August 20, 1942.[111] In the new Fourth Directorate, Filimonov headed the Fourth Department,[112] and Yakov Serebryansky became head of the Special (Terrorist) Group. In May 1943, after the division of the NKVD into the NKVD and NKGB, the Fourth Directorate became the NKGB Fourth Directorate. Sudoplatov headed it until the beginning of 1944.[113] In February 1944, Sudoplatov left to head the NKGB Department "S," created to supervise the analysis of atomic intelligence collected by both the NKGB and the Soviet Military Intelligence (GRU).

Within the NKVD Fourth Directorate, Mairanovsky and Muromtsev each had a laboratory. Both laboratories were under the direct supervision of Commissar Beria and his first deputy, Merkulov (Table 2.1). In 1943–1945, when Merkulov was NKGB commissar, his first deputy, Bogdan Kobulov, whom Beria brought to Moscow from Georgia in 1938, was also in charge of the laboratory. Sudoplatov and his deputy, Eitingon, were well informed about experiments in Mairanovsky's lab. When Sudoplatov was tried in 1958, his involvement with Mairanovsky's "laboratory of death" was one of the charges against him:

> . . . As established [during the court trial], Beria and his accomplices committed terrible crimes against humanity: they tested deadly poisons, which caused agonizing death, on live humans. A special laboratory, which was established for experiments on the action of poisons on living humans, worked under the supervision of Sudoplatov and his deputy Eitingon from 1942 till 1946. They demanded he provide them only with poisons that had been tested on humans . . . [114]

On March 22, 1946, the NKGB was renamed MGB,[115] and on May 4, 1946, the new minister, Viktor Abakumov, replaced Merkulov.[116] Sergei Ogol'tsov, who was appointed the NKGB/MGB first deputy commissar/minister on December 4, 1945, retained his position. Filimonov remained head of the Fourth Department of the MGB Fourth Directorate until June 1946, when the Fourth Department was disbanded.[117] In October 1946, the entire MGB Fourth Directorate was dissolved.[118] Sudoplatov, Eitingon, and their main staff were transferred to the newly organized Department "DR" (Special Service for Diversions and Intelligence) and then, in 1950, to Bureau No. 1 (Terrorist Acts Abroad).[119] The creation of this bureau and Bureau No. 2 (Special Actions Within the Soviet Union) were approved by Stalin himself and then the Politburo (Document 10, Appendix II). Later, in Beria's MVD, on May 30, 1953, Bureau No. 1 became the MVD Ninth Department (Acts of Individual Terror and Diversions) and after Beria's arrest, on July 31, 1953, this department was merged with the MVD Second Main (Foreign Intelligence) Directorate.[120] On August 21, 1953, Sudoplatov was arrested. On November 20, 1953, the Presidium (former Politburo) ordered the creation of a new Special Department 12 within the MVD Second Main Directorate with the same functions as Sudoplatov's former Bureau No. 1: "for terrorist acts at the important military-strategic objects and communications at the territories of the main aggressive states, USA and England, as well as the territories of other capitalist countries."[121]

As Mairanovsky stressed in his letters to Semyon Ignatiev (in 1952), Beria (in 1953), and Khrushchev (in 1955) after he was arrested, Abakumov did not support his laboratory and ideas. After the main reorganization of the MGB, Mairanovsky's lab was included in the newly organized MGB Department of Operational Equipment (OOT),[122] headed by General Fyodor Zhelezov.[123] Therefore, the position of the laboratory within the security service structure became the same as it was in 1937–1938. Head of the NKGB Department "B" (Operational Equipment) Yevgenii Lapshin, with whom Mairanovsky worked, was sent out of Moscow to head the city of Tula regional MGB branch. Department "B" was in charge of making Mairanovsky's and other NKGB scientists' discoveries available for NKGB practice. Lapshin was replaced by Major General A. Kochetkov. Later, in 1951–1953, A. Polkovnikov became head of this department.[124]

In September 1948, Filimonov was dismissed from the MGB headquarters in Moscow (he subsequently became an alcoholic) and sent to head an MGB school in Lvov in the Ukraine. Later, in 1959, long after Mairanovsky's arrest and conviction, his former laboratory (now Laboratory No. 12) ended up as part of the Directorate of Operational Equipment within the KGB. In

1978, under KGB chairman Yurii Andropov, Laboratory No. 12 was included in the newly organized Central Investigation Institute for Special Technology within the KGB Operational-Technical Directorate, or OTU (Table 2.1).

Although the existence of Mairanovsky's lab was a closely held secret, in the late 1940s Sudoplatov lectured about it (without naming Mairanovsky) and its "developments" to the students of the MGB Special School. A former KGB officer, Ilya Dzhirkvelov, who defected to the West in 1980, later recalled:

At his [i.e., Sudoplatov's] lectures we learned about practically every method of organizing sabotage, underground operations and the liquidation, i.e., the murder, of our enemies. He told us that a special Scientific and Technical Department of the KGB [i.e., MGB at the time], with a staff of nameless but exceptionally able doctors, chemists and technologists, was developing and producing new types of weapons and poisons and devices for carrying out "Liter L," which was the code name for liquidation . . . Operations code-named "Liter I," meaning kidnapping, and "Liter L," can be carried out only with the approval of the Secretaries and Politburo members of the Soviet Communist Party . . .

. . . Even in those years the Technical Department of the KGB already had at its disposal fountain pens, cigarette cases and even fake cigarettes which could fire a fatal dose of poison. The poisons used left no traces in the body of the victim and produced the effect of a heart attack, a stroke or suffocation following an asthma attack. In addition, for kidnapping operations they had developed long-acting tranquilizers.[125]

Sudoplatov also gave examples of successful NKVD/MGB assassinations. He proudly described in detail how, on the personal order of Stalin, in 1938 in Amsterdam he killed the Ukrainian nationalist leader Yevhen Konovalets, who lived in Germany and France, using a bomb camouflaged as a candy box.[126]

THE LAB AFTER MAIRANOVSKY

After Mairanovsky's arrest in 1951 and the reorganization of his laboratory, it was not completely disbanded. Laboratory No. 12 continued to exist under the directorship of Mairanovsky's colleague and rival, Vasilii Naumov, and poisons were successfully used for executions abroad. In March 1953, after Stalin's death, MGB minister Semyon Ignatiev wrote to the new USSR leaders Malenkov, Beria, Molotov, Bulganin, and Khrushchev:

The execution of Zalus [a former guard of Leon Trotsky] was conducted through an MGB agent, who gave him a special chemical on February 13, 1953 [in Munich]. The chemical causes the death of a person in 10–12 days. After this Zalus got sick and died on March 4, in one of Munich's hospitals. Using different sources it was found out that the poisoning of Zalus did not provoke the enemy's suspicion. Doctors came to the conclusion that his death was a result of pneumonia.[127]

In the 1950s–1960s, the results of experiments performed at Mairanovsky's former lab, now Special Laboratory No. 12 of the OTU, were used for similar means in Germany. In 1957, Nikolai Khokhlov, a former KGB agent, became deathly ill while attending a convention in Frankfurt. Khokhlov defected in February 1954 after he had arrived in Germany with an order to kill Georgii Okolovich, chief of operations of the anti-Soviet émigré organization the Popular Labor Alliance of Russian Solidarists (NTS).[128] This order had been approved by the Presidium of the USSR Communist Party Central Committee (a new name for the Politburo). The complete anti-NTS operation was ordered by Beria and continued to be important for the Politburo after Beria's arrest and extermination. It was fulfilled under the personal supervision of the new head of the MVD Second Main Directorate, Aleksandr Panyushkin.[129] Khokhlov was a member of the MVD Ninth Department, which succeeded Sudoplatov's Special Bureau No. 1. During the time that Khokhlov was in Germany in 1954, another MVD/KGB team kidnapped and assassinated the NTS Berlin leader, Aleksandr Trushinovich.

Khokhlov was provided with a sophisticated execution weapon—an electrically operated gun with a silencer that fired cyanide-tipped bullets. It was concealed inside a cigarette packet.[130] He received this gun from the head of the Operational Techniques Department, Colonel Khoteyev. This department was located in Kuchino, where Maironovsky's laboratory had moved previously, and included his former lab. The weapon was created with the assistance of Naumov's laboratory.

Instead of killing Okolovich, Khokhlov defected, as Christopher Andrew and Oleg Gordievsky later wrote in their investigation of the KGB, to "an initially skeptical CIA."[131] In 1957, it was discovered that Khokhlov had become ill from poisoning by radioactive thallium.[132] In April 1955, after Khokhlov's defection, "special actions" became the responsibility of the reorganized Thirteenth Department of the KGB First Directorate.[133] Evidently, the KGB specialists from the former Ninth, now renamed Thirteenth, Department of the First Directorate, believed that this substance would not be detected during an autopsy. Due to radiation, the thallium would have already disintegrated. American doctors saved Khokhlov, but he became crippled. He wrote in his memoirs:

I . . . was an exhibit of the achievements of Soviet science. Totally bald, so disfigured by scars and spots that those who had known me did not at first recognize me, confined to a rigid diet, I was nevertheless also living proof that Soviet science, the science of killing, is not omnipotent.[134]

The MVD/KGB was definitely embarrassed that the "traitor" Khokhlov who had refused to kill Okolovich remained alive. Even forty years later, in his memoirs, Sudoplatov described Khokhlov with irritation as an unstable and unreliable person who "claimed that he was poisoned at a cocktail party by the KGB in 1957 and that CIA doctors helped him survive the radioactive thallium used on him."[135]

In 1957, Lev Rebet and, in 1959, Stepan Bandera, both prominent Ukrainian emigrants, were killed in West Germany by another sophisticated weapon: a spray of prussic acid released by a noiseless "pistol."[136] The inhaled gas caused the contraction of blood vessels. The cause of Rebet's death was officially listed as a heart attack. The killer, Bogdan Stashinsky, a member of the same KGB Thirteenth Department, was awarded the Order of the Red Banner in 1959 for these assassinations. However, Stashinsky defected to West Berlin in 1961, one day before the Berlin Wall was sealed. The details of the murders and the secret weapon became known because of Stashinsky's confession. Apparently, there had been serious progress in the killing methods of the MGB since Mairanovsky's time:

A metal tube about as thick as a finger and about seven inches long, and consisting of three sections screwed together . . . A metal lever in the middle section . . . crushes a glass ampoule in the orifice of the tube. This glass ampoule, with a volume of five cubic centimeters . . . contains a poison that resembles water and escapes out of the front of the tube in the form of vapor when the ampoule is crushed. If this vapor is fired at a person's face from a distance of about one and a half feet, the person drops dead immediately upon inhaling the vapor . . . Since this vapor leaves no traces, it is impossible to ascertain death by violence, and . . . the perpetrator suffers no harmful effects from the poison if he swallows a certain kind of tablet beforehand as an antidote and immediately after firing the weapon, crushes an ampoule sewn up in gauze and inhales its vapor.[137]

Stashinsky was tried in Germany and sentenced to eight years' imprisonment. In 1963, "special actions" were handed over to the newly created Department T, and in 1965, to Department V of the First Directorate.[138]

In October 1964, an attempt to assassinate a German counter-audio debugging expert, Horst Schwirkmann, took place in Zagorsky Monastery near Moscow.[139] Schwirkmann was standing in front of an icon he admired in a monastery church, when a middle-aged man who had been praying behind him suddenly left the church. After this, Schwirkmann felt what seemed like ice water on his left buttock and within seconds he was in agonizing pain. This time another chemical from Mairanovsky's arsenal was used. Schwirkmann was sprayed with nitrogen mustard gas. He almost lost his left leg but survived.

In 1978, Mairanovsky's former Laboratory No. 12 was renamed the Central Scientific Investigation Institute for Special Technology, or TsNIIST, within the KGB.[140] It "was attached to Directorate OTU (Operational-Technical) and was under the direct control of the KGB chairman [Yurii Andropov]."[141] This chain of command seems to have been exactly as it was during Beria-Merkulov's time. The laboratory provided the Bulgarian Secret Service with a secret weapon, through a KGB general, Sergei Golubev (Department "K" of the KGB First Main Directorate). This weapon was an umbrella that could shoot small poisoned bullets.[142] The operation was controlled by the head of Soviet Intelligence (the KGB First Main Directorate), Vladimir Kryuchkov (who later became head of the KGB under Mikhail Gorbachev, until the August 1991 coup). Yurii Andropov, at the time the head of the KGB, ordered this operation at the request of Todor Zhivkov, first secretary of the Bulgarian Communist Party. (After Leonid Brezhnev's death, Andropov was for a short time first secretary of the USSR Communist Party, ergo, a Soviet leader). The operation was developed at a meeting chaired by Andropov and attended by Kryuchkov, Vice Admiral Mikhail Usatov (Kryuchkov's deputy) and Oleg Kalugin (at the time head of the First Main Directorate of Counterintelligence).[143]

The Bulgarian emigrant Georgi Markov, who defected to Britain in 1969 and worked for the BBC, was killed by this special weapon. A poisoned pellet was fired from an umbrella on September 7, 1978. The poison used—ricin—was from Mairanovsky's arsenal. For some unknown reason, John Bryden, author of the book *Deadly Allies: Canada's Secret War, 1937–1947*, did not believe that ricin was used for Markov's assassination.[144] Oleg Kalugin, the former KGB general, claimed in an interview given to *Moscow News* in 1991[145] that it had been the third attempt to kill Markov.[146]

At first, Bulgarian agents tried to touch him "accidentally" with a cream that would cause death from a "heart attack" within one to two days. It would be impossible to identify the poison. They then tried to poison Markov with a chemical dissolved in a drink (a method strongly reminiscent of Dr. Mairanovsky's experiments). This attempt also appeared to be unsuccessful. Only the ricin succeeded. Before killing Markov, the Bulgarian Secret Service had successfully tried the method on a convict condemned to death: an umbrella fired a bullet perforated with small holes filled with ricin.[147] In 1978, General Dimitar Stoyanov, Bulgarian interior minister, presented General Kalugin with an expensive Browning hunting rifle as a reward for KGB assistance in killing Markov.[148]

The "umbrella murder" case has not been closed yet. In 1998, Bulgaria's National Investigation Office was still trying to find Francesco Guillino (presumably Markov's killer), to charge him with the murder.[149] Guillino may have settled in Hungary or Romania.

The life of another Bulgarian defector, Vladimir Kostov, was saved because a similar pellet was removed from his back intact, before the ricin had time to escape from the steel bullet. This incident took place in the Paris metro. Seven years later, General Golubev supervised the drugging of a future KGB defector, Oleg Gordievsky, with drugs from Laboratory No. 12 in an attempt to get him to confess.[150] It is known that sometimes dissidents in the Soviet Union were drugged in order to elicit confessions.

Another defector, who moved to the United States in 1992, is Dr. Kanatjan Alibekov, or Ken Alibek, as he is now known. Alibek, former deputy director of a Soviet biological warfare agency called Biopreparat, recently disclosed that the KGB had (and maybe the SVR and FSB still have) close contacts with the Ministry of Health's institutes that specialized in the development of psychotropic and neurotropic biological agents.[151] The network of medical institutions that investigated biological agents that could cause nonlethal and lethal organic and physiological changes useful for the KGB purposes had a name—the Flute Program.[152] Basically, five research institutes in Moscow and the Moscow Region that belonged to the Third Main Directorate of the USSR Ministry of Health (Medstatistika; Institute of Applied Molecular Biology; Institute of Immunology; Scientific and Production Center of Medical Biotechnology; and Center of Toxicology and Hygienic Regulation of Biopreparations) were involved in the Flute Program. In 1989, Valerii Butuzov, who was both a KGB/SVR colonel and a pharmacologist, was put on the staff of Biopreparat formally as an engineer.[153] His job was to provide the former KGB Laboratory No. 12, now TsNIIST, with the new developments at Biopreparat, especially within the Flute Program.

During the reorganizations of 1996–1997, Biopreparat and many former biological weapons facilities seem to have been moved under the Ministry of Economics.[154] The state agency Biopreparat has been transformed into the Russian joint stock company, RAO Biopreparat, with a trading branch, AOOT-Biopreparat-Tsentr, and an international operation branch via a Geneva-based company, Pharmachemtec Limited. At present, the Russian military scientists who control RAO Biopreparat also control the Russian pharmaceutical industry.

The creation of Biopreparat was not possible without the energy and enthusiasm of Academician Yurii Ovchinnikov, who merged molecular genetics achievements at the Academy of Sciences with the interests of the Soviet Ministry of Defense.[155] I have already mentioned Ovchinnikov in Chapter 1; he was the youngest academician and the youngest vice president of the academy. Ovchinnikov was a tall elegant man who easily found a mutual language with academicians and the highest Soviet bureaucrats. He also created a Party career and became a member of the Central Committee. It is interesting to note that his family was a victim of Stalin's regime—his father was arrested and the family was exiled.[156] Ovchinnikov's autocratic and ruthless style of administration was widely known among Soviet biologists.[157]

In 1972, Ovchinnikov asked the Ministry of Defense to support the development of new types of bacteriological and toxicological weapons using genetic engineering methods.[158] This secret program, "The Enzyme," was started under his supervision. Beginning in 1973, a group of research institutes was united under the name Biopreparat. Besides Ovchinnikov's very large Institute of Bioorganic Chemistry, three more Academy of Science institutes in Moscow were involved in the Enzyme project: the Institute of Molecular Biology (Moscow, directed by Academician Andrei Mirzabekov), the Institute of Protein (Pushchino, Moscow Region; directed by Academician Aleksandr Spirin), and the Institute of Biochemistry and Physiology of Microorganisms (Pushchino, Moscow Region; directed by Academician Georgy Skryabin, and after his death, by Professor Aleksandr Boronin). A special commission, the Inter-Agency Scientific and Technical Council, coordinated the secret work of institutions involved in the development of new types of biological weapons: the Academy of Sciences, the Ministries of Health, Agriculture, Defense, and Chemical Industry, and the KGB. It consisted of members from the principal scientific organizations of the Soviet Union, and then Russia, including directors of the academy institutes mentioned above and the secretary academician of the Biochemistry, Biophysics and the Chemistry of Physiologically Active Substances Division (since 1994, Physical-Chemical Biology Division), Academician Aleksandr Baev.[159] Although Academician Baev (1903–1995) spent seventeen years in Stalin's worst labor camps and in exile,[160] he was a devoted supporter of the Soviet regime. In the 1980s–early 1990s, the Inter-Agency Council was headed by a minister of medical industry. It met once every two or three months to discuss the current needs of biological weapon development.

According to Alibek, in 1990, during the peak of Gorbachev's perestroika, the KGB/SVR colonel at Biopreparat, Butuzov, approached Alibek with a plan to assassinate Zviad Gamsakhurdia, the former Soviet political dissident and at the time the newly elected president of Georgia.[161] The KGB authorities (the operation was under the personal control of the KGB chairman Vladimir Kryuchkov) planned to use an aerosol of Ebola virus concealed in an empty box of Marlboro cigarettes for the assassination.[162] An alternative method of killing that Butuzov also considered was spraying the steering wheel of the victim's car with a poisonous agent.[163] It seems that the plan was turned down by the Soviet leaders.

In 1992, Gamsakhurdia was ousted from office, and the former Soviet foreign minister, Eduard Shevarnadze, became Georgian president. The next year, on December 31, 1993, Gamsakhurdia died in mysterious circumstances. Officially his death was announced as a suicide. However, there were rumors that he was killed by Moscow agents.[164] The killing of Gamsakhurdia was the last known assassination plan of Mairanovsky and Muromtsev's KGB successors.

The KGB generously provided their secret service colleagues in many Eastern European countries with Mairanovsky's arsenal of chemicals. In his recently published memoirs, Markus Wolf, chief of the foreign intelligence service of the Ministry of State Security of the German Democratic Republic, recalled:

> One KGB man was dispatched to buyers throughout the Eastern bloc bearing wares such as untraceable nerve toxins and skin contact poisons to smear on doorknobs. The only thing I ever accepted from him was a sachet of "truth drugs," which he touted as "unbeatable" with the enthusiasm of a door-to-door salesman . . . One day, in a fit of curiosity, I asked our carefully vetted doctor to have them analyzed for me. He came back shaking his head in horror. "Use these without constant medical supervision and there is every chance that the fellow from whom you want the truth will be dead as a dodo in seconds," he said. We never did use the "truth drugs."[165]

Even recently, Russia seems to have been engaged in secret scientific work that is prohibited by international law and agreements. In 1991, a group of military chemists was awarded with the prestigious Lenin Prize for the development of a new extremely destructive neuroparalytic weapon.[166] One of the supervisors of this project, Academician Irina Beletskata (b. 1933, became an academy corresponding member in 1974), who heads the Laboratory of Organic Elements Compounds of the Chemistry Department of Moscow University, was elected a full academician in 1992, just after the finalization of the project.[167]

Almost simultaneously, on October 22, 1992, a Moscow chemist, Vil Mirzayanov, was arrested by the police and put into Lefortovo Prison. He was accused of divulging state secrets in newspaper articles published in 1991–1992. In these articles Mirzayanov exposed "the military-industrial complex, which, on the eve of the signing of a Government convention to ban chemical weapons, developed a new type of chemical weapon five to eight times stronger than all known weapons."[168] In 1993, Russia signed the 1993 Chemical Weapons Convention banning chemical weapons.[169] The new type of weapon was a binary nerve agent called Novichok, which means "newcomer" in Russian. The development of Novichok was based on the idea that after the reaction of two neutral chemical compounds, an extremely strong toxic substance can be produced.[170] In this way, the country that keeps the neutral compounds can deny that it has chemical weapons. The binary phospho-organic paralytic nerve gas called Novichok-9 especially has an extremely high toxic activity.[171]

According to Dr. Mirzayanov, Novichok was developed in 1973 by the chemist Pyotr Kirpichev, who worked at the Shikhany (the town of Volsk) branch of the State Scientific Research Institute of Organic Chemistry and Technology (GosNIIOKhT). Another chemist, Vladimir Uglev, joined in the research in 1975. At first Novichok was tested at the Shikhany institute and then, in 1986–1989 near the city of Nukus (Uzbekistan), at a special military testing base. In 1987, a Moscow scientist, Andrei Zhelezov, was accidentally exposed to the residue of the gas during tests. He died in 1992.[172] Mirzayanov made his accusations together with Lev Fedorov, president of the Union of Chemical Safety (Moscow), and one of the inventors of Novichok, Vladimir Uglev.[173] He refused to testify at his own closed trial, which began on January 6, 1994. On February 22, 1994, Mirzayanov was released from prison, and at present he lives in the United States.[174]

In his interviews, Dr. Mirzayanov pointed out that ricin, one of the most dangerous of Mairanovsky's poisons, was produced in Russia as a chemical weapon.[175] Soviet scientists had the same technological problem of dissemination with this toxin in enemy territory as British and American experts had during World War II. Due to the high temperature of the blast from a shell or a bomb, most of the ricin would be inactivated. The idea of putting ricin inside hollow steel needles was then considered by Soviet scientists. During the explosion of a bomb containing such needles, ricin would retain its toxic ability and could easily be introduced into the bodies of numerous victims. Mairanovsky could not have come up with a better solution himself. However, this technology was not introduced into production due to the very high cost of the procedure.

It seems that the Americans did not know about Mairanovsky's experiments with ricin in the late 1930s–1940s and the more recent discussions of Soviet military scientists regarding the use of ricin as a weapon. In an interview with investigative writer David Wise, Benjamin Harris, a former technical director of the Maryland Air National Guard Office at Edgewood Arsenal near Baltimore (one of the main American research facilities on chemical weaponry), said:

> I was aware of one incident where we were asked by the [American] intelligence people to supply information on a toxin that was not a good candidate for use as a weapon. It was ricin. It was considered a toxin because it was produced by a living organism, the castor-bean plant. We did not consider it a good candidate because it was difficult to come by in large quantities and had not been synthesized at that time.[176]

Analyzing Markov's assassination and Harris's information, David Wise came to the wrong conclusion: "Whether the information about ricin was passed to the Soviets, either in the deception phase of SHOCKER [a code name for an FBI/army operation against the Soviet Military Intelligence (GRU) spies who collected information on the development of American nerve gas weaponry] or in a separate, parallel counterintelligence operation, is not clear."[177] Definitely, neither Harris nor Wise knew about Mairanovsky's "achievements" with ricin.

Drs. Mirzayanov and Alibek warned their colleagues and Western politicians that despite all international agreements, Russian scientists would continue to work on chemical and biological weapons. In 1990–1991 in the USSR, eighteen research institutes with 42,000 employed scientists and six plants were working on the problems and production of biological weapons.[178] In 1999, Dr. Mirzayanov was convinced that the only serious problem for the main Russian research institute on chemical weapons, the GosNIIOKhT in Moscow, was lack of funding. If funded, chemists at this institute and its branches will develop new poisonous agents that will be able to penetrate the filters of gas masks.[179] Dr. Alibek pointed to the fact that publications in scientific literature in 1996–1997 showed that Russian scientists have continued the development of genetically engineered strains of virulent viruses and bacteria for biological weapons.[180] These studies were done with the involvement of the Russian Academy of Sciences and under FSB/SVR control. Such scientific work is a definite violation of the Russian agreement with the United States and Britain signed in 1992 that prohibits all work on biological weapons.[181]

Despite the warning, in May 2000 the United States, the European Union, and Japan decided to provide $1.61 million to improve security at the State Research Center for Applied Microbiology in Obolensk (about fifty miles from Moscow), one of the former most secret military installations in the Soviet Union.[182] For the first time, an international conference took place at this center and Western scientists were shown the infamous Building No. 1 where the most top-secret research was previously conducted.[183] General Nikolai Urakov, director of the center, pledged to open the "curtain of secrecy" and convert the center from military to peaceful research. However, the center will still be in the system of military institutions, and there is no guarantee that a group of scientists within this institution will not continue studies in biological weaponry.

In contemporary Russia, academic science is in trouble because of poor governmental funding.[184] At the celebration of the two hundred and seventy-fifth anniversary of the academy in June 1999, President Academician Yurii Semenov declared: "[In 1998] we lived in a state of emergency. All promises of state support for science were not fulfilled."[185] In 2000, the situation became even more desperate. Because of the underfunding of science and miserable salaries, many academic researchers, especially young scientists, have left scientific institutions, and their number in 2000 fell to 910,000, half the figure for 1990.[186] Scientists working in the system of the KGB's secret institutes (since the August 1991 coup, the official name of the KGB has changed several times, but it is easier to refer to it in the old way) never had such a problem, and presumably still do not. In February 1994, after Mirzayanov's release from prison, General Golushko (at the time head of the Federal Counterintelligence Service—alias the KGB) told the journalist Yevgeniya Albats: "The scientific-technical directorate includes institutes for the design of special technology and intelligence equipment. The scientific-technological directorate, along with the designers and the institutes, numbers about ten thousand people. We also work for intelligence and help the Ministry of Internal Affairs."[187] These words are confirmed by the fact that since 1989, special Spetsnaz troops have been armed with guns to shoot bullets that contain neuroparalytic chemicals. These chemicals are produced at a secret research institute in Klimovsk, a town not far from Moscow.[188] Apparently, KGB laboratories are thriving in the economic disaster of contemporary Russia. The general's estimate of 10,000 scientists being involved in secret service work is impressive. The staff at Mairanovsky's laboratory numbered approximately only 20–30.

The legacy of Mairanovsky and his colleagues continues in Russia. There were reports in 1999 to early 2000 that chemical weapons were used by the Russian troops against Chechen rebels and civilians during the fight in Grozny in the North Caucasus.[189] Here is a witness's description:

> Animals were the first who felt the beginning of chemical attacks . . . Poisoned dogs heart-rending howled and whirled strangely as they were try-

ing to bite their own tails. Cats squealed disgustingly like babies when they weep for a long time. Later, after a few hours, people started choking, their skins were covered with red pimples, and their eyes became watering and swollen.[190]

One can only guess what kind of chemical poisons the Russian military experimenters tested in Chechnya that caused these symptoms.

EXPERIMENTS

In or about December 1943 and in or about October 1944 experiments were conducted at the Buchenwald concentration camp to investigate the effect of various poisons upon human beings. The poisons were secretly administered to experimental subjects [Russian prisoners] in their food. The victims died as result of the poison or were killed immediately in order to permit autopsies. In or about September 1944 experimental subjects [who had been condemned to death] were shot with poison bullets [filled with aconitine nitrate projectiles] and suffered torture and death. . . . The defendants Genzken, Gebhardt, Mrugowsky, and Poppendick are charged with special responsibility for and participation in these crimes.

—Charge (K) at "The Case Against the
Nazi Physicians," Nuremberg[191]

I found the first description of Mairanovsky's lab in the literature in a book authored by the KGB defector, Peter Deriabin:

As late as 1953 the interrogations [at the MGB] were backed by a terror device which would have done credit to the worst of the Gestapo professionals. From 1946 until that year, the state security maintained at its Moscow headquarters a quietly notorious laboratory called the "Chamber" (Kamera). Its staff consisted of a medical director and several assistants, who performed experiments on living people—prisoners and persons about to be executed—to determine the effectiveness of various poisons and injections as well as the use of hypnotism and drugs in interrogation techniques. Only the Minister of the State Security and four other high officers were allowed to enter.

The laboratory prospered. The "doctor" in charge was given a special degree of Doctor of Medical Science by Moscow University and nominated for a Stalin Prize for his "research." In October 1953 the Soviet regime announced The Chamber's closing to a select group of State Security officials, after blaming its existence on the Beria excesses. It has probably not been reactivated; but its researchers continue to be exploited by selected personnel of the State Security.

The Chamber, while it lasted, had been under the Commandant's Section in the administrative directorate of the State Security apparatus. It was this section which supervised all executions of political prisoners condemned to death, in addition to its normal physical security duties.[192]

Additional information was published in the former Communist newspaper *Izvestiya* in an interview with the military prosecutor, Colonel Vladimir Bobryonev,[193] who had access to the investigation files on Mairanovsky and Beria, which are still kept at the KGB (FSB) archive. According to the NKVD-MGB-KGB investigation procedure, there were two files for each arrested person. The investigation file contained materials such as transcripts (protocols) of interrogations, and so on. This file was completed before the trial. The prisoner file included documents connected with the life of the arrested person before and after the trial. It contained personal information (the "Anketa"), orders of investigators to move the prisoner within a prison or to another prison, orders to bring the prisoner for interrogations, the trial verdict, the order to transfer the accused prisoner to a labor camp or a prison, and the like. In addition, there was a special file for "operational material" (mainly received from secret informers) on the suspect before the person's arrest and during his or her imprisonment.[194] In his interview, Bobryonev described the laboratory:

A large hall on the first floor of a corner building at Varsonofyevsky Lane [in the central part of Moscow] was provided for the laboratory, which previously had occupied a small room. The hall was divided into five cells with doors facing a large office. The doors had peepholes. During experiments, a member of the laboratory staff was constantly on duty in this office . . . Almost every day a few prisoners condemned to death were brought to the laboratory. The whole procedure was similar to a medical examination. The "doctor" asked the "patient" about his or her health with concern, gave some advice and medication.[195]

At first, mustard gas derivatives were used for experiments. Mustard gas was discovered in 1886 and was used for the first time as chemical weapon by the Germans during World War I in their attack on British troops in July 1917 near Ypres, France.[196] Mairanovsky's results were disappointing: The chemicals were immediately detected during autopsies. This contradicted the main goal of the experiments—to find a chemical without any taste that could not be detected in the victim's body before or after death. Later, various doses of a toxic substance, a protein called ricin, extracted from castor-oil seeds produced by *Ricinus communis,* were tried unsuccessfully for a year. This toxin was discovered at the end of World War I and was regarded as a potential agent for biological warfare.[197] During World War II, in 1942–1943, ricin, under the name Compound W, was considered by British, Canadian, and American experts as a possible biological weapons agent in the war against Japan. By the end of 1943, a pilot project on the production of ricin was developed, and various ricin dispersal methods were tested.[198] In 1944, the Japanese experimented with castor-oil seeds, but not pure ricin, on Russian POWs.[199] Mairanovsky also tried digitoxin[200] on ten prisoners. Eventually a preparation with all the desired properties, called C-2 (carbylomine cholinchloride), was created. Chemicals were given to the victims as "medication," or they were mixed with a meal or drinking water to disguise the taste. These poisons usually brought on great pain and suffering.

Colonel Bobryonev claimed that Mairanovsky's file contains testimonies of witnesses who saw experiments: "Mairanovsky brought to the laboratory people of varying physical conditions, decrepit and full of health, fat and slim. Some died in three-four days, others were racked with pain for a week."[201] According to the witnesses' testimonies, after having taken the preparation C-2, the victim changed physically, seeming to become shorter, quickly weakening and becoming calm and silent. C-2 killed the victim in fifteen minutes.

During the Mairanovsky case investigation in 1954, Mikhail Filimonov testified about the experiments:

> Sudoplatov and Eitingon approved special equipment [poisons] only if it had been tested on humans . . . I witnessed some of the poisoning tests, but I tried not to be present at the experiments because I could not watch the action of poisons on the psyche and body of humans. Some poisons caused extreme suffering. To conceal shouts we even bought a radio set which we turned on [during the experiments].[202]

Mairanovsky's assistant, Aleksandr Grigorovich, and a chemist named Shchegolev were in charge of weighing doses of poisons. However, Mairanovsky himself mixed poisons with food. If poison did not cause death, Mairanovsky injected it using a syringe.[203]

On Eitingon's order, Mairanovsky also experimented with curare. Curare is a blackish, resin-like substance derived from tropical plants of the genus *Strychnos,* especially *S. toxifera.* Also, it can come from the root of the South American vine pareira *(Chondodendron tomentosum),* used by some South

American Indians for poisoning arrowheads. Curare acts by arresting the action of motor nerves. The Soviet secret service had been interested in curare since the time of VCheKa and Yakov Agranov. During the show trial against thirty-four members of the Social Revolutionary Party in Moscow from June 8 to August 7, 1922, the two defendants Grigory Semenov-Vasiliev and Lidiya Konopleva testified that they had provided Faina Kaplan, the unsuccessful assassin of Vladimir Lenin, with bullets poisoned with curare.[204]

This attempt took place on August 30, 1918. Lenin survived, and Kaplan was shot without trial almost immediately after the attempt. The attempt upon Lenin's life provoked the beginning of the Red Terror as a formal response to "counterrevolution activity." The terror was unleashed after two more Bolsheviks, chairman of the Petrograd Bolshevik Committee Moisei Volodarsky and chairman of the Petrograd CheKa Moisei Uritsky, were assassinated on June 20, 1918, and August 30, 1918. After these three assassination attempts, the VCheKa shot approximately 6,185 prisoners and hostages, imprisoned 14,829 persons, put 6,407 into concentration camps, and detained 4,068 as hostages.[205]

However, the testimonies of 1922 sound like a typical fabrication by Agranov and the OGPU. Both defendants, who "repented" of their crime, served in the VCheKa from 1919 and joined the Bolshevik Party in 1921. Moreover, they were acquitted during the trial. It is also unclear whether the very short-sighted Kaplan had shot at all or whether it had been somebody else. In 1992, Boris Petrovsky, a member of the Medical Academy, evaluated the description of Lenin's illness after he had been shot: "There was no poisoning allegedly caused by 'poisoned' bullets . . . One should not talk about poisoned bullets. However . . . the wound was rare and very dangerous for [Lenin's] life."[206]

According to Mairanovsky, after the injection of curare he observed the following symptoms:

Loss of voice and strength, muscular weakness, prostration, labored breathing, cyanosis and death with symptoms of suffocation while retaining complete consciousness. Death was excruciating, but the man was deprived of the ability to shout or move while retaining complete consciousness. Death of the "patient" ensued within 10–15 minutes after a sufficient dosage.[207]

Eitingon testified in 1954:

I was present during experiments at [Mairanovsky's] laboratory. Four Germans, who were condemned to death as active Gestapo men that had taken part in the execution of Soviet people, were the test objects. An injection of curare into blood was used for testing. The poison acted almost immediately, and the men were dead approximately in two minutes . . . [208]

Those in charge of Mairanovsky's work had no doubt about the necessity of experiments on humans. During his interrogation in September 1953, while facing the death penalty, Merkulov testified:

> I believed that since these experiments were being performed on people sentenced by execution as enemies of the Soviet government, and since, in the interests of the Soviet government, these people were turned over to Soviet intelligence in order to provide a reliable means of eliminating enemies through sabotage, then the experiments were not illegal. Furthermore, these experiments were sanctioned by [Commissar] Beria and consequently were considered necessary to the work of the NKVD.[209]

It is worthwhile to add that Merkulov visited Mairanovsky's laboratory once and watched the administration of a poison to a prisoner and the resulting behavior of the prisoner through a peephole in the cell's door. Bogdan Kobulov, who also supervised Mairanovsky's laboratory in the 1940s, had a similar opinion. During his interrogation in 1953, the interrogator, Lieutenant Colonel Bazenko, asked him: "Don't you think that such experiments are crimes against humanity?" Kobulov answered:

> I do not think so, since the end purpose of the experiments was the war against enemies of the Soviet government. The NKVD is an agency that can use such experiments on convicted enemies of Soviet authority in the interests of the Soviet government. As an NKVD employee, I obeyed the orders to perform the experiment, but as a person I believed they were undesirable.[210]

Finally, Beria himself testified about the experiment on August 28, 1953: "I gave orders to Mairanovsky to conduct experiments on people sentenced to the highest measure of punishment, but it was not my idea."[211] The USSR chief prosecutor, Rodion Rudenko, who headed the interrogation, ignored this statement, fearing that Beria would say that these orders came from Stalin and the Politburo. Four days later, in the next interrogation, Beria tried to diminish his role in the experiments:

> I do not know, perhaps experiments were done on 100 people, but I gave the sanction for only three. Merkulov was more involved with it . . .

Mairanovsky reported to me the methods used to poison people. He informed me of the possibility of using the toxic substance ricin to poison people through inhaled air. I proposed that he work on researching this means of poisoning. I was interested in these poisons in connection with an operation that was being planned against Hitler. Then the potency of action of these poisons was tested in experiments on low [sic!] people—convicts . . . I state categorically that I know nothing about this [the results of experiments on subjects].[212]

Later it was not possible to find out the truth. On December 18–23, 1953, Beria, Merkulov, Kobulov, and four others of Beria's closest NKVD-KGB men were tried by a closed session of the Special Session of the USSR Supreme Court chaired by Marshal Ivan Konev.[213] All defendants were found guilty and were shot to death immediately after the trial.[214]

In 1942, Mairanovsky discovered that under certain conditions, ricin had a special effect on subjects, compelling them to become trusting and open. This provoked a two-year series of experiments on obtaining "truthful testimonies" under the administration of chloral scopolamine and phenamine benzedrine. The CIA, which was created in July 1947, started experiments with the same idea ten years later, in 1950–1952.[215] Mairanovsky's series of experiments with "truth drugs" were approved by Merkulov and the head of the NKGB/NKVD Second Main Directorate (Counterespionage), Pyotr Fedotov. Also, Mairanovsky mentioned the involvement of Fedotov's deputy, Lieutenant General Leonid Raikhman.[216] In 1940, Raikhman (alias "Zaitsev"), as head of the NKVD Polish Office, was one of the main organizers of the murder of Polish POWs.[217] In September 1941, as Fedotov's deputy, Raikhman was involved in the deportation of the Volga Germans of the Saratov Region to Kazakhstan and Siberia.[218] After World War II, he worked with Sudoplatov in Lvov (western Ukraine) on "cleansing" the area of Ukrainian and Polish partisans.[219] Raikhman was arrested after Abakumov's arrest and released after Stalin's death. In 1953, during Beria's investigation, Raikhman denied his involvement in the affairs of Mairanovsky. Instead, he named the head of the MGB Investigation Department at the time, Zimenkov, as a source of information about Mairanovsky's experiments.[220]

Mairanovsky's colleague, Vasilii Naumov, an assistant professor at the Pharmacy Department of the Moscow First Medical Institute, who had been mobilized by the NKVD through the Party Central Committee, considered Mairanovsky's attempts to find a truth drug to be useless and without serious results.[221] Nevertheless, in 1946, Soviet MGB "advisers" in Hungary tried actedron pentothal, scopolamine, and morphine on political prisoners.[222]

It is possible that Mairanovsky also worked with narcotics, since some narcotics were used in the 1940s during interrogations to force prisoners to sign
falsified interrogation transcripts. In the late 1980s, the minister and marshal
of aviation, Aleksandr Novikov, recalled that during his arrest in 1945, "I was
given a kind of a cigarette and I lost completely the understanding of where
I was and what was going on."[223] In this state Novikov signed papers given
to him by the MGB interrogator Mikhail Likhachev in the presence of
Minister Abakumov.

In 1966, Sudoplatov claimed that a very narrow circle of people knew
about the results of experiments on humans.[224] These reports were kept in
a concealed envelope that could be opened only on the special order of the
MGB minister or his first deputy. The reports were signed by those who
conducted the experiments and persons who knew about the experiments.
All these documents supposedly disappeared during Sudoplatov's arrest in
August 1953, and their whereabouts are not known. Bobryonev and
Ryazentsev mentioned also that the executioner Vasilii Blokhin had his own
list of names of all people brought for Mairanovsky's experiments. Before he
retired, Blokhin ordered that the notebook be destroyed.[225]

Sudoplatov also mentioned that Arkady Gertsovsky, head of the
Department "A" (Archive) from 1943 to 1953, provided prisoners for exper-
iments. Gertsovsky had the responsibility of carrying out death sentences
and, therefore, could send some prisoners condemned to death to
Mairanovsky's laboratory. In fact, the list of the First Special (later "A")
Department's officers who selected and brought prisoners to Mairanovsky's
laboratory was much longer. Besides Gertsovsky, it included Petrov, Leonid
Bashtakov (in 1940, head of the NKVD First Special Department), A. M.
Kalinin (in 1940, first deputy head of the same department), I. N.
Balishansky, and Vladimir Podobedov.[226]

Later, in 1942–1947, Bashtakov became Head of the special High
NKVD/NKGB/MGB School. Ilya Dzhirkvelov, a former pupil of this
school, recalled: "General Bashtakov [was] an unusually short man for whom
a special chair had been made with legs longer than normal so that when
he was sitting at a table his small stature was less noticeable. General
Bashtakov always delivered his lectures sitting down and when he congratulated us on being accepted for the course he shook our hands without
moving from behind the table."[227] As for Kalinin, his signature appeared
under many reports on executions and cremation of sentenced victims.[228]
In other words, he was present at executions carried out by the main
NKVD/MGB executioner, Vasilii Blokhin.

Along with work on chemicals, it was necessary to develop methods of poison injection. This was done in cooperation with the NKVD Second Special

Department (Operational Equipment) headed by Yevgenii Lapshin. The idea of constructing umbrellas, ballpoint pens, and walking sticks, all of which could shoot very small bullets, seemed to be the best.[229] Special small bullets with holes containing poison were invented. All these tools were tested on humans and cost many lives. On September 23, 1953, Mairanovsky testified:

> During the research we introduced poisons through food, various drinks and used hypodermic needles, a cane, a fountain pen and other sharp objects especially outfitted for the job. We also administered poisons through the skin by spraying or pouring oxime (fatal for animals in minimal doses). But this substance proved not to be lethal for people, causing only severe burns and great pain.[230]

If a prisoner did not die during the first administration of the poison, he was subjected to another one. Filimonov himself shot prisoners with poisoned bullets. These shootings were performed in the basement where executions of prisoners condemned to death took place. According to Bobryonev and Ryazentsev, later, during the interrogations, Mairanovsky testified to the following: "I used one prisoner for two or three experiments. But the last case was a rare one. I want to say in this instance that if there is no lethal outcome after administration of the poison and the subject improves, then another poison is tested on him."[231] Even Muromtsev, Mairanovsky's colleague, who himself used fifteen prisoners or more for his own experiments, said during the interrogation on March 4, 1954, that "Mairanovsky shocked me with his bestial, sadistic treatment of the prisoners."[232]

All these descriptions are similar to materials from the Nuremberg Doctors' trial.[233] Also, one can compare Mairanovsky's attitude to his victims to that of Japanese experimenters: "It is said that some of the doctors associated with the experimentation cried tears of regret when their valuable experimental materials were wasted [e.g., when prisoners died during the experiments]."[234]

However, it seems that today the present Russian secret service is not ashamed of the past. A fountain pen that could fire poisoned bullets is kept at the Historical Demonstration Room (a museum) of the Federal Security Service, or FSB.[235] Sudoplatov used to provide his agents with such pens for the assassination of "anti-Soviet enemies" in Europe.[236]

WARFARE AND SABOTAGE

Mairanovsky's work on mustard gas and other substances requires a general comment. These chemicals appeared in Mairanovsky's laboratory not only because they were known toxins but also because they were chemical and biological weapons.

In the late 1920s to early 1930s, Soviet leaders, military, and security were obsessed with the idea of chemical and toxicological warfare. The first production of poison-gas shells in Russia began earlier, in 1915, during World War I, at a factory in Petrograd and two factories in Moscow.[237] At least one of these installations, the Olgin Chemical Plant two miles from Moscow, was converted in 1927 into a pilot plant for testing new methods of producing poison gases. Professor Ye. Spitalsky, who was previously in charge of a study on poison gases at the Karpov Chemical Institute, was appointed its head. The Karpov Institute, established in 1918 and completely reorganized in 1922, was headed by Academician Bach (later Mairanovsky's supervisor as Director of Institute of Biochemistry) and his deputy, Boris Zbarsky (later a consultant of the OGPU on narcotics and then a victim of the Doctors' Plot case). The Karpov Institute was subordinated to the Presidium of the Supreme Council of National Economy (VSNKh), chaired by Felix Dzerzhinsky. Spitalsky was a specialist on the production of mustard gas and another chemical weapon, phosgene. Early in 1929, he was arrested by the GPU. When Academician Ipatieff went to Krzhizhanovsky, chairman of the State Planning Committee (Gosplan) (who was among the "elected" academicians in 1929, see Chapter 1), and tried to defend Spitalsky, Krzhizhanovsky said that "Spitalsky apparently was a very dangerous man who had planned to poison many outstanding Communists at a large meeting [in 1924] . . . He [i.e., Krzhizhanovsky] showed me [i.e., Ipatieff] a small vial filled with water to demonstrate how little poison Spitalsky needed."[238] At that meeting, Spitalsky gave a speech about chemical weapons and "held a small bottle of water before the audience, and explained that if the liquid were a modern poison gas it would be enough to poison all those present."[239] Unfortunately for Spitalsky, the infamous Iosif Unshlikht, a former deputy of Dzerzhinsky, deputy commissar of defense, and head of the Military Intelligence, presided over that meeting and evidently decided that Spitalsky planned to assassinate the participants of the meeting.

Spitalsky was sentenced to death, but in a year, the death sentence was commuted to ten years' solitary confinement. In fact, Spitalsky was forced to work as a prisoner at the Olgin Plant. He died soon from a heart attack, and his wife was exiled from Moscow. However, a replacement for Spitalsky was found. In November 1929, Professor Kravets, another highly positioned chemist who was a member of the Chemical Committee of the VSNKh, was arrested and sentenced to forced labor at the Olgin Plant.[240] This was the beginning of the *sharashki* system of forced labor by imprisoned scientists.

Before that, in 1923, a special delegation of the German government arrived in Moscow to work out agreements on the cooperative manufacture of guns and poison gases.[241] Germans appointed Dr. Stolzenberg to supervise construction of plants for producing poison gases. A joint Soviet-Russian commission visited a factory built during World War I near Samara on the Volga River. In 1926, before his arrest, Spitalsky actively worked with the commission.[242] The same year, a joint Soviet-German chemical warfare school called Tomka was organized near Saratov, also on the Volga River.[243] It was headed by the German expert Leopold von Sicherer. Both chemical and bacteriological weapons were tested there.[244]

The first Soviet mustard gas factory was set up in 1923 as a joint enterprise of the German firm GEFU with the Soviet corporation Bersol.[245] The Soviet side (called Metakhim) provided the chemical plant and the Germans supplied equipment from the Stolzenberg firm in Hamburg. The contract was signed for twenty years and the project was approved in 1926. The same year, the Stoltzenberg firm built a plant near Volsk on the Volga River (later Volsk-17 or Shikhany-1). Soviet-German cooperation in the production of chemical warfare, testing of chemicals, and training at Tomka ended in July 1933, on Hitler's order.

Later, the Olgin Plant became a basis of the above-mentioned Soviet research institute on chemical weapons, the GosNIIOKhT. The Volsk-17, or Shikhany-1, became the military Central Scientific Research and Testing Institute of Chemical Troops, which until recently produced chemical weapons, and in fact a large store of these chemicals is still located not far from Saratov.[246] Mustard gas was produced at the Kaprolaktam factory in Nizhnii Novgorod.

Chemical weapons were widely tested by Soviet military scientists on enlisted men in the 1930s–1980s.[247] One of the victims, Vladimir Petrenko, testified in 1999 to the Russian branch of the environmentalist group Greenpeace that "these experiments were carried out on dozens of Russian officers in 1982."[248] He had been forced to inhale "unknown toxic substances for 30 seconds" and had since suffered from respiratory, stomach, and thyroid gland illnesses. In the 1980s, chemical tests on unprotected servicemen were held at the secret institute Shikhany-1 by Academician Anatolii Kuntsevich, a future general and deputy commander of the Soviet Chemical Troops.[249] Until April 1994, Kuntsevich was also chairman of the Russian President's Committee on Chemical and Biological Weapons Conventions. Kuntsevich was fired in April 1994 for "numerous and gross violations" of his responsibilities when it became known that he agreed to sell equipment and precursors of chemical weapons to a Syrian laboratory.[250] He was succeeded by Pavel Syutkin. In 2000, Colonel General Stanislav Petrov headed Russia's Radiation-, Chemical-, and Biological-Protection Troops and was in charge of the destruction of toxic chemical substances. At the beginning of 2001, Russia still had around 40,000 tons of these substances, which was almost one-half of the world's stock.[251]

The first biological weapon was developed in Germany also during World War I (in 1915–1918) as a part of the program of biological sabotage against neutral suppliers of the Allied powers.[252] In 1925, the Military Chemical Agency was established by Red Army authorities to take charge of chemical and biological warfare programs. Yakov Fishman (1887–1961) directed this agency until 1937, when he was purged.[253] In 1928, a laboratory on vaccine and serum research was created within this agency in the village of Perkhushkovo not far from Moscow. The microbiologist Ivan Velikanov (1898–1938) was appointed head of this laboratory. The first types of Soviet bacteriological weapons were developed and produced by the microbiologists arrested in 1930–1931; Velikanov was among them. Microbiologists were accused of planning sabotage in the event of war and of giving information to the German professor Heinrich Zeiss, who worked in Moscow in 1928–1933; Zeiss was expelled.[254] In another case, a number of bacteriologists "under the leadership" of Professor Karatygin were tried for allegedly bringing on an epidemic among horses.[255] Many of the condemned microbiologists were imprisoned in a former Pokrovsky monastery in the old town of Suzdal. Scientists who succeeded in their experiments were eventually released, and those who could not produce desirable results were shot.[256]

In 1933, the laboratory in Perkhushkovo was turned into the Red Army's Scientific Research Institute of Microbiology (or Biotechnology). In 1937–1938, many veterinarians and microbiologists involved in military research were arrested and tried. Usually they were charged with sabotage, treason, and espionage for Germany or Japan.[257] The name of the German professor Zeiss was used again. The former director of the Saratov State Institute for Microbiology and Epidemiology S. Nikanorov; deputy director of the Moscow Chemical-Pharmaceutical Scientific Research Institute O. Stepun; deputy director of the Tarasevich Central Scientific Control Institute of Sera and Vaccines Vladimir Lyubarsky (1881–1939); professor of the Institute of Microbiology Iliya Krichevsky (1885–1939); scientific director of the Central Institute of Epidemiology and Microbiology Vladimir Barykin (1879–1939); and director of the Institute of Microbiology Georgii Nadson were arrested and charged with abetting Zeiss's spy scheme. On April 14, 1939, Nadson (arrested on October 29, 1937), Krichevsky (arrested on March 5, 1938), Lyubarsky (arrested on April 15, 1938), and Barykin (arrested on August 22, 1938) were condemned to death by the Military Collegium as members of the same counterrevolutionary organization and were shot the next day. They were rehabilitated in 1955.[258]

On July 6, 1937, head of the Biotechnology Institute Velikanov was arrested again and tried. This time he was condemned to death as a spy and a member of a "counter-revolutionary military plot," and on July 29, 1938, just after the trial, he was shot.[259] During the Bukharin trial, former commissar of agriculture Mikhail Chernov (1891–1938) "testified" that he had instructed the infection of livestock—horses, cattle, and pigs—on the order of German intelligence.[260] He was arrested on November 7, 1937, condemned to death on March 13, 1938, and shot on March 15, 1938. He was rehabilitated in 1988.[261] Also, Yakov Fishman and dozens of his subordinates were among the arrested. A special NKVD commission investigated their alleged "sabotage activity." They were condemned to long terms of imprisonment. Fishman survived the imprisonment and was released only in 1954, after Stalin's death. He was reestablished in the military and became a major general.[262]

In 1942, during World War II, the military Institute of Microbiology was moved to the town of Karol, about 500 miles from Moscow. According to Ken Alibek, a tularemia weapon was developed there and then used against German panzer troops shortly before the Battle of Stalingrad in late summer 1942.[263] However, according to German military intelligence, the Soviet army was immunized against plague.[264] German doctors immediately ordered the vaccine against plague—enough to immunize 1 million men—but never used it. In 1931, another Soviet military laboratory for anthrax *(Bacillus anthracis)* research was established in the city of Tobolsk in Siberia.[265]

During World War II, the threat of chemical war was real. In 1943, the Soviet intelligence radioed to Moscow that the Americans had information that Germany had made active preparations for chemical warfare against the USSR.[266] A former Nazi minister of armaments and war production, Albert Speer, mentioned in his memoirs that "our [e.g., Nazi Germany's] production—until the chemical industry was bombed during the summer of 1944—amounted to 3,100 tons of mustard gas and 1,000 tons of tabun per month."[267] He added that the Allies considered a gas attack on German cities: "On August 5, 1944, Churchill called for a report on England's capability for waging poison-gas war against Germany. According to the report, the available 32,000 tons of mustard and phosgene gas would effectively poison 965 square miles of German territory, more than Berlin, Hamburg, Cologne, Essen, Frankfurt, and Kassel combined." Declassified documents list even higher quantities. A total of 40,719 tons of mustard gas, 1,862,643 bombs filled with mustard gas or phosgene, and 3,394,093 specially designed shells charged with mustard gas were produced during the war in England.[268]

Experiments with mustard gas on the British, Canadian, American, and Australian volunteer servicemen had been carried out since 1940.[269] British experiments were performed at the Chemical and Biological Defence Establishment located in Porton Down in England, in India, and also in Alberta, Canada. Typically, British scientists studied the recuperation period for damage to eyes after the exposure to varying concentrations of mustard gas. Many British volunteers claimed later that they had not been fully aware of the experiment's implications. Canada was a leader in such experiments, and literally hundreds of volunteers were used for testing.[270] Both British and Canadian officials called these men by the misleading term "observers." Unlike the Nazi or Soviet experimenting scientists, many Canadian scientists exposed themselves to the action of gas.[271]

In 1943, American navy officials used the navy's own servicemen (without their knowledge) at least once in experiments with mustard gas at the U.S. Naval Research Laboratory.[272] As many as 60,000 [American] servicemen are believed to have been exposed to varying levels of mustard gas and other chemical agents during the war years to test the effectiveness of protective clothing and treatments as well as the strength of the gas. The main reason for these experiments was the fear that Japan might use mustard gas in the Pacific war theater. In 1991, the U.S. Department of Veterans Affairs approved disability benefits for World War II veterans who, without their knowledge or consent, had been placed in a chamber and exposed to mustard gas and arsenic.[273]

The deployment of mustard gas by the Western Allies led to a tragedy.[274] On December 2, 1943, the British ship *John Harvey* docked in the port of Bari (Italy). The ship had been damaged by a bomb during a German raid. It was loaded with 100 tons of mustard gas in 100-pound bombs. As a result of the action of the released gas, 628 British servicemen suffered terribly, and sixty-nine of them died. The information about this tragedy was covered up for a long time by Allied military officials.

Soviet intelligence was very anxious to find information about the Western Allies' developments in chemical and biological weaponry. In the recently partially declassified letters dated 1941 and 1942, head of the NKVD First Department Pavel Fitin (in the documents, he is mentioned under the code name "Victor") ordered *rezidenti* in New York (Vasilii Zarubin, code name "Maxim"; and his deputy, Gaik Ovakimyan, code name "Gennadii") and in London (Anatolii Gorsky, code names "Vadim" or "Henry") to collect information on the work of American and British scientists in chemical weaponry, military bacteriology, and the uranium-235 problem.[275] Declassified parts of the documents do not contain details on chemical and biological research the NKVD/NKGB was interested in.

The information which was collected by the *rezidenti* has not yet been declassified.[276] However, in 1942–1943, there were official discussions and exchanges in information on the chemical and bacteriological warfare at the diplomatic level and between the NKGB and a part of the British Intelligence Service, the Special Operation Executive or SOE.[277] It seems that both the Soviets and the British used chemical and bacterial poisons for terrorist acts against the Nazis. According to the controversial historian David Irving, in 1942 "Himmler produced a year-old NKVD order covering instructions to the indigenous Russian population on the poisoning— again with arsenic—of German occupation troops."[278] If such an instruction existed, it was definitely produced by Sudoplatov's NKVD Second Department, NKVD/NKGB Fourth Directorate. In 1943, there were cases of charges with poisoning guerrilla activities on Soviet territories occupied by German troops: in the Karachevo Region near the city of Bryansk, and in Kiev. In both cases, a typhus epidemic was spread.[279] In response, the Nazis created a special military-medical inspection team within the Abwehr (German Military Intelligence). Definitely, Sudoplatov's department/directorate was behind these attacks.

At least in 1942–1943, the SOE provided the Polish underground in Warsaw with arsenic and typhoid bacteria (which produces a lethal toxin). In 1943, the Polish liaison officer in Washington, Colonel Mitkewicz, reported to the Western Allied Combined Chiefs of Staff that during the first four months of 1943, 426 Germans were poisoned by the underground, 77 "poisoned parcels" were sent to Germany, and a few hundred Nazis were assassinated by means of "typhoid fever microbes [i.e., *Salmonella typhosa*] and typhoid fever lice."[280] The assassination of the ruthless head of the SD (the SS Intelligence) and Reichsprotektor of Bohemia and Moravia, Reinhard Heydrich, on May 23, 1942, in Prague was successful only because the assassins, the SOE-trained Czechs Jan Kubis and Josef Gabcik, used hand grenades that contained a filling of botulin, a toxin produced by the soil bacterium *Clostridium botulinum* (the British code-name of botulin was "X").[281]

Later, in 1944, an exchange in the same information took place between the NKGB and the American Office of Strategic Services, or OSS.[282] The head of Soviet Foreign Intelligence, Pavel Fitin, informed the Americans about the location of German chemical factories that produced gases for bombs and grenades in Germany and Poland.[283] One can assume that all this information was evaluated by the two NKVD/NKGB experts on chemical and bacteriological toxins, Mairanovsky and his colleague Sergei Muromtsev. In his memoirs, Sudoplatov mentioned that he provided Muromtsev with intelligence information on bacteriological weapons from Israel even after the war.[284]

Possibly, the intelligence on biological and chemical warfare had serious value for the Soviets. According to some memoirs, since 1942 a secret laboratory within the NKVD system located in the Ural Mountains area produced a biological weapon that was tested on prisoners.[285] Supposedly, Arkady Gertsovsky, who was in charge of providing prisoners for Mairanovsky's experiments, headed this secret laboratory. According to not-very-reliable intelligence information obtained by the Americans from the Germans and Japanese, experiments on prisoners and Japanese POWs were also carried out with anthrax, encephalitis, glanders, and plague in Leningrad Prison and in Mongolia near Ulan Bator.[286] If these laboratories in fact existed, Mairanovsky and Muromtsev were definitely involved in their work. Apparently, Merkulov supervised this activity: In May 1941, a month before the German invasion, he signed a detailed review of the show trials of the 1930s against microbiologists and issued a warning regarding bacteriological sabotage by the German and Japanese secret services.[287]

THE VICTIMS

After the war [World War II] began, [German] bioscientists were encouraged to use those who were to die anyway (the inmates of psychiatric asylums and concentration camps) as substitutes for laboratory animals. In fact, German legislation gave animals, such as dogs, more rights than the Jews.

—B. Müller-Hill, *Bioscience in Totalitarian Regimes*

It is difficult to find out who the victims were and how many prisoners were used for Mairanovsky's experiments. In Mairanovsky's lab, prisoners were referred to as *ptichki* (birdies).[288] One can find a parallel to Nazi experiments in this inhuman way of referring to victims: According to a secret memorandum dated June 5, 1942, human beings marked by the SS for death in mobile gas chambers in Auschwitz were always referred to as "the cargo" or "the items."[289] The Japanese military doctors of the notorious Unit 731 regarded the victims of the experiments as *maruta*, or "logs." "They were logs to me," explained a former Japanese officer, Toshimi Mizobuchi, to the correspondent of the *New York Times*.[290] "Logs were not considered to be human. They were either spies or conspirators . . . They were already dead. So now they die a second time [during the experiments]. We just executed a death sentence." It is interesting to note that official Soviet labor camp documents used the same word. Varlam Shalamov, one of the best writers on Soviet labor camps (he spent almost thirty years in the worst of them), later wrote: "Official telegram reads: 'Send 200 trees' [i.e., send 200 new prisoners to the camp]."[291] This was not merely a metaphor. In the permafrost of the tundra, frozen bodies of dead prisoners were used as railroad ties. A survivor of the Vorkuta camps (in northern Russia), A. Kuusinen, later recalled: "Prisoners . . . were fed poorly, and there was no medical help to sick prisoners. Those who fell to the ground [from exhaustion], were left to freeze to death. The dead bodies were used as railroad ties because of a lack in wood; there are no forests in those latitudes."[292]

In their book, Bobryonev and Ryazentsev insisted that some of Mairanovsky's victims were criminals condemned to death; usually that they were picked up at Butyrka Prison. But some were political prisoners, charged with Article 58 of the Russian Criminal Code. Among them there were Soviet citizens, German and Japanese POWs, Poles, Koreans, and Chinese. Japanese POWs, officers, soldiers, and diplomats were used mainly for experiments with tranquilizers.[293] These experiments were performed at Lubyanka No. 2 building (there were two interrogation prisons at the Lubyanka Square in the center of Moscow, Nos. 1 and 2). Mairanovsky's colleague, the pharmaceutical chemist Naumov, testified: "While I was present, experiments were done on spies and saboteurs, as far as I could tell from their interrogations."

During Beria's investigation, the procedure was described by the former commandant of Lubyanka Prison, Vasilii Blokhin, on September 19, 1953:

> I was assigned to deliver the arrested to the special cells. All of the work was directed by Beria or his deputies Merkulov and Kobulov. They gave orders to the First Special Department or Department "A" [i.e., Gertsovsky] to collect the appropriate arrestees from among those sentenced to execution—according to their health, whether ailing or flourishing, according to age, whether young or old, and according to weight, whether thin or fat. In accordance with these orders, Department "A" or the First Special Department selected the appropriate people from among those sentenced to the highest measure of punishment [death] and a list of prisoner's names was given to me. Each time when I received the list, I would personally check with Merkulov or Kobulov whether the names were the right ones and whether they should be delivered to Mairanovsky. After Merkulov or Kobulov confirmed the orders I delivered the prisoners to Mairanovsky.[294]

On October 14, 1953, Gertsovsky testified:

> Before 1942, when I did not work as Head of the First Special Department, in general I had nothing to do with the executions . . . and only knew of Mairanovsky's experiments from [A. M.] Kalinin. He told me

about the experiments in [L. F.] Bashtakov's presence and in his office . . .
I believe only Kalinin, [V. N.] Podobedov, and, I think, Bashtakov had
some relationship to the putting to death of prisoners by Mairanovsky
and Filimonov. But Kalinin died shortly before the war. Podobedov has
been working recently as Head of the First Special Department in the
Ukrainian MVD . . . [295]

Later, on October 23, 1953, Gertsovsky added more detail:

Filimonov [Mairanovsky's superior] usually came to Podobedov and used
the sentences to select the number of prisoners he would need in order to
ask permission from Merkulov or Kobulov to hand them over to him for
the experiments. I do not know if Filimonov would first go to the prison
to select prisoners sentenced to the highest measure of punishment according to Blokhin's criteria. Podobedov could not have gone to the
prison with Filimonov for making such a selection without my authorization . . . The prisoners were handed over to Blokhin in his capacity as
prison warden by the usual orders from Military Tribunals to execute the
sentences. Blokhin's transfer of prisoners to Filimonov was done by verbal
instructions from Merkulov or Kobulov, which were transmitted to
Blokhin through me, and as can be seen from Blokhin's testimony, were
rechecked by him personally with Merkulov and Kobulov.

I understand that Merkulov's and Kobulov's instruction to execute the
sentences by poisoning rather than by shooting, as was indicated by the
court sentence, was a violation of the law. But I considered these violations justified under war conditions.[296]

As noted earlier, the condemned were usually killed by gunshot in the
back of the head, administered by a single executioner—either Blokhin
himself or a member of his small team—in a special basement room of the
Varsonofyevsky Lane building.

Podobedov's name will come up in another case, that of the geneticist
Nikolai Vavilov. His duties at the NKVD/NKGB First Special Department
were very grim—to be present at executions and then register the deaths.
According to the rules, the executioner carried out the verdict, with
Podobedov and a prosecutor in attendance. Additionally, in 1941 Podobedov
was put in charge of contacts with Mairanovsky's laboratory. He and a prosecutor were present when corpses of Mairanovsky's victims were taken from
the laboratory. Both wrote "a protocol" (a report) that the death verdict had
been carried out. The names of the other witnesses of the execution are still
top secret.[297]

At least four German POWs (quite possibly, real Nazi war criminals) were experimented on in 1944.[298] In late 1945, three other Germans were transferred to Mairanovsky's laboratory.[299] This time the prisoners were apparently not Nazis but political emigrants from Nazi Germany. All of them were injected with poisons and died in fifteen seconds. The bodies of two of the victims were cremated, but the third corpse was sent to the Moscow Sklifosovsky Hospital. The autopsy showed that the prisoner died of heart paralysis, but medical examiners did not find any poison in the body.

Probably, the "truth" drugs and other drugs were also widely tested on prisoners. Dr. Charles Schandl, a Hungarian lawyer who had been in contact with the Hungarian underground and British Intelligence in Budapest during the war before being arrested by the Soviets, testified in 1958 to Swedish authorities in Toronto about his experience in Lefortovo Prison in 1946:

> The constant noise from the [hidden] speaker made him dizzy, sometimes he got cramps and after some time he had not been able to determine whether the speaker was on or the voice was his own hallucination. He also noticed that the guards sometimes gave him different food from what the other prisoners received, and he was convinced that the prison authorities had mixed some drug in his food and maybe also in his drinking water since after certain meals he felt an increase in the activity of all his glands and at the same time had an upset stomach.[300]

This description of symptoms echoes that of Mairanovsky's victims. Possibly because of these experiments, Schandl was kept under the highest level of secrecy. After conviction to twenty-five years' imprisonment as an "American spy," Schandl was deprived of his name and became No. 26, under which he was sent to Vladimir Prison.[301] However, Schandl had nothing to do with American espionage: In December 1944, he accompanied a Dutch officer, Hendrik van der Waals, who wanted to contact British Intelligence with information about the German military technical secrets. They ended up in the hands of Soviet Intelligence, which was not interested in their military information at all.[302] It is not clear why Schandl was a numbered prisoner because, as I noted in Chapter 1, only those prisoners involved in the most important political cases that fell under the Department for Investigation of Especially Important Cases were given numbers after conviction.[303]

Although it is not known how many prisoners were used for experiments between 1938 and 1949, in trial testimony Mairanovsky made it clear that there were more than a few. "By my hand many dozens of sworn enemies of Soviet power, including nationalists of all types (including Jewish) were destroyed—this is known to Lt. General P. A. Sudoplatov," Mairanovsky wrote from Vladimir Prison in his appeal to MVD minister Beria on April 21, 1953.[304] Sudoplatov and Grigoriev named at least 150 victims.[305]

EXECUTIONS

Mairanovsky had other victims, not subjects of experiments but of executions. These acts were organized and conducted under the supervision of Sudoplatov and Eitingon and Department "DR" of the NKGB/MGB. In 1966, as part of his appeal for rehabilitation, Sudoplatov wrote about the activity of "DR":

> . . . Following the order of the new Minister Abakumov, in 1946 Eitingon and I were put in charge of organizing and heading the Special Service of the MGB of the USSR [i.e., Department "DR"] . . . Our task included organization of the special intelligence through [a network of] agents abroad and within the country. In particular, following the special order of the Politburo of the C[entral] C[ommittee], we prepared terrorist operations in France, Turkey, and Iran. However, at the last moment we were ordered to postpone them. Within the country during the second part of 1946 and in 1947, four operations were performed.[306]

To fulfill these operations, Abakumov also received orders from the Politburo and the Central Committee. As Sudoplatov stated in his appeal, "Eitingon and I knew very well that Abakumov reported the results of operations conducted by the MGB Special Service [i.e., Department "DR"] to the Central Committee of the Bolshevik Communist Party."[307]

This activity was so secret that Mairanovsky's superior at the time, Zhelezov, was not aware of it. As Mairanovsky put it in a letter to MVD minister Beria on April 21, 1953, from Vladimir Prison, "I had no right to inform my superiors, including the former Department Head Zhelezov, about my additional job, which continued until 1950 (only you, V. N. Merkulov, and P. A. Sudoplatov knew about this job)."[308]

In the summer of 1946, a leader of the Ukrainian nationalistic movement, Aleksandr Shumsky, was killed by Mairanovsky by an injection of curare poison, at a hospital in Saratov (where he was in exile).[309] From 1924 to 1933, Shumsky was Ukrainian commissar of education. In January 1933, he was accused of Ukrainian nationalism and arrested. From 1946, Shumsky lived in exile in Saratov. Before he was executed, Shumsky wrote a personal letter to Stalin in which he protested against the Soviet policy regarding

Ukrainians. He even tried to commit suicide to attract attention to his appeal.[310] Allegedly, in 1946 Shumsky was in contact with Ukrainian nationalists in Kiev and abroad. According to Sudoplatov, this execution of Shumsky was under personal supervision of Abakumov, and the group of executioners consisted of Mairanovsky, his supervisor Ogol'tsov, who was first deputy MGB minister, and Lazar Kaganovich, a Politburo member and the Ukrainian first party secretary from March to December 1947, who had personally known Shumsky.[311]

The next victim was Archbishop Romzha of the Ukrainian Catholic (Uniate) Church. The Ukrainian MGB, under the supervision of Ukrainian MGB minister Sergei Savchenko, staged an unsuccessful car accident in 1947, and the archbishop was taken to a local hospital in the town of Mukachevo.[312] He was killed by an injection of curare provided by Mairanovsky and administered by a medical nurse, an MGB agent.[313] In his memoirs published in Russian, Sudoplatov claimed that before going to Mukachevo for the execution of the archbishop, Mairanovsky and Savchenko were being instructed in Kiev by then by the first Communist Party secretary of the Ukraine, Nikita Khrushchev personally, who supposedly had already received Stalin's approval of the assassination.[314] Savchenko was awarded for the successful execution: He was transferred to Moscow and appointed deputy chairman of the Committee of Information.

The same year a Polish engineer of Jewish origin, Samet, was abducted and killed by Sudoplatov's team in the city of Ul'yanovsk. Samet had been interned in the Soviet Union since 1939 (due to the Hitler-Stalin division of Poland) and according to MGB information, was arranging his defection to Britain in 1947. Mairanovsky again administered the lethal injection of curare.[315] Later, Sudoplatov claimed that Stalin and Minister of Defense Nikolai Bulganin had ordered the killing.[316] Finally, an American citizen and a Gulag prisoner, Isaac Oggins, was killed in Moscow in 1947. Copies of several documents, which evidently came from Oggins's investigation file, were released by the FSB in 1992 and given by the Russian side (Colonel General Dmitrii Volkogonov) of the U.S.-Russia Joint Commission on POW/MIA Affairs to the American side.[317] Although these documents provide some light on the mechanism of Mairanovsky's executions, they also raise unanswered questions.

In the appeal to the Twenty-Third Congress of the Communist Party, Sudoplatov mentioned the killing of Oggins as the fourth assassination he and Eitingon took part in:

> In Moscow, following orders of Stalin and Molotov, an American citizen Oggins was liquidated. Oggins, being imprisoned in a labor camp during

WWII, contacted the American Embassy in the USSR [Moscow]. Many times Americans sent [diplomatic] notes asking for his release from the imprisonment and for a permission for him to leave the USSR for the United States.[318]

According to Sudoplatov's memoirs, "Oggins was a Communist sympathizer and a member of the American Communist Party. He was also a veteran agent of the Comintern and NKVD intelligence in China and the Far East. His wife, Nora, was a member of the NKVD intelligence network in charge of controlling safe apartments in France in the mid-1930s."[319] Oggins was not the only American put into the Gulag during and after World War II.[320] In 1938, Oggins arrived in the Soviet Far East under false Czechoslovak documents and was arrested by the NKVD. Oggins had different aliases. In Bobryonev and Ryazentsev, he is mentioned as "Saines."[321] On the photos released by the FSB and taken, apparently, from his investigation file, there is an inscription: "Egon-Ogens Hain-San Samon" (possibly, the last name was Oggins's NKVD alias in China). This inscription starts with "No. 568," which is probably the number under which Oggins was registered in the prison's Registration Book of Arrested Persons.[322] The "Warrant for the Arrest and Search" No. 2634 was issued for "Hein Egon, also Oggins Isai (Sai) Saimonovich."[323] The "Certificate of Rehabilitation" (dated 1992) was issued to "Oggins–Hein Isai Saimonovich."[324]

The NKVD arrested Oggins on February 20, 1939. At the time, as many members of the Comintern did, he lived in the Moscow Hotel in the center of Moscow (room number 1035).[325] On January 5, 1940, he was tried by the Special Board of the NKVD (OSO). The "Excerpt" from the Protocol [Transcript] No. 1 of the OSO stated:

Hearing: 3. Case No. 85 of the GUGB Investigation Department of the NKVD for Oggins Isai Samoilovich [sic!], born 1898 in Massachusetts (USA), a Jew, an American citizen.

Decision: Oggins Isai Saimonovich [this is in the text] is guilty of spying and was condemned to an imprisonment for 8 years. The term starts from February 20, 1939. The File should be kept in the archive.

Head of the Secretariat of the OSO under the
People's Commissar of the Interior of the USSR Ivanov.[326]

Two letters, "am.," were typed at the left side of the document above the text. Apparently, this meant the "American spy." On January 15, 1940, ten days after the trial, Oggins signed a notification that a NKVD officer had acquainted him with this decision.[327] Another document, a report written by MGB minister Abakumov in May 1947 and addressed to Stalin and Molotov, confirms this information.[328] It also describes the plan Abakumov suggested to deal with Oggins's situation.

Despite the typewritten name "Abakumov" at the bottom of the document, it does not have the MGB letterhead; it was addressed to the USSR Council of Ministers. This is strange because beginning in February 1947, the activity of the MGB was controlled and approved by the Politburo, while the activity of the MVD was controlled by the Council of Ministers.[329] The report was typed with blank spaces indicated by underlines, which later were filled in by hand. Possibly, this was done so that the typist would not see certain key words (this was a routine practice for secret documents in the Soviet Union).[330] The geneticist Nikolai Timofeev-Ressovsky, who in the late 1940s–1950s worked at a secret institute as an imprisoned scientist, described in his memoirs how the secret documents were prepared:

> . . . Even a secret typist [i.e., cleared for secret work] was not allowed to know all secret words. Therefore, the author [of the document] must leave an empty space for these words when he gave the document to a typist. And the typist needed to leave an empty space for a particular number of letters [for each one in the word] (the author was allowed to write by pencil the number of letters, for instance, 5 or 12). Then the author filled the space [on a typed version] with the word, also using a pencil . . . [331]

There is a pattern in these words filled out by hand: American, USA, State Department, Oggins. Two-thirds of the second page of the letter was whited out, evidently before the Xeroxing. The most important part of the letter was also written in by hand (shown in italics):

A Copy No. 4
Strictly Secret
    The USSR Council of Ministers
May 21, 1947
No. 2773/A
    To Comrade I. V. Stalin
    To Comrade V. M. Molotov
I report to you the following:
In April 1942 the *American* Embassy in the USSR informed the USSR Foreign Ministry by a [diplomatic] note that it had information that an *American* citizen *Isai Oggins* was imprisoned in the [labor] camp in [the city of] *Norilsk*. On behalf of the *State Department*,

the Embassy asked for information on the reason of his arrest, the length of the imprisonment term to which *Oggins* was convicted, and about his health.

Because of the insistence of the *American* Embassy, on the order of Comrade MOLOTOV two meetings, on December 8, 1942 and January 9, 1943, between the representatives of the Embassy with the convict *Oggins* were allowed. During these meetings *Oggins* [blank] informed the representatives of the *American* Embassy that he had been arrested as a Trotskyist who had illegally arrived in the USSR, using someone else's passport, for a contact with the Trotskyist underground in the USSR.

Despite this declaration, the *American* Embassy asked MID [i.e., the Foreign Ministry] of the USSR to reconsider his case and to release *Oggins* ahead of schedule. It sent *Oggins*' letters and telegrams to his wife, who is living in the *USA*, as well as informed MID of the USSR that it considered *Oggins* to be an *American* citizen and was ready to repatriate him to his Motherland.

On May 9, 1943 the *American* Embassy was informed that "the proper Soviet organs" [i.e., the MGB] consider it impossible to reconsider the *Oggins* case. On February 20, 1939 *Oggins* [blank] was in fact arrested on the charge of spying and treason.

[A paragraph whited out.]

In the course of the investigation these allegations were not supported and *Oggins* refused to consider himself guilty. However, the Special Meeting [i.e., OSO] under the NKVD of the USSR condemned *Oggins* to 8 years of ITL [i.e., labor camps]. His term started on February 20, 1939.

[Almost a half of the page whited out]

[Blank] the appearance of *Oggins* in the *USA* could be used by persons hostile to the Soviet Union for active propaganda against the USSR.

Based on the given above, the MGB of the USSR considers it necessary *to liquidate* [i.e., to execute] *Isaiya Oggins, to report to the Americans that after the meeting of Oggins with the representatives of the American Embassy in June of 1943, he was returned to the place of confinement in Norilsk and he died there in 1946 in a hospital as a result of an attack of tuberculosis of the spine.*

We will reflect [i.e. falsify] *the process of Oggins' illness in the archives of the Norilsk camp, as well as the medical and other help given to him. Oggins' death will be registered officially in his medical records by an autopsy record and a burial certificate.*

Taking into consideration that *Oggins'* wife [blank] is located in *New York* and appealed to our Consulate about her husband many times, as well as that she knows that he had been arrested [blank], we consider it useful [blank] *to ask her to come to the Consulate and tell her about the death of her husband* [blank].

I'm asking for your instructions.

Abakumov.

Evidently, Stalin and Molotov approved Abakumov's plan because Oggins was killed and his records were falsified. Some documents about Oggins seem to have been kept in Mairanovsky's file: Bobryonev and Ryazentsev wrote that Eitingon brought Mairanovsky to Oggins supposedly for a medical checkup and Mairanovsky killed Oggins by an injection of curare.[332]

However, Oggins's death certificate stated a false date, a false cause, and a false place of death. For some unknown reason, it was dated January 20, 1948, and stated that Oggins died not in Norilsk (as Abakumov proposed) but in Penza in central Russia. It said: "Oggins Isai Saimonovich, 49 years old, died in the town of Penza on January 13, 1947. The death was caused by a heart paralysis aggravated by angiospasm and papillar cancer of the urinary bladder. The death was registered on January 30, 1947."[333]

In 1992, deputy minister of state security V. Frolov wrote to General Dmitrii Volkogonov: "As a result of the investigation it was found that the USA citizen Oggins, who had been groundlessly repressed, was buried at the Jewish cemetery in the town of Penza."[334] But there is no real proof that Oggins was in fact buried in Penza: As of June 2001, the Memorial has still been unable find his grave.

The dates of events mentioned above are significant: on May 21, 1947, Abakumov offered to kill Oggins (who was evidently still alive) and falsify his death date as 1946; the date of Oggins's death on the death certificate was given as January 30, 1947, that is, five months before Abakumov's report; the death certificate date was January 20, 1948. Therefore, the real date of Oggins's death at the hands of Mairanovsky and Eitingon, as well as the real place of his death, cannot be ascertained from these records. The dates of two documents mentioned in the article written by V. Pozniakov on the activity of the Soviet secret services in the United States during the Cold War give some more information.[335] On January 31, 1947 (a day after the official date of Oggins's death), V. Bazykin, a member of the Soviet Foreign Ministry Department in charge of the United States, wrote a memo to Deputy Minister Dekanozov regarding Oggins. Also, on July 10, 1947, Bazykin prepared a document entitled "Questions that could be raised by the US Ambassador [Walter Bedell] Smith in a conversation with Comrade

Molotov." Possibly, the Soviets planned to say that Oggins had died. If so, Oggins seems to have been killed between May 21 (Abakumov's report) and July 10, 1947 (before the meeting between Molotov and Smith). It was not mentioned by Sudoplatov, Bobryonev and Ryazentsev, or Deputy Minister Frolov why Penza was supposedly chosen by the MGB (or Stalin and Molotov) for Oggins's burial. Oggins's real story remains a mystery.

Bobryonev and Ryazentsev suspect that the death of at least two high-ranking Japanese prisoners was a result of the treatment "according to the method of Doctor of Medicine G. M. Mairanovsky."[336] A former head of the Japanese Military Mission in Harbin (in fact, the Harbin Secret Service) and a founder of the Japanese army's spy school, Major General Akikusa Shun, died on March 22, 1949,[337] from general weakness and a heart attack. Akikusa was also commander of the "Scientific Research Division" of the Japanese Secret Service where Soviet POWs and spies were held. Those individuals who did not give information about the Soviet Union to the Japanese (usually under torture) or who tried to escape were sent by the commandant or his deputy to Unit 731, which conducted experiments on humans.[338] The former Japanese general consul in Harbin, Mikayava Funao, died on March 29, 1950, from the same cause. At the time of death, both were in the MGB's Lefortovo Prison. In both cases, the infamous forensic medical expert of Moscow, Dr. P. Semenovsky, signed the autopsy report. The NKVD-MGB often used this doctor to cover up their crimes. He was a member of the Soviet commission that had falsified autopsy reports of Polish officers killed in the Katyn Massacre. Aleksandr Larin, a lawyer who personally knew Semenovsky, characterized him the following way: "Doctor Semenovsky produced his judgment on the merits of the case without an examination of the body . . . Semenovsky had managed to produce purely legal conclusions even in the report of the expert examination: like stating premeditation, ulterior motives and so on and so forth."[339]

It is possible that there was a third high-ranking Japanese victim, Prince Konoe. Bobryonev suspects that he was also subjected to Mairanovsky's and Eitingon's "treatment" in Vladimir Prison.[340] Probably, "Dr. Mairanovsky's method" was used by the MGB more frequently than is yet known. On October 15, 1947, Willy Roedel, who had been the only cell mate of Raoul Wallenberg for the previous two years and possibly cooperated with MGB investigators, suddenly died in Lubyanka Prison.[341] The same Dr. Semenovsky signed an autopsy report stating that Roedel's death was caused by "a heart attack." The Lubyanka Prison commandant, Colonel Aleksandr Mironov,[342] asked the head of the Fourth Department of the MGB Third Directorate (Military Counterintelligence), Colonel Sergei Kartashov, for permission "to cremate [Roedel's] body immediately." This request could have been looked upon as routine except for the fact that Raoul Wallenberg had died "from a heart attack" on February 17, 1947.[343] Roedel was the only person besides a couple of the MGB Fourth Department interrogators, Colonel Kartashov and his superiors, Minister Abakumov and members of the Communist Party Politburo, who knew the details of the Wallenberg case. Currently, these details are still a mystery. Like the two Japanese men mentioned above, Roedel had heart problems before his death.[344] But it is quite possible that these heart problems and, indeed, the deaths of all three were caused by poisoning. Pavel Sudoplatov and his son Andrei created a version of the story (without any documentary proof) that Raoul Wallenberg was poisoned by Mairanovsky.[345]

It seems that in the late 1940s, there were other foreigners who were subjected to Mairanovsky's treatment in Moscow. Mairanovsky himself described the mechanism of "special tasks" carried out in his testimony on August 27, 1953, during Beria's investigation:

> I cannot say who these people were since their names were not given to me, but it was explained that these were enemies that had to be destroyed. I received these orders from L. P. Beria and V. N. Merkulov and Sudoplatov. This relates to the period beginning in 1938 until 1950. During the period that Abakumov was Minister of State Security I was given these orders through Sudoplatov.
>
> When I was given orders to put a certain person to death, it was discussed in the office of L. P. Beria or Merkulov or Sudoplatov, but in all instances with Sudoplatov's participation, and sometimes with the participation of the [Fourth] Department Head, Mikhail Petrovich Filimonov and with M. A. Eitingon, but only as to the question of where the deaths should be arranged, what poison to use and when.
>
> I was never told why a certain person had to be put to death and their names were never mentioned.
>
> After receiving the order, Sudoplatov or Eitingon or Filimonov would schedule a meeting for me in safe houses[346] with the person who was to be put to death and while he was eating or drinking, I would mix poisons into his drink or food. I cannot say how many people were put to death by me but there were several dozen. I do not know their names and I do not know the charges against them. For me the orders from Beria or Merkulov were sufficient. I did not enter into discussion of these orders and obeyed them unconditionally.[347]

One of the main "safe apartments" that belonged to the secret services was in the center of Moscow, in the apartment buildings on Gorky (now

Tverskaya) Street. This apartment was where Sudoplatov and Eitingon met with the MGB agents.[348] Possibly, the same apartment was used by Sudoplatov's Bureau No. 1 for killings. Later on, Kim Philby, a famous former Soviet spy in England, trained future KGB spies in a huge "safe apartment" (perhaps the same one) on Gorky Street.[349]

There is a small discrepancy between this testimony and Sudoplatov's claim that his squad of killers (Sudoplatov-Eitingon-Mairanovsky) assassinated only four victims from 1946 to 1949. It is no wonder that in his memoirs Sudoplatov furiously tried to deny his and Eitingon's involvement in executions, confirming at the same time that both were involved in the killing of Romzha, Samet, Shumsky, and Oggins.[350] Evidently, the number of victims was higher, and killings in Moscow continued during 1950.

It may be that in the early 1950s the Soviet leaders and heads of the MGB were disappointed in the results of Mairanovsky's experiments and therefore turned their attention to more promising bacteriological methods. In 1952, one of the most successful international MGB agents, Iosif Grigulevich (Costa Rican ambassador to Italy and Yugoslavia)[351] was assigned to kill the Communist leader of Yugoslavia, Marshal Iosif Tito, by using a special instrument to infect Tito with plague.[352] In 1940, Grigulevich had already been secretly decorated (along with Sudoplatov and Eitingon) for killing Trotsky.[353] During the planned operation, Grigulevich was named "Max," which was a shortened form of Maximov, the main alias that Grigulevich used, beginning with his cover operations during the Spanish Civil War in the 1930s.[354] The details of Tito's assassination plan were submitted by the MGB to Stalin for his approval:

The MGB USSR requests permission to prepare a terrorist act *(teract)* against Tito, by the illegal agent "Max," Comrade I. R. Grigulevich, a Soviet citizen and member of the Communist Party of the Soviet Union since 1950 . . . "Max" was placed in Italy on a Costa Rican passport, where he was able to gain the confidence and enter the circles of South American diplomats as well as well-known Costa Rican political and trade figures visiting Italy. Using these connections, "Max," on our orders, obtained an appointment as the special plenipotentiary of Costa Rica in Italy and Yugoslavia. In the course of his diplomatic duties, in the second half of 1952, he visited Yugoslavia twice . . . The following options for a terrorist act against Tito were presented.

To order "Max" to arrange a private audience with Tito, during which a soundless mechanism concealed in his clothes would release a dose of pulmonary plague bacteria that would guarantee death to Tito and all present. "Max" himself would not be informed of the substance's nature, but with the goal of saving "Max's" life, he would be given an anti-plague serum in advance.

. . . The terrorist act could be accomplished [in London] by shooting with a silent mechanism concealed as a personal item while simultaneously releasing tear gas to create panic among the crowd, allowing "Max" to escape and cover up all traces.

. . . The terrorist act could be implemented in the same way [in Belgrade] as the second option, to be carried out by "Max" who as a diplomat, accredited by the Yugoslav government, would be invited to such a reception.

In addition, to assign "Max" to work out an option whereby one of the Costa Rican representatives will give Tito some jewelry box, which when opened would release an instantaneously effective poisonous substance . . .

It seems appropriate to use "Max" to implement a terrorist act against Tito. "Max's" personal qualities and intelligence experience make him suitable for such an assignment. We ask for your approval.[355]

Probably, the idea to use plague was based on the data of the Nazi doctors. During the war, Nazi scientists worked on plague intensely, using inmates of concentration camps for experiments.[356] The research papers from the Anatomical Institute in Posen may have fallen into Soviet army hands[357] and subsequently ended up with MGB experts. Muromtsev, Mairanovsky's former colleague and to some extent his rival, was one of these experts. It is probable that his secret MGB laboratory was in charge of the method prepared for Grigulevich. Muromtsev was discharged from the MGB "because of bad health" (Chapter 3) at the end of 1951, approximately at the time Mairanovsky was arrested. An alternative method of killing Tito mentioned in the MGB report to Stalin, a jewelry box with a poison, was definitely from Mairanovsky's arsenal.

Sudoplatov wrote that the plan to murder Tito was prepared by MGB deputy minister Yevgenii Pitovranov.[358] At first Sudoplatov discussed the plan with Stalin, Beria, and Ignatiev (the new MGB minister, see Chapter 3). It was then discussed with the MVD deputy minister Ivan Serov, with the head of the MGB First (Foreign) Directorate, Sergei Savchenko, and with the MGB deputy ministers Vassilii Ryasnoi, General Yepishev, Pitovranov, and Minister Ignatiev. On March 1, 1953, the MGB reported to Stalin that "Max's" attempt to assassinate Tito had, unfortunately, not taken place yet.[359] Possibly, this report was the last document Stalin read before he suffered the fatal stroke in the early hours of March 2.

According to Vitalii Pavlov, a former head of the KGB Foreign Intelligence Institute, Grigulevich refused to fulfill this assignment.[360] He was called back to Moscow and was discharged from the MGB. He was afraid of being killed: He knew too much. Possibly, only Stalin's death and the arrest of Beria saved his life.

3

COLLABORATORS

The diaries, letters, and publications of Nazi doctors of the time . . . contain few elements of idealism . . . Dominating these documents, instead, are small-minded greed for money and privileges, careerism, and a mixture of envy, inflated self-esteem, and contempt for the so-called inferior.
— C. Pross, introduction to G. Aly,
P. Chroust, and C. Pross, *Cleansing the Fatherland: Nazi Medicine and Hygiene*

THIS CHAPTER CONCERNS THOSE scientists who accepted the Soviet regime and successfully used its opportunities to their personal advantage without any concern for morality and ethics. This group includes the Soviet secret service's chief poison investigator, biochemist Grigory Mairanovsky, those who worked in Mairanovsky's lab, those who wrote positive reviews of his dissertation, those who helped to organize slave labor for the Soviet economy, and those who used contacts with the secret services to enhance their professional careers. Also, I will discuss the phenomenon of academic institutions as a place for retirement of former MGB executioners.

MAIRANOVSKY'S CAREER

The Beginning and Success

> *Only incompetent doctors went to work at the MGB. They went to the MGB not because of ideological principles, but because the salary was much higher there than that of normal humane doctors and medical sisters. And after having been hired by the MGB system and having breathed its poisoned air, a person began to lose his or her conscience and turned into a non-human being.*
> — L. Shatunovskaya, *Life in the Kremlin*

I begin with a detailed biography of Grigory Mairanovsky. Only a few documents about Mairanovsky (in the Memorial Archive) are available; the main archival records are still secret. The existence of Mairanovsky's laboratory in 1939–1951 became known during the investigation of Lavrentii Beria, one of the main organizers and administrators of the Soviet secret service and manager of the Soviet atomic project, who was arrested soon after Stalin's death in 1953 and condemned to death during a secret trial. The archival materials concerning this 1953 trial are also still secret. Mairanovsky was arrested even before Beria, in 1951.

The limited materials from Memorial's Archive[1] allow me to reconstruct the scientific career of the head of Laboratory No. 1. Grigory Mairanovsky was born in 1899 in Batumi (Georgia), to a Jewish family and was later identified as a Jew in all official documents. Mairanovsky graduated from Tiflis (Tbilisi) University in 1919 and from the Moscow Second Medical Institute in 1923. In 1929, he became a researcher at the Moscow A. N. Bach Institute of Biochemistry, and from 1933 to 1935 served as head of the Toxicology Department there (Document 11, Appendix II, and Table 3.1). The director of the institute, Academician Aleksei Bach, was well known for his support of the Bolshevik Party. Dr. Zbarsky, who was a consultant of the OGPU/NKVD, was deputy director of the Bach Institute. Both Bach and Zbarsky played an important role in the Sovietization of the academy (Chapter I). Possibly, Mairanovsky's contacts with the NKVD started when he headed the Toxicology Department, since in the USSR, toxicological studies were always secret and controlled by the secret services. The connection with the NKVD also explains why Mairanovsky, who had been working at the Bach Institute as a researcher for only four years, suddenly became deputy director (Document 12, Appendix II). Apparently, he replaced Zbarsky, who in 1933 was appointed chair of the Department of Biochemistry at the Moscow First Medical Institute.

From 1935 until 1937, Mairanovsky headed a special (i.e., secret) laboratory at the All-Union Institute of Experimental Medicine (VIEM). VIEM was created in 1932 in Leningrad on the personal initiative of the Soviet writer Maxim Gorky and the Soviet leaders Stalin and Molotov. It was based on the old Institute of Experimental Medicine, which was established in 1890. In 1934, the main part of VIEM was transferred to Moscow, and only a small branch of it continued to exist in Leningrad.[2] Evidently, Mairanovsky moved to VIEM after the reorganization that followed its transfer from Leningrad to Moscow. He may have been invited to create and head a new secret laboratory. After two years of heading this laboratory, Mairanovsky was demoted to senior researcher and continued to work at this position until 1940 (Document 10, Appendix II). He evidently contin-

Table 3.1 Dates of Mairanovsky's Biography

No.	Event or employment	Date(s)
1.	Birth	1899
2.	Graduation from the Tiflis [Tbilisi] University	1919
3.	Graduation from the 2nd Medical Institute (Moscow)	1923
4.	Post-graduate student, Bach Institute of Biochemistry	1928–29
5.	Researcher, Bach Institute of Biochemistry	1929–32
6.	Senior Researcher, Bach Institute of Biochemistry	1932–33
7.	Head, Toxicology Department, Bach Institute of Biochemistry	1933–35
8.	Deputy Director of Bach Institute	1934–35
9.	Head, Special [Secret] Laboratory, All-Union Institute of Experimental Medicine [VIEM]	1935–37
10.	Senior Researcher, Special [Secret] Laboratory, VIEM	1937–38
11.	Senior Researcher, Pathology [Secret] Department of OV [Poisoning Substances], VIEM	1938–40
12.	Head, Laboratory No. 1, NKVD/NKGB	1938–46
13.	Defence of a doctorate dissertation	1940
14.	Approval of the dissertation	1943
15.	Approval of Professor's title	1943
16.	Assignment to Germany	1945
17.	Assasinations within Sudoplatov's squad	1946–50
18.	Senior Engineer, Laboratory No. 1, OOT, MGB	1946–51
15.	Arrest	December 12, 1951
16.	A letter to MGB Acting Minister Sergei Ogol'tsov	October 17, 1951
17.	A letter to MGB Minister Semyon Ignatiev	December 19, 1952
18.	Trial	February 14, 1953
19.	Imprisonment in Vladimir Prison	March 5, 1953
20.	A letter to MVD Minister Lavrentii Beria	April 27, 1953
21.	Transfer to Lubyanka Prison, Moscow	June 7, 1953
22.	Interrogation by Prosecutor Tsaregorodsky regarding Laboratory No. 1	August 27, 1953
23.	Another interrogation	September 23, 1953
24.	Deprivation of a Doctor degree	December 19, 1953
25.	A letter to Nikita Khrushchev	August 1955
22.	Transfer to Lubyanka Prison, Moscow	March 2, 1957
23.	Participation in Eitingon's trial	March 6, 1957
24.	Transfer to Lubyanka Prison, Moscow	September 6, 1958
25.	Participation in Sudoplatov's trial	September 12, 1958
26.	The release from Vladimir Prison	December 13, 1961
27.	Head, Biochemical Laboratory, Makhachkala	1962–64
28.	A letter to President of the Medical Academy Nikolai Blokhin	May 18, 1964
29.	Academician Blokhin's answer	June 4, 1964
30.	Death	December 1964

ued to work at VIEM, but the NKVD became his main affiliation. The name of his last department at VIEM, the Pathology Department of Poisoning Substances, leaves no doubt that this laboratory worked for the NKVD and, probably, also for the military. In September 1938, Mairanovsky officially joined the NKVD (Document 13, Appendix II), where his Laboratory No. 1 started to function in 1939. Mairanovsky worked in the NKVD/MKGB/MGB system until his arrest in December 1951.

In July 1940, Mairanovsky defended his Doctor of Biological Sciences dissertation at a closed council of scientists at the VIEM who had been authorized to know about the secret work of the NKVD-MGB. Each Soviet and now Russian research institute has a Scientific Council consisting of heads of laboratories and prominent scientists working at the institute. Well-known scientists usually serve on the Scientific Council of several institutes. Besides being in charge of the defense of candidate and doctoral dissertations, the Scientific Council approves the main events of scientific life at the institute—the future plans of different laboratories, reports on ongoing projects, decisions of the administration, and so forth. The scientific secretary of the institute is in charge of the organization of the meetings of the council and all paperwork. Besides the ordinary Scientific Council, whose meetings any employee of the institute can attend, many institutes have a separate special Scientific Council consisting of members who were cleared by the KGB. These special councils are in charge of secret projects of the institute and their meetings are closed to employees without special clearance.

Two scientific degrees, Candidate of Science (which is comparable to the American Ph.D.) and Doctor of Sciences, were introduced in the Soviet Union in 1934. A doctoral dissertation was theoretically a serious scientific contribution in the field of one's expertise. In both cases, a dissertation volume was written. A candidate dissertation was reviewed by two prominent specialists in the field and by an independent institution. Three reviewers and an independent institution reviewed a doctoral dissertation. A dissertation was defended at a meeting of a special Scientific Council of the institute or university's department. The defendant presented materials of the dissertation and answered questions posed by the reviewers and the audience. In the case of secret dissertations (like that of Mairanovsky), only specially selected members of a closed council listened to the defendant. After a successful defense and positive decision of the Scientific Council, the dissertation with all the materials describing the process of the defense was sent to the Highest Attestation Commission. The commission made its own independent review of the dissertation. If the dissertation met the criteria of the commission, it provided the defendant with the diploma of a Candidate or Doctor of

Science, respectively. Usually a doctoral dissertation was written and defended by a person who was already a candidate. This system still exists in Russia.

The title of Mairanovsky's dissertation was *Biological Activity of the Products of Interaction of Mustard Gas with Skin Tissues*.[3] This dissertation included the results of experiments on humans. During later interrogations, Mairanovsky testified: "I did not use mustard gas on prisoners in the special laboratory. Substances similar to mustard gas [i.e., mustard gas derivatives] were taken internally with food. Experiments with mustard gas on the skin were not performed."[4]

It seems that Mairanovsky was a pioneer in experimenting with mustard gas on humans. His Nazi colleagues started their experiments with mustard gas on prisoners of the Sachsenhausen concentration camp in 1939 and also conducted experiments in the Natzweiler camp in 1942–1943.[5] "Wounds were deliberately inflicted on the victims, and the wounds were then infected with mustard gas. Other subjects were forced to inhale the gas or take it internally in liquid form, and still others were injected with the gas," a Nuremberg trial prosecutor stated in 1947.[6] Several experiments were performed as well on women inmates of Ravensbruck.[7] Japanese military researchers experimented with mustard gas on Chinese prisoners in 1940 and 1943.[8] In the Natzweiler camp, the German research project even had a title similar to Mairanovsky's—*The Behavior of Yellow Cross* [a synonym of mustard gas] *in Living Organisms*.[9] At that time, Mairanovsky had already collected materials for his dissertation. In April 1944, after finishing their experiments with mustard gas on inmates of the Natzweiler camp, Dr. August Hirt, professor of anatomy at the Reich University of Strasburg, and Dr. Karl Wimmer, a Luftwaffe doctor, prepared their report *Proposed Treatment for Combat Lesions from Mustard Gas* for publication.[10] By that time, Mairanovsky had already been conferred with the title of doctor as well as professor of pathology (Document 14, Appendix II).

After the war, on August 20, 1947, during the case against the Nazi physicians in Nuremberg, seven Nazi doctors were charged with conducting experiments with mustard gas on inmates at Nazi concentration camps. Of them, four were sentenced to death by hanging, one was sentenced to life imprisonment, and two were acquitted and freed.[11] One of the acquitted physicians, Dr. Kurt Blome, was later recruited by the U.S. military and given a position as physician in the European Command Intelligence Center in Oberursel (Germany).[12] Of two doctors who also experimented with mustard gas and tabun on inmates of the Natzweiler camp, Professor August Hirt committed suicide in 1945, and Dr. Wimmer was never persecuted after he handed over a detailed report about these experiments to American investigators.[13] Not one of the Japanese scientists involved in experiments with mustard gas on humans was tried after the war.[14]

In 1940, the Highest Attestation Commission did not approve Mairanovsky's dissertation. The reason the commission gave was that Mairanovsky's dissertation needed additional experimental research. In February 1943, Mairanovsky arranged for a letter from the NKGB commissar, Vsevolod Merkulov, to be sent to the commission. "Merkulov independently sent a letter in which he said that I had performed a number of assignments of significance to national defense at the Ministry."[15] "Yes, of course the letter helped him. The matter was put on the agenda again at the Presidium of the Highest Attestation Commission with Academician Speransky and Corresponding Member Grashchenkov in attendance and it was decided favorably for Mairanovsky."[16] The official documents at the Memorial Archive do not reflect this story, but it was documented in detail in Bobryonev and Ryazentsev.[17] However, documents show that a meeting of the VIEM Scientific Council on October 20, 1943, approved Mairanovsky's title of professor (Document 10, Appendix II).

Beginning in 1942, in addition to his experiments with poison substances, Mairanovsky had started to work on extracting "truthful testimonies" from interrogated victims. However, these experiments met with failure. Again, this was a complete parallel with his Nazi counterparts in Auschwitz. As Dr. Robert Lifton wrote in his research on the Nazi doctors, "there were other kinds of experiments at Auschwitz. These also combined certain official purposes with individual 'investigative' interests, including the use of drugs (probably mescaline, morphine and barbiturate derivatives) for purposes of extracting confessions, and the use of certain poisons."[18]

After the war, the CIA and the U.S. Office of Naval Intelligence obtained information about Nazi experiments with these types of drugs from one of I. G. Farben's drug experts, Karl Tauboeck.[19] He told Americans that the Gestapo and Abwehr had been looking for a truth drug consisting of barbiturates made from a plant extract. They planned to dope officers who had plotted to kill Hitler and force them to confess. According to Tauboeck, he failed to collect enough plants for the mission.

Mairanovsky was very disappointed with his "truth drugs" failure. As he wrote later (on October 17, 1951) in a letter to MGB acting minister Ogol'tsov,[20] "I would like to propose further elaboration of my methods . . . in solving crimes by putting suspects into a "truth-telling" state . . . This had been approved by an authoritative commission appointed by Minister V. N. Abakumov and Generals Fedotov and Raikhman. For this work I was promised the Stalin Prize." It was naturally very disappointing to miss a chance to receive the most prestigious Soviet prize.

In his memoirs, Sudoplatov claimed that during World War II Mairanovsky played an important role in the anti-German actions of Sudoplatov's terrorist department.[21] According to Sudoplatov, Mairanovsky put to sleep the Abwehr agents, who had been parachuted into the Soviet territory and came to secret "safe apartments." While they were asleep, Mairanovsky supposedly exchanged the poison ampoules hidden in the collars of agents' shirts with ampoules without poisons. This way the agents could not commit suicide when they were later caught by the Soviet secret service. It is unclear whether these apartments were in Moscow or somewhere else. Bobryonev and Ryazentsev mentioned that during the war Mairanovsky went to Tashkent, Chkalovsk, Kuibyshev, and Ulyanovsk.[22] Perhaps these trips were connected with Mairanovsky's service to Sudoplatov. Unfortunately, there is no way to check Sudoplatov's description without access to the SVR and FSB archives.

After World War II, in September–October 1945, Mairanovsky, Naumov, and Smykov[23] were sent to Germany to find specialists who had experimented on humans with poisons and other chemicals in Nazi Germany.[24] The assignment came from then NKGB commissar Merkulov, who received an order from Beria, at the time deputy chairman of Sovnarkom, deputy chairman of the State Committee of Defense (GKO; Stalin was chairman), NKVD minister, and chairman of State Committee No. 1, which had been created to manage the atomic bomb project. Possibly, Mairanovsky's trip was connected with the work of State Committee No. 1—after World War II, many German scientists were taken to the Soviet Union and spent years in captivity working on numerous projects, including that of the A–bomb.[25]

Probably, Beria-Merkulov's instructions also included a wider search for biologists and chemists who were connected with the Soviet Union. Mairanovsky and Smykov were members of one of a few teams who were in charge of this search. At any rate, the Soviet geneticist Nikolai Timofeev-Ressovsky, who in 1929–1945 headed the Genetics and Biophysics Department at the Kaiser Wilhelm Institute for Brain Research in Institute Buch-Berlin, was arrested by the Soviet secret services on September 13, 1945.[26] I will describe this arrest in detail in Chapter 4. The next day, on September 14, 1945, Dr. Heinrich Zeiss, the former head of the Military Hygiene Institute of the German Naval Academy, was arrested.[27] This was the same Dr. Zeiss whom the condemned microbiologists-"traitors" supposedly provided with Soviet state secrets in the 1930s. Later, in 1948, Zeiss was tried and convicted—not as a Nazi criminal but as a German spy and a "wrecker."[28]

After this work, Mairanovsky came to the conclusion that the Nazis' achievements in the field of poisons were "significantly less than ours."[29] I do not know the techniques that Mairanovsky and his team acquired in

Germany, but there definitely were some successful achievements in the field of Mairanovsky's principal expertise—methods of execution that simulated "natural causes" of death. Professor Heissmeyer of the SS hospital in Hohlenlychen developed a technique "of intravenous injections of a suspension of live tubercle bacilli, which brought on acute military tuberculosis within a few weeks. . . . Preliminary tests on the efficacy of this method were performed exclusively on children at the Neuengamme concentration camp."[30] Dr. Sigmund Rascher at Dachau (who was more well known for his freezing and high-altitude experiments)[31] "developed cyanide capsules that could be used either for executions or for suicides."[32]

I think that Mairanovsky can be characterized in the same way that Dr. Josef Mengele was later described by one of the Nazi doctors who worked in Auschwitz: "In my view he [Mengele] was a gifted scientist, but a combination of scientific knowledge, opportunism and ambition, which Mengele had, can lead to anything."[33] Although I would not say that Mengele and Mairanovsky were "gifted scientists," both were professionals motivated by personal ambition who were ready for anything.

Decline and Arrest

In 1946, Colonel of Medical Service Mairanovsky was removed from the directorship of his laboratory. The laboratory was divided into pharmacological and chemical sectors, and Mairanovsky's critics Naumov and Grigorovich (Mairanovsky's former assistant) were appointed to head the new laboratories.[34] The laboratories were moved to Kuchino in the Moscow suburbs. Due to the reorganization of the MGB, Mairanovsky was transferred to the MGB Operational Techniques Department (head: Colonel Fyodor Zhelezov) with the much less prestigious title of senior engineer.

Although Mairanovsky worked from time to time as an executioner together with Sudoplatov and Eitingon (Chapter 2), he hoped that Abakumov, the new MGB minister, would restore his power at the laboratory. Here is how Mairanovsky described his situation in an appeal to First Party Secretary Nikita Khrushchev in August 1955:

Abakumov and Zhelezov promised me [to create] all conditions of my previous work, gave me an order to develop a parallel project within the existing one . . . About 30 persons hired as a staff and a temporary place [for the laboratory] was provided outside of Moscow. Many of the "things" [a code word for poisons] were given to me from my previous work.[35]

In fact, Zhelezov did not support Mairanovsky. It seems that the work on poisons at Mairanovsky's laboratory ended in December 1949 and the laboratory was practically liquidated in 1951. At that time, Mairanovsky tried to revitalize his superiors' interest in ricin. On September 1, 1953, Prosecutor Rudenko presented Beria (who was under investigation) with the following excerpt from a letter Mairanovsky had written to Beria, dated July 17, 1953:

> In 1938, when I was summoned by you [Commissar Beria] concerning the work on using dust-like substances to poison through inhaled air (ricin, a toxic substance from the castor-oil plant), you gave me the order to work in this promising field. Unfortunately, at that time [in 1940–1943] the work with ricin did not yield the expected positive results . . . Recently, our technique has been enhanced by the ability to obtain extremely fine microscopic dispersion. I proposed this topic for research in 1950 along with Major Khoteyev, but it was stopped by Colonel Zhelezov. I have some proposals for using new substances with both sedative and lethal properties to implement your quite correct premise, which you [Minister] gave me . . . [36]

On December 13, 1951, Mairanovsky was arrested (Mairanovsky's prisoner card in Vladimir Prison; Document 11, Appendix II). Before that, on July 12, 1951, Abakumov was arrested on Stalin's order.[37] Abakumov's first deputy, Sergei Ogol'tsov, became MGB acting head for a short time. Merkulov later revealed that he had written a note to Stalin denouncing Abakumov.[38] However, the main allegations were provided by Mikhail Ryumin, at the time senior investigator of the MGB Department for Investigation of Especially Important Cases (OVD). Ryumin reported to the Communist Party Central Committee that Abakumov had known about a Jewish bourgeois nationalistic plot within the MGB linked to American spies.[39] Stalin ordered creation of a special commission for investigation of MGB activity, which consisted of two Politburo members, Beria and Georgii Malenkov, and two Party functionaries, the future MGB minister Semyon Ignatiev and Mikhail Shkiryatov. One of Stalin's devoted followers, Mikhail Shkiryatov (1893–1954) was deputy chairman in 1939–1952, and from 1952–1954, chairman of the Commission of Party Control within the Central Committee.[40] The fate of Abakumov and his men was sealed (Chapter 1).

In August 1951, Ryumin was appointed head of the OVD Department and simultaneously MGB deputy minister. Semyon Ignatiev was appointed the new MGB minister. Before that, Ignatiev headed the Department on the

Party, Trade Union, and Komsomol (Communist Youth Organization) Organs of the Central Committee. Immediately after that, Abakumov's closest MGB associates were arrested.[41] Mairanovsky was among the arrested (Documents 15–17, in Appendix II). Eitingon was also arrested in October 1951 (Eitingon's prisoner card; Document 18, Appendix II) as "a member of a Zionist Plot in the MGB." Like Mairanovsky, he was a Jew by origin. Researchers Petrov and Kasatkina wrote:

> Mairanovsky became one of the victims of a campaign of purges started by Stalin and [the new] MGB Minister, Ignatiev. During those days, in the second part of 1951, all kinds of so-called "plots" within the MGB, in which international intelligence services and "agents of all-world Zionism" supposedly took part, were "discovered." At first, as Mairanovsky said later, he was accused of spying for Japan. The investigation of his case was given to Ryumin and his assistants, who were known for their sadistic cruelty.[42]

From February 1952, Ryumin also headed the "investigation" team that interrogated Abakumov[43] and the arrested Jewish doctors (Chapter 1). The cruelty of Ryumin's "interrogations" was described by Aleksandr Solzhenitsyn in *The Gulag Archipelago*.[44] Later, the investigators rejected the spy version of Mairanovsky's accusation.

There is very little information about the investigation of Mairanovsky's case and his trial. Evidently, poisons played the main role. In his 1955 letter to Khrushchev, Mairanovsky blamed his colleagues for his arrest:

> I . . . was forced to keep some of the "things" [i.e., poisons] at home and even to destroy them . . . Many times Zhelezov and company (Muromtsev, Naumov, Grigorovich, Bukharov) secretly made searches and knew very well that I kept "things" [i.e., poisons], but did not say a word [to me]. As it appeared later, they made [searches] as a provocation because they could take everything from me . . . [45]

Apparently, the investigation started from testimonies of Mairanovsky's colleagues regarding poisons. On January 13, 1952, Colonel Zhelezov testified: "Only after the arrest of Sverdlov, Eitingon and Mairanovsky himself many poisons were found and compensated the shortage found at Mairanovsky [i.e., at his laboratory]. Besides, all these persons possessed absolutely new substances, not registered at the laboratory."[46]

The name of Andrei Sverdlov, the only son of the first Soviet chairman Yakov Sverdlov, had never appeared before in Mairanovsky's story. Not much is known about him. Apparently, Andrei Sverdlov was recruited into the NKVD when he was arrested in 1934 and soon released after Nikolai Bukharin made a personal plea to Stalin.[47] However, the Russian investigative journalist Arkady Vaksberg, who worked at the KGB and other archives, claims that "even as a boy he [Andrei Sverdlov] had worked as a secret informer of the OGPU, writing denunciations of his schoolmates, the children of other Kremlin big shots."[48] In September 1939, Sverdlov interrogated Bukharin's wife, Anna Larina, whom he had known since early childhood.[49] He interrogated her again in 1941. It is known that Sverdlov investigated several more cases in the 1930s–1940s.[50] There is no information available on which assassinations Sverdlov kept poisons for and in which killings he was involved.

Colonel Zhelezov did not name Sverdlov's superior, Yakov Matusov, who was also arrested at the time of the arrests of the Jewish MGB colonels and generals. In 1939, Matusov was a senior investigator of Anna Larina-Bukharina.[51] Before that, in 1937, he signed a warrant for arrest of First Soviet Chief Prosecutor Krylenko.[52] It seems that both Matusov and Sverdlov worked at the Political Secret Department, whose goal was "to combat the anti-Soviet elements"; in 1951, it was the MGB Fifth Directorate.[53] Sudoplatov stated that "Sverdlov had been accused with Mairanovsky and Matusov of, under the leadership of Eitingon, concealing poisons to be used against the leadership of the country."[54] If this was true, this would mean that there was a separate case of "poisoners-plotters within the MGB" under investigation.

What is known for sure is that the names of Eitingon, Matusov, and Sverdlov appeared in the confession of Lev Schwartzman, one of the cruelest NKVD/MGB investigators of the 1930s–1940s (mentioned in Chapters 1 and 4 as one of Nikolai Vavilov's investigators). Schwartzman was arrested immediately after Abakumov, on July 13, 1951.[55] To escape torture, he pretended to be insane and "confessed" that he had had sexual relationships with his own son and daughter, Abakumov, and British ambassador Archibald Clark Kerr. He also declared that in 1945–1946 he had become a Jewish nationalist and organized a group of high-ranking secret service officers of Jewish origin who shared his views. The list of the "members" of the group was long and included the above-mentioned Eitingon, Raikhman, Matusov, and Sverdlov; all these persons were arrested. I have no information about whether Schwartzman mentioned Mairanovsky or whether the connection between Mairanovsky and others was made during the investigation of Mairanovsky's case.

The writer Kirill Stolyarov, who had access to Sverdlov's investigation file, did not mention that Mairanovsky and Eitingon appeared in Sverdlov's case. However, poisonous substances were included in his indictment:

... Together with his accomplices, [Sverdlov] was involved in wrecking activity within the Chekist organs [i.e., MGB] ... secretly kept hostile literature, explosives and poisonous substances [sic!], shells, and a lot of firearms ... [He] completely claimed guilty of [actions according to] Articles 58-10 and 182 pt. I of the RSFSR Criminal Code ... [56]

Therefore, there is no independent data available that Sverdlov's and Matusov's cases were a part of the same investigation as those of Mairanovsky and Eitingon. Moreover, Sverdolov's investigation lasted for nineteen months and he had not been tried before Stalin's death,[57] whereas Mairanovsky had already been convicted and kept in Vladimir Prison.

Mairanovsky appealed in vain during the investigation to new MGB minister Ignatiev. On December 19, 1952, he wrote a letter (cited above) in which he tried to persuade the minister how important his findings in poisons were for the MGB. On February 14, 1953, Mairanovsky was tried secretly by the MGB Special Board (the notorious OSO) and was sentenced to ten years in prison three weeks before Stalin's death (Documents 16 and 17, Appendix II). The final accusation included two points, "abuse of his position" and "illegally keeping strong acting chemicals." According to Bobryonev and Ryazentsev, the first version of the indictment stated:

Mairanovsky, the director of a toxicological laboratory, did not provide guidance to the collective of scientists under him and allowed ongoing work to be disrupted. Having fraudulently obtained his doctoral degree and the title of Professor, Mairanovsky not only hindered the progress of scientific laboratory but due to the incorrect application of special substances because of his ignorance, he personally ruined several important ongoing assignments. In addition, the investigation discovered that the government's procedures for stocking and inventory of poisons, and dangerous substances were created for abuse. In 1946, Mairanovsky was removed from the directorship of the laboratory. After taking a job as a senior engineer at another laboratory, he illegally kept in his possession a large quantity of poisons and dangerous substances ... [58]

Therefore, the investigation accused Mairanovsky not of experimenting on humans (this issue seems never to have been discussed by the investigators, prosecutors, or during the trial itself) but of not conducting better experiments! Also, the fact that he had urged the Highest Commission to approve his doctorate thesis and professor's title by sending a personal letter from Commissar Merkulov was deemed by investigators to indicate that the degree and title had been "fraudulently obtained." Not a word was said about the fact that a group of highly positioned scientists wrote positive reviews of Mairanovsky's work. On December 19, 1953, the Highest Attestation Commission deprived Mairanovsky of his doctorate degree.[59]

Mairanovsky was sent to the most secret political prison in the Soviet Union, which was located in the small town of Vladimir (about 125 miles from Moscow). Ironically, he arrived in Vladimir Prison on March 5, 1953, the day of Stalin's death. I discovered this bit of information while reading Mairanovsky's prisoner card at the archive of Vladimir Prison.[60] Mairanovsky's trial and all the events that followed are still a mystery.

It is not clear whether Eitingon was tried before Stalin's death. In any case, he was released from prison on Beria's order on March 20, 1953.[61] Sverdlov was luckier than Mairanovsky: He had not been tried before Stalin's death. Beria simply closed the case and on May 18, 1953, signed Sverdlov's rehabilitation, prepared by Colonel Aleksandr Khvat (discussed in Chapter 4 as the main investigator in charge of the Nikolai Vavilov case) and approved by Beria's new first deputy, Bogdan Kobulov, and the new head of the OVD Department, Lev Vlodzimersky.[62]

In Vladimir Prison

Although the history of Vladimir Prison started in the eighteenth century during the rule of Catherine the Great, its main buildings were built later, in the middle of the nineteenth century.[63] In 1906, after the 1905 Revolution, it became a special prison for political convicts. From the 1930s on, and increasingly after World War II, Vladimir Prison was used for political prisoners of great state importance. Its official name was "Special MGB Prison No. 2" (Lubyanka Prison was No. 1). In the late 1940s and 1950s, citizens of many countries were kept there. Besides Russians, there were former ministers of the Baltic countries (and their wives, in separate cells without knowledge of the fate of their husbands), Germans, French, Swiss, and others. Among the Baltic prisoners was the former Latvian minister of foreign affairs Wilhelm Munters and his wife Natalia, whom Sudoplatov kidnapped in Riga in June 1940 and secretly transported to Russia.[64] At first Munters and his wife were transferred to Voronezh in central Russia, where Munters was appointed a professor at the local university. On June 28, 1941, six days after the beginning of the war with the Nazis, the couple was arrested. After a trial, they, along with some other former Baltic ministers and their family members, were tried and put in the Kirov Internal Prison. Later, in 1952, all of them were retried, received twenty-five years' imprisonment, and were kept in Vladimir Prison under numbers (Wilhelm and Natalia Munters, under Nos. 7 and 8, correspondingly) from April 1952 until their

A corridor inside Vladimir Prison (1990).
(Photo from Memorial's Archive [Moscow])

release in August 1954.[65] Most of the foreigners were innocent people like Munters, sentenced to ten to twenty-five years' imprisonment according to Article 58 of the Russian Criminal Code. But real Soviet criminals like Mairanovsky, Sudoplatov, Eitingon, and some other Beria men (who were not imprisoned for their real crimes),[66] as well as German and Austrian war criminals, were also there.

According to the memoirs of a former prisoner, a Finn named Unto Parvilahti, among the Russians was Mairanovsky's colleague Professor Grigory Liberman, a chemist who had specialized on poison gases and presumably had a general's rank.[67] Liberman was Academician Ipatieff's pupil at the Artillery Academy laboratory on poison gases and was a specialist on methods of obtaining lewisite.[68] This substance, dichloro (2-chlorovinyl) arsine, was developed in the United States during World War I but was never actually used. As Parvilahti recalled, Liberman, whom he met in prison briefly because of a mistake by the guards, told him that he had been arrested after Lenin's death in 1924 and kept in prisons since then. During some of those years, he was allowed to work in a secret chemical laboratory under NKVD control, but after an accident in the lab, Liberman was put in solitary confinement in Vladimir Prison.

This seems to be true. According to Liberman's prisoner card in Vladimir Prison, he was arrested in 1935 and sentenced five years later, in 1940, on charges of treason against the Motherland and participation in a terrorist organization (Document 19, Appendix II). However, there is a discrepancy between the charges for the arrest (point 14 in the card) and conviction (the back side of the card). In the first case, the following paragraphs of the Criminal Code are mentioned: 58-1a (treason against the Motherland), 58-7 (counterrevolutionary activity in a state institution), 58-8 (terrorist acts against governmental figures), and 58-11 (organization of terrorist acts or a membership in a counterrevolutionary group). In the second, Articles 58-1b (treason against the Motherland committed by a military person), 58-7, and 58-8 are mentioned. The problem is that persons charged with the paragraph 58-1b were punished by death. On May 26, 1947, a special decree of the Presidium of the USSR Supreme Council replaced the punishment by death with twenty-five-year imprisonment (the death penalty was restored in 1950). According to the prisoner card, on October 13, 1947, Liberman was brought to Vladimir Prison. Therefore, it looks as though he was tried again between May and October 1947, sentenced to imprisonment instead of being shot, and put in Vladimir Prison where he was kept in solitary confinement, probably under a number. For some reason, his term was not increased from fifteen to twenty-five years. In January–February 1949, Liberman was brought to Lefortovo Prison in Moscow, possibly to testify against newly arrested colleagues or German specialists. In March 1950, after the end of his fifteen-year term of imprisonment, Liberman was sent into exile to the Krasnoyarsk Region in Siberia.

Among the German prisoners, there was another Mairanovsky colleague, one of the most infamous medical experimenters in Auschwitz, Dr. Carl Clauberg.[69] In 1943, Clauberg reported to Himmler that through the injection of supercooled carbon dioxide into the fallopian tubes, with a staff of ten men he could sterilize as many as 1,000 women per day.[70] Several thousand Jews and Gypsies were sterilized at Auschwitz by this method under his supervision.[71] In 1945, he continued his experiments in Ravensbruck. On June 24, 1945, Clauberg was arrested by the SMERSH Third Directorate (Military Counterintelligence) and sent to Moscow (Clauberg's prisoner card; Document 20, Appendix II). I wonder if his specific knowledge regarding women's sterilization obtained in the medical block of Auschwitz and Ravensbruck, and evidently discussed during interrogations, was later used in Mairanovsky's or some other MGB laboratory.

On July 3, 1948, Clauberg was tried by the OSO and sentenced to twenty-five years' imprisonment according the secret Decree of the Presidium of the USSR Supreme Council *On the Punishment of the Nazi-German Criminals Guilty of Killing and Torturing Soviet Civilians and Prisoners of War, Spies and Traitors of the Motherland and Those Who Helped Them,* dated April 19, 1943. Evidently, there were Soviet citizens among the victims of Clauberg's experiments. The same July, Clauberg was transferred to Vladimir Prison. Possibly, he was kept under a number like Boris Men'shagin (Prisoner No. 29), the other prisoner also punished from April 19, 1943, under the same decree. In 1954–1957, all Germans and Austrians were released irrespective of their crimes and repatriated to their native countries. Clauberg was among them. He returned to Germany in 1955 and for some time practiced medicine under his own name. He openly boasted of his achievements in Auschwitz. Then Clauberg was arrested in the city of Kiel and died in 1957 in a prison hospital waiting for a new trial.

In 1948, sixty-year-old Dr. Heinrich Zeiss, the German specialist on bacteriological weapons whom I mentioned in connection with the 1930s Moscow trials and who had been expelled from Moscow in 1933, also ended up in Vladimir Prison. On July 10, 1948, he was condemned to twenty-five years' imprisonment as a German spy (Zeiss's prisoner card; Document 21, Appendix II). On March 31, 1949, he died there.

Before the mid-1950s, many prisoners were kept in solitary confinement. At that time, Vladimir Prison had cells for approximately 800 prisoners; in 1960, 200 new cells were added. The most prominent prisoners were kept in cells on the first floor of Corpus 2. As I have already mentioned, many of them were given numbers after they had been investigated by the MGB Department for Investigation of Especially Important Cases and convicted by the OSO. I personally knew a former prisoner, Men'shagin, who spent almost twenty-five years in solitary confinement, first in Lubyanka and then in Vladimir Prison. He was found "guilty" in 1951 of having witnessed the German exhumation in 1943 of Polish officers massacred by the NKVD in Katyn in 1940. For seven years, this man was Number 29 instead of having a name.[72] There are two prisoner cards for Men'shagin in the Vladimir Prison file: one without a name but with the No. 29, and another, with Men'shagin's full name.

The conditions in Vladimir Prison in the late 1940s to early 1950s were extremely severe, sometimes almost unbearable. As a former numbered prisoner, Ariadna Balashova, arrested in 1947 in the Allilueva case, told me in 1990, after years in solitary confinement, people forgot how to speak and had to learn to pronounce words again. Others went insane. For a tiny violation of the strict prison rules, a prisoner was put in a punishment cell, or *kartser*. Thomas Sgovio, an American who had already been through the most brutal Soviet labor camps and then spent four months in Vladimir Prison,[73] described in his memoirs his experience of having been kept in such a cell in 1949:

> Three days in the dungeon . . . undressed . . . in my underdrawers . . . four hundred grams of bread and a cup of water . . . it's cold and damp . . . pace back and forth to keep warm . . . all day. Night . . . they give me a board to sleep on . . . I lay down . . . it's too cold . . . I hug my sides . . . no use. Get up, Tommy . . . walk back and forth . . . re-live your life again.[74]

The system of numbered prisoners ended in December 1954.[75] However, those sentenced as members of the Allilueva case were given their real names back and released earlier, in 1953. Also, at the end of 1954, prisoners were given their own clothes instead of the gray uniforms with dark blue stripes introduced in 1948.[76] The length of time allowed for daily walks in the high-walled pen in the prison's yard became longer, about thirty minutes instead of fifteen.

It does not appear that Mairanovsky was kept in the most severe conditions: There is a note on his prisoner's card that in 1953 he was put in the building with mild conditions (into cells of Corpus 3; Documents 16 and 17, Appendix II). Besides Mairanovsky, there were a few other men in Vladimir who had held high positions in Beria's MGB. According to the memoirs of a dissident and former political prisoner, Revolt Pimenov, these Beria men seemed to have received more lenient treatment than other prisoners.[77] A Leningrad mathematician, Pimenov was arrested in 1957, tried on political charges, and sentenced for the first time in February 1958,[78] the year in which Khrushchev boasted that there were no political prisoners in the USSR. After enduring six years of his ten-year term, Pimenov was released due to the intervention of two prominent mathematicians, Academicians Aleksandr Aleksandrov and Mstislav Keldysh. Refused permission to return to Leningrad, Pimenov worked at an institute in the city of Syktyvkar in the northern part of European Russia, where he was elected as a deputy of the Soviet Parliament in 1989. He died in 1990.

According to the memoirs of Eitingon's stepdaughter, Zoya Zarubina (like him, she was also an MGB officer), Eitingon's family was allowed to visit him in Vladimir Prison "once a month, and this was when they took the food parcel . . . Leonid also sent a letter to the family each month."[79] The other prisoners did not recall such privileges.

Pimenov remembered Mairanovsky as a pretentious prisoner. During the short walks in the prison yard, Mairanovsky wore a general's military hat, even on warm days. He was not a general (before his arrest Mairanovsky held the rank of a colonel), but he wanted to be recognized as one. This was ridiculous in those circumstances, since prisoners were deprived of their ranks and awards.

Pimenov recalled another episode. On April 12, 1961, when almost everybody was exulting after the news of Gagarin's space flight, Mairanovsky yelled at Pimenov: "Why don't you smile? You don't like the achievements of the Soviet country, do you?"[80] Eitingon's stepdaughter recalled that Eitingon in prison also remained "a staunch Communist who believed in the system."[81]

In 1990, I myself went to Vladimir Prison as part of an international team of researchers, the Commission on the Fate and Whereabouts of Raoul Wallenberg. Incredibly, the former medical doctor of the Vladimir Prison hospital, Elena Butova, clearly remembered Mairanovsky. She could not forget his words. One day, when he needed some medical treatment and saw a syringe in her hands, Mairanovsky began to shriek: "Do not come up to me! You want to kill me! I know how it could be done!"

On June 7, 1953, Mairanovsky was moved from Vladimir Prison to Lubyanka Prison, Moscow. Evidently this happened after he appealed to the new state security (now MVD) minister, Beria, in a letter dated April 21, 1953. After Stalin's death, in March 1953, Beria merged the MGB and MVD into the new MVD. He also ordered the release of many of his former trusted coworkers who had been imprisoned during the anti-Semitic purges of 1951–1952.[82] Among others, Eitingon, Sverdlov, Matusov, and Raikhman were released. Eitingon and Raikhman received high appointments in the new MVD.[83] Sverdlov also returned to the MVD. Mairanovsky wrote Beria a second time on July 17, 1953, while he was in Butyrka Prison in Moscow.[84] However, it was too late—Beria had already been arrested.

On June 26, Lavrentii Beria, the ruthless head of the new MVD, was arrested by the members of the Presidium of the Communist Party at its session (Table 3.2). This plot was led by Nikita Khrushchev.[85] At the next session of the Presidium, on June 29, a resolution was adopted "On the Organization of the Investigation of the Affair of the Criminal Anti-Party and Anti-Government Activities of Beria." After five secret sessions of the Communist Party Central Committee Plenum that took place on July 2–7, 1953, Beria was denounced at the Plenum along with his cronies.[86] Sergei Kruglov, the newly appointed MVD minister, said at the Second Plenum Session:

Table 3.2 Events Surrounding the Beria and Merkulov Trials

Date in 1953	Event	Source(s)
June 26	Beria's secret arrest	Stickle, *The Beria Affair*, p. 201
June 29	Decision of the Presidium of the Central Committee to start Beria's investigation	Naumov and Sigachev, *Lavrentii Beria*, p. 72; Stickle, *The Beria Affair*, p. 201
July 10	Official announcement of Beria's arrest	Andrew and Gordievsky, KGB, p. 424
Aug. 20	Arrest of Eitingon	Eitingon's Prisoner Card
Aug. 21	Arrest of Sudoplatov	Sudoplatov's Prisoner Card
Aug. 27	Interrogation of Mairanovsky	Bobryonev, "*Doktor Smert*," pp. 365-368 Bobryonev and Ryazentsev, *The Ghosts*, p. 167
Aug. 28	The first interrogation of Beria regarding Mairanovsky's activity	Bobryonev, "*Doktor Smert*," pp. 368-371 Bobryonev and Ryazentsev, *The Ghosts*, pp. 151-153
Aug. 29	Interrogation of Merkulov regarding Mairanovsky's activity	Bobryonev, "*Doktor Smert*," pp. 234-235 Bobryonev and Ryazentsev, *The Ghosts*, pp. 164-166
Sept. 1	Interrogation of Sudoplatov regarding Mairanovsky's activity	Bobryonev, "*Doktor Smert*," pp. 388-389 Bobryonev and Ryazentsev, *The Ghosts*, p. 168
Sept. 1	Interrogation of Beria regarding Mairanovsky's activity	Bobryonev, "*Doktor Smert*," pp. 372-378 Bobryonev and Ryazentsev, *The Ghosts*, pp. 154-161
Sept.	Interrogation of Raikhman, Naumov, Grigorovich, Balishansky, Podobedov regarding Mairanovsky's activity	Bobryonev, "*Doktor Smert*," pp. 380-381 398; Bobryonev and Ryazentsev, *The Ghosts*, pp. 129-131
Sept. 19	Interrogation of Blokhin regarding Mairanovsky's activity	Bobryonev, "*Doktor Smert*," pp. 390-391 396; Bobryonev and Ryazentsev, *The Ghosts*, pp. 129-131
Sept. 23	Interrogation of Mairanovsky	Bobryonev, "*Doktor Smert*," pp. 232-233 389; Bobryonev and Ryazentsev, *The Ghosts*, pp. 70-72, 169
Sept. 29	Interrogation of Merkulov regarding Mairanovsky's activity	Bobryonev, "*Doktor Smert*," pp. 234-235 385; Bobryonev and Ryazentsev, *The Ghosts*, pp. 72-74, 128, 166-170
Oct. 14	Interrogation of Gertsovsky regarding Mairanovsky's activity	Bobryonev, "*Doktor Smert*," pp. 391-392 Bobryonev and Ryazentsev, *The Ghosts*, pp. 170-172
Oct.	Interrogation of B. Kobulov regarding Mairanovsky's activity	Bobryonev, "*Doktor Smert*," pp. 392-394 Bobryonev and Ryazentsev, *The Ghosts*, pp. 172-174
Oct. 23	Interrogation of Gertsovsky regarding Mairanovsky's activity	Bobryonev, "*Doktor Smert*," p. 394; Bobryonev and Ryazentsev, *The Ghosts*, pp. 175-180
Dec. 18–23	Trial of Beria, Merkulov, Kobulov and four other of Beria's men	Petrov, "Sudy protiv NKVD-MGB"; Stickle, *The Beria Affair*, pp. 195-197
Dec. 23	Shooting to death Beria, Merkulov, Kobulov, and other convicts after the trial	Petrov, "Sudy protiv NKVD-MGB"; Naumov and Sigachev, *Lavrentii Beria*, p. 387

Beria pursued the goal of having his own people in the field, without consideration for their political loyalty to the [Communist] Party. As is now clear, we must perceive a number of appointments of such people as Raikhman, Eitingon, Sudoplatov, Meshik, Milstein and others . . . who were expelled from the organs of the MVD prior to his appearance, as a desire to surround himself with people totally faithful to him.[87]

After this, Merkulov and others close to Beria were arrested. Eitingon was arrested again on August 20, 1953.[88] Sudoplatov was arrested in his own office the next day, August 21, 1953 (Sudoplatov's prisoner card; Document 22, Appendix II), by the head of the MVD Seventh (Operative) Directorate and searched like a common criminal.[89] After his arrest, Sudoplatov's deputy, Lev Studnikov, became acting head of the Ninth Department,[90] which was later renamed the Thirteenth Department and then Department V. In 1971, after the defection in England of Oleg Lyalin, an agent of this department, functions of Department V were given to Department S (illegal agents) of the KGB First Main (Foreign Intelligence) Directorate.[91]

Mairanovsky's letter fell into the hands of an OVD investigator, Molchanov. He immediately wrote a report to the new head of the OVD Department, Lieutenant Colonel Kozyrev, who replaced Ryumin. In the report he described Mairanovsky's laboratory and Beria's leading role in its organization and supervision,[92] stating that Mairanovsky's case should be sent to the Chief Prosecutor's Office. At this point, the Presidium of the Central Committee had already put the newly appointed chief prosecutor, Rodion Rudenko[93] in charge of a team of prosecutors to investigate Beria and his men.[94]

On August 27, 1953, Deputy Military Prosecutor Tsaregradsky interrogated Mairanovsky, who gave a detailed testimony. The next day, on August 28, 1953, Rudenko interrogated Beria using Mairanovsky's information. Then everyone who knew about Mairanovsky's activity—Merkulov, Kobulov, Bashtakov, Balishansky, and Gertsovsky—were interrogated (Table 3.2). During the trial, a member of the court, secretary of the Moscow Regional Party Committee Nikolai Mikhailov, asked Beria and Merkulov whether they approved of experiments on humans. Both confirmed their knowledge of the experiments and their approval.[95] However, this episode was not included in the final version of the verdict. Only vague wording appeared such as "the defendant Beria L. P. and his accomplices executed like terrorists those persons who, as they had expected, were potentially capable to expose them."[96]

Immediately after the trial, on December 23, 1953, Beria, Merkulov, Kobulov, and four others condemned to death by the Special Judicial

Session of the USSR Supreme Court were shot. Beria was shot by Colonel General Pavel Batitsky in the presence of Prosecutor Rudenko and General K. S. Moskalenko.[97] After Batitsky, five more officers shot at Beria. In 1954, Batitsky (later marshal and deputy minister of defense) was awarded Hero of the Soviet Union, and three other officers received Orders of the Red Banner for killing Beria.[98] The other convicts were shot by the first deputy MVD minister K. F. Lunev and Deputy Chief Military Prosecutor Yu. D. Kitaev[99] in the presence of Generals Getman, Bakeev, and Sopil'kin.[100] This must have been a unique event: A deputy security minister and a deputy military chief prosecutor personally assassinated former leaders of the state security!

Investigation of Mairanovsky's activity continued after the end of the Beria case. Bobryonev mentions that Tsaregradsky interrogated Mairanovsky again and that Balishansky, Filimonov, Lapshin, Podobedov, Osinkin, Yakovlev, Grigorovich, Naumov, and Muromtsev were also interrogated in February–March 1954.[101] It is possible these interrogations were conducted in connection with the investigations of Sudoplatov and Eitingon. In any event, Eitingon was interrogated regarding Mairanovsky's experiments.[102]

In 1955–1956, when all political cases began to be investigated anew, Mairanovsky appealed for rehabilitation and was brought from Vladimir Prison to Moscow again, but his accusation and term were not changed.[103] In 1957–1958, he was transferred twice to Lubyanka Prison, each time for about two weeks, on March 2, 1957, and on September 6, 1958.[104] Between these dates, from October 1957 until August 1958, Mairanovsky shared Cells 2-2 and 2-52 with an open anti-Semite, Zigurds-Dzierdis Kruminsh.[105] It appears that Mairanovsky testified at the trial of Eitingon, since Eitingon was tried by the Military Collegium of the Supreme Court on March 6, 1957,[106] when Mairanovsky was in Moscow. Sudoplatov was tried by the Military Collegium of the Supreme Court on September 12, 1958,[107] when Mairanovsky was brought to Moscow for the second time. In his memoirs, Sudoplatov described Mairanovsky's appearance and behavior in the courtroom:

> Another witness [besides Sergei Muromtsev] was Mairanovsky, who was escorted to the reception room by guards, looking pale and haunted. Dressed in shabby clothes, he looked like he had just been brought from jail . . . Mairanovsky began to weep the instant he saw me. He didn't expect me to be sitting in an armchair in a good suit with a necktie . . .

. . . He testified that he had consulted me on four cases. With the permission of the chairman,[108] I asked him whether he was subordinated to me, whether the four cases were experiments [on humans] or combat operations [i.e., kidnappings and killings], and from whom he had received the instructions for these specific actions . . . Mairanovsky, answering that he had never worked for me, began to weep. Through his tears he said that these were indeed top-secret combat operations, and he named Khrushchev and Molotov as the source of his instructions. He first told of meeting Molotov in the Committee of Information headquarters, and then, to the wrath of the chairman, mentioned meeting Khrushchev in the railroad carriage on his way to Uzhgorod [where Khrushchev ordered Mairanovsky to poison Archbishop Romzha of the Catholic (Uniate) Church].[109]

Both Eitingon and Sudoplatov were accused of "treason against the Motherland" (which, as in Mairanovsky's case, had nothing in common with the real crimes) and sentenced to twelve and fifteen years of imprisonment, respectively, and three years of disenfranchisement. Now all three could see each other during their daily walks in the prison. Later, Sudoplatov wrote that in Vladimir Prison, Mairanovsky "was a shell of his former self."[110] He was released only at the end of his term, on December 13, 1961.

After Mairanovsky had been released, Eitingon and Sudoplatov shared the same Cell 32 in Corpus 2 from December 25, 1961, until January 12, 1963. Later, they were transferred to Cell 76 in Corpus 1 and then went back to Corpus 2, to Cells 56 and 32 (Documents 18 and 22, Appendix II). In September 1963, Eitingon was moved out. As Pimenov recalled later, "[U]p to the winter of 1962–1963 Sudoplatov and Eitingon were in 'the hospital' [of Vladimir Prison]. When the [prison's] regime became more severe, it was decided that they were not sick anymore and they were transferred to the same floor [as Pimenov] and we met at walks."[111] During these walks, Sudoplatov told Pimenov he should have been tried together with Beria and Merkulov in 1954 when all seven defendants were shot after the trial. Sudoplatov told Men'shagin the same story during their walks in the prison yard.[112] Sudoplatov simulated madness and was put into the Psychiatric Prison Hospital in Leningrad. In the 1980s, Men'shagin recalled Sudoplatov's words:

Sudoplatov's case was postponed and for five years he was kept in Leningrad under psychiatric investigation. He behaved as an idiot. When his wife was brought to him (apparently, on purpose), and called him

"Pashen'ka! Pashen'ka!," he only answered "Mo-o-o!" [as a cow]. When he was taken for a walk, he used to lay on the ground and ate the earth. He did not use the toilet . . . [113]

In 1958, a medical commission decided to transfer Sudoplatov to the Special Psychiatric Prison Hospital in Kazan. Since Sudoplatov knew about sadistic conditions in that hospital, he stopped simulating and was put on trial. Because of this, he was tried only in 1958 and remained alive. (Sudoplatov's version in his book published in 1994 in English differs from this story.)

During the walks in Vladimir Prison, Eitingon tried to simulate madness: As Men'shagin remembered, Eitingon "used to stand in the corner of the pen facing it as if he had been punished and ordered to stand in it."[114] Later, Eitingon's former colleague, a Soviet agent abroad called Matus Steinberg, told Men'shagin (with whom he shared a cell from January 1964 until January 1966)[115] that Eitingon had wanted to attract the attention of prison authorities and be declared a mentally ill person.[116] Eitingon was released from Vladimir Prison in March 1964,[117] and Sudoplatov, in 1968.[118]

The End

In December 1961, Mairanovsky returned to his Moscow apartment in a prestigious house built for the Communist Party, military, and KGB elite. He appealed for rehabilitation again: According to the Soviet bureaucracy, it was better for a former prisoner to have a document stating that a person had been wrongly accused. Instead of being rehabilitated, however, Mairanovsky was ordered to leave Moscow in a few days. He left Moscow for Makhachkala, the capital of the small autonomous North Caucasian Republic of Dagestan on the Caspian seashore near Baku, Azerbaijan. There he became a head of a biochemical laboratory. He died in Makhachkala in 1964.

Mairanovsky's sons tried to appeal for rehabilitation again in 1989–1992. Every time, their request was rejected. "His guilt has been proven by the materials of the case. There are no reasons for reinvestigation of the case," wrote the senior assistant to the USSR general prosecutor, Viktor Ilyukhin, in 1989.[119]

Sudoplatov and Eitingon were luckier. In December 1991, Chief Military Prosecutor General Pavel Boriskin endorsed the decision to rehabilitate both of them.[120] Also, he dismissed the murder charge against General Kalugin for Markov's murder in London. Therefore, at present all three of these executioners are considered innocent according to Russian law.

MAIRANOVSKY'S COLLEAGUES

When Mairanovsky was experimenting on humans, he did not work alone. There were about twenty other scientists who took part in the experiments. In their book, Bobryonev and Ryazentsev mention only a few names: Mairanovsky's assistant Aleksandr Grigorovich; senior chemist V. D. Shchegolev; senior researcher and the head of the bacteriological group, Professor Sergei Muromtsev; pharmaceutical chemist Vasilii Naumov; a technician, Anna Kiriltseva; and Mag, Dmitriev, and Yemelyanov. MGB officials Filimonov, Eitingon, Osinkin, and Lapshin were present at the experiments and even participated in them. Like their Nazi colleagues, the NKVD–MGB used imprisoned scientists to conduct the experiments: Bobryonev and Ryazentsev mentioned at least two names of such prisoners, a biologist Anichkov, and Gorsky.[121] The relationships between the colleagues at this laboratory were the same as those in thousands of regular laboratories: There were serious conflicts between Mairanovsky and his collaborators; especially between himself, Naumov, and Grigorovich. Both considered Mairanovsky to be professionally ignorant.

It would be interesting to know the attitude of these "researchers" toward their work: How did they feel administering lethal poisons to healthy human beings, then observing the subsequent terrible suffering and death? Filimonov started to drink after ten experiments; Muromtsev quit after fifteen.[122] While some executioners became drunkards, others were placed into psychiatric hospitals, and a few committed suicide. What follows is an excerpt from Mairanovsky's letter from Vladimir Prison addressed to the general secretary of the Central Committee, Nikita Khrushchev, regarding how he himself dealt with the situation in 1955:

> This was extremely difficult work with methods that have caused well-deserved doubts and criticism. I and some of the other people who conducted this work had great misgivings: there was the struggle of personal feeling with state necessity. This very difficult state of the nervous system can explain the suicides of Shchigalev and Shchegolev, the psychiatric illness and the acute unrestrained alcoholism of Filimonov, Grigorovich and Yemelyanov and the severe illness of Dmitriev, Mag, and others.[123]

It seems that these Soviet experimenters were not as tough as their Nazi colleagues in concentration camps. Of the group, only Mairanovsky served a term in prison "for the abuse of his position and illegal keeping of poisons." Filimonov was fired from the central MGB in 1947 and transferred from Moscow to Lvov in the Ukraine in 1948, then fired from the MGB in

1954 because of his chronic alcoholism; officially, the reason for firing was "because of the facts discrediting an officer."[124] Seven times he was placed in psychiatric hospitals when he suffered hallucinations of prisoners who had suffered and died during experiments.[125] Naumov and Grigorovich were apparently under arrest for a while during Beria's investigation. In 1964, Naumov, now with the title of professor, still headed a secret KGB laboratory named Military Unit No. 10-55.

Mairanovsky's colleague Sergei Muromtsev (1898–1960), the head of the second secret MGB laboratory, was luckier than Mairanovsky. Muromtsev is an excellent example of the merger between the NKVD-MGB and Lysenko's interests. In 1923, he graduated from the Medical Department of First Moscow University. Like Mairanovsky, he joined the NKVD in 1937, and until 1951, "he was the NKVD-MGB employee as Head and Senior Researcher at several technical facilities."[126] Before that he had served as head of the Microbiology Laboratory at the Institute of Experimental Veterinary Medicine. In 1935, he was given a Doctor of Biology degree without defending his doctorate thesis. This was a mystery because degrees without defense were given only to prominent scientists, and Muromtsev was a microbiologist working in veterinary science, which was not considered a particularly prestigious field of science. Moreover, his publications in 1950–1952 during the time he supported Lysenko revealed his deep ignorance in scientific issues. Possibly, Muromtsev was a good administrator: In 1931, he was one of the organizers of the centralized system of state control of veterinarian vaccines. He continued to work on vaccines until 1943 and in 1946 received a Stalin Prize (for which Mairanovsky was so desperate) for a new method of preparation of vaccines for animals.[127] However, Muromtsev's degree in 1935 might also point to his probable connection with the NKVD as far back as 1935. In 1940, Muromtsev joined the Communist Party.

The goal of Muromtsev's NKVD-MGB bacteriological laboratory was to develop bacterial toxins for the agents' use. In his memoirs, Sudoplatov recalled that in the late 1940s–1950, he provided Muromtsev with spy information from Israel on recent developments in bacteriological weapons.[128] In 1948, while heading the MGB secret lab, Muromtsev was among thirty-five new members of the Agricultural Academy (VASKhNIL) appointed by the USSR Council of Ministers for their support of Lysenko.[129] Stalin himself, as the chairman of the USSR Council of Ministers, signed the list of newly appointed "Academicians." This was a unique event: Academicians were no longer elected but rather appointed by the government and Stalin himself as a reward for their Lysenkoism. Having been an MGB officer (which all biologists were aware of), Muromtsev openly supported Lysenko at Lysenko's triumphant session in August 1948 (Chapter 4) and later, in 1950–1952, during the period of the introduction of Lysenko's ideas into Soviet microbiology. Following the beliefs of Lysenko, Muromtsev stated that microorganism species are unstable, that they can turn into each other.[130] Moreover, according to Muromtsev, viruses and bacteria can appear "from changed proteins of animal, plant, and bacterial cells."[131]

In August 1951, before the arrest of Mairanovsky, Colonel of Medical Service Muromtsev was dismissed from his position as MGB laboratory head and from the MGB, officially because of his "bad health." In fact, his dismissal was evidently connected with the MGB reorganization. In 1956, Muromtsev was appointed acting director of the Gamaleya Institute of Epidemiology and Microbiology (IEM) within the USSR Academy of Medical Sciences. Nobody at the institute knew how this came about.[132] In the terms of that time, it indicated that the KGB was involved in the appointment. Muromtsev was so unpopular with the IEM that even the institute's Communist Party organization raised the issue that a former head of a secret MGB laboratory could not be director of an open scientific institute. The Medical Academy never approved Muromtsev's directorship. Muromtsev died in 1960. Not one staff person from the IEM attended his funeral. But the KGB appears to have been more generous: An article about Muromtsev appeared in 1974 in the *Great Soviet Encyclopedia*.[133] This was a violation of the encyclopedia rules, which specified that only biographies of Academy of Sciences members and not members of the Agricultural or Medical Academies appeared in this publication. Muromtsev was an "appointed" member of the Agricultural Academy, and only a powerful organization such as the KGB could order the encyclopedia staff to publish his biography. Of course, the article made no mention of his cruel command of the secret NKVD-MGB laboratory, the beating up of imprisoned famous scientists (Chapter 4), and experiments on humans that were conducted under his order.

SCIENTISTS WHO KNEW AND APPROVED

No official title or rank in Soviet society enjoyed greater prestige than that of akademik, full membership in the Academy of Sciences of the USSR. Anyone with this title could command an audience at meetings and publish articles in leading newspapers and journals without difficulty.

—L. R. Graham, *What Have We Learned About Science and Technology from the Russian Experience?*

Deciding whether to take part in obvious crimes of the state is one of the main moral choices in the relationship between a scientist and a totalitarian state. Clearly, such involvement is immoral. A subtler problem comes up when it is necessary to approve an obvious crime. Secret scientists in the Soviet Union received scientific degrees. This means many people had knowledge of Mairanovsky's crimes—members of closed scientific councils, the reviewers of his dissertation, and so on. All of them should be considered collaborators in his crimes. I think that this is a moral issue similar to that in Nazi Germany: Not only those doctors who used humans for experiments in concentration camps or ordered prisoners to be killed for their research were guilty; those who used the conditions of the regime to create a successful career were also guilty. Those involved in the crimes "were to a large extent people of long and high standing, university professors and academy members, some of them world famous, authors with familiar names."[134] If I did not know that Max Weinrich wrote these words in his book *Hitler's Professors*, I would think that this was written about Mairanovsky's supporters.

Mairanovsky himself named the supporters of his "scientific" career. Below is a translation of the last document in Memorial's archival file on Mairanovsky.[135] It is a copy of a letter dated May 18, 1964, addressed to the president of the USSR Academy of Medical Sciences in 1960–1968, Academician Nikolai Blokhin:

Dear N. N. Blokhin:

In June 1940, I successfully defended my Doctor of Sciences Dissertation entitled "Biological Activity of the Products of Interaction of Mustard Gas with Skin Tissues." The defense took place at the VIEM. A. D. Speransky, N. I. Grashchenkov, G. M. Frank, B. N. Tarusov, and N. I. Gavrilov were my examiners.

Some details of the mechanism of toxic action of mustard gas on an organism (the pathology and disease development) were analyzed in the dissertation. As a result of the investigation of the mustard gas action I suggested reasonable methods of mustard gas therapy. The mechanism of mustard gas toxic action (its slow action, incubation period and the latent character of its action), general character of the effect (some kind of a "chain" reaction) during usage of a small quantity of the acting preparation has many characteristics in common with the action of malignant tumors.

These principles could be used as well for treatment of some malignant tumors.

The only preserved copy of my dissertation is coincidentally [!—
V.B.] kept in KGB files by Professor V. Naumov. The other copies
were barbarically destroyed during the time of Stalin's Cult. All of
my works connected with "mustard gas" were classified "secret," although there was nothing secret in them.

Academician V. Sanotsky, who was present at my dissertation defense in 1940, knows my work well. If you are interested in my ideas
on the therapy of malignant tumors, I ask you to request my dissertation "for permanent usage" at the following address: Moscow, the
Chief of the Military Unit No. 10-55, V. Naumov. He will send it to
you with pleasure for declassifying because he himself cannot do
this.

I am head of a Biochemical Laboratory in Makhachkala now. In
July I am going to be in Moscow and can meet you. Regretfully, I
could not do this last year.

Sincerely yours, G. M[airanovsky]

On June 4, 1964, Dr. Blokhin replied, "If you are in Moscow, you can
come in for a discussion of your question." In a short letter to the *Moscow
News* in 1990, Academician Blokhin wrote:

I was able to fulfill the request of my correspondent, and I offered to meet
with him in Moscow. When we met, we discussed a plan of experiments
and we planned to meet again in spring, 1965. This meeting did not take
place since G. Mairanovsky passed away in December 1964.

The similarity in the action of mustard gas and malignant tumors on
organisms, which was noted by G. Mairanovsky, has another side. The
mustard gas analogs share a chemical basis with a whole group of preparations with anti-tumor action. Regretfully, G. Mairanovsky's dissertation
has not been known among specialists because of its secrecy. His ideas
were not developed appropriately in his time.[136]

Significant points in this correspondence include verification that the sole
copy of Mairanovsky's dissertation resided with a senior KGB officer,
Mairanovsky's old colleague Professor Naumov, who still headed a secret
KGB laboratory, Military Unit No. 10-55. The president of the Academy of
Medical Sciences, Academician Blokhin, who formally was not connected
with the KGB, could order a copy of this top-secret dissertation from the
organization that had almost unlimited power within the country and
declassify it. Collaboration with the KGB, including collaborating on projects that involved the testing of fatal chemicals on humans, was typical for

Nikolai Blokhin, a supporter of Mairanovsky and president of the Medical Academy of Sciences, shown at a scientific meeting (1956). (Photo from the Russian State Archive of Cinema and Photo Documents [Moscow])

all scientific institutions in the former USSR and, indeed, was necessary to rise to the highest levels within the Academy of Sciences, the Medical Academy, or the university system.

Academician Blokhin wrote his letter to *Moscow News* in 1990 as if he had never heard about the Nuremberg trial and Nazi doctors who experimented on humans with mustard gas exactly as Mairanovsky did. This is not surprising since Blokhin seems to have been one of the most obedient Soviet loyalists. In 1980, a long time after the end of his presidency (from 1960–1968), he signed one of the most scurrilous letters against Academician Andrei Sakharov published in newspapers just before the KGB exiled Sakharov to Gorky (Nizhnii Novgorod).[137]

Who were the examiners of Mairanovsky's dissertation? They, as well as the others present at Mairanovsky's defense, were members of a closed scientific council allowed to know state secrets, including some secrets of the KGB. All of them understood very well what the "objects" of Mairanovsky's experiments were, even if Mairanovsky himself did not mention the "objects." I found all the examiners' names, except N. Gavrilov, in the *Great Soviet Encyclopedia* and *Great Medical Encyclopedia*.

Aleksei Speransky, a member of both the Soviet and the Medical Academy of Sciences and one of the main supporters of Grigory Mairanovsky, shown with students (1952). (Photo from the Russian State Archive of Cinema and Photo Documents [Moscow])

Aleksei Speransky (1888–1961) was a pathologist and physiologist, as well as a member of the Academy of Sciences and Medical Academy of the USSR.[138] From 1923 to 1928, he worked at Ivan Pavlov's laboratory. Later, he headed pathology laboratories at the main institutes of Moscow and Leningrad, then became director of the Institute of General and Experimental Pathology of the USSR Academy. In 1950, he took an active part in the "discussions" at the "Conference on the Problem of the Vital Substances and the Development of Cells"[139] and the "Pavlov Session" joint meeting of the Academy of Sciences and the Academy of Medical Sciences.[140] These meetings, which demolished Soviet physiology, were a continuation of the Lysenko affair, which ultimately annihilated genetics and evolutionary theory in the Soviet Union. The "Pavlov Session" was organized under Stalin's personal order by two Politburo members, Georgii Malenkov and Andrei Zhdanov.[141] The latter was also in charge of Lysenko's "August Session of 1948," which destroyed Soviet genetics. Stalin himself edited texts of Lysenko's speeches for the "August Session" on genetics and that written by Academician Konstantin Bykov for the "Pavlov Session."[142]

In 1950, Academician Speransky was one of the main figures assisting the destruction of physiological science in the USSR. His psychological motivation may have been fear. All his life he was afraid it would be revealed that during the Civil War he had served as a doctor in the White Army of Admiral Aleksandr Kolchak.[143]

Nikolai Grashchenkov (1901–1964) was a neuropathologist and neuro-physiologist, as well as a corresponding member of the Academy of Sciences and a member of the Medical Academy and the Belorussian Academy of Sciences.[144] He joined the Bolshevik (Communist) Party in 1918 and was an ardent Communist ever after. Grashchenkov was the first to describe gas gangrene of the brain caused by a head wound infection. In 1935, he defended his doctorate thesis on epilepsy and immediately afterward went abroad for two years to work at medical schools in Cambridge, England, and New York, New Haven, and Boston. After this, he was appointed a deputy commissar of Narkomzdrav, USSR Health Ministry (1937–1939). From 1939 until 1944, he was director of VIEM, where Mairanovsky worked at the time he defended his thesis. In 1939, he was a member of the commission that dismissed an outstanding biologist, Professor Nikolai Koltsov, as director of the Institute of Experimental Biology, which Koltsov himself created in 1917. After this, Professor Koltsov died of a heart attack.[145] Later, Grashchenkov was a director of the Institute of Neurology (1944–1948) in Belorussia and became president of the Belorussian Academy. In 1951, he returned to Moscow and for a long time served as head of the Neurology Department at the First Medical Institute. In the late 1940s to early 1950s, Grashchenkov was famous because of his numerous attacks in the press on "idealistic" geneticists and physiologists[146] and his support of the pseudoscientific "experiments" of Lysenkoists.[147]

Evidently, both Speransky and Grashchenkov were good professionals and high-level Soviet medical officials who did not care about the true nature of Mairanovsky's "objects." Moreover, Grashchenkov, being deputy minister and head of the VIEM, definitely knew about Mairanovsky's experiments.

Another medical academician, Vladimir Sanotsky, seems to have been the most important expert in terms of Mairanovsky's "experiments." Sanotsky, a corresponding member and later a full member of the Academy of Sciences, was a prominent Soviet toxicologist.[148] From 1934 until 1952, he worked at the Institute of Pathology and Therapy of Intoxication and was for many years a director there. Later, he headed the Toxicology Department at the Veterinary Academy in Moscow and at the same time worked at the Institute of Medical Final Courses. He was a specialist on the action of chemical weapons. As the *Great Medical Encyclopedia* describes him, beginning in 1925, "Sanotsky studied the mechanism of action of some toxic compounds [on humans] and methods of treatment of the results of this action. Most recently [written in 1963] Sanotsky was involved in studies of the pathology and experimental therapy of the effect of radioactive compounds." This man was definitely qualified as a specialist to evaluate Mairanovsky's experiments.

Two more people from Mairanovsky's list, Boris Tarusov and Gleb Frank, were widely known not just in the Russian medical community but also in the biological community. In 1952, Professor Boris Tarusov organized the Biophysics Department in the Biology Faculty of Moscow State University, and in January–February 2001, a conference dedicated to the one-hundredth anniversary of Tarusov was organized by this department. In 1961–1966, I was a biology student there and remember Tarusov as the Biophysics Department head. But I was a young molecular biologist and had no idea of the Biophysics Department's involvement in secret work or that Tarusov was in fact a KGB expert.

Tarusov was not included in Mairanovsky's list of examiners by chance. They worked at the same institutes at the same time: In 1931–1938 Tarusov was at the Bach Institute of Biochemistry, and in 1938–1940, he was the head of a VIEM laboratory.[149] During this time, his main scientific interest was the investigation of the mechanism of action of toxins on cell protoplasm. Later, at the university, he specialized in the biophysical aspects of the action of radiation.

Gleb Frank (1904–1976) was a Soviet biophysicist, a member of the Academy of Sciences, and a foreign member of the East German and Hungarian Academies, as well as of a few international organizations.[150] As a young scientist, he worked with the well-known cytologist Aleksandr Gurvich, the discoverer of mitogenetic radiation, first at Moscow University and then at the Physicotechnical Institute and Leningrad branch of VIEM, where he headed the Biophysics Department, and finally at the Institute of Experimental Biology (under the Gurvich's directorship).[151] In 1948, Frank organized the Institute of Biophysics within the Medical Academy of the USSR. Later, from 1957 until his death in 1976, he was director of the Academy Institute of Biophysics. In 1964, this institute moved from Moscow to the Academy Center in the town of Pushchino, about eighty miles from Moscow.[152] But there is another detail in Frank's biography tracing his connection to Mairanovsky: In 1933–1946, he worked at the same VIEM, where he headed the Department of Biophysics.

The Institute of Biophysics within the Medical Academy was first established in 1946 as the Radiation Laboratory, on the initiative of Academician Igor Kurchatov,[153] head of the secret Laboratory No. 2, which was in charge of the Soviet atomic project. Later, Laboratory No. 2 became the Kurchatov Institute of Atomic Energy within the Academy of Sciences. The goal of the Radiation Laboratory and then the Institute of Biophysics was to create

Academician Gleb Frank (1951), another supporter of Mairanovsky, was a prominent biophysicist and director of the Institute of Biophysics within the Medical and then the Soviet Academy of Sciences. (Photo from the Russian State Archive of Cinema and Photo Documents [Moscow])

principles of safe work with radioactive elements and to construct radiation dosimeter equipment.[154]

Academician Frank is remembered by the Russian biological scientific community as being among those directors who supported independent scientists.[155] One of the scientists who worked in Frank's Institute of Biophysics, Simon Schnol, wrote about Frank: "He combined a vivid, sincere interest in science with a complete understanding of the 'rules of the game' [of the Communist Party officials]."[156] "A director [of an academy institute] should have had specific talents . . . It was necessary to be in good relationships with the Party high-ranking officials and the KGB," added Dr. Schnol.[157] As already noted, the KGB controlled every institution in the former Soviet Union and exercised this control in many different ways. First, the head of the personnel department in every institution was usually a retired KGB officer. Second, a special "First Department" in every institution was in charge of "secrets." No scientific papers (or books) could be published in any Russian or international journal without the approval of the head of the First Department of the Institute. These people were connected with a higher body, a special Academy First Department headed by a KGB general. Another KGB general headed the Academy Department of Foreign Relationships, which controlled and approved contacts with foreign colleagues. Moreover, the details of everyday life in all academy institutes were controlled by a KGB "curator," located at KGB headquarters.

Besides all this, institutes that were working on the problems of atomic energy were under the control of a special Counterintelligence Department. It was created within the NKGB/MGB in 1945 (Department "K"); after several reorganizations, it became the KGB First Special Department (1954–1959), then the KGB Fifth Directorate (1959–1960), and finally, its functions were transferred under the KGB Second Main Directorate.[158] Evidently, this department collected materials from informers among scientists: The recently published secret "Report on Academician Lev Davydovich Landau," signed by head of the KGB First Special Department Ivanov and dated December 19, 1957, was based completely on the materials from scientist-informers.[159] As for Academician Frank, as a KGB expert, he would have had his own connection with this organization.

The obedience of Dr. Frank to orders from the Communist Party was absolute. On August 29, 1973, a letter against Academician Sakharov, with the signatures of forty scientists, was published in the main Soviet newspaper, *Pravda*.[160] The letter stated that Sakharov's "utterances align him with highly reactionary circles that are working against peaceful coexistence among nations, and against the policies of our Party and state designed to promote scientific and cultural cooperation and world peace."[161] Signing the letter against Sakharov was a test of academicians' loyalty to the "Party line." Dr. Frank, who had signed the letter, did not see his name in the newspaper. Terrified, he went to the secretary of the academy to find out the extent of the intrigue against him. The secretary assured him that it was simply a printer's error.[162]

The last opponent, Dr. Nikolai Gavrilov, was definitely Mairanovsky's colleague. He was director of the State Scientific Research Institute of Organic Chemistry and Technology (GosNIIOKhT) or a "post office [a name used in the USSR for secret facilities] No. 702" located at 23 Shosse Entuziastov in Moscow.[163] A plant for the production of such chemical weapons as mustard gas and lewisite was hidden behind the scientific-sounding name of this organization. Apparently, this was a successor of the Olgin Chemical Plant of the 1920s–1930s. Experiments on humans were a routine part of this "institute's" work. Formally, the experiments were said to be performed on "volunteers." The "volunteers" were young rural men who were desperately trying to escape from their villages (where there was hunger and no work), hoping to receive permission to live and work in Moscow (which was not allowed for villagers).[164] In exchange for permission to live in Moscow at the plant's hostel and to work at the "institute," as well as receiving a very small fee, these "volunteers" were glad to allow a chemical to be applied to their skin or to receive an injection. The experimenters did not tell them that the application or injection could result in cancer or other terrible diseases.

The list of names of Mairanovsky's thesis opponents clearly shows that specialists who knew about Mairanovsky's experiments were officially respectable scientists who eventually became high-ranking members in the hierarchy of the Academy of Sciences and the Medical Academy. In fact, some of them have since become widely known in the Western scientific community. Besides these scientists, there were the members of the Scientific Council who listened to Mairanovsky's presentation of his dissertation. It seems that the number of specialists who knew and understood what was going on was rather large. Not one of the scientists and doctors who knew about Mairanovsky's work asked him about the objects of his experiments or how his data had been obtained. Even much later, Academician Blokhin did not ask these questions, although it was evident that the results, which were described by Mairanovsky in his letter to Blokhin, must have been obtained by experimenting on human beings. It was their moral choice and a compromise with their conscience to play a role in Mairanovsky's crimes.

THE GULAG'S "ACADEMICIANS," GIDROPROEKT AND DALSTROI

> There—row on row, according to years,
> Kolyma, Magadan,
> Vorkuta and Narym
> Marched in invisible columns.
> > —Aleksandr Tvardovsky, "Tyorkin in
> > Another World" (a poem in Russian)

Due to the specific nature of the work of Mairanovsky, Muromtsev, and their colleagues, research facilities of this sort are still secret. However, after Stalin's death some of the secret MGB-KGB institutes were declassified and their heads became academicians. Academician Sergei Zhuk is a good example of such a scientist.[165]

Zhuk started his career as one of the organizers of the White Sea–Baltic Canal construction project, the first such Soviet project (1931–1934) to involve hundreds of thousands of prisoners. It is estimated that 200,000 prisoners died during the construction of this canal. Aleksandr Solzhenitsyn mentioned Zhuk as one of "6 main murderers each of whom accounted for thirty thousand lives" (the other five were NKVD-Gulag officials).[166] In 1940, Zhuk was appointed deputy head of the NKVD Main Directorate of Camps for Hydrotechnical Construction (Glavgidrostroi).[167] On October 24, 1941, Glavgidrostroi was reorganized into the Department for Hydrotechnical Construction within the NKVD Main Directorate of Camps for Industrial Construction (Glavpromstroi or GULPS), and Zhuk became head of this department. On March 13, 1950, a new MVD Directorate for Projecting, Planning, and Research (Gidroproekt), again headed by Major General Zhuk, was established. Gidroproekt existed in the MVD system until the reorganizations of the MVD and MGB following Stalin's death on March 5, 1953. Another "main murderer" of the White Sea–Baltic Canal construction, Major General Yakov Rapoport, became deputy director of Zhuk's institute when he retired from the MVD in 1956.[168]

Between 1947 and 1951, Glavgidrostroi and Volgostroi (another system of MVD labor camps) was in charge of the construction of the Volga-Don Canal, which connected the Volga and Don Rivers.[169] Chief Engineer Zhuk received a special high salary for managing the slave labor on this project.[170] After the reorganization of Glavgidrostroi in the late 1950s, Zhuk continued his career as a member of the Academy of Sciences (elected in 1953).[171] The construction plans for the dams and canals that caused so much environmental damage to the Volga, Angara, and Yenisei river basins were developed under his guidance at this institute. Praise for people like Zhuk continues in Russia today.

For instance, in 1993, the official journal of the Russian Academy, *Vestnik Rossiiskoi Akademii Nauk*, congratulated geologist Academician Nikolai Shilo on his eightieth birthday.[172] A short biography written in the style of the Brezhnev period declares that "besides his scientific research work, N. A. Shilo made a tremendous contribution to the organization of science in the northeastern region of the country [Russia]." It was not explained that Shilo started his career in the Far East as a high-ranking functionary of the MVD system in charge of countless gold-mining labor camps. In 1949, he was appointed director of the All-Union Research Institute One for Gold and Rare Metals (VNII-1), one of the main branches of the MVD system in the Soviet Far East.[173] In Stalin's Russia, the geographic names Magadan and Kolyma, where Shilo worked, were the predecessors of Auschwitz and Buchenwald. The writer Georgii Demidov, who spent fourteen years in several of the worst Kolyma labor camps, named Kolyma "Oswiecim [Auschwitz] without ovens."[174] Shilo's biography also mentions him as "an honorable citizen of the city of Magadan and the city of Winnipeg (Canada)," as well as "an honorable Doctor of Science of Ohio State University" (apparently he received an honorary degree there as a consequence of some joint scientific project during Soviet times).

In 1964, Shilo was elected a corresponding member and in 1970 he became a full member of the academy. In 1960, he was appointed director of the Academy North–Far Eastern Scientific Center (in Magadan), and in 1977, he became head of the presidium of this center.[175] After many years of work in the Academy of Sciences system, Shilo was known among Russian scientists as a person who still used the language of Gulag functionaries. Even in the 1990s, when inviting a person into his office, Shilo continued to say "Vvedite," which is an order to bring a prisoner in, instead of "Voidite," which means an invitation to come in.

Another academician and commissar/minister of marine transport (in 1941–1948), Pyotr Shirshov (1905–1953), was in charge of transportation of prisoners to the Dalstroi (Main Directorate for Building in the Far East), shipments of supplies for them, and transportation of the slave labor products back to the "main" land. Before his career as a Soviet minister, Shirshov took part in several expeditions to the Arctic, including the first expedition on a drifting scientific station called "The Northern Pole" in 1937–1938.[176] The Soviet press of the time presented the first explorers of the Northern Pole as national heroes. Shiroshov was elected academician in 1939, when Stalin himself, Vyshinsky, and many other officials became members of the academy.

I found out about the involvement of Academician Shirshov in Gulag activity only in recently published archival materials, in the catalog of the formerly top-secret Special Files of Beria.[177] In 1949, Shirshov, who at the time was characterized as a "Soviet patriot and a true son of the Party of Lenin and Stalin,"[178] headed a state commission that worked on speeding up the transportation of the MVD prisoners to the Dalstroi. He was personally responsible for transport ships (including the dreaded *Dzhurma*)[179] that were infamous for their inhuman conditions.[180] In 1946, Shirshov organized transportation of Japanese POWs from Korea to different USSR labor camps for "work at industrial sites of different ministries."[181] Later, Shirshov was involved in other movements of prisoners[182] and personally asked Beria not to reduce the number of prisoners working at Latvian ports.[183] In 1946, he became director of the Academy Institute of Oceanology. After Shirshov's death, this institute was given his name: P. P. Shirshov Institute of Oceanology, Russian Academy of Sciences. Besides the institute, a bay on Franz Josef Land and an underwater ridge in the Bering Sea bear the name of this Gulag manager and academician.

Psychologically, Shirshov's involvement in Dalstroi work is not easy to imagine. He knew very well what transportation meant for scores of thousands of prisoners. His own wife, the thirty-three-year-old actress Yevgeniya Garkusha, was arrested in 1946 and sent to the Kolyma gold mines, where she died almost immediately.[184] Shirshov was never told the reason for her arrest.

Magadan and Kolyma (the Dalstroi region) were the main areas for gold-mining labor camps in the Soviet Union during Stalin's time. Dalstroi's gold was no less bloody than the "Jewish" gold from the Nazi extermination camps that the Swiss banks held for so long.[185] The life span of prisoners in the Kolyma mines was about one year. To stay alive was even worse. There were special labor camps for thousands of frostbitten invalids without fingers, hands, feet, noses, or ears.[186] In 1940, the Dalstroi mines produced about 300 tons of gold.[187] Of the 10,000–12,000 Polish POWs sent to Kolyma in 1940–1941 after the occupation of Poland by Nazi and Soviet troops (according to the Stalin-Hitler agreement of 1939), only 583 were still alive in 1942–1943.[188] The number of Polish victims who died in the Dalstroi area is approximately the same as that of Polish officers killed in the Katyn Massacre. It is unfortunate that there is no movement to compensate the relatives of these Polish forced laborers as is now being pursued for Jewish forced labor in Nazi Germany.

Perhaps it is not hard to understand how "scientists" like Shilo evaded exposure for so long, as even many Americans of the era did not want to see what was going on. In summer 1944, the vice president of the United States, Henry A. Wallace, and a group of advisers headed by Professor Owen Lattimore and representing the Office of War Information visited the Kolyma area.[189] This trip was apparently the result of political intrigues. President Franklin D. Roosevelt "simply wanted Wallace out of the country so he could select a more popular running mate for the fall election."[190] The NKVD officials of the Dalstroi reported personally to Stalin about the trip of the American delegation.[191]

The American delegation was completely fooled by the Soviet and NKVD-NKGB authorities. Members of the delegation did not notice the telltale signs of labor camps (such as the ubiquitous barbed wire) and were charmed by the most dreadful NKVD officials.[192] In an article published by *National Geographic Magazine* at the end of 1944, Lattimore wrote:

> Magadan is . . . a part of the domain of a remarkable concern, the Dalstroi (Far Northern Construction Company), which can be roughly compared to a combination of Hudson's Bay Company and TVA [Tennessee Valley Authority]. It constructs and operates ports, roads, and railroads, and operates gold mines and municipalities, including, at Magadan, a first-class orchestra and a good light-opera company . . . As one American remarked, high-grade entertainment just naturally seems to go with gold, and so does high-powered executive ability.
>
> Mr. Nikishov, the head of Dalstroi, had just been decorated with the Order of Hero of the Soviet Union for his extraordinary achievements.[193] Both he and his wife have a trained and sensitive interest in art and music and also a deep sense of civic responsibility.
>
> We visited gold mines operated by Dalstroi in the valley of the Kolyma River, where rich placer workings are strung out for miles. It was interesting to find, instead of the sin, gin, and brawling of an old-time gold rush, extensive greenhouses growing tomatoes, cucumbers, and even melons, to make sure that the hardy miners got enough vitamins![194]

I felt uncomfortable while writing down these paragraphs. Knowing what Magadan and the Kolyma gold mines were for millions of prisoners who perished, the words of the sophisticated American professor sounded blasphemous to me. I can only leave it to Lattimore's conscience to rectify his comparison of the Dalstroi land of slavery with the "combination of Hudson's Bay Company and TVA."

Ivan Nikishov (1894–1958), Communist Party functionary, member of the Supreme Soviet, and candidate member of the Central Committee, was head of the Dalstroi in 1940–1946. In 1942, he married Aleksandra Gridasova, who became head of the Maglag, a complex of labor camps (including a camp for women) in Magadan and the surrounding area.[195] The Nikishovs' "extraordinary achievements" left a considerable mark in the history of the Soviet Gulag: as with Rudolf Hoess and Elsa Koch for Nazi Germany, the Nikishovs are remembered as NKVD officials with no boundaries to their cruelty.[196] Vegetables were raised by slaves in permafrost soil not for themselves but only for their masters (the Nikishovs' mansion in Magadan was surrounded by a garden), and the "first-class orchestra and a good light-opera company" consisted of slave musicians and actors, who any minute could end up in a gold, tin, or uranium mine.[197] As in the Nazi camps, the "first-class orchestra" provided "high-grade entertainment" every day at 5:00 A.M. in the dark frozen tundra to gloomy columns of exhausted prisoners, surrounded by ruthless guards and barking dogs, when the prisoners were about to leave the concentration camps to work in the inhuman conditions of the Kolyma area.

As for the Nikishovs' "trained and sensitive interest in art," there were in fact famous imprisoned painters in this slave empire. Every government holiday, such as the May 1, November 7 (the day of the Bolshevik Revolution), and so on, they were obliged to paint copies of the official portraits of Soviet leaders. One of the copies was made by Vasilii Shukhaev, a famous painter who was arrested by the NKVD just after he had lived in Paris. Here is a typical scene:

> Nikishov . . . a master of the region, who personally inspected the portrait [at a special exhibition in Magadan], flew into a rage: "Who did dare to show Iosif Vissarionovich [Stalin] with a dirty collar?!" The answer was: "This is not dirt, this is a shade. You can see that the light [on the portrait] is coming from a side." "What shade are you talking about?" Nikishov roared. Vasilii Ivanovich [Shukhaev], who did not even know about this emotional fight, was sent from a barrack [of the concentration camp] to a kartser [a punishment building without heat and with a low food ration in the permafrost of tundra].[198]

One of Alexandra Nikishova's factories of enslaved women produced embroideries. Vice President Henry Wallace admired the embroideries:

> . . . We remember the wife of Ivan Nikishov, a plump woman of about forty, whom we first met in Magadan at an extraordinary exhibit of paintings in embroidery, copies of famous Russian landscapes. The landscapes were made by a group of local women who gathered regularly during the severe winter to study needlework, an art in which Russian peasants have long excelled. As we walked along, Ivan stopped before two of the paintings I admired very much. The work was in colored threads. He took them down and handed them to me as a gift. These two wall pictures now convey to visitors at my home in Washington rich impressions of the beauty in Russia's rural landscape.[199]

No wonder that the embroideries were of the highest quality: Shukhaev's wife, who worked as a fashion designer in Paris before she was arrested, was in charge of the team of craftswomen, who were political prisoners. I wish Mr. Wallace would have seen this "group of local women who gathered regularly during the severe winter to study needlework" in the barracks of

Magadan labor camps and the conditions of their work. I think that if the two embroideries given to Wallace have survived, they should be displayed at the Holocaust Memorial Museum in Washington together with the drawings of Jewish artists who worked in the ghettos and Nazi camps.

Nikishova also authorized programs of enslaved opera. Ida Varpakhovskaya, a singer at Nikishovs' opera house who survived the imprisonment, recalled: "One day Gridasova . . . sent an instruction to L. V. [the enslaved director of the opera, the famous theater director Leonid Varpakhovsky], in which she ordered to include 'the song of Doreadot' [she meant the toreador's aria from Charles Bizet's *Carmen*] into the program of a concert."[200]

I cannot believe that all the members of the American delegation were so naive that they did not notice at all what was going on around them. Besides Magadan, the delegation visited other centers of the Gulag system in the cities of Karaganda and Komsomolsk-on-Amur.[201] It would have been practically impossible not to see the countless labor camps with their barracks surrounded by barbed wire fences from the plane when the delegation arrived in these cities.

Elinor Lipper, a Swiss ex-Communist and inmate of the Kolyma camp at the time of Wallace's mission, wrote later: "Mr. Wallace went home and published his enthusiastic report on Soviet Asia. The watch towers were put up again, the prisoners sent out to work again, and in the empty shop windows there were to be seen nothing but a few dusty and mournful boxes of matches."[202]

In 1945, Wallace sent articles from the Soviet press he and his staff collected during his trip to Russia to the American geneticist Leslie C. Dunn, who, together with Theodosius Dobzhansky, was preparing an English translation of Lysenko's book *Heredity and Its Variability* (published in 1946).[203] Dunn and Dobzhansky believed "the best way to deal with Lysenko's influence is to make known his ideas and evidence in the form in which he himself has published them."[204] Wallace supported publishing Lysenko's book, possibly in the hope that American geneticists would accept the new type of supposedly "progressive" Soviet genetics.[205]

Probably, Mr. Wallace simply did not want to confront the truth: He was a Communist sympathizer whom the FBI considered to be a Soviet spy.[206] In this instance, the suspicion was based on real facts. After his governmental career (U.S. vice president, 1941–1945, and U.S. secretary of commerce, 1945–1946), Wallace campaigned in 1948 for his own third party, a pro-Soviet "Progressive Party," with the help of American Communists and their Soviet controllers.[207] The "Communist sympathizer" reputation finally cost Wallace his political career.[208] Another American prisoner of Kolyma camps during the Wallace and Lattimore visit, Thomas Sgovio, added the last detail to the picture: "Before his death, Mr. Wallace admitted he had been naive and gullible. Lattimore has never admitted he was duped. I shall leave it to the American people to judge the Professor."[209]

The historian and Gulag survivor Anton Anotonov-Ovseenko described Nikishov's end.[210] He died in a bath in 1956, after he wrote a detailed report to Party officials about the atrocities in the Dalstroi. Like the Nazi war criminals, he claimed that he had only followed orders:

> . . . Yezhov and Beria demanded to fulfill the plan of gold production by any cost: "Do not be sorry for prisoners. You will receive workers always when steamers can bring them [to Kolyma] . . . "
>
> I do not feel guilty . . . I was only an executor. Here are copies of Yezhov's and Beria's orders. I kept them because I knew that I might be asked . . . [211]

THE "ACADEMICIANS" BRIDGING SECURITY AND POLITICS

In contemporary Russia, the connection between the academy and the former KGB structures remains tight. Academician Yevgenii Primakov, formerly director of the Institute for Oriental Studies (IVAN) and the Institute for World Economy and International Relations (IMEMO), in 1991 headed the KGB First Main Directorate and then, in 1991–1996, the Foreign Intelligence Service (the SVR, a new agency that was previously the KGB First Main Directorate).[212] Primakov's close contact with the KGB started in the late 1950s, when he served as a Middle East correspondent for *Pravda*. As he told the investigative journalist Yevgeniya Albats privately, "no one who wanted to work abroad got away without some contact with the organs."[213] His KGB code name at that time was "Maxim," and he was sent frequently on intelligence missions to the Middle East and the United States.[214] According to Primakov himself, these missions were ordered by the Central Committee.[215] During his years as a *Pravda* correspondent, Primakov published a series of anti-American and anti-Israeli propaganda brochures: *Who Is Behind Israel?* (1959), *The USSR Is a True Friend of Arab Nations* (1969), and *The Middle East Crisis Is a Threat to the World Peace* (1969).[216]

In 1970, Primakov was appointed vice director of IMEMO.[217] This institute was created in 1956. Anushavan Arzumyan, son-in-law of the Politburo member Anastas Mikoyan, was its first director. He died in 1966 and Academy Corresponding Member Nikolai Inozemtsev (elected in 1964), vice chief editor of *Pravda*, was appointed IMEMO director. In 1968, he became an academician. Inozemtsev's main duty was to write speeches for

General Secretary Leonid Brezhnev. Having known Primakov through the work in *Pravda,* Inozemtsev invited him to IMEMO. Inozemtsev and Primakov changed the work of the institute from academically oriented research to the analysis of current political international events. IMEMO prepared secret reviews of the events to inform the Central Committee and Politburo. With the support of Inozemtsev, in 1974 Primakov was elected corresponding member of the Academy.[218]

In December 1977, Primakov was appointed director of the IVAN.[219] Under his guidance, the institute became more involved in political than in academic studies. Primakov was especially interested in the study of Islam and the Middle East. In 1978 in Beirut, he published in Arabic the propaganda book *USA Politics in the Middle East.*

In 1979, Primakov was elected academician. It was widely known that he became an academician not as a scientist but because of his position as director of an academy institute.[220] Academician Inozemtsev, who had many contacts within the Central Committee, as well as within the academy, personally asked academicians—representatives of the natural sciences—to vote for his protégé. Although he was not an economist, Primakov joined the Economic Division of the academy: there was no separate division on international affairs. Inozemtsev died in 1982, and Primakov was appointed director of the IMEMO in 1986, now with the support of Aleksandr Yakovlev, the new head of the Propaganda Division of the Central Committee.[221]

In 1986, Primakov became a nonvoting (alternate) member of the Communist Party's Central Committee, and in 1989, he was named nonvoting member of the Politburo. At the same time, in 1988–1989, Primakov was academic secretary of the Academy Presidium. In 1995–1997, when Primakov headed the SVR, an official three-volume historical book published by the SVR, *Essays on the History of the Russian Foreign Intelligence,*[222] was provided with his name as an honorary "editor in chief," although his role in writing this book "can scarcely have been much more than nominal." In fact, according to Primakov's biographer Leonid Mlechin, this book was edited by Lolly Zamoysky, an analyst of the KGB First Directorate and later SVR, known as a fanatic believer in a global Masonic-Zionist plot.[223] It seems that Primakov principally changed the orientation and working style of Russian foreign intelligence. He moved the main goal of intelligence from targeting "the main enemy," meaning the United States, to targeting international problems such as weapons of mass destruction, organized crime, drug traffic, and terrorism.[224]

On January 9, 1996, Primakov was appointed Russian foreign minister. Primakov's first SVR deputy, Vyacheslav Trubnikov, was appointed head of the SVR. Trubnikov's professional career within the KGB began in the 1960s, after he graduated from Moscow State Institute of International Relations.[225] Later, in 2000, Trubnikov was appointed first deputy foreign minister. In August 1998, Primakov became Russian prime minister for nine months. The respected science magazine *Nature* seemed very impressed by his academician status: "A former economist, Middle East expert, head of two research institutes, spymaster and diplomat, Primakov caps his impressive range of expertise with Russia's highest scientific rank: that of academician."[226]

Primakov was never an economist. Besides, I would like to remind the "C. L." who signed this article that beginning in 1929, the Soviet nomenklatura often used the academician rank as a perk for those willing to do its dirty work. Alexander Vucinich wrote about these people in his study of the Soviet Academy: "Such individuals made it impossible for the Academy to justify its claim to be the true forum of the best representatives of Soviet scholarship."[227]

In addition, Soviet dictator Josef Stalin was an honorary academician. The notorious Andrei Vyshinsky, the Soviet chief prosecutor who organized and directed the show trials in the 1930s (including Bukharin's trial) and then became foreign minister, was also an academician. Moreover, beginning in 1949, the Soviet press officially named Stalin "the main coryphaeus in all branches of science."[228] Some scientists wrote in their papers: "I. V. Stalin teaches us,"[229] and so forth. Obviously, all this does not mean that the poorly educated Stalin (after one year at a seminary, he quit to become head of a gang, which robbed banks to fund the Bolshevik Party) was in fact a scientist. I have already mentioned examples of Soviet academicians who were simply appointed on the order of the Central Committee of the Communist Party. In 1946, Stalin's main official Marxist philosopher and head of the Directorate of Agitation and Propaganda (Agitprop) of the Central Committee, Georgii Aleksandrov (1908–1961), was "elected" and became an academician and his deputy, Mikhail Iovchuk,[230] became corresponding member.[231] The "input" of Academician Aleksandrov has nothing to do with science. His articles were simply a eulogy for the leading role of the Party opinion in Soviet science:

> The followers of progressive opinions and trends in science, supported by the Communist Party and by public opinion, gain the leading posts in science, direct its development, help to overcome errors and defects in the activities of various scientists and the wrong opinions which arise in isolated individuals among the Soviet intelligentsia under the influence of bourgeois ideologies.[232]

In 1932, Aleksandrov graduated from the Moscow Institute of History and Philosophy and soon began to work in the Comintern Executive

Committee.[233] In 1940, the thirty-two-year-old Aleksandrov was appointed head of Agitprop within the Central Committee after Andrei Zhdanov formally became the Central Committee secretary of ideology.[234] In 1943, Aleksandrov received a Stalin Prize for his editorship of the third volume of *Istoriya filosofii* [History of Philosophy]. At the same time, he started an anti-Semitic campaign against Jewish artists and intellectuals. On July 15, 1943, he and his deputy, Tatiyana Zueva, sent a note to secretaries of the Central Committee, in which they claimed that "the leading staff [of the Bolshoi Theater] had been selected only because of their national origins, and with the prevalence of Jewish names."[235] In April 1944, the Politburo unexpectedly criticized Aleksandrov's third volume of the *History of Philosophy*. Apparently, Aleksandrov's chauvinism was too much even for Stalin at that time. From 1945, Aleksandrov played one of main roles in denouncing the Jewish Anti-Fascist Committee and its members. This was easy for Aleksandrov, especially because he was chief editor of Agitprop's magazine *Kul'tura i zhizn* [Culture and Life].

In 1947, Stalin demoted Aleksandrov to director of the Academy Institute of Philosophy. However, Aleksandrov retained his contacts with Politburo members Malenkov and Suslov and his influence in official philosophy.[236] In 1954, Aleksandrov was appointed minister of culture. After Aleksandrov's supporter Georgii Malenkov was dismissed as chairman of the Council of Ministers, Aleksandrov was exiled to Minsk, the capital of Belorussia, where he worked at a local institute of philosophy.

In 1960, another of Aleksandrov's deputies, Pyotr Fedoseev, also became an academician. Until 1947, he had been Aleksandrov's deputy at Agitprop and later was appointed chief editor of *Bolshevik* magazine. In 1952, Fedoseev was dismissed and *Bolshevik* was renamed *Kommunist*.[237] Despite the fact that a few popular brochures about the "harm" of religion published by Fedoseev were his only "contribution" to science, in the 1970s–1980s, he was vice president of the academy, headed the academy's Publishing Council and the Scientific Council on the Studies of Problems of Peace and Disarmament. No wonder it was Fedoseev who awarded General Secretary of the Communist Party Konstantin Chernenko (who had no training in any field of science at all) with the highest Soviet Academy prize in 1985, a golden Karl Marx medal.[238] It is at best naive to present the KGB/SVR head and a former Russian foreign and prime minister Primakov as a serious scientist. A talented administrator, he obtained his academician title while holding one of the highest positions in the Soviet hierarchy.

Yevgenii Primakov is an example of both the merger of the KGB with the academy and the merger of Soviet (now Russian) espionage with diplomacy. This alliance has a long history. During the last years of Stalin's dictatorship, in 1947–1949, the MGB's First (Foreign or Espionage) Directorate and the Military Intelligence were simply combined with the Foreign Ministry into a governmental structure, the Committee on Information, or KI.[239] The KI was in charge of political, economic, and scientific-technical intelligence operations, and the Soviet ambassadors were in charge of intelligence and illegal (i.e., spy) networks. A good example is Aleksandr Panyushkin, who was the Soviet ambassador to the United States at the beginning of the Cold War, in 1947–1952.[240] Documents recently released from the KGB archives show that besides his diplomatic duties, Panyushkin (under the alias "Vladimir") also controlled and coordinated the activity of Soviet spies, including Americans involved in Wallace's election campaign in 1948.[241] In 1952–1953, he was also deputy chair of the "Small" Committee on Information, called the "Small KI," under the USSR Foreign Ministry.[242] The Small KI was the Foreign Ministry merged with a small group of intelligence service after the Military Intelligence (GRU) had returned to the Ministry of Defense and the Foreign Intelligence had moved back to the MGB.[243] It is not surprising that after this job, former Ambassador Panyushkin headed in 1954–1956 the KGB First Main Directorate, which after the fall of the Soviet Union became the SVR, headed by Primakov (in 1991–1996). Before 1991, not less than 50 percent of the staff of Soviet embassies and companies abroad were represented by KGB officers from the First Directorate.[244] Currently, the percent of intelligence officers under diplomatic cover seems to have grown because of the smaller number of real diplomats, that is, the employees of the Russian Foreign Ministry.[245]

On May 12, 1999, Primakov was sacked by Russian president Boris Yeltsin and replaced by First Deputy Prime Minister Sergei Stepashin.[246] The FSB head, Vladimir Putin (later prime minister and then president), visited the former prime minister and gave him a traditional KGB gift,[247] a hunting rifle, as "a reward for his help in protecting Russia's security."[248] According to the Russian press, in the summer of 2000, Primakov was moved back to the presidential administration.[249]

"HONORARY RETIREMENT"
FOR EXECUTIONERS

In 1990 I became Vice-Chancellor for International Relations [of St. Petersburg University]. I was, as we [i.e., the KGB/FSB/SVR officers] put it, in active reserve.

—Vladimir Putin, former KGB officer and
director of the FSB, later Russian president[250]

After Stalin's death it became typical that retired MGB-KGB functionaries were appointed to work in science. This was not really anything new (more on this in Chapter 4). In the 1950s, science simply became a place for retired MGB/KGB veterans. This was more than the collaboration of individual scientists with the secret services; it was a general collaboration of academic institutions with the KGB system.

The example of Mairanovsky's colleague Muromtsev, who became acting director of the Academy Gamaleya Institute of Epidemiology and Microbiology, has already been discussed. Another good example is Iosif (Joseph) Romual'dovich Grigulevich, who had been involved in many assassination cases, including that of Leon Trotsky and a plan to assassinate the Yugoslavian leader Tito. In 1960, after his deportation from Latin America, the experienced killer Grigulevich received another assignment: He was appointed to work as a "scientist" at the Academy Ethnography Institute in Moscow.[251] Without any special education, he "worked" there until his death in 1988. In 1979, he even became a corresponding member of the academy, which was unquestionably due to his KGB connections and not to his scientific knowledge.[252] Another former "diplomat," Semyon Gonionsky, who during World War II was living (and spying) in the United States, was a "scientist"—and a party secretary—at the same institute in the 1960s–1970s. But the case of Vladimir Boyarsky is perhaps the most famous.

Until recently, this former NKVD-MGB investigator worked as a scientist at the Academy Institute of Problems of Complex Exploitation of Natural Resources. In 1958, Boyarsky was made a senior editor of the Academy of Sciences Press (Nauka) and a year later became editor in chief. Very few people knew that he had never been trained in chemistry and that his "scientific" career had been organized by an old friend, Academician Mikhail Agoshkov.[253] In 1933–1941, Agoshkov, a mining expert, worked at the North Caucasus Mining Metallurgical Institute[254] and became friends with Boyarsky. In 1941, Agoshkov moved to the academy's Moscow Institute of Mining and in 1952 became its deputy director. He was head of the Academy Foreign Section (which was completely controlled by the KGB) until 1960. In 1961, he became deputy and in 1962 acting chief scientific secretary of the academy. It is interesting that during all of his "brilliant" career in academy administration, Agoshkov was only a corresponding (elected in 1953) and never a full member (he became an academician only in 1981). He had to have very powerful connections (evidently, with the KGB) in order to hold such high positions within the academy without being an academician. Agoshkov was Boyarsky's coauthor of the textbook *Development of Ore and Loose Deposits,* which was the basis of Boyarsky's doctoral dissertation.[255]

In the 1980s, the "chemist" Dr. Boyarsky was still a member of the Nauka Publishing House Editorial Council and made decisions on which scientists' books should be published. In 1989, he was finally exposed in the mass media.[256]

It was revealed that Boyarsky had left a bloody trail in Czechoslovakia in 1950–1951 during the preparation of the anti-Semitic Rudolf Slansky trial.[257] Boyarsky was senior adviser within a group of thirty MGB officers who in 1950 supervised the organization of the Czechoslovak Security Service, the StB.[258] The first task of the StB was the Slansky trial. Boyarsky's instruction was simple: "Our greatest enemy is international Zionism, [which has at its disposal] the most elaborate espionage organizations."[259] It is not surprising that for this purpose the fanatical Czech anti-Semite Andre Keppert was appointed director of the StB's Department for the Search for Enemies of the State. Keppert had a primitive method of identifying his enemies: "[W]henever he saw a hooked nose he either opened a file on the owner or put him in jail."[260] According to both Nazi propaganda and Soviet anti-Semites, a hooked nose is a characteristic feature of the Jews (the Jews as an ethnic, not religious, group).

Ironically, Boyarsky's career in Czechoslovakia ended because his deputy, Yesikov, started to suspect that Boyarsky was a Jew himself! Yesikov informed Moscow that Boyarsky "had behaved improperly in connection with the materials . . . regarding the hostile activity of Jewish bourgeois nationalists."[261] MGB deputy minister Yevgenii Pitovranov himself looked into the matter: "According to the allegations of a number of USSR MGB workers, Comrade Boyarsky has incorrectly reported his ethnic background as Ukrainian, although his manner and appearance show him to be a Jew . . .Verification of Boyarsky's biographical data did not confirm these allegations."[262]

Despite this, Stalin's decision was negative for Boyarsky: "Experience with Boyarsky's work in Czechoslovakia has shown that he is not well qualified enough to discharge responsibly the obligations of an adviser."[263]

But Boyarsky's previous actions in Russia were more impressive and showed that in fact he was very experienced in NKVD-MGB work. In 1939, as a NKVD lieutenant, he falsified a case against 103 persons, fifty-one of whom were shot to death on the basis of his work. During his interrogations he used sophisticated torture on both men and women. His former NKVD colleague, Investigator Sheshikov, testified about Boyarsky's methods of interrogation:

> From prolonged standing, the detainee's body was very swollen, and she weakened and, unable to stand, began to fall. Then Boyarsky proposed that Zarubin [another investigator] and I tie her to the wall. For that purpose he put handcuffs on the detainee's hands himself, with her hands

crossed behind her back, and said we should tie a rope from the handcuffs to a hook stuck in the wall. In addition, Boyarsky said we should string a rope across the detainee's chest, under her arms, and tie it to a nail in the wall. After that, Boyarsky himself grabbed her braids and tied them to a nail, so that she could not lower her head to her chest or let it rest on her shoulders. . . . We did not give food or drink to the detainee, we did not take her to the bathroom, and a strong odor began to come from her. Boyarsky came in from time to time and demanded testimony from her, but she did not give any, after which Boyarsky said, "You'll hang here till you rot, or till you give us testimony." Toward the end, the detainee began to hallucinate; she groaned, at first loudly, then more and more quietly. At around four or five in the morning, the detainee died.[264]

Only after Boyarsky was exposed in 1990–1991 in the press (and then at the institute) as a former executioner was he deprived of his scientific degree.

However, exposure of another former MGB investigator in the mass media, Pavel Grishaev,[265] did not result in his dismissal. In 1946, he was a member of the SMERSH-MGB team[266] that brought a few German witnesses and the testimony of other high-ranking Germans kept in Moscow prisons to the Nuremberg trial. Two years later, Grishaev became one of the most notorious investigators involved in anti-Semitic trials and purges. He was a member of the team that tortured the arrested members of the famous Jewish Anti-Fascist Committee.[267] Maryana Zaitseva, a victim of the Allilueva case that preceded the JAC case, later described Grishaev's style of "interrogation":

He behaved as an executioner beating me up with a rubber truncheon. As a result I used to faint and was repeatedly given medical assistance. Grishaev showed the truncheon covered with blood to my husband [he had also been arrested and Grishaev also "worked" on him] saying that "this is the blood of your wife" . . . All interrogations took place at night . . . Knowing that according to the rules of Lefortovo Prison it was prohibited to sleep during the day, he deprived me of normal sleep for a month . . . Other investigators of the Department for Investigation of Especially Important Cases were present during my night interrogations— Komarov, Rassypinskii, Likhachev, and others, including former Minister of Security Abakumov, who accused them of being incapable of handling interrogations . . . [268]

When the seemingly all-powerful Minister Abakumov had been arrested in 1951 in his turn, Lieutenant Colonel Grishaev became deputy head of the Department for Investigation of Especially Important Cases and was appointed an investigator of the Abakumov case. Abakumov was kept constantly handcuffed and with the help of Grishaev was subjected to many types of tortures, which he had used before to interrogate his own victims, including a cold cell with a refrigerating system.[269]

Grishaev successfully escaped any punishment, whereas many of his colleagues were shot to death after short trials after Stalin's death. Moreover, after Stalin's death he worked as a teacher of law for thirty-five years, became a professor of law and then an "Honored Public Figure" (a special title in the Soviet Union). What a cruel joke! In 1964, after appeals of his former victims to the Communist Party offices, he received "a Party reprimand," which was erased in 1967. In 1990, he was defended by the officials of the All-Union Institute of Law following newspaper articles about his past: "The article in the newspaper was written with a contemporary evaluation of the past; it does not take into consideration all his [Grishaev's] later life and scientific and teacher's careers. His 35-year work at the institute was irreproachable."[270]

Another Grishaev colleague, Daniil Kopelyansky, who interrogated Raoul Wallenberg, preferred the career of an architect after he lost his job at the MGB during the purge of Jews from the organs after Abakumov's arrest in 1951. In the 1990s, he was frequently seen at the library of the Architects' Club House in Moscow. In 1991–1997, he refused to release any information about the fate of Wallenberg.

Of course, Boyarsky and Grishaev, as well as the other numerous investigators who are still alive, deny participation in any crime.[271] Mysteriously, they do not remember details of interrogations or the names of victims. (Nazi war criminals often suffered a similar type of amnesia.) They are proud of their secret service careers and will keep the secrets of the organs until their death. (When KGB officers resigned, they signed a special document promising to never release details of their work.)

Many NKVD/MGB/KGB officers mentioned in this book considered science a prestigious job for their children. Sons and daughters of Mairanovsky, Boyarsky, Khvat, Kruzhkov, Solovov, and Sudoplatov became scientists at Moscow University and research institutes within the Soviet (now Russian) Academy of Sciences. Like children of Nazi functionaries in Germany, all of them believe that their fathers were only following orders from above.

INFORMERS

In our country every worker is on the staff of the NKVD.
—Anastas Mikoyan, commissar of foreign trade, from
a speech at the twentieth anniversary of the VCheKa[272]

Some of the Soviet scientists, usually devoted Communist Party members, had few qualms about working with the OGPU/NKVD/MGB/KGB. Analysis of the secret KGB textbook *History of the Soviet Security Service* shows that the work of the Soviet secret services would not be possible without secret agents.[273] Thus, a Special Letter of the Secret Operational Directorate of the OGPU from July 20, 1928, plainly said that a "qualified fight" against "anti-Soviet counterrevolutionaries" should be based on a well-organized network of informers and secret agents.[274] In the late 1920s, OGPU deputy head Yagoda boasted:

> We can turn anyone into a secret informer [*seksot* in Russian] . . . Who does want to die of hunger? If the OGPU starts to work on a person with the goal to force him to be an informant, his resistance is useless. Eventually, he will be in our hands: we will force to kick him out from his job and he will not be accepted anywhere else without a secret approval of our organization [*organy*]. Especially if the person has a family, a wife, and children, he is forced to capitulate soon.[275]

Basically, there were three types of secret agents and informers: special agents *(spetsagenty)*, special informers *(spetsosvedomiteli)*, and informers *(osvedomiteli,* or *seksoty).*[276] Special agents were professionals or semiprofessionals who temporarily or permanently served at the NKVD/MGB/KGB. Special informants were recruited to the secret service for special assignments only. However, informants were the most numerous group and were recruited for collecting information about alleged anti-Soviet activity within all of Soviet society. All these secret collaborators signed special agreements with the OGPU-KGB, were given pseudonyms for their reports, and kept secret their contacts with the security service. In the late 1950s–1970s, the KGB additionally introduced the category of "trusted persons" *(doverennye litsa).*[277] These individuals made their connections with the KGB widely known but kept secret the type of information they provided to the KGB. Their work with the KGB was based on their enthusiasm; they did not sign agreements with the KGB and had no special KGB alias.

As Sudoplatov wrote in his memoirs, the whole Soviet system was based on information received from the security service:

> Security offices and administrative agencies provide the leadership with a monthly report on developments in the country. This report includes a summary of internal difficulties and failures of performance at various institutions and enterprises, based on informers' reports. Under Stalin's rule

it was almost impossible to meet an informer during the daytime; we met our sources almost every evening.[278]

Of course, everyone in the Soviet Union knew that someone among his or her friends and colleagues was a secret informer (if he or she was not an informer him- or herself). Even now I still have an unpleasant feeling about my close friends in Moscow who might have been informers. I also witnessed a more open form of connection between informers and the KGB "friends" (this was the name used for KGB personal supervisors of informers).

It was at the end of 1984. I went to the KGB Reception Room (the corner of the Furkasov Lane and Malaya Lubyanka in downtown Moscow) because of my problems with the KGB. After I opened the first door, I saw a huge mailbox to my left. Here any Soviet citizen could deposit an anonymous letter to the KGB, supposedly without being noticed. But that was not so: There was a TV camera pointed at the entrance door. The second door led into a big hall, the right part of which was full of small open booths with telephones. I watched several people sneaking into the booths. I heard the high voice of a woman in the nearest booth. She was complaining about her colleague at work who had been allowed to go for a trip abroad. The woman said that the colleague should not go for the trip because she was a speculator and an anti-Soviet element.

I knew exactly what would happen to that unfortunate woman the informer was reporting on. This was still in the time when every trip abroad by a Soviet citizen was approved or disapproved by both the Party and KGB officials. I received such disapproval in 1975. The director of the institute where I worked at the time gathered at his office members of the Soviet delegation to a scientific international conference in Yugoslavia. I was important to the delegation because I spoke English, and the others did not. We had already gone through all necessary Party and other commissions, which had checked us for loyalty, and we had tickets for the trip in our hands. During the meeting, suddenly a phone rang on the director's desk. The director picked up the receiver and listened without saying a word. His face became pale. He put the receiver down and told me: "The organs (i.e., KGB) are against your trip."

In the KGB hall, there was a small flight of stairs in front of me leading to the next floor. A short sergeant in KGB uniform, who stood near the stairway, was staring at me suspiciously. He asked me to show him my passport. After he had inspected my passport, he told me that the Reception Room was upstairs. I followed his instructions, went upstairs, and joined a line of approximately ten men and women; men predominated.

I will never forget these people. Most of them were silent and looked very tense. One man, definitely a native of Uzbekistan in a traditional Uzbek hat, loudly boasted how he would hand over the anti-Soviet "saboteur" fellows from his kolkhoz in Central Asia to the KGB. Some men were trembling. I had never before seen adults shivering from fear. While waiting in the line, one more detail struck me. A group of twelve- to fourteen-year-old kids led by two KGB officers walked in front of our line. Each of them held a notebook. They definitely felt very comfortable in this notorious building. They were "young followers of Felix Dzerzhinsky" and the future KGB recruits.

When my turn came, I was ordered to enter a room with several file cabinets. A big muscled woman in plainclothes asked for my name and then for some time searched the files. After she found what she was looking for, she asked me what I wanted. I told her my story: Because of KGB intervention, I had lost my job at the Academy of Sciences and could not find another one. I had sent a letter to the KGB chairman, Viktor Chebrikov, in which I had asked about the reasons for the KGB actions against me. I had never received an answer, which was a violation of Soviet rules: Officials were obligated to answer the inquiries from citizens within one or two months. She sent me to another room, where a guy who looked like a professional wrestler was waiting for me. He went through the documents in the file the woman had provided him with and said that the KGB had nothing to do with my problems and that I should immediately leave their headquarters. So I did, looking for the last time at people coming into the big hall with telephones on the first floor. The KGB (now FSB) Reception Room is still open all hours of the day and night.

The system worked well, especially with persons who volunteered for cooperation with the secret service. In September 1945, a physicist from Moscow University, Yakov Terletsky, was appointed as a secret scientific adviser (evidently, a special informer) to Sudoplatov's Department "S" of the NKGB (in charge of intelligence materials on A-bomb development by the American and British teams).[279] Department S was established within the NKVD on September 27, 1945, with the goal of "obtaining and analyzing the intelligence on the creation of the A-bomb."[280] Sudoplatov was appointed head of this department, and Eitingon and General Nikolai Sazykin became his deputies. On January 10, 1946, Department S was reassigned under the NKGB/MGB. Terletsky was the NKVD/MGB's point person to contact the famous physicist Niels Bohr in Denmark in 1946 concerning the A-bomb project.[281] Terletsky's mission was under personal control of Stalin.[282] In 1990, Terletsky wrote in his memoirs:

Although I myself happened to be connected with the secret intelligence service, I was absolutely shocked when I heard that Niels Bohr could be named an agent of the [British] Intelligence Service. For us, the Soviet people, it was a natural duty to our Motherland (but for many individuals a very unpleasant one) to help the Soviet secret organs. But the "Intelligent Service"! Always, even when the English were our allies, it seemed to have been an organization guarding interests of the bourgeoisie, which is our class enemy.[283]

Terletsky's notes show that even professors of the leading Soviet University in Moscow had been heavily brainwashed by the Soviet ideology propaganda machine. It comes as no surprise that Academician Sakharov mentioned Terletsky as "a theoretical physicist and self-appointed champion of ideological purity . . . Terletsky apparently envied Lysenko's laurels, as did many at the time."[284]

There was additionally a very strong psychological motivation for a scientist to collaborate with the NKVD/KGB: secret power and, as we will see in the Vavilov case in the next chapter, the opportunity to destroy a hated scientific opponent through nonscientific methods.

It has become even easier now to inform the FSB. According to deputy head of the FSB Counterintelligence Department Nikolai Volobuev, in 2001 the FSB has set up a special phone line for scientists who are in contact with foreign colleagues and suspect them to be spies.[285] In April 2001, the Russian Supreme Court supported the FSB regulation to use anonymous denunciations from citizens for investigation.[286] Since 1988, this practice has been officially banned in the Soviet Union.

SOME BITTER THOUGHTS

Almost all German scientists eagerly accepted offers to become the successors of their Jewish colleagues who had been fired. The simple acceptance of such offers in the name of science made them loyal to the regime.
—B. Müller-Hill, *Science, Truth and Other Values*

I have already discussed the possible motivations of Mairanovsky and his colleagues who worked in the secret system of NKVD/MGB installations. No doubt such scientists as Tarusov and Frank and the others from Mairanovsky's list of thesis opponents rationalized their collaboration with the KGB just as did their colleagues in 1930s Germany who did not hesitate to follow Nazi orders. Usually these people were motivated by moral weakness and fear and would have reasoned something along the following lines: I could not refuse. My refusal would be dangerous for my family and people who depend on me. A scoundrel could replace me and my colleagues would suffer, and so on.

Only the KGB successors know how many "scientists" with the same "excellent service" in the past are still working at or are affiliated with the Russian Academy, and with other scientific institutions. At present, there are numerous secret services in Russia instead of one KGB: the Federal Security Service (FSB), Federal Government Communications and Information Agency (FAPSI), the Foreign (or External) Intelligence Service (SVR), Federal Border Service, State Tax Police, and Federal Guard Service. All of them represent different branches of the former KGB.[287]

The FSB, FAPSI, and SVR are tightly connected with scientific research. In 1997–1998, the FSB had 76,500 employees. Its power became even wider than that of the KGB in the past. This agency has the authority to search homes and businesses without a prosecutor's warrant and to gather intelligence on political groups deemed a threat to the state. It can run its own prison system, infiltrate foreign organizations or organized crime, create front enterprises, and demand information from private companies. It controls all state secrets and provides security for the armed forces and the federal government.[288]

Another domestic agency, FAPSI, has a staff of 54,000. It is responsible for electronic communication security and surveillance and controls the most crucial Russian computer and communication networks.[289] There is growing public concern that the FSB and FAPSI are working on the development of monitoring e-mail messages by linking their offices with all Internet providers in Russia.[290]

The involvement of the KGB First Main Directorate, now SVR, in "dirty tricks," including assassinations, has already been described in previous chapters. Ken Alibek claims in his recent book *Biohazard* that assassinations using bacteriological agents were planned by the KGB even in 1989–1990, during Gorbachev's tenure.[291]

Today, the three systems, the Russian Secret Service (FSB and FSK), the Academy of Sciences, and the military (Ministry of Defense), are still interrelated. In 1992–1994, Kuntsevich, an academician and a general, testified as an expert on chemical weapons against Dr. Mirzayanov during the investigation performed by the FSB, which is the former KGB. Dr. Mirzayanov was released from the FSB's Lefortovo Prison only because of international pressure applied by human rights activists.[292] Like the former KGB high official Sudoplatov, Russian military experimenters such as Kuntsevich, who was in charge of chemical warfare tests on unprotected servicemen in the 1980s,[293] have no regrets about their experiments on humans.

Many of the facts I uncovered while researching this book were a personal shock to me. For instance, I knew several scientists who worked with

Academician Shirshov. Did they know that Shirshov had been in charge of the transportation of prisoners, including those sent to Magadan, Kolyma, and the other death camps of the Dalstroi? Possibly they did not, because this part of his life and activity was top secret. But if they knew, what would be their reaction to this knowledge and would their attitude toward him change? Would they think that the goal of Soviet dominance of world affairs justified the means? I do not know. But I suspect that most of them would think so.

Recent Russian publications on the history of the Soviet atomic project show that Russian historians and scientists think that the creation (by all means) of the Soviet A-bomb was crucial to the existence of the Soviet Union because of the American threat in the late 1940s. One author, Yurii Smirnov, wrote: "The A-bomb was created during that dangerous USSR and USA confrontation period which began in the summer of 1946, when the war between the former allies could have started at any moment."[294]

I found a more typical and old Soviet-style point of view in the memoirs written in 1977 by the former deputy minister of health, A. Burnazyan:

... An atomic blackmail, heated by the [bombing of] Hiroshima and Nagasaki, was a threat to the world. Harry Truman amused himself by the idea that during at least his presidency the United States would have an absolute monopoly on the atomic bomb ... On the appeal of the government, Soviet scientists and engineers ought to create in a short period of time their atomic bomb to defend their Motherland from the new threat and not allow the "Cold War," which had just started, to turn into a "hot" atomic war.[295]

A young historian, N. Kuznetsova, concluded:

I cannot reproach those [Soviet scientists] who in the 1940s created the atomic weapon ... And one cannot apply moral evaluation to the atomic espionage. It was not possible to buy these secrets in Los Alamos for any money. But the anxiety about the future of mankind, i.e., pure idealistic ideas, forced some to risk their lives and to organize transfer of the top secret information to Moscow [from Los Alamos].[296]

I can only add to this phrase that the names of these "idealists" who "cared about mankind's future" are very well known: Stalin and Beria. The latter supervised most of the atomic espionage in the United States and was put in charge of the Soviet atomic project in 1945.

What the Russian historians are not saying is that the Soviet A-bomb project and the first steps of the H-bomb project were under complete NKVD-MGB control. This meant that the laboratory work of scientists was based on the work of an army of prisoners who built the laboratories, mined the uranium without any protection, and so on. In 1945, Stalin himself decided that the atomic project should be under the NKVD:

> The NKVD has substantial building and construction organizations, an army of construction workers [i.e., Gulag prisoners], good qualified specialists and managers. The NKVD has also a branched network of local posts, as well as a network of organizations at railroads and waterways [i.e., the labor camps again].[297]

After this pronouncement, the system of labor camps located throughout the country and slave labor became the basis of both the A-bomb and the H-bomb projects.

I believe that one must not have two moral standards in one's attitude toward or evaluation of the crimes committed by Nazi or Soviet scientists and their NKVD-MGB managers. There was no difference in what Mairanovsky and his colleagues and the Nazi doctors in camps did or in how the Nazi V-rockets and Soviet H-bomb were created. There was no difference for prisoners if they were sent into slave labor in the German military industry or to the Soviet gold mines of Kolyma. For me, the only difference is that the Nazi regime has been dead for a long time and scientists who helped it to flourish were condemned by the international community, whereas what was going in the Soviet Union is poorly known. I feel that there is very little understanding by the international community of the profound extent of the penetration of Soviet (and now Russian) science by the secret services and the involvement of Soviet/Russian academic science in the work of these secret services.

Each time when I read about the achievements of Soviet physics in the late 1940s–1950s, I recall materials from the Memorial Archive. Old, poor-quality photos show women prisoners somewhere in the Dalstroi labor camps. These prisoners are sitting at tables on which there are heaps of ore. It is uranium ore, and the women are working with the ore with their bare hands. It is difficult even to imagine how short the life of these women was and how terrible their death was after the radiation they had been exposed to.

I cannot believe that the whole glory of Soviet science, and Soviet physics in particular, was worth the life of these enslaved women.

4

RESISTANCE

. . . I feel the exclusion of Jewish scientists to be an injustice . . . I there-fore prefer to forgo this appointment [to replace fired Jewish professor Philip Ellinger], though it is suited to my inclinations and capabilities, rather than having to betray my convictions.
>   —Otto Krayer, associate professor of physiology
>   (Götingen), letter to the Prussian minister for
>   science, art, and national education

You are of course personally free to feel any way you like about the way government acts. It is not acceptable, however, for you to make the practice of your teaching profession dependent upon those feelings. You would in that case not be able in the future to hold any chair in a German univer-sity. . . . I forbid you, effective immediately, from entering any govern-mental academic institution, and from using any State libraries or scien-tific facilities.
>   —Minister Stukart's answer to Krayer[1]

THE PROTEST OF PROFESSOR Otto Krayer against the Nazi Party's policy of anti-Semitism was a rare occurrence. Most of his colleagues had no qualms about taking over the position of an expelled Jewish colleague. The same situation existed in the Soviet Union. Comparing Nazi Germany and the Soviet Union, Paul Josephson, a researcher on science in both coun-tries, wrote: ". . . Nazi and Soviet biology shared transformationist visions of changing society through the dedicated application of the science. . . . Direct and indirect political interference in the activities of scientists gave these transformationist visions their brutality and dominance."[2]

I am absolutely convinced that there can be no excuse for a scientist who collaborated with the NKVD-KGB. Certainly, it was impossible to live in the Soviet system without a certain compromise of one's morals. But the level of compromise could be kept to a minimum. There were choices. The first choice was whether to join the Communist Party. Membership imparted clear career opportunities unavailable to nonmembers. The next choice was whether to cooperate with the KGB (every scientist was approached for cooperation in some form by the KGB). In Mairanovsky's case, it is not merely the chemists who synthesized poison chemicals and the doctors who implemented and studied them who are guilty. The guilt also belongs to those scientists who approved his results and supported his dissertation.

These scientists could have held back their approval. Even among Soviet high-ranking biologists there were individuals who refused to follow KGB or Communist Party orders both during the time when Mairanovsky worked for the KGB and afterward. To prove my point, I will only give some examples, since this issue is complex and deserves a separate study.

NIKOLAI KOLTSOV'S STUDY IN 1920

As I described in Chapter 1, Nikolai Koltsov, director of the Institute of Experimental Biology, was one of those accused during the first Soviet show trial—the case against the supposedly anti-Soviet Tactical Center. Professor Koltsov, whom his Western colleagues considered "probably the best Russian zoologist of the last generation,"[3] established his institute in the middle of 1917 just before the Bolshevik Revolution.[4] A prediction of the crossing over in 1902 and later, in 1927, of the submicroscopic structure and template process of reproduction of the chromosome's macromolecular structure was among Koltsov's scientific achievements.[5] Private Moscow donors funded the organization of Koltsov's institute. Prior to that, Professor Koltsov had problems with official scientific institutions that were under the control of St. Petersburg imperial bureaucrats. In 1906, he refused to defend his doctorate thesis at Moscow University during the student strike. Moreover, the same year, he published a brochure in memory of students killed by Cossacks[6] during the first revolt in Moscow of the Russian Revolution in October–December 1905. The brochure included names of the murdered students, and Koltsov planned to donate money received for the brochure to those university students who had been arrested.[7] The authorities immediately confiscated the brochure. Finally, Koltsov was among 123 Moscow University professors who left the university protesting the order of the tsar's minister of education, Lev Kasso, to deprive Moscow University of its independent status. A prominent zoologist, Mikhail Menzbir, had been elected (and not appointed from St. Petersburg) as Moscow University's rector. In 1911, Minister Kasso ordered the restoration of imperial rules and an end to the electoral procedure. Professor Menzbir was dismissed from his post, and 123 professors left the university.[8] Koltsov was invited to two private Moscow colleges and returned to Moscow University only in 1917. At that point he had already been elected corresponding member of the Russian Academy of Sciences in St. Petersburg. No wonder the new Soviet regime was suspicious of this independent scientist.

In 1920, when Koltsov was arrested, the VCheKa was as yet inexperienced in the details of show trials and treated the defendants during the trial rather mildly. On March 8, 1920, Koltsov's colleagues and pupils wrote a letter to the VCheKa in Koltsov's defense.[9] Because of this letter, Koltsov was not arrested and from August 16 to 20, he attended the court trial as a defendant. He was accused of keeping money to help families of arrested members of the nonexistent Tactical Center.[10] He also supposedly allowed his apartment and office at the institute to be used for meetings of members of the Moscow branch of the Tactical Center, the National Center.[11] After the trial, Koltsov published a scientific paper that included a detailed description of the physiological changes to a defendant's body caused by the stress of a death sentence:

During the first days of the trial I slept at home and every morning checked my weight. It was the same until the morning of August 19. In the evening of that day, after the Prosecutor demanded the death penalty for four defendants and different prison terms for the others, I was arrested and spent a night in the VCheKa Special Department custody. On August 20, after four hours of waiting, the verdict was announced. According to the verdict, 24 of the accused must be shot. However, another verdict, with lighter punishment, replacing this one, was immediately announced. Half of the accused were released immediately. I was among the released. After coming back home at midnight, I checked my weight again and found out that . . . during the last 38 hours I lost 5 pounds. . . . During the next three days of rest I slept a lot and moved a lot (I walked for about 15 km with a weight of 20–30 lb.) and ate 2,500 calories a day. On the morning of August 24, my weight increased by 4 lb., i.e., I gained 7 lb. in three days.[12]

Koltsov's scientific study on changes in his own body during this terrifying time was a remarkable response to the violence of the state. But the courageous response from Koltsov's colleagues and pupils, who defended him despite the danger of bringing on their own deaths by doing so, is far more remarkable.

In the 1920s, Koltsov's institute (which was within the Commissariat of Health, the Narkomzdrav) became one of the leading genetic institutions of its time.[13] In 1927, Koltsov described the duplicate structure of genetic material (the "double helix," although he didn't call it that) for the first time.[14] But the OGPU–NKVD did not leave Koltsov and his institute alone. In 1929, the head of the Genetics Laboratory, the outstanding geneticist Sergei Chetverikov, was arrested by the OGPU and sent into exile without a trial.[15] In 1932, Vladimir Efroimson, who had been both Koltsov's and Chetverikov's pupil, was arrested. The investigator demanded that Efroimson testify in the investigation against Koltsov.[16] Efroimson managed to withstand the pressure of the interrogation and refused to comply. He was then condemned to three years' imprisonment in a labor camp. This was his first term in the camps. Efroimson's second term of seven years started in 1949, after he protested publicly against Lysenko.

In 1937, the Lysenkoists published a series of articles against Koltsov.[17] On May 20, 1937, in his speech at the Annual Session of the Academy, the Secretary Academician Nikolai Gorbunov connected Koltsov with Nikolai Vavilov and called them Fascists: "The Institute of Genetics [headed by Vavilov] of the Academy of Sciences not only did not criticize Professor Koltsov's fascistic nonsense, but even did not dissociate itself from his 'theories' which support the racial theories of the fascists."[18]

On June 29, 1937, a month after this session, Gorbunov, who was Lenin's former secretary, was arrested by the NKVD and shot on September 7, 1938, immediately following the "trial."[19] The same year the Medical Genetics Institute was disbanded. This institute had been modeled after the laboratory of medical genetics at Koltsov's institute. A medical doctor, Solomon Levit (1884–1934) joined the Bolshevik (Communist) Party in 1919.[20] From 1926 until 1930, he was a high-ranking bureaucrat at the Communist Academy. This academy (at first the Socialist Academy of the Social Sciences) was founded in 1919 as a competitor to the Academy of Sciences but was incorporated in 1936 into the Academy of Sciences.[21] From 1928, Levit worked at the Medical Genetics Institute and in 1930 was appointed its director. During 1931, Levit and another Party member, the geneticist Isaac Agol, worked in the United States at the laboratory of the prominent geneticist (and later a Nobel laureate) Hermann J. Muller. In 1938, both Levit and Agol were arrested by the NKVD and shot.[22]

In January 1939, Koltsov and another outstanding biologist, Lev Berg,[23] were nominated by the biology branch of the Academy of Sciences to become full members of the academy (both were corresponding members). But the day before the election, the official Communist newspaper, *Pravda*, published an article against both scientists entitled "Pseudo-Scientists Should Not Be Members of the Academy of Sciences."[24] In this article, Koltsov was described as "a counterrevolutionary" and "a fascist," and Berg was called "an idealist" who sympathized with Hitlerism. The article was signed by

Academicians Aleksei Bach and Boris Keller; Professor Khachatur Koshtoyanst; and Candidates of Biological Sciences A. Shcherbakov, R. Dozortseva, Ye. Polikarpova, N. Nuzhdin, S. Kraevoi, and K. Kosikov. I have already described the role of Academician Bach in the Sovietization of the academy. Boris Keller (1874–1945), a member of the Agricultural Academy (VASKhNIL), was one of only six VASKhNIL Academicians (there were forty-seven full members of VASKhNIL in the 1930s) who had strongly supported Lysenko since 1935. Keller's devotion to Lysenko was rewarded in 1938, when the Academy Presidium issued an order to establish a Laboratory of Evolutionary Ecology for him within the Institute of Genetics.[25]

Two of the signers, Dozortseva and her husband, Nuzhdin, had begun their careers as geneticists and coworkers of Vavilov. Obviously, there were plenty of careerists in the scientific community who were ready to follow any order of the Bolshevik (Communist) Party. Dozortseva was awarded almost instantly for her deed. In March 1939, she was appointed scientific secretary of the academy's biological branch. Her husband, Nikolai Nuzhdin (1904–1972), was elected a corresponding member of the academy in 1953, after he had published many articles supporting Lysenko. Still, he never became a full member. In 1964, when Nuzhdin's name was suggested for nomination at the Academy General Assembly, at first the molecular biologist Academician Vladimir Engelhardt spoke against his candidacy.[26] But the words of Academician Andrei Sakharov, who informed the assembly about the destructive role Nuzhdin had played as one of Lysenko's closest cronies, were the most important:

Together with Academician Lysenko, he [Nuzhdin] is responsible for the shameful backwardness of Soviet biology and of genetics in particular, for the dissemination of pseudoscientific views, for adventurism, for the degradation of learning, and for the defamation, firing, arrest, even death, of many genuine scientists. I urge you to vote against Nuzhdin.[27]

In his short speech, another prominent physicist, Academician Igor Tamm, supported Sakharov.[28] In vain, Lysenko tried to defend his protégé. The third physicist, Academician Yakov Zeldovich, openly announced that he would vote against Nuzhdin. Nuzhdin's career was over. After Sakharov's statement, he was not elected. This was quite an unusual event at the academy: According to Soviet practice, all candidates were approved by the Science Department of the Communist Party Central Committee before elections.[29] This practice started in 1927, when a Special Commission of the Sovnarkom (Council of People's Commissars) was formed to control Academy of Sciences activity and election of academicians.[30] All materials of this commission were "top secret." After the academy meeting, Sakharov wrote two letters about Lysenkoism and Lysenko's attempt to nominate Nuzhdin to *Izvestiya* and to Nikita Khrushchev personally.[31] As a punishment for voting against Nuzhdin, Nikita Khrushchev wanted to disband the academy, but he was dismissed from his post as first secretary of the Party during a bloodless coup and was replaced by Leonid Brezhnev before he could act against the academy.[32]

Lysenko, who was seated at the meeting near Sakharov, was furious: "People like Sakharov should be locked up and put on trial!"[33] As we now know, Lysenko's wish became a reality in 1980, when Sakharov was exiled to Gorky (Nizhnii Novgorod) without a trial, under heavy KGB guard. It would have been a triumphant victory for Lysenko, had he not died four years before.

But all these events happened much later than the tragic days of 1939. On January 23, 1939, Trofim Lysenko and his crony Nikolai Tsitsin were elected to the Academy of Sciences instead of Koltsov and Berg. This was the second time Koltsov had not been elected because of Party disapproval. Tsitsin's career started in the early 1930s.[34] In 1935, with Stalin's personal support, Tsitsin became director of the West Siberian Experimental Station in Omsk, and the station was promoted to the Siberian Institute of Grain Culture. In 1938, he was appointed director of the Academy Botanical Garden in Moscow. From the late 1940s to early 1950s, during the time of Lysenko's greatest power, Tsitsin was chairman of the "Court of Honor" of the Academy of Sciences. These "courts," which existed within the ministries and the central state committees, were created in the late 1940s to try scientists who refused to follow Lysenko's pseudoscience or for officials who did not follow the instructions of Communist Party leaders.[35] In November 1947, the "Court of Honor" of the Academy of Sciences condemned anti-Lysenkoist geneticist Anton Zhebrak (1901–1965). The "court trial" was supervised by the Politburo main ideologist, Mikhail Suslov. As a result, Zhebrak was dismissed from his post as president of the Belorussian Academy of Sciences. The MGB tried to arrest him at his apartment in Minsk, but Zhebrak's friends hid him and the MGB did not find him.[36] But it seems Lysenko did not inspire loyalty. In February 1948, Tsitsin wrote a letter to Stalin criticizing Lysenko,[37] and in the late 1950s, he became Lysenko's rival as the leader of Michurin's biology.

In 1939, after the elections, the president of the Academy of Sciences, botanist Vladimir Komarov, welcomed Lysenko and Tsitsin as "the most deserving scientists" joining the academy. Stalin himself, as well as Chief Prosecutor Andrei Vyshinsky, were also "elected" as honored full members. The chairman of the Council of Ministers and Politburo member

The main building of the Presidium of the Soviet Academy of Sciences (from 1934 on), as it looked in the 1950s. Annual meetings of the academy took place in this eighteenth-century palace. (Photo from the Russian State Archive of Cinema and Photo Documents [Moscow])

Vyacheslav Molotov was "elected" an academy full member later, in 1946. Stalin himself sent him a telegram (Molotov was in New York): "19.9.46. The academicians ask you not to object to your election to honorary membership in the Academy of Sciences. Please do agree. Druzhkov [i.e., With friendship]."[38] Understanding that the situation with the elections was "a death sentence" for his institute, Koltsov wrote an appeal to Stalin,[39] to no avail. The article in *Pravda* against Koltsov and Berg meant that the highest Soviet and Party authorities, including Stalin himself, approved Lysenko's and Tsitsin's election.

Koltsov was also attacked by Communist Party members in his own institute. At an institute meeting on January 15, 1939, one of his most talented pupils, Nikolai Dubinin, accused Koltsov of supposedly racist and Fascist views because in the 1920s, Koltsov had been an enthusiastic supporter of eugenics (which meant simply human genetics in Russia in the 1920s). As Dubinin recalled later, Koltsov responded that "he did not take back a single word he had ever spoken about genetics."[40] However, the resolution of the meeting was in support of Koltsov, and it said that the article in *Pravda* signed by Academician Bach and others "gave a wrong image of N. K. Koltsov as a scientist and a citizen."[41] This was almost an uprising against "the Party line"! Of course, the problem was not Koltsov's scientific opinions but his independence and the impossibility of controlling him and his institute ideologically.

A special commission was sent to Koltsov's institute. It included Academician Lysenko, newly elected, as well as Academician Bach and one of Mairanovsky's supporters, Academician Grashchenkov. As a result of the commission's "inspection," Koltsov lost his institute. On June 3, 1939, Koltsov, one of the best biologists of the twentieth century, begged his colleague and old friend, Secretary Academician Leon Orbeli:

> It seems that I will not be pushed out from my apartment and my small laboratory room (both are completely separated from the other rooms of the same building of the Institute). . . . Do I still have a salary? Will my wife, M. P. Koltsova (Doctor of Biological Sciences), and my personal technician, E. P. Kumakova, be allowed to continue to work with me? How will we be paid and funded (I need very small sums for experiments which I can cover from my salary)? I would prefer to receive this money from the Academy, but if this is not possible, you can attach my small laboratory (three persons) to any institute within the Academy . . . [42]

Koltsov died of a heart attack on December 2, 1940, in Leningrad, where he arrived with his wife, Maria Sadovnikova-Koltsova, to give a lecture. The same night, his wife (who was also his research assistant) committed suicide.[43] She left a letter to colleagues at the Institute of Experimental Biology. In it, she cited the last words of Koltsov. Before he died, Koltsov suddenly opened his eyes and said: "I would like everything and everybody to wake up." He definitely meant the nightmare with his institute, Lysenko, and the whole regime. Koltsov and his wife were buried together in the same grave at Vvedenskoe Cemetery in Moscow.

In 1940, Koltsov's institute was transferred from the Commissariat of Health to the Academy of Sciences and renamed the Institute of Histology, Cytology, and Embryology (now Severtsov Institute of Ecology and Evolutionary Problems of the Russian Academy of Sciences). The histologist Georgii Khrushchov, quite loyal to Lysenko, was appointed director of the renamed institute. Only in 1967, one of Koltsov's devoted pupils, Boris Astaurov, managed to create the Koltsov Institute of Developmental Biology within the academy, which to some extent continued Koltsov's tradition in science.

Lev Berg became an academician in 1946. After 1939, he was nominated again for the elections in 1943 and 1946. In 1946, Berg was recommended for the geography (and not the biology) branch of the academy. The second nominee for the same position, Dr. Baransky, refused to compete with Berg. In a letter addressed to the Academy Presidium, he wrote: "No one can be an Academician if Berg isn't one."[44] Berg was elected.

After Koltsov's death, censors struck his name from all Soviet scientific literature for the following twenty-five years. Lysenkoists sometimes mentioned Koltsov as the author of "the most reactionary and insane delirium."[45] Generations of Soviet biologists never heard the name of this brilliant zoologist, geneticist, and evolutionist. However, Koltsov at least died a free man. The second major enemy of the "people's scientist" (as Lysenko was known in the Soviet press), Academician Nikolai Vavilov, died in the hands of the NKVD. Lysenko himself denounced Vavilov to the secret service.

PROTESTORS OF THE 1930S–1940S: VAVILOV AND PRYANISHNIKOV

Every time he [Nikolai Vavilov] was brought in, Khvat [the NKVD investigator] asked him the same question:
"Who are you?"
"I am Academician Vavilov."
"You're a load of shit and not an Academician."
—M. Popovsky, *The Vavilov Affair*

As one can see from the investigation materials, they [the geneticist Grigory Levitsky and botanist Konstantin Flyaksberger] were arrested [in 1941] in fact because of their sharp criticism of Lysenko and because of their belief (which they announced at a meeting of the Institute's Scientific Council) that one should not support scientific theories by political slogans.
—Senior prosecutor of the Leningrad
Region I. V. Katukova[46]

From the 1920s–1950s, one needed to have courage to withstand the ideological pressure of the Soviet state and to retain one's scientific and human beliefs. Biologists could be punished for two "crimes"—nonacceptance of Lysenko's doctrine and protests against the arrests of colleagues. The second was especially dangerous.

Before he was arrested in 1940, Nikolai Vavilov had tried to help those members of his institute's staff who had been arrested (at least eighteen had been arrested between 1934 and 1940) by sending letters to various state departments and approaching the head of the Leningrad NKVD.[47] Vavilov, one of the most talented botanists and geneticists of the twentieth century, was well known in the international scientific community for his discoveries of the law of homologous series in hereditary variation[48] and of centers of origin of cultivated plants.[49] In 1924, he created the All-Union Institute of Applied Botany and New Cultures in Leningrad, which in 1930 was renamed the All-Union Institute of Plant Breeding (VIR).[50] Vavilov was director of the VIR until his arrest in 1940. Also, in 1929 he formed the All-Union Academy of Agricultural Sciences (VASKhNIL). He served as president of VASKhNIL until 1935, when Vavilov was replaced by Aleksandr Muralov and then Lysenko. From 1930 until 1940, Vavilov also headed the Academy Institute of Genetics.

Vavilov tried to defend colleagues who had been arrested by the OGPU–NKVD even during the early 1930s. He wrote letters in defense of forty-four arrested agricultural colleagues and, in 1934, on the behalf of two arrested scientists, V. M. Kreps and Sergei Sobolev.[51] When Vavilov himself was arrested, four members of the institute staff, Drs. Nina Bazilevskaya, Nikolai Kovalev, Maria Rozanova, and Yelena Stoletova, wrote letters to the Central Committee of the Bolshevik (Communist) Party and the NKVD defending him.[52] Due to the political atmosphere of the time, this was almost suicidal. But these scientists could not stay silent.

During the 1990s, the FSB allowed Nikolai Vavilov's son, the physicist Yurii Vavilov, and the historian Yakov Rokityansky to look through Vavilov's Investigation File of Case No. 1,500 and some other files that contained materials regarding Vavilov. Yurii Vavilov and Rokityansky published several documents declassified by the FSB.[53] They included more documents in the book *A Trial of an Executioner: Nikolai Vavilov in the Torture Chamber of the NKVD. A Biographical Sketch. Documents,* which was published in Russian in 1999.[54] Together with the materials published earlier by Mark Popovsky in his book *The Vavilov Affair,* these documents provide a unique opportunity to recreate Vavilov's fate in the hands of the NKVD. This is the only case where almost complete NKVD/NKGB investigation documents on a Soviet political prisoner have been released to the public.

The arrest of Vavilov in 1940 was approved at the highest state level. On July 16, 1939, only a couple of months after Lysenko, Tsitsin, and Stalin himself became academicians, NKVD commissar Lavrentii Beria in an official letter addressed to Chairman of the Council of Commissars Vyacheslav Molotov asked for permission to arrest the scientist:

> The NKVD has reviewed the materials about the fact that after T. D. Lysenko was appointed President of the Academy of Agricultural Sciences,

N. I. Vavilov and the bourgeois school of so-called "formal genetics," which he heads, organized a systematic campaign aimed to discredit Lysenko as a scientist. . . . That is why I ask for your approval to arrest N. I. Vavilov.[55]

Beria's arrest of Vavilov was directly related to Stalin's personal interest in Lysenko, his "theories," and his fight against Vavilov. Less than a year before Vavilov's arrest, on November 20, 1939, Stalin sent for Vavilov. The meeting was scheduled for 11:00 P.M. However, the dictator forced Vavilov to wait until 2:00 A.M. This was their last meeting. Stalin was very rude toward Vavilov during the conversation: "Well, citizen Vavilov, how long are you going to go on fooling with flowers and other nonsense? When will you start raising crop yields?" Vavilov tried to describe the importance of basic science for "raising crop yields." The dictator interrupted him: "You may go."[56] Apparently, this conversation sealed Vavilov's fate and Stalin ordered Beria to act.

Evidently, the review Beria mentioned meant a special report prepared by Bogdan Kobulov, at the time head of the NKVD Main Economic Directorate. According to materials on the official FSB web site, this directorate was established within the VCheKa on January 21, 1921, and after the reorganization of the VCheKa in 1922, became a directorate within the OGPU.[57] By 1923, 75 percent of all institutions in the country were under the secret control of this directorate. The first known OGPU detailed information about the "counter-revolutionary ramified network of Vavilov," prepared by the Eighth Department of this directorate and signed by its head, Lev Mironov, was dated March 14, 1932.[58]

In 1934, the Economic Department became a part of the Main Directorate of State Security (GUGB) within the NKVD, but in 1936, in Yezov's NKVD, it was merged with the GUGB Counterintelligence Department.[59] In 1938, under Beria, the Main Economic Directorate (GEU) for "fighting against sabotage and wrecking in the people's industry and agriculture" became a separate unit within the NKVD, and Kobulov was appointed its head. Kobulov's report on Vavilov was entitled "The Campaign Waged by Reactionary Scholars Against Academician T. D. Lysenko."[60] Vavilov and his teacher, Academician Dmitrii Pryanishnikov, were named in it as "defenders of genetics against Lysenko's attacks" who were "trying hard to discredit Lysenko as a scholar." The report also included a list of other opponents of Lysenko, beginning with the name of the botanist and president of the academy, Vladimir Komarov.

It is evident now that the GEU and not the GUGB, which was in charge of political cases, collected materials for the future Vavilov case. From

September 4, 1939, until the division of the NKVD into two institutions—the NKVD and the NKGB—on February 3, 1941, there were two separate NKVD Investigation Departments within the GUGB and GEU. The GEU was kept at the NKVD until April 1943, when it became a part of the NKGB Second Directorate.[61]

Apparently, Molotov sanctioned the arrest of Vavilov, because on August 6, 1940, Beria approved the "Order [Warrant] for Arrest" issued for Vavilov.[62] On August 7, 1940, the warrant was also approved by USSR deputy general prosecutor G. Safonov. The warrant was prepared by NKVD officer V. Ruzin (head of the Third Division of the GEU Third Department) and signed by two of his supervisors, Stepan Reshetnikov and Bogdan Kobulov. It was dated August 5, 1940.

The warrant stated that "from the first days of [the existence of] the Soviet Union N. I. Vavilov was against the current [political] regime and expressed slander [regarding] leaders of the Party and Soviet Government."[63] One of the main accusations was that Vavilov was allegedly connected with the so-called Labor Peasant Party (TKP), one of the OGPU's fabrications. Many outstanding Russian agricultural scientists, such as the well-known economists Nikolai Kondratiev and Aleksandr Chayanov, were arrested by the OGPU between 1930–1933 for being TKP "members." According to the OGPU's fantasy, the TKP consisted of 200,000 members, and 1,000 people were arrested for allegedly being a part of this fictional group. The development of the TKP case was under Stalin's personal supervision. He read the OGPU reports and transcripts of interrogations and wrote directions to the OGPU chair Menzhinsky and then Yagoda.[64] He ordered Menzhinsky: "Run Messrs. Kondratiev, Yurovsky [an arrested member of the Finance Commissariat], Chayanov, etc. through the [OGPU] mill."[65]

According to Stalin, the TKP was a branch of a widespread plot that included other groups of "wreckers" who were convicted during other show trials (the Promparty case, Torgprom case, and the like). The plot was supposedly controlled from abroad by Russian emigrants.[66] The arrested "TKP members" were condemned to various terms of imprisonment in labor camps or were exiled. Later, in 1938, most of them were shot. On July 16, 1987, the Soviet Supreme Court rehabilitated Chayanov, Kondratiev, and a number of other scientists and stated that the TKP never existed in reality.[67]

My grandfather, the agronomist Georgii Luppo, was among those arrested. Despite torture, he did not sign false testimony until the OGPU investigators threatened to arrest his daughter (i.e., my mother) and give her to the OGPU soldiers. Such cases are documented. When Stanislav Kossior, the deputy chair of the Sovnarkom and Politburo member, was arrested in 1938 and refused to sign a false testimony written by the NKVD interrogators, his sixteen-year-old daughter was brought to Lubyanka for an "investigation" and raped by the NKVD interrogators in the presence of her father. She committed suicide immediately after this "interrogation."[68] My grandfather was never allowed to return to Moscow after he served his term in one of the northern labor camps. He died in 1941 of a heart attack after a new round of interrogations at the NKVD.

Some of the arrested scientists, evidently after torture, gave testimonies against Vavilov. The warrant mentioned four scientists: the cytologist Nikolai Avdulov (1899–1938), the VIR's employee Kuleshov, the plant breeder Viktor Talanov (1871–1938), and the plant breeder and geneticist Viktor Pisarev (1882–1972).[69] Avdulov worked at the VIR from 1928–1932 and was arrested twice, in 1932 and 1937. He died in imprisonment. A corresponding member of the academy (elected in 1931), Talanov worked at the VIR from 1926–1931 and was arrested for the first time in 1931. Later, after he was arrested for the third time, he died in prison. Finally, Pisarev, who was director of the VIR Central Genetics and Selection Experimental Station near Leningrad from 1923 to 1933, was arrested in 1933. He was released and in 1934 continued to work at the VIR. Later on, Pisarev worked at the Scientific Research Institute of Agricultural Sciences.

The NKVD warrant for Vavilov stated:

After the arrest of the main functionaries of the TKP, VAVILOV did everything possible for their [i.e., the TKP members'] rehabilitation. He took petitions from the accused and their wives and wrote appeals stating the innocence of the arrested. He handled a list of the 44 arrested persons whom he considered should be released to [Commissar of Agriculture Yakov] Yakovlev, who later was arrested as an enemy of the people.[70]

Definitely, in the Soviet Union of the 1930s, the defense of arrested colleagues was regarded as a crime against the state. The warrant also allegedly connected Vavilov with Nikolai Bukharin and his followers. Bukharin was a proponent of gradual and peaceful involvement of peasantry in Soviet agricultural management through cooperative farms. He strongly opposed the Five Year Plan proclaimed by Stalin (and supported by Molotov) in 1929. Under this plan, peasants were forced to join Soviet cooperative farms (kolkhozes). During the process of collectivization, millions of peasants (and members of their families) were arrested and sent to labor camps. The collectivization also caused the famine of 1932–1933, during which about 12 million perished in the Ukraine and the Volga River region.[71] For his opposition to collectivization, in November 1929 Bukharin was expelled from the Politburo and he and his followers were labeled "right-wingers."[72]

Several persons arrested in 1937 were forced to sign "testimonies" about the alleged Vavilov-Bukharin connection. The warrant cited the words of the deputy director of the VIR in charge of science, Arkadii Aleksandrov (1898–?), accused of being a member of a "right-wing" organization (which existed in the imagination of the NKVD investigators only), who testified on July 13–14, 1937: "[The arrested acting president of VASKhNIL] MURALOV and VAVILOV recommended that I should join their conspiracy and ordered me to contact some other members of the [anti-Soviet] organization within the VIR. Vavilov pointed to [I.] LAPIN and [Nikolai] KOVALEV."[73]

In the 1930s, A. K. Lapin headed the VIR Bureau on Experimental Studies. As for the agronomist Nikolai Kovalev (1888–1959), he directed the Nikitsky Botanical Garden from 1928 to 1930, then, from 1931–1936, he was deputy director of the VIR, and from 1936–1941, director of the VIR Experimental Station in the city of Maikop. Arkadii Aleksandrov died in imprisonment during the investigation of his case.

The former president of VASKhNIL, Academician Georgii Meister, who was arrested as an alleged member of a rightist-Trotskyist organization, supposedly also testified against Vavilov on October 19, 1937:

> During meetings with the former participants of the "TKP," Vavilov, Talanov, Shekhurdin, David, and Samarin, I repeatedly had anti-Soviet discussions with them, knowing that they continued to stand on the anti-Soviet position. All of them, as well as myself, became later members of a rightist-Trotskyist organization . . . [74]

Like Vavilov, one of these scientists, the agronomist and VASKhNIL member Aleksei Shekhurdin (1886–1951), was an open anti-Lysenkoist. Together with two other prominent plant breeders, VASKhNIL academicians Pyotr Lisitsin and Pyotr Konstantinov, Shekhurdin declared in 1936 in public, at the Fourth Session of the VASKhNIL, that Lysenko's agronomic methods had no value.[75] It was not possible simply to dismiss the opinion of these scientists. For instance, in 1921, Lisitsin had drafted a decree "On Seed Production," which was later signed by Lenin. The decree required that seed testing and production be performed at special scientific stations.[76] In 1948, a few days before the August 1948 Session of VASKhNIL, Konstantinov sent a letter to Stalin criticizing Lysenko.[77]

Academician Rudolf David (1887–1939), one of the founders of agricultural meteorology in the USSR and director of the Institute for the Study of Drought located in Saratov, who was mentioned by Meister, was arrested after he publicly defended Academician Nikolai Tulaikov, who had already been arrested.[78] On November 27, 1937, he testified:

> A large nucleus of prominent Academy [i.e., VASKhNIL] members, headed by VAVILOV, KOLTSOV [sic!], MEISTER, KONSTANTI-NOV, LISITSYN, and SEREBROVSKY [sic!], actively opposed Lysenko's revolutionary theory of vernalization and intravarietal cross-breeding. . . . They were undoubtedly united in a single anti-Soviet organization . . .[79]

It is known now that all these testimonies against Vavilov were signed only after torture. Academician Georgii Meister called Vavilov "a wrecker," but later on he withdrew his charges.[80] He lost his mind during the investigation, but the NKVD investigators still used his "testimonies." However, Nikolai Gorbunov (permanent secretary academician before arrest) and Yakov Yakovlev, who, as commissar of agriculture, had frequently publicly criticized Vavilov and supported Lysenko, refused to testify against Vavilov during interrogations.[81]

Molotov and Stalin had heard of Vavilov's "Bukharin connection" before. On March 9, 1938, during the Bukharin trial, in a secret letter about the discussion of the trial among various groups of people (such information, based on reports from NKVD informers, was prepared for the Soviet leaders every few days), NKVD commissar Yezhov wrote: "Academician Vavilov N. I. in a conversation with the scientific staff of the VIR said: 'N. I. Bukharin is a smart man, he has a wide vision; I traveled with him abroad. The trial is a long tale for small children.'"[82] One can only guess which one of the VIR's informers reported Vavilov's words to the NKVD. Despite facts to the contrary, the accusation of connections with Bukharin stayed even in the verdict of the Vavilov case, dated July 5, 1941: "Following the orders from BUKHARIN, VAVILOV was engaged in a direct anti-Soviet connection with White Russian emigrants abroad and used his scientific trips abroad for this purpose."[83]

The NKVD warrant directly mentioned the names of Lysenko and Tsitsin, "elected" to the academy a year before Vavilov's arrest:

> Pushing forward hostile theories, VAVILOV is fighting against the theory and work of LYSENKO, TSITSIN, and MICHURIN, which have the crucial importance for agriculture in the USSR. He declares that "we were, are and will be the 'anti' [i.e., anti-Lysenkoists]; we will go to the fire for our [scientific] views and will not surrender our positions to anybody. It is not possible to give up the position. One must fight to the end."[84]

Definitely, the mentioning of Vavilov's comparison of his situation to Galileo's stand against the Inquisition in his arrest warrant—that is, "we will go to the fire for our views"—illustrates that the NKVD considered its role similar to that of the Inquisition. To arrest, torture, and execute opponents of scientists whose professional opinion was supported by the Party and the state was the OGPU/NKVD/NKGB method of solving professional disagreements in science. This phrase was taken, evidently, from the report of an informer and was cited in another document described below—the Memorandum.

On August 6, 1940, Vavilov was arrested by the NKVD while he was on an expedition in the Carpathians collecting plants.[85] Thus, he was arrested before the warrant for his arrest was approved in Moscow by Beria (August 6) and Deputy General Prosecutor Safonov (August 7). In other words, an oral order to arrest Vavilov must have preceded the finalization of the NKVD paperwork in Moscow. The "Record of Personal Search of Nikolai Ivanovich Vavilov" has the same date.[86] It is interesting that in the next "Record of the Search," the date was changed to August 7.[87] A devoted Lysenkoist, the agronomist Johann Eikhfeld replaced Vavilov as director of the VIR. In December 1940, Lysenko's deputy, VASKhNIL vice president V. Mosolov, signed a decree excluding Vavilov from membership at VASKhNIL.[88]

The same day, on August 7, 1940, the NKVD searched Vavilov's apartments in Moscow and Leningrad, his country house (dacha), and his office in the VIR.[89] The NKVD confiscated twenty-three items from his Moscow apartment.[90] Included was a copy of a letter addressed to Stalin giving Vavilov's scientific reasons for his disagreement with Lysenko (No. 3 on the list of confiscated items). No. 21 on the list was approximately 2,500 pages of Vavilov's scientific manuscripts in nineteen folders. Forty-four items were confiscated from his Leningrad apartment.[91] Item 38 mentioned twenty-two folders of manuscripts and notes from various expeditions. On August 9, 1940, the search continued in Vavilov's office. The list of the twenty-one confiscated items again contained many manuscripts (nineteen folders).[92]

Later, on June 21, 1941, NKGB investigator A. Koshelev and deputy head of the First Division of the NKGB Investigation Department, Lieutenant Aleksandr Khvat, issued an order to destroy twenty-six of the listed items. They included ninety-two folders of Vavilov's materials about expeditions and trips to Africa, the United States, and England; ninety notebooks; eight folders of Vavilov's unpublished manuscripts "in Russian and foreign languages"; numerous photos brought by Vavilov from expeditions; nine folders of Vavilov's letters; two folders of letters to Vavilov; 157 professional books; 123 issues of professional journals; four books written by Bukharin;

a book of memoirs by the Russian anarchist Pyotr Kropotkin; and a photo of the head of the Russian Provisional Government, Aleksandr Kerensky; among other things. According to the opinion of the investigators, only four professional books were to be saved, to be given to the VASKhNIL library. The NKGB acquired two items: two rifle cartridges and "an old flint-lock gun decorated with a plaque made of white metal," that is, an antique pistol. Deputy head of the NKGB Investigation Department Major Lev Schwartzman[93] approved this order on June 29, 1941.[94] Vavilov's scientific legacy disappeared into the NKGB furnaces.

On August 10, 1940, head of the Third Economic Department of the Leningrad Region NKVD Branch Zakharov and head of the Fourth Division of this department, N. Makeev, signed a long top-secret document called the Memorandum.[95] It described the main accusations listed in the warrant in detail. Vavilov's alleged "anti-Soviet group" supposedly consisted of twenty-four members of the VIR staff. Five persons from this list (the botanists Leonid Govorov, Konstantin Flyaksberger, and Aleksandr Maltsev, and the geneticists Georgii Karpechenko[96] and Grigory Levitsky[97]) were arrested later, in 1941. This group was supposedly a remnant of the TKP and other anti-Soviet organizations.

The document stated that "the anti-Soviet activity of VAVILOV connects him with the interests of capitalistic states: England, USA, Germany." Among these "hostile" connections, the Memorandum declared: "It is known that Vavilov had many meetings with the German General Consul Zechlin which took place in the private apartment of a member of the group, Emme. According to known information, Zechlin was interested in all problems of economy and agriculture . . . "[98]

Later, Zechlin's name surfaced during many interrogations of Vavilov.[99] As proof of the accusations of anti-Soviet activity and "wrecking," the Memorandum cited long excerpts from "testimonies of scientists arrested and tried between 1932–38." The end of the Memorandum is the most interesting: It consists of citations of Vavilov's statements against Lysenko, evidently collected by NKVD informers. The last citation says: "LYSENKO himself is weak, but there is support of the Party and government leaders behind him, which guarantees him the victory in the fight against the truth in science. . . . We were, are and will be the 'anti' [i.e., anti-Lysenkoists]; we will go to the fire for our [scientific] views and will not surrender our positions to anybody. It is not possible to give up the position. One must fight to the end.'" Definitely, the last two sentences impressed the NKVD officers: They cited them in two documents. An independent professional opinion about a Party-supported colleague was considered to be a serious offense against the state.

The reaction of Academician Dmitrii Pryanishnikov, who in 1940 was already seventy-five years old, to Vavilov's arrest was the most courageous.[100] From the spring of 1941 until the end of 1943, he unsuccessfully fought in defense of his best pupil, Vavilov. In February 1941, Pryanishnikov did what was considered impossible—he had an appointment with State Security Commissar Lavrentii Beria at the NKVD headquarters at Dzerzhinsky (Lubyanka) Square and tried to defend Vavilov.[101] After this meeting, he found out that not only Vavilov but two other talented plant geneticists, Georgii Karpechenko and Leonid Govorov, had also been arrested by the NKVD. Pryanishnikov immediately wrote letters to Beria and to the president of the Academy, the botanist Vladimir Komarov.

In the letter to Beria, Pryanishnikov openly criticized Lysenko and his followers and the slander they had spread, which led to the NKVD actions.[102] He even described the behavior of an NKVD informant, the botanist Shlykov, who had denounced Vavilov in a secret letter to the NKVD:

> One can conclude that Vavilov's enemies consider that his scientific disagreements with Lysenko caused Vavilov's arrest from the fact that Shlykov (an employee at the VIR who had been accepted on Lysenko's demand against Vavilov's will) boasted that he "forced Vavilov to be arrested." He repeatedly said that he wrote secret information on Vavilov [to the NKVD] and that he was proud of this action.[103]

In fact, Shlykov informed on Vavilov to the NKVD at least twice.[104] And on March 2, 1939, he wrote to the Central Committee Science Department.[105] Shlykov proposed to replace Vavilov as director of the VIR with the NKVD agent Shundenko, who was already deputy director despite his professional incompetence.

Pryanishnikov started his fight to save Vavilov during a very difficult time—the autumn of 1940 through the spring of 1941. On August 10, 1940, Vavilov was brought to the dreaded Lubyanka Prison in Moscow.[106] At 1:30 P.M. on August 12, 1940, the deputy head of the GEU Investigation Department, the ruthless interrogator Aleksandr Khvat, started his first interrogation of Vavilov, which went on for five hours.[107] Vavilov was in the hands of this sadist until the end of the "investigation." Two long interrogations, on August 13 and 14, were held at night.[108] On August 16, 1940, Vavilov signed a document stating that he was accused of conducting crimes according to Paragraph 58-1a (treason against the Motherland), 58-7 (wrecking in the interest of former owners or foreign countries), 58-9 (destroying state property for a counterrevolutionary purpose), and 58-11 (membership in a counterrevolutionary organization) of the Russian Criminal Code.[109] The document was prepared and signed by Khvat and approved by the acting head of the GEU Investigation Department, Lev Schwartzman.[110]

In a period of six months, due to the efforts of Khvat and another investigator, Albogachiev, Vavilov had changed from a strong fifty-three-year-old into a doddering old man. According to KGB (FSB) archival documents, from August 10, 1940, until June 14, 1941, Khvat interrogated Vavilov approximately 215 times, Albogachiev interrogated him thirteen times, and Schwartzman (who approved the destruction of Vavilov's manuscripts and library) interrogated him twice.[111] Schwartzman specialized in writing false transcripts of interrogations and usually worked in a pair with another ruthless investigator who tortured the interrogated person until he or she would sign materials prepared by Schwartzman. On the whole, Vavilov was interrogated by the NKVD investigators for approximately 900 hours. Some of the interrogations lasted twelve to thirteen hours.

For a better understanding of the NKVD/NKGB involvement in Vavilov's fate, it is necessary to mention that from 1939–1943, the NKVD/NKGB structure had changed several times.[112] From December 1938 and until February 1941, there were three Investigation Departments within the NKVD (under Commissar Beria) in the GUGB, GEU, and GTU (Main Directorate of Transportation). The Vavilov case was started by the GEU (head, Bogdan Kobulov; head of the Investigation Department, Pavel Meshik). Schwartzman was first deputy head of the GEU Investigation Department, Khvat was deputy head, and Albogachiev was senior investigator.

In February 1941, the NKVD was divided into two organizations: the NKVD (under Commissar Beria), without the Investigation Department, and the NKGB (under Commissar Vsevolod Merkulov), which included the Investigation Directorate headed by Lev Vlodzimersky. This structure existed until July 20, 1941, when the NKVD and NKGB were merged once again, into the NKVD (Commissar Beria, First Deputy Commissar Merkulov). Therefore, from February until Vavilov's trial, the NKGB Investigation Department, headed by Vlodzimersky, with Schwartzman as his deputy and later acting head, was in charge of the Vavilov case. In March 1941, Khvat became deputy head of the First Department of the NKGB Investigation Directorate. His documents were approved by the head of the First Department of the NKGB Investigation Directorate, A. Zimenkov (i.e., Khvat's direct superior), by the head of the NKGB Investigation Directorate, Vlodzimersky, and by the deputy NKG commissar, Kobulov. Prosecutor Bochkov and Military Prosecutor Vasiliev also signed decisions to continue the investigation.[113] Vavilov's verdict was signed by Khvat, approved by Schwartzman, Vlodzimersky, and first deputy NKGB commissar Ivan Serov. Besides these persons, investigators of the Fourth Division of the First

Department of the NKGB Investigation Directorate, D. Konoplev and Kopylov, and Shukshin, the senior investigator of the same division, signed minutes of confrontations of Vavilov with the arrested Govorov, Panshin, Karpechenko, and Zaporozhets.[114]

Evidently, in the Vavilov case, Khvat used materials that the OGPU/NKVD had been collecting since 1931. These materials had been kept in special secret Operational File No. 268615, opened by the OGPU on Vavilov. In 1931, a special Instruction on the Registration of Anti-Soviet and Counterrevolutionary Elements (No. 298/175) was issued by the OGPU.[115] Two types of registration were introduced: Group A for persons who had already been under secret surveillance and Group B for persons for whom information was received for the first time. A special card was created for each person, but secret reports on them were kept in the files of informants. With some changes, this system existed until the end of the Soviet Union. For simplification, I use here the name "operational file." Such operational files were created by the OGPU-NKVD-MGB-KGB on individuals who attracted the attention of the secret service. By the time of Vavilov's arrest, there were seven volumes of NKVD reports in his operational dossier.[116]

There were NKVD informers in the VIR. Academician Ivan Yakushkin started to provide the OGPU/NKVD with secret information on his colleagues in 1931.[117] A noble by origin, Yakushkin tried unsuccessfully at the end of the Civil War to escape from the Crimea to Turkey with the retreating White Russian Army of Baron Pyotr Wrangel. He was arrested in 1930 as a member of the fictitious Labor Peasant Party (TKP) but was released from imprisonment after he agreed to work for the OGPU as an informer. The above-mentioned KGB textbook directly pointed to the role of secret agents (informers) in the creation of the TKP case: "A group of members of the counterrevolutionary 'Labor Peasant Party' (TKP) with a center at the Narkomzem [Commissariat of Agriculture] was disclosed and unmasked with the help of [our] agents."[118]

Aleksandr Kol, head of the Department of Plant Introduction of the VIR agreed, as Yakushkin had, to be a secret NKVD informer after he had been arrested in 1933.[119] However, others voluntarily wrote secret reports on Vavilov and his closest coworkers to the NKVD—among them were VIR employees Fyodor Sidorov, Fyodor Teterev, and the inspector of VASKhNIL, Kolesnikov.[120]

Moreover, the NKVD secretly assigned its officers to the VIR. From the late 1930s, NKVD major Stepan Shundenko worked at Vavilov's institute as a scientist. As A. Zubarev, a member of the NKVD expert commission that decided Vavilov's fate, recalled in 1955, Shundenko based his work on the

"Michurin-Lysenko view."[121] The level of his professional incompetence in biology was well known in the institute, and his example is an illustration of how deep the NKVD-KGB penetration of an academic institution could be. Geneticist and Communist Party member Dr. Mikhail Khadzhinov recalled later:

> On one occasion [in 1937] I received a reprimand from the party committee [of Vavilov's institute] because my [graduate] student, Shundenko, had not submitted his thesis to the examiners. I replied that Shundenko was simply not capable of writing a thesis and he had neither the necessary theoretical knowledge nor the experimental data. "Nevertheless he must receive a degree," I was told. "If you can't teach him, write it for him yourself." And, however ashamed I am to admit it now, I did in fact dictate a thesis for Shundenko for which he very soon received his doctorate.[122]

This was a common practice during the Soviet years. In this way secret service officers and party functionaries (including members of the Central Committee) became scientists and even academicians. After Shundenko left the KGB in the 1960s, he abandoned his biology "career" and became an assistant professor specializing in the history of the Communist Party at Leningrad State University.[123]

In the spring of 1938, despite the protest of director of VIR Vavilov, the half-educated Shundenko was appointed deputy director in charge of science.[124] Immediately after, he declared that he did not share Academician Vavilov's "incorrect" views on genetics and plant breeding and started talking about the "enemies" at the institute who would soon be exposed by Academician Lysenko.

Just as Vavilov was dismissed from the VIR, Shundenko disappeared from the institute. As he wrote in 1988 in a letter to the Russian magazine *Ogonyok*, "following the decision of the Secretariat of the Central Committee of the Bolshevik (Communist) Party [which meant the involvement of Stalin himself], [in 1939] I was transferred from the VIR Deputy Director position to the State Security [NKVD] organs, where I worked irreproachably for 40 years."[125] While at VIR, he pretended to be a loyal supporter of Vavilov and one of his closest friends. In fact, in 1941, Shundenko reappeared at the VIR in the uniform of a NKVD major, heading the commission that investigated imprisoned biologists and agronomists.

Another NKVD secret agent and a graduate student, Grigory Shlykov, continued Shundenko's work at the institute, actively helping the new director, the agronomist Eikhfeld, who was a devoted Lysenkoist, to destroy the scientific staff. He was arrested after World War II, sentenced, and spent several years in labor camps. He was released after Stalin's death in 1953. In 1962, he submitted a Doctor of Agriculture Sciences dissertation to the Georgian Agricultural Institute (Tbilisi) for defense. In it, he spoke about Vavilov almost as a personal friend,[126] completely ignoring the role he had played in his destruction.

As mentioned in Chapter 1, according to secret service procedures, an investigation file was started after a person had been arrested. It contained the materials that reflected the investigation and supposedly supported the accusations, including original transcripts of interrogations signed by the arrested person. This file was closed before the trial. One more file, a prisoner file, included documents connected with the imprisonment—the movement of the prisoner through different cells in the same prison and between prisons, investigator's warrants for interrogations, and so on. This file was sent together with the condemned person after the trial to the labor camp (the usual way of punishment) where the prisoner was assigned to serve his or her term. It was kept at the administration of the camp until the end of the prisoner's term. All documents connected with the life of the prisoner in the camp, including records about work, confiscated letters from and to the prisoner, and so on were put in this file.

Evidently, a undated letter addressed to Stalin written approximately from the end of 1933 until the beginning of 1934, long before Vavilov's arrest, was moved from his operational (prior to arrest) to his investigation file.[127] It was signed by the head of the Economic Department and deputy chairman of the OGPU, Georgii Prokofiev, and head of the OGPU Economic Directorate Lev Mironov. The letter accused Vavilov, Tulaikov, and Director of the All-Union Institute of Animal Breeding E. Liskun of counterrevolutionary activity. Practically everything Vavilov was accused of later during his trial appeared in this letter: the membership in an anti-Soviet organization, anti-Soviet political views, "wrecking," unapproved contacts with "foreign and emigrant groups," connections with the French minister of education, who supposedly was close to the French military headquarters, and so forth. In the letter, the two Chekists referred to the testimonies of persons arrested who had been interrogated between February 1932 and March 1933 in connection with the fictional TKP. The authors concluded:

> Therefore, on the basis of the data given above, it was discovered that VAVILOV and TULAIKOV had been members of the counterrevolutionary organization in agriculture, the so-called Labor Peasant Party (TKP) which was destroyed by the OGPU in 1930. After the consolidation of counterrevolutionary groups, [they] became active leaders of the counterrevolutionary plot against the Soviet leadership in agriculture.

This letter explains why and how the Economic Directorate of the NKVD prepared the warrant for Vavilov's arrest. Evidently, Vavilov's operational file was kept at the Economic Directorate of the OGPU/NKVD, and authors of the warrant simply used the letter as a draft. In addition, they added some information from the coerced statements of scientists arrested and investigated in 1937–1938. After Vavilov's arrest it was easy for Khvat and his team to take testimonies of Muralov, Avdulov, and others from Vavilov's operational file and update them with the testimonies of scientists and officials who were arrested after Vavilov (such as Karpechenko, Flyaksberger, and Bondarenko).[128]

During the review of the Vavilov case by the new Military Collegium in 1955 (a part of his rehabilitation), it became clear that some materials in the investigation file were simply falsified by Khvat and other investigators.[129] There were copies of transcripts of interrogations of Chayanov, Sidorov, Trifonov, Iordanov, and Zicherman in Vavilov's investigation file, but no originals were found. Even more obvious was the fact that Vavilov's file contained a copy of a transcript of the interrogation of Academician Muralov dated August 7, 1940, even though Muralov had been shot in 1937. In its 1955 decision, the collegium stressed the involvement of "the former employee of the NKVD Khvat, on whom the Special Inspection Department of the KGB has materials confirming that he falsified the Investigation Files."[130]

The main goal of investigator Khvat and his team was to force Vavilov to admit he was guilty of the accusations leveled against him. During the first interrogation on August 12, 1940, Vavilov strongly denied everything: "I declare categorically that I had never been engaged in espionage or any other kind of anti-Soviet activity."[131] However, Lieutenant Khvat was quite experienced, and on August 14, he started to interrogate Vavilov during the night, sometimes for ten to thirteen hour sessions. After ten days, on August 24, Vavilov signed his first confession: "I admit that I was guilty of being from 1930 a participant in the anti-Soviet organization of right-wingers that existed in the People's Commissariat of Agriculture. I am not guilty of espionage activity."[132] As co-plotters involved in "anti-Soviet activity," he named persons who had already been arrested, tried, and executed: Commissars of Agriculture Yakovlev and Mikhail Chernov, Deputy Commissar Nikolai Muralov, VASKhNIL vice presidents Gorbunov, Moisei Volf, Aron Gaister, Chernykh, Tulaikov, and Meister, and members of the VASKhNIL staff, Secretary Academician Lev Margolin (1895–1938),[133] and Khodorovsky. However, Khvat was persistent, and on September 11, 1940, Vavilov confessed to being a "wrecker" and signed a document entitled "The Wrecking [Activity] in the System of the Institute of Plant Breeding That I Directed from 1920 Until My Arrest on August 6, 1940."[134] Khvat stopped interrogations for a couple of weeks. Vavilov was even allowed to start writing a book, *History of the Development of Agriculture,* in his cell.[135]

Then, on September 28, 1940, Vavilov signed another document, "My Organizational Role in the Anti-Soviet Organization in the Institute of Plant Breeding."[136] The interrogations in October–November were not frequent, but evidently they were intense. Vavilov was exhausted, and on December 25 and 27 he wrote more documents: "Testimonies About My Anti-Soviet and Wrecking Activity" and "The Establishment of an Anti-Soviet Connection with the TKP."[137] Although Vavilov had already pleaded guilty of "wrecking," anti-Soviet activity, and having been the head of anti-Soviet scientists, Khvat continued to ask questions about Vavilov's international connections with his scientific colleagues and about colleagues at the institute. The interrogation on January 7, 1941, centered around a Bulgarian geneticist and politician Doncho Kostov, whom Vavolov invited in 1932 to work at the Academy Laboratory of Genetics.[138] Together with the famous anti-Fascist Georgi Dimitrov, who allegedly was later "killed" by Jewish doctors, Kostov was a cofounder of the Bulgarian Communist Party. In Bulgaria, he was jailed from 1924 to 1929. As a geneticist, Kostov worked in the USSR until 1939; from 1935 to 1939, he headed the Laboratory of Plant Hybridization in the Academy Institute of Genetics.

In 1939, Kostov returned to Bulgaria and led the partisan struggle against the Nazis during World War II.[139] In 1942, he was arrested and sentenced to life in prison; his five codefendants were condemned to death. Partisans released Kostov in 1944, and from that time on, he was second only to Dimitrov in the Bulgarian Communist Party.

During the interrogation in January 1941, Vavilov characterized Kostov as a capable scientist. Khvat was interested in Kostov's connections with Western colleagues and his opinion about the Soviet Union. These questions had a long-term goal: In December 1948, Kostov disappeared from public view, and on July 20, 1949, he was arrested by the Bulgarian MVD on charges of economic sabotage and espionage for imperialist powers. During the investigation, a special method of torture was created for him— he was put in a cell with a small window on the ceiling. From time to time cold water was pumped into the cell. Finally he "confessed." From December 7 to 14, 1949, he and ten codefendants were "tried" in a show trial. Kostov openly denied all charges. He was condemned to death; others were sentenced to imprisonment. On December 16, Kostov was hanged. Stalin, who personally hated Kostov, was behind the trial that was organized by Stalin's puppet—Kostov's Communist Party rival Vulko Chervenkov.[140] The minutes of Vavilov's interrogation regarding Kostov indicate that the arrest of Kostov might have been planned much earlier, in the late 1930s.

During interrogations from December 1940 to January 1941, Khvat also asked Vavilov about Professors Govorov, Karpechenko, Flyaksberger, Levitsky, and other colleagues listed as members of his anti-Soviet group. Evidently, these questions had a particular goal: Khvat was busy preparing warrants for the arrest of Vavilov's alleged accomplices, Professors Karpechenko and Govorov and a former VASKhNIL deputy president, Aleksandr Bondarenko. Govorov and Karpechenko were arrested on February 15, 1941,[141] and Bondarenko, on February 8, 1941.[142]

Georgii Karpechenko (1899–1941) was an outstanding plant geneticist. The warrant for his arrest stated that he "had been exposed as a participant of an anti-Soviet plot" and "under the leadership of N. I. Vavilov had conducted an open struggle against the vanguard methods [of scientific work] and the treasured achievements of Academician Lysenko in obtaining high crop yields."[143] These accusations bring to mind the last conversation of Vavilov with Stalin when the dictator referred to "crop yields." Possibly, an official report about the work of the VIR written by Karpechenko after the arrest of Vavilov and dated September 1940 also played a role in Karpechenko's arrest. He had plainly stated that the results of experiments performed at the VIR for checking Lysenko's theories did not confirm them.[144]

Leonid Govorov (1885–1941), a botanist and plant breeder, was an old and close friend of Vavilov. Like Pryanishnikov, he could not remain silent after Vavilov's arrest. He went to Moscow with the intention of meeting Stalin or Georgii Malenkov (a member of the Politburo) to plead Vavilov's case. Of course, this effort was for naught, as Govorov could not get into the Kremlin.[145] He was arrested after he got back to Leningrad and was brought back to Moscow for interrogation.

In 1935, when Bondarenko was the first vice president of VASKhNIL, he wrote a secret letter with the Party secretary of the VASKhNIL, Klimov (later head of the Investigation Group of the NKVD's Leningrad Regional Department) addressed to Stalin personally, in which they denounced Vavilov.[146] The letter claimed that "Vavilov always defends wreckers," "at the moment he has a 'minus' value as President [of the VASKhNIL]," and the like. But the main accusation was that "Academician Vavilov constantly and publicly declares that *any* [Communist Party] *checking of the work of highly qualified scientists is* simply offensive and 'personally unacceptable to him'" (italics in the original).

Stalin read the letter, and the original bears Stalin's note: "To the members of the PB. St.[alin]." The letter was immediately copied (on April 5, 1935) and given to all members of and candidates to the Politburo, as well as to the state security commissar of the time, Nikolai Yezhov.[147] Apparently, the letter was the reason that Bondarenko was arrested in 1941 and investigated in connection with Vavilov. It is known now that during interrogations he signed testimonies against the cytogeneticist Grigory Levitsky, who was later arrested.[148]

On February 18, 1941, Vavilov signed a document entitled "What I Know About Aleksandr Stepanovich Bondarenko."[149] Numerous standard bureaucratic NKVD expressions such as "wrecking activity" and "wrecking selection of the cadres to the leading positions within the Academy" reveal that this document was, apparently, prepared by Khvat. Bondarenko was described in it as a protégé of Commissar Yakovlev, who had already been executed. Also, this document mentioned, among others, Director of the Institute of Agrochemistry and Agrotechnique Anton Zaporozhets, whom Vavilov hardly knew. Soon Zaporozhets and Professor Boris Panshin (director of the All-Union Institute of Sugar Beets located in Kiev), whose name cropped up during many previous interrogations of Vavilov, were also arrested.[150] On March 3, 1941, Vavilov was interrogated regarding both Bondarenko and Zaporozhets.[151]

In March 1941, Khvat concentrated his efforts on forcing Vavilov to admit that he had spied for different Western countries.[152] Vavilov strongly denied this accusation: "I did not have espionage contacts with anybody."

At this point Khvat decided to use another NKVD tactic—a stool pigeon, Prokopy Lobov, was put in Vavilov's cell. On March 21, 1941, Lobov wrote a letter addressed to the Investigation Directorate in which he described Vavilov as "a convinced enemy of the Soviet Power."[153] On April 24, Senior Investigator Marisou of the First Department of the NKGB Investigation Directorate interrogated Lobov regarding Vavilov.[154] Evidently, most of the text of the minutes was written by the interrogator himself. It is difficult to believe that a simple peasant like Lobov would have knowledge of so many scientists and their problems.

Finally, Khvat decided (or was ordered) to create a commission of scientific experts who would evaluate "the wrecking activity" of Vavilov. He suggested that this commission would be approved by Lysenko and Commissar of Agriculture Benediktov. Vlodzimersky approved Khvat's idea.[155] Lysenko received the following letter from deputy NKGB commissar Kobulov:

USSR People's Commissariat of State Security
May 5, 1941
No. _____
Moscow
To: President of the Lenin All-Union Academy of Agriculture
    Com.[rade] LYSENKO

Because of the necessity to create an expert commission for documentation of the wrecking activity of the arrested former Director of the All-Union Institute of Plant Breeding, Academician Vavilov N. I., I ask you to agree to include the following candidates in the expert commission:

MOSOLOV, V. P., Vice President of the Lenin All-Union Academy of Agriculture [Lysenko's deputy]

CHUENKOV, S. V., Deputy Commissar of Agriculture

YAKUSHKIN, I. V., Academician of the Academy of Sciences and of Lenin All-Union Academy of Agriculture [an NKVD informer]

VODKOV, A. P., Deputy Head of the Glavsortupr [Main Directorate of Seed Varieties] of Narkomzem [Commissariat of Agriculture] of the USSR

ZUBAREV, A. K., Scientific Secretary of the Section of Plant Breeding of the Lenin All-Union Academy of Agriculture [an NKVD agent]

> Deputy of the People's Commissar of
> State Security of the Union of SSR
> Kobulov[156]

Lysenko noted on the document: "I agree with the candidates. Lysenko, May 9, 1941." During the interrogation on June 23, Khvat informed Vavilov about the commission, its members, and a list of sixteen questions that the investigation asked the commission to answer.[157] Vavilov asked that Vodkov be replaced, whom he did not know personally, by either Pyotr Zhukovsky, of the Timiryazev Agricultural Academy, or Pyotr Lisitsin. Apparently Vavilov did not know that there was no difference between Vodkov and Zhukovsky, who, like Yakushkin and Kol, had been secretly reporting on him to the OGPU/NKVD long before his arrest. Later, from 1951 to 1960, Zhukovsky was director of the VIR.[158] And Khvat and his superiors, of course, did not want to include the openly anti-Lysenkoist Lisitsin in the commission. The next day Khvat refused to make the change. The negative decision was approved by Schwartzman.[159]

In 1987, Khvat recalled: "I put together an experts' commission, with an Academician at its head, and went to see Trofim Lysenko. They—that is, the Academicians and professors—confirmed the sabotage."[160] In 1955, a member of the commission and longtime NKVD informer Academician Yakushkin testified during Vavilov's rehabilitation proceedings: "The members of the expert commission—Vodkov, Chuenkov, Mosolov, and Zubarev—were all very hostile to Vavilov."[161] Vodkov simply hated him. Chuenkov was very much under Lysenko's influence and was a natural opponent of Vavilov. Zubarev was a colleague of Lysenko and also much under his influence. Mosolov, Lysenko's assistant, was also an opponent of Vavilov. The expert commission was formed with the specific purpose of providing a deliberately prejudiced and negative opinion of Vavilov's work.

In 1955 the Military Collegium concluded:

> Yakushkin had a special assignment from the OGPU-NKVD-MGB of the USSR and provided [the OGPU-NKVD] with some documents about Vavilov. Therefore, he could not be an expert on the case. . . . When interrogated during the reviewing [of the case], Yakushkin . . . said that he followed the NKVD orders and could not be objective in his evaluation of Vavilov's activity. He signed the "opinion" of the expert group, although he did not know who wrote it. He did not agree before and does not agree now with many conclusions of the "opinion."[162]

Another member of the commission, Zubarev, testified in 1955 that the commission did not check Vavilov's activity but "only signed a conclusion that had been written by somebody."[163] The commission worked under the supervision of NKVD major S. Shundenko.

After the outbreak of the war on June 22, 1941, the NKGB investigators received instructions to speed up the transfer of the cases to the court. For Vavilov, the last and possibly the most difficult period of interrogations started. Khvat organized a series of confrontations between the arrested scientists. On June 23, 1941, Vavilov was brought face-to-face with Boris Panshin; on June 24 with Karpechenko; on June 26 with Zaporozhets; and on June 29 with Bondarenko.[164] It is difficult to read the minutes of these meetings. It is clear that Vavilov was exhausted physically and morally. Definitely, Karpechenko and Panshin had already been intimidated by Khvat and his team. Vavilov and Karpechenko disagreed only on the date when Vavilov had supposedly "recruited" Karpechenko to his anti-Soviet organization. Vavilov insisted on 1931–1932, while Karpechenko said that it happened in 1938.[165] Panshin also doubted that he had been involved in Vavilov's anti-Soviet wrecking activity. Some of Zaporozhets's statements, by contrast, were similar to the opinion of investigators and definitely helped them:

> First of all I would like to stress that fact that VAVILOV had a special attraction to old anti-Soviet specialists, in particular to those who were re-

leased from imprisonment (who had been arrested earlier by the NKVD). He hired them to work at the All-Union Institute of Plant Breeding, which he directed. . . . During VAVILOV's visits to Moscow, to the Agricultural Academy when he was its President, a large number of persons usually visited him with requests to help those who had been arrested by the NKVD or to hire those who had been convicted of anti-Soviet activity and finished their terms . . . [166]

Bondarenko "confessed" that he in fact "belonged to the anti-Soviet organization within the Agricultural Academy headed by Vavilov. However, he insisted that VAVILOV was especially hostile to scientists-Communists, considering them ignorant and [he] always preferred old specialists and those who had anti-Soviet views . . . "[167]

According to the recollection of the artist Grigorii Fillipovsky in 1968, who was kept together with Vavilov in Cell 27 of Butyrka Prison in Moscow in June 1941, Vavilov's physical condition after Khvat's interrogations was terrifying:

Every night Vavilov was taken off for questioning. At dawn a warder would drag him back and throw him down at the cell door. Vavilov was no longer able to stand and had to crawl on all fours to his place on the bunk. Once there his neighbors would somehow remove his boots from his swollen feet and he would lie still on his back in his strange position for several hours.[168]

On June 28, 1941, four more of Vavilov's colleagues were arrested in Leningrad: cytologist, geneticist, and corresponding member of the academy Grigory Levitsky; head of the VIR Wheat Department Konstantin Flyaksberger; former deputy director of the VIR Nikolai Kovalev; and academician and head of the VIR Bureau of Herbs Aleksandr Maltsev. Copies of transcripts of Flyaksberger's testimonies were included in the Vavilov case.[169] Drs. Nina Bazilevskaya, Yevgeniya Sinskaya, and Maria Shebalina were driven out of the institute.[170] The NKVD investigators used innocuous information received from Vavilov during long interrogations as the material for creating "cases" against his colleagues. Four pupils of Levitsky, famous specialists in different fields—Drs. Nikolai Avdulov (died in 1938 in a labor camp), Boris Vakar, Vladimir Chekhov, and Ya. Ellengor—had already been arrested by the NKVD.[171]

On June 29, 1941, Khvat claimed materials taken during the search of Vavilov's apartment—a photo of Aleksandr Kerensky, copies of letters defending Professor Ivan Makarov (arrested July 29, 1931) and Professor Sergei Sobolev (arrested April 9, 1934)—exposed his anti-Soviet activities.[172] The investigation head, Schwartzman, approved.

Finally, on July 4, 1941, Vavilov signed a document entitled "My Attitude to Espionage Activity."[173] It is difficult to say which part of the document was written by Vavilov himself and which was prepared by Khvat. Definitely, Vavilov included the phrase that in Germany between 1930–1933 he met "the geneticist Timofeev-Ressovsky, who from 1926–1927 went to Germany to work at the Brain Institute [directed] by Dr. Vogt (who treated V. I. Lenin). He constantly renewed his Soviet passport and **desired to go back** to the USSR. I have informed the Presidium of the Academy about this . . . " (bold in the original). Insisting on Timofeev's "desire to go back" to the Soviet Union, Vavilov tried to help him because obviously the NKGB considered Timofeev to be an anti-Soviet defector. But Khvat did not succeed in his main goal: Vavilov never admitted he was a spy. He only wrote that "unintentionally and without desire, in fact I helped spies to sneak into the USSR under the cover of scientists, and this way I helped their hostile spy activity, to which I plead guilty."

The verdict prepared by Khvat, approved by Schwartzman, Vlodzimirsky, and First Deputy Commissar Serov, was dated the next day, July 5, 1941.[174] Basically, it included all points of the arrest warrant. The same day, the head of the Medical Department of Lubyanka Prison inspected Vavilov and found that he had myocarditis.[175] No wonder Vavilov developed heart problems after the investigation. Apparently, Khvat wanted to know whether Vavilov could physically withstand the accusation. The next day, on July 6, Khvat officially showed Vavilov the verdict.

The text of the verdict contains three notes by Vavilov after Khvat's main statement. Vavilov definitely understood that Khvat falsified "testimonies" about his spy activity. Khvat included the notes (in brackets):

> The defendant Vavilov N. I. . . . confirms his testimonies given during the investigation and declares that he had no political connections and even meetings with Bukharin except their mutual trip to England in 1931 to a congress on the history of science and techniques. [Testimonies of Tulaikov about this are not true. I reject testimonies of Avdulov N. P. and Savich about my espionage activity. I absolutely do not know Kuznetsov I. V. and Ushakova, who testified about my spy work.]
> (Signature of the accused)   N. Vavilov [176]

On July 8, 1941, the Military Collegium of the USSR Supreme Court decided to hear the Vavilov case "in a closed trial, without participation of the prosecution and defense."[177] A trial lasting only a few minutes took place on July 9, 1941. The collegium was chaired by Military Jurist Suslin and included Military Jurists Dmitriev and Klimin and Secretary Mazurov. Vavilov plead guilty of membership in the TKP before 1930. He strongly denied the accusations of espionage activity. But he admitted that he had headed a terrorist organization whose members were Bondarenko, Karpechenko, Govorov, Zaporozhets, and Panshin (in other words, those who, as he knew, had been arrested). He appealed to the court: "During the period of my arrest [i.e., the detention] I understood that I have made a serious mistake. I want to work and ask you to give me a chance to serve our country."[178]

The members of the Military Collegium were not moved and signed the verdict without revision. It repeated points on Vavilov's arrest warrant:

During the preliminary investigation and in the court it was established that from 1925 Vavilov was one of the leaders of an anti-Soviet organization known as the "Labor Peasant Party." Beginning in 1930, he was an active participant in an anti-Soviet organization of right-wingers operating within the Narkomzem system and several other scientific institutions of the USSR. Vavilov used his positions as the President of the Academy of Agricultural Sciences, Director of the Plant Breeding Institute, Deputy President of the Lenin Academy of Agricultural Sciences, and a member of the USSR Academy of Sciences, in the interests of the anti-Soviet organization. His widespread wrecking activity aimed to disrupt and liquidate kolkhozes [collective farms] and to bring about the collapse of socialist agriculture in the USSR. Besides pursuing anti-Soviet aims, Vavilov maintained contacts with White émigrés abroad and supplied them with information which is considered top secret in the Soviet Union.[179]

On the basis of Paragraphs 58-1a, 58-7, 58-9, and 58-11 of the Russian (RSFSR) Criminal Code, the Military Collegium condemned Vavilov to the supreme penalty, death by shooting. His personal property was ordered to be confiscated. The sentence was final and was not open to appeal. Despite the last phrase in the verdict, the same day Vavilov was allowed to write an appeal to the Presidium of the Supreme Soviet of the USSR, the only body that could stop the carrying out of the death sentence. Vavilov requested a pardon:

To the Presidium of the Supreme Soviet of the USSR:
. . . I beg the Presidium of the Supreme Soviet to grant me a pardon and to give me the opportunity to atone by my work for my guilt in the eyes of the Soviet regime and the Soviet people.

Having devoted 30 years to research work in the field of plant breeding (recognized by the award of the Lenin Prize, etc.), I beg to be granted at least a possibility to complete work for the benefit of the Socialist agriculture of my Motherland.

As an experienced educator I pledge myself to give myself over entirely to the training of Soviet specialists. I am 53.

20.00 hours.

9.VII.1941

Person under sentence:

N. Vavilov

Former Academician, Doctor of Biology and Agronomy.[180]

Seventeen days later, on July 26, 1941, the Presidium of the Supreme Soviet rejected Vavilov's appeal.[181] Vavilov was transferred to death row in Butyrka Prison.[182] But he was not shot. On August 8, "a convict, former Academician, Doctor of Biological and Agronomical Sciences Vavilov" (as he named himself) appealed once again, now to NKVD commissar Beria. A week before, on July 20, 1941, the NKVD had merged with the NKGB, and Beria became commissar of the new NKVD, and Merkulov, his first deputy.[183] Vavilov wrote:

I am taking the liberty of appealing to be given the possibility of concentrating my work on tasks of the most immediate importance at the present time in my specialty—*plant breeding*. I could complete in *six months* the writing of a *Practical Handbook for Selection of Varieties of Cereal Plants Resistant to Main Diseases*. By intensive work over six or eight months I could complete a *Practical Handbook for Selection of Cereal Plants for Conditions in Various Regions of the USSR*.

I am also well acquainted with the problems of subtropical plant breeding, including plants of importance for *the country's defense*, such as the tung-oil tree, the cinchona and others, as well as plants rich in vitamins.

All my experience in the field of plant breeding and all my knowledge and strength I would like to devote to the Soviet regime and my Motherland wherever I can be of maximum use.

Nikolai Vavilov

8.08.1941

Butyrka Prison, Cell No. 49[184]

When I think about this point in Vavilov's life, I ask myself: Why was Vavilov not shot immediately after the conviction? Why was he allowed to appeal several times? I have a strong feeling that Stalin, Beria, Molotov, and others who were behind his case did not plan to kill Vavilov immediately but wanted at first to simply demoralize this proud scientist to the extent where he would beg his executioners for his life. It was a continuation of the confrontation of Russian subcultures that started at the moment of the Bolshevik Revolution—one side represented brutal, half-literate power-mongers (almost all Politburo members of the time had not even finished high school) who understood only ruthless Mafia-like methods, and the other represented humanistic values and education.

Of course, July 1941 was a period of Soviet military disasters, and Stalin, Beria and other Politburo members were busy restructuring the Red Army and economy. But Vavilov's last appeal definitely attracted Beria's attention.

In the meantime, Pryanishnikov continued his efforts to save Vavilov. In 1942, he tried to submit Vavilov's works for the highest civil award of the state, a Stalin Prize.[185] This was an incredible gesture: After Vavilov's arrest, people were afraid to even mention his name. Pryanishnikov also forced the president of the academy, Komarov, to talk with the academician and USSR general prosecutor Andrei Vyshinsky, as well as with Molotov about Vavilov.[186] The appeals had no success.

At the beginning of 1943, Pryanisnikov persuaded Komarov to write a letter to Stalin inquiring about Vavilov's fate and his whereabouts.[187] Independently, Vavilov's brother, the physicist and academician Sergei Vavilov (who later replaced Komarov as academy president) approached Komarov with the same request.[188] He even wrote a draft of the letter. No reply followed until the autumn, when Komarov asked his assistant to call Stalin's personal secretary Aleksandr Poskrebyshev. This was the right man to get through to Stalin. "Stalin used to pace up and down while dictating," recalled Khrushchev. "He couldn't stay seated when he was thinking. He dictated while walking around. . . . He always dictated to Poskrebyshev, and then Poskrebyshev would read it back to him."[189] Poskrebyshev answered Komarov that the letter had been transferred to Beria.

At the end of 1943, Pryanishnikov tried again. He secured a second appointment with Beria at NKVD headquarters. According to Pryanishnikov's daughter, Beria told the academician (pointing at the thick volumes of Vavilov's case documents on his desk): "There he [Vavilov] writes in his own hand that he sold himself to the British intelligence service."[190] Evidently, Beria meant "My Attitude to Espionage Activity," which Vavilov signed during the last days of the investigation. Probably, Beria also remembered that the order for arrest that he approved contained a long list of Vavilov's alleged "spy contacts." In the presence of Beria, Pryanishnikov looked through the volumes of the Vavilov case. He refused to admit that his pupil was a spy or a "wrecker." "I shall believe it only if he [Vavilov] tells me it himself," said Pryanishnikov to the commissar, and left.[191]

What Commissar Beria did not tell Pryanishnikov was that his attempts to save Vavilov were too late. Nikolai Vavilov had already died of dystrophy in Saratov Prison hospital on January 26, 1943.[192] The medical records gave a false cause of death: pneumonia.[193] Beria also did not inform Pryanishnikov that in August 1941, he himself had petitioned the Presidium of the USSR Supreme Soviet to commute Vavilov's death sentence. The direct intervention of Beria (possibly, on Stalin's order) in the fate of Vavilov became known from a letter written by Vavilov to Beria later, on April 25, 1942:

> On August 1, 1941, i.e., three weeks after I was sentenced, I was informed in Butyrka Prison by your representative in your name that you had petitioned the Presidium of the Supreme Soviet of the USSR for the sentence in my case to be abolished and for my life to be spared.
>
> On October 4, 1941, I was transferred on your order from Butyrka Prison to the NKVD Internal [Lubyanka] Prison and on October 5 and 15 I had conversations with your representative about my attitude to the war and to Fascism and about my employment as a scientist with long experience. I was informed on October 15 that I would be offered every possibility of carrying out scientific work as an Academician and that the matter would be settled finally in the course of the next two or three days.[194]

It is clear from this letter that there was a plan to transfer Vavilov to a secret institute for imprisoned scientists, a *sharashka*. It may have been Pavel Sudoplatov who talked to Vavilov, because Sudoplatov was the next person to appear in the documents of the file. The events of the war interrupted these meetings. The evacuation of prominent prisoners from Sukhanovo and Lefortovo Prisons in Moscow started in May 1941.[195] Contrary to Stalin, Beria definitely believed in the numerous reports from the NKVD agents abroad that Hitler would start a war against the Soviet Union in June 1941. Prisoners were moved to an old prison in the city of Orel and executed there on September 11, 1941, a month before the Nazi troops occupied Orel on October 8.[196]

Vavilov was luckier: He was among the inhabitants of Lubyanka Prison who were put on trains on October 16 and transported to three other cities. The most important prisoners, including Vavilov, were brought to Saratov. Levitsky and Flyaksberger were moved to the city of Zlatoust. Vavilov arrived in Saratov Prison on October 29, 1941, and was put into Block 3, which was used for the most important political prisoners. He was kept in solitary confinement.[197] There he got sick and was taken to the prison hospital.

After his release from the hospital, Vavilov was kept with another academician, the historian Ivan Luppol, and an engineer from Saratov, Ivan Filatov, in a cell for persons sentenced to death. Ivan Filatov was sentenced to death in 1942 after he signed false testimonies. Later, his death sentence was commuted to ten years in a labor camp, but he was so weak that he was sent home to die. After Filatov was released, the two academicians continued to share the same cell. There were no orders from Moscow regarding Vavilov. On April 25, 1942, after Vavilov's many requests, the warden of the prison, Lieutenant Irashin, allowed Vavilov to send a letter to Beria. Vavilov ended his last appeal to the "deeply respected Beria" with the following words:

> I am 54, with a vast experience and knowledge in the field of plant breeding, with a good command of the principal European languages, and I would be happy to devote myself entirely to the service of my country. . . . I would be glad at this difficult time to be used to improve the country's defenses in my specialty as a plant breeder, increasing the output of plants, foodstuff and industrial crops . . .
>
> I request and beg you to make my lot easier, to decide on my future and to allow me to work in my special field even at the lowest level . . . and to permit me to contact my family . . . about which I have no information more than year and a half.
>
> I am sincerely requesting a rapid resolution of my case.[198]

The letter has the signature of an NKVD official mentioned in Chapter 2: "True: Deputy Head of the 1st NKVD Special [Statistics] Department, Captain of Security Service Podobedov." Podobedov was one of the people who supplied Mairanovsky's Kamera with "birdies," that is, victims for experiments. At this point, a still unknown decision concerning the fate of Vavilov had been made by Beria or, perhaps, Stalin. This decision was connected in some way with one of the main persons involved in the Mairanovsky affair, Sudoplatov. The following document was recently declassified:

INFORMATION

VAVILOV Nikolai Ivanovich, born 1887 in Moscow, before his arrest was Vice President of the Lenin Academy of Agriculture.

He was arrested on August 7, 1940, and accused in accordance with article 58 part 1a, article 58 parts 7–9 and 11 of the RSFSR Criminal Code.

The Military Collegium of the USSR Supreme Court condemned him to death by shooting.

The execution of the penalty was postponed. N. I. VAVILOV was enlisted under the 4th NKVD Directorate by Comrade Sudoplatov [sic].

Deputy Head of the 1st NKVD Special Department,

Security Captain Podobedov

May 19, 1942[199]

The original of this document has two handwritten penciled notes: "Com.[rade] Merkulov, I'd like to talk to you. L. P. Beria. 31/V–42," and "Com.[rade] Sudoplatov. Report to C[omrade] Beria. I'd like to talk to you. M[erkulov]. 9/VI."[200] In other words, on May 19, 1942, Vavilov was put under the control of Sudoplatov's NKVD Fourth Directorate, but he was still not pardoned. On May 31, NKVD commissar Beria had a conversation about Vavilov with his deputy, Merkulov. Sudoplatov reported to Beria on Vavilov's transfer soon after June 9, 1942. Apparently, Sudoplatov also had a conversation with Merkulov about Vavilov shortly after June 9.

After conversations between Beria, Merkulov, and Sudoplatov on June 13, 1942, Merkulov sent a special letter to Vasilii Ulrich, chairman of the Military Collegium of the Soviet Supreme Court, regarding Vavilov and Luppol. The letter requested their sentences be commuted: "In view of the fact that the men under sentence referred to above *might be used in work of importance for the country's defense*, the NKVD of the USSR petitions for death sentence to be commuted to detention in the corrective labor camps of the NKVD for a period of 20 years each" (emphasis added).[201]

On June 27, 1942, in a special letter, Ulrich personally informed Gertsovsky, head of the NKVD First Special Department, that the Presidium of the Supreme Court had changed the sentence on June 23, 1942.[202] The excerpt from the transcript of the meeting stated: "Due to the change in decision of the Presidium of the Supreme Soviet on July 26, 1941 No. 9/124cc, Paragraphs 283 [i.e., Vavilov] and 316 [Luppol], the death sentence of I. K. Luppol and N. I. Vavilov was commuted to detention in the corrective labor camps for a period of 20 years each."[203] On July 4, 1942, Vavilov was officially informed about the change in his sentence.[204]

It is necessary to remember that in 1942 Sudoplatov was head, and later Eitingon was deputy head, of the new NKVD Fourth Directorate (Intelligence, Terror and Sabotage in the Enemy's Rear) created in January 1942.[205] One can only guess how Sudoplatov and his supervisors planned to involve Vavilov in terrorist activity. Did Beria (or Stalin) want to use Vavilov's wide knowledge of foreign countries and many languages to assist Sudoplatov's spies and guerrillas? Or would Vavilov, an excellent botanist, have been assigned to work at Mairanovsky's laboratory as an expert on poisonous plants? Did Mairanovsky and Sudoplatov hope to find and test other plant poisons beyond ricin, and new narcotics and plant-derived "truth drugs"? The spring of 1942 was exactly the time when Mairanovsky was conducting his experiments with "truth drugs." Or did Beria have information about Hitler's plan to cultivate the Russian dandelion, *Taraxacum koksaghyz*, for producing natural rubber,[206] and think Vavilov should have been used for checking this idea, which was unrealistic for Germany? The NKVD/NKGB knew that in 1942 Germany did not have natural rubber and used only a synthetic substitute.[207]

And what happened between July 4, 1942, when Vavilov was officially informed about the change in his sentence, and January 24, 1943, when he was moved from his cell to the prison hospital? Had he started to work for Sudoplatov from his cell? If so, what kind of work was it? There is nothing about Vavilov in Sudoplatov's book: The KGB even now keeps its secrets.

Apparently, in 1944 Pryanishnikov found out about Vavilov's death.[208] But he continued fighting for Karpechenko. On July 20, 1945, Pryanishnikov appealed to Beria again.[209] He asked Beria for an amnesty for Karpechenko because of the end of the war with Nazi Germany. "If it is not possible to apply the amnesty to G. D. Karpechenko, it is necessary at least to put him in conditions favorable for his work in the Narkomvnudel [i.e., the NKVD] system. His knowledge and talents should work for our Motherland," wrote Pryanishnikov.

The old academician did not know that he was trying to help a dead person. As became known recently, on July 7, 1941, Karpechenko was tried along with Vavilov, Govorov, and Bondarenko.[210] The primary materials about the investigation and the trial are still in the closed KGB/FSB archives. The four defendants were found guilty of "anti-Soviet activities" and "wrecking." According to Vavilov's testimony at the trial, Karpechenko "had supported his [i.e., Vavilov's] program of wrecking which had diverted institutes [i.e., the VIR] from practical tasks of Soviet agriculture."[211]

Like Vavilov, Karpechenko was tortured during his NKGB investigation. In his last plea to the court Karpechenko said: ". . . I cannot confess my guilt. During the preliminary deposition, I did confess to all the charges brought against me. But I made this confession under duress of the methods used during the deposition."[212] On July 9, 1941, Karpechenko was condemned to death. His plea was denied, and on July 28, 1941, he was shot.[213]

During the trial, Bondarenko, like Karpechenko, repudiated his previous testimonies against Vavilov.[214] He had been accused that "since 1937 [he] was one of the leaders of an anti-Soviet wrecking organization in the system of the Agricultural Academy and was connected with agents of the American intelligence."[215] On July 9, 1941, the Military Collegium condemned Bondarenko to death, and he was shot on July 27, 1941, a day before Karpechenko.[216]

The dates of the rejection of Vavilov's appeal (July 26, 1941) and the death of Bondarenko (July 27, 1941) and Karpechenko (July 28, 1941) are almost identical. It seems that their appeals were reviewed by the Military Collegium the same day. It is still a mystery why Vavilov was left alive for a while, while the other two defendants were immediately shot. Either Beria or Stalin intervened, or the whole scenario was planned in advance. For some reason, Govorov was also kept alive. He died in 1943 in imprisonment.[217]

The trial of Vavilov's four colleagues arrested in Leningrad was postponed until the end of the war. On January 3, 1942, Senior Investigator Kuksinsky and head of the Investigation Group of the NKVD Leningrad Regional Department Klimov (the same Klimov who signed the above-mentioned secret letter to Stalin) signed the "Decision to Postpone the Investigation Because of the Impossibility of an Expert Evaluation."[218] Levitsky died in Zlatoust Prison on May 20, 1942, and Flyaksberger died in the same prison on September 13, 1942.[219] In 1943, only Kovalev and Maltsev were still alive in imprisonment and their interrogations started again in May–June.[220] The same "expert" commission that had worked on Vavilov's case, consisting of A. Vodkov, A. Zubarev, V. Mosolov, and S. Chuenkov (minus Shundenko), gave its opinion on the Kovalev-Maltsev case. It is interesting that Lysenko himself wrote favorably about Maltsev in a *kharakteristika* (characterization) document he sent to the NKVD on February 20, 1940.[221] Nevertheless, Kovalev and Maltsev were tried and convicted. They were released only in the mid-1950s.[222]

It is likely that in 1940 the NKVD plan was to organize a show trial with numerous defendants and to focus it on a conspiracy of geneticists and basic biology scientists out to sabotage Soviet agriculture. Possibly, it planned to arrest many of the scientists about whom Vavilov was asked during his interrogations. Evidently, the Nazi invasion on June 22, 1941, prevented the show trial and therefore Vavilov and the other three defendants were simply tried in chamber by the Military Collegium.

As incredible as it may seem, the war of the Leningrad NKVD/NKGB against scientists and other representatives of the intelligentsia did not stop with the arrest of the leading geneticists and agronomists of the VIR. From 1941–1943, the NKVD and its branches had the Third (Secret-Political) Directorate with its Second Department, whose goal was "to combat anti-Soviet formations among the Academic, scientific-technical, humanitarian, and medical intelligentsia, artists and writers," which consisted of five special divisions.[223] In 1943, this directorate became a part of the NKGB Second Directorate (Counterintelligence). The war against the intelligentsia continued even during the horrors of the 900-day Nazi siege of Leningrad, when 800,000 of Leningrad's inhabitants died of cold and starvation. Here is a scene from the NKVD prison in Leningrad in 1942:

> Of 15 men imprisoned in a cell, only three or five remained alive within a week, and the dead ones were replaced by new prisoners. Professors, officers, historians, writers, persons who had worked at the local Communist Party Committee, and even prosecutors were especially numerous among prisoners. . . . After the trial [and before being sent to a labor camp], I was put in another cell where there were about 100 inmates. The convicts' ages ranged from 10 to 80 years. . . . On the top row of a wooden bunk, which was built from one wall of the cell to the other, lay those men who were not cannibals, while under the bunk, on the floor, there were about 15–20 cannibals. They used to crawl out from their "hole" during the night, drag a live person from the bunk to their place underneath, kill and eat him. We tried to appeal to the guards to take measures against the cannibals, but they used to reply that the more prisoners had been eaten, the better it would be for them since they would have less work. Each day about 10–15 prisoners died in that cell.[224]

The name of only one of the NKVD/MGB officers working during the Nazi blockade of the city, Lieutenant Nikolai Kruzhkov, is known. He specialized in torturing imprisoned skeletal scientists.[225] In besieged Leningrad, the NKVD/NKGB officers (as well as members of the Communist Party elite) were provided with a special food ration. In fact, Leningrad party boss (first secretary) Andrei Zhdanov was so obese that a special tennis court in a bunker was constructed so he could exercise to lose weight. In the late 1950s, Kruzhkov, promoted to the rank of MGB colonel, was tried not as a torturer but as a "saboteur" and sentenced to fifteen years in a labor camp.[226]

I do not know how long Kruzhkov was imprisoned, but usually high-ranking MGB officers were released long before the end of their term. In the early 1990s, his son, a scientist working at Moscow University, tried to persuade Moscow journalists that his father had been a kind and decent man.[227]

There was one more victim, now largely unknown, connected with the Vavilov case—an old German diplomat, Erich Zechlin. Zechlin was born in 1883 and in 1907 received a Ph.D. in literature.[228] In 1918, he started to work at the German Foreign Office. From 1928 to 1933, he was German general consul in Leningrad and then served in Lithuania. Finally, in

September–November 1944, he was second German envoy to Finland. On June 13, 1945, Zechlin was arrested by the Soviet Military Counter-intelligence (SMERSH) and sent to Moscow.[229] After a few interrogations, the military intelligence lost interest in Zechlin and he was transferred to the NKGB Second Directorate (Counterintelligence). He was accused of having been a spy a long time before the war, when he was a consul in Leningrad. NKGB commissar Merkulov approved the verdict. In June 1946, the Military Collegium sentenced Zechlin to "10 years of imprison-ment in a correction labor camp" for "spying for Germany from 1928 until 1933. . . . He gathered intelligence he was interested in through his agents." During Vavilov's interrogations, Khvat tried to force Vavilov to say he was one of Zechlin's agents. In vain, Zechlin asked the USSR Supreme Council to pardon him:

> . . . I am requesting the USSR Supreme Council to pardon me and to permit me to leave [the USSR] for my Motherland Germany . . .
>
> During my work as a Consul and Envoy I had never fulfilled any spy action or recruited any spy agent and never collected any secret informa-tion. Besides, I request that you would take into consideration that all these incriminating circumstances occurred 14 years ago. . . . I am 63 years old, in bad health, and I cannot do physical work . . .
>
> In my Motherland I could participate in a creation of a new demo-cratic state. I was never a member of the Nazi Party and never followed the Nazi ideology. . . . After WWI I joined the Democratic Party and I was a member of it until it was disbanded in 1932. Now I would like to take part in the work of this party again; the goal of this party is to de-Nazify and democratize Germany.
>
> My brother, Walter Zechlin, . . . shared my democratic views. He was deprived of his German citizenship during the Fascist regime . . . [230]

In fact, Walter Zechlin was not only an anti-Fascist, but in 1941 he pro-vided Arvid Harnak (alias "Corsican"), one of the leaders of the Soviet spy network in Germany known as the Red Orchestra, with secret informa-tion.[231] Erich Zechlin was repatriated to Germany only in December 1953. He died soon after his return.

For a long time, most of Vavilov's colleagues did not know what had hap-pened to him. Besides having held many positions in biology, Vavilov had also been president of the Geographic Society. After he was arrested in 1940, Lev Berg was elected the new president. In 1947, the society celebrated its hundredth anniversary. Berg wrote a history of the society and devoted one of the chapters to Vavilov. Naturally, a censor demanded he take this chapter out. Berg refused to publish the book without the chapter about Vavilov. Finally, the book appeared with the chapter. Possibly, this was the only example when a chapter about an arrested scientist who died in NKVD hands was published in the 1940s. In 1950, after Berg died, the library of the Geographic Society was closed and Vavilov's name was blacked out from the materials of the society.[232]

When Pryanishnikov recalled Vavilov in the 1940s, he could not keep from crying. "Dmitrii Nikolaevich started to cry and he was still wiping his tired eyes with a handkerchief for a long time, even after we had turned to other subjects of conversation," Professor Aleksandr Kuptsov, one of Pryanishnikov's pupils, wrote in 1958 about his conversation with Pryanishnikov in January 1944.[233] Fortunately for him, the courageous Academician Pryanishnikov died before the August 1948 Session and did not see the triumph of Lysenko.

WITHIN THE ATOMIC PROJECT

There is not much information about the *sharashki* in which imprisoned biologists worked. The only history available is on the *sharashka* created within the Soviet atomic project for one of Koltsov's pupils, the convicted geneticist Nikolai Timofeev-Ressovsky.[234] In fact, the unusual life and personality of this scientist attracted the attention of two novelists.[235]

In 1925, as a young Soviet geneticist working on the fruit fly *Drosophila*, Timofeev, along with his geneticist wife, Yelena, went to Germany to Oscar Vogt's Institute of Neurology in Berlin as part of a Soviet-German scientific cooperation effort. He remained in Germany until the conquest of Berlin by the Soviet army in 1945. From 1935 to 1945, Timofeev headed the Laboratory of Genetics at the Kaiser Wilhelm Institute in Berlin. Timofeev's encyclopedic knowledge of biology influenced the German atomic physicists, including Karl Zimmer and Max Delbrück, with whom he coauthored several papers. The pioneering article on gene size published in 1935 was the most famous and eventually provoked the idea of DNA structure.[236] In 1944, Timofeev's eldest son, Dmitrii, was arrested by the Gestapo as a member of the anti-Nazi underground group that helped foreign slave workers to escape and hide. On May 1, 1945, he perished in the Nazi concentration camp Mauthausen. Although Timofeev was not directly involved in the anti-Nazi underground, he employed several Russian POWs and half-Jewish scientists and saved them from death. He also helped the outstanding geneticist Charlotte Auerbach escape from Nazi Germany to England in 1933. However, Timofeev's work in Nazi Germany caused a controversial discussion in the scientific community between 1990–1992.[237]

The complete official rehabilitation of Timofeev by Russian authorities in 1991 ended these discussions. Academician Nikolai Dubinin, director of the Institute of Genetics within the Soviet/Russian Academy of Sciences, who betrayed his teacher Koltsov in 1939, was one who worked to prevent the rehabilitation.[238]

Before continuing Timofeev's story, however, it is necessary to review briefly the organization of the Soviet A-bomb program.[239] The Special Committee on the Atomic Bomb was established on August 20, 1945, under the chairmanship of Lavrentii Beria, who was no longer the NKVD head but, as a Politburo member, continued to be in charge of security services. This committee consisted of two high-ranking Party functionaries, three industrial managers, and two physicists. Georgii Malenkov and Nikolai Voznesensky represented the Politburo. Voznesensky held many posts: From 1938, he headed the Gosplan (State Planning Committee); in 1941, he became first deputy chairman of the Sovnarkom/Sovmin; in 1943, he was elected academician; and in 1947, he was promoted to Politburo member. However, in 1949 he was arrested and tried and was shot in 1950.[240] Boris Vannikov (1897–1962, at the time commissar of armaments), Avraamii Zavenyagin (one of the highest NKVD/MVD functionaries), and Mikhail Pervukhin (1904–1978, at the time commissar/minister for chemical industry and Politburo member, 1952–1957) were the three industrial managers. Later, in 1957–1958, Pervukhin became minister of medium machine building (i.e., of atomic industry). At first, two physicists, Igor Kurchatov (1903–1960) and Pyotr Kapitsa, headed the scientific part of the project. Kurchatov had cooperated with the NKVD on the A-bomb project since 1943. As for Kapitsa, as I have already described, in August 1946 he was dismissed and put under house arrest. After this, Kurchatov became the leading physicist of the project. The committee's secretariat was headed by NKVD major general V. Makhnev.

The First Main Directorate of the Sovnarkom/Sovmin was put in charge of managing mines, industrial plants, and research establishments (including *sharashki*) necessary for the project. Vannikov was dismissed from his commissar position and appointed head of this directorate; Zavenyagin was appointed his first deputy; and Pavel Meshik, one of Beria's main men, became one of his four deputies. Also, the Scientific-Technical (or simply Technical) Council was created under the First Directorate. It was chaired by Vannikov with Pervukhin, Zavenyagin, and Kurchatov as deputies and included industrial managers (commissars/ministers) and scientists. Among the first members were physicists Isaak Kikoin (1908–1984), Abram Alikhanov (1904–1971), and Abram Ioffe.[241] Sudoplatov's Department S (S meant "Sudoplatov") within the NKVD (on January 10, 1946, it was transferred to the NKGB) was in charge of intelligence on the development of the atomic weapon abroad.[242] Eitingon, Nikolai Sazykin, and Amayak Kobulov were appointed deputy heads of this department.[243] Later it was renamed the Second Bureau of the Council. The project was a merger of Party, state, and scientific efforts, with the involvement of slave labor in the USSR, Czechoslovakia, Bulgaria, and East Germany.

As Timofeev recalled, after the Soviet troops occupied Berlin, he negotiated with Academician Leon Orbeli, at the time secretary academician of the Academy Biology Division, about his possible work in Russia: "[Avraamii] Zavenyagin and [Igor] Kurchatov wanted to include me, together with my German co-workers, the physicist [Karl] Zimmer, radiochemist [Hans] Born, and radiobiologist [Alexander] Katsch, into the atomic project. Zavenyagin prepared a special installation in the Ural Mountains."[244] Despite the negotiations, on September 13, 1945, Timofeev-Ressovsky was arrested in Berlin.[245] Later he said: "But some other NKVD department [not Zavenyagin's] arrested me."[246] Aleksandr Solzhenitsyn described how Timofeev was arrested. General Ivan Serov, at the time deputy head of the Soviet Military Administration in Germany and a future KGB chairman, asked Timofeev at the Buch Institute in Berlin: "'Who are you?' offensively using the familiar form of address. And the scientist . . . replied, using the same familiar form: 'And who are you?' Serov corrected himself, this time using the formal address: 'Are you a scientist?'"[247] In fact, Timofeev was arrested on NKGB order and the sinister Pavel Sudoplatov was in charge of his arrest.

On August 20, 1945, the deputy head of the NKGB Second Directorate (Counterintelligence), Major General I. Ilyushin, sent a note to the head of the NKGB Fourth Directorate (Organization of Terrorist Acts on the Occupied Territories), Lieutenant General Sudoplatov, regarding Timofeev.[248] General Ilyushin claimed that Timofeev had been "tightly . . . associated with the Gestapo [and] actively worked against the USSR." The note also mentioned that two of Timofeev's brothers, Dmitrii and Vladimir, "had been arrested by the NKGB several times for their anti-Soviet activity." In the end, Ilyushin asked for the urgent arrest of Timofeev. Evidently, Sudoplatov did not hesitate. On October 10, 1945, Warrant No. 2567 for Timofeev's arrest was signed by first deputy NKGB commissar Bogdan Kobulov and approved by USSR deputy prosecutor Vavilov.[249] A month later, on September 13, Timofeev was arrested by a group of NKVD operatives, and on October 8, 1945, he was brought to Moscow for investigation.[250]

Timofeev was interrogated by investigators of the Eleventh (Interrogation) Department of the NKGB Second Directorate.[251] He was accused of not returning to the Soviet Union from Germany in 1937 (the accusation that appeared during Vavilov's interrogations), contacts with Russian emigrants (including the philosopher Semyon Frank), and "help to the German

[Military] intelligence." On March 5, 1946, Timifeev's case was merged with the case of his colleague Sergei Tsarapkin. Tsarapkin had joined Timofeev in Berlin in 1926 and worked with him until both were arrested in 1945. While being kept in Lubyanka and Butyrka Prisons, Timofeev involved his cell mates in lectures:

> . . . In Lubyanka, I organized a colloquium. There [Vadim] Vasyutinsky, a professor, gave a course of talks on ancient history [he was a specialist in the history of England and Scotland]. . . . Then it [the colloquium] was in Butyrka, where I was a cell mate of Solzhenitsyn.[252] He also took part in our colloquium. And then [the colloquium] was in the camp. In Butyrka Prison, there were seventeen participants [in Cell 75]. There were three priests, two of them were the Orthodox, and one a Uniate. . . . I was the only biologist. There were four physicists, four engineers, and an economist. I gave presentations on the biophysics of ionizing radiation, on the chromosome theory of inheritance, on the Copenhagen general methodology principles, on the importance of these principles for the philosophy. . . . Then the physicists lectured on their issues. Of seventeen prisoners only [the physicist Viktor] Kagan and I remained alive.[253]

However, Zavenyagin did not forgot Timofeev. On February 4, 1946, he wrote a letter to NKGB commissar Merkulov asking to transfer Timofeev to the NKVD Ninth Directorate. This Directorate of Special Institutes was established within the NKVD on January 26, 1946. Lieutenant General and Deputy Commissar Avraamii Zavenyagin was appointed its head, and Major General Valentin Kravchenko, the former supervisor of Maironovsky's laboratory, became its deputy head.[254] Merkulov ordered the head of the Second Directorate, Pyotr Fedotov, to speed up the investigation, and Fedotov, in turn, ordered his subordinates to do so.[255] In the meantime, Timofeev's German colleagues—Zimmer, Born, Katsch, and Wilhelm Pütz (a former head of the Personnel Department and a representative of the Abwehr at the Kaizer Wilhelm Institute)—were intensively interrogated from November 1945 until May 1946 about Timofeev's work in Berlin.[256] Timofeev himself was interrogated in detail about his work in Germany, especially in April 1946.

On May 25, 1946, the head of the Second NKGB Directorate, Lieutenant General Fedotov, approved the accusation against Timofeev (and Tsarapkin) of treason against the Motherland (Article 58-1a of the Russian Criminal Code). On July 4, 1946, the Military Collegium of the USSR Supreme Court sentenced Timofeev as a traitor to ten years' imprisonment in labor camps, an additional five years of disenfranchisement, and property confiscation. He was sent to the Karlag group of labor camps in Kazakhstan, where he was kept from August to November 1946. The conditions of life and work there were inhuman—the political convicts were constantly terrorized by the criminal convicts.[257] Like Timofeev, Tsarapkin was sentenced to ten years in labor camps.

Finally, Zavenyagin personally ordered Timofeev to be found in the Gulag and brought to the *sharashka* built on the shore of Sungul Lake near the town of Kasli in the Chelyabinsk Region (the southern Ural Mountains). This special *sharashka*, "Object B," was created in 1946 within the MVD Ninth Directorate. In November 1947, Object B became Laboratory B, and in official documents it was mentioned as P.O. Box 0215, with a mailing address of Kasli, P.O. Box 33/6.

When Timofeev was found and brought to Butyrka Prison in Moscow, he was dying of pellagra. The trip was awful. Later, Solzhenitsyn wrote down what Timofeev told him:

> . . . Timofeev–Ressovsky traveled from Petropavlovsk to Moscow in a compartment [for six prisoners] that had *thirty-six* people in it! For several days he hung suspended between other human beings and his legs did not touch the floor. Then they started to die off and the guards hauled the corpses out from under their feet (Not right away, true; only on the second day). That way things became less crowded. The whole trip to Moscow continued in this fashion for *three weeks*.[258]

As Solzhenitsyn continued, "in Moscow . . . a miracle took place. . . . Officers carried out Timofeev-Ressovsky from the prisoner transport in their arms, and he was driven away in an ordinary automobile." However, he was still a convict and was brought to the MVD hospital. Timofeev recalled that "I remembered only that the name of my wife was Lyol'ka [a nickname], but I forgot her full name. I forgot the names of my sons. I forgot everything. I forgot my last name. I remembered only that Nikolai was my first name."[259] Timofeev suffered the consequences of pellagra for the rest of his life: He could not read any more, and his wife had to read scientific articles to him. The German scientists Zimmer, Born, and Katsch "were brought to Moscow and for a year and a half were waiting in [the town of] Elektrostal [near Moscow] for me [i.e., Timofeev] to be found and treated for pellagra."[260] Also, "while I [Timofeev] was improving, physicists and biologists were found among imprisoned intelligentsia through all [camps of] the Soviet Union. They were brought to Butyrka Prison in Moscow and shown to me."[261]

Despite the treatment, Timofeev was very weak when he was brought to the *sharashka*. "I could hardly climb a stair. When I put a foot on the next step, I had no strength to pull the second foot," Timofeev recalled.[262] His wife, Yelena, joined him in the Sungul. Tsarapkin was also transferred to Laboratory B.

In January 1948, the work of Laboratory B was discussed for the first time at a meeting of the Special Committee in Moscow.[263] In August 1948, the whole MVD Ninth Directorate, including Laboratory B, was transferred from the MVD to the First Main Directorate.[264] Later the lab became Institute B, and then the secret "Object No. 0211." On the whole, the installation operated from 1946 until 1955. In 1955, construction of the new research nuclear physics institute was started at the same location, and the secret town of Chelyabinsk-70, or Snezhinsk, was built near the institute. In 1992, the institute was renamed the Russian Federation Nuclear Center (RFYaTs-VNIITF).

In May 1946, MVD colonel Aleksandr Uralets-Ketov was appointed director of Object B. Before that he was deputy head of the Tagil Labor Camp, and then the Chelyabinsk Metallurgic Construction Labor Camp, two huge Gulag industrial centers.[265] In December 1952, Uralets was transferred to Moscow and a candidate of chemical sciences, Gleb Sereda, was appointed director of Laboratory/Institute B. Timofeev headed the Radiobiological Department, and Professor Sergei Voznesenksy (1892–1958) headed the Chemical Department.[266] The staff consisted of imprisoned biologists and physicists, as well as approximately thirty free scientists brought from Germany, including Zimmer, Born, Katsch, and the radiochemist Nikolaus Riehl, who later wrote memoirs about his experience in the Soviet Union.[267] This was an unusual *sharashka*: It was located in a very picturesque place and even imprisoned scientists lived in houses and not in barracks or a prison.

Timofeev's laboratory studied the effect of radiation on different organisms and on groups of different species (usually called natural cenozis), as well as the effect of radioactive pollution on the biosphere and the geochemical behavior of radioisotopes.[268] Timofeev was forced to focus his experiments on the investigation of "the influence of the emissions of radioactive materials on the growth of useful plants."[269] Timofeev's long-term colleague Tsarapkin refused to leave genetics even in imprisonment. At Laboratory B, "he closed himself off and worked exclusively on theoretical problems of genetics." Members of the German group experimented in their previous fields: Zimmer worked in radiation dosimetry, Born dealt with radiochemistry, Katsch "focused primarily on the problems of developing methods to extract radionucleotides that had been incorporated in various organs."[270]

Timofeev was formally released from imprisonment only in 1951. In March 1955, he received a document with a resolution from the Supreme

Soviet that he had been mistakenly charged and tried. However, Timofeev and Tsarapkin were fully rehabilitated only in 1991, after their deaths, and Timofeev was never allowed to live in Moscow. In 1955, he was appointed head of a laboratory and then of the Department of Biophysics of the academy's Ural Division in Sverdlovsk. In 1957, Timofeev formally defended his doctorate thesis at the Botanical Institute in Leningrad, but it was not approved by the Highest Attestation Commission! He became a doctor of biological sciences only in 1964, after the second defense.

In 1964, the Timofeevs moved to the town of Obninsk (about 100 miles from Moscow), and Timofeev organized the Department of Genetics and Radiology at the newly created Institute of Medical Radiology within the Medical Academy. In 1971, this department was closed on the order of the KGB. From 1972 until his death in 1981, Timofeev was professor-consultant at the Institute of Medical-Biological Problems in Moscow. His last years were difficult. His wife, with whom he worked in Berlin and in the Sungul *sharashka*, predeceased him, in 1973.

Those who met Timofeev (his nickname was "the Bison") never forgot him. Here is how the Russian writer Daniil Granin saw Timofeev when he met him at the Fourteenth International Congress of Genetics in Moscow in 1978:

> In that far corner the Bison sat in a chair. His powerful head was pulled into his shoulders, and his small eyes glittered sharply. . . . His lower lip protruding, he snorted, roared either in approval or in outrage. His thick mane of gray hair was shaggy. He was old, of course, but his years had not worn him out; on the contrary. He was as heavy and solid as a petrified oak.[271]

SOME OPPOSITION

Lysenko's destruction of genetics and geneticists would not have been complete without the destruction of the evolutionary theory that is based upon genetics. After World War II, Lysenko and his ideologist, Prezent, started a crusade against this theory. On June 28, 1946, Lysenko published an article in *Pravda* entitled, "Do Not Sit in the Sledge Which Does Not Belong to You,"[272] in which he attacked a famous botanist, Academician Pyotr Zhukovsky, who "dared" not to accept Lysenko's new theory: his denial of intraspecies competition, the basis of Darwin's evolutionary theory. Lysenko repeated his position in another popular newspaper, *Literaturnaya Gazeta*, on October 18, 1947. As usual, Lysenko did not bother to give any scientific proof to confirm his thesis:

There is no intraspecies competition in nature. There is only competition between species: the wolf eats the hare; it [the hare] eats the grass. Wheat does not hamper wheat. But couchgrass, goose-foot, pastor's lettuce are all members of other species, and when they appear among wheat or *kok-saghyz* [Russian dandelion], they take away the latter's food, and struggle against them.

Bourgeois biology, by its essence, because it is bourgeois, neither could nor can make any discoveries that have to be based on the absence of intraspecies competition, a principle it does not recognize. . . . By means of the fabricated intraspecies competition, "the eternal laws of nature," they [American scientists] are attempting to justify the class struggle and the oppression, by white Americans, of Negroes. How can they admit absence of competition within a species?[273]

This was enough for some biologists. On November 4, 1947, at the open meeting of the Scientific Council of the Biological Faculty of Moscow University, three prominent scientists—Academician Ivan Schmalhauzen, the zoologist Aleksandr Formozov, and the botanist Dmitrii Sabinin—gave detailed presentations on the problem of intraspecies competition.[274] They showed that Lysenko's own examples of the hare and *kok-saghyz* were excellent for understanding intraspecies competition. Lysenko simply did not know the scientific facts.[275]

The Scientific Council sent the resolution of the meeting, signed by its twenty-four members, to *Literaturnaya Gazeta* for publication. However, it was published two weeks later, as an article entitled, "Our Objections to Academician Lysenko," with the signatures of only Schmalhauzen, Formozov, Sabinin, and the dean of the biology faculty, Sergei Yudintsev.[276] For Yudintsev, who was a Party member, the inclusion of his signature was especially dangerous. The same issue of *Literaturnaya Gazeta* included an article, "For Creative Darwinism, Against Malthusianism," by five ardent Lysenkoists, Artavazad Avakian, Donat Dolgushin, Neo Belen'ky, Ivan Glushchenko, and Fyodor Dvoryankin. Two weeks later, the newspaper published three more articles written by the Lysenkoists. The editorial board of *Literaturnaya Gazeta* was clearly on Lysenko's side.

The academy also tried to stop Lysenko. On December 11, 1947, the Bureau of the Biological Division held a meeting presided over by Academician Orbeli.[277] Besides Orbeli, Lysenko's enemies were represented by Academicians Schmalhausen, Vladimir Sukachev (director of the Institute of Forestry), Pavel Baranov (deputy director of the Institute of Botany), and Yevgenii Pavlovsky (director of the Institute of Zoology). Lysenko and his crony Artavazad Avakian represented the opposite side. Also, there was the philosopher Mark Mitin, who, like Vyshinsky and Stalin, was appointed an academician in 1939. Mitin had already been involved in biological "discussions" between the geneticists and Lysenkoists in the late 1930s. The bureau's resolution confirmed the existence of intraspecies competition and denounced the Lysenkoists' accusation of Malthusianism. It was a usual trick of Lysenkoists to say that geneticists and evolutionists followed the "bourgeois" theory of Thomas R. Malthus (1766–1834). This English economist stated at the beginning of the nineteenth century that human population tends to increase faster, at a geometrical ratio, than the means of supply, which increases at an arithmetical ratio. This social theory was quite simple and was introduced long before Darwin's theory of evolution, but it definitely influenced the formulation of Darwin's natural selection theory.[278] However, it had nothing in common with genetics. A report about the bureau's meeting was sent to the Party Central Committee.

From February 3–8, 1948, a wider conference on evolutionary problems took place at Moscow University.[279] Academician Schmalhausen opened the conference, and more than thirty-six specialists in genetics and evolution presented their data. Among others, my father gave a talk, "The Evolutionary Rates of Marine and Freshwater Fauna," in which he outlined the conclusions of his doctoral dissertation. He was lucky: He defended the dissertation at the end of 1947 and Academician Schmalhausen was his main thesis opponent. A year later, the defense of such a dissertation and this opponent would have been impossible. Academician Sukachev stated: "The existence of intraspecies competition in nature was not invented by scientists, but it is a conclusion based on a hundred years of observations by botanists and forestry specialists."[280]

After the February 1948 conference, the newly appointed head of the Science Department of the Central Committee, the twenty-eight-year-old Yurii Zhdanov, son of the Central Committee secretary Andrei Zhdanov and husband of Stalin's daughter, Svetlana, invited Academician Schmalhausen to the Kremlin and told him that the discussion around the problem on intraspecies competition would be "archived."[281] On April 10, 1948, Yurii Zhdanov even delivered a lecture, "On Issues of Modern Darwinism," at the Moscow Polytechnic Museum in support of Lysenko's opponents.[282]

THE AUGUST 1948 SESSION: GENERAL FACTS

Lysenko did not participate in the conferences at Moscow University. He was waiting for Stalin's reaction, and he knew "The Master" (an epithet for Stalin in the 1940s–1950s in common conversation) much better than young Zhdanov. After a series of Kremlin intrigues, the text of Yurii

Zhdanov's lecture was given to Stalin. Dr. Nikolai Krementsov, who saw this document at the Party Archive, writes that there are "numerous remarks in the margins. The essence and style of these remarks strongly suggest that they were Stalin's: 'Ha-ha-ha,' 'Nonsense,' 'Get out!' and similar comments mark numerous pages of the text."[283] The involvement of Stalin personally in the issue had crucial consequences for Soviet biology.

On July 10, 1948, a draft of the Central Committee resolution entitled "On the Situation in Soviet Biological Science," prepared by a special commission (Dmitrii Shepilov, the Central Committee member, and Mitin), was sent to all members of the Politburo for editing.[284] This resolution was not published in the media. Instead, the Politburo decided to hold a meeting of the Agricultural Academy, VASKhNIL, with Lysenko's report on the same subject.

On July 12, Lysenko sent a list of his most devoted supporters, the "leading representatives of the Michurinist trend" as he wrote, to Georgii Malenkov, a member of the Politburo.[285] On July 15, Stalin signed a decree of the Council of Ministers that appointed thirty-five new academicians to VASKhNIL. Eleven names were taken from Lysenko's list, including his chief ideologist, Isaak Prezent. On July 28, *Pravda* published this list of the new "Academicians." Mairanovsky's colleague, the MGB officer Sergei Muromtsev, was among them. A pseudotheory that some microorganisms can change into others was his main "scientific achievement," besides his secret work on poisons for the execution of the "enemies" of the Soviet Union.

On July 31, the August 1948 Session of VASKhNIL began. It continued until August 7. I will not go into a detailed description of the session; this has been done by many authors.[286] Instead, I want to follow the fate of those scientists whom I mentioned above.

Lysenko opened the session with the speech, "On the Situation in Soviet Biological Science." The text was edited by Stalin himself and had Stalin's numerous notes in the margins.[287] Stalin deleted seven pages of the original Lysenko manuscript. Some of the deleted phrases indicated that Stalin considered Lysenko's statements stupid. He underlined the phrase "any science is class-oriented by its very nature" and wrote in the margin: "Ha-ha-ha!!! And what about mathematics? And what about Darwinism?" Through the whole text, Stalin changed "bourgeois" to "reactionary" and "the Soviet" to "scientific" biology or genetics.[288]

Lysenko's speech targeted basically "Mendelist-Morganist genetics." However, Lysenko did not forget the evolutionists who dared to confront him. He condemned those scientists who followed Darwin's view on Malthusian theory:

Highly regarding the significance of Darwin's theory, Marxist classicists at the same time indicated the errors allowed by Darwin. Darwin's theory, appearing indisputably materialistic in its basic features, contains within itself a series of substantial errors. . . . It was a great blunder for Darwin to introduce reactionary Malthusian ideas into his theory of evolution. . . . At present it is quite intolerable to accept the erroneous parts of Darwinian theory. . . . So much the more intolerable is it to project the erroneous parts of Darwin's doctrine as the foundation stone of Darwinism (I. I. Schmalhausen, B. M. Zavadovsky, P. M. Zhukovsky).[289]

Lysenko returned to these names later. He accused Schmalhausen of introducing "formalistic, auto-mystical" theories that had "long been smashed by the progressive movement of advanced science."[290] Academician Zhukovsky became guilty of the acknowledgment "that the chromosome theory of heredity is freely offered from university platforms."[291]

The above-mentioned philosopher Mitin was even more aggressive toward Academician Schmalhausen. Mitin concluded: ". . . In effect, the methodology on which [Schmalhausen's] book [*Factors of Evolution*][292] is built has nothing in common with dialectical materialism. This book is metaphysical and idealistic."[293] Both Lysenko and Mitin mentioned Professor Koltsov, who had already been dead for many years, as one of their main targets among "our native Mendelists-Morganists" who "share the chromosome theory of heredity, its Weismannist basis and idealistic conclusions in entirety."[294] Lysenko's main ideologist, Prezent, a skilled demagogue, also attacked Schmalhausen: "As the fundamental principle in Schmalhausen's pseudoscientific construction, it is Weismann's autonomization of the organism . . ."[295]

Mairanovsky's colleague Sergei Muromtsev, a recently appointed full member of the Agricultural Academy, also got a chance to accuse the Mendelists-Morganists: "If the representatives of the Mendelist-Morganist school fail to understand the need for a creative approach to the solution of the problems facing biological science, if they fail to appreciate their responsibility to the field of practice, they will be left behind not only by socialist science, but also by the practice of socialist construction in this country."[296]

We know well in what field of "practical work" Muromtsev succeeded: the development of biological toxins for MGB assassinations. And Muromtsev's personal experience of the "creative approach" was the labor of imprisoned scientists forced to work on biological poisonous agents. Muromtsev was especially outraged by Professor Iosif Rapoport's defense of genetics at the session: ". . . We [the Michurinists-Lysenkoists] differ in principle as to method and general approach to the solution of scientific problems. And if you do not realize the difference, Professor Rapoport, your cytogenetic research will prove as sterile as the entire school of formal genetics."[297]

At the beginning of "Concluding Remarks" on August 7, 1948, Lysenko openly declared that he was a tool of the Party: "The Central Committee of the Party has examined my report and approved it."[298] The same day, *Pravda* published a letter from Yurii Zhdanov to Stalin in which Zhdanov confessed that he had been mistaken in his previous critique of Lysenko.[299] In "Concluding Remarks," Lysenko again condemned Academician Zhukovsky: "Academician P. M. Zhukovsky, as is worthy of a Mendelist-Morganist, cannot imagine a transmission of heredity characteristics without a transmission of chromosomes. . . . He cannot see the possibility of producing hybrids in plants by means of grafting; hence he cannot visualize the possibility of the inheritance of the acquired characteristics by plants and animals . . ."[300]

Zhukovsky was devastated: As a Party member, he was expected to follow orders. And he followed them in contradiction to his professional knowledge: "I admit that I took an erroneous stand . . . I declare: I will fight—and sometimes I am very capable at it—for the Michurinist biological science. . . . I appeal to all Michurinists, among whom are both my friends and my foes, and declare that I will honestly fulfill all that I have stated here today . . ."[301]

After these words, Academician Zhukovsky lost all credibility as a scientist. There were two more members of the Party who also cooperated: Corresponding Member of the Ukrainian Academy of Sciences Professor Ivan Polyakov and Moscow geneticist Sos Alikhanyan.[302] A few months before the session, in his talk at the February 1948 conference at Moscow University, Professor Polyakov had discussed intraspecies competition as a basis of formation of new species.[303] But this time he stated:

> . . . One must make an absolute rupture with false views and resolutely criticize the metaphysical, idealistic, Weismannist views in the works of certain Soviet scientists. We must help our Party to expose this reactionary, pseudoscientific rot which is spread abroad by our enemies. . . . The Michurinist movement in science, led by T. D. Lysenko, is a broad and great national scientific movement, a movement which promotes a more rapid passage on the great path of the triumphant construction of Communist society . . .[304]

However, these words did not win the sympathy of the Lysenkoist audience, and Polyakov's speech was the only one at the session that was not followed by applause.

As for Alikhanyan, in the late 1930s he was appointed to the biology faculty of Moscow University without any training in biology. He lectured on genetic theory and was an activist in the Party organization.[305] During World War II, he lost a leg. His renunciation at the August 1948 Session was especially undignified:

> From tomorrow, I will begin to rid not only my own scientific activity of old, reactionary, Weismannist-Morganist views, but will also begin to remake, to break in two, all of my students and comrades. . . . I, for my part, categorically declare to my comrades that henceforth I will fight my adherents of yesterday who will not understand and join the Michurinist movement. I will not only criticize the vicious Weismannism-Morganism which appeared in my works, but will also take an active part in the progressive movement forward of Michurinist science.[306]

The speech did not help. Like the other staff members of the Department of Genetics, Alikhanyan was dismissed after the August 1948 Session. But he fulfilled his promise, became a Lysenkoist, and even defended a doctoral dissertation on so-called vegetative hybridization in microorganisms.[307] Several times he tried to become a corresponding member of the Armenian Academy and the USSR Academy. In the 1960s, he turned around and became a "normal" microbiologist again. From 1958, he headed the Laboratory of Genetics and Selection of Microorganisms at the Radiobiological Department of the Kurchatov Institute of Atomic Energy. I was a graduate student in that laboratory, and I met Dr. Alikhanyan frequently. Then, in the 1970s, he became director of the All-Union Research Institute of Genetics and Selection of Microorganisms (VNII Genetika) and professor in the Department of Genetics and Selection at Moscow State University. As director, Alikhanyan was a member of the Inter-Agency Commission that played an important role in the development of Soviet military biological programs.[308]

The end of the August 1948 Session turned into the beginning of administrative actions against Lysenko's numerous enemies. On August 27, 1948, *Pravda* published "A Letter to Stalin from the Presidium of the Academy of Sciences," in which the Presidium promised "to rectify the errors we permitted, to reorganize the work of the Division of Biological Sciences [of the Academy] and its institutes, and to develop biological science in a true materialistic Michurinist direction."[309] The Presidium also reported on its recent actions: Secretary Academician Leon Orbeli had been dismissed and replaced by an enthusiastic supporter of Lysenko, Academician Ivan Oparin.

Academician Schmalhausen was dismissed from his post as director of the Institute of Evolutionary Morphology.[310]

An editorial article in the same issue of *Pravda*, evidently prepared with the involvement of the Politburo, pointed to the "errors" in biology:

> This occurred above all because the Presidium of the Academy of Sciences and the Bureau of the Biological Division forgot the most important principle in any science—the Party principle. . . . Meanwhile, it must be noted that questions of scientific leadership are not limited to biology. The Presidium of the Academy of Sciences and the Bureau of the Biology Department, having admitted errors in the leadership of biological science, must draw for themselves the necessary conclusions not only in the sphere of biology, but in all other spheres of scientific activity.[311]

There is no doubt in my mind that Stalin and the Party wanted to extend the control they had gained over biological science to all branches of science. Stalin was concerned that some academicians remained independent even twenty years after the Bolshevization of the academy. At any rate, discussions similar to those at the August session occurred in physiology in June 1950, in organic chemistry against the resonance theory in June 1951, and in geology (lithology) in 1951–1952.[312] Another discussion, against Albert Einstein's theory of relativity, was planned in theoretical physics in 1949.[313] Like Mendelist genetics, cybernetics was officially pronounced "a bourgeois pseudoscience."

Numerous orders of the minister of higher education, Sergei Kaftanov, followed the August 1948 Session.[314] Academician Vasilii Nemchinov, who dared to support geneticists at the August session (although he was not a biologist but an economist), was dismissed from his post as director of the Timiryazev Agricultural Academy, and Academician Zhebrak was removed as chair of the Department of Genetics of this academy. Zhebrak was replaced by Lysenko himself. According to Order No. 1208 from Kaftanov, the whole staff of the Department of Darwinism and its chair, Academician Schmalhausen, as well as the staff of the Department of Genetics, Professor Sabinin (chair of the Department of Plant Physiology), Yudintsev, and many others were dismissed from the Biology Faculty. Later, the same Kaftanov fought against chemists who followed the resonance theory. In 1952, after he had become director of the Karpov Institute of Physical Chemistry, he appealed to the minister of chemical industry to order the firing of those who worked on "the vicious resonance theory, which had been rejected by Soviet chemists."[315]

In 1948, Lysenko did not forget any of those who opposed him. Order No. 1259 dismissed Professor Boris Zavadovsky, whom Lysenko mentioned in his speech, as chair of the Department of Darwinism of the Moscow Pedagogical Institute (i.e., College). In 1949, Professor Zavadovsky lost his last job, director of the Timiryazev Biological Museum, and he died in 1949.[316] The whole staff of the Departments of Darwinism and Genetics at Moscow University (as well as those in Leningrad and other cities) was replaced by Lysenkoists. On September 8, 1948, Minister Kaftanov proudly reported in *Izvestiya* about the staff changes at the universities and concluded: "The struggle in the field of biology has ended in a complete triumph of Michurin's doctrine, preserving a new stage in the development of materialistic biology."[317]

As a result of these actions, thousands of biologists lost their jobs. "I remember 1948," recalled the Russian biologist Nikolai Vorontsov.[318] "That fall, in all universities, in all institutions, three thousand biologists lost their jobs and all possibility of research—three *thousand*."[319] Lysenko's main ideologist, Prezent, was appointed Biology Faculty dean and chair of the Department of Darwinism at both Moscow and Leningrad Universities.

THOSE WHO LOST AND THOSE WHO GAINED

The fates of the three scientists who started the fight against Lysenko in 1947—Schmalhausen, Formozov, and Sabinin—were different. When Academician Ivan Schmalhausen (1884–1963) was dismissed from his university and academy positions in 1948, he was an internationally recognized scientist.[320] Until 1937, he lived in Kiev, where he headed the Institute of Zoology and Botany of the Ukrainian Academy of Sciences, which he had organized in 1930. In 1935, he was elected to the USSR Academy of Sciences, and in 1936 he was appointed director of the academy's A. N. Severtsov Institute of Evolutionary Morphology in Moscow. In 1939, he also became professor and chair of the Evolutionary Department at Moscow State University. He was a recognized specialist in evolutionary morphology of vertebrates and the author of fundamental monographs on evolution. But in the Lysenkoist Moscow of 1948, he could not find a job.

With great difficulty, because of the opposition of Party officials, the director of the Zoological Institute in Leningrad, Academician Pavlovsky, added Academician Schmalhausen to the staff of his institute as senior researcher on December 1, 1948.[321] Later, in 1952, Academician Pavlovsky could not hire another anti-Lysenkoist, Professor Polyansky, because two anti-Lysenkoists, Academician Schmalhausen and Professor A. Strelkov, were already working there. In 1955, Schmalhausen was given a small group of junior researchers. Before his death in 1963, Schmalhausen wrote two more fundamental monographs, *The Origin of Terrestrial Vertebrates*[322] and *Regulation of Form Development During Individual Development*.

As a result of Minister Kaftanov's order, in 1948 Professor Aleksandr Formozov (1899–1973), the well-known naturalist, ecologist, and vertebrate zoologist, lost his job at Moscow University. He was also dismissed from the editorial board of the *Zoological Journal*.[323] This was punishment for Formozov's presentation, "Observation on Intraspecific Competition for Survival in Vertebrates," at the November 1947 conference. Fortunately, Professor Formozov was also an employee of the Academy Institute of Geography, where he headed the Biogeography Department from 1945 until 1963. The orders of the Academy Presidium and Minister Kaftanov targeted biological institutions only, and this saved Professor Formozov. He successfully continued to work on ecological and evolutionary problems of mammals and birds at the Institute of Geography. He was involved as well in the organization of a network of nature reserves in the USSR.

The fate of Professor Dmitrii Sabinin (1889–1951) was the most tragic.[324] His fundamental monograph on plant physiology was withdrawn from the publishing house. Lysenko could not forget that in the November 1947 conference, Sabinin presented the lecture "On Intraspecies Competition in Artificially Planted and Naturally Growing Plants," in which he completely destroyed Lysenko's theoretical inventions, using Lysenko's own examples of species. After two years of unemployment, Sabinin was accepted at the Academy Soil Institute. However, the new, pro-Lysenkoist secretary academician Oparin did not approve Sabinin's appointment, and Sabinin became an outcast in Moscow. Finally, Sabinin left Moscow for the Crimea and started to work on algae of the Black Sea. But all the pressure was too much for him, and on April 22, 1951, he shot himself.

Isaak Prezent (1902–1969) was triumphant. In 1948 Prezent, who had no training in biology, became an academician of the Agricultural Academy (he was on Stalin's list of appointees), dean of the Biology Faculty in Moscow, and chair of the Departments of Darwinism at both Moscow and Leningrad Universities. At the August 1948 Session of VASKhNIL, Prezent's speech (thirty pages) was only a little bit shorter than Lysenko's (thirty-nine pages). His conclusion was:

> . . . Our Soviet biologists, armed with the Michurinian doctrine, have already demonstrated the fallaciousness of Morganism up to the hill. Nobody will be led astray by the Morganists' false analogies between the invisible atom and the invisible gene. Far closer would be the analogy

between the invisible gene and the invisible spirit. . . . We shall continue to expose them [the Morganists] as adherents of an essentially false scientific trend, a pernicious and ideologically alien trend, brought to our country from foreign shores. (Applause.) We, Michurinists, will . . . develop this remarkable [Michurinist] doctrine by the efforts of the entire body of the many thousands of Michurinists. . . . The future in biology belongs to Michurin, and only to Michurin.[325]

A Party member since 1921, Prezent graduated from the Faculty of Social Sciences of Leningrad University in 1925 or 1926.[326] After that, it seems he worked for a year at Vavilov's All-Union Institute of Plants.[327] By 1930, he was a senior staff member at the Leningrad Division of the Communist Academy, president of the Society of Materialist Biologists, and a docent at Leningrad Pedagogical Institute (College).[328] In 1931, Prezent was appointed chair of the Department of Dialectics of Nature and Evolutionary Theory, which he created at Leningrad University. The goal of this department was to connect biology with Marxist dialectic materialism, or simply to introduce Party control in biology.

In 1930–1931, Prezent participated in the campaign against Boris Raikov, a professor at Leningrad Pedagogical Institute.[329] Professor Raikov (1880–1966) was also president of the Society for the Propagation of Natural Science Education. Prezent denounced Professor Raikov as an "agent of the world bourgeoisie" and accused him and the society of teaching "a passive 'love of nature.'" Professor Raikov was arrested in 1931, tried, and exiled to the north. He returned to Leningrad only in 1945 and was elected a member of the Academy of Pedagogical Sciences.[330]

In 1929, Prezent met Lysenko for the first time at the First All-Union Congress of Geneticists and Breeders.[331] In May 1932, Prezent, with a group of students, visited Lysenko's Institute of Genetics and Breeding in Odessa (now in the Ukraine).[332] Then, in May 1933, Prezent and Lysenko went together to Askaniya Nova, a nature reserve located at the mouth of the Dnieper River (Khersonsky Region, currently the Ukraine).[333] Their negative attitude to the complex research of the reserve ecosystem (the reserve preserved a part of the natural steppe) was fruitful: In August of the same year, an OGPU commission arrived in Askaniya Nova to investigate the director of the reserve, the ornithologist and zoogeographer Professor Vladimir Stanchinsky (1882–1941) and his staff.[334]

Evidently, Prezent could not forget Professor Stanchinsky's humiliating response at the Fourth All-Union Meeting of Zoologists in 1930. In a commentary on Stanchinsky's presentation, Prezent expressed doubts that ecology should be considered a science without the approval of Party leaders.

Stanchinsky's answer to Prezent was quick and sharp.[335] In autumn of 1933, the OGPU commission arrested three leading scientists of the reserve, the zoologists S. Medvedev and A. Gunali and the veterinarian F. Orlovsky. On February 24, 1934, Professor Stanchinsky was also arrested by the NKVD. He was condemned to five years' forced labor and served his term as an imprisoned veterinarian at the NKVD agricultural farms. Stanchinsky was released in 1936 and managed to get a job at the Central Forest Reserve in Central Russia. On June 29, 1941, he was arrested again (most former political prisoners were arrested once more after the Nazi invasion on June 22). Stanchinsky died in Vologda Prison soon after he had been tried by the OSO, which condemned him to ten years' forced labor as "a socially dangerous and a former condemned person."

In 1934, Prezent was fired from Leningrad University and moved to Lysenko's Institute of Genetics and Breeding in Odessa.[336] He immediately became Lysenko's close collaborator as the ideologist and philosopher of "Michurinist biology."[337] In 1935, he was also appointed coeditor of Lysenko's journal *Vernalization*.[338] Later, he lectured again on his "purified" Soviet Darwinism to the students of Leningrad University.[339]

After Prezent became chair of the Darwinism Departments at Moscow and Leningrad Universities in 1948, Lysenko's supporters replaced serious scientists. Notorious Lysenkoists became professors of Darwinism (Fyodor Dvoryankin) and genetics (Noi Feiginson and Faina Kuperman) at Moscow University. Professor Sabinin was replaced by the Lysenkoist Boris Ruban. Others, like the ichthyologist Nikolai Lebedev, moved to the "purified" Department of Darwinism. At Leningrad University, famous zoologists, embryologists, and evolutionists like Professors Nikolai Gerbil'sky, Yurii Polyansky, Pavel Terent'ev, and Pavel Svetlov lost their jobs.[340] The chair of the Genetics Department, Mikhail Lobashov, was replaced by the Lysenkoist Nikolai Turbin.

Prezent introduced his own course of "Darwinism" at both faculties. I remember clearly this thick mimeographed volume. It was a real struggle to read because of the unwieldy demagogic language and terminology of the "truly Marxist dialectics." Of course, all Lysenko's inventions were presented as real facts. Not only students but also professors were obliged to attend Prezent's lectures for "re-education" in the Party-approved Michurinist biology.[341]

The exams at the end of this course had a specific reputation among students: Prezent preferred to invite female students to his apartment for the exam. Knowing this, strong male students accompanied their female classmates to the apartment of Professor Prezent and stayed there until the end of the exam.[342] Prezent clearly suffered from the psychological complex of a short man. He wore shoes with very high heels and a tall green hat.[343]

The fall of Prezent at Moscow University was quick and unexpected. It had nothing to do with biology. The anti-Semitic wave that had become, since 1947, step by step, the new "Party line" played the main role. Beginning in late 1949, letters with complaints about Prezent (usually unsigned) overflowed the Ministry of Higher Education, the Council of Ministers, and the Party Central Committee's Department on Science. Gennadii Kostyrchenko, a researcher on anti-Semitism during Stalin's era, found the following unsigned appeal in one of the Moscow archives:

[Prezent] does nothing but deprive the youth in many ways. . . . He dismissed from Moscow University widely-known Russian scientists: Academicians M. M. Zavadovsky, I. I. Schmalhausen; Professors D. A. Sabinin, A. A. Paramonov; and many others. They were replaced by ignorami of the Jewish nationality, such as N. I. Feiginson, F. M. Kuperman, . . . and others. These sorts of replacements are deeply subversive actions. The university that bears the name of the great Russian scientist Lomonosov has no room for real Russian scientists; whereas the Jewish ignorami develop Russian science.[344]

Of course, only a few Lysenkoists were of Jewish origin (more precisely, of the "Jewish nationality," as was written in Soviet passports). Others were Russians, and some were Armenians or Ukrainians like Lysenko. But in the atmosphere of the late 1940s, during the "fight against the Cosmopolitans," such letters worked well. On May 26, 1950, Prezent was dismissed by resolution of the Central Committee.[345] Another Lysenkoist, Dvoryankin, was appointed to chair the Department of Darwinism. Prezent remained a full member of the Agricultural Academy and from time to time continued his attacks on the hated Mendelists-Morganists.

I remember Prezent in the middle of the 1950s. Sometimes my father took me to dinner at the restaurant at the Moscow Scientists Club. Only doctors of science could join this organization, and their family members had the right to attend the numerous events and performances at this elite place.[346] It was (and still is) located in an old, partly reconstructed prerevolutionary mansion, and some of its rooms had old richly decorated interiors. The restaurant was located in a former winter garden with walls made of deep yellow marble with bronze decorations attached to them. An additional glass wall divided the whole space into two rooms of uneven size. According to rumors, this enormous glass was brought from Venice. There were about twelve tables in the main part of the restaurant behind the glass wall, and usually the same people had dinner there almost every day.

One day a short man with a square figure, curly half-gray hair, and mustache appeared at one of the tables. I had the impression that the mustache gave this person a resemblance to Charlie Chaplin. He tried hard to escape meeting my father or coming close to him even accidentally. My father told me that this man was Prezent. Prezent was afraid not only that a Michurinist-Mendelist would not give him his hand, but that this Mendelist-Morganist would slap his face. Sometimes such things happened to Prezent.

In 1969, a few days before he died of cancer, Prezent was expelled from the Agricultural Academy.[347] Shortly before his death, he visited one of his enemies, Professor Roskin. Later Dr. Kalinnikova, one of Roskin's coworkers, recalled:

> One day, when the whole [Roskin's] laboratory staff gathered [at Roskin's office], somebody knocked at the door and a little bit strange head of a short man appeared. The expression on Grigorii Iosifovich [Roskin's] face changed immediately and he asked us to leave the office for a while. We understood that something unusual had happened. After we returned to his office, there was anger on Professor's face: "Do you know who had just come to me? Bloody Prezent! He asked me to provide him with *cruzin*. I did not give it to him . . ."[348]

Academician Aleksandr Oparin (1894–1980) was another who gained significantly from the August 1948 Session. In 1949, he became secretary academician of the Biology Division instead of Academician Orbeli. In contrast to Prezent, he was a serious scientist and the author of a theory on the origin of life. The first version of his book *Origin of Life* was published in Russian in 1924, and the English edition that appeared in 1938 was widely read by Western scientists.[349] He became corresponding member of the academy in 1939, academician in 1946, and director of the Bach Institute of Biochemistry in 1946. But from the 1940s–1960s, Oparin was more a Soviet official than a scientist. Besides his positions at the academy, in 1950 he was appointed a member of the International Council for Peace, and in 1952 and 1962, he was elected vice president of the International Federation of Scientists.[350]

During his years of power, Academician Oparin was an open pro-Lysenkoist. I have already mentioned his role in the tragic fate of Sabinin. He became even more famous as a supporter of Olga Lepeshinskaya and her pseudotheory on "the origin of cells from noncellular matter."

Lepeshinskaya (1871–1963), an old Bolshevik, a personal friend of Lenin, and an active Party functionary, started her biological studies in the 1920s, when she was over fifty years old.[351] In the 1930s, she published a few papers on "the origin of the cells from non-cellular matter," which were seriously criticized by many scientists, including Professor Koltsov.[352] It was evident

that all Lepeshinskaya's "discoveries" were simply based on artifacts (i.e., arti-
ficial substances or structures formed during the preparation of microscop-
ic slides) obtained because of poorly and nonprofessionally made histology
preparations (she worked at home with her daughter, granddaughter, and
daughter's husband, who assisted her). It is funny that Lepeshinskaya's husband, Panteleimon, also an old Bolshevik, was the only person who understood very well what was going on. He told their mutual acquaintance,
Yakov Rapoport: "Do not listen to her: She does not know anything about
science and says complete nonsense."[353]

Finally, with the help of another old Bolshevik, F. Petrov, in 1945
Lepeshinskaya managed to publish a monograph under the same title as her
theory. It had a foreword written by Lysenko and one of his closest coworkers, the VASKhNIL academician Ivan Glushchenko. The book described
Lepeshinskaya's experiments in which, for instance, red blood cells "were
developed" from yolk.

After Lysenko's victory in 1948 and using her Party connections in the
Central Committee, Lepeshinskaya initiated a joint meeting of the Academy
Biology Division, the Medical Academy, and representatives of the
Agricultural Academy. This meeting took place on May 22–24, 1950.
Academician Oparin presided over the commission that organized it. He
formulated the goal of the meeting:

> The attempts to create living systems are possible . . . only in the Soviet
> Union. Such attempts are not possible anywhere in capitalist countries
> because of the ideological position. . . . I think that the goal of the meet-
> ing should be the criticism and destruction of . . . the last basics of the
> Mendelism in our country, the Virchowian description of the cell theory
> [i.e., that a cell can be originated only from another cell].[354]

Twenty-seven speakers praised Lepeshinskaya's alleged discovery, including one of Mairanovsky's supporters, Academician Speransky. Some of them
were forced to speak by personal order from the Central Committee.[355]

The same year (1950), Lepeshinskaya received the highest Soviet award,
the Stalin Prize. Two years later, in 1952, with the involvement of Oparin, a
second joint conference of the Medical Academy and the Academy Biology
Division on the problem of cell origin was organized. As Lepeshinskaya
declared, "[U]sing experimental methods . . . a new dialectical-materialistic
theory on the origin of all cells from non-living matter has been developed."[356]

All this nonsense was stopped only after Stalin's death. However, Oparin
continued to be an admirer of Lysenko. In 1954, he wrote:

The August 1948 Session of the VASKhNIL and the joint session of the USSR Academy of Sciences and the USSR Academy of Medical Sciences [i.e., the session of 1950 on physiology] had a profound influence on the development of Soviet biological science. They were turning points after which all branches of biology in our country started to be developed on the basis of materialistic principles of the Michurinist biology and Pavlov physiology. . . . Our duty is to continue to guard biological science from the influence of foreign reactionary concepts of Morganism and vitalism.[357]

Finally, in 1956 Oparin was dismissed from his secretary academician position after three Leningrad anti-Lysenkoists, Vladimir Aleksandrov, Dmitrii Lebedev, and Yurii Olenov, wrote a letter addressed to the Presidium (former Politburo) of the Communist Party.[358] The letter was signed by 297 biologists, including academicians, corresponding members of the academy, and professors. Some were Party members and even pro-Lysenkoists. The letter consisted of five points, including "change the leadership of the Biology Division of the Academy," that is, dismiss Oparin. Academician Engelhardt, the anti-Lysenkoist, replaced Oparin as the new secretary academician.

Besides his duties at the academy, Oparin was a professor at Moscow University. For us students, he seemed a "model" academician: Large and tall, with a mustache and a small beard, Oparin dressed smartly and always wore a bow tie. When I was a fourth-year student, he taught a course on technical biochemistry. Despite his impressive and pretentious appearance, the lectures were quite dull. It is very difficult to say why, but after the second lecture, students refused to attend them. There was something false in Oparin's manner that students did not like. This refusal created a serious scandal: Such a famous and highly positioned scientist found an hour per week to come to the university, but ungrateful students did not want to listen to his lectures!

A TYPICAL LYSENKOIST

In the late 1940s, the Lysenkoist style of argument was introduced in all spheres of biology. In 1948, Nikolai Lebedev, a professor at the Lysenkoist Department of Darwinism at Moscow University, started to destroy the work of invertebrate zoologists of that faculty.

Fifteen years before that, in 1934, my father and his professor at the time, Lev Zenkevich (later secretary academician of the Academy Division of Oceanology, Atmosphere Physics, and Geography),[359] published a paper in which they proposed to introduce a worm, *Nereis succinea*, from the Azov into the Caspian Sea.[360] For an unknown reason, the benthic invertebrates that lived on the bottom of the Caspian Sea began to die out in the 1930s, and the peak of their death was in 1937. The sharp depletion in these organisms, which were the food of many fish, especially caviar-producing sturgeons, strongly affected the number of all fish in the Caspian Sea. Urgent measures were needed. After several years of experiments, it was shown that the Sea of Azov worm *Nereis* could be a candidate for survival in the Caspian Sea. From 1939–1941, on the order of the Politburo member Anastas Mikoyan, special expeditions transported the worm from the Sea of Azov to three locations in the Caspian Sea.

By 1946, the success of the project was evident: Not only had the worm become a common member of the Caspian Sea benthic fauna, but fish (especially sturgeons) had started to feed on it.[361] The introduction was considered a serious scientific development, and in 1948, a group of scientists from the Zoological Museum of Moscow University (my father and Professor Zenkevich) and from the All-Union Scientific Research Institute of Fisheries and Oceanography (VNIRO) was recommended by the USSR Ministry of Fisheries for the prestigious Stalin Prize. Nikolai Lebedev, who did not participate in the work, also wanted to be among the awarded, but the real participants rejected his request.

Out of spite, Lebedev wrote a strongly negative review of the *Nereis* project addressed to the State Committee on Stalin Prizes, which he thought would be kept secret. His main point was that the introduced worm was a carnivore invertebrate that depleted the fauna. This was a lie—anyone who ever opened a textbook on invertebrate zoology and read about oligochaet worms knows this. In his review, Lebedev simply invented data that did not exist in scientific papers he cited and falsified maps of animal distribution in the Caspian Sea. To persuade those who did not know anything about invertebrates, Lebedev filmed a "documentary" about *Nereis*. An ugly worm enlarged to a dimension of the whole movie screen looked as if it might really be a terrible carnivore.

The campaign against my father and Professor Zenkevich started. The decision of the Biology Faculty Party Bureau (the Communist Party organization in every Soviet institution elected its bureau and its secretary, and the bureau and its secretary controlled all details of life of the institution) recommended their dismissal. During those years, such a decision was the precursor of an MGB investigation.[362] All types of accusations were used, from the label "Morganists" to "Cosmopolitans" (Jews). The last was not true in the case of Professor Zenkevich, since he was a descendant of Polish nobility. But, of course, the fact that Zenkevich was arrested by the OGPU for a short time in 1933[363] was used against him. As a result of the campaign, my father was forced to leave the university for several years. He became a professor at the Pedagogical Institute in the city of Yaroslavl, about 200 miles north of Moscow. During those days, many scientists and professors who lost their jobs because of persecutions or Jewish names were accepted in the institutes in small towns around Moscow.

The fight continued. In 1953, a special conference on the problem of acclimatization of *Nereis* took place. New scientific data supported the previous results that had indicated the success of the project.[364] The materials of the conference were published as a book, *Acclimatization of Nereis in the Caspian Sea*. It received an award from the Moscow Society of Naturalists (MOIP), at the time the only organization free of the Lysenkoists. The authors of the *Nereis* project were recommended for the Stalin Prize for the second time but, of course, did not get it because of the pressure of the Biology Faculty Party organization.

On January 29, 1955, Valentin Kaverin, who was a famous Soviet writer and the brother of well-known epidemiologist and virusologist Lev Zilber, published an article entitled, "On Honesty in Science," in the newspaper *Literaturnaya Gazeta*.[365] Kaverin described in detail the falsifications and insinuations Lebedev had used in the attempt to destroy the *Nereis* project. The article had no effect on Lebedev. He published a new paper in which he simply repeated his previous manipulation of data. Lebedev's paper was criticized in a series of serious scientific publications.[366] My father wrote: "The question of the reason why N.V. Lebedev tried to prove [the negative effect of *Nereis* in the Caspian Sea] is outside of this article."[367] Most of the readers knew the answer—greed and desire for more power were Lebedev's motivations.

I met Lebedev for the first time in the early 1960s when he played the role of inquisitor in a student scandal. Three students secretly put a huge portrait of Lysenko into the women's bathroom and attached it to the water tank above the toilet. The next morning, nobody noticed that Lysenko's portrait was missing from the wall: There were many portraits of different officials along the corridors of the faculty. But a woman who entered the bathroom and saw the portrait hanging from the top became hysterical. The Party Bureau of the Biology Faculty immediately turned this stupid student prank into a "political case."

In 1962, Lysenko was still in power and enjoyed the complete support of General Party Secretary Nikita Khrushchev. The Party Bureau started its investigation, and as a member of the bureau, Professor Lebedev was put in charge of it. After lengthy interrogations of many students, the three "insurgents" were found. The ironic side of the story was that Dmitrii P., the son of a pro-Lysenkoist professor, Vasilii P., was the organizer of the prank. The

Party Bureau wanted to expel the three students from the university with the label of anti-Soviet political enemies. In order to do this, the students first had to be expelled from the Komsomol (Communist Youth Union) membership, and this could only be done at a Komsomol meeting of the biology students of our year. In the Soviet Union, almost every young person was a member of the Komsomol. It was almost impossible for a non-Komsomol member to be accepted to the university as a student.

But at this point, the whole procedure, which was so easily practiced during Stalin's years, suddenly stopped. At the meeting, students refused to vote to expel the "insurgents" from the Komsomol. Professor Lebedev shrieked uselessly at the disobedient audience: "You must vote! All workers of the world, even the Japanese, know Comrade Lysenko! He is a member of the Supreme Council of our Government! Those students who humiliated him must be punished!" In fact, Lysenko was deputy head of the USSR Supreme Soviet earlier, from 1938 till 1956.[368] Lebedev looked very strange during his tirades. For some reason, in those days he always wore a huge "Rembrandt" beret. Despite all the pressure, the students refused to vote against the three pranksters at this and at a later organized meeting.

Finally, the administration expelled the three from the university without a political charge for two years. Using his friendly connections, the pro-Lysenkoist professor put his son into a mental hospital for several months (where he was not treated). This boy was readmitted to the university the next year, and the other two were readmitted two years later.

During those years, Lebedev lectured on the so-called creative Darwinism. There were two teachers of this Darwinism, Department Chair Fyodor Dvoryankin and Lebedev. Dvoryankin looked the part of a fanatic—extremely thin, frequently dressed up in a Russian folk shirt (in contrast to the "bourgeois" professors of nonproletarian or peasant origin). He energetically tried to persuade students of the reality of all Lysenko's "miracles," including the lack of intraspecies competition and the existence of a kind of solidarity within plant species. Lebedev was also very emotional. I cannot forget his last lecture of the course. He plainly stated that the modern discoveries of molecular biology did not prove the physical existence of genes and that DNA had nothing to do with inheritance. He ended the lecture by drawing the main postulate of molecular biology on the board: The word "DNA," with an arrow pointing to the word "RNA," and a second arrow pointing from RNA to the word "protein." Then Lebedev said: "Professor Belozersky tells you that DNA codes proteins through RNA. This is not true." Suddenly he raised his voice and screamed: "This *does not* exist!" And he angrily crossed out the drawing several times with a piece of chalk.

Naturally, Lebedev's role in the *Nereis* saga and in the story of Lysenko's portrait and his lectures on "creative Darwinism" were not mentioned in his obituary, which presented him only as a prominent ichthyologist.[369]

THE *CRUZIN* CASE

The so-called *cruzin,* or KR, case was one of the most famous in the history of Soviet biology and medicine of the late 1940s. Academician Vasilii Parin (1903–1971), a well-known physiologist, was tried in 1948 as a "traitor" and condemned to twenty-five years' imprisonment as an "American spy" (Document 23, Appendix II).[370] He was found guilty of giving a copy of a manuscript of a book about a new anti-cancer preparation, *cruzin,* written by two Moscow researchers, Professors Grigory Roskin and Nina Klyueva, to American colleagues. Roskin (1892–1964) was a prominent protozoologist and cytologist, a pupil of Nikolai Koltsov. From 1930, he headed the Department of Histology and Embryology at Moscow State University.[371] Beginning in 1927, he studied the difference between malignant and normal cells, and in 1931, his research focused on the anti-cancer effect of the parasitic protozoan *Trypanozoma cruzi.* Together with his wife, the microbiologist Klyueva (1898–1971) of the Institute of Epidemiology, Microbiology, and Contagious Diseases within the Medical Academy, Dr. Roskin developed a method of extraction of the anti-cancer substance from this parasite. Evidently, a specific surface membrane glycoprotein of *Trypanozoma* acts as a tumor suppressor.[372]

At first the substance was named KR, and then *cruzin.* "'K' and 'R' turned out to be wife and husband, charming, modest, and obviously devoted to each other and to their work," wrote American ambassador Walter Bedell Smith in his memoirs about meeting the scientists at Klyueva's institute on June 20, 1946.[373] The book, titled *The Biotherapy of Malignant Tumors,* which summarized the results of fifteen years of experiments with *cruzin,* was published in Russian in 1946.[374] Its second edition was translated into English and published in England only in 1963.[375] In 1946, Roskin and Klyueva's research was approved and supported by the highest level of the Soviet state, the Politburo members.[376] *The Biotherapy of Malignant Tumors* had already been in print when Professor Parin, at the time secretary academician of the Medical Academy, gave the manuscript to American colleagues during his visit to the United States in 1947.

Dr. Parin started his career in physiology at Kazan University (1925–1928), then continued his work at Perm University (1928–1932). From 1933–1940, he headed the Department of Normal Physiology at the Sverdlovsk (now Ekaterinburg) Medical Institute and in 1940 was promoted to director there.[377] In 1941, the thirty-eight-year-old Parin was appointed director of the First Moscow Medical Institute and then, in 1942, became deputy USSR commissar (minister) of health in charge of science. Professor Parin was the main organizer of the Medical Academy, which was created on December 20, 1944, mainly to oppose VIEM.[378] Mairanovsky's supporters, the academicians Speransky and Grashchenkov (VIEM director), were against establishing this new academy. Parin alone wrote a draft of the structure of the academy and its institutions. Nikolai Burdenko (1876–1946) was appointed president (1944–1946), and Parin was to be secretary academician of the new academy.

The *cruzin* case attracted Stalin's personal attention. He ordered the creation of a special commission of the Politburo, and Beria and Andrei Zhdanov were appointed the heads. On January 28, 1947, Zhdanov summoned Klyueva to the Kremlin for an interrogation. He was especially interested in "how it could happen that they [Klyueva and Roskin] were unable to maintain priority in the hands of Soviet scientists and [that] the secret of producing the preparation became known to the Americans."[379] Also, Zhdanov asked Klyueva about the visit of Ambassador Smith to her laboratory. On February 17, 1947, Parin, Roskin, and Klyueva were ordered to come to the Kremlin to attend a meeting of the commission. As Roskin recalled later, the meeting took place in a highly charged atmosphere.[380] They were kept waiting for a long time, and the tension and nervousness were extreme when Stalin finally appeared and started to walk back and forth in the room. It was clear that Stalin had studied the book by Roskin and Klyueva attentively. When he addressed the audience, he read the detailed notes that he had made in the margins of the book.

During the meeting, members of the Politburo commission reported that Academician Parin had proven that he had had permission from Minister of Health Georgii Miterev to publish Roskin and Klyueva's papers in American scientific journals, but Minister Miterev stated that he had not given such permission.[381] Miterev burst into tears and said that he was not guilty of anything. However, Stalin's words were decisive. He said: "I do not trust him [i.e., Prof. Parin]."[382] The fate of Professor Parin was determined, and he was arrested. Minister Miterev was replaced by Efim Smirnov.

Following Stalin's recommendations, Roskin and Klyueva were not arrested but officially named as "traitors," "anti-patriots," and so on in the press and at Communist Party meetings.[383] This was easy to do in 1947, due to the fact that Professor Roskin was a Jew, and the anti-Semitic campaign in the USSR against the "cosmopolitans" was underway. Roskin and Klyueva were tried by a Court of Honor on June 5, 1947, in the overcrowded club hall of the Council of Ministers.[384] The main Party ideologist, Politburo member, and Central Committee secretary Andrei Zhdanov personally wrote the scenario of the court trial and the text of the speech of the public prosecutor.[385] Zhdanov also directed the rehearsals of the trial.

From June 5–7, 1947, the open sessions of the court took place at the Variety Theater in Moscow.[386] Thousands of specially selected spectators came to watch the show. During the first day, Roskin and Klyueva were publicly interrogated. The second day was devoted to the testimonies of the "witnesses," members of the court, and representatives of the audience. On the third day, the public prosecutor presented his accusation. Roskin and Klyueva were announced to have been guilty of "anti-patriotic behavior," "treason against the Motherland," and they were publicly reprimanded.

The detailed transcripts of all speeches were sent to the Politburo every day. Members of the Politburo attentively followed the first trial of the Court of Honor. Professor Nikolai Blokhin, who later became president of the Medical Academy and supported Mairanovsky, played an active role in the persecution of the two scientists. Academicians Boris Zbarsky and Ivan Strashun were among those who, during the second day of the trial, especially attacked the two "murderers in white coats,"[387] as Roskin and Klyueva were called, for treason against the Motherland. Zbarsky finished his speech by saying: "Clean yourselves of the disgrace and shame that you have inflicted upon yourselves by your unworthy deeds—you have never been patriots."[388] This detestable speech did not save Zbarsky from his fate: Five years after this incident, he was arrested as a Jewish member of the "Doctors' Plot."

Surprisingly, Roskin and Klyueva were not arrested. Moreover, a month later, on July 12, 1947, the Soviet Council of Ministers ordered all ministries involved in the *cruzin* project "to help Professor Klyueva with materials and equipment to build her laboratory."[389] Evidently, the whole show was organized to frighten the intelligentsia, especially scientists.

On June 17, the Central Committee of the Party issued a secret letter, "On the Case of Professors Klyueva and Roskin," to the Party organizations of all the country's institutions. It started the propaganda campaign against the "anti-patriots fawning before the West," which from the beginning had a clear anti-Semitic character. Before being arrested, Parin was named as a spy over 100 times during the same procedure of the Court of Honor by a chairman of this court, Professor A. Shabanov.[390] In the middle of July, the Central Committee ordered a halt to publishing the English translation of such Soviet scientific journals as *Journal of Physics* and *Acta Physica-Chemica*, and even the translated contents of the Russian versions of the journals and abstracts of the articles.[391]

After a yearlong "investigation," on April 8, 1948, Academician Parin was convicted by the OSO as "a traitor of the Motherland" (Article 58-1a) and sentenced to twenty-five years' imprisonment.[392] At first he was sent to the city of Norilsk, at the time a center of labor camps famous for their terrible conditions. Fortunately, he was recalled on the way to Norilsk and incarcerated in Vladimir Prison, where he was kept as an "American spy." For part of his term here, Parin shared Cell No. 13 with professor of history Lev Rakov and the writer Daniil Andreev.[393] Together, these cell mates managed to secretly write a book, *The Newest Plutarch*, which was eventually published in 1991.[394] Parin wrote forty-four stories for the book.

Parin was released after Stalin's death, in November 1953. He successfully continued his scientific and administrative career. In 1960, he became director of the Institute of Normal and Pathologic Physiology of the Medical Academy, and from 1965 to 1969, he was director of the newly organized Institute of Medical-Biological Problems. In 1966, he was elected to the USSR Academy of Sciences, and from 1967 until his death in 1971, Academician Parin was vice president of the Medical Academy. As for Professor Roskin, in 1956 he received a personal letter from the new leader of the state and the Communist Party, Nikita Khrushchev.[395] In this letter Khrushchev apologized for the persecution of Roskin and Klyueva (surely a unique gesture from a Communist Party leader to a nonmember of the Party). After this, Roskin was able to continue his work at Moscow University.

I remember the two main figures of the "cruzin affair," Professor Roskin and Academician Parin. As a student, I met Professor Roskin from time to time at the Biology Faculty of Moscow University. With a mustache, smartly dressed, he looked like a typical representative of the old Russian prerevolutionary intelligentsia. Sometimes I saw him talking to my father; they had a lot in common, especially their passion for invertebrate zoology. During those days I knew about the history of cruzin in general, but I became aware of the details much later, after Professor Roskin and my father had already died and, unfortunately, I had no opportunity to question them.

For a couple of years, in the early 1960s, Dr. Parin's youngest son, Aleksei, was my close friend, and I frequently visited his huge apartment full of books in a building not far from downtown Moscow. Several times I met Aleksei's father, an extremely polite and educated person with a kind facial expression, who never showed that he held a high-level official position in the Soviet scientific hierarchy. Of course, I knew that he had been arrested during the Stalin years. Also I knew that because of his arrest, Aleksei's eldest brother, Vasilii, was expelled from the Medical Institute and was forced to work as a mover for a while (later he became a famous Moscow surgeon). And I knew that the whole family (Aleksei's other brother, his sister, and especially his mother) had a very difficult time before Stalin died. But I did not know the details of the story described above. During those days, it was not polite to talk about somebody's arrest and imprisonment.

TWO WHO DID NOT BOW

One person, Iosif Rapoport (1911–1990), spoiled the triumph of Lysenko at the August 1948 Session of VASKhNIL. This short, thin geneticist with an eye patch over his left eye dared to interrupt Lysenko and his cronies with sharp comments. The stenographers were so frightened that only twenty years later one of them told Rapoport: "We stenographers decided not to put your sharpest phrases in writing."[396] However, they did include the bit where Rapoport screamed "Obscurantists!" in the middle of Lysenkoist Nikolai Turbin's speech.[397]

Real geneticists were not invited to the session, and it was clear that the organizers of the session would do everything in their power to pretend that every biologist had finally accepted Lysenko's ideas. "Most people of the audience," Rapoport wrote later, "were those whom Lysenko promised to put quickly in high positions, making them 'Generals' and 'Admirals' (his own words)."[398] Rapoport, who received his ticket from an acquaintance, gave the only speech in opposition to the Lysenkoists. The journalist Mark Popovsky recalled later:

> . . . I can still see the figure of Iosif Rapoport, with his black curls and boyish expression. He looked very handsome in his military tunic without shoulder boards but with rows of medal ribbons on his chest. Even the black bandage over an empty eye socket did not disfigure him, but lent a keener expression to his pale nervous face. His address, too—he was a candidate of science at the time—was nervous but firm in tone. He confined himself in the main to purely scientific points: that genes were a physical reality, that mutations could be controlled, that genetics had been of great benefit to mankind and could produce many more useful results. He ended with the blameless statement that "only on the basis of honesty and criticism of our own mistakes can we advance toward the great success to which our country calls us."[399]

After five minutes, Rapoport was interrupted by Pavel Lobanov, chairman of the session, deputy minister of agriculture, and newly appointed VASKhNIL academician. Later, in April 1956, Lobanov replaced Lysenko as VASKhNIL president.[400] As Popovsky recalled, after Rapoport's speech, "the applause was mingled with hostile whistling."[401] The speech was published in *Pravda* with unauthorized changes.[402] Rapoport's letter to the newspaper requesting it to publish his authorized changes was not answered. When Rapoport called the chief editor (and Central Committee member) Pyotr Pospelov, the editor answered: "*Pravda* never makes a mistake."[403]

The punishment was immediate. In September 1948, Rapoport was fired from the Academy Institute of Cytology, Histology, and Embryology (Koltsov's former institute). On January 5, 1949, the Party organization of this institute expelled him from the Communist Party.[404] According to Party rules, the decision was approved by the bureau of the regional Party organization. This meeting, as described by a participant, was quite unusual and colorful:

> At the meeting of the Regional Party Bureau Comrade Mityaev gave a political evaluation of Comrade Rapoport's behavior. In particular, he pointed to his [Rapoport's] demagogic anti-Party statements that the formal geneticists had supposedly been punished. In this way he [Rapoport] agreed with the bourgeois scientists of Britain and the United States. During [Mityaev's] speech Rapoport screamed and banged on the table and tried to confront the speaker. Therefore, at the Bureau meeting, as at the Party meeting at the Institute, Rapoport did not even try to accept his errors. On the contrary, out of bravado he claimed that he had his own point of view and was not afraid to defend it. But this point of view did not correspond to our Party line . . . [405]

All copies of the institute's journal with his last papers on the action of chemical mutagens were taken out of circulation and destroyed.[406] Rapoport found work as a geology technician, in which capacity he worked for years. He returned to genetics only in 1958.[407]

Rapoport started his scientific career as a postgraduate student of Professor Koltsov. However, World War II interrupted his research. In 1941, he volunteered for the Moscow People's Militia and spent five years of the war at different fronts. The People's Militia troops were formed in 1941 mainly in Moscow and Leningrad when the German Nazis were at the outskirts of these cities. These troops consisted of volunteers who were too old or were unqualified for the draft. Because of the disastrous situation at the fronts in autumn 1941, these troops were sent into battle with very little military training or equipment. Very few survived the first days of battle.

As an officer, Rapoport became legendary within the troops for his courage and was nominated three times for the highest military award, Hero of the Soviet Union. He did not receive it, however, because he often confronted higher commanders whose behavior he considered cowardly or unethical.[408] At the front, he joined the Communist Party. He defended his dissertation when he visited Moscow for a few days in 1943. He returned to the front even after he was wounded and lost his left eye.

In 1958, academician and Nobel laureate Nikolai Semenov organized the Department of Chemical Mutagenesis in his Academy Institute of Chemical Physics. Semenov, like Gleb Frank, was a typical prominent Soviet scientist who basically followed the demands of the regime.[409] But despite his successful career and conformism, Semenov also knew the dark side of Soviet science—during the 1940s–early 1950s he was falsely accused of plagiarism.[410] Additionally, he was a personal lifelong friend of the courageous academician Kapitsa.[411] Sometimes Semenov surprised his Party supervisors, and his inviting Rapoport to the institute was an example of this behavior. Rapoport was appointed head of the new Department of Chemical Mutagenesis only after an eight-month-long fight between Semenov and Party officials, who did not want this troubled geneticist to work in his field of expertise.[412]

In 1963, Rapoport and the English geneticist Charlotte Auerbach were nominated for the Nobel Prize for their developments in chemical mutagenesis. The Science Department of the Central Committee told Rapoport the condition under which the USSR Academy of Sciences would support his nomination—an appeal to the Party condemning his behavior toward Lysenko and the August 1948 Session. Despite the intense pressure, Rapoport categorically refused to write such an appeal. Following the Central Committee instruction, academy officials wrote to the Nobel Prize Committee that they would not support Rapoport's nomination.[413] Probably, this was the only case when a Nobel Prize in science was not given to a nominee because of his professional and human integrity. In 1979, Rapoport received the official Soviet recognition. He was elected a corresponding member of the academy. The life of this remarkable person ended in 1990 in a traffic accident. Because Rapoport had only one eye, he did not notice a car when he was crossing the street.

Another Koltsov pupil, Vladimir Efroimson (1908–1989), also strongly opposed the August 1948 Session. His action had more severe consequences. He was arrested by the MGB. I have already mentioned Efroimson's name above in connection with his first arrest in 1932, when the OGPU considered preparing a political case against Koltsov. After he was released from a labor camp in 1936, Efroimson worked until 1938 in Tashkent.[414] On the basis of experiments with the silkworm, he wrote a fundamental monograph on the genetics of this insect. The monograph had already been submitted to the publishing house, but it was not published because Efroimson was a former political prisoner. He moved to the All-Ukrainian Station of Silkworm Breeding in the Ukraine. There he wrote a new version of the monograph *Problems of Genetics, Selection, and Hybridization of the Silkworm.* The book was not published again. Moreover, Efroimson was fired. In the summer of 1941, a few days before the outbreak of war, Efroimson managed to defend his candidate dissertation.[415]

Efroimson served in the Red Army as an epidemiologist and a medical doctor from August 1941 until November 1945. He also volunteered for the military intelligence and took part in operations to capture German soldiers for interrogation. He knew exactly what would happen to him, a Jew and a Soviet officer, if he was caught by the Nazis. But German was his second language (he had graduated from Moscow German School), and he believed that because of his excellent German, it was his duty to be involved in intelligence.

At the August 1948 Session, Efroimson did not try to confront the Lysenkoists. As he usually explained, his wife (who was also a geneticist) had forbidden him to do so. She was too frightened by Lysenko's triumph. Yet Efroimson did act in his own eccentric way. After the session, he sent a written analysis of Lysenko's activity to the Science Department of the Communist Party Central Committee. Efroimson's second arrest by the MGB was the only response of Party officials to his letter.

When he was arrested in 1949, Efroimson was officially accused of "slandering the Soviet Army." In 1945, he wrote a report to army headquarters about having witnessed atrocities by Soviet soldiers against German civilians. I remember Efroimson's vivid description of a small German town after the conquest by the Red Army. Efroimson could not forget, for the rest of his life, how during the first night after the conquest, German women secretly sneaked out of town with young girls in an attempt to protect them from multiple rapes by Soviet soldiers.[416] But this was in 1945, and Efroimson's revolt against the atrocities had nothing to do with his letter against Lysenko in 1949 when he was taken to the MGB headquarters at Lubyanka Prison.

In fact, Efroimson was arrested because of his openly anti-Lysenkoist position. During the investigation, he even tried a hunger strike to force the MGB interrogator to change the accusation to the real anti-Lysenkoist issue. Finally, Efroimson was condemned to seven years' imprisonment in a labor camp, which he spent in the terrible Dzhezkazgan camps in Kazakhstan. Like prisoners of the Nazi camps, the inmates of Dzhezkazgan Special Camps had numbers on their clothes. "The numbers were painted on by prisoners with brushes and pots of black paint," the American Alexander Dolgun, who was in the same barrack with Efroimson, recalled later.[417]

After his release, even before he was rehabilitated in 1956, Efroimson wrote again from scratch his huge anti-Lysenko report, "On the Undermining of Soviet Agriculture and the International Prestige of Soviet Science." The first version of this manuscript had been confiscated during his arrest in 1949. Efroimson sent it now not to the Central Committee but to the USSR Chief Prosecutor's Office.[418] The biologist Zhores Medvedev, who in the 1960s wrote the first book on Lysenko and his crimes, *The Rise and Fall of T. D. Lysenko,* used this material for his research. Medvedev's book appeared as a *samizdat* (self-published) manuscript in Russian and was disseminated among scientists in 1962. The English version was published by Columbia University Press in 1969. There was no answer from the prosecutors, and Efroimson published several anti-Lysenko articles in different scientific journals. This was very difficult to do because of Lysenko's still overwhelming power in Soviet biology. Not only Efroimson but the editors of the journals as well needed great courage to publish such papers.

After Efroimson was released from the labor camp and returned to Moscow, as a former political prisoner he could not find a professional job as a geneticist. After terms in labor camps, former convicts accused of political crimes under Article 58 of the Russian Criminal Code needed to submit an appeal to the Prosecutor's Office for rehabilitation. Before being rehabilitated, former political prisoners were treated as criminals who had been convicted of real crimes. As such, former convicted scientists, of course, could not find a job as scientists or publish their scientific papers. Despite this, Efroimson was accepted at the newly opened Library of Foreign Literature. The director of this library, Margarita Rudomino, was a unique person. She managed to give jobs to many former political prisoners, which was not appreciated by Party officials. In 1961, working as a bibliographer, Efroimson wrote the first book in Russian on medical genetics, *Introduction to Medical Genetics.* It was published in 1964 only after the energetic intervention of Academician Vasilii Parin and physicist Academician Axel Berg on behalf of the book.[419]

In 1962, Efroimson received his Doctor of Biological Sciences diploma, fifteen years after he defended his thesis in 1947. It was not given to him before that because of his arrest. Finally, in 1967 Efroimson was accepted at the Moscow Institute of Psychiatry, where he headed the Genetics Department. In 1975, he was forced to retire from this post, and from then until his death, he was professor-consultant at the academy's N. K. Koltsov Institute of Developmental Biology.[420] This institute was organized in 1967 by another Koltsov pupil, Boris Astaurov.[421]

Efroimson's last two monographs, *Genetics of Ethics and Esthetics* and *Genius and Genetics,* were published in 1995 and 1998, unfortunately only in Russian, after his death.[422] These books have no parallel in scientific literature. Their analysis of human history, interpreted by a geneticist with the understanding of biological mechanisms of aspects of human behavior, required outstanding erudition and the ability to collect and analyze data in many fields. And Efroimson had these abilities. He could talk about history and literature for hours, and he was a workaholic, able to spend eighteen hours a day at his desk. He believed that human history showed that such characteristics as altruism, heroism, conscience, respect for old people, parental love, intellectual curiosity, and so on "have entered into the basic stock of man's inherited characteristics."[423]

Efroimson created a theory that he believed could help to select genetically gifted children. He naively thought that the Soviet authorities would be interested in finding such kids and creating the most favorable conditions for the development of their talents. It is sad that he valued this theory so much that he was afraid of meeting his former mate at the labor camp, the American Alexander Dolgun, after the latter had been released from imprisonment. This was understandable. Meetings with foreign citizens unsupervised by the KGB were still forbidden for Soviet citizens even during the late 1950s–1960s, and Efroimson did not want to jeopardize the theory he was working on. Later, Dolgun recalled: "We became very friendly in prison, although years later when I tried to look him up in Moscow he refused to see me because I was American and he feared a third term. But . . . in Dzhezkazgan, on our first meeting, he gave me some extra food he had saved and began to explain the camp routine to me. He seemed a man who knew his way around, and I decided to stick close to him at first, as long as I needed his help."[424]

Emotionally, it was not easy for me to write about Vladimir Pavlovich Efroimson. During the last years of his life, I spent many hours in his kitchen listening to his memories and discussing many scientific topics with him. When I received a telegram about his death, I was thousands of miles away from Moscow, above the Arctic Circle.[425] It was difficult for me to get to Moscow in time for his funeral. At first I persuaded somebody who had a car to take me through 300 miles of tundra to Murmansk. Then I almost had a fistfight with people standing in a long line in Murmansk for plane tickets to Moscow.

I felt strongly that I ought to pay my last respects to Vladimir Pavlovich: He was the only scientist who tried to help me when I lost my job and was not accepted at any institute because of my confrontation with the KGB. Efroimson did not ask me what my problem was; he had too much knowledge about the NKVD-MGB-KGB and figured out what was going on without questioning me. He simply said that he would accompany me to the Leninsky Region Party Committee and would demand they find a professional job for me (the main academy research institutes and Moscow University were located in this region of Moscow). And he did. Together we had an appointment with an official at the Science Department of the committee. Efroimson said: "I want him [i.e., me] to continue what I'm working on. For this purpose he must have a job." Of course, nothing came of this attempt. But Efroimson was the only one who tried to help. The others whom I asked for help refused.

MORE OPPOSITION IN MOSCOW

In 1952, two scientific magazines, the *Botanical Journal* and *Bulletin of the Moscow Society of Naturalists*, started to publish papers that strongly criticized Lysenko's "creative Darwinism." Academician Vladimir Sukachev (1880–1967), director of the Academy Institute of Forestry, chief editor of the *Botanical Journal*, president of the Botanical Society since 1948, and president of the Moscow Society of Naturalists since 1955, was behind this anti-Lysenko campaign.[426] Sukachev was elected corresponding member in 1920, and academician in 1943. His Institute of Forestry had worked on the problem of intraspecies competition since 1925.[427] During the 1940s–1950s, Sukachev was a member of the bureau of the Academy Biology Division. This high position within the academy structure helped him to become a leader of the campaign against Lysenko. However, many years before his uncompromising fight against Lysenko, in the early 1930s, Sukachev had used Marxist political slang against his scientific rivals, calling them counterrevolutionaries, and so on.[428] Evidently, this was because he was a member of the Bolshevik Party.

In 1952, the *Botanical Journal* started the campaign with a paper written by one of the main former supporters of Lysenko, Nikolai Turbin. After the August 1948 Session, Turbin was appointed chair of the Department of Genetics and Selection at Leningrad University. Now he openly wrote that Lysenko's experiments were unsubstantiated.[429] Among other Lysenkoists, at the beginning of 1953, Academician Oparin published a furious answer to the attack of the *Botanical Journal* under the title "I. V. Stalin, the Inspirer of the Leading Biological Science":

For all Soviet biologists, this document [the text of Lysenko's speech at the August 1948 Session], personally reviewed by I. V. Stalin, is a precious program for the creative development of biology, one that defines its course and goals. Soviet creative Darwinism constitutes the granite foundation, the solid base on which all branches of biology are tempestuously developing.[430]

It was a little bit late to use Stalin's name to defend Lysenko. On March 5, 1953, Stalin died.

The *Botanical Journal* invited Lysenko to write an article about his views. The paper "A New Departure in the Science of Biological Species" was published in the first 1953 issue of the journal.[431] It repeated Lysenko's usual statements about species transformations. Sukachev's paper "On the Intraspecies and Interspecies Relationships Among Plants" followed Lysenko's article. Sukachev analyzed Lysenko's arguments in detail and revealed their scientific weakness.[432] After that, methodically, one after another, anti-Lysenkoist articles appeared in the *Botanical Journal*.[433]

In 1954, the Moscow Society of Naturalists (MOIP) also started to publish a series of anti-Lysenkoist articles in its *Bulletin*. Established in 1805, the MOIP was the oldest Russian scientific society.[434] It was possibly the only scientific institution in the Soviet Union that managed to continue and maintain ethical traditions in science. In 1931, the then president of MOIP, the zoologist Menzbir, wrote a letter to Molotov in defense of an arrested member of the society, physicist academician Pyotr Lazarev, and Lazarev was released.[435] Although it was a part of the Moscow University structure, the society managed to withstand Lysenkoism with minor losses. According to the memoirs of the geologist academician Aleksandr Yanshin, in 1949 the president of MOIP, the chemist and academician Nikolai Zelinsky (1861–1953), in response to the August 1948 Session of VASKhNIL organized the Genetics Section within the society.[436] Zelinsky was one of the founders of organic synthesis and oil chemistry. Also, in 1915, during World War I, he invented a gas mask with a charcoal filter. He was elected to the academy in 1929.

In 1950–1951, three employees of the society with Jewish last names were dismissed.[437] One of them, the MOIP scientific secretary, the outstanding botanist and historian of biology Sergei Lipschitz (1905–1983), was in charge of publishing the multivolume *Dictionary of Russian Botanists*. The publication was stopped in 1952 after four volumes had been published. Four more volumes, prepared by Lipschitz, have never been printed. Academician Sukachev, chief editor of the *Dictionary*, and the MOIP vice president, Corresponding Member Pavel Baranov, were ordered to report to the Central Committee about the *Dictionary*.[438] The meeting was presided over by the Politburo main ideologist, Mikhail Suslov. The highest Party officials could not believe the information they heard—in 1952, during the peak of the "fight against cosmopolitans," an author with the Jewish name Lipschitz dared to publish a dictionary that contained biographies of the enemies of people, emigrants, and so forth. Lipschitz even tried to include the biography of Lysenko's archenemy Nikolai Vavilov in the second volume with information about his death. The date was given as January 23, 1943, which is wrong. But one can only guess how difficult it must have been during Stalin's time when the fate of Vavilov was kept completely secret for Dr. Lipschitz to even find out that Vavilov had died.

No wonder the Central Committee was angered by Lipschitz. Lipschitz had personally met Vavilov and Lysenko, and his attitude toward Lysenko was known among biologists. Later, Lipschitz recalled his last meeting with Vavilov at the Commissariat of Agriculture (Narkomzem) in 1938 or 1939:

Vavilov was very gloomy. No doubt, with his bright mind, he understood the approaching threat and saw that a storm would come. . . . One could hear Lysenko's hoarse voice in the next hall. It reminded me [of the] barking of a dog who caught cold. In a dictator's style he pronounced non-logical, "true" ideas, disconnected with each other, about the transition of the dandelion [*Taraxacum officinale*] into the kok-saghyz [*T. koksaghyz*] and back. Lysenko's appearance and the style of his speeches were very similar to those of Hitler's. (It is a mystery that nobody has noticed this similarity before.) In my opinion, the coincidence was not accidental. Both were paranoiacs.[439]

At the beginning of 1953, during a search at Lipschitz's apartment, the MGB confiscated all materials prepared for the *Dictionary*. It seems that only Stalin's death saved Lipschitz from arrest. Both Sukachev and Baranov helped Lipschitz to find a job at the Academy Botanical Institute in Leningrad.

Academician Sukachev was elected MOIP president in 1955, but the anti-Lysenkoist publications in the society's *Bulletin* started earlier.[440] It is difficult to even imagine how the society managed to persuade a censor (in the Soviet Union, every scientific article was approved for publication by a censor) in 1956 not to stop publication of the anti-Lysenko article written by Efroimson, who was just released from a labor camp.[441]

The vertebrate zoologist (mammologist) Veniyamin Tsalkin (1903–1970), who was vice chief editor of the *Bulletin*, helped Sukachev to continue the society's anti-Lysenkoist campaign. In fact, Tsalkin was the campaign's strategist. He was a specialist on the evolution of mammals, especially artyodactyls.[442] Since 1940, Tsalkin had worked at the Biological Faculty of Moscow University, but in 1950 he was forced to leave the university because of an anti-Semitic campaign and pressure from the Lysenkoists. He started to work at the Academy Archaeology Institute, where he organized the Paleozoology Laboratory. At the Archaeology Institute, Tsalkin could continue his study on the evolution of domestic animals. He was safe from the Lysenkoists' attacks, and at the same time, he himself could attack Lysenko and his cronies. Later, in 1966, Professor Tsalkin was elected vice president of MOIP.

As a child, I liked it when my father told me we were going to visit Dr. Tsalkin. Nonofficial discussions of MOIP actions against Lysenkoists took place at this apartment during the mid-1950s. Academician Sukachev and Dr. Tsalkin frequently invited my father to participate in the discussions. As for me, I was taken to see my friend, Dr. Tsalkin's daughter.

Everything that surrounded Dr. Tsalkin was unusual and exciting, the location of the building (the entrance to it was from Red Square), the building itself (one of the oldest in Moscow), the apartment with its skinny corridor and a bathtub in the kitchen behind a curtain. There was an antique rack for overcoats standing in the middle of the corridor. One had to pass this rack with care: A big mean Siamese cat used to hide on its top hat-shelf. He was waiting for a victim. If someone was not attentive enough, a huge clawed paw struck the intruder of the apartment on the head from above.

But most of all I liked to meet the host of the apartment—not very tall, thin, with a completely bald head and very attentive eyes behind round glasses—he looked impressive. He had a good sense of humor and told a lot of jokes. The jokes were sharp, and I knew that many of Tsalkin's opponents were afraid of his sharp tongue.

In 1958, the Central Committee ordered the Academy Presidium to include some Lysenkoists on the editorial board of the *Botanical Journal*.[443] After this, the journal stopped publishing anti-Lysenkoist articles. But MOIP continued to withstand the pressure and in 1958 organized a session on genetics. For the first time since 1948, the geneticists had an opportunity to give presentations on real genetics.

Unfortunately, later on, MOIP was taken under the complete control of the Party and KGB. In September 1970, the Central Committee banned a scientific conference dedicated to the seventieth anniversary of the prominent geneticist, a pupil of Koltsov and Chetverikov, Nikolai Timofeev-Ressovsky, whose unusual life I have already described. Despite the ban, the *Bulletin* published a biographical article about Timofeev written by two biologists, Nikolai Vorontsov and Aleksei Yablokov.[444] After this the Central Committee issued a special instruction that publishing of scientists' biographies must be approved by the "directive organs," meaning the Central Committee and the KGB.[445]

Lysenko did not forget how much Sukachev damaged his reputation by publications in the *Botanical Journal* and the MOIP *Bulletin*. Lysenko used his connections in the Central Committee and in the academy, where in 1959 his supporter, Norair Sisakyan, replaced the anti-Lysenkoist academician Engelhardt as secretary academician of the Biology Division. In 1960, Sisakyan was appointed chief scientific secretary of the academy.[446] At the August 1948 Session, Sisakyan pledged his loyalty to Lysenko:

> For us biochemists the value of the heritage of the great scientist Michurin, the effectiveness and transformative character of Michurin's theory, which has been further developed in the works of T. D. Lysenko, are determined not only by the magnificent quality of the varieties they have created, not only by the distinguished contribution they have made to biological science, but also by the fact that the Michurin theory has opened new vistas, has created wide opportunities also for biochemical research.[447]

In the mid-1950s, Sisakyan became not only a high-ranking bureaucrat within the academy but also an important Soviet official abroad: In 1956, he was elected a member and vice president of the International Astronautical Academy.[448] He could easily help Lysenko.

Indeed, Stalin's time was over, and Sukachev could not be arrested. But in 1961, a decision was made at the Academy Biological Division to move the Institute of Forestry, which Sukachev had created and headed for thirty years, from Moscow to Krasnoyarsk in Siberia. Sukachev was too old and sick to leave Moscow. As a result, only a small laboratory was left to the former head of a big institute.[449]

The same year, in August 1961, Lysenko was reinstalled as president of the Agricultural Academy with the help of Nikita Khrushchev and without election.[450] But in October 1964, Khrushchev was dismissed from his positions in the course of the "bloodless coup." Leonid Brezhnev became general secretary of the Party and the Soviet leader. In February 1965, Lysenko was not reelected as president of VASKhNIL or even as a member of its presidium.[451] Although Lysenko retained his membership in the USSR Academy of Sciences, the Ukrainian Academy of Sciences, and VASKhNIL, his glorious days were in the Stalinist past. He died in 1976.

DISSENT FROM THE LATE 1950S TO THE 1970S

After Stalin's death, a number of protests against KGB control of scientific biological institutions came out into the open. In 1956, Sergei Muromtsev, a former colleague of Mairanovsky and head of a secret MGB laboratory, was appointed director of the Gamaleya Institute of Epidemiology and

Microbiology (IEM) within the USSR Academy of Medical Sciences. A former political prisoner, Academician Pavel Zdrodovsky, refused to work under his guidance.[452] Beginning in 1937, Academician Zdrodovsky was arrested several times[453] and finally ended up at Muromtsev's secret MGB lab *(sharashka)* as an imprisoned scientist. In 1956, Dr. Zdrodovsky quit the IEM, returning to the institute only after Muromtsev's death in 1960.

Another former political prisoner, Academician Lev Zilber (1894–1966), the author of the virus theory of cancer, continued his work at the same institute after a "serious conversation" with Muromtsev. It was well known at the institute that during this dialogue chairs were broken.[454] Both Zdrodovsky and Zilber knew the brutality of Muromtsev very well. When they were forced to work as imprisoned scientists at the secret bacteriological MGB *sharashka* headed by Muromtsev, they were abused so much that Zilber asked the MGB administration to transfer him to a common labor camp, where he had no chance of survival. Later, at the Gamaleya Institute, Muromtsev tried to tell Zilber that he "had to" beat both him and Zdrodovsky up at the MGB *sharashka* because otherwise, the other MGB officers would have beaten them more severely.[455]

It is worth mentioning the history of Dr. Zilber's virus theory of cancer. Like Academician Zdrodovsky, Academician Zilber was arrested by the NKVD-MGB three times: in 1931, 1937–1939, and 1940–1944.[456] In 1931, he was accused of "a deliberate attempt to infect the population" of the city of Baku with the plague virus and, in 1937, of attempting to disseminate the virus of Japanese encephalitis. In 1940, he was accused of "high treason against the Motherland." In spite of torture during interrogations in 1937 and 1940, Zilber never signed the false papers prepared by his NKVD interrogators. His arrest in 1940 prevented the publishing of a monograph on encephalitis, which he wrote before his second arrest in 1937.

In 1940, after spending some time in the terrible labor camps in the Pechora River area in the northern part of European Russia, Dr. Zilber was brought to Moscow, where he was offered a transfer to a secret bacteriological laboratory within the NKVD-MGB system (possibly Laboratory No. 1). Dr. Zilber refused and was sent to a NKVD-MGB chemical laboratory (another *sharashka*). He was forced to work on the production of alcohol from reindeer moss. Here, hiding from the MGB agents and informers at the laboratory, Dr. Zilber managed to write *The Virus Theory of Cancer Etiology* on very thin sheets of rice paper. Dr. Zilber smuggled these sheets secretly to Dr. Zinaida Ermol'eva, the discoverer of Soviet penicillin in 1942. She was allowed, together with Dr. Zilber's brother, the writer Valentin Kaverin, to visit him every two or three months. After this, a group of high-ranking members of the Soviet biological and medical establishment, including

Academicians Nikolai Burdenko, Leon Orbeli, and Vladimir Engelhardt, wrote a letter to Stalin defending Dr. Zilber, who was then released from prison in March 1944. Between that time and his death in 1966, Academician Zilber worked on the problem of cancer etiology. In 1952, during the hysterical anti-Semitic campaign against "cosmopolitans" and "doctor-killers," Dr. Zilber expected to be arrested again. Only the death of Stalin prevented the arrest of his colleagues and himself.

Unfortunately, Dr. Zilber did not prevent a KGB colonel and later general, Oganes Baroyan, from becoming director of the same IEM after Muromtsev's death, although he knew about Baroyan's affiliation with the KGB.[457] In the late 1940s, Baroyan headed a Soviet hospital in Tehran, capital of Iran, and was on good terms with the shah, whom he treated. Through Baroyan, Soviet Intelligence influenced some of the Shah's political decisions.[458] Later, as a KGB agent, Baroyan worked at the World Health Organization from which he was finally expelled. As director of the Gamaleya Institute, he was elected a member of the Medical Academy. Baroyan was well known within the scientific community for abusing his subordinates.[459]

There were other examples of those who resisted Party and KGB control. Boris Astaurov, a geneticist, academician, and director of the Koltsov Institute of Developmental Biology, refused to dismiss Professor Aleksandr Neyfakh (1926–1997) from his position as head of a laboratory after Neyfakh had been expelled from the Communist Party for demonstrating sympathy toward participants in the Red Square demonstration against the Soviet invasion of Czechoslovakia in 1968.[460] Even when he was young, Astaurov showed unusual courage. In 1930, he openly refused to vote for the death penalty for the defendants of the Promparty case.[461] According to the ritual of Stalin's time, everyone was forced to vote against the defendants at meetings organized during show trials. This way the Party officials pretended that the decisions at show trials were supported by the whole population. To save Astaurov from arrest, Koltsov sent him to Central Asia to work with the silkworm. Astaurov, along with two famous physicists, Academicians Sakharov and Pyotr Kapitsa, actively defended biologist Zhores Medvedev, who in late May 1970 was diagnosed as suffering from "creeping schizophrenia" and was placed, by force, in a psychiatric hospital in the town of Kaluga (about 100 miles from Moscow) because of his dissident activity and for publishing the book *The Rise and Fall of T. D. Lysenko* in the United States. As Sakharov recalled later, "Medvedev's work in two disparate fields—biology and political science— was regarded as evidence of a split personality, and his conduct allegedly exhibited symptoms of social maladjustment. In fact, his detention was the Lysenkoites' revenge for his book attacking them . . . "[462]

Academician Sakharov "went to the Institute of Genetics, where an international symposium on biochemistry and genetics was in progress. Many scientists had come from the socialist countries and twenty to thirty from the West."[463] Before the session began, he wrote on the blackboard: "I am collecting signatures in defense of the biologist Zhores Medvedev, who has been forcibly and illegally placed in a psychiatric hospital for his writings. Contact me during the break or reach me at home. A. D. Sakharov."

The director of the Institute of Genetics, Academician Nikolai Dubinin (who in 1939 betrayed his teacher, Nikolai Koltsov), erased the announcement. Despite this, many dissidents signed the letter to Soviet authorities drafted by Sakharov. The academic establishment was outraged by Sakharov's action. "I was called in by [Mstislav] Keldysh, president of the Academy," continued Sakharov in his memoirs, "and reprimanded for my behavior. I argued with him, and he promised to talk to the Minister of Health, Academician Boris Petrovsky."[464] The mathematician Mstislav Keldysh (1911–1978) was president of the Academy of Sciences from 1961 to 1975.

At the meeting at the USSR Ministry of Health, presided over by Minister Petrovsky, the infamous director of the Serbsky Institute of Forensic Psychiatry, Georgii Morozov, "delivered a carefully worded medical report on Medvedev's condition."[465] Astaurov, Kapitsa, and Sakharov argued with Morozov. After Sakharov spoke, the physicist and Academician Anatolii Aleksandrov, who represented President Keldysh and later, in 1975–1986, succeeded Keldysh as president of the academy, said that Sakharov's appeals to Western scientists showed that Sakharov himself "was in need of psychiatric attention." Later, in 1973, during the anti-Sakharov campaign, Aleksandrov did not sign a letter written on behalf of the academy against Sakharov. "Keldysh had signed, but his successor as president of the Academy, Aleksandrov, avoided doing so. When they called his home, the person who answered said, "Anatoly Petrovich [Aleksandrov] is drunk and can't come to the phone," wrote Sakharov in his *Memoirs*.[466] Sakharov asked the deputy minister of health: "How could you sign the order to put Zh. Medvedev into a mental institution?" The vice minister's answer was: "What do you want from me? I cannot do anything, since every year I am forced to sign *scores* of blank [without names] commitment papers on the order of the KGB!"[467]

As a result of the defense by Astaurov, Sakharov, and Kapitsa, as well as of the protests of numerous Soviet writers and filmmakers, on June 17, 1970, Medvedev was released from the hospital.[468] He later emigrated to England.

For Academician Kapitsa, one of the best physicists of the twentieth century (awarded the Nobel Prize in 1978), the defense of Zhores Medvedev was a continuation of his behavior during the late 1930s–1940s, when he tried to help several arrested colleagues. In the 1930s, his letters to Soviet leaders saved the lives of two outstanding physicists, Vladimir Fok (1898–1974) and Lev Landau (1908–1968), who had been arrested.[469] Academician Fok was arrested twice, in 1935 and 1937.[470] In 1937, NKVD commissar Yezhov interrogated Fok himself, but Fok was released after Kapitsa wrote to Stalin. After that Academician Fok, in his turn, also wrote letters to Soviet leaders defending the arrested physicists D. I. Yeropkin and Landau. Landau (arrested in 1938) spent a year in prison. He was released after Kapitsa wrote letters to Stalin, Beria, and Molotov; Niels Bohr also wrote a letter of support.[471] Landau was elected academician in 1946, and in 1962 he became a Nobel laureate.

Other physicists arrested in 1937 in connection with Landau's "case" were not so fortunate. Vadim Gorsky (1906–1937), Lev Shubnikov (1901–1937), and Lev Rozenkevich (1905–1937) were condemned to death and shot in alphabetical order on November 8, 9, and 10, 1937, after a short NKVD investigation and a trial by the OSO.[472] Two arrested foreign scientists who worked at the same Physical-Technical Institute in Kharkov, the Austrian Communist Alexander Weissberg and the German Friedrich Houtermans, were handed over by the NKVD to the Gestapo shortly after the Soviet-German Pact of August 1939.[473]

Another physicist arrested in 1938, corresponding member of the academy (elected academician later, in 1956) Ivan Obreimov, tried in vain to defend his three pupils. In 1940, he wrote a letter about them from a labor camp near the town of Kotlas to a deputy of the Soviet Supreme Council and director of the Academy Physics Institute, Academician Sergei Vavilov (Nikolai Vavilov's brother). In 1941, Obreimov was released from a labor camp after Kapitsa's letter to Molotov.[474] In 1944, Obreimov wrote another appeal regarding Gorsky to NKGB commissar Merkulov. In answering this letter, the head of the NKGB Archival Department Gertsovsky (whose name appeared earlier in connection with Mairanovsky and Nikolai Vavilov), produced the usual lie. In June 1944, he wrote that Gorsky had died on November 25, 1941, "of pneumonia in a punishment NKVD labor camp."[475] In fact, Gorsky had already been dead for years. He was shot on November 8, 1937.

It is not known why the NKVD/MGB/KGB always lied about the death date of its victims. Only from the late 1950s to early 1960s, during the period of official mass "rehabilitation" of the NKVD/MGB/KGB victims, and in the 1990s, when the KGB/FSB started to give investigation files from their archives to the relatives of victims, did it became clear that a common NKVD/MGB formula "the arrested was condemned to 10 years of imprisonment without a right of writing letters" in fact meant that the victim had already been shot to death.

During the 1970s–1980s, Academician Andrei Sakharov was almost unique in his moral stance against the crimes of an amoral regime. Sakharov began his fight after he already had a high position at the academy. Lower-level scientists who raised their voice against state crimes immediately lost their jobs and were excluded from the scientific community. A good example of this is the fate of the physicist and corresponding member of the Armenian Academy of Sciences Yurii Orlov, who was expelled from his scientific job after he joined the dissident movement in the 1970s.[476] He was arrested in 1978 when he headed the Moscow Helsinki Watch Group. Orlov was given the maximum sentence for political crimes, seven years in labor camps and five years of exile. Just as in Stalin's time, the Armenian Academy Presidium expelled Orlov from its ranks in a secret session.[477] Orlov returned to scientific work only after he had been released from imprisonment and emigrated to the United States.

That hot spring and summer of 1978, everyone in Moscow who listened to the BBC or Radio Free Europe or knew about the events from friends was terrified. For the first time after Stalin's death, there were so many political trials in the country—against Orlov in Moscow; against Zviad Gamsakhurdia and Merab Kostava, members of the Georgian Helsinki Group in Tbilisi; against writer Aleksandr Ginzburg in Kaluga (not far from Moscow, where Ginzburg lived in exile after his first sentence in 1967); and finally, against the Jewish activist and refusenik Anatoly Shcharansky, again in Moscow.

Orlov's trial was held on May 15–18 in the Moscow suburb of Lyublino. Temporary barriers were erected around the courthouse, and scores of KGB men guarded the entrance of the courthouse. A group of Orlov's friends and supporters was always standing outside the building during the trial, directly in front of the KGB cordon. These people attended despite the danger of losing their professional jobs, risking possible searches after the trial, and so forth. The KGB photographers openly came up to every newcomer and took photos. Here I met Academician Sakharov for the first time.

The next day, after the end of Orlov's trial, I received a telephone call. Without introducing himself, a man's voice told me that he got my telephone number from our mutual friend, a scientist in Novosibirsk, the main center of scientific research in Siberia. The man who called asked me for an urgent meeting. He arrived soon. He did not give me his name and refused to come into my apartment. He handed me an envelope and said: "Do not ask me about anything, please. This is the only thing we can do for Irina [Yurii Orlov's wife]. We know that you can give this to her." There were banknotes in the envelope.

He turned around and rushed downstairs without waiting for the elevator to come. The fear of being connected with any kind of dissident was deep in every professional scientist. But I recall that event with a warm feeling. In the political environment of 1978, people who collected money for the wife of a political prisoner were definitely courageous.

Later, at the end of July, Lyusya Kovaleva, wife of the biologist and human rights activist Sergei Kovalev, brought me to the apartment of Academician Sakharov. It was not easy to get there. Two KGB men in plain clothes were standing across the hallway and watched everyone who came up to the door of this "special" apartment.

At that time Kovalev was serving a term in a labor camp for political prisoners. In 1970, Kovalev, a well-known electrophysiologist, was forced out of Moscow State University after he became a founding member of the Initiative Group for Human Rights in Moscow. In 1974, he and several other human rights activists reestablished publishing the Chronicle of Current Events, an unofficial underground magazine devoted to descriptions of human rights violations in the USSR (the first issue was published in 1968). At the end of 1974, Kovalev was arrested by the KGB, and in December of 1975, he was tried in Vilnius, Lithuania. He was accused of editing Issues 28–34 of the Chronicle. Kovalev received the maximum punishment for Soviet political prisoners (Article No. 70 of the Soviet Criminal Code), seven years in a special labor camp and three years in exile. He returned to Moscow in the late 1980s.

When Lyusya and I entered Sakharov's apartment, Andrei Dmitrievich asked me to keep him informed on the events at the Fourteenth International Congress of Genetics scheduled for the next month, August. August 1978 was a special date—thirty years after Lysenko's triumph at the August 1948 Session and ten years after the oppression of the Prague Spring by Soviet troops. It had already become known that many foreign geneticists had refused to go to the Moscow congress because of the trials against Orlov and Shcharansky.

However, the congress sessions went smoothly. I had a feeling that the number of plainclothes KGB agents exceeded the number of foreign scientists who attended the meeting. There was only one unsuccessful attempt to show solidarity with the imprisoned Kovalev. During the last general session, the Soviet embryologist Aleksandr Neyfakh came up to the microphone and started to read a letter in defense of Kovalev signed by some of the participants of the congress. Immediately, biochemist Academician Aleksandr Baev, who himself spent seventeen years in Stalin's camps and exile, rushed to the microphone and interrupted Neyfakh's effort. Most participants did not even notice or understand what had happened.

I visited Academician Sakharov at his dacha. He was sitting at an outside table in front of the dacha writing something. I noticed that he was left-handed. I apologized for the intrusion and told him my impressions about the congress and Neyfakh's attempt.

GENERAL REMARKS

It is evident that against all odds during the existence of the Soviet Union, moral opposition to the regime was expressed by at least some scientists. During the 1920s–1930s, it was basically in the form of letters to the highest Party and state officials in defense of arrested colleagues. For this form of protest, a person needed to have courage. Each letter could be used by the secret services as a reason to arrest the defender. Despite the danger, these letters, especially those written by academicians elected before the Bolshevik Revolution, were not rare. Thus, Academician Vernadsky, who was already a famous scientist and politician before the revolution (he was even a member of the Provisional Government), was not aware of the fact that the OGPU/NKVD had been preparing a case against him. For this, the NKVD used "testimonies" of several scientists arrested in 1933–1934 among a hundred intellectuals accused of having been members of the Russian National Party (RNP).[478] This "Party" never existed and was invented by the OGPU/NKVD. Vernadsky sent numerous letters to the heads of the OGPU/NKVD, Molotov, and other Soviet functionaries in defense of the hydrologist Boris Lichkov (1888–1960), who was among the alleged RNP members.[479] After spending almost six years in labor camps, Lichkov was released and lived in Samarkand until 1945, when he was allowed to return to Leningrad. Vernadsky constantly wrote friendly letters to Lichkov when he was in labor camps and exile, despite the danger of being in contact with a political convict. Besides Lichkov, Vernadsky tried to save other arrested scientists—the historian and corresponding member Vladimir Beneshevich (1874–1943), Dmitrii Shakhovskoi (1861–1939), the geologist professors Anatolii Boldyrev (1883–1946) and Vladimir Arshinov, Veniamin Zilbermints, chemists Bruno Brunovsky and Aleksandr Simorin. Of all of them, only Arshinov was released, in 1940. After Vernadsky's letter to Chief Prosecutor Vyshinsky and letters from other scientists, Boldyrev was also released from one of the Kolyma labor camps. However, he was allowed to work only in the same area, in the Dalstroi system. In 1946, Boldyrev froze to death on the way to one of the Kolyma mines.[480]

There are many other examples. As mentioned, before Nikolai Vavilov was arrested, he defended his imprisoned coworkers. And after Vavilov had been

arrested, his teacher, Academician Pryanishnikov, and some of Vavilov's colleagues tried to defend him. In the 1930s, Lysenko's rise to power was
accompanied by the arrests of many geneticists. Lysenko, whose weird theories became the Party line and were approved by Stalin himself, simply
used his connections at the highest Party level and the OGPU/NKVD to
eliminate opponents such as Vavilov. The numerous attacks of Prezent, who
from 1932 became the main ideologist of Lysenko, on biologists working in
different fields usually ended with the arrests of his opponents.

The triumphal procession of Lysenko to complete power over biology
was temporarily interrupted by World War II. As a high-ranking bureaucrat
stated later, "the [Soviet] geneticists were saved by the Nazis. If not for the
war [against Germany], we would destroy you [the geneticists] in 1941."[481]
After the August 1948 Session of VASKhNIL, not only the defense of arrested colleagues but even the expression of a professional opinion that contradicted the Party-approved Lysenko "biology" became a crime and was punished. The form of punishment had also changed. The arrests of biologists
because of their anti-Lysenkoist views became rare, and the open anti-
Lysenkoists were simply fired without hope of finding a new professional
position. This meant professional unemployment for years, sometimes for
the rest of one's days.

According to Soviet rules, to be employed, a professional needed to have
a good reference *(kharakteristika)* from the former place of work signed by
the director of the institution, the secretary of the institution's Party organization, and the chair of the institution's trade union organization. Trade
unions formally existed in the Soviet Union, but in fact they were simply an
additional mechanism of Communist Party control. A biologist who was
described in his or her reference as a person who did not follow the Party-
approved line in biology had almost no chance of finding a new job, especially in the main scientific centers of Moscow or Leningrad. A *kharakteristika* was needed also for keeping the job of researcher or teacher, because
once every several years, a contest for the position was announced and only
a person with a loyal political background and behavior had a chance of
winning it. But even so, most biologists refused to accept Lysenko's nonsense.

It is amazing that decisions about Soviet biology and theoretical medicine
were made at the highest Party and state level. Stalin expressed his views on
genetics to Vavilov at personal meetings, edited texts of Lysenko's speeches,
and read the book about *cruzin* written by Drs. Roskin and Klyueva. He recommended how to deal with opposition to Lysenko and how to punish
Academician Parin. All these actions were approved by the Politburo. Thus,
any scientist who defended an arrested colleague or even refused to accept

Lysenko's doctrine automatically became a political enemy of the state. The arrest of such a person was simply a matter of time. I think that only Stalin's death prevented the mass arrests of those who withstood Lysenko during the late 1940s and early 1950s.

Unfortunately for Soviet science, the biologists arrested in the 1930s and those who lost their jobs in the late 1940s and early 1950s were replaced by people with low professional qualifications, such as the VASKhNIL academicians appointed in 1948 (including Mairanovsky's colleague Muromtsev), Party functionaries (for example, Lepeshinskaya), or simply those who had low moral standards. Academician Oparin, who played a crucial role at the Academy of Sciences after the August 1948 Session, was a good example of the last group.

Together with Thomas Jukes,[482] I strongly disagree with Stanley Miller and his colleagues, who justified Oparin's behavior as the condition necessary for his survival: "It is clear that Oparin and many others went along with Lysenkoism and apparently supported it fully. However, even given the advantages of hindsight, it seems disingenuous to criticize these Soviet researchers for their accommodation with Lysenko, since their survival was dependent on it."[483]

In fact, nothing threatened Oparin's survival. He was an academician and director of the Institute of Biochemistry, which then was not directly involved in the study of genetics or evolutionary theory. He was not attacked by Lysenko or Prezent in the press. He simply was an opportunist who saw his chance to advance his career in exchange for support of Lysenko. It was his choice and desire for power. Academician Schmalhausen, Professors Formozov and Sabinin, and 3,000 other biologists, victims of the August 1948 Session, lost their professional jobs because of their integrity and moral principles and because they would not make compromises with their consciences. Academician Orbeli, whom Oparin replaced as secretary academician, not only refused to fire two geneticists, Rose Manzing and Ivan Kanaev, from his Institute of Evolutionary Physiology and Pathology of the Highest Nervous Activity within the Medical Academy after the August 1948 Session, but instead hired a third geneticist, Mikhail Lobashov, who had just been fired from Leningrad University as a "Mendelist-Morganist."[484]

The Lysenkoists needed to work much harder to destroy Academician Orbeli. To begin with, the joint Academy of Sciences and Medical Academy "Pavlov Session" was organized in 1950. It brought "Lysenko in physiology," as Academician Konstantin Bykov was called, to power. After that a special Scientific Council on the Problems of Physiology Theory of Academician I. P. Pavlov (under Bykov's chairmanship) was created in 1951. As secretary academician, Oparin cooperated closely with Bykov against

Orbeli. Oparin definitely belonged to the same category of scientists as Grashchenkov, Speransky, Frank, and Blokhin, all of whom had no problem supporting Mairanovsky's experiments.

To return to the comparison of the situation in the Soviet Union and Nazi Germany, it is evident that in Germany there were groups of people with basically two opposite types of behavior. There were rare German scientists who refused to replace their Jewish colleagues or those Germans who tried to save Jews or even joined the anti-Nazi underground. Most of them were executed by the Nazi regime or perished in concentration camps. These people had motivations similar to the Russian scientists who tried to save their colleagues and maintained their moral and professional integrity. There was also a rather numerous group of Nazi scientists who gained from taking over the positions of their Jewish colleagues or the SS doctors who profiteered from gold teeth and the belongings of the victims killed in extermination camps. For the most part, these people survived the war, became wealthy, and obtained good professional jobs.[485] I can compare this type of German with the functionaries, including Oparin, who profiteered from the Party line in Soviet biology. I do not think that profiteering in critical circumstances should be considered a decent mode of survival.

It is worth mentioning that the other above-mentioned active and important supporter of Lysenko, Norair Sisakyan, was praised by the international scientific community and politicians even higher than Oparin. As well as being elected a member and vice president of the International Astronautical Academy, in 1964 Sisakyan was elected president of the Thirteenth UNESCO General Assembly (1964–1966) and a crater on the Moon was named after him. After Sisakyan's death, a plaque in his memory was placed on the fourth UNESCO administrative building in Paris.[486]

The dismissal of Oparin as a result of the appeal of hundreds of scientists was a unique event that had not been possible in Stalin's years. It definitely showed a change in the mindset of Soviet scientists—the understanding by many of the necessity of civil actions against Party control of science. This change was later extended by the dissident movement to moral issues and human rights.

However, the introduction of Lysenkoism as the Party line in biology and biomedicine caused a selection of persons without moral integrity in these fields. Moreover, almost all Lysenkoists and their supporters kept their positions even after the fall of Lysenko in 1964–1965. Those real scientists who lost their jobs because they rejected Lysenkoism never had the opportunity to realize their scientific talents and potential. Such scientists of the highest moral determination and integrity as Drs. Rapoport and Efroimson wasted their talents during years of persecution without a professional job. The

Soviet society that killed countless citizens in labor camps was not interested in talented scientists unless they were completely under the ideological control of the Party. Even when Rapoport and Efroimson were able to continue their work, they were dependent on more conformist scientists like Academician Semenov.

All these circumstances created a climate of tolerance and acceptance of any Party order, especially if it was connected with KGB work, by the academy functionaries without questioning the moral aspects of the issue. Academician Blokhin did not ask Mairanovsky about the source of his results when Mairanovsky appealed to him in 1964. In the meantime, it is evident for any professional that Mairanovsky's data were obtained on humans. It does not seem that Academicians Speransky, Grashchenkov, Frank, and other opponents of Mairanovsky's doctoral thesis, who knew about his experiments, ever had a problem with their conscience. In these terms, Academicians Zilber and Zdrodovsky's refusal to accept Mairanovsky's colleague, the Lysenko-devoted supporter and "academician" Muromtsev, as director of VIEM was unusual in the atmosphere of tolerance of immoral actions at the Academy of Science and Medical Academy. The lack of moral standards resulted later, from the 1970s–1990s, in the appearance of the next generation of scientists, such as the high-level functionary Academician Ovchinnikov, who had no doubts about the moral implications of the work on the development of biological weapons and poisons for the KGB.

But people such as Koltsov, his pupils Rapoport and Efroimson, and many others described in this chapter (as well as others not mentioned in this book) will remain forever examples of scientific integrity and human dignity. Very few of them became academicians or corresponding members of the academy because of their moral choice not to follow the Party line against their beliefs. It was impossible for them to make a compromise with their conscience, to accept Lysenkoism, or to betray and deliver another scientist into the hands of the ruthless NKVD/MGB interrogators.

A cytologist, Professor Vladimir Aleksandrov, wrote in his memoirs about the late 1940s: "Lysenko's biology made an immense experiment in social psychology. . . . The experiment revealed the limits of moral firmness in various persons."[487] Dr. Aleksandrov, a Jew by origin, was one of the most uncompromising fighters against Lysenko. In 1949, Professor Boris Tokin of Leningrad University accused Aleksandrov of being an aide to the alleged Jewish Masonic Lodge's "Grand Master," Professor Aleksandr Gurvich, director of the Institute of Experimental Biology (IEB) within the Medical Academy of Sciences.[488] All the accusations were complete nonsense. But the accusations even worked against the Institute's next director, cytologist Dmitrii Nasonov, a Russian noble by origin.[489] In July 1950, after a special commission from the Medical Academy investigated the "anti-Lysenkoist activity" at the IEB, Professor Aleksandrov and twenty of his colleagues were fired, and Professor Nasonov's laboratory was closed.[490] In 1955, Professor Aleksandrov and two other biologists from Leningrad, Dmitrii Lebedev and Yurii Olenov, wrote a letter to the Central Committee of the Communist Party protesting Lysenko's monopoly in biology based on the Party's support for Lysenko. This letter was signed by 300 biologists, and it was the first collective protest by numerous scientists against the policy of the Communist Party in Soviet history.

Another fighter against Lysenko, Corresponding Member of the Academy Yurii Polyansky (1904–1993), a gifted protozoologist, was more lenient than Aleksandrov in his evaluation of the compromises some biologists made concerning Lysenko.[491] Polyansky himself did not compromise with the officials, despite being a Party member. Although as a professor he should not have been drafted, like Rapoport and Lobashov, he voluntarily joined the People's Militia at the beginning of the war with Germany in 1941.

After World War II, Polyansky returned to Leningrad State University, where he was appointed proctor and taught at the Pedagogical Institute [College]. However, in 1947, in cooperation with the Leningrad geneticist Yurii Olenov, he organized an anti-Lysenkoist seminar. Lysenko did not forget this. During the August 1948 Session, Lysenko's ideologist, Isaak Prezent, attacked Polyansky personally.[492] As a result, Polyansky lost his job both at the university and the Pedagogical Institute and became unemployed. Finally, he was accepted at the academy's Murmansk Biological Station, located on the shore of the Barents Sea above the Arctic Circle. In 1952, Polyansky returned to Leningrad and helped Professor Nasonov to organize the Institute of Cytology. Later, he chaired the Department of Invertebrate Zoology at Leningrad University and headed a laboratory at the Institute of Cytology.

Before he died in 1993, Polyansky finished his memoirs. He wrote: "I, who lived through that horrible time, cannot blame those [biologists] who 'repented of their errors' and 'accepted' Lysenko and [Olga] Lepeshinskaya because usually each of these persons headed a group of colleagues and pupils, and these people would lose their jobs if their boss was dismissed. Therefore, it was literally a 'struggle for life.' Among a very few 'recalcitrant' cytologists first of all I would like to name D. N. Nasonov and V. Ya. Aleksandrov."[493] So, giving the examples of Nasonov and Aleksandrov, Polyansky concluded himself that it was possible to withstand the Party line and not to accept orders that contradicted one's conscience.

However, later, at the academy meeting in 1952, Nasonov was forced to repent of the "sin" of disagreeing with Lepeshinskaya. Prominent doctor

Yakov Rapoport (later, in 1953, arrested as a member of "Doctors' Plot") recalled: "Then he [Nasonov] rushed out into the foyer covering his face with hands and screaming: 'I'm so ashamed, so ashamed!' I tried to comfort him, citing the phrase of M. S. Vovsi [another doctor, later accused of being a member of the "Doctors' Plot"]: 'At present, nothing is shameful!'"[494]

Of course, the defenders of arrested colleagues, especially in the 1920s–1930s, were not only among biologists. As I described above, Academician Kapitsa was an outstanding example among physicists. But the situation in physics and technology in the late 1940s differed from that in biology. Basically, research in these fields was secret, and numerous imprisoned physicists and engineers worked in the system of special institutes, the so-called *sharashki*. As mentioned in Chapters 1 and 2, special institutes for imprisoned scientists existed from the late 1920s. However, a system of secret *sharashki* under the NKVD Department of Special Design Bureaus was established in the late 1930s, on September 29, 1938.[495] Even arrested NKVD specialists, especially those from the Foreign Intelligence, were transferred under the NKVD Special Bureau for some time for teaching and writing textbooks.[496] Later, they were tried and usually executed. In July 1941, this department was renamed the NKVD/MVD Fourth Special Department, in which 489 imprisoned scientists and 662 NKVD officers worked.[497] Aleksandr Solzhenitsyn gave a fictional description of a typical physical-technological *sharashka* of the late 1940s in his *The First Circle*,[498] while Lev Kopelev and Dimitri Panin gave a nonfictional account of the same institution.[499] There are memoirs of scientists and engineers who worked in aviation construction *sharashki*.[500] In March 1953, after Stalin's death, the NKVD/MVD Fourth Special Department was disbanded.[501]

One of the former imprisoned *sharashka* workers, Lev Kopelev (who, like Efroimson, tried to protest against Soviet atrocities in Germany and was accused of "slandering the Soviet Army"), gave a psychological analysis (through the words of his friend, the imprisoned engineer Panin) of how the MGB turned free scientists into slaves in the *sharashki*:

> Everything is set up very simply. Professors, engineers with higher degrees, inventors—they're all used to being spoiled. . . . On the outside, your head is rarely concerned only with work. . . . A person like that can be helped only by our Soviet security organs. They grab him by the scruff of the neck, drag him to Lubyanka, Lefortovo or Sukhanovka[502]—confess, bastard, who did you spy on, how did you wreck, where did you sabotage. . . . They lower him once or twice into the cooler when it's freezing, when there's water in it. They'll hit him on the face, the ass, the ribs—not to kill or maim, but so that he will feel pain and shame, so that

he will know that he is no longer a human being but just a nothing and that they can do whatever they want to him. The prosecutor will explain the articles [of the Russian Criminal Code] to him and promise him the maximum. The investigator threatens to arrest his wife if he doesn't confess. And then, after all that, they will give him a magnanimous ten years . . .

So they're preparing the cadres for the *sharashki.* . . . No days off. Vacation is a foreign word. Overtime is sheer pleasure; anything's better than sleeping in the cell. You chase away thought of freedom, of home—they only bring on depression and despair. And work is no longer a duty but the only meaning of life, the substitute for all pleasures and all comforts . . .

. . . In the *sharashki* . . . they address you by your name and patronymic, feed you decently, better than many eat on the outside; you work in warmth, sleep on a straw mattress with a sheet. No worries—just make sure to use your brain, think, invent, perfect, advance science and technology.[503]

Kopelev and Panin worked at the *sharashka* Marfino located in the suburbs of Moscow, described by Solzhenitsyn in *The First Circle.* Some of the German POWs also worked there in 1949. One of the Germans who had had training in radio engineering and who was released from the Soviet captivity in 1950 concluded that this secret institute was organized for high-frequency research,[504] which was true.

Compared to the *sharashki* involved in theoretical and applied physics, biological *sharashki* such as Muromtsev's laboratory were not so numerous or of the same economic and military importance. Possibly, only the *sharashka* created for Timofeev-Ressovsky within the Soviet atomic project was as important as the technical *sharashki.*

I think that the existence of *sharashki* during Stalin's regime, especially during and after World War II, had a profound effect on the entire Soviet scientific community. Even those theoretical physicists who were free still worked in the same secret system as imprisoned scientists under the most powerful person in the Soviet Union after Stalin, Lavrentii Beria (head of the atomic project) and his NKVD/MVD managers such as Zavenyagin. There were Beria's personal representatives, the special "plenipotentiaries of the Council of People's Commissars," at each research facility and nuclear plant involved in the atomic bomb project.[505] This was the beginning of the First Departments and "curators" within each research institution. It was not possible for free scientists like young Sakharov to overlook that the secret atomic center where the Soviet A-bombs and H-bombs were created,

Arzamas-16 (constructed from 1946–1951), was built by approximately 10,000 inmates of labor camps located within this town.[506] The NKVD/MVD Main Directorate of Camps for Industrial Construction (Glavpromstroi) with its network of labor camps was in charge of the construction of all buildings for the atomic project. The Spetsmetupravlenie within the NKVD/MVD Main Directorate of Camps of the Mining-Metallurgic Industry (GUILGMP) was in charge of the prospecting, mining, and enriching of the uranium. Many of the inmates of labor camps in Arzamas-16 were political prisoners condemned on the basis of Article 58 of the Russian Criminal Code. The head of the A-bomb project, Academician Kurchatov, had no problem with the use of slave labor. On March 25, 1947, he sent Beria (together with Beria's "plenipotentiary Pavlov") a request for "POWs construction workers" to build the secret Laboratory No. 2.[507]

On the whole, the A-bomb and H-bomb projects completely depended on the work of prisoners. The whole uranium industry was controlled by the Gulag system. I think that the involvement of physicists in work based on slave labor seriously influenced the moral atmosphere at the academy after many of the physicists who participated in secret projects became its members. And those scientists who went through the camps and *sharashki* never recovered from their horrifying experiences. Analyzing the memoirs of survivors of the Soviet and Nazi camps, the historian Mikhail Heller concluded: "Even those who [physically] survive in a camp, die [emotionally and morally]. Only few of them manage to resurrect again later."[508]

However, partly due to all these negative aspects and as a moral response to them, the main critic of the Soviet regime, the physicist Academician Sakharov, emerged within the Academy of Sciences. I would like to remind the reader what "completely altered" Academician Sakharov's thinking.[509]

After the successful test of the thermonuclear bomb on November 22, 1955, Marshal Mitrofan Nedelin (military director of the test and deputy minister of defense from 1955–1960) gave a banquet for selected scientists, technicians, ministry, and military officials. Sakharov recalled:

> The brandy was poured. The bodyguards stood along the wall. Nedelin nodded to me, inviting me to propose the first toast. Glass in hand, I rose, and said something like: "May all our devices explode as successfully as today's, but always over test sites and never over cities."
>
> The table fell silent, as if I had said something indecent. Nedelin grinned a bit crookedly. Then he rose, glass in hand, and said: "Let me tell a parable . . ." The point of his story (half lewd, half blasphemous, which added to its unpleasant effect) was clear enough. We, the inventors, scien-

tists, engineers, and craftsmen, had created a terrible weapon, the most terrible weapon in human history; but its use would lie entirely outside our control. The people at the top of the Party and military hierarchy would make the decisions. Of course, I knew this already—I wasn't that naive. But understanding something in an abstract way is different from feeling it with your whole being, like the reality of life and death.[510]

Marshal Nedelin did not want to offend Sakharov. For him, there was simply no question about moral issues: The Party and its military and KGB naturally should have used scientists and products of their work for its own purposes without the scientists' consent. Sakharov had never forgotten this lesson: "Many years have passed, but I still feel as if I had been lashed by a whip. . . . [Nedelin] wanted to squelch my pacifist sentiment, and to put me and anyone who might share these ideas in our place."[511]

EPILOGUE

I am not aware that any of the thousands who served in that vast build-
ing on Lubyanka Square [i.e., the KGB] has gone insane, committed
suicide, or publicly spoken out in tears of repentance, horror and mortal
anguish.

—L. Razgon, *True Stories*

After World War II, many of the Nazi doctors and pseudo-geneticists continued their careers without any problem or remorse about the victims of
their experiments during their Nazi past.[1] In the Soviet Union and Russia,
the details of these secrets of the past are still kept in closed archives. It is
interesting that many of the former NKVD/MGB/KGB officers who survived Stalin ended up in the fields of science and law. The Soviet regime did
even more for their former servants. During the last days of the Soviet
Union, such killers as Mairanovsky's colleagues Sudoplatov and Eitingon
were rehabilitated as if they were as innocent as their victims.

But I cannot forget. I imagine. Almost every day trucks with innocent
signs—"Bread," "Provisions," or "Toys"—left Lubyanka or Lefortovo. After a
short trip, they stopped in the center of Moscow in front of an ordinary old
house. The "cargo" of these trucks were individuals on the edge of sanity.
After many months of abuse, torture, and a five- to ten-minute parody of a
trial ending with the words "condemned to death," after being held for an
indeterminate time in special death-row cells, they were brought to a place
with medical personnel. The "doctors" asked questions about their health.
The condemned did not know that they were only the "birdies," and it was
the final act of a brutal play that would end with terrible suffering and death
at the hands of these "doctors."

A second scenario comes to mind. The highly educated, multilingual
Naum Eitingon invites a person (usually a foreigner) to visit his friend,
whose apartment is in the center of Moscow. It appears that Eitingon's
friend is a doctor, and his name is Mairanovsky. Doctor Mairanovsky insists

that he must make a medical examination of the guest (of course, for free). Then he insists that the guest urgently needs a shot. The rest we already know.

It happened in the Moscow of my childhood. It happened when anyone could be arrested, day or night. And my parents could have been among the victims.

In 1987, the investigative journalist Yevgeniya Albats interviewed an old family man, a loving father of four children. The only unusual detail was that this man was the former NKVD investigator Aleksandr Khvat, who tortured Academician Nikolai Vavilov and created the Vavilov case in 1940. The journalist asked Khvat: "Didn't you feel any compassion for Vavilov? After all, he was facing the death penalty. Didn't you feel pity for him, as a human being?" "Khvat laughed out loud," Albats writes in her book. "What do you mean, compassion? . . . It wasn't like he [Vavilov] was the only one, or anything."[2] No wonder that Khvat made a good career within the NKVD/MGB and before Stalin's death headed MGB Department "T," charged with combating "persons expressing threats to the Party and Soviet leaders."[3]

This was not the opinion of just one old person. As I have already described, the NKVD arrested Vavilov after Trofim Lysenko had signed a secret report to the NKVD. In 1989, Lysenko's son, Yurii, wrote to the editors of the popular Russian magazine *Ogonyok:* "I . . . am against having even a kopek of my money go to the construction of a 'memorial to the victims of Stalinism.' I think fanning hatred for Stalin is harmful and unfair."[4]

There is an unusual logic in the attitude of the current Russian officials to the ghosts of the past. Mairanovsky and many of the OGPU/MGB leaders mentioned in this study and eliminated by Stalin (Abakumov, Agranov, Beria, Amayak and Bogdan Kobulov, Komarov, Likhachev, Merkulov, Meshik, Prokofiev, Ryumin, Schwartzman, Stepanov, Tsanava, Vlodzimersky, Yagoda, Yezhov, Zhupakhin) were not rehabilitated by the Soviet/Russian Chief Military Prosecutor's Office. As for Abakumov and the persons who were tried with him (including Likhachev and Komarov), in 1994 the Military Collegium of the Russian Supreme Court changed the old verdict that qualified them as persons who committed crimes against the state to those who committed crimes "using their positions in the military."[5] In December 1997, the Russian Supreme Court revised the verdicts again and changed the death penalty of Abakumov, as well as Likhachev, Makarov, and their supervisor Aleksandr Leonov, to a twenty-five-year term of imprisonment. This is really an Orwellian situation: to change the punishment of persons who were shot forty-four years ago! At the same time, Sudoplatov and Eitingon were rehabilitated, despite their evident involvement in the deaths of numerous victims. Sudoplatov wrote in his memoirs that his and Eitingon's rehabilitation was based on the fact that they "did not fabricate false cases against the 'enemies of people.'"[6] The appeal of Beria's relatives in 2000 for his political rehabilitation was rejected by the Military Collegium of the Russian Supreme Court.[7]

This demonstrates the approach of the Soviet/Russian military prosecutors. It is true that all former VCheKa/MGB officials who were not rehabilitated were involved in the creation of falsified materials of the cases. This was the basic difference between the Nazi and Soviet secret services. The Gestapo tortured its detainees because it wanted to know the truth, whereas the VCheKa/MGB tortured victims to force them to sign falsified testimonies. Aleksandr Solzhenitsyn gives an example of a person, Yevgenii Divnich, who was tortured by both the Gestapo and MGB:

> The Gestapo accused him of Communist activities among Russian workers in Germany, and the MGB charged him with having ties to the international bourgeoisie. . . . The Gestapo was nonetheless trying to get at the truth, and when the accusation did not hold it, Divnich was released. The MGB wasn't interested in the truth and had no intention of letting anyone out of its grip once he or she was arrested.[8]

The Soviet security services had three goals: first, to create an impression that foreign and inner "enemies" threatened the existence of the country; second, to control the Soviet population through the myth that the organs knew everything; and third, to turn its helpless victims into slaves who could be used in all branches of the Soviet economy. But still, Sudoplatov and Eitingon were serial killers. Evidently, the Russian military prosecutors in charge of rehabilitation did not consider the assassination of innocent victims in the name of the Soviet Union and on the order of the Politburo to be crimes. The FSB/SVR officers also consider Sudoplatov to be a hero, not a killer. When on December 23, 1993, Sudoplatov appeared at the meeting of the SVR in Moscow, all the officers stood up and applauded.[9]

The idea that military prosecutors are in some way superior to civilian prosecutors goes back to Stalin's time, when the Military Court tried many political cases. In the current Russia, only the Chief Military Prosecutor's Office has access to the files of such persons as Beria, Abakumov, and other former high-ranking members of the MGB staff. Only military prosecutors decide whether the rehabilitation of these persons is possible or not. This is why only military prosecutor Bobryonev, and not civilian and independent researchers, had an opportunity to investigate Mairanovsky's MGB/KGB file.

Some activities of the secret services, such as Mairanovsky's experiments with poisons, were similar in both Nazi Germany and the Soviet Union. However, one needs to keep in mind that experimentation was not the only usage of persons condemned to death *(rasstrel'niki)* in the Soviet Union. According to the former Soviet military intelligence officer Viktor Suvorov, physically strong *rasstrel'niki* were used for training in hand-to-hand fighting.[10] In the VCheKa, these persons were called "gladiators"; in the NKVD, "volunteers"; in SMERSH, "Robinsons"; and in the Special Troops (Spetsnaz) of the 1990s, "dolls" *(kukly)*.

Mairanovsky's experiments on POWs and political prisoners in the unsuccessful search for "truth drugs" bring to mind secret and similarly unsuccessful studies conducted by the CIA during the late 1940–1950s.[11] At least the American guinea pigs were not POWs or political prisoners but, usually, volunteers. Experiments with radioactive substances were also conducted on volunteer convicts and servicemen, as well as on cancer patients.[12] The British secret experiments with nerve gases from the 1940s–1960s were performed on volunteer military personnel.[13] The point is: Uncontrolled secret research performed by secret services or the military tends to end up with experiments on humans, no matter what country is involved.

During the last decade, the attitude of the Russian population to the history of the VCheKa/KGB and to the current secret services has turned from negative to positive. On December 4, 1998, the lower house of the Russian parliament, the Duma, voted in favor of restoring the statue of the creator of the first Soviet political police (VCheKa), "Iron Felix" Dzerzhinsky.[14] This statue was dismantled on August 21, 1991, when large crowds of Muscovites protested against CheKa/NKVD/MGB/KGB repression. But by late 1998 and early 1999, the attitude of many officials and Muscovites to Dzerzhinsky and the CheKa/KGB had changed. On February 23, 1999, the official day of the Red (Soviet) Army, Moscow witnessed a demonstration of radical Communists and nationalists with slogans "Stalin, Beria, Gulag."[15] The ominous ghosts of the past are rather popular again in Russia. During the Duma election in 1999, one of the political parties was named the "Stalin Bloc." It was led by the arch-leftist Viktor Anpilov and included Stalin's grandson Yevgenii Dzhugashvili.[16] According to a poll conducted in December 1999, 66 percent of Russians considered Stalin's rule more good than bad or equally good and bad.[17]

Beginning in 1997, many key positions in the Russian government, including that of prime minister (Yevgenii Primakov, Sergei Stepashin, and then Vladimir Putin), were taken by former high-ranking KGB functionaries. The list of these people is rather long,[18] but perhaps the most unusual was the meteoric career of the former FSB head and current president,

Vladimir Putin. In July 1998, President Boris Yeltsin appointed the former KGB officer Putin to the offices of FSB head and secretary of the policy-making Security Council of Russia. On August 9, 1999, Yeltsin suddenly promoted him to prime minister.[19]

Putin joined the KGB in 1975, and until 1984, he and his FSB first deputy Viktor Cherkesov (formerly head of the St. Petersburg branch of the FSB) served in the notorious Fifth Main Directorate of the KGB Leningrad branch, which targeted dissidents and human rights activists.[20] After spending years in Germany (Putin had been transferred to the KGB First Main Directorate), in 1990 he returned to Leningrad and worked under the cover of the St. Petersburg University International Department. At the university, Putin participated in meetings on external economic politics.[21] That same year, Putin left the KGB and joined the staff of the reformist mayor of Leningrad, Anatoly Sobchak. In 1994, he became first deputy head of St. Petersburg's city government, and in 1996, he moved to Moscow as deputy to Pavel Borodin, manager of the office that administered the property of President Yeltsin's administration.[22] Later, as acting president, Putin sacked Borodin, evidently because of allegations of corruption and international money laundering.[23]

As the FSB Head, Putin became well known to Russian and international environmentalists. Before the trial of the environmentalist Aleksandr Nikitin,[24] charged by the FSB with treason and leaking state secrets to the Norwegian environmentalist group Bellona, even began, Putin declared in a press interview that Nikitin would be convicted, but the punishment would be softened due to international attention.[25] Putin also claimed that foreign intelligence services largely use various environmental organizations for their work and therefore these organizations would remain under the strict control of the FSB. On April 17, 2000, the Russian Supreme Court finally acquitted Nikitin.[26] On September 13, 2000, the Supreme Court rejected a bid by prosecutors to reopen the case.[27]

In November 1997, Nikitin's arrest was followed by the arrest of another environmentalist, the military journalist Grigory Pasko, in the Russian Far East. The reason was the same—the disclosure of information on nuclear waste pollution. Pasko was amnestied on July 20, 1999, but he continued to claim that he was innocent.[28] In 2000, he published a book in Russian entitled *Case No. 10: Grigory Pasko Against the FSB.*[29] Pasko maintains that the FSB and other secret services used his trial to create a "spy mania" to justify their inflated numbers. He also accused President Putin of putting the rights of the state above the rights of citizens. On November 22, 2000, the Military Tribunal of the Russian Supreme Court sent Pasko's case back to another military court for a new trial. Pasko called this decision "a death sentence" for him. Longtime Russian human rights activist Sergei Grigoryants commented: "It is not just that the human rights situation is drastically deteriorating in Russia. . . . War has been officially declared on civil society in Russia."[30]

At the beginning of 1998, thousands of scientists wrote letters to the FSB in support of their colleagues Vladimir Borodin and Mikhail Galaktionov of the Institute of Acoustics in Moscow, whom the FSB had been considering accusing of passing state secrets to the American company Lockheed.[31] However, in 1999 the FSB opened a new case, this time against nuclear physicist and environmentalist Dr. Vladimir Soyfer, who researched nuclear contamination in the Pacific Ocean. He was accused of mishandling classified documents.[32]

The uncertainty of Russian law on state secrets allows the FSB to interpret any environmental activity as spying. Again, the whole situation is quite Orwellian: Thirty-six Russian ministries and departments compile their own lists of secret information that may be classified and can be used by the FSB to bring charges of espionage.[33]

Despite the fact that Viktor Cherkesov was the main organizer of the Nikitin case, as well one of those involved in persecutions of dissidents during the Soviet years, in May 2000 President Putin appointed his old crony to a prestigious federal post.[34] Cherkesov's appointment was met mostly negatively in St. Petersburg. The role of the FSB in the life of the city and its university has become almost the same as that of the KGB during Soviet times—FSB officers openly attend seminars at St. Petersburg University in order to evaluate the students. Surprisingly, Yurii Saveliev, rector of St. Petersburg University, supported this interference. In August 2000, in an interview with *Washington Post* correspondent Daniel Williams, he said: "The FSB is very active in our university. They get 20 to 30 graduates from us every year. I am very happy about this, because the organization like this needs prepared staff."[35]

In his nationally televised 2000 New Year's Eve address, Putin declared, "The potential of the special services will not just be maintained but increased."[36] Before that, on December 15, 1999, the day of the tenth anniversary of Academician Sakharov's death, Putin cynically put flowers on Sakharov's grave. The Russian journalist Juliya Kalinina sadly wrote: "If Andrei Dmitrievich could see Putin approaching him, he would die a second time."[37]

Almost immediately, in the first days of the new century, Putin started to fulfill this promise. He signed legislation giving nine major security and law enforcement bodies (FSB, SVR, MVD, tax police, Border Guards, Customs Committee, Kremlin Security Service, Presidential Security Service, and

Parliamentary Security Service) the right to control the Internet.[38] Now Internet service providers must link their computers, using special technology developed by the FSB, with those at the FSB headquarters. In response, the famous human rights activist and wife of the late Academician Sakharov, Yelena Bonner, said, "This means Russia has officially become a police state."

In October 2000, President Putin signed an official thirty-seven-page document entitled, "Doctrine of Information Security of the Russian Federation," aimed at protecting Russia's national security in view of the information revolution.[39] The whole document is full of Cold War phraseology. It is not clear to what extent this control and censorship will be applied to scientific information.

Amazingly, some Russian scientists (connected with military production) demand even more strict control over state secrets. On November 10, 2000, the state Russian news agency ITAR-TASS published a letter signed by Corresponding Member of the Academy Barrickad Zamyshlyaev of the Central Institute of Physics and Technology and Academicians Vladimir Kiryukhin, Fyodor Mitenkov, Ashot Sarkisov, and Nikolai Khlopkin. They wrote:

> Russia has something in the military, technical, and scientific areas to be proud of and something to protect against uninvited guests. The latter take advantage of our openness, economic difficulties and sometimes mercenary interests of some representatives of the military-industrial complex in a bid to obtain Russian know-how and breakthrough technologies for next to nothing.[40]

The Russian Nobel Prize winner of 2000, Zhores Alfyorov, academician and director of the Ioffe Physical-Technical Institute in St. Petersburg, appealed to Putin personally to improve funding for Russian science. "With Vladimir Vladimirovich's help there will be a new impulse from politics in science and cutting-edge technologies," Alfyorov said after a meeting with Putin.[41] I am not sure that after this meeting Russian science will be properly funded, but I am positive that the security service structures in charge of science will be. Unfortunately, Alfyorov belongs to the Communist faction in the Russian Duma and, therefore, apparently believes in the Soviet system of organization of science, including KGB/FSB control.

The financial crisis of Russian science could be potentially dangerous in two ways. First, Russian nuclear, chemical, and biological warfare technology could be sold or smuggled to such countries as Iran and Iraq, despite American programs to help former Soviet military scientists to destroy stockpiles of these substances.[42] Terrorism is an additional problem. Thus, enriched uranium has already been smuggled out of the former Soviet Union by the Russian Mafia.[43] Although the threat of chemical and biological terrorist attacks is not high (there have been seventy-one actual attacks from 1900 until May 1999, with 123 fatalities and 3,774 injuries), such substances from the Soviet past as cyanide were among the tools used.[44] In one case within the United States, even Mairanovsky's beloved ricin was prepared for assassination attacks. In 1991, four members of the Minnesota Patriots Council acquired ricin for use in a plot to assassinate Internal Revenue Service officials, a U.S. deputy marshal, and local law enforcement officers. The FBI arrested the terrorists before the attacks were carried out. However, many modern agents such as VX nerve gas, anthrax, salmonella bacteria, and the HIV virus were also among international terrorists' tools.

Second, in violation of international agreements, work on chemical and biological weapons in Russia might be intensified because the state funding for military technology will be increased. The law on state secrets can be easily used to cover up such research. This brings to mind the ghosts of Mairanovsky, Muromtsev, Eitingon, and Sudoplatov and their work on poisons.

This is not only a guess. In July 2000, when I visited Moscow, my molecular biology colleagues said that Academician A. S. had offered President Putin's administration a new project on biological warfare, the Biological Shield of Russia, for consideration. If accepted, mainly institutes of the Russian Academy of Sciences located in the town of Pushchino would be involved in the project. I understand that this academician is trying to find a solution to keep his institute alive and employees paid (their salaries are so miserable that the employees can hardly survive). But this short-term solution can have serious consequences for the whole world.

After Putin's appointment, the former political prisoner and famous Russian human rights activist (and also former president Yeltsin's adviser on human rights and a deputy of the Duma), the biologist Sergei Kovalev, said that only when Russians admitted collective guilt for the past would they reject those with a KGB past.[45] The Russian journalist Anna Politkovskaya expressed the same opinion, but more emotionally: "We are living through the darkest time of the last scores of years. The authorities in power went crazy trying to cover up their own crimes and pretending to be irreconcilable [in the war with the Chechens]. For this purpose they are using neo-Stalinism. This [reverse to the past] occurred at once and naturally because the country has the same feeling."[46] On April 27, 2001, Politkovskaya received an award from the New York-based Overseas Press Club for her courageous reports on the war in Chechnya.[47] I hope her warning about the return of Russian politics to the Soviet past will be heeded.

A monument to the memory of the victims of Stalin's terror (a stone brought from the first Soviet concentration camp in the Solovetsky Islands). The dedication ceremony by Memorial took place on October 30, 1990, in front of the current FSB headquarters. (Photo by Vadim Birstein [New York], 1997)

During Yeltsin's years in power, the Russian government did almost nothing for the still-living victims of Stalin's regime or to commemorate those who had perished in the Gulag. On October 30, 1999 (the Day of Remembrance of Victims of Political Persecution in Russia), Moscow Memorial summarized the situation. In the last ten years, there has been no serious government help for the victims; the full list of names of the arrested, imprisoned, and executed persons was not disclosed; the KGB/FSB archives continued to be closed to independent research; the location of only 20–30 percent of the mass graves of the executed was officially released; no memorials to the victims of the terror were erected; and no information about the Soviet terror was included in textbooks on Russian history.[48] Memorial's final conclusion: "On the whole, the authorities do not pay any attention to the problems of the totalitarian past."

The National Memorial in remembrance of Stalin's victims that was planned in 1989–1990 has never been built. I doubt it ever will be. On the contrary, under Putin, for the first time since his death in 1953, Stalin was commemorated by a plaque attached to a wall at the Kremlin Palace in Moscow.[49] Simultaneously, a special 100-ruble coin with the faces of the "Big Three"—Stalin, former U.S. president Harry Truman, and former British prime minister Winston Churchill—was minted.[50] It is not surprising that Russian human rights activists were extremely concerned. Grigory Yavlinsky, the leader of the democratic party Yabloko, wrote on January 30, 2001:

> The most characteristic trait of today's government, which it unabashedly demonstrates, is the absence of any notion of the value of human life, any idea that there are inalienable rights and freedoms. It is senseless to try to explain this to the authorities: They don't allow these simple ideas into their consciousness . . . [51]

The foundation of a new political system is being laid—a twenty-first-century national socialism. There is no guarantee that in this neo-Stalinist Russia, controlled by secret services and the military, new "Mairanovskys" and "Muromtsevs" will not test on humans—for instance, on the Chechen rebels or other targets—the sophisticated chemical compounds and genetically engineered biological products developed with the help of scientists from the Russian Academy of Sciences.

NOTES

INTRODUCTION

1. Josephson, Paul R., *Totalitarian Science and Technology* (Atlantic Highlands, NJ: Humanities Press, 1996); Krementsov, Nikolai, *Stalinist Science* (Princeton, NJ: Princeton University Press, 1997); Tolz, Vera, *Russian Academicians and the Revolution: Combining Professionals and Politics* (New York: St. Martin's Press, 1997); Roberg, Jeffrey L., *Soviet Science Under Control: The Struggle for Influence* (New York: St. Martin's Press, 1998); Kolchinsky, Eduard I., *V poiskakh sovetskogo "soyuza" filosofii i biologii* [In Search of the Soviet "Union" Between Philosophy and Biology] (St. Petersburg: Dmitrii Bulanin, 1999) (in Russian); Romanovsky, Sergei I., *Nauka pod gnyotom rossiiskoi istorii* [Science Under the Pressure of Russian History] (St. Petersburg: Izdatel'stvo St. Petersburgskogo Universiteta, 1999) (in Russian).

2. Kandel, F., *Essays on Events in the History of Russian Jews (Until the Second Part of the Eighteenth Century)* (Jerusalem: Tarbut, 1988) (in Russian).

3. See documents from the Police Department Archive currently kept in the State Archive of the Russian Federation (GARF) in Moscow, published in Volkov, A. V., and M. V. Kulikova, "Rossiiskaya professura: 'pod kolpakom' u vlasti" [Russian Professors: Under surveillance of the authorities], *Vestnik Instituta Istorii Estestvoznaniya i Tekhniki* 2 (1994):65–75 (in Russian). The similarity between the Police Department documents and those from the VCheKa/KGB files is striking.

4. See, for instance, Chapter 4 ("The Bolsheviks and the Intelligentsia") in Koenker, Diane P., William G. Rosenberg, and Ronald G. Suny, eds., *Party, State, and Society in the Russian Civil War: Explorations in Social History* (Bloomington: Indiana University Press, 1989), pp. 239–318.

5. See, for instance, Heller, Mikhail, and Aleksandr M. Nekrich, *Utopia in Power: The History of the Soviet Union from 1917 to the Present,* translated from Russian by Phyllis B. Carlos (New York: Summit Books, 1986), pp. 114–136, 211–221.

6. Kokurin, A. I., and N. V. Petrov, *Lubyanka: VChK-OGPU-NKVD-MGB-MVD-KGB, 1917–1960, Spravochnik* [Lubyanka: VChK-OGPU-NKVD-MGB-MVD-KGB, 1917–1960, a Reference Book] (Moscow: MFD, 1997) (in Russian).

7. Smirnov, Mikhail B., ed., *Systema ispravitel'no-trudovykh lagerei v SSSR, 1923–1960: Spravochnik* [The System of Correction Labor Camps in the USSR, 1917–1960: A Reference Book] (Moscow: Zven'ya, 1998) (in Russian).

8. Petrov, Nikita V., and Konstantin V. Skorkin, *Kto rukovodil NKVD 1934–1941: Spravochnik* [Who Directed the NKVD, 1934–1941: A Reference Book] (Moscow: Zven'ya, 1999) (in Russian).

9. On Lysenko, see, for instance, Medvedev, Zhores A., *The Rise and Fall of T. D. Lysenko* (New York: Columbia University Press, 1969); Popovsky, Mark, *The Vavilov Affair* (Hamden, CT: Archon Books, 1984); Joravsky, David, *The Lysenko Affair* (Chicago: University Chicago Press, 1986); Graham, Loren R., *Science, Philosophy, and Human Behavior in the Soviet Union* (New York: Columbia University Press, 1987), pp. 102–156; and Soyfer, Valery N., *Lysenko and the Tragedy of Soviet Science*, trans. L. Gruliow and R. Gruliow (New Brunswick, NJ: Rutgers University Press, 1994).

10. About Memorial and its work, see Adler, Nanci, *Victims of Soviet Terror: The Story of the Memorial Movement* (Westport, CT: Praeger, 1993); Hochschild, Adam, *The Unquiet Ghost: Russians Remember Stalin* (New York: Viking, 1994), pp. 17–20, 24–27, 40, 121, 139.

11. GULAG is the Russian acronym for the Main Directorate of [Labor] Camps, Glavnoe Upravlenie Lagerei, within the OGPU (i.e., United State Directorate under the Council of Commissars, or SOVNARKOM), which in 1934 became the NKVD (Commissariat of Internal Affairs). The GULAG system of labor camps was established on April 25, 1930, for economic purposes, i.e., as a source of slave labor. It united separate systems of camps and prisons that existed under the OGPU and NKVD. Later, many additional separate systems of labor camps were created within the NKVD, which in 1946 became the MVD (Ministry of Internal Affairs): the Main Directorate of Camps for Railroad Building, the Main Directorate of Camps for Roads Building, the Main Directorate of Camps for the Mining and Metallurgic Industry, the Main Directorate of Camps for Logging, the Main Directorate for Building at the Far North (Dalstroi), etc. Practically all types of Soviet industry had their own systems of labor camps (see details in Jacobson, Michael, *Origins of the Gulag: The Soviet Camp System 1917–1934* (Lexington: University Press of Kentucky, 1993); Jacobson, M., and M. B. Smirnov, "Systema mest zaklyucheniya v RFSR i SSSR, 1917–1930" [The imprisonment system in the RSFR and USSR, 1917–1930], in Smirnov, *Systema ispravitel'no-trudovykh lagerei*, pp. 10–24; Smirnov, M. B., S. P. Sigachev, and D.V. Shkapov, "Systema mest zaklyucheniya v SSSR, 1929–1960" [The imprisonment system in the USSR, 1929–1960], in Smirnov, *Systema ispravitel'no-trudovykh lagerei*, pp. 25–74; Kokurin and Petrov, *Lubyanka*, pp. 76–142. After Aleksandr Solzhenitsyn published his book *The Gulag Archipelago* in 1973, the word "Gulag" became a generic name for the whole system of slave labor of political prisoners in the Soviet Union.

12. During the time of "perestroika," in 1988–1990, Vadim Bakatin (b. 1937) was Minister of the Interior (MVD). In 1991 he was appointed head (chairman)

of the KGB (see Wise, D., "Closing Down the KGB," *New York Times Magazine*, November 24, 1991). In December 1991, Bakatin was replaced by Viktor Barannikov. Despite all Bakatin's efforts to solve the mystery of Wallenberg's death, the KGB stopped independent archival investigation on this issue.

13. Petrov, N., and T. Kasatkina, "Ekspertiza 'Memoriala'" [Memorial's expertise], *Moscow News* 39 (1990) (in Russian); Gevorkyan, N., and N. Petrov, "Terakty [Terrorist acts], *Moscow News* 31 (1992) (in Russian); Gevorkyan, N., and N. Petrov, "Priznat' tselesoobraznym osushchestvlenie aktov terrora" [Carrying out terrorist acts should be recognized as expedient], *Moscow News* 35 (1992) (in Russian).

14. Bandura, Yu., and S. Bura, "Grigorii Mairanovskii: gipotezy i fakty" [Grigory Mairanovsky: Hypotheses and facts], *Moscow News* 39 (1990) (in Russian); Burbyga, N., "Prigovoryen k 'medosmotru'" [Condemned to a "medical examination"], *Izvestiya* 114, April 16, 1992 (in Russian).

15. The manuscript was translated from Russian by the well-known translator Catherine Fitzpatrick.

16. Bobrenjow, Wladimir, und Waleri Rjasanzew, *Das Geheimlabor des KGB: Gespenster der Warsanowjew-Case* (Berlin: Edition Verlags-Gmb-H, 1993).

17. Bobryonev, Vladimir, *"Doktor Smert," ili Varsonofievskie prizraki* ["Doctor Death," or the Ghosts of Varsonofyevsky Lane] (Moscow: Olimp, 1997) (in Russian).

18. For example, see Weinreich, Max, *Hitler's Professors* (New York: Yiddish Scientific Institute, 1946); Lifton, Robert J., *The Nazi Doctors: Medical Killings and the Psychology of Genocide* (Basic Books, 1986); Deichmann, Ute, *Biologists Under Hitler*, trans. Thomas Dunlap (Cambridge: Harvard University Press, 1996).

19. Müller-Hill, Benno, "Bioscience in Totalitarian Regimes: The Lessons to Be Learned from Nazi Germany," in Roy, D. J., B. E. Wynne, and R. W. Old, eds., *Bioscience and Society* (Chichester: John Wiley, 1991), pp. 67–76; Müller-Hill, Benno, "Science, Truth and Other Values," *Quarterly Review of Biology* 68 (3) (1993):399–407.

20. The first publication of the book was in 1988; here I use the latest version: Müller-Hill, Benno, *Murderous Science: Elimination by Scientific Selection of Jews, Gypsies, and Others in Germany, 1933–1945* (Cold Spring Harbor, MI: Cold Spring Harbor Laboratory Press, 1998).

21. *Materials of the Trial of Former Servicemen of the Japanese Army Charged with Manufacturing and Employing Bacteriological Weapons* (Moscow: Foreign Languages Publishing House, 1950); Williams, Peter, and David Wallace, *Unit 731: Japan's Secret Biological Warfare in World War II* (New York: Free Press, 1989); Harris, Sheldon H., *Factories of Death: Japanese Biological Warfare, 1932–45, and the American Cover-Up* (London: Routledge, 1997); Parker, John, *The Killing Factory: The Top Secret World of Germ and Chemical Warfare* (London: Smith Gryphon Publishers, 1996), pp. 85–89.

22. Andrew, Christopher, and Oleg Gordievsky, *KGB: The Inside Story* (New York: Harper Perennial, 1991), pp. 644–645; Kalugin, Oleg, "Tipichno 'bolgar-

skoe' ubiistvo Interviyu Olega Kolugina zhurnalistke 'Moskovskikh Novoste:' N. Gevorkyan" [A typical "Bulgarian" murder: An interview of Oleg Kalugin by the *Moscow News* journalist, N. Gevorkyan], *Moscow News* 17 (1991) (in Russian). Markov's biography and a detailed description of his murder are given in: Bereanu, Vladimir, and Kalin Todorov, *The Umbrella Murder* (Oxford: TEL, 1994), pp. 13–46.

23. Harris, Robert, and Jeremy Paxman, *A Higher Form of Killing: The Secret Story of Chemical and Biological Warfare* (New York: Hill and Wang, 1982), pp. 226–237; Ranelagh, J., *The Agency: The Rise and Decline of the CIA* (New York: Simon and Schuster, 1987), pp. 202–216; Marks, John, *The Search for the "Manchurian Candidate"* (New York: McGraw Hill, 1991).

24. These experiments continued even later. In her book *Secret Agenda* (p. 171), Linda Hunt wrote: "Thousands of American soldiers, seven thousand of them between 1955 and 1975 alone, were used as unwitting guinea pigs in the tests. They were gassed, maced, and drugged in the search for the ultimate mind-control weapon" (Hunt, Linda, *Secret Agenda: The United States Government, Nazi Scientists, and Project Paperclip, 1945 to 1990* [New York: St. Martin's Press, 1991]).

25. Marchetti, Victor, and John D. Marks, *The CIA and the Cult of Intelligence* (New York: Alfred A. Knopf, 1974).

26. Colby, William, and Peter Forbath, *Honorable Men: My Life in the CIA* (New York: Simon and Schuster, 1978), pp. 317–319.

27. Originally published by John Marks as *The Search for the "Manchurian Candidate": The CIA and Mind Control* (New York: Times Books, 1978). In this study I have used the latest edition of his book, published in 1991.

28. See details in Welsome, Eileen, *The Plutonium Files: America's Secret Medical Experiments in the Cold War* (New York: Dial Press, 1999).

29. The nerve gases tabun, sarin, and soman were discovered and synthesized in 1936–1938 by Dr. Gerhard Schrader at I. G. Farben in Nazi Germany. After World War II, the Soviets dismantled the gas-producing plant in Breslau (Poland) and reassembled it in the Soviet Union. Dr. Schrader was captured by the Americans, and American scientists learned from him about the production of these gases in Germany. In the 1950s, British and American military scientists developed a new powerful nerve gas, VX (Harris, Robert, and Jeremy Paxman, *A Higher Form of Killing*, pp. 57–61, 70–71, 151–152, 203–204).

30. Gilligan, A., and R. Evans, "Soldiers Tricked into Chemical Tests," *Electronic Telegraph* 892, November 2, 1997 (on-line version) Syal, R., "Porton Down Faces Criminal Inquiry into Airman's Death," *Electronic Telegraph* 1528, August 1, 1999 (on-line version); Evans, R., "Scandal of Nerve Gas Tests," *Observer*, September 3, 1999.

31. Parker, *The Killing Factory*, p. 196.

32. Gilligan, A., and R. Evans, "MoD Admits Airborne Germ Warfare Tests," *Electronic Telegraph*, November 16, 1997 (on-line version).

33. In 1991, I gave a talk on Mairanovsky at the Conference on International Aspects of Ethical and Social Issues in Human Genome Research, Washington,

DC. In 1996, I included new data in my presentation at another meeting, the Third World Congress of Bioethics: Bioethics in an Interdependent World, San Francisco, November 20–25.

34. See Vavilov, Yurii N., and Yakov G. Rokityansky, "Golgotha: Arkhivnye materialy o poslednikh godakh zhizni akademika N. I. Vavilova" [Golgotha: Archival materials on the last years of Academician Vavilov's life (1940–1943)], *Vestnik Rossiiskoi Akademii Nauk* 63 (1993):830–846 (in Russian).

35. About the structure of the Politburo, see Löwenhardt, John, *The Soviet Politburo* (Canongate: Thomson Litho, 1982).

36. See, for instance, "O tak nazyvaemom 'Dele Evreiskogo Antifashistskogo Komiteta'" [On the so-called "Jewish Anti-Fascist Committee Case"], *Izvestiya TsK KPSS* 12 (1989):35–40 (in Russian); Rapoport, Louis, *Stalin's War Against the Jews: The Doctor's Plot and the Soviet Solution* (New York: Free Press, 1990), pp. 80–97. First Deputy MGB Minister Sergei Ogoltsov (1900–1977) was awarded the Order of the Red Banner for carrying out the organization of the assassination of Mikhoels. On April 3, 1953, Ogoltsov was arrested, charged with carrying out the assassination, and deprived of his position as first deputy minister and the award. He was released on August 6, 1953, and discharged from the MVD in January 1954. See Petrov and Skorkin, *Kto rukovodil NKVD*, p. 323.

37. See Stetsovsky, Yurii, *Istoriya sovetskikh repressii* [History of Soviet Repressions] (Moscow: Znak-SP, 1997), vol. 1, pp. 485–486 (in Russian).

38. Kostyrchenko, Gennadi, *Out of the Red Shadows: Anti-Semitism in Stalin's Russia* (Amherst, NY: Prometheus Books, 1995), pp. 258–276.

39. At least four prominent Academicians were members of this council (Alibek, Ken, with Stephen Handelman, *Biohazard: The Chilling True Story of the Largest Covert Biological Weapons Program in the World—Told from the Inside by the Man Who Ran It* [New York: Random House, 1999], p. 158).

40. After I finished writing this book, a new source was published: Yesakov, V. D., ed., *Akademiya Nauk v resheniyakh Politburo TsK RKP(b)-VKP(b), 1922–1952* [The Academy of Sciences in Resolutions of the Central Committee of the Russian/All-Union Communist (Bolshevik) Party, 1922-1952] (Moscow: Rosspan, 2000) (in Russian). It contains numerous additional documents showing the complete control over academy life in the 1930s–1950s by the Politburo and Stalin himself.

41. Loren R. Graham, *What Have We Learned About Science and Technology from the Russian Experience?* (Stanford: Stanford University Press, 1998), pp. 133–134.

CHAPTER ONE

1. A note from Vladimir Grum-Grzhimailo dated July 18, 1928, Academy of Sciences Archive, F. 518, Op. 2, D. 14, L. 47–48, cited (pp. 178–179) in Perchenok, F. F., "Akademiya Nauk na 'velikom perelome'" [The Academy of Sciences at the "great rupture"], in Okhotin, Nikita, and Arsenii Roginsky, eds., *Zven'ya: Historical Almanac* [The Links] (Moscow: Progress; Phoenix: Atheneum, 1991), vol. 1, pp. 163–238 (in Russian).

2. Tolz, *Russian Academicians*, p. 37.

3. A copy of the letter from the Academy of Sciences Archive in St. Petersburg, cited (pp. 93–95) in Samoilov, V. O., and Yu. A. Vinogradov, "I. P. Pavlov: 'Ne odin zhe ya tak dumayu . . . '" [I. P. Pavlov: "Am I alone in thinking this way? . . . "], in Glinka, M. S., ed., *Sovremennye mysli, ili proroki v svoem otechestve* [Well-Timed Thoughts, or Prophets in Their Own Fatherland] (Leningrad: Lenizdat, 1989), pp. 92–101 (in Russian); another translation is in Tolz, *Russian Academicians*, p. 37.

4. Perchenok, "Akademiya Nauk," p. 190.

5. A copy of Molotov's letter to Academician Pavlov from the Academy of Sciences Archive in St. Petersburg, cited (pp. 95–96) in Samoilov and Vinogradov, "I. P. Pavlov: 'Ne odin zhe ya tak dumayu . . .'"

6. See Sobolev, V. S., "Utochnim fakty" [Let's correct the facts], *Vestnik Akademii Nauk* 8 (1990):146–147 (in Russian); Fainstein, M. Sh., "Ob'edinenie dvukh akademii" [The merger of two academies], *Vestnik Instituta Istorii Estestvoznaniya i Tekhniki* 2 (1999):40–55 (in Russian). For general information on the early history of the St. Petersburg Academy, see, for instance, Vucinich, Alexander, *Science in Russian Culture: A History to 1860* (Stanford: Stanford University Press, 1963); a short version is in Vucinich, Alexander, *Empire of Knowledge: The Academy of Sciences of the USSR* (1917–1970) (Berkeley: University of California Press, 1984), pp. 6–71.

7. Romanovsky, S. I., "Pervyi demokraticheski izbrannyi prezident akademii nauk" [The first democratically elected president of the Academy of Sciences], *Vestnik Rossiiskoi Akademii Nauk* 66 (12) (1996):1095–1110 (in Russian).

8. Ibid., p. 1097.

9. The whole list of names is given in Tolz, *Russian Academicians*, pp. 188–189.

10. Ibid., p. 17.

11. See the biography of Pavlov, for instance, in Vucinich, Alexander, *Science in Russian Culture, 1867–1917* (Stanford: Stanford University Press, 1970), pp. 298–327; and a detailed description of Pavlov's studies, in Babkin, Boris P., *Pavlov: A Biography* (Chicago: University of Chicago Press, 1949).

12. Babkin, *Pavlov*, p. 214.

13. See, for instance, Vucinich, *Science in Russian Culture, 1867–1917*, pp. 115 and 285; Salensky, W., "Recherches sur le développement du sterlet *(Acipenser ruthenus)*," *Archives de Biologie* 2 (1881): 233–341.

14. Vucinich, *Science in Russian Culture, 1867–1917*, pp. 282–283.

15. Ipatieff, Vladimir N., *The Life of a Chemist*, trans. Haensel and Lusher (Stanford: Stanford University Press, 1946).

16. Vucinich, *Science in Russian Culture, 1867–1917*, pp. 358–361.

17. Ibid., pp. 341–343.

18. Ipatieff, *The Life of a Chemist*, pp. 566–567.

19. Vucinich, *Science in Russian Culture, 1867–1917*, pp. 96–97.

20. Ibid., pp. 416–421.

21. Bailes, Kendall E., *Technology and Society Under Lenin and Stalin: Origins of the Soviet Technical Intelligentsia, 1917–1941* (Princeton: Princeton University Press, 1978), p. 41; Bailes, Kendall E., *Science and Russian Culture in an Age of Revolutions: V. I. Vernadsky and His Scientific School, 1863–1945* (Bloomington: Indiana University Press, 1990); Tolz, *Russian Academicians,* pp. 153–168.

22. Ipatieff, *The Life of a Chemist,* pp. 220 and 234.

23. Kozlov, B. I., and B. V. Levshin, "V kontse 'Serebryanogo veka'" [At the end of the "Silver Age"], *Vestnik Rossiiskoi Akademii Nauk* 68 (7) (1998):579–595 (in Russian).

24. Arskaya, L. P., "Dvenadtsatyi prezident akademii nauk" [The twelfth president of the Academy of Sciences], *Vestnik Rossiiskoi Akademii Nauk* 64 (1) (1994):56–68 (in Russian).

25. Sobolev, "Utochnim daty," p. 147.

26. Koltsov, Anatolii V., *Sozdanie i deyatel'nost' Komissii po izucheniyu estectvennykh proizvoditel'nykh sil Rossii, 1915–1930 gg.* [The Creation and Activity of the Commission for the Study of Natural-Productive Forces of Russia, 1915–1930] (St. Petersburg: Nauka, 1999), p. 41 (in Russian).

27. Kozlov and Levshin, "V kontse," p. 579.

28. Cited in ibid., p. 582.

29. Soloviev, Yu. G., "Nepremennyi sekretar'—voploshchenie blagorodstva" [The permanent secretary as personified decency], *Vestnik Rossiiskoi Akademii Nauk* 64 (7) (1994):637–649 (in Russian); Alpatov, V. M, and M. A. Sidorov, "Dirizher akademicheskogo orkestra" [A conductor of the academy orchestra], *Vestnik Rossiiskoi Akademii Nauk* 67 (2) (1997):164–173 (in Russian).

30. A medical Professor replaced Oldenburg as minister (Kozlov and Levshin, "V kontse," p. 583). Later, in 1919, Oldenburg was arrested and detained by the CheKa for two weeks (Alpatov and Sidorov, "Dirizher akademicheskogo orkestra," p. 168).

31. According to the calendar used in Russia before 1918, the date of the Bolshevik Revolution was October 25, 1917.

32. For details, see Aksenov, Gennadii P., *Vernadsky* (Moscow: Soratnik, 1994), pp. 227–235 (in Russian).

33. See, for instance, Gerson, Lennard D., *The Secret Police in Lenin's Russia* (Philadelphia: Temple University Press, 1976), pp. 15–25; Leggett, George, *The CHEKA: Lenin's Political Police* (Oxford: Clarendon Press, 1981), pp. 1–4.

34. Bailes, *Science and Russian Culture,* pp. 146–148; more details are given in Aksenov, *Vernadsky,* pp. 239–260.

35. Vernadsky, V. I., "Iz dnevnikov 1921 goda" [Excerpts from the 1921 diary], in Okhotin and Roginsky, *Zven'ya,* vol. 1, pp. 475–487.

36. Ipatieff, *The Life of a Chemist,* p. 271.

37. See p. 289 in Bailes, Kendall E., "Natural Scientists and the Soviet System," in Koenker, Rosenberg, and Suny, *Party, State, and Society in the Russian Civil War,* pp. 267–295.

38. For the English translation of the decree, see Babkin, *Pavlov,* p. 165.

39. McClelland, James C., "The Professorate in the Russian Civil War," in Koenker, Rosenberg, and Suny, *Party, State, and Society in the Russian Civil War,* pp. 243–266; Bailes, "Natural Scientists," pp. 287–289; Revyakina, I. A., and I. N. Selezneva, "Trudnye gody rossiiskoi nauki" [Difficult years for Russian science], *Vestnik Rossiiskoi Akademii Nauk* 64 (10) (1994):931–937 (in Russian).

40. Ipatieff, *The Life of a Chemist,* pp. 271–272.

41. Texts of two of Vernadsky's reports are given in Bastrakova, M. S., "Akademiya nauk i sozdanie issledovtel'skikh institutov (dve zapiski V. I. Vernadskogo)" [The Academy of Sciences and the organization of research institutes (two reports of V. I. Vernadsky)], *Vestnik Instituta Istorii Estestvoznaniya i Tekhniki* 1 (1999):157–167 (in Russian).

42. Bailes, "Natural Scientists," p. 279.

43. Aksenov, *Vernadsky,* pp. 325–326. In 1922, Vernadsky left Russia and worked abroad until 1926. For the reasons he returned, see Kolchinsky, E. I., "Pochemu V. I. Vernadsky vernulsya v Sovetskuyu Rossiyu? (Bremya vybora: 1922–1926) [Why did V. I. Vernadsky return to Soviet Russia? (The burden of choice, 1922–1926)], appendix in Kolchinsky, *V poiskakh sovetskogo "soyuza,"* pp. 218–251.

44. For details, see Bailes, "Natural Scientists," pp. 280–281, and Krementsov, *Stalinist Science,* pp. 17–23.

45. Romanovsky, "Pervyi demokraticheski izbrannyi prezident," p. 1099; Koltsov, *Sozdanie i deyatel'nost',* p. 68.

46. Vernadsky, Vladimir I., *Publitsisticheskie stat'i* [Publicist Papers] (Moscow: Nauka, 1995), p. 249 (in Russian).

47. Cited in Koltsov, *Sozdanie i deyatel'nost',* p. 63.

48. "O reforme deyatel'nosti uchenykh uchrezhdenii i shkol vysshikh stupenei v Rossiiskoi Sotsialisticheskoi Federativnoi Sovetskoi Respublike" [On the reform of activity of scientific institutions and high schools in the Russian Soviet Socialist Republic], *Vestnik Narodnogo Prosvyashcheniya Soyuza Kommun Severnoi Oblasti* 6–8 (1918):69 (in Russian). Cited in Kolchinsky, *V poiskakh "soyuza,"* p. 32.

49. Only one issue of this magazine was published. Cited in Chernov, V., "Krovavye psikhozy" [Blood psychoses], in *Che-Ka: Materialy po deyatel'osti chrezvychainykh kommissii* [Che-Ka: Materials on the Activity of Extraordinary Commissions] (Berlin: Orfei, 1922), pp. 15–16 (in Russian).

50. Kokurin and Petrov, *Lubyanka,* p. 8.

51. See, for instance, Leggett, *The CHEKA,* pp. 250–254.

52. Kokurin and Petrov, *Lubyanka,* p. 9.

53. See "The Organization of the GPU," among Pavlovsky's papers in the Hoover Institution Archives, Stanford University, the B. I. Nikolaevsky Collection, Box 217, Folder 6 (published in Felshtinsky, Yuri, *VCHK-GPU* (Benson, VT: Chalidze Publications, 1989), pp. 148–149 (in Russian). On the establishing

of the OAU, see Leggett, *The CHEKA*, p. 230; on the financial autonomy of the VCheKa, see Gerson, *The Secret Police*, pp. 281–282.

54. Leggett, *The CHEKA*, p. 27. See also biographies of Artuzov, Gerson, Lander, and Pavlunovsky in Leggett, *The CHEKA*, pp. 403, 443–444, 452–453, and 456. On Artuzov, see Petrov and Skorkin, *Kto rukovodil NKVD*, pp. 93–94.

55. Kokurin and Petrov, *Lubyanka*, p. 143; Petrov and Skorkin, *Kto rukovodil NKVD*, pp. 82–83.

56. Leggett, *The CHEKA*, pp. 287–288.

57. On Krylenko, see Conquest, Robert, *The Great Terror: A Reassessment* (New York: Oxford University Press, 1990), pp. 249, 420–421; see also Vaksberg, Arkady, *Stalin's Prosecutor: The Life of Andrei Vyshinsky* (New York: Grove Weidenfeld, 1991), pp. 133–142; Yeremina, L. S., and A. B. Roginsky, eds., *Rasstrel'nye spiski: Moscow, 1937–1941, "Kommunarka," Butovo* [Lists of the Executed: Moscow, 1937–1941, Kommunarka and Butovo] (Moscow: Obshchestvo "Memorial," 2000), p. 225 (in Russian). On the style of Krylenko's treatment of "enemies of the people" see, for instance, the memoirs of Marie Avinov (Chavchavadze, Paul, and Marie Avinov, *Pilgrimage Through Hell* [Englewood Cliffs, NJ: Prentice-Hall, 1968], pp. 111–119).

58. Cited in Babkov, V. V., "N. K. Koltsov: Bor'ba za avtonomiyu nauki i poiski podderzhki vlasti "N. K. Koltsov: The fight for the autonomy of science and search for the authorities' support," *Voprosy Istorii Estestvoznaniya i Tekhniki* 3 (1989):3–19 (in Russian).

59. *Krasnaya kniga VCheKa* [The VCheKa Red Book], vol. 2, 2nd ed. (Moscow: Izdatel'stvo politicheskoi literatury, 1989) (in Russian).

60. Cited in Babkov, "N. K. Koltsov," p. 5.

61. *Krasnaya kniga VCheKa*, vol. 2, p. 35.

62. Reformatskaya, M. A., "Yunye gody rovesnikov veka" [The early years of persons born in 1900], in Timofeev-Ressovsky, N. V., *Vospominaniya: Istorii, napisannye im samim, s pis'mami, fotografiyami i dokumentami* [Memoirs: Stories Written by Himself with Letters, Photos, and Documents] (Moscow: Soglasie, 2000), pp. 659–686 (in Russian).

63. Golinkov, D. L., *Krakh vrazheskogo podpolia (Iz istorii borby s kontrrevolyutsiei v Sovetskoi Rossii v 1917–1924 gg.)* [The End of the Enemy's Underground: From the History of Combat Against the Counterrevolution in Soviet Russia, 1917–1924] (Moscow: Politizdat, 1971), p. 287 (in Russian).

64. Tolstoy, Alexandra, *I Worked for the Soviet,* translated by the author, in collaboration with Roberta Yerkes (New Haven: Yale University Press, 1935), p. 96.

65. Cited in Babkov, "N. K. Koltsov," p. 5.

66. Yeremina and Roginsky, *Rasstrel'nye spiski*, p. 208.

67. Tolstoy, *I Worked for the Soviet,* pp. 95–96.

68. Babkov, "N. K. Koltsov," pp. 5–6.

69. Cited in Grigoryan, N. A., "Sotsialno-politicheskie vzglyady I. P. Pavlova" [The social-political views of I. P. Pavlov], *Vestnik Akademii Nauk SSSR* 10 (1991):74–87 (in Russian).

70. Voznesenskii, I., "Iz rannikh svidetel'stv o 'Dele PBO' [On the early testimonies regarding the "PBO case"], in Okhotin and Roginsky, *Zven'ya,* vol. 1, pp. 464–474.

71. Selezneva, I. N., and Ya. G. Yanshin, "Tsel'yu byla russkaya nauka" [Russian science was the target], *Vestnik Rossiiskoi Akademii Nauk* 64 (9) (1994):821–834 (in Russian).

72. Perchenok, F. F., "Spisok rasstrelyannykh" [A list of the executed], *Novyi Mir* 4 (1989):263–269 (in Russian).

73. See Lenin's and Dzerzhinsky's letters cited in Selezneva and Yanshin, "Tsel'yu byla russkaya nauka," pp. 823–824.

74. Voznesenskii, "Iz rannikh svidetel'stv," p. 464.

75. Later, millions of children of "enemies of the people" ended up this way. Tagantsev's children were lucky: They were finally adopted by relatives.

76. Before the Bolshevik Revolution, Anna Kad'yan (1860–?) was a librarian and the treasurer of the High Women's (Bestuzhev) Courses in St. Petersburg/Petrograd. See Sergeev, V. A., "Iz Khvalynska v Petrograd: Pis'ma K. A. Posse k N. S. Tagantsevu i V. A. Steklovu [1917–1918]" [From Khvalynsk to Petrograd: Letters of K. A. Posse to N. S. Tagantsev and V. A. Steklov (1917–1918)], in Dobkin and Roginsky, *Zven'ya,* vol. 2, pp. 378–394.

77. Academician Tagantsev's letter to Lenin dated June 16, 1921, and Mrs. Kad'yan's letter to Lenin dated July 29, 1921 (Russian Center for the Preservation and Study of Documents of Most Recent History, RTsKhIDNI, F. 5, Op. 1, D. 2594, L. 4). Cited in Selezneva and Yanshin, "Tsel'yu byla russkaya nauka," pp. 825–826.

78. Dzerzhinsky's letter to Lenin dated June 19, 1921. Cited in Selezneva and Yanshin, "Tsel'yu byla russkaya nauka," pp. 823–824.

79. Bazhanov, Boris, *Bazhanov and the Damnation of Stalin,* trans. and commentary by D. W. Doyle (Athens: Ohio University Press, 1990), p. 240.

80. Cited in Selezneva and Yanshin, "Tsel'yu byla russkaya nauka," p. 824.

81. Voznesenskii, "Iz rannikh svidetel'stv," pp. 466–469.

82. Gerson, *The Secret Police,* pp. 183–184. More details in Avrich, P., *Kronstadt, 1921* (Princeton: Princeton University Press, 1970).

83. Gerson, *The Secret Police,* p. 183.

84. Serge, Victor, *Memoirs of a Revolutionary: 1901–1941,* trans. Peter Sedgwick (London: Oxford University Press, 1963), p. 131.

85. This was the beginning of the wide purges against the Red Army officers. According to recent data, approximately 43,000 officers were executed in 1937–1938. The number of executed generals was much higher than the number of Soviet generals killed in 1941–1945 during World War II. After Stalin's death, it became clear that the accusation of Tukhachevsky and the other generals was based on forged documents created by the SD (the SS intelligence) under the supervision of the SD head, Reinhard Heydrich. See Conquest, *The Great Terror,* pp. 182–213; Volkogonov, Dmitri, *Stalin: Triumph and Tragedy,* trans. Harold Shukman (New York: Grove Weidenfeld, 1991), pp. 316–329.

86. Voznesenskii, "Iz rannikh svidetel'stv," p. 468.

87. Ibid., pp. 469–470.

88. From a letter by Kyrtenkov, Chugaev, and Chernyaev to chairman of the Council of Commissars dated August 26, 1921 (RTsKhIDNI, F. 2. Op. 1. D. 20625. L. 1). Cited in Selezneva and Yanshin, "Tsel'yu byla russkaya nauka," p. 826. On Gorbunov, see Parkhomenko, A. A., "Akademik N. P. Gorbunov: Vzlet i tragediya" [Academician N. P. Gorbunov: Ascension and tragedy], in Yaroshevskii, M. G., ed., *Repressirovannaya nauka* [Repressed Science] (Leningrad: Nauka, 1991), pp. 409–423 (in Russian); Yeremina and Roginsky, *Rasstrel'nye spiski*, p. 112.

89. Lenin, Vladimir I., *Polnoe sobranie sochinenii* [Collected Works] (Politizdat: Moscow), vol. 53, p. 169 (in Russian). The note was cited in Selezneva and Yanshin, "Tsel'yu byla russkaya nauka," p. 824.

90. Voznesenskii, "Iz rannikh svidetel'stv," p. 474.

91. Cited in Melgunov, S. P., *Krasnyi terror v Rossii, 1918–1923* [The Red Terror in Russia, 1918–1923] (Moscow: Puico, 1990), p. 141 (in Russian). The first edition of this book was published in Berlin in 1923.

92. Cited in Selezneva and Yanshin, "Tsel'yu byla russkaya nauka," p. 823.

93. Karpinsky's letter to Lenin dated September 21, 1921 (RTsKhIDNI, F. 2, Op. 1, D. 20969, L. 1–2). Cited in Selezneva and Yanshin, "Tsel'yu byla russkaya nauka," pp. 826–827.

94. Cited in Romanovsky, "Pervyi demokratichesky izbrannyi," p. 1099.

95. See Agranov's report about arrests, dated October 26, 1921. Reproduced in Revyakina and Selezneva, "Trudnye gody rossiiskoi nauki," p. 937.

96. Voznesenskii, "Iz rannikh svidetel'stv," pp. 472–473.

97. Chebrikov, V. M., G. F. Grigorenko, N. A. Dushin, and F. D. Bobkov, eds., *Istoriya sovetskikh organov gosudarstvennoi bezopasnosti: Uchebnik, "Sovershenno sekretno"* [History of the Soviet Security Service: A Textbook, "Top Secret"] (Moscow: Vysshaya Shkola KGB, 1977), pp. 147–149 (in Russian).

98. Details in Latyshev, A. G., *Rassekrechennyi Lenin* [Declassified Lenin] (Moscow: Mart, 1996), pp. 201–226 (in Russian).

99. Petrov and Skorkin, *Kto rukovodil NKVD*, pp. 82–83 and 349–350.

100. Latyshev, *Rassekrechennyi Lenin*, p. 221.

101. The text of Unshlikht's report is cited in ibid., p. 215, and Volkov and Kulikova, "Rossiiskaya professura," p. 73.

102. Latyshev, *Rassekrechennyi Lenin*, p. 214.

103. Volkov, A. V., "'Preussen' plyvet: K istorii vysilki iz Rossii 'antisovetskoi intelligentsii' 1922" [The "Preussen" swims: On the history of deportation of the "anti-Soviet intelligentsia" from Russia in 1922], *Priroda* [Nature] 5 (1999):124–128 (in Russian).

104. For more details, see Kassow, Samuel D., *Students, Professors, and the State in Tsarist Russia* (Berkeley: University of California Press, 1989), pp. 288–298.

105. Ibid., pp. 353–357; Bailes, *Science and Russian Culture*, pp. 116–118.

106. Schnol, Simon E., *Geroi i zlodei rossiiskoi nauki* [Heroes and Villains of Russian Science] (Moscow: Kron-Press, 1997), pp. 15–36 (in Russian).

107. Astaurov, Boris L., and Pyotr F. Rokitsky, *Nikolai Konstantinovich Koltsov* (Moscow: Nauka, 1975), p. 18 (in Russian).

108. Lenin, Vladimir I., *Collected Works*, vol. 44 (Moscow: Progress Publishers, 1970), p. 284: in a letter from Petrograd dated September 15, 1919.

109. Letter of Vladimir Vernadsky to his son George, dated 1921. Columbia University, Bakhmeteef's Humanities, Vernadsky Collection, box 11. Cited in Kolchinsky, *V poiskakh*, p. 224.

110. Lenin, *Polnoe sobranie sochinenii*, vol. 54, p. 270.

111. The Entente was the anti-Bolshevik coalition of Britain, United States, and France. In spring 1918, approximately 5,000 Allied troops occupied the city of Arkhangelsk in the northern part of European Russia (see, for instance, Lincoln, W. Bruce, *Red Victory: A History of the Russian Civil War* [New York: Touchstone, 1989], pp. 163–193).

112. Lenin, *Polnoe sobranie sochinenii*, vol. 54, pp. 265–266.

113. Ibid., p. 364.

114. Possibly, Varvara Yakovleva (1884–1941?) was put in charge of the high school because she was more educated than other Bolshevik leaders; at least she had studied math and physics.

115. In February 1922, the VCheKa (All-Russian Extraordinary Commission), which since December 1917 was under the Sovnarkom (Council of People's Commissars), was merged with the NKVD and renamed GPU (State Political Directorate) within the NKVD. On December 30, 1922, after the creation of the Soviet Union from the RSFSR (Russian Federation), the GPU was reorganized into the OGPU (United State Political Directorate) within the NKVD. See Kokurin and Petrov, *Lubyanka*, pp. 8–11.

116. Recently discovered at the Archive of the Bureau of the Secretariat of the Bolshevik (Communist) Party Central Committee, the "Draft Resolution" of the Politburo Meeting is now kept at the Russian Center for the Preservation and Study of Documents of Most Recent History (RTsKhIDNI) in Moscow (F. 17, Op. 86, D. 17, L. 50–51). Cited in Selezneva, I. N., "Dokumenty iz fonda Byuro Sekretariata TsK VKP(b)" [Documents from the Archive of the Bureau of the Secretariat of the Central Committee of the Bolshevik Party], *Vestnik Rossiiskoi Akademii Nauk* 66 (10) (1996):927–931 (in Russian), document no. 5 (p. 930).

117. From Agranov to Dzerzhinsky, Top Secret, June 1, 1922. Cited in Selezneva, "Dokumenty iz fonda Byuro Sekretariata TsK VKP(b)," pp. 927–929, document no. 1 (RTsKhIDNI, F. 17, Op. 86, D. 17, L. 55–59).

118. Excerpt from the Protocol No. 10 of the Politburo meeting on June 8, 1922. Cited in Selezneva, "Dokumenty iz fonda Byuro Sekretariata TsK VKP(b)," pp. 927–929, document no. 3 (RTsKhIDNI, F. 17, Op. 86, D. 17, L. 49).

119. Selezneva, I. N., "'Tsel' GPU" [The GPU's target], *Vestnik Rossiiskoi Akademii Nauk* 66 (10) (1966):925–927 (in Russian).

120. For details, see McClelland, "The Professorate in the Russian Civil War," pp. 251–256.

121. Draft Resolution of the Presidium of VtsIK dated June 1922. In Selezneva, "Dokumenty iz fonda Byuro Sekretariata TsK VKP(b)," p. 931, document no. 7 (RTsKhIDN, F. 17, Op. 86, D. 17, L. 53).

122. The Politburo resolution dated June 12, 1922 (Izvestiya VtsIK, 1922, No. 1573), cited in Selezneva, "Dokumenty iz fonda Byuro Sekretariata TsK VKP(b)," p. 931.

123. Rokityansky, Ya. G., "Dva pis'ma akademika I. P. Pavlova" [Two letters of Academician I. P. Pavlov], *Vestnik Akademii Nauk SSSR* 10 (1991):87–89 (in Russian).

124. Mochalov, I. I., "V. I. Vernadsky i Glavlit" [V. I. Vernadsky and Glavlit], *Vestnik Instituta Istorii Estestvoznaniya i Tekhniki* 2 (1999):150–163 (in Russian).

125. For details, see Blyum, Arlen V., *Sovetskaya tsenzura v epokhu total'nogo terora, 1929–1953* [Soviet Censorship During the Epoch of Total Terror, 1929–1953] (St. Petersburg: Akademicheskii Proekt, 2000), pp. 89–93 (in Russian). A photo of the first page of copy no. 785 of "The Combined List of Books That Should Be Taken from Libraries and Bookstores," dated 1973, is given in King, David, *The Commissar Vanishes: The Falsification of Photographs and Art in Stalin's Russia* (New York: Henry Holt, 1999), p. 12.

126. Dzerzhinsky's notes of his conversation with Lenin on September 5, 1922, and an instruction to Unshlikht from Dzerzhinsky's diary are given in Latyshev, *Rassekrechennyi Lenin*, pp. 213–214.

127. See the history of reorganizations of this department in Kokurin and Petrov, *Lubyanka*, p. 126. On changes during and after "perestroika," see Waller, J. Michael, *Secret Empire: The KGB in Russia Today* (Boulder: Westview Press, 1994), pp. 16, 71.

128. Reiss, Albert, ed., *Molotov Remembers: Inside Kremlin Politics. Conversations with Felix Chuev* (Chicago: Ivan R. Dee, 1993), p. 121.

129. Ibid., p. 237.

130. Koltsov, *Sozdanie i deyatel'nost*, p. 69.

131. Graham, Loren R., *The Soviet Academy of Sciences and the Communist Party, 1927–1932* (Princeton: Princeton University Press, 1967), pp. 80–153; Levin, A. E., "Expedient Catastrophe: A Reconsideration of the 1929 Crisis at the Soviet Academy of Sciences," *Slavic Review* 47 (2) (1988):261–279; Aleksandrov, D. A., and N. L. Krementsov, "Opyt putevoditelya po neizvedannoi zemle: Predvaritelnyi ocherk sotsialnoi istorii sovetskoi nauki (1917–1950-e gody)" [An attempt at a guidebook for unknown territory: Preliminary outline of the social history of Soviet science (1917–1950s)], *Voprosy Istorii Estestvoznaniya i Tekhniki* 4 (1989):67–80 (in Russian); Brachev, V. S., "Ukrashchenie stroptivoi ili kak Akademiya Nauk obuchali" [The taming of an obstinate character, or how the Academy of Sciences was taught obedience], *Vestnik Akademii Nauk SSSR* 2 (1990):120–127 (in Russian); Perchenok, "Akademiya Nauk," pp. 163–238; Orel, V. M., "Bitva so zdravym smyslom: Kak prinimalsya ustav Akademii 1930

goda" [A fight against common sense: How the statute of the academy was accepted], *Vestnik Rossiiskoi Akademii Nauk* 64 (1994):366–375 (in Russian); Tolz, *Russian Academicians,* pp. 26–67.

132. Popovsky, Mark, *Manipulated Science: The Crisis of Science and Scientists in the Soviet Union Today,* trans. P. S. Falla (Garden City, NY: Doubleday, 1979), p. 29.

133. Romanovsky, "Pervyi demokraticheski izbrannyi prezident," pp. 173–175.

134. Document 1 in Malysheva, M. P., and V. S. Poznansky, "Partiinoe rukovodstvo Akademiei nauk: Sem' dokumentov iz byvshego arkhiva Novosibirskogo obkoma KPSS" [The Party leadership of the Academy of Sciences: Seven documents from the former archive of the Novosibirsk Regional Committee of the Communist Party], *Vestnik Rossiiskoi Akademii Nauk* 64 (11) (1994):1033–1041 (in Russian).

135. Cited in Grigoryan, "Sotsialno-politicheskie vzglyady." Vera Tolz wrongly attributes this letter to the 1930s (Tolz, *Russian Academicians,* p. 130).

136. Yeremina and Roginsky, *Rasstrel'nye spiski,* p. 290. Other members of the same case are mentioned in Chapter 2.

137. Koltsov, A. V., "Vybory v Akademiyu Nauk SSSR v 1929 g." [The elections to the Academy of Sciences in 1929], *Vestnik Instituta Istorii Estestvoznaniya i Tekhniki* 3 (1990):53–66 (in Russian).

138. Perchenok, "Akademiya Nauk," p. 190; Tolz, *Russian Academicians,* p. 45.

139. Krementsov, *Stalinist Science,* p. 302.

140. Ibid.

141. Antonova, N. S., and N. V. Drozdova, "Rossiiskie uchenye—akademiku A. V. Lunacharskomu" [From Russian academicians to Academician A. V. Lunacharsky], *Vestnik Rossiiskoi Akademii Nauk* 64 (3) (1994):253–265 (in Russian).

142. Volgin replaced Academician Oldenburg, who was permanent secretary from 1904. In 1935, the Politburo replaced Volgin with Lenin's former secretary Nikolai Gorbunov (Krementsov, *Stalinist Science,* p. 41).

143. On Vavilov, see Adams, Mark, "Vavilov, Nikolai Ivanovich," in Gillispie, Charles Coulston, ed., *Dictionary of Scientific Biographies,* vol. 15, supp. 1 (New York: Charles Scribner's Sons, 1978), pp. 505–513; Crow, James F., "N. I. Vavilov, Martyr of Genetic Truth," *Genetics* 134 (1) (1993):1–4.

144. Koltsov, *Sozdanie i deyatel'nost,* p. 110.

145. Brachev, "Ukroshchenie stroptivoi," pp. 120–125; Koltsov, "Vybory."

146. Smagina, G. I., and V. M. Orel, "Novye dokumenty o deyatelnosti Komissii po istorii znanii AN SSSR (k 70-letiyu organizatsii)" [New documents on the activity of the AN USSR Commission on the History of Knowledge (up to its 70th anniversary)], *Voprosy Istorii Estestvoznaniya i Tekhniki* 2 (1993):54–66 (in Russian).

147. Tugarinov, I. A., "VARNITSO i Akademiya nayk" [VARNITSO and the Academy of Sciences], *Voprosy Istorii Estestvoznaniya i Tekhniki* 4:46–55 (in Russian).

148. Heller and Nekrich, *Utopia in Power,* pp. 208–209, 211–212, 228.

149. Lyons, Eugene, *Assignment to Utopia* (New Brunswick, NJ: Transaction Publishers, 1991), p. 127.

150. Perchenok, "Akademiya Nauk," pp. 228–230.

151. Published in Yanshina, F. T., "Neizvestnyi Vernadsky" [The unknown Vernadsky], *Vestnik Rossiiskoi Akademii Nauk* 63 (9) (1993):822–829 (in Russian).

152. Brachev, "Ukroshchenie stroptivoi," p. 195.

153. Perchenok, "Akademiya Nauk," pp. 204–205.

154. Tolz, *Russian Academicians,* p. 51.

155. Ibid.

156. A transcript of the meeting is given in Perchenok, "Akademiya Nauk," pp. 226–230.

157. Perchenok, "Akademiya Nauk," pp. 214–215.

158. Brachev, V. S., "Opasnaya professiya—istorik: Stranitsy zhizni akademika S. F. Platonova" [Historian—a dangerous profession: Episodes from the life of S. F. Platonov], *Vestnik Akademii Nauk SSSR* 9 (1991):65–73 (in Russian); Brachev, V. S., "Ispoved' uznika OGPU (neizvestnaya rukopis' akademika S. F. Platonova)" [The confession of an OGPU prisoner (an unknown manuscript of Academician S. F. Platonov], *Vestnik Rossiiskoi Akademii Nauk* 9 (1992):118–128 (in Russian).

159. Pokrovsky's letter to the OGPU Secret Department dated September 29, 1932, Russian Center for the Preservation and Study of Documents of Most Recent History (RTsKhIDNI), F. 147, Op. 2, D. 11, L. 3. Reproduced in Yesina, A. V., "'Mne zhe oni sovershenno ne nuzhny' (Sem' pisem iz lichnogo arkhiva akademika M. N. Pokrovskogo)" ["I do not need them" (Seven letters from the personal archive of Academician M. N. Pokrovsky)], *Vestnik Rossiiskoi Akademii Nauk* 6 (1992):103–114 (in Russian).

160. Chebrikov et al., *Istoriya,* p. 274; Rossi, Jacques, *The Gulag Handbook: An Encyclopedia Dictionary of Soviet Penitentiary Institutions and Terms Related to the Forced Labor Camps* (New York: Paragon House, 1989), p. 453.

161. Antonova and Drozdova, "Rossiiskie uchenye—akademiku A. V. Lunacharskomu," p. 265.

162. See details about the commission in Perchenok, "Akademiya Nauk," p. 174.

163. The transcript of the General Meeting of the Academy of Sciences, Academy of Sciences Archive, F. 3, Op. 4, D. 7, L. 98. Cited in Perchenok, "Akademiya Nauk," p. 230.

164. Stetsovsky, *Istoriya,* vol. 2, p. 170.

165. For instance, Soyfer, *Lysenko,* and Krementsov, *Stalinist Science.*

166. Soyfer, *Lysenko,* pp. 132–135.

167. See details, for example, in Joravsky, *The Lysenko Affair,* pp. 229–243.

168. Soyfer, *Lysenko,* pp. 8–42.

169. Graham, *What Have We Learned,* pp. 17–28.

170. Gaisinovich, A. E., and K. O. Rossianov, "'Ya gluboko ubezhden chto ya prav': N. K. Koltsov i lysenkovshchina" ["I am deeply convinced that I am right": N. K. Koltsov and Lysenko], *Priroda* 6 (1989):95–103 (in Russian).

171. Graham, *What Have We Learned,* p. 20.

172. Dobzhansky, Theodosius, "The Crisis in Soviet biology," in Simmons, Ernest J., ed., *Continuity and Change in Russian and Soviet Thought* (Cambridge: Harvard University Press, 1955), pp. 329–344. On Dobzhansky, see, for instance, Adams, Mark B., ed., *The Evolution of Theodosius Dobzhansky: Essays on His Life and Thought in Russia and America* (Princeton: Princeton University Press, 1994).

173. Fyodorovich, V., "The Winter Fields," *Pravda,* August 7, 1927 (in Russian).

174. Details in Soyfer, *Lysenko,* pp. 12–31.

175. Popovsky, *The Vavilov Affair,* pp. 41–51.

176. Manevich, E. D., "Takie byli vremena" [It was a special time], *Voprosy Istorii Estestvoznaniya i Tekhniki* 2 (1993):119–132 (in Russian). Manevich mentioned that Dr. Joseph Needham and not Eric Ashby attended the lecture with Julian Huxley. But Huxley wrote that he possessed a copy of the summary of this lecture written by Ashby. See Huxley, Julian, *Soviet Genetics and World Science: Lysenko and the Meaning of Heredity* (London: Chatto and Windus, 1949), p. 101.

177. Huxley, *Soviet Genetics,* pp. 101–102.

178. Cited in Zonn, S. V., "Akademik Vladimir Nikolaevich Sukachev (1880–1967) kak prezident Moskovskogo Obshchestva Ispytatelei Prirody" [Academician Vladimir Nikolaevich Sukachev (1880–1967) as the president of the Moscow Society of Naturalists], *Bulletin Moskovskogo Obshchestva Ispytatelei Prirody, Otdelenie biologicheskoe* 101 (3) (1996):97–102 (in Russian).

179. Lysenko, T. D., "Novoe v nauke o vide" [News in the science of species], *Agrobiologiya* [Agrobiology] 6 (1950):15–25 (in Russian).

180. Lysenko, Trofim D., *Agrobiologiya* [Agrobiology] (Moscow: Selkhozgiz, 1952), p. 552 (in Russian).

181. Ibid., p. 604.

182. Ibid., p. 662.

183. Lysenko, "The Situation in Biological Science," in *The Situation in Biological Science: Proceedings of the Lenin Academy of Agricultural Sciences of the USSR, July 31–August 7, 1948: Complete Stenographic Report* (New York: International Publishers Co., 1949), p. 132.

184. Soyfer, *Lysenko,* p. 210.

185. Dobzhansky, Theodosius, "Lysenkoist's 'Michurinist' genetics," *Bulletin of Atomic Scientists* 8 (1952):40–44.

186. Cited in Soyfer, *Lysenko,* p. 58.

187. Ibid., p. 121.

188. Ibid., p. 61.

189. A short history of the creation of kolkhozes is given, for instance, in Heller and Nekrich, *Utopia in Power,* pp. 232–244.

190. Rossianov, K. O., "Editing Nature: Joseph Stalin and the "New" Soviet Biology," *Isis* 84 (1993):728–745.

191. Huxley, Julian, *Evolution in Action* (New York: Harper and Brothers, 1953), p. 169.

192. Cook, R. C., "Lysenko's Marxist Genetics: Science or Religion?" *Journal of Heredity* 40 (7) (1949):169–202.

193. Adams, Mark B., "Science, Ideology, and Structure: The Koltsov Institute, 1900–1970," in Lubrano, Linda L., and Susan G. Solomon, eds., *The Social Context of Soviet Science* (Boulder: Westview Press, 1980), p. 199.

194. Cited in Blyum, *Sovetskaya tsenzura*, p. 112.

195. Yakovlev, B., *Kontsentrastionnye lageri SSSR* [Concentration Camps in the USSR] (München: Institute for the Study of the History and Culture of the USSR, 1955), p. 69 (in Russian).

196. Lifton, *The Nazi Doctors*, pp. 292–293.

197. See, for instance, Hilberg, Raoul, *The Destruction of the European Jews* (New York: Holmes and Meier, 1985), pp. 27–37.

198. Müller-Hill, "Science, Truth and Other Values," p. 405.

199. Grekova, T. I., and K. A. Lange, "Tragicheskie stranitsy istorii Instituta Eksperimental'noi Meditsiny (20-30-e gody)" [The tragic pages of the Institute of Experimental Medicine history, the 1920s-1930s], in Yaroshevskii, M. G., ed., *Repressirovannaya Nauka, Vypusk II* [Repressed Science, issue 2] (St. Petersburg: Nauka, 1994), pp. 10–11 (in Russian).

200. Shatunovskaya, Lidiya, *Zizn' v Kremle* [Life in the Kremlin] (New York: Chalidze Publications, 1982), pp. 197–200 (in Russian).

201. Rapoport, Yakov, *The Doctor's Plot of 1953,* trans. N. A. Petrova and R. S. Bobrova (Cambridge: Harvard University Press, 1991), p. 32.

202. Conquest, *The Great Terror*, p. 58.

203. Radzinsky, Edvard, *Stalin*, trans. H. T. Willetts (New York: Anchor Books, 1996), pp. 292 and 422.

204. Petrov and Skorkin, *Kto rukovodil NKVD*, pp. 357–358.

205. Radzinsky, *Stalin*, p. 423.

206. Volkogonov, *Stalin*, pp. 339–340.

207. Radzinsky, *Stalin,* pp. 293–294.

208. Ibid., p. 421.

209. Volkogonov, *Stalin,* p. 340.

210. Allilueva, Svetlana, *Twenty Letters to a Friend,* trans. Priscilla Johnson McMillan (New York: Harper and Row, 1967), p. 196.

211. Mlechin, Leonid, *Predsedateli KGB: Rassekrechennye sud'by* [The KGB Chairmen: Declassified Biographies] (Moscow: Tsentrpoligraf, 1999), p. 171 (in Russian).

212. Stolyarov, Kirill, *Palachi i zhertvy* [Executioners and Victims] (Moscow: Olma-Press, 1997), pp. 66–67 (in Russian).

213. Hodos, George H., *Show Trials: Stalinist Purges in Eastern Europe, 1948–1954* (New York: Praeger, 1987), pp. 106–107.

214. From an interview with Anna's son Vladimir by Rosamond Richardson. Cited in Richardson, Rosamond, *Stalin's Shadow: Inside the Family of One of the World's Greatest Tyrants* (New York: St. Martin's Press, 1994), pp. 232–233.

215. Ibid., p. 233, from an interview with Yevgeniya's son Sasha by Rosamond Richardson.

216. There were two prisoner cards for Molochnikov in the file of Vladimir Prison, with his full name and as Prisoner No. 21 (Documents 3 and 4 in Appendix II).

217. Personal communication in 1990.

218. Vaksberg, Arkady, *Stalin Against the Jews*, trans. A. W. Bouis (New York: Alfred A. Knopf, 1994), pp. 156–157.

219. Kostyrchenko, *Out of the Red Shadows*, p. 79.

220. Vaksberg, *Stalin Against the Jews,* p. 217.

221. Kostyrchenko, *Out of the Red Shadows*, pp. 82–83.

222. The text is reproduced as Document No. 6 in Naumov, V., and Yu. Sigachev, *Lavrentii Beria, 1953* (Moscow: Mezhdunarodnyi Fond "Demokratia," 1999), pp. 23–25 (in Russian).

223. See, for instance, Kostyrchenko, *Out of the Red Shadows*, pp. 31–34.

224. Beria's letter to the Presidium (Politburo), dated April 2, 1953. Reproduced in Naumov and Sigachev, *Lavrentii Beria,* pp. 25–28 (document no. 7).

225. Shatunovskaya, *Zhizn' v Kremle,* p. 335.

226. A description of Komarov in his Prisoner File cited in Stolyarov, *Palachi i zhertvy,* p. 26.

227. Memoirs of Iosif Turko, cited in Demidov, V., and V. Kutuzov, "*Poslednii udar*" [The final blow in], Leningradskoe delo "*The Leningrad Case*" (Leningrad: Lenizdat, 1990), pp. 5-157 (in Russian).

228. Shatunovskaya, *Zhizn' v Kremle,* p. 284.

229. Ibid., pp. 300–308.

230. Stolyarov, *Palachi i zhertvy,* p. 27.

231. Loebl, Eugen, *My Mind on Trial* (New York: Helen and Kurt Wolff, 1976), p. 62.

232. Soyfer, *Lysenko,* p. 348.

233. Shatunovskaya, *Zhizn' v Kremle,* pp. 257–260 (in Russian); Kostyrchenko, *Out of the Red Shadows,* p. 87.

234. Prisoner cards of Mariyana Zaitseva and Vitalii Zaitsev.

235. Prisoner card of Tatyana Fradkina (Memorial's Archive [Moscow], fond 171; prisoner cards from Vladimir Prison).

236. Morozov, Grigory, "Pis'ma iz seifa" [Letters from a safe], *Obshchaya Gazeta* 6, February 6, 2000 (on-line version, in Russian).

237. Prokopenko, A. S., *Bezumnaya psikhiatriya: Sekretnye materialy o primenenii v SSSR psikhiatrii v karatel'nykh tselyakh* [Mad Psychiatry: Secret Materials on the Use of Psychiatry for Punishment in the USSR] (Moscow: Sovershenno Secretno, 1997), pp. 20, 24–27 (in Russian).

238. Zakharov,V. E., "Rekviem po M. L. Levinu" [Requiem for M. L. Levin], *Priroda* 2 (1996):122–126 (in Russian).

239. Sakharov, Andrei *Memoirs*, translated by R. Lourie (New York: Alfred A. Knopf, 1990) p. 550. For Levin's description of his trips to Sakharov, see Levin, M. L., "Iz vystuplenii na Sakharovskikh chteniyakh" [From speeches at Sakharov's hearings], *Priroda* 8 (1990): 124–126 (in Russian).

240. Rapoport, *The Doctor's Plot of 1953*, pp. 143–244;Vaksberg, *Stalin Against the Jews*, pp. 226–227; Kostyrchenko, *Out of the Red Shadows*, pp. 248–305.

241. See, for instance, Turkevich, J., "Stern, Lina Solomonovna (Physiologist)," in *Soviet Men of Science: Academicians and Corresponding Members of the Academy of Sciences of the USSR* (Princeton: D.Van Nostrand, 1973), pp. 348–349.

242. Kostyrchenko, *Out of the Red Shadows*, pp. 79–81.

243. See details in ibid., pp. 83–85.

244. Cited in ibid., p. 85.

245. An excerpt from the "testimony," dated January 9, 1948, is given in Kostyrchenko, *Out of the Red Shadows*, pp. 85–86.

246. See "O tak nazyvaemom 'Dele.'"

247. Reiss, *Molotov Remembers*, p. 325.

248. Molotov's top-secret note to Stalin, dated January 20, 1949, from the President's Archive published in Radzinsky, *Stalin*, p. 533.

249. Vaksberg, *Stalin Against the Jews*, p. 189.

250. Rapoport, *Stalin's War Against the Jews*, p. 125.

251. See the court record in Rubenstein, Joshua, and Naumov,Vladimir P., eds., *Stalin's Secret Pogrom: The Postwar Inquisition of the Jewish Anti-Fascist Committee*, trans. Laura Esther Wolfson (New Haven:Yale University Press, in association with the United States Holocaust Memorial Museum, 2001).

252. The translation of Cheptsov's statement written on August 15, 1957, is given inVaksberg, *Stalin Against the Jews*, pp. 227–236.

253. Naumov and Sigachev, *Lavrentii Beria,* p. 497.

254. See memoirs of Esther Markish, the wife of one of the executed (Markish, Esther, *The Long Return,* with a foreword by David Roskies [New York: Ballantine Books, 1978], pp. 176–230).

255. "O tak nazyvaemom "Dele," p. 40.

256. See, for instance, Batygin, G. S., and I. F. Devyatko, "Evreiskii vopros: khronika sorokovykh godov, chast' pervaya" [The Jewish question: The chronicle of the 1940s, part one], *Vestnik Rossiiskoi Akademii Nauk* 63 (1) (1993):61–72; Batygin, G. S., and I. F. Devyatko, "Evreiskii vopros: Khronika sorokovykh godov, chast' vtoraya" [The Jewish question: The chronicle of the 1940s, part two], *Vestnik Rossiiskoi Akademii Nauk* 63 (2) (1993):143–151 (in Russian).

257. Stolyarov, *Palachi i zhertvy*, p.11.

258. An excerpt from a transcript of the interrogation of Isaak Fefer on April 22, 1949, given in Kostyrchenko, *Out of the Red Shadows*, p. 259.

259. Rapoport, *The Doctors' Plot of 1953*, p. 57.

260. Naumov and Sigachev, *Lavrentii Beria*, p. 434.

261. Kostyrchenko, *Out of the Red Shadows*, pp. 260–261.

262. Viktorova's prisoner card, Memorial's Archive (Moscow), fond 171; prisoner cards from Vladimir Prison.

263. Stolyarov, *Palachi i zhertvy*, p. 26.

264. Etinger, Ya., "Kogda nachalos' 'delo vrachei'?" [When did the "Doctors' Case" start?], in Okhotin and Roginsky, *Zven'ya*, vol. 1, pp. 555–559 (in Russian).

265. Kostyrchenko, *Out of the Red Shadows*, p. 264.

266. Ibid., pp. 273–274.

267. Rapoport, *The Doctor's Plot of 1953*, pp. 74–75; Kostyrchenko, *Out of the Red Shadows*, p. 291.

268. Naumov and Sigachev, *Lavrentii Beria*, p. 491.

269. Kostyrchenko, *Out of the Red Shadows*, p. 285.

270. Ibid., p. 283.

271. Ibid., p. 275.

272. Ibid., p. 296.

273. Rapoport, N., *To li byl', to li nebyl'* [This Might or Might Not Have Happened] (St. Petersburg: Izdatel'stvo Pushkinskogo Fonda, 1998), p. 15 (in Russian).

274. Heller and Nekrich, *Utopia in Power*, pp. 503–504.

275. Khrushchev's radio announcement on July 19, 1964. Cited in Reiss, *Molotov Remembers*, p. 236.

276. Kostyrchenko, *Out of the Red Shadows*, p. 275.

277. Stolyarov, *Palachi i zhertvy*, pp. 200–201.

278. Beria's top-secret note to Georgii Malenkov, no. 17/B, dated April 1, 1953. The text was published as document no. 5 in Naumov and Sigachev, *Lavrentii Beria*, pp. 21–23. The secret resolution no. P3/1 regarding the so-called Doctors' Plot case was approved by the Presidium on April 3, 1953 (document no. 6 in Naumov and Sigachev, *Lavrentii Beria,* pp. 23–25). Beria, Voroshilov, Bulganin, Pervukhin, Kaganovich, Saburov, Mikoyan, Khrushchev, Molotov, and Malenkov were present at the meeting.

279. Vasilieva, Larissa, *Kremlin Wives,* translated from Russian by Cathy Porter (New York: Arcade Publishing, 1994), pp. 154–155.

280. Ibid., p. 155.

281. Vaksberg, *Stalin Against the Jews,* p. 192; Vasilieva, *Kremlin Wives,* p. 159.

282. Vasilieva, *Kremlin Wives,* p. 159.

283. Materials from Ekaterina Kalinina's NKVD Investigation File are cited in ibid., pp. 116–135.

284. Kokurin and Petrov, *Lubyanka,* pp. 72–77.

285. Documents nos. 5 and 6 in Naumov and Sigachev, *Lavrentii Beria,* pp. 21–25.

286. Viktorova's prisoner card, Memorial's Archive (Moscow), fond 171; prisoner cards from Vladimir Prison.

287. Beria's top-secret letter to Malenkov no. 128/B, dated June 25, 1953, published as document 22 in Naumov and Sigachev, *Lavrentii Beria*, pp. 64–66.

288. Stolyarov, *Palachi i zhertvy*, pp. 16–18.

289. Ibid., p. 239.

290. Ibid., p. 299.

291. Petrov, N., "Sudy protiv chlenov NKVD-MGB" [Trials against NKVD-MGB members], in Okhotin and Roginsky, *Zven'ya*, vol. 1, pp. 430–436 (in Russian).

292. In her memoirs, Dr. Raissa Berg describes in detail her frightening experience when she was called to the Special Department of the Automation Institute of the Novosibirsk Branch of the academy (Berg, Raissa L., *Acquired Traits: Memoirs of a Geneticist from the Soviet Union* [New York: Viking, 1988], pp. 368–371).

293. Albats, Yevgenia, *The State Within a State* (New York: Farrar, 1994), p. 195.

294. Popov, F., *Arzamas-16: Sem' let s Andreem Sakharovym. Vospominaniya kontrrazvedchika* [Arzamas-16: Seven Years with Academician Sakharov. The Recollections of a Counterintelligence Officer] (Murmansk: Pazori, 1998), p. 190 (in Russian).

295. Popov, *Arzamas-16*, p. 207.

296. Aleksandrov, Vladimir Ya., *Trudnye gody sovetskoi biologii: Vospominaniya sovremennika* [Hard Years of Soviet Biology: Memoirs of a Contemporary] (St. Petersburg: Nauka, 1993), pp. 224–225 (in Russian).

297. Maksimov, V., "Po obyknoveniyu general Zdanovich otlil pulyu" [As usual, General Zdanovich lied], *Novaya Gazeta*, March 13, 2000 (on-line version, in Russian).

298. "Akademiku V. Ye. Sokolovu 70 let" [Academician V. Ye. Sokolov is seventy years old], *Vestnik Rossiiskoi Akademii Nauk* 68 (5) (1998):467 (in Russian).

299. There were Councils of Deputies (Parliaments) in each Soviet republic, including the Russian Federation, and the Soviet Council, which consisted of separately elected deputies. This system had nothing to do with real democracy because there was only one Communist Party–approved candidate for the deputy position during all elections.

300. Domaradsky, I. V., *"Perevyortysh" (Rasskaz "neudobnogo" cheloveka)* ["Troublemaker" (The Story of an "Inconvenient" Person)] (Moscow: N.p., 1995), pp. 72–76 (in Russian).

301. Rimmington, Anthony, "Biotechnology," in Berry, Michael J., ed., *Science and Technology in the USSR* (Burnt Mill, UK: Longman, 1988), pp. 233–245.

302. Alibek, *Biohazard*, pp. 43–44.

303. Dr. Goldfarb's attempt to smuggle a nonpathogenic strain of *Escherichia coli* through the Soviet border (about which I was not aware of during the interrogation) and his "case" are briefly described in Daniloff, N., *Two Lives, One Russia* (New York: Avon Books, 1988), pp. 171–177.

304. See, for instance, Schnol, *Geroi i zlodei,* pp. 312–339.

305. Polyansky, Yu. I., *Gody prozhitye: Vospominaniya biologa* [The Years I Lived Through: Memoirs of a Biologist] (St. Petersburg: Nauka, 1997), pp. 126–137 (in Russian).

306. Birstein, Vadim J. *Tsitogeneticheskie i molekulyarnye osnovy evolutsii pozvonochnykh* [Cytogenetic and Molecular Aspects of Vertebrate Evolution] (Moscow: Nauka, 1987), (in Russian).

307. Novik, I. B., "Normal'naya 'pseudonauka'" [A normal "pseudoscience"], *Voprosy Istorii Estestvoznaniya i Tekhniki* 3 (1990):3–16 (in Russian).

308. Smirnov, Yu. N., "Stalin i atomnaya bomba" [Stalin and the atom bomb], *Voprosy Istorii Estestvoznaniya i Tekhniki* 2:125–130 (in Russian). On Axel Berg, see Siforov, V. I., and V. I. Neiman, "Shturman otechestvennoi radio-electroniki: K 100-letiyu co dnya rozhdeniya akademika A. I. Berga" [A navigator of national radioelectronics: To the 100th anniversary of the birth of Academician A. I. Berg], *Vestnik Rossiiskoi Akademii Nauk* 63 (11) (1993):1018–1023 (in Russian).

309. Kapitsa's letter to Stalin on the organization of works on the A-bomb project, including his resignation from the Special Committee, dated November 25, 1945. Reproduced in Ryabev, L. D., ed., *Atomnyi proekt SSSR: Dokumenty i materialy,* tom 2, kniga 1 [The Atomic Project in the USSR: Documents and Materials, vol. 2, bk. 1] (Moscow: Nauka, 1999), pp. 613–620 (in Russian).

310. Rubinin, P. E., "Svobodnyi chelovek v nesvobodnoi strane" [A free man in a non-free country], *Vestnik Rossiiskoi Akademii Nauk* 64 (1994):497–523 (in Russian).

311. Boag, J. W., P. E. Rubinin, and J. Shoenberg, eds., *Kapitza in Cambridge and Moscow: Life and Letters of a Russian Physicist* (New York: North-Holland, 1990), p. 368.

312. Gevorkyan and Petrov, "Terakty."

313. Cited in Stetsovsky, *Istoriya,* vol. 2, p. 243.

314. Unpublished memoirs of Yu. V. Adamchuk, cited in Antonov-Ovseenko, Anton, *Beria* (Moscow: Izdatel'stvo AST, 1999), pp. 403–404 (in Russian).

315. Medvedev, R. A., "Yuri Andropov i Andrei Sakharov" [Yurii Andropov and Andrei Sakharov], *Vestnik Rossiiskoi Akademii* 69 (1) (1999):72–80 (in Russian).

316. Stolyarov, *Palachi i zhertvy,* p. 327.

317. The Communist International, or Comintern, an international Communist organization, was created at the First Meeting in Moscow on March 2–6, 1919. The Comintern's goal was to coordinate activities of the Communist Parties in different countries for the world Communist revolution. From 1926 to 1929, Nikolai Bukharin headed the Comintern. Dr. Varga was a candidate to the Executive Committee of the Comintern and an editor of its magazine. In 1943, Stalin ended the activity of the Comintern, and the members of its staff were employed by the newly created Department on International Information of the Central Committee of the Bolshevik Party. The Comintern's structure is described in Adibekov, G. M., E. N. Shakhnazarova, and K. K. Shirinya, *Organi-*

zatsionnaya struktura Kominterna: 1919–1943 [Organizational Structure of the Comintern, 1919–1943] (Moscow: Rosspen, 1997), (in Russian).

318. Mlechin, *Predsedateli,* p. 372.

319. Holloway, David, *Stalin and the Bomb: The Soviet Union and Atomic Energy, 1939–1956* (New Haven: Yale University Press, 1994), p. 289.

320. Politkovskaya, Anna, "Kontslager' s kommercheskim uklonom" [A concentration camp with a commercial trend], *Novaya Gazeta* 14, February 2, 2001 (on-line version, in Russian).

CHAPTER TWO

1. Cited in Stetsovsky, *Istoriya,* vol. 2, p. 62.

2. Mairanovsky's laboratory is also mentioned in another book by the same authors: Bobryonev, Vladimir A., and Valerii B. Ryazentsev, *Palachi i zhertvy* [Executioners and Victims] (Moscow: Voenizdat, 1993), p. 170 (in Russian).

3. Details of the biography of Leonid (or Naum) Eitingon (1899–1981) in Costello, John, and Oleg Tsarev, *Deadly Illusions* (New York: Crown, 1993), pp. 237, 279–280, 298; Parrish, Michael, *The Lesser Terror: Soviet State Security, 1939–1953* (Westport, CT: Praeger, 1996), pp. 312–320; Kokurin and Petrov, *Lubyanka,* p. 46; West, Nigel, and Oleg Tsarev, *The Crown Jewels: The British Secrets at the Heart of the KGB Archive* (London: HarperCollins, 1998), p. 209.

4. *Murder International, Inc.: Murder and Kidnapping as an Instrument of Soviet Policy* (Washington, DC: U.S. Government Printing Office, 1965), pp. 1–52.

5. The text of "Plan of the Agent-Operational Actions in the 'Duck' Case" is given in Primakov, Yevgenii, ed., *Ocherki istorii Rossiiskoi Vneshnei Razvedki* [Essays on the History of the Russian Foreign Intelligence] (Moscow: Mezhdunarodnye Otnosheniya, 1997), vol. 3, p. 93 (in Russian). Only one copy of this document was produced, and it was kept in Beria's personal file. In 1955, it was transferred from the General Prosecutor's Office to the Archive of the First Main KGB Directorate (now the SVR Archive).

6. Cited in Gevorkyan and Petrov, "Terakty."

7. Haynes, John Earl, and Harvey Klehr, *Venona: Decoding Soviet Espionage in America* (New Haven, CT: Yale University Press, 1999), pp. 276–283.

8. Sudoplatov, Pavel, Anatoli Sudoplatov, Jerrold L. Schecter, and Leona P. Schecter, *Special Tasks: The Memoirs of an Unwanted Witness—a Soviet Spymaster* (Boston: Little, Brown and Co., 1994).

9. Andreev, A. V., and A. B. Kozhevnikov, "Kopengagenskaya operatsiya sovetskoi razvedki" [The Copenhagen operation of the Soviet Intelligence], *Voprosy Istorii Estestvoznaniya i Tekhniki* 2 (1994):18–21 (in Russian); "Unsubstantiated Charges of Treason," *Nature* 368 (1994):779–780; "Spying Is Bad Business," *Nature* 369 (1994):2; Goldansky, Vitalii, "Russian Bomb," *Nature* 372 (1994):399; Knight, Amy, "The Man Who Wasn't There," *New York Times,* May 3, 1994; Rhodes, R., "Atomic Spies, or Atomic Lies?" *New York Times,* May 3, 1994; Smirnov, Yurii N., "Dopros Nielsa Bohra: Arkhivnye svidetel'stva" [An interrogation of Niels Bohr: The archival evidence], *Voprosy Istorii Estestvoznaniya i*

Tekhniki 4 (1994):111–117 (in Russian); Terletsky, Yakov P., "Operatsiya 'Dopros Nielsa Bohra'" [The operation "The Interrogation of Niels Bohr"], *Voprosy Istorii Estestvoznaniya i Tekhniki* 2 (1994):21–44 (in Russian); Ulam, A. B., "Murder Was Part of the Job Description," *New York Times Book Review*, May 22, 1994. See also Holloway, *Stalin and the Bomb*, pp. 82–84, 90–95, 103–108, 138, 174, and 222–223. The most detailed criticism of Sudoplatov's version of the Soviet atomic espionage is given in Zubok, Vladislav, "Atomic Espionage and Its Soviet 'Witnesses,'" *Bulletin of Cold War International History Project* (CWIHP) 4 (1994), available at http://cwihp.si.edu/cwihplib.nsf/ (quick search: "Atomic Espionage").

10. Barkovsky, V. B., "S kakoi tsel'yu 'doprashivali" Nielsa Bohra? "[For what purpose was Niels Bohr "interrogated"?], *Voprosy Istorii Estestvoznaniya i Tekhniki* 4 (1994):122–123 (in Russian); Macilwain, C., "Manhattan Physicists Cleared by FBI Inquiry," *Nature* 374 (1995):581.

11. Cited in Jeffery, Inez Cope, *Inside Russia: The Life and Times of Zoya Zarubina* (Austin, TX: Eakin Press, 1999), p. 17.

12. Holloway, David, "Charges of Espionage," *Science* 264 (1994):1346–1347.

13. Chapters 4, 8, and 9 in Sudoplatov, P., et al., *Special Tasks*, pp. 65–86 and 221–284.

14. Ibid., pp. 270–271, 278–279, and 407–408.

15. Revolt Pimenov (Volin, O., "S berievtsami bo Vladimirskoi Tuyr'me" [With Beria's men in Vladimir Prison], in *Minuvshee* [The Past] [Paris: Atheneum], no. 7 [1989]:363–374 [in Russian]) and Boris Men'shagin (Men'shagin, Boris G., *Vospominaniya: Smolensk . . . Katyn . . . Vladimirskaya Tur'ma . . .* [Memoirs: Smolensk . . . Katyn . . . Vladimir Prison . . .] (Paris: IMCA-Press, 1988) (in Russian) and my personal conversation with Men'shagin in 1980 in Moscow described identical versions of what Sudoplatov told them about his arrest and investigation during his imprisonment.

16. Sudoplatov, Pavel, *Spetsoperatsii: Lubyanka i Kreml, 1930–1950 Gody* [Special Operations: Lubyanka and the Kremlin, the 1930s–1950s] (Moscow: Olma-Press, 1998), pp. 595–601 (in Russian).

17. The documents published in Prokopenko, *Bezumnaya psikhiatriya*, pp. 81–89 (in Russian).

18. Sudoplatov, P., et al., *Special Tasks*, pp. 265–284.

19. Sudoplatov, P., *Spetsoperatsii,* pp. 455–456.

20. Bobryonev and Ryazentsev, *The Ghosts*, p. 136.

21. Sudoplatov, Andrei, *Tainaya zhizn' generala Sudoplatova: Pravda i vymysly o moem otse* [The secret life of General Sudoplatov: The Truth and Lies About My Father] (Moscow: Sovremennik, 1998), vol. 2, p. 275.

22. Zbarsky, Ilya, and Samuel Hutchinson, *Lenin's Embalmers* (London: Harvill Press, 1998), p. 54.

23. On Lenin's body embalming, see ibid., pp. 65–66, 77–91, 110–111, 114–115, 119–122.

24. Ipatieff, *The Life of a Chemist,* p. 432.

25. Gevorkyan and Petrov, "Terakty."

26. Petrov and Skorkin, *Kto rukovodil NKVD*, p. 380.

27. Sudoplatov, P., et al., *Special Tasks,* pp. 58–59.

28. Andrew Christopher, and Vasilii Mirokhin, *The Sword and the Shield: The Mitrokhin Archive and the Secret History of the KGB* (New York: Basic Books, 1999), p. 41.

29. Petrov and Skorkin, *Kto rukovodil NKVD*, p. 381.

30. Weinstein, Allen, and Alexander Vassiliev, *The Haunted Wood: Soviet New York Espionage in America—the Stalin Era* (New York: Random House, 1999), p. 89.

31. Andrew and Mitrokhin, *The Sword and the Shield*, p. 41.

32. Zbarsky and Hutchinson, *Lenin's Embalmers,* pp. 101–102.

33. Andrew and Mirokhin, *The Sword and the Shield*, p. 75.

34. Petrov and Skorkin, *Kto rukovodil NKVD,* pp. 46 and 380–380.

35. Gevorkyan and Petrov, "Terakty."

36. Vaksberg, *Stalin Against the Jews*, p. 35.

37. Levitsky, Boris, *The Uses of Terror: The Soviet Secret Police, 1917–1970* (New York: Coward, McCann and Geoghegan, 1972), p. 74.

38. Petrov and Skorkin, *Kto rukovodil NKVD*, pp. 459–460.

39. Leggett, *The CHEKA*, p. 275.

40. Conquest, Robert, *The Great Terror*, p. 380.

41. Orlov, Alexander, *The Secret Story of Stalin's Crimes* (New York: Random House, 1953), pp. 261–270; Tucker, Robert C., and Stephen F. Cohen, eds., *The Great Purge Trial* (New York: Grosset and Dunlap, 1965), pp. 686–687.

42. Tucker and Cohen, *The Great Purge Trial*, pp. 481–482.

43. Ibid., p. 480.

44. Cited in Mlechin, *Predsedateli KGB*, p. 132.

45. Tucker and Cohen, *The Great Purge Trial*, pp. 686–689.

46. Ibid., pp. 506–509.

47. Shentalinsky, Vitaly, *Arrested Voices: Resurrecting the Disappeared Writers of the Soviet Regime*, trans. John Crowfoot, introduction by Robert Conquest (New York: Free Press, 1996), pp. 262–264.

48. Kostyrchenko, *Out of the Red Shadows*, p. 277.

49. Katkov, Georgy, *The Trial of Bukharin* (New York: Stein and Day, 1969), p. 171.

50. Tucker and Cohen, *The Great Purge Trial*, p. 511.

51. Topolyansky, V. D., "Doctor D. D. Pletnev," in Yaroshevsky, *Repressirovannaya Nauka*, pp. 315–316.

52. Ibid., p. 309.

53. The letter is given in Radzinsky, *Stalin*, pp. 379–380. In prison, Bukharin wrote four letters to Stalin, dated April 15, September 29, November 14, and December 10, 1937 (Radzinsky, *Stalin*, pp. 374–381); all of them are now kept in the Presidential Archive.

54. Soon after the Bukharin trial, NKVD Captain Lazar Kogan was arrested and shot (Cohen, "Introduction," p. xviii).

55. Cited in Frezinsky, B., "Golos iz bezdny (Tyuremnye stranitsy Nikolaya Bukharina)" [A voice from the abyss (Nikolai Bukharin's writings in prison)], in Bukharin, Nikolai, *Vremena* [The Times] (Moscow: Progress-Kul'tura, 1994), pp. 3–20 (in Russian).

56. The famous painter Konstantin Yuon "liked them so much that he told Nikolai Ivanovich [Bukharin], 'Give up politics. Politics promises nothing good in the future. Take up painting. Landscapes, that's your calling!' (Larina, Anna, *This I Cannot Forget: The Memoirs of Nikolai Bukharin's Widow* [New York: W. W. Norton, 1994], p. 82). Bukharin's son Yurii became a professional artist.

57. For a discussion of the complexity and controversy of Bukharin's ideas see, for instance, Laqueur, Walter, *Stalin: The Glasnost Revelations* (New York: Charles Scribner's Sons, 1990), pp. 19–43.

58. Zbarsky and Hutchinson, *Lenin's Embalmers,* pp. 108–109.

59. Katkov, *The Trial of Bukharin,* pp. 164–166, 228–229; Conquest, *The Great Terror,* pp. 375–390; Andrew and Gordievsky, *KGB,* pp. 135–136.

60. Zbarsky and Hutchinson, *Lenin's Embalmers,* p. 110.

61. For details, see Katkov, *The Trial of Bukharin,* pp. 122–123, 224; Conquest, *The Great Terror,* pp. 375–390.

62. Petrov and Skorkin, *Kto rukovodil NKVD,* p. 460.

63. Mlechin, *Predsedateli KGB,* pp. 133–134.

64. Reiss, *Molotov Remembers,* p. 264.

65. Yeremina and Roginsky, *Rasstrel'nye spiski,* pp. 64, 68, 179, and 241.

66. Roginsky, A. B., "Posleslovie" [Concluding remarks], in ibid., pp. 485–501.

67. Tucker and Cohen, *The Great Purge Trial,* pp. 688–689.

68. Shentalinsky, *Arrested Voices,* pp. 274–275.

69. Conquest, *The Great Terror,* p. 395.

70. Davies, Joseph E., *Mission to Moscow* (New York: Simon and Schuster, 1941), pp. 261-280.

71. Koppes, Clayton R., and Gregory D. Black, *Hollywood Goes to War: How Politics, Profits, and Propaganda Shaped World War II Movies* (New York: The Free Press, 1987), pp. 190-191.

72. Davies, *Mission to Moscow,* pp. 270-271.

73. Ibid., p. 272.

74. According to Howard Koch's memoirs, at a dinner at the White House in the presence of Davies President Roosevelt personally suggested that Jack Warner make this movie (Koch, Howard, *As Time Goes By: Memoirs of a Writer* [New York: Harcourt Brace Jovanovich, 1979], p. 101). However, later former White House officials and Davies denied that such a meeting took place (Fariello, Griffin, *Red Scare: Memoirs of the American Inquisition* [New York: W. W. Norton, 1995], p. 273).

75. Koppes and Black, *Hollywood,* p. 193.

76. MacLean, Elizabeth Kimball, *Joseph E. Davies. Envoy to the Soviets* (Praeger: Westpoint, CT, 1992), pp. 106-107; Hoberman, J., *The Red Atlantis. Communist Culture in the Absence of Communism* (Philadelphia, PA: Temple University Press, 1998), pp. 161-162.

77. Hoberman, *The Red Atlantis*, p. 162.

78. MacLean, *Joseph E. Davies*, p. 179.

79. Koch, *As Time Goes By*, p. 169.

80. MacLean, *Joseph E. Davies*, p. 93.

81. Fariello, *Red Scare*, p. 276.

82. Costello and Tsarev, *Deadly Illusions*, p. 299. See also Orlov, *The Secret Story*, pp. 237–238; Andrew and Gordievsky, *KGB*, pp. 138–139; and Conquest, *The Great Terror*, p. 409.

83. According to the writer Edvard Radzinsky, the record of a closed Military Collegium session on February 3, 1940, is the last item in the NKVD Yezhov File (Case File 510) at the KGB/FSB Archive (Radzinsky, *Stalin*, p. 431).

84. The postmortem report dated December 2, 1938, is cited in ibid., p. 422.

85. Ibid., p. 427. The declassified "History of Comrade Krupskaya's Illness" is now kept at the Party Archive in Moscow.

86. Conquest, *The Great Terror*, pp. 408–409.

87. For details, see, for instance, Poretsky, Elisabeth K., *Our Own People: A Memoir of "Ignace Reiss" and His Friends* (Ann Arbor: University of Michigan Press, 1970), pp. 208–242.

88. Primakov, *Ocherki istorii*, vol. 3, pp. 82–84.

89. Andrew and Mitrokhin, *The Sword and the Shield*, pp. 75–76.

90. Ibid., pp. 69–71.

91. Kokurin and Petrov, *Lubyanka*, pp. 20–21.

92. Mlechin, *Predsedateli KGB*, p. 144. The mechanisms of listing the victims and of the approval of the lists of persons condemned to death by Stalin, Molotov, Yezhov, his deputy Frinovsky, Vyshinsky, and his deputy Grigorii Roginsky are described in detail in Petrov, N.V., and A. B. Roginsky, *"Pol'skaya operatsiya" NKVD 1937–1938* [The NKVD's "Polish operation" in 1937–1938], in Gur'yanov, A. E., ed., *Repressii protiv polyakov i pol'skikh grazhdan* [Repressions Against Poles and Polish Citizens] (Moscow: Zven'ya, 1997), pp. 77–113 (in Russian), and Okhotin, N., and A. Roginsky, "Iz istorii 'nemetskoi operatsii' NKVD 1937–1938 gg." [From the history of the NKVD's "German operation" in 1937–1938], in Shcherbakova, Irina L., ed., *Repressii protiv rossiiskikh nemtsev: Nakazannyi narod* [Repressions Against the Russian Germans: The Punished Nation] (Moscow: Zven'ya, 1999), pp. 35–74 (in Russian).

93. Kokurin and Petrov, *Lubyanka*, p. 147.

94. Mlechin, *Predsedateli KGB*, p. 174.

95. Andrew and Gordievsky, *KGB*, p. 244.

96. NKVD Order No. 00362, dated June 9, 1938 (Kokurin and Petrov, *Lubyanka*, pp. 19–20).

97. According to Bobryonev, Osinkin was a Party functionary appointed to work at the NKVD (Bobryonev and Ryazentsev, *The Ghosts*, pp. 140–141; Bobryonev, *"Doktor Smert,"* p. 39).

98. Kokurin and Petrov, *Lubyanka*, pp. 22–23.

99. Gevorkyan and Petrov, "Terakty." See also Table 2.1.

100. Petrov and Skorkin, *Kto rukovodil NKVD*, p. 421.

101. From biographies of Lapshin and Filimonov (Petrov and Skorkin, *Kto rukovodil NKVD*, pp. 263–264 and 421–422).

102. Bobryonev, *"Doktor Smert,"* p. 38.

103. The Regional Moscow VCheKa had its own prison and a place for executions in the building Bol'shaya Lubyanka 14, a former eighteenth-century palace located across the street. See Nezhdanov, F., "Tyur'ma Vserossiiskoi Chrezvychainoi Komissii (Moskva, B. Lubyanka, 11)" [Prison of the All-Russian Extraordinary Commission (Moscow, B. Lubyanka, 11)], in *Che-Ka: Materialy po deyatel'osti chrezvychainykh komissii* [Che-Ka: Materials on the Activity of Extraordinary Commissions] (Berlin: Orfei, 1922), pp. 152–163 (in Russian), and Leggett, *The CHEKA*, pp. 219–220. Currently, this building belongs to the Regional Moscow FSB.

104. Povartsov, Sergei, *Prichina smerti—rasstrel* [Execution Was the Cause of Death] (Moscow: Terra, 1996), p. 179 (in Russian).

105. Sudoplatov, P., *et al.*, *Special Tasks*, pp. 64–69.

106. Primakov, *Ocherki istorii*, vol. 3, p. 93.

107. "A Plan" of Trotsky's assassination cited above. See ibid.

108. For details, see, for instance, Andrew and Gordievsky, *KGB*, pp. 168–172; Primakov, *Ocherki istorii*, vol. 3, p. 90–109.

109. Primakov, *Ocherki istorii*, vol. 3, pp. 105–108.

110. Kokurin and Petrov, *Lubyanka*, pp. 31 and 33.

111. Ibid., p. 33.

112. Petrov and Skorkin, *Kto rukovodil NKVD*, p. 421.

113. Sudoplatov, P., *et al.*, *Special Tasks*, p. 184; Kokurin and Petrov, *Lubyanka*, p. 35.

114. The secret "Verdict" of the Military Collegium of the USSR Supreme Court on the accusation of Pavel Anatol'evich Sudoplatov of crimes under Articles 17-58-1b of the RSFSR [Russian Federation] Criminal Code dated September 12, 1958. Published in Sudoplatov, A., *Tainaya zhizn'*, vol. 2, pp. 433–434.

115. NKGB Order No. 00197 dated March 22, 1946, issued following the Decision of the Soviet Supreme Council, dated March 15, 1946 (Kokurin and Petrov, *Lubyanka*, p. 35).

116. According to the Politburo's Resolution P 51/IV, dated May 4, 1946 (Kokurin and Petrov, *Lubyanka*, p. 35).

117. Petrov and Skorkin, *Kto rukovodil NKVD*, p. 421.

118. MGB Order No. 0047, dated October 6, 1946 (Kokurin and Petrov, *Lubyanka*, p. 35).

119. MGB Order No. 00532, dated September 28, 1959 (Kokurin and Petrov, *Lubyanka*, p. 38).

120. Kokurin and Petrov, *Lubyanka*, pp. 75–76.

121. Document 158 in Kudryavtsev, I. I., ed., *Arkhivy Kremlya i Staroi Ploshchadi: Dokumenty po "Delu KPSS"* [Archives of the Kremlin and Old Square: Documents on the "Communist Party Case"] (Novosibirsk: Sibirskii Khronograf, 1995), pp. 26–27 (in Russian).

122. Politburo Decision P 53/59, dated August 20, 1946. Cited in Kokurin and Petrov, *Lubyanka*, p. 36.

123. Kokurin, A., and N. Petrov, "MGB: Struktura, funktsii, kadry: Statiya pyataya (1946–1953)" [The MGB: Structure, function, and cadre: The fifth article (1946–1953)], *Svobodnaya Mysl* 11 (1997):111 (in Russian); Bobryonev and Ryazentsev, *The Ghosts*, pp. 142–144.

124. Kokurin and Petrov, "MGB," p. 120.

125. Dzhirkvelov, Ilya, *Secret Servant: My Life with the KGB and the Soviet Elite* (New York: Harper and Row, 1987), pp. 50–51.

126. Ibid., pp. 55–60. Dzhirkvelov incorrectly names Konovalets "Ivan Konovalenko." His memoirs were published in 1986, eight years before Sudoplatov published his own description of events (Sudoplatov, P., et al., *Special Tasks*, pp. 12–29).

127. Gevorkyan and Petrov, "Terakty."

128. Khokhlov, Nikolai, *In the Name of Conscience* (New York: David McKay, 1959), pp. 242–279.

129. Ibid., pp. 221–224.

130. Ibid., p. 232. See a photo of this weapon in Melton, H. K., *The Ultimate Spy Book* (New York: DK Publishing, 1996), p. 153.

131. Andrew and Gordievsky, *KGB*, p. 464.

132. Khokhlov, *In the Name of Conscience*, pp. 349–362.

133. Andrew and Mitrokhin, *The Sword and the Shield*, p. 359.

134. Khokhlov, *In the Name of Conscience*, p. 363.

135. Sudoplatov, P., et al., *Special Tasks*, pp. 246–247.

136. Seth, Ronald, *The Executioners: The Story of SMERSH* (New York: Hawthorn Books, 1967), pp. 144–183; Rositzke, Harry, *The KGB: The Eyes of Russia* (Garden City, NY: Doubleday, 1981), pp. 108–109. Andrew and Gordievsky, *KGB*, pp. 464–465.

137. From the Written Motivation of the Verdict in the Stashinsky Trial before the Federal High Court in Karlsruhe (West Germany), cited in Seth, *The Executioners*, p. 24. See a photo of this weapon in Melton, *The Ultimate Spy*, p. 154.

138. Andrew and Mitrokhin, *The Sword and the Shield*, p. 374.

139. Rositzke, *The KGB*, p. 109; Wise, David, *Cassidy's Run: The Secret Spy War over Nerve Gas* (New York: Random House, 2000), p. 78.

140. Kalugin, O., "Tipichnoe 'bolgarskoe' ubiistvo.

141. Andrew and Gordievsky, *KGB*, pp. 644–645.

142. See a photo of the shooting device of the umbrella in Melton, *The Ultimate Spy*, p. 152.

143. Andrew and Mitrokhin, *The Sword and the Shield*, pp. 388–389.

144. Bryden, John, *Deadly Allies: Canada's Secret War, 1937–1947* (Toronto: McClelland and Stewart, 1990), pp. 295–296. I hope that after my disclosure of Mairanovsky's activity there will be no uncertainty that the KGB executioners in fact used ricin as a deadly poison.

145. Kalugin, "Tipichno 'bolgarskoe' ubiistvo."

146. In his book published in 1994, Kalugin gives fewer details on Markov's murder than in his newspaper interview (Kalugin, Oleg, *The First Directorate: My 32 Years in Intelligence Against the West* [New York: St. Martin's Press, 1994], pp. 178–186).

147. Kalugin, "Tipichno 'bolgarskoe' ubiistvo."

148. Kalugin, *The First Directorate*, p. 186; Andrew and Mitrokhin, *The Sword and the Shield*, p. 389.

149. "Bulgaria to See Interpol," *Financial Times*, September 9, 1998.

150. Andrew and Gordievsky, *KGB*, p. 645.

151. Alibek, *Biohazard*, pp. 171–172.

152. Ibid., p. 302.

153. Ibid., pp. 171–174.

154. Rimmington, A., "Fragmentation and Proliferation? The Fate of the Soviet Union's Offensive Biological Weapons Programme," *Contemporary Security Policy* 20 (1) (April 1999):86–100.

155. Popovsky, *Manipulated Science*, pp. 57–58.

156. This is according to Ovchinnikov's sister, who was also an organic chemist and worked at the Belozersky Institute of Bioorganic Chemistry within the Moscow State University.

157. Schnol, *Geroi i zlodei*, pp. 403–418.

158. Alibek, *Biohazard*, pp. 40–41.

159. Domaradsky, *"Perevyortysh,"* pp. 58–65; Alibek, *Biohazard*, pp. 42, 158.

160. Baev, A. A., "Moya biografiya" [My biography], *Vestnik Rossiiskoi Akademii Nauk* 64 (4) (1994):356–365 (in Russian).

161. Alibek, *Biohazard*, pp. 174–176.

162. Ibid., p. 177.

163. Ibid.

164. Ibid., p. 176.

165. Wolf, Markus, and Anne McElvoy, *Man Without a Face: The Autobiography of Communism's Greatest Spymaster* (New York: Times Books, 1997), pp. 212–213.

166. Beletskaya, I. P., and S. S. Novikov, "Khimicheskoe oruzhie Rossii" [Chemical weapons of Russia], *Vestnik Rossiiskoi Akademii Nauk* 65 (2) (1995):99–111 (in Russian).

167. According to the Russian press, Academician Beletskaya recently funded a pyramid scam, the Moscow company Alma Mater Libera established by her son, Sergei Shakirov, and two of his friends. All three are graduates from the

Chemical Faculty of Moscow University and have tight connections with the university. In her interview for the newspaper *Novaya Gazeta*, Academician Beletskaya did not deny her participation in the scam and approved the racketeering, beatings of, and extortion of expensive cars from the unfortunate "debtors" by her son (Voloshin, P., "Sitsiliiskaya sem'ya akademika" [Academician's Sicilian family], *Novaya Gazeta* 58, October 23, 2000 (on-line version, in Russian).

168. *New York Times*, January 28, 1994.

169. Krauss, C., "U.S. Urges Russia to End Production of Nerve Gas," *New York Times*, February 6, 1997. On October 31, 1997, the Russian State Duma ratified the ban ("Russia Ratifies Chemical Arms," *Russia Today Report*, November 6, 1997 (on-line version, in Russian). According to the Russian officials, in 1999, of the 24 former poison-gas factories, 6 were planned to be destroyed, and 18 had already been destroyed or converted to peaceful use (Miller, J., "Russia Discloses Details of Its Former Chemical Arms Program," *New York Times*, November 30, 1999). Poorly kept in warehouses, chemical weapons and the wastes from their production are a very serious threat to the environment in many areas of Russia and the Central Asian republics. On the pollution from mustard-gas derivatives, see, for instance, Hoffman, David, "Russia's Forgotten Chemical Weapon," *Washington Post*, August 16, 1998.

170. A review on the binary agents and their production in the USSR in the 1980s–1990s is given in Tucker, J. B., "Converting Former Soviet Chemical Weapons Plants," *Nonproliferation Review* 4 (1) (1996):1–15 (on-line version).

171. Bulatov, Valerii I., *Rossia: Ekologia i armia* [Russia: Ecology and the Army] (Novosibirsk: TsERIS, 1999), p. 57 (in Russian).

172. Wise, *Cassidy's Run*, pp. 191–195.

173. Albats, *The State*, pp. 325–328; Hoffman, David, "Soviets Reportedly Built Weapon Despite Pact," *Washington Post*, August 16, 1998.

174. "Update on Mirzayanov," *Surviving Together* 12 (1) (1994):20; Wise, *Cassidy's Run*, pp. 194–195.

175. From a documentary movie: *Poisons*, Discovery Magazine Series, 1996, Discovery Communications, Inc.

176. Wise, *Cassidy's Run*, p. 60.

177. Ibid., p. 61.

178. Bulatov, *Rossia*, p. 62.

179. Interview with Dr. Mirzayanov in Smithson, A. E., "Toxic Archipelago: Preventing Proliferation from the Former Soviet Chemical and Biological Weapons Complexes," *Henry L. Stimson Center*, Report no. 32 [1999]:1–117; available at http://www.stimson.org/cwc/toxic.htm), p. 47.

180. Alibek, *Biohazard*, pp. 258–269.

181. A detailed analysis of the current situation with the institutions involved in the research on chemical and biological weapons, including Biopreparat, Vector, GosNIIOKhT, etc., is given in Smithson, "Toxic Archipelago," and *Biological Weapons: Effort to Reduce Former Soviet Threat Offers Benefits, Poses New Risks*

(Washington, DC: U.S. General Accounting Office, April 2000), GAO/ NSIAD-00-138.

182. Heintz, J., "Russia Germ Lab Security Gets Boost," *Washington Post*, May 24, 2000.

183. Miller, J., "Russia Opens Doors to Lab That Created Deadly Germs," *New York Times*, May 24, 2000.

184. See, for instance, Graham, Loren R., *Science in Russia and the Soviet Union: A Short History* (Cambridge: Cambridge University Press, 1993), pp. 190–196; Aldhous, P., "A Scientific Community on the Edge," *Science* 264 (1994):1262–1264; Stone, R., "New Minister Sets Lofty Goals," *Science* 282 (1998):1979–1980; Levitin, C., "Aim for Better Business Sense to Bolster Russian Science," *Nature* 401 (1999):628.

185. "Obshchee sobranie Rossiiskoi Akademii Nauk prizvalo Akademika Primakova stat' prezidentom" [The Russian Academy of Sciences' General Assembly called for Primakov to become president], *Nezavisimaya Gazeta*, June 3, 1999 (in Russian).

186. "Minister Sounds Alarm for Russian Science," Agence France Presse, February 15, 2001 (on-line version).

187. Albats, *The State*, p. 352.

188. Anonymous, "Smert' ego organizatsii" [Death to his organization], *Obshchaya Gazeta*, December 25, 1997 (in Russian).

189. According to unconfirmed reports from Chechnya, on December 5, 1999, the Russian troops used chemical weapons against the Chechen civilians ("Chemical Weapons Used in Chechnya—Claim," *ITN Online*, December 7, 1999 [on-line version]). The second alleged usage of chemical weapons and napalm by the Russian troops against Chechens was on December 30, 1999 ("Russians, Chechens Trade Charges Over Chemical Weapons," Agence France Presse, December 31, 1999 (on-line version).

190. Abdulaeva, M., "Lyudi i zveri" [People and beasts], Novaya Gazeta, June 15, 2000 23 (d) (on-line version, in Russian).

191. "Judgment and Aftermath," in Annas, George J., and Michael A. Grodin, eds., *The Nazi Doctors and the Nuremberg Code: Human Rights in Human Experimentation* (New York: Oxford University Press, 1992), pp. 94–105. Two of the defendants, Gebhardt and Mrugowsky, were sentenced to death by hanging; Genzken and Poppendick were sentenced to imprisonment for 20 and 10 years, respectively (Mitscherlich, Alexander, and Fred Mielke, "Epilogue: Seven Were Hanged," in Annas and Grodin, *The Nazi Doctors*, pp. 105–107).

192. Deriabin, Peter, and Frank Gibney, *The Secret World* (Garden City, NY: Doubleday and Co., 1959), p. 137.

193. Burbyga, "Prigovoryen k 'medosmotru'"; see also Bobryonev and Ryazentsev, *The Ghosts*, pp. 47–50.

194. See more information about files in Chapter 4.

195. Burbyga, "Prigovoryen k 'medosmotru.'"

196. Harris and Paxman, *A Higher Form of Killing,* pp. 25–28; Bryden, *Deadly Allies,* pp. 17–18.

197. Bryden, *Deadly Allies,* p. 223.

198. Ibid., p. 223; Endicott, Stephen, and Edward Hagerman, *The United States and Biological Warfare: Secrets from the Early Cold War and Korea* (Blooming-ton: Indiana University Press, 1998), p. 33.

199. Harris, *Factories of Death,* p. 93.

200. A mixture of cardiac glycosides obtained from plants belonging to the genus *Digitalis.*

201. Burbyga, "Prigovoryen k 'medosmotru.'" See also Bobryonev and Ryazentsev, *The Ghosts,* p. 49.

202. A transcript of the interrogation is cited in Bobryonev, *"Doktor Smert,"* pp. 409–411.

203. A testimony of Aleksandr Grigorovich in 1954, cited in ibid., p. 409.

204. For details, see Litvin, A. A., *Krasnyi i belyi terror v Rossii, 1918–1921gg.* [The Red and White Terror in Russia, 1918–1921] (Kazan: Tatarskoie knizhnoe izdatel'stvo, 1995), pp. 172–196 (in Russian).

205. Ibid., p. 64.

206. Petrovsky, B. V., "Ranenie i bolezn' Lenina [Lenin's wounding and ill-ness]," *Pravda,* November 25, 1990 (in Russian).

207. A testimony of Mairanovsky, cited in Bobryonev, *"Doktor Smert,"* pp. 256–257; translated in Bobryonev and Ryazentsev, *The Ghosts,* p. 78.

208. Cited in Bobryonev, *"Doktor Smert,"* p. 409.

209. A transcript of the interrogation of Vsevolod Merkulov by investigator Col. Uspensky on August 29, 1953. Cited in Bobryonev, *"Doktor Smert,"* pp. 385–390; translated in Bobryonev and Ryazentsev, *The Ghosts,* pp. 169–170.

210. A transcript of the interrogation of Bogdan Kobulov by investigator Lt. Col. Bazenko, October 1953. Cited in Bobryonev, *"Doktor Smert,"* pp. 393–394; translated in Bobryonev and Ryazentsev, *The Ghosts,* p. 173.

211. A transcript of the interrogation of Lavrentii Beria by Chief Prosecutor Roman Rudenko on August 28, 1953. Cited in Bobryonev, *"Doktor Smert,"* p. 370; translated in Bobryonev and Ryazentsev, *The Ghosts,* p. 153.

212. A transcript of the interrogation of Lavrentii Beria by Chief Prosecutor Rudenko on September 1, cited in Bobryonev, *"Doktor Smert,"* pp. 372–378, and translated in Bobryonev and Ryazentsev, *The Ghosts,* p. 155–158. Beria's words about Hitler are on p. 374 of *"Doktor Smert."*

213. According to the Decree of the Presidium of the USSR Supreme Council dated December 10, 1953, the Special Court consisted of the Chair Marshal I. S. Konev and the following members: chairman of the VTsSPS N. M. Shvernik, first deputy of the chairman of the USSR Supreme Council Ye. L. Zeidlin, army general K. S. Moskalenko, secretary of the Moscow Regional Communist Party Committee N. A. Mikhailov, chairman of the Moscow City Court L. A. Gromov, first deputy of the MVD Minister K. F. Lunev, and

chairman of the Georgian Republic Council of Trade Unions M. I. Kuchava. The Decree was signed by chairman of the Presidium of the USSR Supreme Council Kliment Voroshilov and secretary of the Presidium of the USSR Supreme Council N. Pegov. The Presidential Archive, F. 3, Op. 24, D. 473, L. 1–7, cited as a part of Document No. 6 in Naumov and Sigachev, *Lavrentii Beria*, p. 386.

214. Petrov, "Sudy protiv chlenov NKVD-MGB."

215. Marks, *The Search for the "Manchurian Candidate"*, pp. 23–36.

216. Mairanovsky's letter to MGB Minister Ignatiev, dated October 17, 1951. Cited in Bobryonev *"Doktor Smert,"* pp. 315–316, and translated in Bobryonev and Ryazentsev, *The Ghosts,* pp. 126–130.

217. See Abarinov, V., *The Murders of Katyn* (New York: Hippocrene Books Inc., 1993), pp. 153–172.

218. Repressions against the Russian Germans started in 1937 (Okhotin and Roginsky, "Iz istorii"). However, the mass deportations were organized after the invasion of the USSR by Nazi troops and the beginning of the war on June 22, 1941. From September 3 to 20, 1941, more than 440,000 Volga Germans were deported to Kazakhstan and Siberia. The operation was headed by Serov. On the whole, 1,209,430 Germans from the Volga River area, the Moscow and Leningrad regions, the Crimea, the North Caucasus, and the Kuban River region were deported to Central Asia in 1941–1942 (Pohl, J. Otto, *The Stalinist Penal System: A Statistical History of Soviet Repression and Terror, 1930–1953* (Jefferson, NC: McFarland, 1997), pp. 72–90. Later, in 1944, more Germans were deported from the Crimea (Stetsovsky, *Istoriya*, vol. 1, pp. 457–458).

219. Parrish, *The Lesser Terror*, pp. 312–313.

220. Abarinov, *The Murders of Katyn*, pp. 153–172.

221. An interrogation of Vasilii Naumov regarding Mairanoivsky in 1954. Cited in Bobryonev, *"Doktor Smert,"* p. 325, and translated in Bobryonev and Ryazentsev, *The Ghosts*, pp. 83–84.

222. Felix, Chistopher, with James McCagar, *A Short Course in the Secret War* (Lanham: Madison Books, 1992), p. 188.

223. Cited in Kutuzov, V., "Gryaznaya kukhnya Abakumova" [Abakumov's dirty kitchen], in *"Leningradskoe delo"*, pp. 400–412 (in Russian).

224. Gevorkyan and Petrov, "Terakty"; see also Sudoplatov, P., *et al.*, *Special Tasks*, p. 411.

225. Bobryonev and Ryazentsev, *The Ghosts,* p. 64.

226. Bobryonev, *"Doktor Smert,"* p. 205; Bobryonev and Ryazentsev, *The Ghosts*, pp. 59, 108–109.

227. Dzhirkvelov, *Secret Servant*, p. 45.

228. See, for instance, reports on the execution and cremation of the famous Soviet/Russian writer Isaak Babel given in Povartsov, *Prichina smerti,* p. 178.

229. Photos of such a cane and a pen are given in Melton, *The Ultimate Spy*, pp. 149 and 152.

230. An interrogation of Mairanovsky by the investigator Tsaregradsky on September 23, 1953, cited during the interrogation of Merkulov on September 29, 1953, by Chief Prosecutor Rudenko (Bobryonev, *"Doktor Smert,"* p. 389; translated in Bobryonev and Ryazentsev, *The Ghosts,* p. 169).

231. Bobryonev, *"Doktor Smert,"* p. 177; Bobryonev and Ryazentsev, *The Ghosts,* p. 52.

232. Special Prosecutor Tsaregradsky's interrogation of Muromtsev on March 4, 1954 (cited in Bobryonev, *"Doktor Smert,"* p. 409, and translated in Bobryonev and Ryazentsev, *The Ghosts,* p. 83).

233. See, for instance, a letter written by a Nazi doctor, Joachim Mrugowsky, in September 1944 and presented at the Nuremberg trial on December 9, 1946 (cited in Taylor, Telford, "Opening Statement of the Prosecution, December 9, 1946," in Annas and Grodin, *The Nazi Doctors,* pp. 83–84).

234. Cited in Harris, *Factories of Death,* p. 71.

235. "KGB Shows Off Its Past—and Present," *Russia Today Report,* August 7 (1998) (on-line version).

236. Khokhlov, *In the Name of Conscience,* pp. 135–136.

237. Ipatieff, *The Life of a Chemist,* p. 232.

238. Ibid., p. 469.

239. Ibid., p. 399.

240. Ibid., p. 487.

241. Ibid., p. 382–388.

242. Ibid., p. 423.

243. See details in Dyakov, Yuri, and Tatyana Bushuyeva, *The Red Army and the Wehrmacht: How the Soviets Militarized Germany, 1922–33, and Paved the Way for Fascism* (Amherst, NY: Prometheus Books, 1995), pp. 21–23, 178–189, and 193–203.

244. Bojtzov, Valentin, and Erhard Geissler, "Chapter 8: Military Biology in the USSR, 1920–45," in Geissler, Erhard, and John Ellis van Courtland Moon, eds., *Biological and Toxin Weapons: Research, Development, and Use from the Middle Ages to 1945* (New York: Oxford University Press, 1999), pp. 152–167.

245. See details in Nekrich, A. M., *Pariahs, Partners, Predators: German-Soviet Relations, 1922–1941* (New York: Columbia University Press, 1997), pp. 52–60; Rowland, R. H., "Russia's Secret Cities," *Post-Soviet Geography and Economics* 37 (7) (1996):426–462.

246. "Russia Gets EU Money to Destroy Chemical Weapons," Reuters, March 2, 2000 (on-line version).

247. Voronov, Vladimir, "Prazdnik na obochine: Dlya chego Rossii nuzhno khimicheskoe oruzhie?" [A Party on a Roadside: For What Purpose Does Russia Need Chemical Weapons?], *Sobesednik* 20 (1997):9–10 (in Russian).

248. "Soviet Officer Had to 'Volunteer' as Chemical Weapon Guinea Pig," Agence France Presse, April 23, 1999 (on-line version).

249. Voronov, "A Party on a Roadside."

250. Efron, S., "Russia Investigates Alleged Chemical Arms Smuggling," *Los Angeles Times*, October 25, 1995.

251. "Chemical Sale Plan to Fund Russian Arms Scrapping," Reuters, February 9, 2001 (on-line version).

252. Wheelis, M., "Chapter 3: Biological Sabotage in the First World War," in Geissler and Moon, *Biological and Toxin Weapons*, pp. 35–62.

253. Bojtzov and Geissler, "Chapter 8," pp. 156 and 162.

254. Ibid., pp. 160–161.

255. Heller and Nekrich, *Utopia in Power*, p. 228.

256. Popovsky, *Manipulated Science*, p. 10.

257. Bojtzov and Geissler, "Chapter 8," pp. 160–162.

258. Yeremina and Roginsky, *Rasstrel'nye spisky*, pp. 36, 223, 256, and 290.

259. Ibid., p. 78.

260. Tucker and Cohen, *The Great Purge Trial*, pp. 102–104.

261. Yeremina and Roginsky, *Rasstrel'nye spisky*, p. 435.

262. Bojtzov and Geissler, "Chapter 8," p. 162.

263. Alibek, *Biohazard*, pp. 29–32. See also Bojtzov and Geissler, "Chapter 8," p. 164.

264. Report on the interrogation of the German Professor Heinrich Kliewe, head of the working group Blitzableiter under the Wehrmacht: "Bacterial War," in Alsos Mission MIS, WD, c/o G-2 Ho ETOUSA APO 887, 13 May 1945, Report No. A-B-C-H-H/149, p. 7. National Archives, Washington, DC (NAW) RG 319, Box 3, Folder BW 14. I am grateful to Professor Geissler for kindly providing me with a copy of this document.

265. Rimmington, A., "From Military to Industrial Complex? The Conversion of Biological Weapons Facilities in the Russian Federation," *Contemporary Security Policy* 17 (April 1996):81–112; Bozheyeva, G., Y. Kunakbayev, and D. Yeleukenov, "Former Soviet Biological Weapons Facilities in Kazakhstan: Past, Present, and Future," *CNS Occasional Papers* 1 (1999):1–27, available at http://cns.edu/pubs/opapers/op1/op1.htm.

266. Cables No. 843 (dated April 23, 1943) and 1804 (dated July 31, 1943) from Washington to Moscow in *Venona Historical Monograph* No. 5, "The KGB and GRU in Europe, South America, and Australia"; available at http://www.nsa.gov/docs/venona/docs/Apr43/23_Apr_1943_R4_ml_p1.gif and http://www.nsa.gov/docs/venona/docs/July43/31_July_1943_R4_m2_p1.gif.

267. Speer, Albert, *Inside the Third Reich* (New York: Macmillan, 1990), p. 489; see also Harris and Paxman, *A Higher Form of Killing*, pp. 62–63.

268. Harris and Paxman, *A Higher Form of Killing*, pp. 117–147; Parker, *The Killing Factory*, p. 50.

269. Bryden, *Deadly Allies*, pp. 167–178; Parker, *The Killing Factory*, pp. 52–57.

270. Bryden, *Deadly Allies*, p. 176.

271. Ibid., pp. 168–171.

272. Annas, George J., and Michael A. Grodin, "Where Do We Go from Here?" in Annas and Grodin, *The Nazi Doctors*, pp. 307–314.

273. "Pentagon to End Secrecy About Poison Gas Tests," *New York Times*, March 11, 1993. Also reproduced in Harris, *Factories of Death*, p. 239.

274. Bryden, *Deadly Allies*, pp. 162–166.

275. Excerpts from the "Letter No. 1 on XY [Scientific-Technical Intelligence] from January 27, 1941" (to: "Gennadii" and signed "Victor"); the "Letter No. 4 [to A. Gorsky] from March 15, 1942" (signed "Victor"); the "Letter No. 7 (XY) dated March 27, 1942" (to "Maxim" and signed "Victor"). The excerpts are reproduced in Ryabev, *Atomnyi proekt SSSR*, pp. 223–224 (document no. 91); p. 259 (document no. 117), pp. 259–260 (document no. 118) (in Russian).

276. The official Russian history of the Foreign Intelligence mentions information on "some types of chemical warfare agents" among other spy achievements of Gaik Ovakimyan in the United States (Primakov, *Ocherki istorii*, vol. 3, p. 177).

277. Smith, Bradley F., *Sharing Secrets with Stalin: How the Allies Traded Intelligence, 1941–1945* (Lawrence, KS: University Press of Kansas, 1996), p. 127.

278. Irwing, David, *Hitler's War* (London: Hodder and Stoughton, 1977), p. 463.

279. Bojtzov and Geissler, "Chapter 8," p. 163.

280. Report on the Polish Secret Army for the period 1942 to April 1943, submitted to the CCS (Combined Chiefs of Staff) on September 7, 1943. US National Archives, CCS.381. Poland (6630–43), sec. 1; cited in Harris and Paxman, *A Higher Form of Killing*, pp. 97, 275–276.

281. Harris and Paxman, *A Higher Form of Killing*, pp. 98–102.

282. About the short cooperation between the NKGB and the OSS, see, for instance, Deane, John R., *The Strange Alliance: The Story of Our Efforts at Wartime Co-operation with Russia* (New York: Viking Press, 1947), pp. 50–59; Smith, *Sharing Secrets*, pp. 169–170; Weinstein and Vassiliev, *The Haunted Wood*, pp. 238–264, and many documents in *The OSS-NKVD Relationships* (New York: Garland Publishing, 1989).

283. See Pavel Fitin's letter to Maj. General John R. Deane, dated September 27, 1944; reproduced as Document 69 in *The OSS-NKVD Relationships*.

284. Sudoplatov, P., *Spetsoperatsii*, p. 619.

285. Memoirs of O. G. Shatunovskaya, cited in Antonov-Ovseenko, *Beria*, pp. 312–313.

286. A top-secret letter of NKGB Commissar Merkulov to the State Security Commissars of the Soviet and autonomous republics, 1941, German translation by the German Intelligence, in the Moscow Region Central Archive, fond 500, Op. 21452, d. 1. Cited in Bojtzov and Geissler, "Chapter 8," p. 163. I am grateful to Professor Geissler for providing me with a copy of this document.

287. Bojtzov and Geissler, "Chapter 8," pp. 160–161, 165.

288. Bobryonev, *"Doktor Smert,"* p. 98; Bobryonev and Ryazentsev, *The Ghosts*, p. 66.

289. Todorov, Tzvetan, *Facing the Extreme: Moral Life in the Concentration Camps*, trans. Abigail Pollak and Arthur Denner (New York: Henry Holt, 1996), p. 161.

290. Blumenthal, R., and J. Miller, "Japan Rebuffs Requests for Information About Its Germ-Warfare Atrocities," *New York Times*, March 4, 1999.

291. Shalamov, Varlam, *Kolyma Tales* (New York: Penguin Books, 1994), p. 157.

292. Smolentsev, L. N., *Golgofa Rossii* [The Golgotha of Russia] (N.p.: Syktyvkar, 1993), p. 350 (in Russian).

293. Bobryonev and Ryazentsev, *Palachi i zhertvy*, p. 114.

294. Blokhin's testimony (p. 392 in Bobryonev, *"Doktor Smert"*) in a transcript of the interrogation of Arkady Gertsovsky on October 14, 1953, by Deputy Military Chief Prosecutor Uspensky (Bobryonev, *"Doktor Smert,"* pp. 391–394; translated in Bobryonev and Ryazentsev, *The Ghosts*, pp. 176–177).

295. The same transcript (Bobryonev, *"Doktor Smert,"* pp. 394–395; translated in Bobryonev and Ryazentsev, *The Ghosts*, pp. 176–177).

296. A transcript of the interrogation of Arkady Gertsovsky on October 23, 1953, by Deputy Military Chief Prosecutor Uspensky (Bobryonev, *"Doktor Smert,"* pp. 394–398; translated in Bobryonev and Ryazentsev, *The Ghosts*, pp. 176–177).

297. Bobryonev, *"Doktor Smert,"* pp. 207–208.

298. Gertsovsky's testimony on October 14, 1953 (cited in Bobryonev, *"Doktor Smert,"* p. 391; translated in Bobryonev and Ryazentsev, *The Ghosts*, pp. 170–171).

299. Balishansky's testimony on February 4, 1954 (cited in Bobryonev, *"Doktor Smert,"* p. 398; translated in Bobryonev and Ryazentsev, *The Ghosts*, p. 179).

300. Swedish Foreign Office White Books on Raoul Wallenberg (Stockholm), vol. 35, report regarding conversation with Dr. Charles W. Schandl, which took place in Toronto, Sunday February 2, 1958, Consul Folke Persson, February 5, 1958, New York. Translated into English by Jacob Wallenberg (New York), 1991.

301. Charles Schandl's prisoner card in Vladimir Prison (Memorial's Archive [Moscow], fond 171; prisoner cards from Vladimir Prison).

302. Two more persons who worked with van der Waals for the British Intelligence, the Hungarian lawyer Raphael Rupert and RAF warrant officer Reginald Barratt, whom Ruppert hid at his house, were also arrested by the Soviets. Barratt was soon killed, and Van der Waals died in the Butyrka Prison Hospital in 1948, whereas Rupert survived a long imprisonment. See Veress, Laura-Louise, *Clear the Line: Hungary's Struggle to Leave the Axis During the Second World War* (Cleveland, OH: Prospero Publications, 1995), pp. 229–230.

303. Schandel was described as "Charlie" in the memoirs of Lucien Gouaze: Serbet, Jean-Paul, *Polit-Isolator* (Paris: Robert Lafont, 1961), pp. 375–378. J.-P. Serbet was the pseudonym of French intelligence officer Lucien Gouaze, who was kidnapped by the MGB officers in 1948 in Austria. He was accused of espi-

onage and condemned to twenty-five years' imprisonment. He was kept in Vladimir Prison from 1949 and released in 1956.

304. Cited in Bobryonev, *"Doktor Smert,"* p. 343; translated in Bobryonev and Ryazentsev, *The Ghosts,* p. 34.

305. Sudoplatov's testimony on September 1, 1953 (cited in Bobryonev, *"Doktor Smert,"* p. 389, and translated in Bobryonev and Ryazentsev, *The Ghosts,* p. 155) and Grigoriev's testimony in 1954 (cited in Bobryonev, *"Doktor Smert,"* p. 409).

306. Sudoplatov's appeal to the Twenty-Third Congress of the Communist Party. Cited in Gevorkyan and Petrov, "Terakty."

307. Cited in ibid.

308. The text of the whole letter is given in Bobryonev, *"Doktor Smert,"* pp. 342–345.

309. Bobryonev, *"Doktor Smert,"* pp. 278–279; Bobryonev and Ryazentsev, *The Ghosts,* pp. 80–81.

310. Kozlov, V. A., and S. V. Mironenko, eds., *Arkhiv noveishei istorii Rossii. Tom I. "Osobaya papka" I. V. Stalina, Iz materialov Sekretariata NKVD-MVD SSSR 1944–1953. Katalog dokumentov* [Archive of Contemporary Russian History. Vol. I. The "Special Files" for I.V. Stalin. From Materials of the NKVD-MVD of the USSR, 1944–1953] (Moscow: State Archive of the Russian Federation, 1994) (in Russian), p. 184.

311. Sudoplatov, P., *Spetsoperatsii,* pp. 408–409.

312. Sudoplatov, P., et al., *Special Tasks,* pp. 252–253.

313. Bobryonev and Ryazentsev, *The Ghosts,* p. 113.

314. Sudoplatov, P., *Spetsoperatsii,* pp. 413–414.

315. Bobryonev, *"Doktor Smert,"* p. 278; Bobryonev and Ryazentsev, *The Ghosts,* pp. 77–78.

316. Gevorkyan and Petrov, "Terakty."

317. The documents (TFR 18/19 through 28) are kept at the archive of the Commission in Washington, DC. I am very grateful to Mr. Albert Graham of the commission, who kindly sent me copies of the documents.

318. Cited in Gevorkyan and Petrov, "Terakty."

319. Sudoplatov, P., et al., *Special Tasks,* pp. 281–282.

320. See, for instance, Alexander Dolgun's memoirs: Dolgun, Alexander, and Patrick Watson, *An American in the Gulag* (New York: A. Knopf, 1975).

321. Bobryonev, *"Doktor Smert,"* pp. 203, 253; Bobryonev and Ryazentsev, *The Ghosts,* p. 56.

322. Document TFR 18–19.

323. The NKVD "Warrant for Arrest and Search" No. 2634 dated February 20, 1939. There is a page No. 4 handwritten in the right upper corner of the document (Document TFR 18–23).

324. A Certificate of Rehabilitation No. 13/3-3940-92 dated July 28, 1992, and signed by Deputy Prosecutor of the Russian Federation G. F. Vesnovskaya (TFR 18–26).

325. The "Warrant for Arrest and Search" No. 2634 (TFR 18-23).

326. The "Excerpt" from the Protocol [Transcript] No. 1 of the OSO dated January 5, 1940. It has two handwritten page numbers: 145 (crossed out) and 162 (Document TFR-24).

327. The reverse side of the same document (Document TFR-25).

328. There are handwritten page numbers 284–286 at the right upper corner of the pages (Document TFK 18-20).

329. A Joint Decision of the Central Committee and USSR Council of Ministers No. 251, dated February 8, 1947.

330. The same system was used, for instance, in the letter of Beria (then minister of the interior, i.e., MVD) to G. M. Malenkov, dated April 2, 1953: the name of Stalin was written by hand through the whole letter (see document no. 7 in Naumov and Sigachev, *Lavrentii Beria*, pp. 25–28).

331. Timofeev-Ressovsky, Nikolai, *Vospominaniya* [Memoirs] (Moscow: Pangeya, 1995), p. 344 (in Russian).

332. Bobryonev, *"Doktor Smert,"* pp. 198–203; Bobryonev and Ryazentsev, *The Ghosts,* pp. 55–56.

333. A death certificate issued by the Northern Regional Bureau of Registration (ZAGS) of the town of Penza on January 20, 1948 (TFR 18-28).

334. A letter from the Russian Federation Security Ministry (currently the Federal Security Service, FSB), addressed to "The Adviser of the Russian President on the Defense Matters, D. A. Volkogonov," signed by Deputy Minister V. Frolov and dated September 9, 1992 (TFR 18-27).

335. Pozniakov, V. V., "Tainaya voina Iosifa Stalina: Sovetskie razvedyvatel'nye sluzhby v SShA nakanune i v nacale kholodnoi voiny, 1943–1953 [Josef Stalin's secret war: Soviet intelligence services in the United States before and during the early Cold War, 1943–1953]," in Gaiduk, I. V., N. I. Yegorova, and A. O. Chubaria, eds., *Stalinskoe desyatiletie kholodnoi voiny: Fakty i gipotezy* [Stalin's Decade of the Cold War: Facts and Hypotheses] (Moscow: Nauka, 1999], pp. 188–207 (in Russian).

336. Bobryonev and Ryazentsev, *Palachi i zhertvy*, pp. 169–170; Bobryonev, *"Doktor Smert,"* pp. 271–272; Bobryonev and Ryazentsev, *The Ghosts,* pp. 115–117.

337. Akikusa's prisoner card in Vladimir Prison (Memorial's Archive [Moscow], fond 171; prisoner cards from Vladimir Prison).

338. Williams and Wallace, *Unit 731,* pp. 34–35.

339. Abarinov, *The Murders of Katyn*, pp. 244–245.

340. Bobryonev, *"Doktor Smert,"* p. 273; Bobryonev and Ryazentsev, *Palachi i zhertvy*, p. 170.

341. Copies of original documents from Roedel's Prisoner File released by the KGB.

342. Aleksandr Mironov (1896–1968) was the Inner (Lubyanka) Prison commandant from 1939 until 1953.

343. The so-called Smoltsov's Report cited in USSR Foreign Minister Andrei Gromyko's note, dated February 6, 1957.

344. A "Medical Report" dated September 12, 1947, and signed by head of the Medical Department of Lubyanka Prison, Medical Major Kuzmin. Released by the KGB.

345. Sudoplatov, P., et al., Special Tasks, pp. 270–271; Sudoplatov, P., Spetsoperatsii, pp. 441–442; Sudoplatov, A., Tainaya zhizn', vol. 2, pp. 276.

346. Meetings with the agents or informers in "safe apartments" or hotels was a usual practice of the NKVD/MGB/MVD/KGB officers.

347. Mairanovsky's testimony on August 27, 1953, cited in Bobryonev, "Doktor Smert," pp. 366–367; translated in Bobryonev and Ryazentsev, The Ghosts, pp. 152–153.

348. Khokhlov, In the Name of Conscience, pp. 122–124.

349. Gordievsky, Oleg, Sleduyushchaya ostanovka—rasstrel [Shooting to Death Is the Next Step] (Moscow: Tsentrpoligraf, 1999), pp. 256–257.

350. Sudoplatov, P., Spetsoperatsii, pp. 450–451; Sudoplatov, A., Tainaya zhizn, vol. 2, p. 284.

351. The unusual career of one of the most successful Soviet agents, Iosif Grigulevich, was described recently by Andrew and Mitrokhin in The Sword and the Shield, pp. 99–101, 162–163, and 357–358. However, the authors mistakenly wrote that Grigulevich was a Jew. In fact, he was a Karaim: see Anokhin, G. I., "Luis, brat ubiitsy Trotskogo" [Luis, Leon Trotsky's assassin's brother], Vestnik Rossiiskoi Akademii Nauk 66 (6) (1996):530–535 (in Russian); Pavlov, Vitalii, Operatsiya "Sneg" [Operation "Snow"] (Moscow: Geya, 1996), pp. 156–161 (in Russian); and Primakov, Ocherki istorii, vol. 3, pp. 148–154. The Karaims are a Judaic sect (Karai), but ethnically they are not related to the Jews: They are people of Turk descent who have adopted Karaism. There are three groups of Karaims: the largest in the Crimea (the original location) and two others, in Lithuania and Poland. The western communities have existed since the early fifteenth century, when Grand Duke of Lithuania Witold brought 483 Karaim families to his country (see Karaim home page, http://www.turkiye.net/sota/karaim.html). Grigulevich was born in Lithuania.

352. Anokhin, "Luis, brat ubiitsy Trotskogo." See also Pavlov, Operatsiya "Sneg," pp. 159–161.

353. Gevorkyan and Petrov, "Terakty."

354. Pavlov, Operatsiya "Sneg," pp. 156–159.

355. Volkogonov, D., "Plan Stalina ubit' Tito" [Stalin's plan to assassinate Tito], Izvestiya, June 11, 1993 (in Russian). Translation of the document into English available at http://cwihp.si.edu/cwihplib.nsf.

356. Deichmann, Biologists Under Hitler, pp. 287–288.

357. Ibid., p. 417.

358. Sudoplatov, P., et al., Special Tasks, pp. 336–339.

359. Andrew and Mitrokhin, The Sword and the Shield, p. 358.

360. Pavlov, Operatsiya "Sneg," p. 159.

CHAPTER THREE

1. Mairanovsky's letter with his biography, addressed to Academician Nikolai Blokhin (dated May 18, 1964); Archival Record from the USSR Medical Academy Archive (January 5, 1962); an archival excerpt from a transcript of a meeting of the Scientific Council of the All-Union Institute of Experimental Medicine, VIEM (July 3, 1963); Certificate No. 82061 from Vladimir Prison (April 10, 1962); and a copy of a certificate issued by the KGB (January 26, 1962) (Memorial's Archive [Moscow], fond 1, op. 1, d. 2872). Also see Appendix II.

2. For the history of the VIEM, see Grekova, T. I., and K. A. Lange, "Tragicheskie stranitsy istorii Instituta Eksperimental'noi Meditsiny (20–30-e gody)" [The tragic pages of the history of the Institute of Experimental Medicine, the 1920s–30s], in Yaroshevskii, *Repressirovannaya nauka*, issue 2, pp. 9–44 (in Russian); Grigoryan, N. G., "50-letie Meditsinskoi Akademii" [The 50th anniversary of the Medical Sciences Academy], *Vestnik Roissiiskoi Akademii Nauk* 65 (2) (1995):176–179 (in Russian).

3. Mairanovsky's letter to Blokhin, May 18, 1964.

4. A transcript of Mairanovsky's interrogation on September 23, 1953 (cited in Bobryonev, *"Doktor Smert,"* pp. 231–232, translated in Bobryonev and Ryazentsev, *The Ghosts,* pp. 70–72).

5. Mitscherlich, Alexander, and Fred Mielke, *Doctors of Infamy: The Story of the Nazi Medical Crime,* trans. Heinz Norden, with statements by Andrew C. Ivy, Telford Taylor, and Leo Alexander, and a note by Albert Deutch (New York: Henry Schuman, 1949), pp. 75–80; Kogon, Eugen, *The Theory and Practice of Hell: The Shocking Story of the Nazi S.S. and the Horror of the Concentration Camps,* trans. Heinz Norden (New York: Berkeley Books, 1982), p. 173.

6. Taylor, "Opening Statement of the Prosecution," p. 76.

7. Hunt, *Secret Agenda,* p. 153.

8. Williams and Wallace, *Unit 731,* pp. 45–46; Harris, *Factories of Death,* p. 71.

9. Deichmann, *Biologists Under Hitler,* p. 257.

10. Mitscherlich and Mielke, *Doctors of Infamy,* pp. 79–80.

11. On the whole, six convicts were hanged, five were sentenced to life imprisonment and three to imprisonment from ten to twenty years, and seven were acquitted ("Publisher's Epilogue: Seven Were Hanged," in ibid., p. 146).

12. Hunt, *Secret Agenda,* pp. 179–181.

13. Bower, Tom, *The Paperclip Conspiracy: The Hunt for the Nazi Scientists* (Boston: Little, Brown, 1987), pp. 93–97.

14. Williams and Wallace, *Unit 731,* pp. 235–253.

15. A transcript of the interrogation of Mairanovsky on September 23, 1953 (cited in Bobryonev, *"Doktor Smert,"* pp. 232–233, translated in Bobryonev and Ryazentsev, *The Ghosts,* pp. 70–71).

16. A transcript of the interrogation of Merkulov on September 29, 1953 (cited in Bobryonev, *"Doktor Smert,"* pp. 234–235, translated in Bobryonev and Ryazentsev, *The Ghosts,* pp. 73–74).

17. See the transcripts cited in Notes 15 and 16.

18. Pp. 219–220 in Lifton, Robert J., "Medicalized Killing in Auschwitz," in Gutman, Y., and A. Saf, eds., *The Nazi Concentration Camps: Structure and Aims; The Image of the Prisoner; The Jews in the Camps* (Jerusalem: Yad Vashem, 1984), pp. 207–234.

19. Hunt, *Secret Agenda*, pp. 163–164.

20. Cited in Bobryonev, *"Doktor Smert,"* p. 315, translated in Bobryonev and Ryazentsev, *The Ghosts*, p. 126.

21. Sudoplatov, P., *Spetsoperatsii*, p. 630.

22. Bobryonev and Ryazentsev, *The Ghosts*, p. 75.

23. I could not find any specific information about Smykov.

24. According to Bobryonev, this information is in the transcript of Merkulov's interrogation by the investigator Uspensky (Bobryonev, *"Doktor Smert,"* pp. 400–401; Bobryonev and Ryazentsev, *The Ghosts*, p. 181).

25. Riehl, Nikolaus, and Frederick Seitz, *Stalin's Captive: Nikolaus Riehl and the Soviet Race for the Bomb* (Washington, DC: American Chemical Society and Chemical Heritage Association, 1996).

26. "Osnovnye daty zhizni N. V. Timofeev-Ressovsky" [The main dates in the life of N. V. Timofeev-Ressovsky], in Timofeev-Ressovsky, *Vospominaniya: Istorii, napisannye im samim* (2000), pp. 819–822.

27. Heinrich Zeiss' prisoner card in Vladimir Prison. Memorial's Archive (Moscow), fond 171 (Document 21 in Appendix II).

28. Articles 58–6, pt.1, and 58–9. Zeiss's prisoner card.

29. Mairanovsky's report to Merkulov, mentioned in Bobryonev, *"Doktor Smert,"* p. 401; Bobryonev and Ryazentsev, *The Ghosts*, p. 181.

30. Statement by Dr. Leo Alexander, in Mitscherlich and Mielke, *Doctors of Infamy*, pp. 27–34.

31. Taylor, "Opening Statement of the Prosecution."

32. Proctor, Robert N., *Racial Hygiene: Medicine Under the Nazis* (Cambridge: Harvard University Press, 1988), p. 221.

33. Cited in Posner, Gerald L., and John Ware, *Mengele: The Complete Story* (New York: Cooper Square Press, 2000), p. 42.

34. Bobryonev, *"Doktor Smert,"* p. 292; Bobryonev and Ryazentsev, *The Ghosts*, pp. 138–139.

35. The text of the letter is given in Bobryonev, *"Doktor Smert,"* pp. 294–296.

36. Bobryonev, *"Doktor Smert,"* pp. 346 and 374; Bobryonev and Ryazentsev, *The Ghosts*, pp. 159–160 and 183–184.

37. For details, see Stolyarov, *Palachi i zhertvy*; Knight, *Beria*.

38. Knight, *Beria*, p. 158.

39. The report also contained other accusations of Abakumov: that he violated the MGB interrogation process by ordering not to write transcripts of interrogations and, therefore, concealed from Stalin and the Party facts of sabotage by the imperialistic forces, that after the war he acquired a lot of trophy stuff, and so on (Stolyarov, *Palachi i zhertvy*, pp. 13–15).

40. Naumov and Sigachev, *Lavrentii Beria*, pp. 496–497.

41. Some of them (Raikhman and Pitovranov) have already been mentioned above. But the most important persons were the head of the MGB Department for the Investigation of Especially Important Cases, Aleksandr Leonov, and his two deputies, Vladimir Komarov and Mikhail Likhachev, as well as the head of the MGB Secretariat, Ivan Chernov, and his deputy, Yakov Broverman. All these individuals, except Chernov, worked during the war in the Military Counterintelligence SMERSH under Abakumov, who headed SMERSH.

42. Petrov and Kasatkina, "Ekspertiza 'Memoriala.'"

43. Before that, until February 1952, Abakumov was kept in a special prison of the Central Committee of the Communist Party, "Matrosskaya Tishina," and his case was investigated by Deputy Chief Prosecutor K. Mokichev (Stolyarov, *Palachi i zhertvy*, pp. 15–37).

44. Solzhenitsyn, A. I., *The Gulag Archipelago, 1918–1956,* vol. 1 (New York: Harper and Row, 1973), pp. 126–127.

45. Mairanovsky's letter to Khrushchev. The text of the letter is given in Bobryonev, *"Doktor Smert,"* pp. 294–296.

46. Bobryonev, *"Doktor Smert,"* p. 290–291.

47. Larina, *This I Cannot Forget*, p. 241.

48. Vaksberg, *Stalin Against the Jews*, p. 101.

49. Larina, *This I Cannot Forget*, pp. 240–246.

50. Three names are known: Pavel Vasiliev, a poet; P. Petrovsky, the son of an old Bolshevik; and a military historian named P. Meshcheryakov (Parrish, *Lesser Terror*, p. 310). Arkady Vaksberg claims that Sverdlov "beat them [prisoners] mercilessly" during interrogations (Vaksberg, *Stalin Against the Jews*, pp. 101–102).

51. Larina, *This I Cannot Forget*, pp. 170 and 239–241.

52. Vaksberg, *Stalin's Prosecutor*, p. 133.

53. Changes in subordination of the Secret-Political Department from 1934 till 1954 are given in Kokurin and Petrov, *Lubyanka*, p. 126.

54. Sudoplatov, P., *et al.*, *Special Tasks*, p. 348.

55. Kostyrchenko, *Out of the Red Shadows*, p. 126.

56. Stolyarov, *Palachi i zhertvy,* p. 338.

57. Ibid., p. 338.

58. Bobryonev and Ryazentsev, *The Ghosts,* p. 27.

59. Kokurin and Petrov, "MGB," p. 111.

60. There are two cards for Mairanovsky in Vladimir Prison's file: one written on March 6, 1953, by V. Danilova (secretary of the prison's archive), and a second one, written on July 6, 1956, by I. Shchelanova (Documents 16 and 17 in Appendix II). The first card includes information from Mairanovsky's arrival to the prison on March 5, 1953, until his departure for Lubyanka Prison in Moscow on June 7, 1953. The second card contains information from Mairanovsky's return to Vladimir Prision on July 4, 1956, until his release on December 13, 1961.

61. Eitingon's prisoner card (Document 18 in Appendix II).

62. Stolyarov, *Palachi i zhertvy*, pp. 338–339.

63. Zaretsky, Ye., *"Vladimirskii Tsentral"*: *Istoriya stroitel'stva, znamenitye uzniki, den' segodnyashnii (po muzeinoi ekspozitsii)* [Vladimir Prison: History, Famous Prisoners, and Today (museum exposition)] (Vladimir: AOZT "Kaleidoskop," 1997) (in Russian).

64. Sudoplatov, P., et al., *Special Tasks*, pp. 101–102.

65. Wilhelm and Natalia Munters's prisoner cards in Vladimir Prison (Memorial's Archive [Moscow], fond 171; prisoner cards from Vladimir Prison).

66. See Volin, "S berievtsami vo Vladimirskoi Tuyr'me," and Men'shagin, *Vospominaniya.*

67. Parvilahti, Unto, *Beria's Gardens* (New York: E. P. Dutton, 1960), pp. 147–150.

68. Ipatieff, *The Life of a Chemist*, p. 441.

69. In his memoirs, Lucien Gouaze mentioned Clauberg as one of the inhabitants of Cell 45 in Corpus 3 in 1954 (Serbet, *Polit-Isolator*, p. 368).

70. Proctor, Robert N., "Nazi Doctors, Racial Medicine, and Human Experimentation," in Annas and Grodin, *The Nazi Doctors*, pp. 17–31.

71. Taylor, "Opening Statement of the Prosecution," p. 80. See also Weinreich, *Hitler's Professors*, pp. 197, 218; Lifton, *The Nazi Doctors*, pp. 271–278, and Lifton, R. J., and A. Hackett, "Nazi Doctors," in Gutman, Israel, Michael Berenbaum, Yisrael Gutman, and Raul Hilberg, eds., *Anatomy of the Auschwitz Death Camp* (Bloomington: Indiana University Press and U.S. Holocaust Memorial Museum, 1994), pp. 301–316.

72. Men'shagin, *Vospominaniya*, p. 100; Menshagin's prisoner card in Vladimir Prison.

73. From March 24, 1949, until July 21, 1949 (Sgovio's prisoner card, Memorial's Archive [Moscow], fond 171; prisoner cards from Vladimir Prison).

74. Sgovio, Thomas, *Dear America! Why I Turned Against Communism* (Kenmore, NY: Partners' Press: 1979), p. 280.

75. Men'shagin, *Vospominaniya*, p. 100.

76. Parvilahti, *Beria's Gardens,* p. 138; Men'shagin, *Vospominaniya*, p. 100.

77. Volin, "S berievtsami vo Vladimirskoi Tur'me." O. Volin was the pseudonym of a former Soviet dissident and political prisoner, Revolt Pimenov (see Sakharov, *Memoirs* pp. 314–318).

78. Revolt Pimenov's prisoner card in Vladimir Prison (Memorial's Archive [Moscow], fond 171; prisoner cards from Vladimir Prison).

79. Jeffery, *Inside Russia* pp. 56–57.

80. Volin, "S berievtsami vo Vladimirskoi Tur'me."

81. Jeffery, *Inside Russia*, p. 57.

82. A Decree of the Presidium of the USSR Supreme Council "On Amnesty" dated March 27, 1953, included paragraph 2, which amnestied this type of prisoners.

83. Raikhman was appointed head of the Control Inspection to Check the Fulfillment of Orders of the Minister, and Eitingon was appointed deputy of Sudoplatov, who now headed the Ninth MVD Department. On July 31, 1953,

this department was placed under the Second Main (Foreign Intelligence) MVD Directorate (Kokurin and Petrov, *Lubyanka*, pp. 72 and 129; Naumov and Sigachev, *Lavrentii Beria*, p. 498).

84. Cited in Bobryonev, *"Doktor Smert,"* p. 346; translated in Bobryonev and Ryazentsev, *The Ghosts,* pp. 181–182.

85. See Khrushchev's own description of the events in *Khrushchev Remembers,* with an introduction, commentary, and notes by Edward Crankshaw, trans. and ed. Strobe Talbott (New York: Bantam Books, 1971), pp. 357–369.

86. Resolution on the Criminal, Anti-Party and Anti-Government Activities of Beria of the Plenum of the Central Committee CRSU. Adopted anonymously at the Session of the Plenum of the CC CSPU, July 7, 1953 (Stickle, D. M., ed., *The Beria Affair: The Secret Transcripts of the Meeting Signalling the End of Stalinism* (New York: Nova Science Publishers, 1992), pp. 183–191.

87. Ibid., p. 95.

88. Eitingon's prisoner card at Vladimir Prison (Document 18 in Appendix II). The MGB/MVD investigator Pavel Grishaev prepared the arrest of Eitingon and Ryumin (Vaksberg, *Stalin Against the Jews*, p. 279). Grishaev was one of investigators of Abakumov (his former boss) and applied terrible methods of torture to Abakumov.

89. Khokhlov, *In the Name of Conscience*, p. 184.

90. Ibid., p. 185.

91. Murphy, David E., Sergei A. Kondrashov, and George Bailey, *Battleground Berlin: CIA vs. KGB in the Cold War* (New Haven: Yale University Press, 1997), pp. 109 and 470.

92. Bobryonev, *"Doktor Smert,"* pp. 347–348, and 363–364.

93. On June 29, 1953, at the Presidium of Central Committee meeting, Stalin's chief prosecutor (from 1948–1953) G. Safonov (1904–1972) was dismissed and Rodion Rudenko was appointed the new chief prosecutor (Naumov and Sigachev, *Lavrentii Beria*, pp. 216–217 and 418).

94. A top-secret decision of the Presidium of the Central Committee "On the organization of investigation of the case on criminal anti-Party and anti-Government [i.e., anti-Soviet] activity of Beria" dated June 29, 1953. The text is given in Naumov and Sigachev, *Lavrentii Beria*, p. 72.

95. A transcript of the Special Court Meeting of the USSR Supreme Court on December 18–23, 1953; Mikhailov's inquiry cited in Bobryonev, *"Doktor Smert,"* pp. 399–400; translated in Bobryonev and Ryazentsev, *The Ghosts*, pp. 372–378.

96. Official information "In the USSR Supreme Court" published in the daily *Pravda* on December 24, 1953. Cited as document no. 9 in Naumov and Sigachev, *Lavrentii Beria*, pp. 387–391. See the English translation in Stickle, *The Beria Affair*, pp. 195–197.

97. Document 8 ("Act [Report]" dated December 23, 1953) in Naumov and Sigachev, *Lavrentii Beria*, p. 387.

98. Mlechin, *Predsedateli*, p. 357.

99. In December 1953, Kitaev closed investigation of the Abakumov case (Stolyarov, *Palachi i zhertvy*, p. 101).

100. "Act [Report] dated December 23, 1953," reproduced in Popov, B. S., and V. G. Oppokov, "Berievshchina," *Voenno-Istoricheskii Zhurnal* 10 (1991):56–62 (in Russian).

101. Bobryonev, *"Doktor Smert,"* pp. 408–411. Translations of excerpts from transcripts of interrogations of Balishansky (on February 4, 1954) and Muromtsev (on March 3, 1954) are given in Bobryonev and Ryazentsev, *The Ghosts,* pp. 83.

102. Bobryonev, *"Doktor Smert,"* pp. 409.

103. Decision of the Commission of the USSR Supreme Council Presidium, transcript no. 135 from September 3, 1956.

104. Mairanovsky's second prisoner card at Vladimir Prison (Document 17 in Appendix II).

105. Dates of the cell occupancy on Kruminsh's prisoner card (Memorial's Archive [Moscow], fond 171; prisoner cards from Vladimir Prison).

106. Eitingon's prisoner card at Vladimir Prison (Document 18 in Appendix II).

107. Sudoplatov's prisoner card at Vladimir Prison (Document 22 in Appendix II).

108. Deputy Chairman of the Military Collegium, Major General Kostromin (Sudoplatov, P., *et al.*, *Special Tasks*, p. 399).

109. Ibid., pp. 400–401.

110. Ibid., p. 407.

111. Volin, "S berievtsami vo Vladimirskoi Tur'me," pp. 370–371.

112. Men'shagin, *Vospominaniya*, pp. 124–125.

113. Ibid., p. 125.

114. Ibid., p. 126.

115. Ibid., pp. 94, 118–119. Men'shagin's memory was phenomenal: According to prisoner cards, Men'shagin shared cells 2-30, 2-45, and 2-26 with Steinberg from 1964 until January 1966. On January 8, 1966, Steinberg was released (Menshagin's and Steinberg's prisoner cards, Memorial's Archive [Moscow], fond 171; prisoner cards from Vladimir Prison).

116. Men'shagin, *Vospominaniya*, pp. 123–125.

117. Eitingon was transferred to Vladimir Prison on March 16, 1957, and released from it in March 1964 (from his prisoner card).

118. After that Sudoplatov became a translator and a ghost writer. He died in 1996 (Naumov and Sigachev, *Lavrentii Beria*, pp. 486–487).

119. A copy of Ilyukhin's letter to F. G. Mairanovsky dated September 18, 1989 (Memorial's Archive [Moscow], fond 1, op. 1, d. 2862).

120. Sudoplatov, P., *et al.*, *Special Tasks*, pp. 430–443.

121. Bobryonev, *"Doktor Smert,"* pp. 42, 240; Bobryonev and Ryazentsev, *The Ghosts,* p. 85.

122. Bobryonev and Ryazentsev, *The Ghosts*, p. 162.

123. Mairanovsky's letter to Khrushchev, dated August 1955, cited in Bobryonev, "*Doktor Smert*," p. 294; translated in Bobryonev and Ryazentsev, *The Ghosts*, p. 146.

124. Petrov and Skorkin, *Kto rukovodil NKVD*, pp. 422–423.

125. Bobryonev and Ryazentsev, *The Ghosts*, pp. 142–143.

126. The "'Archival Information' from the KGB Central Archive," given in 1988 to Muromtsev's daughter, Natalia Tolmacheva. Cited in "Eta gor'kaya pravda" [This bitter truth], *Ogonyok* 29 (1988):23–24.

127. Sudoplatov, A., *Tainaya zhizn'*, vol. 2, pp. 521–522.

128. Sudoplatov, P., *Spetsoperatsii*, p. 617.

129. *Pravda*, July 28, 1948.

130. Muromtsev, Sergei N., *Problemy sovremennoi mikrobiologii v svete michurinskogo ucheniya* [Problems of Current Microbiology in the Light of Michurin's Ideas] (Moscow: Pravda, 1950) (in Russian).

131. Muromtstev, S. N., "Novye raboty o nasledstennosti i ee izmenchivosti y mikrooganizmov" [New works on inheritance and its variability in microorganisms], *Zhurnal Mikrobiologii, Epidemiologii and Immunologii* 3 (1951):7–13 (in Russian).

132. Abelev, G. I., I. N. Kryukova, and V. N. Gershanovich, "Pis'mo v redaktsiyu zhurnala *Ogonyok*" [A letter to the Editorial Board of the magazine *Ogonyok*], *Ogonyok* 29 (1988):24 (in Russian).

133. "Muromtsev, Sergei Nikolaevich," *Great Soviet Encyclopedia: A Translation of the Third Edition* (New York: Macmillan, 1974), vol. 17, p. 245.

134. Weinreich, *Hitler's Professors*, p. 7.

135. Memorial's Archive (Moscow), fond 1, op. 1, d. 2872.

136. Blokhin, N., "Akademik N. Blokhin daet pokazaniya" [Academician N. Blokhin testifies], *Moscow News* 39 (1990) (in Russian).

137. Sakharov, *Memoirs*, p. 515.

138. "Speransky, A. D.," in *Bol'shaya Meditsinskaya Entsiklopedia* [The Great Medical Encyclopedia] (Moscow: Sovetskaya Entsiklopedia, 1976), vol. 24, p. 308 (in Russian).

139. Rapoport, *The Doctor's Plot of 1953*, pp. 262–266.

140. Kulaev, B. S., "'Pavlovskaya sessiya' i sud'ba sovetskoi fiziologii" [The "Pavlov Session" and the fate of the Soviet physiology], *Voprosy Istorii Estestvoznaniya i Tekhniki* 3 (1988):138–141 (in Russian); Arshavsky, M. A., "O sessii 'dvukh akademii'" [On the session of "two academies"], in Yaroshevsky, *Repressirovannaya nauka*, issue 2, pp. 239–242.

141. Yaroshevskii, M. G., "'Pavlovskaya sessiya,'" pp. 129–136; Krementsov, *Stalinist Science*, p. 273.

142. Yaroshevskii, "'Pavlovskaya sessiya,'"; Arshavsky, "O sessii 'dvukh akademii,'" p. 239.

143. Kulaev, B. S., "'Pavlovskaya sessiya.'"

144. "Grashchenkov, N. I.," in *Bol'shaya Meditsinskaya Entsiklopedia*, vol. 8, pp. 198–201 (in Russian).

145. Aleksandrov, *Trudnye gody*, pp. 17–18.

146. Grigoryan, "50-letie Akademii Meditsinskikh Nauk," pp. 176–179.

147. Aleksandrov, *Trudnye gody*, p. 35.

148. "Sanotsky, V. A.," in *Bol'shaya Meditsinskaya Entsiklopedia*, vol. 29, p. 363 (in Russian).

149. "Tarusov, B. N.," in *Bol'shaya Meditsinskaya Entsiklopedia*, vol. 31, pp. 1144–1145 (in Russian).

150. "Frank, Gleb Mikhailovich," in *Great Soviet Encyclopedia*, vol. 27, p. 319.

151. Belousov, L. V., A. A. Gurvich, S. Ya. Zalkind, and N. N. Kannegiser, *Aleksandr Gavrilovich Gurvich* (Moscow: Nauka, 1970), pp. 50, 55, and 69 (in Russian).

152. In 1990, this institute was divided into the Institute of Theoretical and Experimental Biophysics (Director L. Chailakhyan), and the Institute of Cell Biophysics (Director Yevgenii Fesenko) (Schnol, *Geroi i zlodei*, p. 440).

153. Burnazyan, A. I., "Fantasticheskaya real'nost'" [The fantastic reality], *Vestnik Rossiiskoi Akademii Nauk* 63 (3) (1993):243–257 (in Russian).

154. In the early 1950s, the Department of Medical Radiology at the Central Institute of Final Medical Education (TsIU) of the Medical Academy was another site of secret medico-biological studies on radiation effect within the Soviet atomic project. These studies were supervised by the MGB and Special Directorate of the Medical Academy (Schnol, *Geroi i zlodei*, pp. 301–304).

155. Abelev, G. I., "The 'Alternative' Science. From the Life of Science During the Period of Stagnation," *Ontogenez* 22 (1991):659–672 (in Russian; English translation in *Russian Journal of Developmental Biology* 22 [1992]:413–424).

156. Schnol, *Geroi i zlodei*, p. 391.

157. Ibid.

158. Kokurin and Petrov, *Lubyanka*, pp. 125–126. The specificity of the work of the First, Second, and Seventh MGB/KGB Departments in a secret center of the Soviet atomic project Arzamas-16 in the 1940s–1950s is described in Popov, *Arzamas-16*, pp. 50–65.

159. The report was reproduced in Krivonosov, Yu. I, "Landau i Sakharov v 'razrabotkakh' KGB" [Landau and Sakharov in the "investigative materials" of the KGB], *Voprosy Istorii Estestvoznaniya i Tekhniki* 34 (1993):124–132 (in Russian).

160. Sakharov, *Memoirs*, pp. 386–388.

161. Ibid., pp. 632–633.

162. Popovsky, *Manipulated Science*, p. 31.

163. Dr. Vil Mirzayanov (personal communications). The GosNIIOKhT in Moscow and its branches in Shikhany, Volgograd, and Novocheboksarsk continue to be the main potential reasearch centers on chemical weaponry in Russia (see Smithson, "Toxic Archipelago").

164. A special police permit, called a "propiska," is still needed for Russian citizens living in Moscow.

165. A short biography of Zhuk (1892–1957): "Zhuk, Sergei Yakovlevich," in *Great Soviet Encyclopedia*, vol. 9, p. 646.

166. Solzhenitsyn, *The Gulag Archipelago, 1918–1956,* vols. 3–4, p. 99.

167. Kokurin and Petrov, *Lubyanka,* pp. 31, 62, 120, 122, 138.

168. Petrov and Skorkin, *Kto rukovodil NKVD,* p. 357.

169. Kozlov, V. A., and S. V. Mironenko, eds., *Arkhiv Noveishei Istorii Rossii. Tom IV. "Osobaya Papka" L. P. Berii. Iz Materialov Sekretariata NKVD-MVD SSSR 1946–1949. Katalog Dokumentov* [Archive of Contemporary Russian History. Vol. IV. The "Special Files" for L. P. Beria. From Materials of the NKVD-MVD of the USSR, 1946–1949] (Moscow: State Archive of the Russian Federation, 1996), pp. 342 (Document D. 205, L. 195–241), 516 (D. 244, L. 47–142).

170. Ibid., p. 452.

171. Vorontsov, Nikolai N., "Nature Protection and Government in the USSR," *Journal of the History of Biology* 25 (1992):369–383.

172. "Akademiku N. A. Shilo 80 let" [Academician N. A. Shilo is now 80], *Vestnik Rossiiskoi Akademii Nauk* 63 (1993):948 (in Russian).

173. In 1946, gold mines (and labor camps of prisoners working in them) were gathered under the new MVD Special Main Directorate (SGU) *Glavspetstsvetmet.* In 1951, the new MVD Geological Directorate became in charge of coordinating all MVD mining camp activity, including SGU, Dalstroi, and countless others (Kokurin and Petrov, *Lubyanka,* pp. 50–51, 63).

174. In 1946, Georgii Demidov (1908–1986) received his second term in labor camps for this statement. Demidov was under KGB surveillance until his death. In 1980, during the search of apartments of Demidov's friends in different cities, the KGB confiscated manuscripts of all Demidov's unpublished works (Shentalinsky, *Arrested Voices,* pp. 132–134).

175. "Shilo, Nikolai Alekseevich," in *Great Soviet Encyclopedia,* vol. 29, pp. 596–597.

176. See "Shirshov, Pyotr Petrovich," in *Great Soviet Encyclopedia,* vol. 29, p. 603.

177. Kozlov and Mironenko, *"Osobaya Papka" L. P. Berii,* pp. 122, 128, 187, 207–208, 232, 452, 507, 596, 601, 603, and 628. It is interesting that some oil was brought to the Dalstroi and its labor camps from the United States (pp. 207–208).

178. "P. P. Shirshov [an obituary]," *Vestnik Akademii Nauk SSSR* 23 (2):45–46 (in Russian).

179. Excerpts from the memoirs of the Gulag's survivors with a description of transportation are given in Conquest, Robert, *Kolyma: The Arctic Death Camps* (New York: Viking Press, 1978), pp. 25–35.

180. Kozlov and Mironenko, *"Osobaya Papka" L. P. Berii,* p. 344.

181. Ibid., p. 515.

182. Ibid., p. 249.

183. A letter addressed to L. Beria and dated July 29, 1947 (Kozlov and Mironenko, ibid., pp. 274–275).

184. Radzinsky, *Stalin*, pp. 523–525.

185. See, for instance, Bower, Tom, *Nazi Gold: The Full Story of the Fifty-Year Swiss-Nazi Conspiracy to Steal Billions from Europe's Jews and Holocaust Survivors* (New York: HarperCollins, 1997).

186. A survivor of Kolyma prisoner camps, the American Thomas Sgovio described in detail conditions of the "work" in the Kolyma gold mines (Sgovio, *Dear America,* pp. 209–211).

187. Anders, Wladyslaw, *An Army in Exile* (Nashville, TN: Battery Press, 1981), p. 76.

188. Conquest, *Kolyma*, pp. 218–219.

189. Wallace, Henry A., *Soviet Asia Mission* (New York: Reynal and Hitchcock, 1946).

190. Newman, Robert P., *Owen Lattimore and the "Loss" of China* (Berkeley: University of California Press, 1992), p. 107.

191. Reports dated May 29 and June 8, 1944, in Kozlov and Mironenko, *"Osobaya papka" I. V. Stalina*, pp. 30 and 32.

192. Conquest, *Kolyma*, pp. 204–213; Newman, *Owen Lattimore*, pp. 109–110; Hochschild, *The Unquiet Ghost*, pp. 268–272.

193. In fact, on January 20, 1944, Ivan Nikishov was awarded the Order of Hero of Socialist Labor, a civilian analogue of the military Order of Hero (Kokurin, A., and N. Petrov, "NKVD-NKGB-SMERSH: struktura, funktsii, kadry: Stat'ya chetvertaya (1944–1945)" [NKVD-NKGB-SMERSH: Structure, function, and cadre: The fourth article, 1944–1945], *Svobodnaya Mysl* 9 (1997):94 (in Russian).

194. Lattimore, O., "New Road to Asia," *National Geographic Magazine* 86 (6) (1944):657.

195. Conquest, *Kolyma*, pp. 68–69. It is possible that later, in 1953, Gridasova-Nikishova worked on the staff of Vladimir Prison: Some of the prisoner cards were signed "Gridasova" by a person who filled out the card (see Viktorova's prisoner card).

196. Conquest, *Kolyma*, pp. 206–212.

197. Solzhenitsyn, *The Gulag Archipelago*, vol. 2, pp. 497–500. Ida Varpakhovskaya, a Kolyma survivor, an actress, and the wife of the famous imprisoned theater director Leonid Varpakhovsky, published memoirs with many details on the life of the Nikishovs' slaves (Varpakhovskaya, I., "Iz vospominanii kolymskoi 'Traviaty'" [From the memoirs of Kolyma's "Traviata"], in Korallov, M. M., ed., *Teatr Gulaga* [The Gulag's Theater] (Moscow: Memorial, 1995), pp. 65–79 (in Russian).

198. Varpakhovskaya, "Iz vospominanii," p. 73.

199. Wallace, *Soviet Asia Misson*, p. 127.

200. Varpakhovskaya, "Iz vospominanii," p. 73.

201. Lattimore, "New Road to Asia," pp. 648, 673.

202. Lipper, Elinor, *Eleven Years in Soviet Prison Camps* (Chicago: Henry Regnery, 1951), pp. 266–269.

203. Lysenko, Trofim D., *Heredity and Its Variability*, trans. Theodosius Dobzhansky (New York: King's Crown Press, 1946).

204. Dunn's letter to Michael Lerner, dated June 29, 1945; cited in Krementsov, *Stalinist Science*, p. 122.

205. Krementsov, N. L., "'Amerikanskaya pomoshch' sovetskoi genetike, 1945–1947" ["American help" to Soviet genetics, 1945–1947], *Vestnik Instituta Istorii Estestvoznaniya i Tekhniki* 3 (1996):25–41 (in Russian); Krementsov, N. L., "A 'Second Front' in Soviet Genetics: The International Dimension of the Lysenko Controversy, 1944–1947," *Journal of the History of Biology* 29 (1996):229–250.

206. A letter of J. Edgar Hoover, the FBI director, to George E. Allen, dated May 29, 1946, reproduced in Moynihan, Daniel P., *Secrecy: The American Experience* (New Haven: Yale University Press, 1998), pp. 63–68.

207. Weinstein and Vassiliev, *The Haunted Wood*, pp. 68–69, and 234–235.

208. Moynihan, *Secrecy*, p. 124.

209. Sgovio, *Dear America*, pp. 250–251.

210. Antonov-Ovseenko, Anton, *Vragi naroda* [Enemies of People] (Moscow: Intellekt, 1996), pp. 286–288 (in Russian).

211. Ibid., p. 287.

212. About the new situation within the former KGB see Waller, *Secret Empire*, and Knight, Amy, *Spies Without Cloaks: The KGB's Successors* (Princeton: Princeton University Press, 1996).

213. Albats, *The State*, p. 462.

214. Andrew and Mitrokhin, *The Sword and the Shield*, p. 13.

215. Mlechin, Leonid, *Yevgenii Primakov: Istoriya odnoi kar'ery* [Yevgenii Primakov: History of the Career] (Moscow: Tsentrpoligraf, 1999), p. 51 (in Russian).

216. Ibid., p. 61.

217. Ibid., pp. 64–79.

218. Ibid., p. 89.

219. Ibid., pp. 81–86.

220. Ibid., pp. 86–88.

221. Ibid., pp. 98–110.

222. Primakov, Yevgenii, ed. *Ocherki Istorii Rossiiskoi Vneshnei Razvedki* [Essays on the History of the Russian Foreign Intelligence] (Moscow: Mezhdunarodnye Otnosheniya, 1995–1997), vols. 1–3 (in Russian). The fourth volume of this series was published in 1999 under the editorship of Vyacheslav Trubnikov.

223. Mlechin, *Yevgenii Primakov*, pp. 21, 573.

224. Ibid., pp. 218–223.

225. Knight, *Spies*, pp. 115–117.

226. C. L., "Hopes Ride on Manager with a Scientist's Mind," *Nature* 395 (1998):209.

227. Vucinich, *Empire of Knowledge*, p. 364.

228. Tolz, *Russian Academicians*, p. 136.

229. For instance, Nikolskii, G. V., "O nekotorykh obshchikh voprosakh biologii" [On some general questions of biology], *Bulletin Moskovskogo Obshchestva Ispytatelei Prirody, Seriya biologicheskaya* 18 (2) (1953):48–56 (in Russian).

230. Iovchuk was the propaganda secretary of the Belorussian Communist Party Central Committee. In summer 1949, he was demoted to a post at the Department of Dialectic and Historical Materialism at the Urals State University in the city of Sverdlovsk (Kostyrchenko, *Out of the Red Shadows*, p. 218).

231. Yaroshevsky, M. G., "Stalinism i sud'by sovetskoi nauki" [Stalinism and the fate of Soviet science], in Yaroshevskii, *Repressirovannaya Nauka*, p. 29. During the same election of 1946, Chairman of the USSR Council of Ministers Vyacheslav Molotov also gained the status of Honorable Academician (Reiss, *Molotov Remembers*, p. 316). Like most Bolshevik leaders, Molotov was poorly educated: He was dismissed from his gymnasium, then graduated from a *reaschulle* (a secondary school), and in 1916 enrolled in the Saint Petersburg Polytechnic Institute. However, he did this only in order to avoid the draft and as a cover for underground revolutionary activity (Reiss, *Molotov Remembers*, p. xiii).

232. Aleksandrov, G. F., "Bor'ba mnenii i svoboda kritiki—zakon razvitiya peredovoi nauki" [A struggle of opinions and freedom of criticism—a law of the development of progressive science], *Priroda* 6 (1952):3–12 (in Russian).

233. Kostyrchenko, *Out of the Red Shadows*, p. 24.

234. In May 1941, Zhdanov was replaced in this position by the First Secretary of Moscow Regional and Moscow City Committees Andrei Shcherbakov. At the time Shcherbakov also headed the Main Political Directorate of the Red Army and the Sovinformburo and was a secretary of the Central Committee. Zhdanov continued to be the first secretary of the Leningrad Regional Party Committee and a Politburo member. In summer 1944, Zhdanov moved to Moscow and actively intrigued against Aleksandrov. After Shcherbakov's death in 1945, Zhdanov resumed his position as the Central Committee's secretary of ideology. In July 1948, Stalin criticized Zhdanov at a Politburo meeting, and Zhdanov was removed from his position as second secretary. He died soon after this meeting.

235. Cited in Kostyrchenko, *Out of the Red Shadows*, p. 23. See also Stetsovsky, *Istoriya*, vol. 1, pp. 465–486.

236. For more details see, for instance, *Out of the Red Shadows*, pp. 212–218.

237. Ibid., p. 218.

238. Yaroshevsky, M. G., "Stalinism i sud'by sovetskoi nauki," p. 29.

239. Zubok, Vladislav, and Constantine Pleshakov, *Inside the Kremlin's Cold War* (Cambridge: Harvard University Press, 1996), pp. 87–88; Murphy *et. al.*, *Battleground Berlin*, pp. 40–41, 447–448.

240. Andrew and Gordievsky, *KGB*, pp. 425–426.

241. Weinstein and Vassiliev, *The Haunted Wood*, pp. 68–69, 291–297.

242. Dzhirkvelov, *Secret Servant*, pp. 136–139.

243. Zubok, V., "Soviet Intelligence and the Cold War: The 'Small' Committee of Information in 1952–1953," *Diplomatic History* (Winter 1995).

244. Mlechin, *Yevgenii Primakov*, p. 209.

245. Ibid., p. 211. Under President Putin, Russian diplomacy became completely controlled by the SVR: In May 2000, the SVR Head Vyacheslav Trubnikov (see Table I.1) was dismissed and appointed the first deputy foreign minister of Russia.

246. "Sacked Primakov Was Reluctant Premier," Reuters, May 12 (1999) (on-line version).

247. This tradition has a long history. Thus, in 1945 Beria tried to give an expensive rifle to Academician Kapitsa after Kapitsa sent Stalin a letter in which he complained about the rudeness of Beria and other high Party leaders toward scientists involved in the A-bomb project (Antonov-Ovseenko, *Beria*, p. 396).

248. "Security Service Rewards Ex-PM with Rifle," Reuters, May 18 (1999) (on-line version).

249. "Primakov Is Back," *Moskovskii Komsomolets*, July 28, 2000 (in Russian).

250. Gevorkyan, N., and A. Kolesnikov, "Interview with Acting President Vladimir Putin," *Kommersant-Daily*, March 10, 2000 (on-line version).

251. Anokhin, "Luis, brat ubiitsy Trotskogo."

252. The same year, Yevgenii Primakov, later head of the SVR (Foreign Intelligence) and Russian prime minister, was elected a full member of the academy.

253. Albats, *The State*, p. 156.

254. Turkevich, J., "Agoshkov, Mikhail Ivanovich (Mining Expert)," in *Soviet Men of Science*, pp. 2–3. Also see "Agoshkov, Mikhail Ivanovich," in *Great Soviet Encyclopedia*, vol. 1, p. 141.

255. Investigative journalist Yevgeniya Albats found out that Boyarsky's candidate dissertation was entitled "Defeat of the Interventionists and White Guards" and the title of his doctoral dissertation was "Development of the Scientific Technical Bases for Open Ore Mining in the USSR: The Experience of Historical Research" (Albats, *The State*, p. 153). One can only guess who the real author(s) of such different manuscripts were.

256. Petrov, "Sudy protiv NKVD-MGB."

257. About the trial, see Hodos, *Show Trials*, pp. 73–92; Andrew and Gordievsky, *KGB*, pp. 415–416.

258. Kaplan, K., "Sovetskie sovetniki v Chekhoslovakii v 1949–1956" [Soviet advisers in Czechoslovakia in 1949–1956], *Problemy Vostochnoi Evropy* 11–12 (1983):41–57 (in Russian).

259. Kaplan, Karel, *Report on the Murder of the General Secretary* (Columbus: Ohio State University Press, 1990), p. 134.

260. Cotic, Meir, *The Prague Trial: The First Anti-Zionist Show Trial in the Communist Block* (New York: Herzl Press/Cornwall Books, 1987), p. 219.

261. Cited in Kaplan, *Report on the Murder*, p. 128.

262. Cited in Albats, *The State*, p. 147.

263. Ibid., p. 146.

264. Ibid., pp. 129–130.

265. Vaksberg, A., "Zasluzhennyi deyatel'" [An honored public figure], *Literaturnaya Gazeta*, March 15, 1989 (in Russian); Vaksberg, A., "Golos 'ottuda'" [A voice "from there"], *Literaturnaya Gazeta*, August 1, 1990, p. 13 (in Russian); Abarinov, V., "V kuluarakh dvortsa yustitsii" [In the lobby of the Palace of Justice], *Gorizont* 9 (1989):61–70 (in Russian); Abarinov, V., "K voprosu o tendentsioznosti" [On the question of tendentiousness], *Gorizon* 5 (1990):43–45 (in Russian).

266. The Main Directorate of Counterespionage SMERSH (an abbreviation of the Russian "smert shpionam," i.e., death to spies] was organized on the basis of Special Departments of the NKVD within the Soviet Ministry of Defense in 1943. In 1946, it was merged with the NKGB into the MGB. Viktor Abakumov headed SMERSH (1943–1946) and then the MGB (1946–1951) (Kokurin and Petrov, *Lubyanka*, p. 143). The horrifying style of "interrogations" of POWs or suspected innocent civilians by SMERSH's officers, when the arrested man or woman could be simply tortured to death, was described in Sinevirskii, N., "SMERSH: God v stane vraga" [SMERSH: A year in the enemy's camp], *Grani* (Munich), November (1948):1–135 (in Russian).

267. See, for instance, "O tak nazyvaemom 'Dele,'" p. 40.

268. A copy of a letter of Maryana Zaitseva to the First Deputy of the Head of the Communist Party Control Commission, Z. Serduk, dated April 17, 1964 (Memorial's Archive [Moscow], fond 1, op. 1, d. 1745).

269. Stolyarov, *Palach i zhertvy*, pp. 66–67.

270. Kutafin, O. E., and E. S. Frolov., "V redaktsiyu *Literaturnoi Gazety*" [To the Editorial Office of *Literaturnaya Gazeta*], *Literaturnaya Gazeta,* April 4, 1990 (in Russian).

271. Vaksberg, "Zasluzhennyi deyatel'"; Albats, *The State*; my own conversations with these people in 1990–1991.

272. Cited in Radzinsky, *Stalin*, p. 402.

273. Chebrikov *et al.*, *Istoriya,* pp. 143–145, 201–202, 237–241, 356, 432, and 558.

274. Ibid., p. 201.

275. Stetsovsky, *Istoriya*, vol. 2, p. 67.

276. Chebrikov *et al.*, *Istoriya*, pp. 239–240.

277. Ibid., p. 558.

278. Sudoplatov, P., *et al.*, *Special Tasks*, pp. 10–11.

279. Holloway, *Stalin and the Bomb*, pp. 135–136.

280. Kokurin and Petrov, *Lubyanka*, p. 46.

281. Sudoplatov described this "interrogation" of Bohr as an extremely successful MGB operation (Sudoplatov, P., *et al.*, *Special Tasks*, pp. 206–207).

282. On November 8, 1945, the NKVD sent Stalin a special report about the meeting of Terletsky with Bohr, which included a list of questions, Bohr's answers, and Igor Kurchatov's comments on the answers. See Kozlov and Mironenko, *"Osobaya Papka" I. V. Stalina*, p. 150.

283. Terletsky, "Operatsiya 'Dopros Nielsa Bohra.'"

284. Sakharov, *Memoirs*, p. 328.

285. "Russia Spy Case Resumes, FSB Warns of 'Shady' Links," Reuters, February 26, 2001 (on-line version).

286. "Russian Court Allows FSB to Probe Anonymous Denunciations," Agence France Presse, April 25, 2001 (on-line version).

287. Waller, J. M., "Russia's Security Services: A Checklist for Reform," *Perspective* 8 (1) (September–October 1997) (on-line version).

288. See details in Knight, *Spies*.

289. Agence France Presse, September 25, 1998.

290. See *Moscow Libertarium*, August 11 (1998) (on-line version).

291. Alibek, *Biohazard*, pp. 174–176.

292. Albats, *The State*, pp. 326–327.

293. See Voronov, V., "Prazdnik na obochine."

294. Smirnov, "Stalin i atomnaya bomba."

295. Burnazyan, "Fantasticheskaya real nost." Burnazyan (1906–1981) was deputy minister of health in charge of radiation security.

296. Kuznetsova, N. I., "'Atomnyi sled' v VIET (kak zapreshchali nash zhurnal)" [The "atomic trial" in the VIET (the story of how our journal was banned)], *Voprosy Istorii Estestvoznaniya i Tekhniki* 4 (1997):59–79 (in Russian).

297. Cited in Smirnov, "Stalin i atomnaya bomba."

CHAPTER FOUR

1. Krayer's letter to Stukart, dated June 15, 1933, and Stukart's answer, dated June 20, 1933, are cited in Goldstein, A., "Otto Krayer," in *National Academy of Sciences, Biographical Memoirs* (Washington, DC: National Academy Press, 1987), vol. 57, pp. 151–255. Later Prof. Krayer departed Germany and finally moved to the United States. He died in 1982 as a retired full professor at Harvard Medical School.

2. Josephson, *Totalitarian Science and Technology*, p. 18.

3. Goldschmidt, Richard B., *The Golden Age of Zoology. Portraits from Memory* (Seattle: University of Washington Press, 1956), p. 106.

4. Astaurov and Rokitsky, *Nikolai Konstantinovich Koltsov*, pp. 22–40.

5. Zalkind, S. Y., "Koltzoff, Nikolai Konstantinovich," in Gillispie, C. C., ed., *Dictionary of Scientific Biography* (New York: Scribner's Sons, 1973), vol. 7, pp. 454–457.

6. Cossacks (the most devoted of the Tsar's troops) were used before 1917 against any civilian unrest. These troops were infamous for their cruelty.

7. Koltsov, Nikolai K., *Pamyati pavshikh: Zhertvy iz sredy moskovskogo studentchestva v oktyabr'skie i dekabr'skie dni* [In Memory of the Fallen: Students—Victims of October and December Days] (Moscow: Burche, 1906) (in Russian).

8. See, for instance, memoirs of the geneticist Nikolai Timofeev-Ressovsky: Timofeev-Ressovsky, N. V., "O prozhitom (iz vospominanii, zapisannykh v 1977 g. M. Adamsom" [Memories of the past (noted by M. Adams in 1977)], in

Vorontsov, Nikolai N., ed., *Nikolai Vladimirovich Timofeev-Ressovsky* (Moscow: Nauka, 1993), pp. 18–50 (in Russian).

9. Babkov, "N. K. Koltsov," p. 5.

10. *Krasnaya kniga VCheKa*, vol. 2, p. 50.

11. Ibid., pp. 49–50, 377.

12. Koltsov, N. K., "Ob izmenenii vesa cheloveka pri nestabil'nom balanse" [On the change of a human's weight under unstable balance], *Izvestiya Instituta Eksperimental'noi Biologii* 1 (1921):25–30 (in Russian).

13. For instance, Adams, "Science, Ideology, and Structure."

14. Koltsov, Nikolai K., *Fiziko-Khimicheskie osnovy morfologii* [The Physical-Chemical Basis of Morphology. A speech given at the 3rd All-Union Meeting of Zoologists, Anatomists, and Histologists, Leningrad, December 12, 1927] (Moscow-Leningrad: Gosizdat, 1929) (in Russian); Koltsov, N. K., "Molekuly nasledstvennosti (stat'ya, datirovannaya 1935 i soprovozhdaemaya redaktorskimi zamechaniyami)" [Molecules of inheritance (paper dated 1935 and supplied with the editorial notes)], *Bulletin Moskovskogo Obshchestva Ispytatelei Prirody, Otdelenie Biologicheskoe* 70 (4) (1965): 75–114 (in Russian). On the transmission of Koltsov's ideas among German physicists through his pupil, Nikolai Timofeev-Ressovsky, see Perutz, M. F., "Physics and the Riddle of Life," *Nature* 326 (1987): 555–558; also, Olby, Robert, *The Path to the Double Helix* (New York: Dover Publications, 1994), p. 17.

15. On Chetverikov, see Dobzhansky, Th., "Sergei Sergeevich Tschetverikov, 1880–1959," *Genetics* 55 (1967):1–3; Astaurov, B. L., "Zhizn' S. S. Chetverikova" [The life of S. S. Chetverikov], *Priroda* 2 (1974):57–67 (in Russian); Adams, M. B., "Sergei Chetverikov, the Kol'tsov Institute, and the Evolutionary Synthesis," in Mayr, E., and W. B. Provine, eds., *The Evolutionary Synthesis* (Cambridge: Harvard University Press, 1980), pp. 242–278; Babkov, V.V., "Uchenyi ob uchenom" [A scientist speaks about another scientist], *Priroda* 10 (1991):96–97 (in Russian).

16. Golubovsky, Mikhail D., "Vvedenie" [Introduction], in Efroimson, V. P., *Genetika etiki i estetiki* [Genetics of Ethics and Esthetics] (St. Petersburg: Talisman, 1995) (in Russian).

17. Babkov, "N. K. Koltsov."

18. The text of the speech is given in Soloviev, Yu. I., "Zabytaya discussiya o genetike" [The forgotten discussion on genetics], *Vestnik Rossiiskoi Akademii Nauk* 64 (1) (1994):46–55 (in Russian).

19. Parkhomenko, "Akademik N. P. Gorbunov." The execution was sanctioned by Stalin himself (Volkogonov, *Stalin*, p. 292).

20. Adams, M. B., "Levit, Solomon Grigorevich," in Gillispie, C. C., ed., *Dictionary of Scientific Biographies* (New York: Charles Scribner's Sons, 1990), vol. 18, supp. 2, pp. 546–549.

21. Vucinich, *Empire of Knowledge*, pp. 81–90; Soyfer, *Lysenko*, pp. 317–318.

22. More details about Levit, Agol, and the Medical Genetics Institute are in Adams, M. B., "The Politics of Human Heredity in the USSR, 1920–1940,"

Genome 31 (2) (1989):879–884; Adams, Mark B., "Eugenics in Russia," in Adams, Mark B., ed., *The Wellborn Science: Eugenics in Germany, France, Brazil, and Russia* (New York: Oxford University Press, 1989), pp. 153–229.

23. On Berg, see Sokolov, N. N., "Lev Semenovich Berg," in Pavlovskii, E. N., ed., *Pamyati akademika L. S. Berga* [In Memory of Academician L. S. Berg] (Moscow: Izdatelstvo Akademii Nauk SSSR, 1955), pp. 18–60 (in Russian); Birstein, V. J., and W. E. Bemis, "Leo Semenovich Berg and the Biology of Acipenseriformes: A dedication," in Birstein, Vadim J., John R. Waldman, and William E. Bemis, eds., *Sturgeon Biodiversity and Conservation* (Dordrecht: Kluwer Academic Publishers, 1997), pp. 15–22.

24. *Pravda*, January 11, 1939.

25. Joravsky, *The Lysenko Affair*, pp. 379–380 and 382.

26. Bolotovsky, "Ugolovnoe delo" [A criminal case], *Priroda* 8 (1990): 114–118 (in Russian). On Engelhardt, see Engelhardt, V. A., "Life and Sscience," *Annual Review of Biochemistry* 51 (1982):1–19; Gottih, B. P., "Organizator nauki" [An organizer of scientific research], *Vestnik Rossiiskoi Akademii Nauk* 64 (12) (1994):1120–1127 (in Russian).

27. Sakharov, *Memoirs*, p. 233–236.

28. Bolotovsky, B. M., "Ugolovnoe delo."

29. Roberg, *Soviet Science Under Control*, pp. 41–42.

30. Yurieva, M., and D. Rezlina, "M. N. Pokrovskii: K otchyotu o dey-atel'nosti Akademii Nauk za 1926 g." [M. N. Pokrovskii: On the report of the Academy of Sciences for 1926], in Dobkin and Roginsky, *Zven'ya*, vol. 2, pp. 580–599.

31. Bolotovsky, "Ugolovnoe delo."

32. Afiani, V. Yu., and S. S. Ilizarov, " . . . 'My razgonim k chertovoi materi Akademiyu Nauk,' zayavil 11 iyulya 1964 goda pervyi secretar' TsK KPSS N. S. Khrushchev" ["We will disband the Academy of Sciences to hell," the first secretary of the Central Committee of the Communist Party N. S. Khrushchev declared on July 11, 1964], *Voprosy Istorii Estestvoznaniya i Tekhniki* 1 (1999): 167–173 (in Russian).

33. Sakharov, *Memoirs*, p. 233–236.

34. Joravsky, *The Lysenko Affair*, pp. 81–82, 160.

35. Resolution of the USSR Council of Ministers and Central Committee of the Communist Party on March 28, 1947. See Kostyrchenko, *Out of the Red Shadows*, p. 70; Murin, Yu., "Sudy chesti" [Courts of honor], *Izvestiya TsK KPSS* 11 (1990):135–137 (in Russian).

36. Soyfer, *Lysenko*, pp. 166–167.

37. The letter was reproduced in Andreev, L. N., "Neizvestnyi dokument akademika N. V. Tsitsina" [An unknown document written by Academician N. V. Tsitsin], *Vestnik Rossiiskoi Akademii Nauk* 68 (12) (1998):1096–1108 (in Russian).

38. This telegram, Molotov's reply, and others that followed are kept in the President's Archive in Moscow (Radzinsky, *Stalin*, p. 527).

39. Koltsov's letter to Stalin, in Gaisinovich and Rossianov, "'Ya gluboko ubezhden chto ya prav.'"

40. Dubinin, Nikolai P., *Vechnoe dvizhenie* [The Movement Forever] (Moscow: Politicheskaya Literatura, 1973), p. 71 (in Russian).

41. Detlaff, T. A., "Institut experimentalnoi biologii" [Institute of Experimental Biology], *Ontogenez* 19 (1) (1988):94–112 (in Russian).

42. The letter was given in Grigoryan, N. A., "N. K. Koltsov i experimental'-naya genetika vysshei nervnoi deyatel'nosti" [N. K. Koltsov and the genetics of high nervous activity], *Priroda* 6 (1992):93–97 (in Russian). On Orbeli, see Grigorian, N. A., "Uchenyi i vlast'" [A scientist and state power], *Vestnik Akademii Nauk SSSR* 4 (1991):60–70 (in Russian).

43. Babkov, "N. K. Koltsov."

44. Berg, *Acquired Traits*, p. 283.

45. Academician Mikhail Mitin's speech at the August Session (1948) of the Agricultural Academy (VASKhNIL) (see Zirkle, Conway (ed.), *Death of a Science in Russia. The Fate of Genetics as Described in* Pravda *and Elsewhere* (Philadelphia (PA): University of Pennsylvania Press: 1949), p. 151).

46. An excerpt from the resolution, dated March 29, 1989, and signed by Senior Prosecutor of the Leningrad Region I. V. Katukova. The complete text is given in Levitskaya, N. G., and T. K. Lassan, "Materialy k biografii Grigoriya Andreevicha Levitskogo" [Materials for the biography of Grigorii Andreevich Levitsky], *Tsitologiya* 34 (8) (1992):102–123 (in Russian).

47. Popovsky, *The Vavilov Affair*, pp. 96–98.

48. Vavilov, N. I., "The Law of Homologous Series in Variation," *Journal of Genetics* 12 (1) (1922):47–89.

49. Vavilov, Nikolai I., *Centers of Cultivated Plants* (Leningrad: 1926) (in Russian and English).

50. For a short biography of Vavilov, see Dobzhansky, Th., "N. I. Vavilov, a martyr of genetics," *Journal of Heredity* 38 (1946):226–232; Adams, M. B., "Vavilov, Nikolai Ivanovich," in Gillispie, C. C., ed., *Dictionary of Scientific Biography* (New York: Charles Scribner's Sons, 1978), vol. 15, supp. 1, pp. 505–513. For more details, see Popovsky, *The Vavilov Affair*; and Rokityansky, Ya. G., "Golgofa Nikolaya Vavilova: Biograficheskii ocherk" [The Golgotha of Nikolai Vavilov: A biographical sketch], pp. 4–141 in Rokityansky, Ya. G., Yu. N. Vavilov, and V. A. Goncharov, eds., *Sud palacha: Nikolai Vavilov v zastenkakh NKVD. Biograficheskii ocherk. Dokumenty* [The Trial of an Executioner: Nikolai Vavilov in the Torture Chamber of the NKVD. A Biographical Sketch. Documents] (Moscow: Academia, 1999) (in Russian).

51. Vavilov, Yu. N., and Ya. G. Rokityansky, "Znaniya broshennye v ogon'" [Knowledge thrown into the fire], *Vestnik Rossiiskoi Akademii Nauk* 66 (1996):625 (in Russian). Vavilov's letter regarding Sobolev addressed to the OGPU is given in the appendix, pp. 631–632. The original is kept at the FSB Central Archive, p-2311, t. 8, pp. 230–231.

52. Popovsky, *The Vavilov Affair*, p. 162.

53. Vavilov,Yu. N., and Ya. G. Rokityansky, "Golgotha: Arkhivnye materialy o poslednikh godakh zhizni akademika N. I.Vavilova" [Golgotha: Archival materials on the last years of Academician Vavilov's life (1940–1943)], *Vestnik Rossiiskoi Akademii Nauk* 63 (1993):830–846 (in Russian); Vavilov and Rokityansky, "Znaniya broshennye v ogon'."

54. Rokityansky et al., *Sud palacha*.

55. The text is given in Vavilov and Rokityansky, "Golgotha," p. 832.

56. Lebedev, D. V., "Iz memuarov antilysenkvtsa s predvoennym stazhem" [From the memoirs of an anti-Lysenkoist with a pre-war period of service], in Yaroshevsky, *Repressirovannaya Nauka*, p. 280.

57. Mozokhin, O. B., "Ob organizatsii ekonomicheskikh podrazdelenii OGPU" [On the organization of the OGPU economic departments], in *Istoricheskie chteniya na Lubyanke 1999 god: Otechestvennye sluzhby v 20–30-e gody* [History Lectures at the Lubyanka, 1999: The State Services during the 1920s–30s], available at: http://www.fsb.ru/history/read/1999.html.

58. Rokityansky et al., *Sud palacha*, pp. 142–158 (document 1). Signed by Head of the OGPU Economic Directarate (EKU) Lev Mironov (see biography in Petrov and Skorkin, *Kto rukovodil NKVD*, pp. 300–301) and approved by First Deputy Head of the OGPU A. Akulov (Akulov was at this position only for a year, in 1931–1932; see Conquest, *Inside Stalin's Secret Police,* pp. 13–14).

59. Kokurin and Petrov, *Lubyanka*, pp. 12, 17, and 21.

60. Popovsky, *The Vavilov Affair*, pp. 143–144.

61. Kokurin and Petrov, *Lubyanka*, p. 23.

62. Rokityansky et al., *Sud palacha*, pp. 197–207 (document 8).

63. Document 1 in the appendix to Vavilov and Rokityansky, "Golgotha," p. 835.

64. Stalin's letter to Menzhinsky and letters to Molotov, dated August 2 and 23, 1930 (nos. 56, 57, and 59) in Lih, Lars T., Oleg V. Naumov, and Oleg V. Khlevniuk, eds., *Stalin's Letters to Molotov, 1925–1936* (New Haven: Yale University Press, 1995), pp. 195–196, 199–201, and 203–204.

65. Ibid., p. 196.

66. Ibid., pp. 191–197.

67. Stetsovsky, *Istoriya*, vol. 2, p. 166.

68. Ibid., vol. 1, p. 164.

69. Document 1 in the appendix to Vavilov and Rossianov, "Golgotha," pp. 838–840.

70. Appendix to Vavilov and Rossianov, "Golgotha," p. 837.

71. See, for instance, Conquest, Robert, *The Harvest of Sorrow: Soviet Collectivization and the Terror-Famine* (New York: Oxford University Press, 1986).

72. Heller and Nekrich, *Utopia*, pp. 222–223.

73. Appendix to Vavilov and Rossianov, "Golgotha," p. 839.

74. Ibid., p. 839.

75. Popovsky, *The Vavilov Affair*, p. 80.

76. Joravsky, *The Lysenko Affair*, pp. 190–191; Soyfer, *Lysenko*, pp. 33, 82.

77. Krementsov, *Stalinist Science*, p. 183.

78. Popovsky, *The Vavilov Affair*, p. 142; Soyfer, *Lysenko*, p. 98.

79. Ibid., pp. 142–143. David's testimonies were cited in the warrant for Vavilov's arrest (appendix to Vavilov and Rokityansky, "Golgotha," p. 840).

80. Soyfer, *Lysenko*, pp. 135–136.

81. Ibid., p. 145.

82. I am very grateful to my colleagues from Memorial (Moscow) who directed my attention to this report.

83. Document 110 in Rokityansky et al., *Sud palacha*, pp. 507–511.

84. Appendix to Vavilov and Rokityansky, "Golgotha," p. 840.

85. Popovsky, *The Vavilov Affair*, pp. 128–129.

86. Document 9 in Rokityansky et al., *Sud palacha*, pp. 207–208.

87. Document 12 in ibid., pp. 211–212.

88. Popovsky, *The Vavilov Affair*, p. 158.

89. Documents 16–21, 14–26 in Rokityansky et al., *Sud palacha*, pp. 215–228.

90. Document 17 in ibid., pp. 216–218. The original is kept in the FSB Central archive, no. P-2311, t. 4, l. 47–49.

91. The list (document no. 4) is given in the appendix to Vavilov and Rokityansky, "Znaniya, broshennye v ogon'," pp. 633–634, and in Rokityansky et al., *Sud palacha*, pp. 220–222 (document 20). The original is kept in the FSB Central Archive (no. P-2311, t. 4, l. 23–24).

92. Document 26 in Rokityansky et al., *Sud palacha*, pp. 226–228.

93. From July 1940 to February 26, 1941, Schwartzman was acting head of this department (Petrov and Skorkin, *Kto rukovodil NKVD*, p. 52).

94. Document 106 in Rokityansky et al., *Sud palacha*, pp. 492–493.

95. Document 28 in ibid., pp. 228–251.

96. On Karpechenko, see Lebedev, D. V., "Georgii Dmitrievich Karpechenko," in Belyaev, Dmitrii K., and Vladimir I. Ivanov, eds., *Vydauyshchesya sovetskie genetiki* [Outstanding Soviet Geneticists] (Moscow: Nauka, 1980), pp. 37–48 (in Russian).

97. On Levitsky, see Prokofieva-Bel'govskaya, A. A., "Grigorii Andreevich Levitsky," in ibid.; Adams, M., "Levitskii, Grigorii Andreevich," in Gillispie, *Dictionary of Scientific Biographies* (1990), vol. 18, supp. 2, pp. 549–553.

98. In the Russian text, the name is written as Zeikhlin, but the correct German spelling is Zechlin.

99. Transcripts of interrogations: dated November 16, 1940; January 9, March 11, and May 27, 1941 (documents 56, 64, 75, and 92 in Rokityansky et al., *Sud palacha*, pp. 351–359, 382–383, 404–407, and 451–453, respectively).

100. In 1931, Academician Pryanishnikov unsuccessfully tried to save another arrested scientist, agronomist S. Gerken (Solov'ev, S. S., "Muzhestvo akademika D. N. Pryanishnikova" [The courage of Academician D. N. Pryanishnikov], *Vestnik Rossiiskoi Akademii Nauk* 9 (1992):128–137 (in Russian).

101. Rossianov, K. O., "Iz istorii bor'by akademika D. N. Pryanishnikova za genetiku" [From the history of Academician D. N. Pryanishnikov's fight for genetics], in Yaroshevskii, *Repressirovannaya Nauka*, p. 528.

102. Ibid., pp. 529–530.

103. Ibid., p. 529.

104. Shlykov gave the first testimony against Vavilov on July 13, 1937, cited in the Information on Vavilov prepared by Deputy Head of the Eighth Division of the Fourth (Special) Department GUGB NKVD Ya. Vostrikov before Vavilov's arrest (document 6 in Rokityansky et al., *Sud palacha*, pp. 187–195). Then, on July 7, 1938, Shlykov wrote his secret letter addressed to the head of the Leningrad Regional NKVD Department (Soyfer, *Lysenko*, p. 532). Full texts of the letters are given in Soyfer, *Lysenko*, pp. 117–120.

105. Medvedev, *The Rise and Fall*, pp. 260–261.

106. Document 29 in Rokityansky et al., *Sud palacha*, pp. 251–254.

107. Document 31 (minutes of the interrogation) in ibid., pp. 255–258.

108. Documents 32 and 34 (minutes of interrogations) in ibid., pp. 258–261, 263–264.

109. Document 35 in ibid., p. 265.

110. In fact, Schwartzman was acting head of this department.

111. Vavilov and Rokityansky, "Golgotha," p. 833; Vavilov and Rokityansky, "Znaniya broshennye v ogon'," pp. 628–629. A list of interrogations from Vavilov's Investigation File is given as document 97 in Rokityansky et al., *Sud palacha*, pp. 462–468. Transcripts of many interrogations are also given in the same book.

112. Kokurin and Petrov, *Lubyanka*, pp. 20–35.

113. Documents 74, 80, 86, and 93 in Rokityansky et al., *Sud palacha*, pp. 402–404, 413–414, 441–443, and 453–455.

114. Documents 82, 98, 101, 102 in ibid., pp. 432–435, 468–475, 481–484, and 484–489.

115. Chebrikov et al., *Istoriya*, pp. 240–241.

116. Popovsky, *The Vavilov Affair*, pp. 136–137. For comparison: In the 1980s, the KGB Operational File on Academician Sakharov consisted of 540 volumes (Stetsovsky, *Istoriya*, vol. 2, p. 72).

117. See "A Decision of the Military Collegium of the USSR Supreme Court No. 4 n-011514/55," dated August 20, 1955. The text is given in the appendix to Vavilov and Rokityansky, "Golgotha," p. 844.

118. Chebrikov et al., *Istoriya*, p. 257.

119. Popovsky, *The Vavilov Affair*, pp. 138–139.

120. Ibid., pp. 139–140; Levitskaya and Lassan, "Materialy k biografii," p. 115.

121. Popovsky, *The Vavilov Affair*, p. 152.

122. Cited in ibid., p. 153.

123. Soyfer, Valery, *Vlast i Nauka. Istoriya razgroma genetiki v SSSR* [Power and Science: A History of the Destructon of Genetics in the USSR] (Tenafly, NJ: Hermitage, 1989), pp. 351 and 362 (in Russian).

124. Medvedev, *The Rise and Fall*, pp. 56–57; Popovsky, *The Vavilov Affair*, p. 153.

125. "Eta gor'kaya pravda."

126. Soyfer, *Lysenko*, p. 157.

127. The letter is cited in Vavilov and Rokityansky, "Znaniya, broshennye v ogon'," p. 626.

128. These names are given in "Decision of the Military Collegium of the USSR Supreme Court No. 4 n–011514/55," dated August 20, 1955. The text is given (document No. 10) in the appendix in Vavilov and Rokityansky, "Golgotha," pp. 844–845.

129. Vavilov and Rokityansky, "Golgotha," p. 844.

130. The "Decision of the Military Collegium" (document no. 10) in the appendix in Vavilov and Rokityansky, "Golgotha," p. 845.

131. Document 31 in Rokityansky et al., *Sud palacha*, p. 257.

132. Document 38 in ibid., p. 269.

133. Margolin was shot in 1938 (Joravsky, *The Lysenko Affair*, p. 324; Levitskaya and Lassan, "Materialy k biografii," p. 115).

134. Document 43 in Rokityansky et al., *Sud palacha*, pp. 288–295.

135. Popovsky, *The Vavilov Affair*, p. 147.

136. Document 49 in Rokityansky et al., *Sud palacha*, pp. 300–303.

137. Documents 58 and 371 in ibid., pp. 361–371.

138. Document 63 in ibid., pp. 378–381.

139. Hodos, *Show Trials*, pp. 17–18.

140. Ibid., pp. 18–23.

141. Soyfer, *Lysenko*, p. 357.

142. Vavilov and Rokityansky, "Znaniya, broshennye v ogon'," p. 635.

143. Soyfer, *Lysenko*, p. 357. Dr. Soyfer received notes about Karpechenko's Investigation File No. 981251 from Dr. Daniil Lebedev (St. Petersburg), whom the FSB allowed to examine this file in 1993.

144. Levina, Ye. S., "Tragediya N. I. Vavilova" [The tragedy of N.I. Vavilov], in Yaroshevsky, *Repressirovannaya Nauka,* p. 235. The report is kept in the Archive of the VIR, D. 143a, pp. 79–82.

145. Popovsky, *The Vavilov Affair*, p. 147.

146. A secret letter addressed "To the Central Committee of the Communist (Bolshevik) Party. To C.[omrade] I. V. Stalin," signed by Vice President Bondarenko and Party Secretary Klimov and dated March 27, 1935. The text is given (document no. 2) in the appendix to Vavilov and Rokityansky, "Znaniya broshennye v ogon'," pp. 632–633. The original is kept at the Russian Federation Presidential Archive, F. 3, Op. 30, D. 63, pp. 142–146.

147. A "Strictly Secret" letter of the Head of the Special Sector of the Central Committee to the members of and candidates to the Central Committee, dated April 5, 1935. The copy has a note: "Should be returned to the Second Department of the Special Sector of the Central Committee." The list of names included the following persons: Andreev, Chubar', Eikhe, Kaganovch, Kalinin, Kossior,

Mikoyan, Molotov, Ordzhonikidze, Petrovsky, Postyshev, Stalin, Voroshilov, and Zhdanov. Of all these persons, Vlas Chubar', Robert Eikhe, Stanislav Kossior, and Pavel Postyshev were arrested and shot in 1937–1938; Sergei Ordzhonikidze committed suicide (Conquest, *The Great Terror*, pp. 167–173, 419–420). The text of the letter is given (document no. 3) in the appendix to Vavilov and Rokityansky, "Znaniya broshennye v ogon'," p. 633. The original is kept at the Russian Federation Presidential Archive, F. 3, Op. 30, D. 63, p. 141.

148. Levitskaya and Lassan, "Materialy k biografii," p. 119.

149. Document 71 in Rokityansky et al., *Sud palacha*, pp. 394–397.

150. Levitskaya and Lassan, "Materialy k biografii," p. 148.

151. Document 76 in Rokityansky et al., *Sud palacha*, pp. 407–408.

152. Interrogations on March 11 and 20 (documents 75 and 77 in ibid., pp. 404–406 and 409–410).

153. Document 78 in ibid., pp. 410–411.

154. Document 85 in ibid., pp. 438–441.

155. Document 88 in ibid., pp. 444–445.

156. Document 89 in ibid., pp. 445–446.

157. Document 99 in ibid., pp. 475–480.

158. Soyfer, *Vlast' i nauka*, pp. 148, 298.

159. Document 100 in Rokityansky et al., *Sud palacha*, pp. 480–481.

160. Albats, *The State*, p. 77.

161. Popovsky, *The Vavilov Affair*, p. 151.

162. Appendix in Vavilov and Rokityansky, "Golgotha," p. 845.

163. From the "Resolution of the Military Collegium of the USSR Highest Court" No. 4 n-011514/55 (dated August 20, 1955). The text is cited in Vavilov and Rokityansky, "Znaniya broshennye v ogon'."

164. Documents 98, 101, 102, and 108 in Rokityansky et al., *Sud palacha*, pp. 468–475 481–484, 495–500.

165. Document 101 in ibid., p. 483.

166. Document 102 in ibid., p. 485.

167. Document 108 in ibid., p. 499.

168. The recollection is given in Popovsky, *The Vavilov Affair*, p. 150.

169. Flaksberger was mentioned in the "Decision of the Military Collegium of the USSR Supreme Court No. 4 n-011514/55" dated August 20, 1955. The text is given (document no. 10) in the appendix in Vavilov and Rokityansky, "Golgotha," p. 844.

170. Popovsky, *The Vavilov Affair*, p. 164; Soyfer, *Lysenko*, p. 357n.

171. Levitskaya and Lasson, "Materialy k biografii," p. 114.

172. Document 105 in Rokityansky et al., *Sud palacha*, pp. 491–492.

173. Document 109 in ibid., pp. 501–507.

174. Document 110 in ibid., pp. 507–510.

175. Document 111 in ibid., pp. 510–512.

176. Document 112 in ibid., p. 512.

177. Document 113 in ibid., pp. 513.

178. Minutes of the Closed Court Session of the Military Collegium on July 9, 1941 (document 115 in Rokityansky et al., *Sud palacha*, pp. 514–515).

179. Document 116 in Rokityansky et al., *Sud palacha*, pp. 515–516.

180. Popovsky, *The Vavilov Affair*, p. 156; document 117 in Rokityansky et al., *Sud palacha*, pp. 516–517.

181. "An Excerpt No. 9/124cc from the Transcript of the Meeting of the Supreme Soviet on July 26, 1941." Signed by Secretary of the Military Collegium of the USSR Supreme Court Mazur (document 117 in Rokityansky et al., *Sud palacha*, p. 517).

182. Popovsky, *The Vavilov Affair*, p. 156.

183. Kokurin and Petrov, *Lubyanka*, pp. 28–30.

184. Document 119 in Rokityansky et al., *Sud palacha*, p. 518.

185. Popovsky, *The Vavilov Affair*, p. 528.

186. Ibid., pp. 168–169.

187. Ibid., p. 170.

188. On Sergei Vavilov, see, for instance, Joravsky, D., "The Vavilov Brothers," *Slavic Review* 24 (1965):381–394; Kojevnikov, A., "President of Stalin's Academy: The Mask and Responsibility of Sergei Vavilov," *Isis* 87 (1996):18–50; Solov'ev, Yu. I, "Akademik S. I. Vavlov: Drama russkogo intelligenta" [Academician S. I. Vavilov: The tragedy of a Russian intellectual], *Voprosy Istorii Estestvoznaniya i Tekhniki* 1 (1999b):132–156 (in Russian).

189. Crankshaw, *Khrushchev Remembers*, p. 292.

190. Popovsky, *The Vavilov Affair*, p. 171.

191. Ibid., p. 171.

192. "A Report of Doctor P. Sychenko to the Head of the Hospital," dated January 26, 1943. The text is given (document no. 7) in the appendix to Vavilov and Rokityansky, "Golgotha," p. 842; document 130 in Rokityansky et al., *Sud palacha*, p. 526.

193. "An Excerpt from the Medical Register No. 5 of Prisoners of Saratov Prison No. 1 Who Died." The text is given (document no. 9) in the appendix to Vavilov and Rokityansky, "Golgotha," p. 843; document 133 in Rokityansky et al., *Sud palacha*, p. 528.

194. Vavilov's letter to Beria from Saratov Prison No. 1, dated April 25, 1942 (document 120 in Rokityansky et al., *Sud palacha*, pp. 519–521).

195. Vaksberg, *Stalin's Prosecutor*, pp. 224–225.

196. Parrish, *The Lesser Terror*, pp. 69–71.

197. Popovsky, *The Vavilov Affair*, p. 176–177.

198. Document 120 in Rokityansky et al., *Sud palacha,* pp. 520–521.

199. Document no. 5 in the appendix to Vavilov and Rokityansky, "Znaniya broshennye v ogon'," p. 634; document 122 in Rokityansky et al., *Sud palacha,* p. 522.

200. Vavilov and Rokityansky, "Znaniya broshennye v ogon'," p. 629.

201. Document no. 4 in the appendix to Vavilov and Rokityansky, "Golgotha," p. 841; document 124 in Rokityansky et al., *Sud palacha,* p. 523.

202. Document 126 in Rokityansky et al., *Sud palacha,* pp. 524–525.

203. "An Excerpt from the Transcript of the Meeting of the Presidium of the USSR Supreme Soviet No. 10/4c on June 23, 1942," paragraph 325. Signed by Podobedov, Deputy Head of the First Special NKVD Department (document no. 5 in Appendix to Vavilov and Rokityansky, "Golgotha," p. 842; document 125 in Rokityansky et al., *Sud palacha,* p. 524).

204. Document 127 in Rokityansky et al., *Sud palacha,* p. 525.

205. The Fourth Directorate, charged with "spying, terror and sabotage in the enemy's rear," was created out of the former Second Department of the NKVD on January 18, 1942 (Kokurin and Petrov, *Lubyanka,* pp. 32–33).

206. Speer, Albert, *Infiltration,* trans. Joachim Neugroschel (New York: Macmillan, 1981), pp. 190–193.

207. See a telegram from "Maxim" (Vasilii Zarubin, New York) to "Victor" (Pavel Fitin, Moscow), dated May 21, 1943 (The Venona Project; available at http://www.nsa.gov/docs/venona/docs/May43/21_May_1943_p2.gif).

208. Rossianov, "Iz istorii bor'by akademika D. N. Pryanishnikova," p. 531.

209. Ibid.

210. Soyfer, *Lysenko,* p. 357.

211. Materials from Vavilov's Investigation File, cited in ibid.

212. Materials from Karpechenko's Investigation File cited in ibid.

213. Ibid.; Yeremina and Rokityansky, *Rasstrel'nye spiski,* p. 188.

214. Popovsky, *The Vavilov Affair,* p. 83.

215. Vavilov and Rokityansky, "Znaniya broshennye v ogon'," p. 629.

216. Yeremina and Rokityansky, *Rasstrel'nye spiski,* p. 56.

217. Levitskaya and Lassan, "Materialy k biografii," p. 114.

218. Ibid., p. 121.

219. The dates of death were given in the "Decision of the Change in the Decision on Canceling the Criminal Case," signed by Senior Deputy Prosecutor of the City of Leningrad I. V. Katukov, dated March 29, 1989 and cited in Levitskaya and Lassan, "Materialy k biografii," pp. 123–124.

220. Ibid., p. 115.

221. Ibid.

222. Soyfer, *Lysenko,* p. 357.

223. "The NKVD Structure on May 20, 1942" (document no. 27 in Kokurin and Petrov, *Lubyanka,* pp. 271–304).

224. Voloshin, S. V., "Iz vospominanii" [From the memoirs], in Okhotin and Roginsky, *Zven'ya,* vol. 1, pp. 45–46.

225. Albats, *The State,* p. 78.

226. Ibid., pp. 117–118.

227. Ibid., p. 78.

228. "An Informational Note from the Politisches Archiv des Auswartigen Amts (Bonn)." I am very thankful to Ms. Maria Keipert of this archive, who provided me with the information on German diplomats.

229. Zechlin's Prisoner File (fond 541 at the Former Special Archive, now the Center of Keeping Historic-Documentary Collection, Moscow).

230. Ibid.

231. Documents nos. 161 and 173 in Stepashin, S.V., ed., *Organy gosudarstvennoi bezopasnosti SSSR v Velikoi Otechestvennoi Voine* [The USSR State Security Service During the Great Patriotic War] (Moscow: Kniga i Biznes, 1995), vol. 1, pp. 45–46, 70–73 (in Russian).

232. Berg, *Acquired Traits*, pp. 287–288.

233. Kuptsov, A. I., "In Memory of Nikolai Ivanovich Vavilov" (Moscow, June 22, 1958). A manuscript cited in Popovsky, *The Vavilov Affair*, p. 171.

234. See Timofeev's biography in Glass, B. Timofeeff-Ressovsky, Nikolai Vladimirovich, in F. L. Holmes, ed., *Dictionary of Scientific Biographies* (New York: Charles Scribner's Sons, 1990), vol. 18. supp. 2; Vorontsov, N. N., ed., *Nikolai Vladimirovich Timofeev-Ressovsky*; Timofeev-Ressovsky, *Vospominaniya* (1995); Timofeev-Ressovsky, *Vospominaniya: Istorii, napisannye im samim* (2000).

235. Welt, Elly, *Berlin Wild* (New York: Viking, 1986), and Granin, Daniil, *The Bison: A Novel About a Scientist Who Defied Stalin*, trans. A. W. Bouis (New York: Doubleday, 1989).

236. Timofeeff-Ressovsky, N. W., K. C. Zimmer, and M. Delbrück, "Uber die Natur der Genmutation und der Genstructur," *Nachr. Ges. Wiss. Göttingen. Biologie* 1 (13) (1935): 189–245. See also Perutz, "Physics and the Riddle of Life," and Olby, *The Path to the Double Helix*, pp. 231 and 147.

237. Berg, R. L., "In defense of Timofeeff-Ressovsky," *Quarterly Review of Biology* 65 (4) (1990):457–479; Yakovlev, A. A., "Kto vy, doktor Timofeev?" [Who are you, Dr. Timofeev?], *Vestnik Akademii Nauk* 5 (1990):133–134 (in Russian); Paul, D. B., and C. B. Krimbas, "Nikolai V. Timofeeff-Ressovsky," *Scientific American* (February 1992):86–92.

238. Sakanyan, E. S., "Lyubov' i zashchta" [Love and defense], in Timofeev-Ressovsky, *Vospominaniya: Istorii, napisannye im samim* (2000), pp. 707–800.

239. See, for instance, Holloway, *Stalin and the Bomb*, pp. 134–138; Bondarev, N. D., A. A. Keda, and N.V. Selezneva, "U istokov sovetskogo atomnogo proekta (novye arkhivnye materialy)" [At the beginning of the Soviet Atomic Project (new archival materials)], *Voprosy Istorii Estestvoznaniya i Tekhniki* 2 (1994):116–119 (in Russian). Most of the documents on the project are reproduced in Ryabev, L. D., ed., *Atomnyi proekt SSSR: Dokumenty i materialy. Tom II, Atomnaya bomba, 1945–1954, Kniga 1* [The Atomic Project in the USSR: Documents and Materials. Vol. 2, Atomic Bomb, 1945–1954, Part 1] (Moscow: Nauka, 1999) (in Russian).

240. See Volkogonov, *Stalin*, pp. 520–524.

241. See short biographies of all these individuals in Holloway, *Stalin and the Bomb*, pp. 447–452.

242. Kokurin and Petrov, *Lubyanka*, pp. 35, 46.

243. Kokurin and Petrov, "NKVD-NKGB-SMERSH."

244. Timofeev-Ressovsky, *Vospominaniya: Istorii, napisannye im samim* (2000), p. 350.

245. "Osnovnye daty zhizni N.V. Timofeev-Ressovsky" [Main Dates of N.V. Timofeev-Ressovsky's Life], in Timofeev-Ressovsky, *Vospominaniya: Istorii, napisannye im samim* (2000), pp. 819–822.

246. Timofeev-Ressovsky, *Vospominaniya: Istorii, napisannye im samim* (2000), p. 350.

247. Solzhenitsyn, *The Gulag Archipelago*, vol. 1, p. 149.

248. The text of the note is partly cited in Goncharov, V. A., and V. V. Nekhotin, "Neizvestnoe ob izvestnom: Po materialam arkhivnogo sledstvennogo dela na N. V. Timofeeva-Ressovskogo" [Unknown information about known facts: materials from the archival Investigation File of N.V. Timofeev-Ressovsky], *Vestnik Rossiiskoi Akademii Nauk* 70 (3) (2000):249–257 (in Russian).

249. A photo of the warrant is given in Goncharov and Nekhotin, "Neizvestnoe ob izvestnom," p. 250.

250. Ivanov, V. I., "Net proroka v svoyom otechestve" [There is no prophet in his own country], *Priroda* 9 (1990):71–77 (in Russian).

251. Goncharov and Nekhotin, "Neizvestnoe ob izvestnom," pp. 250–251.

252. Timofeev-Ressovsky, *Vospominaniya: Istorii, napisannye im samim* (2000), p. 355.

253. Aleksandr Solzhenitsyn described the inhabitants of Cell 75 in *The Gulag Archipelago*, vol. 1, pp. 597–605.

254. Kokurin and Petrov, *Lubyanka*, p. 47.

255. Goncharov and Nekhotin, "Neizvestnoe ob izvestnom," p. 252.

256. Excerpts from transcripts of interrogations are given in Goncharov and Nekhotin, "Neizvestnoe ob izvestnom," pp. 253–255.

257. Timofeev-Ressovsky, *Vospominaniya: Istorii, napisannye im samim* (2000), pp. 351–355.

258. Solzhenitsyn, *The Gulag Archipelago*, vol. 1, p. 493.

259. Timofeev-Ressovsky, *Vospominaniya: Istorii, napisannye im samim* (2000), p. 360.

260. Ibid., p. 351. For the presentation of events by the German scientists, see Riehl and Seitz, *Stalin's Captive*, pp. 89–104.

261. Timofeev-Ressovsky, *Vospominaniya: Istorii, napisannye im samim* (2000), p. 362.

262. Ibid., p. 351.

263. Document no. 50 in Ryabev, *Atomnyi proekt SSSR*, vol. 2, pt. 1, pp. 236–237.

264. Document no. 68 in ibid., pp. 305–306.

265. Smirnov, *Systema ispravitel'no-trudovykh lagerei*, pp. 180–181 and 473.

266. Ryabev, *Atomnyi proekt SSSR*, vol. 2, pt. 1, p. 662.

267. Timofeev-Ressovsky, *Vospominaniya* (1995), pp. 323–341; Riehl and Seitz, *Stalin's Captive*, pp. 121–132.

268. Ivanov, V. I., "Prirodookhrannye idei 'Zubra'" [The environmental ideas of the "Bison"], *Vestnik Rossiiskoi Akademii Nauk* 12 (1992):40–49 (in Russian).

269. Riehl and Seitz, *Stalin's Captive*, p. 128.

270. Ibid.

271. Granin, *The Bison*, p. 2.

272. The title is a Russian proverb meaning one should not work in a field in which one is not competent.

273. Reproduced in Lysenko, *Agrobiologiya*, pp. 602–606.

274. The text of these lectures was published as a brochure *Vnutrividovaya bor'ba u zhivotnykh i rastenii* [Intraspecies Competition in Animals and Plants] (Moscow: Moscow University, 1947).

275. Manevich, "Takie byli vremena," pt. 2.

276. Krementsov, *Stalinist Science*, pp. 150–151.

277. Ibid., pp. 151–152.

278. See, for instance, Mayr, Ernst, *The Growth of Biological Thought: Diversity, Evolution, and Inheritance* (Cambridge: Belknap Press, 1982), pp. 478–479, 484, 491–493.

279. Polyansky, V., and A. Zelikman, "Moskovskaya konferentsiya po problemam darwinizma" [Moscow Conference on the Problems of Darwinism], *Priroda* 6 (1948):85–87 (in Russian).

280. Ibid., p. 86.

281. Krementsov, *Stalinist Science*, p. 153.

282. Ibid., p. 165.

283. Ibid.

284. Ibid., p. 168.

285. Ibid.

286. For details, see Medvedev, *The Rise and Fall*, pp. 103–140; Joravsky, *The Lysenko Affair*, pp. 97–143; Soyfer, *Lysenko*, pp. 183–204; Krementsov, *Stalinist Science*, pp. 158–190.

287. Rossianov, "Editing Nature."

288. Ibid., pp. 732–738.

289. The translation of Lysenko's speech in Zirkle, *Death of a Science*, pp. 99–101.

290. Ibid., pp. 112–113.

291. Ibid., pp. 129–130.

292. The English translation: Schmalhausen, Ivan I., *Factors of Evolution: The Theory of Stabilizing Selection,* trans. I. Doridick (Chicago: University of Chicago Press, 1986).

293. In Zirkle, *Death of a Science*, pp. 151–154.

294. Lysenko, in ibid., p. 109.

295. Zirkle, *Death of a Science*, pp. 240–243.

296. Lysenko, *The Situation in Biological Science*, p. 332.

297. Ibid., p. 334.

298. Zirkle, *Death of a Science*, p. 249.

299. See the text of the letter in ibid., pp. 267–170. It is also given in Soyfer, *Lysenko*, pp. 190–191.

300. Soyfer, *Lysenko*, 250–251.

301. In Zirkle, *Death of a Science*, pp. 271–272.

302. The research activity of Sos Alikhannyan (1906–1985) started in 1932 at Moscow State University. His career is discussed in the text.

303. Polyansky and Zelikman, "Moskovskaya konferentsiya," p. 86.

304. In Zirkle, *Death of a Science*, pp. 275–276.

305. Joravsky, *The Lysenko Affair*, pp. 221–223; Soyfer, *Lysenko*, pp. 156–157.

306. The text is in Zirkle, *Death of a Science*, pp. 273–275.

307. Soyfer, *Lysenko*, pp. 156–157.

308. Domaradsky, *"Perevyortysh,"* p. 59.

309. Manevich, "Takie byli vremena," pt. 2. The text is in Zirkle, *Death of a Science*, pp. 283–285.

310. Resolution, August 26, 1948, the text is in ibid., pp. 285–290.

311. The text is in ibid., pp. 290–294.

312. Sonin, A. S., "Pechal'nyi yubilei odnov kampanii" [A sad jubilee of one of the campaigns], *Vestnik Akademii Nauk* 8 (1991):96–106 (in Russian); Romanovsky, S. I, "Na puti k teoreticheskoi litologii (diskussiya 1950-kh godov)" [On the way to theoretical lithology (a discussion of the 1950s)], *Voprosy Istorii Estestvoznaniya i Tekhniki* 2 (1992):28–37 (in Russian).

313. Sonin, A. S., "Soveshchanie, kotoroe ne sostoyalos'" [The meeting that did not take place], *Priroda* 3 (1990a):97–102, 4 (1990b):91–98, and 5 (1990c):93–99 (in Russian).

314. Medvedev, *The Rise and Fall*, pp. 122–124.

315. Kovner, M. A., "Moi repressirovannye uchitelya" [My repressed teachers], *Voprosy Istorii Estestvoznaniya i Tekhniki* 4 (1997):113 (in Russian).

316. Manevich, "Takie byli vremena," pt. 2.

317. Kaftanov, S., "V podderzhku michurinskoi biologii v vysshei shkole" [In support of Michurin's biological theory in higher institutions of learning], *Izvestya*, September 8, 1948 (in Russian); translation in Zirkle, *Death of a Science*, pp. 294–300.

318. One of Timofeev-Ressovsky's pupils, Nikolai Vorontsov (1934–2000) was a zoologist, geneticist, and evolutionist, the author of more than 550 scientific publications, a foreign member of the Swedish and American National Academies of Sciences. In 1989, he was appointed minister of the newly created USSR Nature Protection Ministry, which was disbanded after the fall of the USSR in 1991. Later, Vorontsov participated in several international actions of Greenpeace. Until his death in 2000, he headed a laboratory at the Koltsov Institute of Developmental Biology in Moscow. I was on the staff of this laboratory in 1984 and from 1990 to 1998.

319. Vorontsov, N. N., "Current State of Evolutionary Theory in the USSR," in Leonard Warren and Hilary Koprovski, eds., *New Perspectives of Evolution* (New York: John Wiley and Sons, 1991), pp. 65–75.

320. Makhotin, A. A., "Ivan Ivanovich Schmalhausen (1884–1963)," *Zoologicheskii Zhurnal* 58 (2) (1964):297–302 (in Russian).

321. Polyansky, *Gody prozhitye*, p. 136.

322. The English translation: Schmalhausen, Ivan I., *The Origin of Terrestrial Vertebrates*, trans. L. Kelso (New York: Academic Press, 1968).

323. Nasimovich, A. A., "Pamyati Aleksandra Nikolaevicha Formozova" [In memory of Aleksandr Nikolaevich Formozov], *Bulletin Moskovskogo Obshchestva Ispytatelei Prirody, Otedelenie Biologicheskoe* 80 (1) (1975):5–18 (in Russian).

324. Medvedev, *The Rise and Fall*, pp. 126–127; Trubetskova, "Nauchnaya i pedagogicheskaya deyatelnost'."

325. Lysenko, *The Situation in Biological Science*, pp. 602–603.

326. Kremenetsov, *Stalinist Science*, p. 304; Kolchinsky, *V poiskakh*, p. 56.

327. Soyfer, *Lysenko*, pp. 122–123; Kolchinsky, *V poiskakh*, pp. 58–59, 178–180.

328. Ryzhkova, E. V., "Akademik Isai Izrailevich Prezent," *Vestnik Leningradskogo Gosudarstvennogo Universiteta* 10 (1948):98–101 (in Russian).

329. Kolchinsky, *V poiskakh*, p. 202.

330. Medvedev, *The Rise and Fall*, pp. 10–11; Weiner, Douglas R., *Models of Nature: Ecology, Conservation, and Cultural Revolution in Soviet Russia* (Bloomington: Indiana University Press, 1988), pp. 124, 132–133, 270; Soyfer, *Lysenko*, pp. 62–63.

331. Soyfer, *Lysenko*, p. 63.

332. Kolchinsky, *V poiskakh*, pp. 204–205.

333. Nechaeva, N. T., and V. V. Stanchinsky, Jr., "Pervyi ekolog strany" [The first Russian ecologist], *Priroda* 12 (1991):90–95 (in Russian). This reserve was organized in 1898 by Fridrich Fal'ts-Fein on his estate (Weiner, *Models of Nature*, p. 17).

334. For details of Vladimir Stanchinsky's biography, see Weiner, *Models of Nature*, pp. 79–82; Nechaeva, N. T., and V. S. Shishkin, "V poiskakh estestvennykh system (nauchnoe nasledie V. V. Stanchinskogo" [In the search of natural systems (the scientific heritage of V. V. Stanchinsky)], *Voprosy Istorii Estestvoznaniya i Tekhniki* 2 (1994):87–97 (in Russian).

335. Nechaeva and Shishkin, "Pervyi ekolog strany."

336. Kolchinsky, *V poiskakh*, pp. 205–206.

337. Joravsky, *The Lysenko Affair*, pp. 92–93, 238–240.

338. Soyfer, *Lysenko*, p. 64.

339. Joravsky, *The Lysenko Affair*, p. 120. According to the scholar Valery Soyfer, in 1937 Prezent was arrested for seducing a minor. After the intervention of Lysenko, Prezent was released and continued his attacks on the hated "Mendelists-Morganists," including Professor Koltsov and Academician Vavilov (Soyfer, *Lysenko*, p. 64).

340. Ginetsinskaya, T. A., "Biofak Leningradskogo Universiteta posle sessii VASKhNIL" [The biology faculty of Leningrad University after the VASKhNIL session], in Yaroshevskii, *Repressirovannaya Nauka*, pp. 114–125.

341. Schnol, *Geroi i zlodei*, p. 321.

342. This is not a rumor. One of my father's pupils, M.V., currently academician and director of a big institute within the academy, told me that he accompanied his female classmates to Prezent's apartment several times.

343. Schnol, *Geroi i zlodei*, p. 255.

344. Kostyrchenko, *Out of the Red Shadows*, pp. 250–251. Only the name of the archive (Russian Center for the Preservation and Study of Documents of Modern History) but not the code of the document is given.

345. Ibid., pp. 250–251.

346. The Moscow Scientists Club (Dom Uchenykh) was organized in June 1920 [Savina, G. A., "Napisano v podvalakh OGPU" [It was written in the OGPU basement], *Vestnik Rossiiskoi Akademii Nauk* 65 (5) (1995):452–460 (in Russian)].

347. Soyfer, *Lysenko*, p. 332.

348. Kalinnikova, V. D., "Tsitolog Grigorii Iosifovich Roskin" [The cytologist Grigory Iosifovich Roskin], *Priroda* 8 (1994: pp. 62–74 (in Russian).

349. Miller, S. L., J. W. Schopf, and A. Lazcano, "Oparin's *Origin of Life*: Sixty years later," *Journal of Molecular Evolution* 44 (1997):351–353. See details in Graham, *Science, Philosophy, and Human Behavior*, pp. 70–96.

350. Oparin, Aleksandr Ivanovich, in Turkevich, *Soviet Men of Science*, pp. 275–276.

351. Aleksandrov, *Trudnye gody*, pp. 125–128.

352. Gaisinovich, A. E., and E. B. Muzrukova, "'Otryzhka' kletochnoi teorii" ["The belching" of the cell theory], *Priroda* 11 (1989):92–100 (in Russian).

353. Rapoport, Ya., "Nedolgaya zhizn' 'zhivogo veshchestva'" [The short life of a "living substance"], in Glinka, M. S., ed., *Sovremennye mysli, ili proroki v svoem otechestve* [Well-Timed Thoughts, or Prophets in Their Own Fatherland] (Leningrad: Lenizdat, 1989), p. 130 (in Russian).

354. Cited in Gaisinovich and Muzrukova, "'Otryzhka' kletochnoi teorii," p. 98.

355. Rapoport, "Nedolgaya zhizn' 'zhivogo veshchestva,'" p. 139.

356. Details in Soyfer, *Lysenko*, pp. 216–218.

357. Oparin, A. I., "Otchet Biologicheskogo otdeleniya AN SSSR" [The report of the Biology Division of the USSR Academy], *Izvestiya Akademii Nauk SSSR, Seriya Biologicheskaya* 3 (1955):3 (in Russian).

358. Aleksandrov, *Trudnye gody*, pp. 165–169. It is amazing that Dmitrii Lebedev and Yurii Olenov were Party members.

359. Bogorov, V. G., "Lev Aleksandrovich Zenkevich (1889–1970)" [L. A. Zenkevich (1889–1970)], *Bulletin Moskovskogo Obshchestva Ispytatelei Prirody, Otdelenie Biologicheskoe* 76 (3) (1971):9–12 (in Russian).

360. Zenkevich, L. A., and J. A. Birstein, "O vozmozhnykh meropriyatiyakh po povysheniyu proizvoditel'nykh svoistv Kaspiya i Arala" [On possible measures for enhancing the productivity of the Caspian and Aral seas], *Rybnoe Khozyaistvo* 3 (1934):38–40 (in Russian).

361. Zenkevich, L. A., J. A. Birstein, and A. F. Karpevich, "Pervye uspekhi rekonstruktsii fauny Kaspiiskogo morya" [First steps in reconstruction of the Caspian Sea fauna], *Zoologicheskii Zhurnal* 24 (1) (1945):31 (in Russian).

362. According to the rumors, the university rector at the time, Academician Aleksandr Nesmeyanov (rector in 1948–1951), was against the arrest.

363. Laius, Yu. A., "'Sel'dyanaya problema Barentsova morya': vzaimoot-nosheniya nauki, praktiki I politiki" ["The herring problem of the Barents Sea": relationships between science, practical application, and politics], in *Na Perelome* [At the Turning Point], vol. 1 (St. Petersburg, 1997), pp. 177–199 (in Russian).

364. For instance, Birstein, J. A., and N. N. Spasskii, "Donnaya fauna Kaspi-iskogo morya do i posle vseleniya *Nereis succinea*" [The bottom fauna of the Caspian Sea before and after the introduction of *Nereis succinea*], in *Akklimatizat-siya nereis v Kaspiiskom more* [Acclimatization of *Nereis* in the Caspian Sea] (Moscow: Izdatel'stvo MOIP, 1953), pp. 36–114 (in Russian).

365. Kaverin, V., "O chestnosti v nauke" [On honesty in science], *Literatur-naya Gazeta*, January 29, 1955 (in Russian).

366. Saenkova, A. K., "K voprosu o vzaimootnosheniyakh *Nereis succinea* s donnymi organizmami severnogo Kaspiya" [On the relationships of *Nereis succinea* with the other benthic organisms of the northern Caspian Sea], *Bulletin Moskovskogo Obshchestva Ispytatelei Prirody, Otdelenie Biologicheskoe* 61 (1) (1956):45–50 (in Russian); Vinogradov, L. G., "O meste *Nereis succinea* v bentose severnogo Kaspiya" [On the position of *Nereis succinea* in the benthos of the northern Caspian Sea], *Bulletin Moskovskogo Obshchestva Ispytatelei Prirody, Otde-lenie Biologicheskoe*, 60 (6) (1956):61–76 (in Russian); and others.

367. Birstein, J. A., "Rezultaty akklimatizatsii *Nereis succinea* v Kaspii i ikh kri-tika" [Results of the *Nereis succinea* acclimatization in the Caspian Sea and their critics], *Bulletin Moskovskogo Obshchestva Ispytatelei Prirody, Otdelenie Biologich-eskoe* 61 (1) (1956):23–44 (in Russian).

368. Krementsov, *Stalinist Science*, p. 302.

369. Chugunova, N. I., et al., "Pamyati N. V. Lebedeva (26 noyabrya 1902–8 oktyabrya 1970)" [In memory of N.V. Lebedev, November 26, 1902–October 8, 1970]," *Voprosy Ikhtiologii* 11 (3) (1971):518–519 (in Russian).

370. Meerson, F. Z., "Glava iz istorii russkoi fiziologii" [A chapter in Russian physiology history], *Priroda* 12 (1988): 83–96 (in Russian).

371. Brodsky, V. Ya., "Grigory Iosifovich Roskin (k 100-letiyu so dnya rozh-deniya)" [Grigory Iosifovich Roskin (to his 100th birthday)], *Tsitologiya* [Cytol-ogy] 35 (4) (1993):139–142 (in Russian); Kalinnikova, V. D., "Tsitolog Grigory Iosifovich Roskin."

372. Latif, F., et al., "Identification of the von Hippel-Lindau Disease Tumor Suppressor Gene," *Science* 260 (5112) (1993):1317–1320.

373. Smith, Walter Bedell, *My Three Years in Moscow* (Philadelphia: J. B. Lippincott Co., 1950), p. 292.

374. Klyueva, Nina G., and Grigorii I. Roskin, *Bioterapiya Zlokachestvennykh Opukholei* [Biotherapy of Malignant Tumors] (Izdatel'stvo AMN SSSR: Moscow, 1946) (in Russian).

375. Klyueva, N. G., and G. I. Roskin, *Biotherapy of Malignant Tumors* (New York: Macmillan, 1963).

376. Krementsov, *Stalinist Science*, pp. 132–134.

377. Meerson, "Glava iz istorii russkoi fiziologii."

378. Grigoryan, "50-letie Meditsinskoi Akademii."

379. Cited in Krementsov, *Stalinist Science*, p. 134.

380. Kalinnikova, "Tsitolog Grigorii Iosifovich Roskin."

381. Meerson, "Glava iz istorii russkoi fiziologii."

382. Krementsov, N. L., "Sovetskaya nauka na poroge kholodnoi voiny:'Delo KR'" [Soviet Science at the Break of the Cold War: The "KR Case"], in *In Memoriam: Istoricheskii sbornik pamyati F. F. Perchenka* [In Memoriam: A Collection of Historical Studies in the Memory of F. F. Perchenok] (Moscow-St. Petersburg: Feniks-Atheneum, 1995), p. 283 (in Russian).

383. Meerson, "Glava iz istorii russkoi fiziologii."

384. Kostyrchenko, *Out of the Red Shadows*, pp. 70–71.

385. Krementsov, "Sovetskaya nauka na poroge," pp. 282–284.

386. Ibid., p. 283.

387. A term used in the Soviet mass media in the late 1940s–early 1950s for doctors of Jewish origin.

388. Kostyrchenko, *Out of the Red Shadows*, p. 71.

389. Order No. 44-3 of the USSR Council of Ministers, entitled "On the Measures Necessary to Help the Laboratory of Professor Klyueva" dated July 12, 1947 (Krementsov, "Sovetskaya nauka na poroge," p. 290).

390. Meerson, "Glava iz istorii russkoi fiziologii."

391. Krementsov, "Sovetskaya nauka na poroge," p. 288.

392. Parin's prisoner card (Document 23 in Appendix II).

393. In his memoirs Lucien Gouaze mentioned Parin under the name Barine as one of the inhabitants of Cell 45 in Corpus III in 1954 (Serbet, *Polit-Isolator*, p. 369).

394. Andreev, D. L., V. V. Parin, and L. L. Rakov, *Noveishii Plutarkh* [The Newest Plutarch] (Moscow: Moskovskii Rabochii, 1991) (in Russian).

395. Kostyrchenko, *Out of the Red Shadows*, p. 71.

396. Rapoport, I. A., "Vystuplenie: 'Kruglyi stol.' Stranitsy istorii sovetskoi genetiki v literature poslednikh let" [A speech at the meeting "Round Table." Pages in the history of Soviet genetics in the literature of the last several years], *Voprosy Istorii Estestvoznaniya i Tekhniki* 4 (1987):126–131 (in Russian).

397. Lysenko, *The Situation in Biological Science*, p. 487.

398. Rapoport, I. A., "Akademik N. N. Semenov i genetka" [Academician N. N. Semenov and genetics], *Priroda* 3 (1992):99–103 (in Russian).

399. Popovsky, *Manipulated Science*, p. 149.

400. Soyfer, *Lysenko*, p. 242.

401. Popovsky, *Manipulated Science*, p. 149.

402. See the official translation of the speech in Zirkle, *Death of a Science*, pp. 139–142.

403. Rapoport, "Vystuplenie: 'Kruglyi stol.'"

404. Schnol, *Geroi i zlodei*, pp. 266–267.

405. Ibid., p. 268.

406. Stroeva, O. G., "Iosif Abramovich Rapoport v zerkale svoikh trudov" [Iosif Abramovich Rapoport as mirrored in his works], *Priroda* 1 (1997):3–12 (in Russian).

407. Rapoport, "Akademik N. N. Semenov."

408. The text of three recommendations is given in Schnol, *Geroi i zlodei*, pp. 260–265.

409. On Semenov's voting in favor of Vladimir Vinogradov, a KGB officer and deputy director of the Academy Foreign Department, see Popovsky, *Manipulated Science*, pp. 37–38.

410. Solov'ev, Yu. I., "Mest' obscuranta: Mrachnyi epizod iz zhizni akademika N. N. Semenova" [Revenge of an obscurantist: The gloomy period in the life of Academician N. N. Semenov], *Vestnik Rossiiskoi Akademii Nauk* 64 (9) (1994b):840–847 (in Russian).

411. Boag et al., *Kapitza*, p. 427.

412. Rapoport, "Akademik N. N. Semenov."

413. Ibid.

414. See, for instance, pp. 118–120 in Adams, Mark B., "The Soviet Nature-Nurture debate," in Graham, Loren R., ed., *Science and the Soviet Social Order* (Cambridge: Harvard University Press, 1990), pp. 94–140.

415. Schnol, *Geroi i zlodei*, pp. 278–279.

416. About the atrocities committed by the Soviet troops and Stalin's personal favorable attitude to them, see Naimark, Norman M., *The Russians in Germany: A History of the Soviet Zone of Occupation, 1945–1949* (Cambridge: Belknap Press, 1995), pp. 69–140.

417. Dolgun and Watson, *An American in the Gulag*, p. 167.

418. Published as Efroimson, V. P., "O Lysenko i lysenkovshchine" [On Lysenko and Lysenkoism], *Voprosy Istorii Estestvoznaniya i Tekhniki* 1–4 (1989) (in Russian).

419. Schnol, *Geroi i zlodei*, p. 280.

420. See Efroimson's detailed scientific biography in Vorontsov, N. N., M. D. Golubovsky, and E. A. Izyumova, "Vladimir Pavlovich Efroimson—vydayushchiisya otechestvennyi genetik (k 80t-letiyu so dnya rozhdeniya)" [Vladimir Pavlovich Efroimson as an outstanding Soviet geneticist (to his 80th

birthday)], *Bulletin Moskovskogo Obshchestva Ispytatelei Prirody, Otdelenie Biologicheskoe* 94 (3) (1989):96–109 (in Russian).

421. Solovieva, Yu. I., "Belye odezdy akademika Astaurova" [The white clothes of Academician Astaurov], *Vestnik Rossiiskoi Akademii Nauk* 69 (2) (1999):151–158 (in Russian).

422. Efroimson, *Genetika etiki i estetiki*; Efroimson, Vladimir P., *Genial'nost' i genetika* [Genius and Genetics] (Moscow: Russkii Mir, 1998) (in Russian).

423. Efroimson, V. P., "Rodoslovnaya al'truizma (Etika s pozitsii evolutsionni genetiki cheloveka)" [The genealogy of altruism: Ethics from the evolutionary human genetics point of view], *Novyi Mir* 10 (1971):204 (in Russian). This article (briefly described in Graham, *Science, Philosophy, and Human Behavior*, pp. 226–230) presented the main outlines of Efroimson's books *Genetics of Ethics and Esthetics* and *Genius and Genetics*.

424. Dolgun and Watson, *An American in the Gulag*, p. 166.

425. See Chapter 1, "Memories."

426. Zonn, "Akademik Vladimir Nikolaevich Sukachev."

427. Kolchinsky, *V poiskakh*, p. 81.

428. Ibid., pp. 177–178.

429. Turbin, N. V., "Darwinizm i novaya teoriya proiskhozhdeniya vidov" [Darwinism and the new theory of species], *Botanicheskii Zhurnal* 37 (6) (1952):798–818 (in Russian).

430. Oparin, A. I., "I. V. Stalin—vdokhnovitel' peredovoi biologicheskoi nauki" [I. V. Stalin, the inspirer of the leading biological science], *Zhurnal Obshchei Biologii* 14 (2) (1953):90–95 (in Russian).

431. Lysenko, T. D., "Novoe v nauke o biologicheskom vide" [New data in the science of the biological species], *Botanicheskii Zhurnal* 38 (1) (1953):44–54 (in Russian).

432. Sukachev, V. N., "O vnutrividovykh i mezhvidovykh vzaimootnosheniyakh sredi rastenii" [On the intraspecies and interspecies relationships in plants], *Botanicheskii Zhurnal* 38 (1) (1953):55–96 (in Russian).

433. For more details, see Soyfer, *Lysenko*, pp. 229–231.

434. Gur'yanov, B. P., "K istorii vozniknoveniya Moskovskogo obshchestva ispytatelei prirody" [On the establishment of the Moscow Society of Naturalists], *Bulletin Moskovskogo Obshchestva Ispytatelei Prirody, Otdelenie Biologicheskoe* 58 (2) (1953):93–96 (in Russian).

435. Savina, "Napisano v podvalakh OGPU."

436. Rokityansky, Ya. G., "Geolog bozhiei milost'yu" [The geologist from God], *Vestnik Rossiiskoi Akademii Nauk* 64 (12) (1994):1081–1094 (in Russian). For more details, see Weiner, Douglas R., *A Little Corner of Freedom: Russian Nature Protection from Stalin to Gorbachëv* (Berkeley: University of California Press, 1999), pp. 214–216.

437. Kostyrchenko, *Out of the Red Shadows*, p. 251.

438. Fainstein, M. Sh., "Sud'ba 'Slovarya russkikh botanikov'" [The fate of the "Dictionary of Russian Botanists"], *Priroda* 8 (1992):126–128 (in Russian).

439. Lipschitz, S. J., "Nikolai Ivanovich Vavilov," *Bulletin Moskovskogo Obshchestva Ispytatelei Prirody, Otdelenie Biologicheskoe* 102 (4) (1997):67–70 (in Russian).

440. See, for instance, Kozo-Polyansky, B. M., "Ob otnoshenii 'novogo v nauke o biologicheskom vide' k ucheniyu Darwina" [On the relationship of "new data in the science of the biological species" to Darwin's theory], *Bulletin Moskovskogo Obshchestva Ispytatelei Prirody, Otdelenie Biologicheskoe* 59 (3) (1954):85–87 (in Russian).

441. Efroimson, V. P., "O roli eksperimenta i tsifr v selskokhozyaistvennoi biologii" [On the role of experiment and the data in agricultural biology], *Bulletin Moskovskogo Obshchestva Ispytatelei Prirody, Otdelenie Biologicheskoe* 61 (5) (1956):83–91 (in Russian).

442. Novikov, G. A., "Pamuyati Veniamina Iosifovicha Tsalkina" [In memory of Veniamin Iosifovich Tsalkin], *Bulletin Moskovskogo Obshchestva Ispytatelei Prirody, Otdelenie Biologicheskoe* 76 (1) (1971):5–17 (in Russian).

443. Zonn, "Akademik Vladimir Nikolaevich Sukachev."

444. Vorontsov, N. N., and A. V. Yablokov, "K 70-letiyu N. V. Timofeeva-Resovskogo" [To the 70th birthday of N. V. Timofeev-Ressovsky], *Bulletin Moskovskogo Obshchestva Ispytatelei Prirody, Otdelenie Biologicheskoe* 75 (5) (1970):144–148 (in Russian).

445. Vorontsov, N. N., "Raznolikii Timofeev-Ressovsky" [The many faces of Timofeev-Ressovsky], *Priroda* 10 (1995):90–105 (in Russian).

446. Soyfer, *Lysenko*, pp. 306–307; Gazenko, O. G., and A. A. Gyurdzhyan, "U istokov kosmicheskoi biologii i meditsiny: K 90-letiyu so dnya rozhdeniya akademika N. M. Sisakyana" [At the beginning of cosmic biology and medicine: The 90th anniversary of Academician N. M. Sisakyan], *Vestnik Rossiiskoi Akademii Nauk* 67 (1) (1997):82–87 (in Russian).

447. Lysenko, *The Situation in Biological Science*, p. 134.

448. Gazenko and Gyurdzhyan, "U istokov kosmicheskoi biologii."

449. Zonn, "Akademik Vladimir Nikolaevich Sukachev."

450. Soyfer, *Lysenko*, p. 270.

451. Ibid., p. 283.

452. Abelev et al., "Pis'mo." Also see Golinevich, E. M., "Pis'mo v redaktsiyu *Ogon'ka*" [A letter to the Editorial Board of the magazine *Ogonyok*], *Ogonyok* 29:24 (in Russian).

453. Razgon, Lev, *True Stories* (Dana Point, CA: Ardis, 1997), pp. 175–179.

454. Abelev et al., "Pis'mo."

455. Soyfer, *Lysenko*, pp. 335–336.

456. Kiselev, L. L., G. I. Abelev and F. L. Kiselev, "Kak Sirano de Bergerak, on mog gordit'sya belym perom na shleme: K 100-letiyu akademika L. A. Zilbera" [Like Cyrano de Bergerac, he could be proud of the white plume on his battle helmet: To the 100th anniversary of Academician L. A. Zilber], *Priroda* 6 (1994):66–84 (in Russian).

457. Popovsky, *Manipulated Science*, pp. 38–39.

458. Dzhirkvelov, *Secret Servant*, pp. 68–69.

459. Popovsky, *Manipulated Science*, p. 39.

460. See Abelev, "The Alternative Science"; Neyfakh, A. A., "Address at the session of the Scientific Council of the Kol'tsov Institute of Developmental Biology, Russian Academy of Sciences, dedicated to the 70th birthday of A. A. Neyfakh," *Ontogenez* 29 (5) (1998):387–393 (in Russian; English trans. in *Russian Journal of Developmental Biology* 29 (5) (1998):217–223).

461. Babkov, "N. K. Koltsov," p. 10.

462. Sakharov, *Memoirs*, pp. 309–312.

463. Ibid., pp. 310–311.

464. Ibid., p. 311.

465. Ibid., p. 312.

466. Ibid., p. 386.

467. Fainberg, V. Ya., "Osnovatel' novoi morali" [A founder of the new morality], *Voprosy Istorii Estestvoznaniya i Tekhniki* 4 (1990):84–92 (in Russian).

468. For details, see Medvedev, Zh. A., and R. A. Medvedev, *A Question of Madness* (New York: Alfred A. Knopf, 1971).

469. Rubinin, P. E., "Svobodnyi chelovek v nesvobodnoi strane" [A free man in a non-free country], *Vestnik Rossiiskoi Akademii Nauk* 64 (6) (1994):497–523 (in Russian).

470. Gorelik, G. E., "V. A. Fok: Filosofiya tyagoteniya i tyazhest' filosofii" [V. A. Fok: The philosophy of gravity and the weight of philosophy], *Priroda* 10 (1993):81–93 (in Russian).

471. Ginzburg, V. L., "Unikal'nyi fizik and Uchitel' fizikov" [A unique physicist and a master among physicists], *Priroda* 2 (1993):92–103 (in Russian).

472. Holloway, *Stalin and the Bomb*, p. 44; Rubinin, P. E., "Rukopis' I. V. Obreimova iz arkhiva P. L. Kapitsy" [I. V. Obreimov's manuscript from P. L. Kapitsa's archive], *Vestnik Rossiiskoi Akademii Nauk* 64 (3) (1994):243–246 (in Russian).

473. Weissberg, Alex, *The Accused* (New York: Simon and Schuster, 1951), pp. 505–506.

474. Rubinin, "Rukopis' I. V. Obreimova." Before he was released, in 1940–1941 Obreimov worked as an imprisoned physicist in Moscow.

475. Reproduced in the appendix in Rubinin, "Rukopis' I. V. Obreimova," p. 247.

476. Orlov, Yury, *Dangerous Thoughts: Memoirs of a Russian Life* (New York: William Morrow, 1992).

477. Sakharov, *Memoirs*, p. 483.

478. Ashin, F. D., and V. M. Alpatov, "'Rossiiskaya natsional'naya partiya'— zloveshchaya vydumka sovetskikh chekistov" ["The Russian National Party," an ominous invention of the Soviet Chekists], *Vestnik Rossiiskoi Akademii Nauk* 64 (10) (1994):920–930 (in Russian)].

479. Vernadsky,V. I., "Iz pisem raznykh let" [From letters written in different years], *Vestnik Akademii Nauk SSSR* 5 (1990):93–94, 97–98, 100, 102, 104, and 106–107.

480. For letters in defense, see Vernadsky, V. I., "Iz pisem," pp. 82,105, 106–108, 111, 113, and responses to them.

481. Rapoport, "Vystuplenie."

482. Jukes, T. H., "Oparin and Lysenko," *Journal of Molecular Evolution* 45 (1997):339–341.

483. Miller et al., "Oparin's *Origin of Life*."

484. Leibson, L. G., "'Pavlovskaya sessiya' 1950 g. i sud'by sovetskoi fiziologii" [The "Pavlov Session" of 1950 and the fate of Soviet physiology], *Voprosy Istorii Estestvoznniya i Tekhniki* 4 (1988):147–152 (in Russian).

485. See, for instance, Müller-Hill, *Murderous Science*, about the former Nazi doctors.

486. Gazenko and Gyurdzhyan, "U istokov kosmicheskoi biologii i meditsiny."

487. Aleksandrov, *Trudnye gody*, p. 73.

488. Kostyrchenko, *Out of the Red Shadows*, p. 249.

489. Nikolsky, N. N., and D. L. Rozental, "Sud'ba tsitologii eto sud'ba issledovatelya" [The fate of cytology is the fate of a reseacher], *Vestnik Rossiiskoi Akademii Nauk* 65 (10) (1995): 938–944 (in Russian).

490. Aleksandrov, *Trudnye gody*, pp. 42–47.

491. Polyansky, *Gody prozhitye*, pp. 72–126.

492. See Zirkle, *Death of a Science*, pp. 246–247.

493. Polyansky, *Gody prozhitye*, p. 163.

494. Papoport, "Nedolgaya zhizn," p. 143.

495. Kokurin and Petrov, *Lubyanka*, p. 129.

496. Khaustov,V. N., "Razvitie sovetskoi spetssluzhby (1917–1941)" [The development of the Soviet special service, 1917–1941], in *Stanovlenie i razvitie otechestvennykh spetssluzhb* [Establishing and Development of the Soviet Special Services], 1997 (in Russian), available at http://www.fsb.ru/history/read/1997/haustov.html.

497. Kokurin and Petrov, "NKVD-NKGB-SMERSH," p. 95.

498. Solzhenitsyn, Aleksandr I., *The First Circle*, trans. T. P. Whitney (New York: Harper and Row, 1968).

499. Kopelev, Lev, *Ease My Sorrows* (New York: Random House, 1983); Panin, Dmitri, *The Notebooks of Sologdin*, trans. John Moore (New York: Harcourt Brace Jovanovich, 1976), pp. 262–285.

500. Kerber, L. L., *Stalin's Aviation Gulag: A Memoir of Andrei Tupolev and the Purge Era* (Washington, DC: Smithsonian Istitution Press, 1996), pp. 149–240; Hartford, *Korolev*, pp. 49–63.

501. Kokurin and Petrov, "NKVD-NKGB-SMERSH," p. 95.

502. The NKVD-MGB investigation prisons in Moscow.

503. Kopelev, *Ease My Sorrows*, pp. 4–5.

504. Cawthorne, Nigel, *The Iron Cage* (London: Fourth Estate, 1993), p. 184.

505. Holloway, *Stalin and the Bomb*, p. 135; document no. 100 in Ryabev, *Atomnyi proekt*, vol. 2, pt. 1, pp. 430–433.

506. Goleusova, L. P., "'Arzamas-16': Kak vsye nachinalos' . . . " [Arzamas-16: How it all began], *Voprosy Istorii Estestvoznaniya i Tekhniki* 4 (1994):89–97 (in Russian).

507. Kozlov and Mironenko, *"Osobaya Papka" L. P. Berii,* pp. 161–162 (Document D. 177, L. 118).

508. Heller, Mikhail, *Kontsentratsionnyi mir i sovetskaya literatura* [The World of Concentration Camps and Soviet Literature] (Moscow: MIK, 1996), p. 255 (in Russian).

509. Sakharov, *Memoirs*, p. 195.

510. Ibid., pp. 194–195.

511. Ibid., p. 194.

EPILOGUE

1. See, for instance, Müller-Hill, *Murderous Science.*

2. Albats, *The State*, p. 77.

3. Kokurin and Petrov, "MGB," p. 120; Kokurin and Petrov, *Lubyanka*, p. 36.

4. Cerf, Christofer, and Marina Albee, eds., *Small Fires: Letters from the Soviet People to Ogonyok Magazine, 1987–1990* (New York: Summit Books, 1990), pp. 250–251.

5. Mlechin, *Predsedateli KGB*, p. 306.

6. Sudoplatov, *Spetsoperatsii*, p. 667.

7. "Russian Court Rejects Pardon for Stalin Henchman," Reuters, May 30, 2000 (on-line version).

8. Solzhenitsyn, *The Gulag Archipelago*, vol. 1, p. 145.

9. Voskresenskaya, Z., *Pod psevdonimom Irina* (Under the Pseudonym Irina) [Moscow: Sovremennik, 1997], p. 286 (in Russian).

10. Cited in Stetsovsky, Yu., *Istoriya sovetskikh repressii* [History of Soviet Repressions] (Moscow: Znak-SP, 1997), vol. 2, p. 151 (in Russian).

11. Marks, *The Search for the "Manchurian Candidate."* Dr. Sidney Gottlieb, who headed the Chemical Division of the CIA's technical services in the 1950s and experimented with LSD (he was the real "Manchurian Candidate" of Marks's book), died on March 7, 1999 (Hodgson, G., "The real Manchurian Candidate," *Guardian*, March 11, 1999 (on-line version).

12. Welsome, *The Plutonium Files.*

13. Evans, Rob, "Scandal of Nerve Gas Tests," *Observer*, September 3, 1999.

14. Filipov, D., "Repositioning 'Iron Felix' 7 Years Later," *Boston Globe*, December 7, 1998.

15. "Anti-Yeltsin Protesters Stage Rallies," Reuters, February 24, 1999.

16. "Stalin Returns to Russian Political Scene," Reuters, December 17, 1998 (on-line version).

17. Goble, Paul, "Memory and Forgetfulness," *1999 Radio Free Europe/Radio Liberty, Inc.,* December 23, 1999 (on-line version).

18. See, for instance, Pinsker, D., "Poslednii rezerv" [The last reserve], *Itogi,* February 16, 1999, pp. 12–19 (in Russian); Shleinov, R., "Byvshikh generalov ne byvaet? Beglyi perechen' sotrudnikov spetssluzhb, rabotayushchikh vo vliyatel'nykh strukturakh" [Can generals be "former"? A brief list of secret service persons working at important structures], *Novaya Gazeta* (7), February 22, 1999 (on-line version, in Russian); "Russian Secret Service Opens Doors to Powerful Posts," Agence France Presse, August 10, 1999; Boyle, Jon, "The Rise of Secret Services in Russia," Agence France Presse, March 10, 2000 (on-line version).

19. Landsberg, M., "Yeltsin Taps KGB for New Premier," Associated Press, August 10, 1999.

20. Knight, Amy, "Crime, But No Punishment," *Washington Post,* December 6, 1998; "Parliament Chiefs Named to Security Council," Reuters, April 13, 1999. Those who worked at the Leningrad (St. Petersburg) University remember Putin as a KGB "curator" of the university. In 1995–1996, Cherkesov became known as a key FSB figure in the persecution of the former navy officer Aleksandr Nikitin (discussed later in the text).

21. In his official biography, Putin presents this work for the KGB as his intention to write his doctoral thesis (Putin, Vladimir, *First Person* [New York: PublicAffairs, 2000], pp. 86–87).

22. "Profile of Vladimir Putin, Russia's new PM," Reuters, August 9, 1999.

23. Wines, Michael, "The Kremlin's Keeper, the World at His Fingers, Is Under a Cloud," *New York Times,* September 16, 1999.

24. The former naval captain Aleksandr Nikitin was arrested in 1996 on charges of treason and leaking state secrets to the Norwegian environmentalist group Bellona. The FSB's charges were dismissed during the trial at the beginning of 1999, but in November 1999, Nikitin was charged for the eighth time. The new FSB indictment was based on secret and retroactive normative acts. On December 29, 1999, the court in St. Petersburg acquitted Nikitin on charges that he had revealed state secrets while working for Bellona. Judge Sergei Golets stated that the accusations were a violation of the Russian Constitution because they were based on secret orders from the Defense Ministry that Nikitin could not have known about. Judge Golets also cited the European convention on human rights, to which Russia is a signatory. Details are available at http://www.bellona.no.

25. Kudrik, I., "FSB Chief Publicly Convicts Nikitin," *Bellona,* July 9, 1999, available at http://www.bellona.no.

26. The Russian Supreme Court confirmed the St. Petersburg City Court acquittal of Nikitin (Kudirk, I., T. Nilsen, and R. Forseth, "Supreme Victory!" *Bellona,* April 17, 2000, available at http://www.bellona.no/imaker?id= 16538&sub=1).

27. "Russia Acquits Nuclear Dissenter Nikitin," Reuters, September 14, 2000 (on-line version).

28. Gordon, Michael R., "Russia Frees Journalist Who Exposed Nuclear Dumping," *New York Times*, July 21, 1999.

29. "Russia Gripped by 'Spy Mania,'" Reuters, November 21, 2000 (on-line version).

30. Hoffman, David, "Court Orders New Trial for Journalist," *Washington Post*, November 23, 2000.

31. Levitin, Carl, "Russian Acoustics Scientists Defended on 'Secrets' Charges," *Nature* 392 (1998):638.

32. "Russian Environmental Researcher Falls Foul of Security Services," *Nature* 400 (1999):300.

33. Gessen, Maria, "Russians, Young and Old, Are Forced Back to Uniform," *New York Times*, February 29, 2000; Badkhen, Anna, "When Is a Spy Really a Spy?" *St. Petersburg Times* 615, October 27, 2000 (on-line version).

34. "Predstavlenie nachalos" [The show has begun], *Kommersant*, May 22, 2000.

35. Williams, Daniel, "Russian Case Ignites Fears of Soviet Past," *Washington Post*, August 3, 2000.

36. Tracy, Jen, "Russia's Electronic Police Get Carte Blanche," *St. Petersburg Times*, January 14, 2000 (on-line version).

37. Cited in Piontkovsky, Andrei, "Preemnik po rezhimu" [The successor of the regime], *Novaya Gazeta*, December 23, 1999 (on-line version, in Russian).

38. Tracy, "Russia's Electronic Police."

39. Cohen, Ariel, "Analysis: Russian New Information Security Doctrine—An Orwellian Deja Vu," UPI, October 10, 2000 (on-line version).

40. A part of the letter was cited in "Russian Scientists Demand Stricter Control over State Secrets," *BBC Monitoring*, November 10, 2000 (on-line version).

41. "Russian Nobel Winner Meets Putin, Asks for Funding," Reuters, October 13, 2000 (on-line version).

42. See, for instance, Smithson, "Toxic Archipelago" and *Biological Weapons.*

43. Friedman, Robert I., *Red Mafia: How the Russian Mob Has Invaded America* (Boston: Little, Brown and Co., 2000), p. 156.

44. Tucker, Jonathan B., and Amy Sands, "An Unlikely Threat," *Bulletin of the Atomic Scientists* 55 (4) (July/August 1999):46–52.

45. "Russians Mostly Shrug Off Putin's KGB Past," Reuters, August 11, 1999.

46. Politkovskaya, Anna, "Esli smotret' cherez pritsel, to deti pokhozhi na boevikov: Reportazh s mesta otsutstviya gumanitarnoi katastrofy" [In hindsight, children look like terrorists: A report from the location where "there is no humanitarian catastrophe"], *Novaya Gazeta*, October 15, 1999 (on-line version, in Russian).

47. "Zhurnalist *Novoi Gazety* Anna Politkovskaya nagrazhdena v N'yu-Iorke premiei imeni Artyoma Borovika" [The *Novaya Gazeta* journalist Anna

Politkovskaya was awarded the Artyom Borovik Prize in New York], *NTV Channel,* April 27, 2001 (on-line version).

48. "Oktyabr' 30, 1999: Den' pamyati zhertv politicheskikh repressii: Itogi desyatiletiya pozitsii obshchestva 'Memorial'" [October 30, 1999: A day of commemorating the victims of political repressions: A summary, the position of the "Memorial" society]," *Polit.ru,* November 2, 1999 (on-line version, in Russian).

49. "Putin Commemorates Kremlin Plaque Featuring Stalin," Agence France Presse, May 10, 2000 (on-line version).

50. "Stalin Depicted on Russian Money for First Time," Agence France Presse, May 5, 2000 (on-line version).

51. Yavlinsky, Grigory, "Sham Reform Leads to National Bolshevism," *Moscow Times,* January 30, 2001.

APPENDIX II

1. Memorial's Archive (Moscow), fond 171. Prisoner cards from Vladimir Prison.

2. Ibid.

3. There are two cards for Molochnikov in the file of Vladimir Prison, one with No. 21, and the second without a number.

4. Memorial's Archive (Moscow), fond 171. Prisoner cards from Vladimir Prison.

5. Ibid.

6. This document and the following documents No. 8 and 23 represent shortened versions of prisoner cards rewritten in 1990 by the former member of Vladimir Prison administration, Mrs. V. Danilova (during the late 1940s–1950s she was in charge of the prison's card file), for the local museum in the city of Vladimir. Evidently, such information as the movement of a prisoner through diferent cells in Vladimir Prison was still considered secret in 1990.

7. Tumerman, like with his wife Shatunovskaya (Document 6), was released and rehabilitated "because of the lack of evidence of his criminal activity" (a phrase commonly used for the rehabilitation of Soviet political prisoners).

8. As in ibid.

9. Memorial's Archive (Moscow), fond 171. Prisoner cards from Vladimir Prison.

10. From the Presidential Archive (Moscow), F. 3. Phrases shown in italic are handwritten.

11. There are two cards for Mairanovsky in the file of Vladimir Prison.

12. From the file of Vladimir Prison.

13. Memorial's Archive (Moscow), fond 171. Prisoner cards from Vladimir Prison.

14. This decision was taken on the basis of an appeal by Zoya Zarubina, Eitingon's stepdaughter, to Chief Military Prosecutor Borisoglebsky (Jeffery, *Inside Russia,* p. 62).

15. Memorial's Archive (Moscow), fond 171. Prisoner cards from Vladimir Prison.

16. Ibid.

17. Ibid.

18. Usually if a patronymic name is mentioned for foreigners in MGB documents, that meant the foreigner spoke Russian.

19. Memorial's Archive (Moscow), fond 171. Prisoner cards from Vladimir Prison.

20. See Note 6.

APPENDIX I:
BIOGRAPHICAL
SKETCHES

Biographies of some key individuals are given below. "Not rehabilitated" in the biographies of state security individuals means that they were considered for rehabilitation in the late 1980s–1990s but were not rehabilitated because of the crimes they committed as NKVD/MGB officers.

Abakumov, Viktor (1908–1954) joined the OGPU (Economic Department) in 1932. Until 1934, in different NKVD departments. Head of the city of Rostov-on-Don NKVD Regional Branch (1939–1941), head of the NKVD Special Department and deputy NKVD commissar (1941–1943), head of the Main Directorate SMERSH ("death to spies") of Ministry of Defense (1943–1946), MGB minister (1946–1951). Arrested on August 12, 1951, and on December 19, 1954, sentenced to death and shot. Not rehabilitated (Petrov and Skorkin, *Kto rukovodil NKVD*, pp. 80–81).

Agoshkov, Mikhail (1905–?), mining specialist. Graduated from the Far East Polytechnic Institute in Vladivostok (1931). At the North Caucasus Mining Metallurgical Institute (1933–1941); later at the Academy Institute of Mining; deputy director there from 1952. Corresponding member (1953), academician (1981). Until 1960, head of the Academy Foreign Section, then deputy and acting chief scientific secretary of the academy. Stalin Prize in 1951. Coauthored the textbook *Development of Ore and Loose Deposits* with NKVD/MGB investigator Vladimir Boyarsky, who had never been trained in geology. Later Boyarsky received a Doctor of Sciences degree and became a senior editor at the Academy of Sciences press, *Nauka*.

Agranov, Yakov (1893–1938) joined the VCheKa in 1919. Plenipotentiary and deputy head of the Special Department (1919), head of the Special Bureau for Deportation of Anti-Soviet Elements and Intelligentsia (1921–1923). From 1923 on, key positions within the GPU/OGPU. Head of the Moscow OGPU (1931–1934), first deputy NKVD commissar (1934–1937). Supervised all main Moscow show trials of the 1930s. In 1937, transferred to the city of Saratov. Arrested; executed on August 1, 1938. Not rehabilitated (Petrov and Skorkin, *Kto rukovodil NKVD*, p. 82–83).

Alekhin (Smolyarov), Mikhail (1902–1939) joined the CheKa in the city of Nikolaev in 1921. From 1931, in Moscow, then Leningrad (1934–1937). Deputy head of the Twelfth Department of the NKVD Main State Security Directorate (from 1937), and acting head of the Second Special (Operational Equipment) Department (1938). Arrested on September 13, 1938. On February 22, 1939, sentenced to death and shot. Not rehabilitated (Petrov and Skorkin, *Kto rukovodil NKVD*, p. 88).

Aleksandrov, Georgii (1908–1961), philosopher. Joined the Party in 1928. Graduated from the Moscow Institute of History and Philosophy (1932). Head of the Directorate of Propaganda and Agitation (Agitprop) within the Central Committee (1940–1947), director of the Academy Institute of Philosophy (1947–1954). Academician (1946). Played an important role in the Soviet anti-Semitic propaganda during the 1940s and early 1950s. Minister of culture (1954–1955), then at the Institute of Philosophy (1956–1961). Stalin Prize in 1943 and 1946.

Andropov, Yuri (1914–1984), KGB chairman and Party general secretary. Second secretary of the Petrozavodsk City Committee, then second secretary of the Central Committee of the Karelo-Finnish Republic (1944–1952). From 1952, at the Central Committee in Moscow, then head of the Fourth European Department in the Foreign Ministry. Ambassador to Hungary (1953–1957). Organizer of the military suppression of the Hungarian Revolution in 1956. KGB chairman (1967–1982), Party general secretary and chairman of the Presidium of the USSR Supreme Council (1982–1984) (Volkogonov, Dmitri, *Autopsy for an Empire: The Seven Leaders Who Built the Soviet Regime*, ed. and trans. Harold Shukman [New York: Free Press, 1998], pp. 329–382).

Antonov-Ovseenko, Anton (b. 1920), historian and writer. The son of a Bolshevik military leader and Commissar of Justice Vladimir Antonov-Ovseenko (executed in 1938). Arrested in 1940 and spent 13 years in different labor camps.

Astaurov, Boris (1904–1974), embryologist and geneticist. At Nikolai Koltsov's Institute of Experimental Biology since 1935. Corresponding member (1956); academician (1966). Active anti-Lysenkoist. Director of the Academy Institute of Developmental Biology, which he created as a continuation of Koltsov's institute (1967–1974).

Bach (or **Bakh**), **Aleksei** (1857–1946), biochemist and revolutionary. From 1885, in emigration in France, United States, Switzerland. Returned to Russia in 1917 after the Bolshevik Revolution. From 1918, headed the Central Chemical Laboratory under the All-Union Council of People's Industry (VSNKh), which in 1935 became the Karpov Physical-Chemical Institute. In 1920, organized the Institute of Biochemistry within the Commissariat of Health, and in 1935, another one, within the academy. From 1927, head of the All-Union Association of Workers of Science and Technique to Assist the Socialist Construction (VARNITSO), which played the crucial role in the Sovietization of the academy. Academician (1929), secretary academician of the Academy Chemistry Department (1939–1945).

Baev, Aleksandr (1904–1994), molecular biologist. Graduated from the Medical Faculty of Kazan University. From 1935, at the Bach Institute of Biochemistry in Moscow. Arrested in 1937. Released in 1944; lived in the cities of Norilsk and Syktyvkar. Defended a Candidate of Science thesis in Leningrad (1947) with the help of Vladimir Engelhardt and Leon Orbeli. Rehabilitated in 1954. From 1959, at the Institute of Molecular Biology (Moscow). Corresponding member (1969), academician (1970). Secretary academician of the Academy Biophysics, Biochemistry, and Chemistry of Physiologically Active Compounds Division (1970–1988). From 1988, adviser to the Academy Presidium; a member of the USSR Inter-Agency Scientific and Technical Council, which coordinated secret development of new types of biological weapons. Honorable member of the European and American academies and societies. President and past president of the International Biochemical Union (1976–1982).

Bashtakov, Leonid (1900–1970) joined the OGPU in 1923. From 1938, head of different divisions within the NKVD First Special Department (in charge of registration). Head of the NKVD First Special Department (1940–1941), head of the NKGB Second Department (1941–1942). Together with Vsevolod Merkulov and Bogdan Kobulov, responsible for the Katyn Massacre in 1940. Head of the High School of the NKVD/NKGB/MGB (1942–1947). Retired in 1951. Head of the Secret Enciphering Department of the USSR Ministry of Geology (Petrov and Skorkin, *Kto rukovodil NKVD*, pp. 101–102).

Belozersky, Andrei (1905–1971), biochemist, specialist in nucleic acids chemistry. Established the presence of nucleic acids in plants and bacteria (from the 1930s–1950s); later specialized in molecular evolution. Corresponding member (1958), academician (1962). Secretary academician of the Academy Biochemistry, Biophysics, and the Chemistry of Physiologically Active Compounds Division (1970–1971). Organizer and head of the Moscow University Inter-Faculty Laboratory of Bioorganic Chemistry (now Belozersky Institute of Physico-Chemical Biology).

Berg, Axel (1893–1979), a marine officer and radiophysicist, the main Soviet expert in military radio technical equipment and a pioneer in the development of the Soviet theory of information, computers, electronic industry, and applied aspects of information theory in biology and medicine. From 1943, deputy minister of electronic industry, and in 1953, deputy defense minister. Academician (1946). In 1953 organized the Academy Institute of Radiotechnology and Electronics. Retired from the army in 1960. Chair of the Scientific Council on the Complex Problem "Cybernetics" under the Academy Presidium.

Berg, Lev (or **Leo**) (1876–1950), zoologist, ichthyologist and a geographer. Graduated from Moscow University (1898). From 1917, at Petrograd (Leningrad) University and other colleges. Head of the Special Ichthyology

Laboratory within the Institute of Zoology in Leningrad (1934–1950). Corresponding member (1928), academician (1946). Published more than 1,509 papers and monographs in different languages on 17 main topics. Anti-Lysenkoist. His theoretical books *Nomogenesis or Evolution Determined by Law* (1922 in Russian; translated into English in 1969) was furiously criticized by Soviet philosophers and Lysenkoists. Stalin Prize post mortem (1951).

Beria, Lavrentii (1899–1953), the main organizer of the Soviet state security system. In 1915, joined an underground Marxist group in the city of Baku (Azerbaijan) and in 1921, the Azerbaijan CheKa. Chairman and then commissar of the Georgian GPU/NKVD (1926–1931), chairman of the Caucasian GPU (included three republics, Azerbaijan, Armenia, and Georgia) (1931), first secretary of the Georgian Republic and the Tbilisi City Committees (1931–1938). First deputy NKVD commissar (1938), then NKVD commissar (1938–1945), deputy chairman of the Council of People's Commissars (Sovnarkom) (1941–1946), chairman of the State Committee No. 1 and deputy chair Council of Ministers (Sovmin) (1945–1953), MVD minister and deputy chair of the Sovmin (March 5, 1953–June 26, 1953). Arrested during the meeting of the Presidium of the Central Committee. Tried in a closed secret meeting of the USSR Supreme Court, condemned to death, and shot immediately after the trial on December 23, 1953. Not rehabilitated.

Blokhin, Vasilii (1895–1955) joined the VCheKa in 1921. Head of a special group of the VCheKa/NKVD/MGB executioners: commandant of the OGPU (1926–1938); head of the Commandant Department of the NKVD Administrative-Economic Directorate (1938–1943), head of the Commandant Department of the NKGB Administrative-Economic Directorate (1943–1946), head of the Commandant Department of the MGB Management Directorate (1946–1952), commandant of the MGB (1952–1953). Provided Mairanovsky with prisoners for experiments. Discharged in 1953 "because of bad health." In 1954 deprived of major general rank (1945) (Petrov and Skorkin, *Kto rukovodil NKVD*, p. 112).

Bondarenko, Aleksandr (1893–1941), Party and state figure. Member of the Agricultural Academy (VASKhNIL) (1931). Vice president (1931–1935), scientific secretary of the VASKhNIL (1935–1936), head of the Institute of Beet Planting of the VASKhNIL (1936–1937) and of a department at the Academy Institute of World Industry and World Politics. Arrested on February 8, 1941, sentenced to death (the Vavilov case), and shot on July 27, 1941. Rehabilitated in 1956.

Braunstein, Aleksandr (1902–1986), biochemist. Graduated from the Kharkov Medical Institute (1925). At the Bach Institute of Biochemistry (1930–1936). From 1936, head of the Section of Metabolism at the All-Union Institute of Experimental Medicine and later at the Institute of Biological Medical Chemistry of the Medical Academy, of a laboratory at the Institute of Molecular Biology (1959–1986). Member of the Medical Academy (1945) and of the USSR Academy (1964). Hero of Socialist Labor, Stalin Prize (1941) and Lenin Prize (1980).

Bukharin, Nikolai (1888–1938), one of the Bolshevik Party leaders and the main theorist. Joined the Party in 1906. A Central Committee member (from 1917), and a Politburo member (1924–1929). Head of the Communist International (Comintern) (1926–1929), chief editor of the Bolshevik daily *Pravda* (1918–1929) and of the daily *Izvestia* (1934–1937). Academician (1929). Director of the Academy Institute of the History of Natural Sciences and Technology (1932–1938), head of the Scientific-Research Section of the All-Union Council of People's Industry (VSNKh) and then of the Commissariat of Heavy Industry (1934–1938). Arrested on February 27, 1937. On March 15, 1938, shot after a show trial. Rehabilitated.

Chayanov, Aleksandr (1888–1938), agrarian, economist, historian and writer. Member of the Collegium of the USSR Commissariat of Agriculture (1921–1923), director of the Institute of Agricultural Economy (1922–1928). Author of the theory of cooperative farming. Also published the utopian work *Journey of My Brother Aleksei to the Land of the Peasant Utopia* (1920) and some other novels. In *Journey*, predicted that in 1984 Russia would be a free peasant country (he chose the date 1984 long before George Orwell, who published *1984* in 1948). Soviet officials considered the *Journey* to be a secret plan of an anti-Soviet organization. In 1930 arrested as a leader of the Labor Peasant Party, tried, and sentenced to exile (to Kazakhstan). Arrested for the second time in 1937 and on October 3, 1937, condemned to death. Shot in 1938. Rehabilitated in 1987.

Chernov, Ivan (1906–1991), head of the Secretariat of the Main SMERH Directorate (1943–1946), head of the MGB Secretariat (1946–1951). In 1951 arrested along with Abakumov and his men and in 1954 was condemned to 15 years' imprisonment. Rehabilitated in 1992 (Naumov and Sigachev, *Lavrentii Beria*, p. 494; Stolyarov, *Palachi i zhertvy*, pp. 32–37, 141).

Chernov, Mikhail (1891–1938), Party and state figure. Commissar of agriculture (1934–1937). On November 7, 1937, arrested and tried in March 1938 as a German spy. His alleged mission was to infect horses destined for the Red Army. On March 13, 1938, at the Bukharin show trial, was sentenced to death and two days later was shot. Rehabilitated in 1988 (Bojtzov and Geissler, "8. Military biology," p. 161; Yeremina and Roginsky, *Rasstrel'nye spiski*, p. 435).

Chetverikov, Sergei (1880–1959), one of the founders of population genetics. Worked at Nikolai Koltsov's Institute of Experimental Biology. In 1929 exiled to the city of Sverdlovsk (now Yekaterinburg) for five years. Worked as a mathematics teacher in a technical school in the town of Vladimir, then moved to the city of Gorky (Nizhnii Novgorod). Dean of the Biology Department at Gorky University, where he organized the Department of Genetics. Dismissed from his post in 1948 after the August 1948 session.

Clauberg, Carl (1898–1957), SS physician infamous for his experiments on female inmates of concentration camps. Born in Wupperhoff. During World War I, served in the infantry. Later studied medicine at the universities of Kiel, Hamburg, and Graz. Qualified as doctor in 1925. From 1937, professor of gynecology and obstetrics at the University of Koenigsberg. Joined the Nazi Party in 1933; SS Gruppenfuhrer. In 1942, Heinrich Himmler entrusted him with the implementation of an experimental sterilization program at Auschwitz. Injected acid liquids into the uterus of Jewish and Gipsy victims. Continued experiments in Ravensbruck. Sterilized approximately 700 women. Captured by the Soviets in 1945 and in 1948 sentenced to 25 years' imprisonment. Kept in Vladimir Prison. Like other German POWs, released in 1955. In November 1955, arrested in the city of Kiel. Died in prison shortly before the new trial.

Deborin, Abram (1881–1963), leading Marxist philosopher in the 1920s. Joined the Bolshevik Party in 1928. Chief editor of the Party magazine *Pod znamenem marxisma [Under the Banner of Marxism]* (1922–1930), deputy director of the Marx and Engels Institute in Moscow under the Central Committee (1926–1931). In 1930, became the main target of the discussion in philosophy initiated by Stalin, who named Deborin and his followers "the Menshevik idealists." Continued to work at the academy, while his colleagues were arrested (Rokityansky,Ya. G., "Nesostoyavsheesya samoubiistvo" [The suicide that did not happen], *Vestnik Rossiiskoi Akademii Nauk* 63 (5) (1993):458–461 (in Russian).

Dekanozov, Vladimir (1898–1953) joined the local CheKa in Azerbaijan in 1921. In the CheKa/OGPU of Azerbaijan and Georgia until 1932. From 1932–1938, in the Georgian government. Head of the Fifth (Foreign Intelligence) and Third (Counterintelligence) Departments of the NKVD Main State Security Directorate (GUGB) and deputy NKVD commissar (1938–1939). Deputy commissar/minister of foreign affairs (1939–1947), and Soviet ambassador to Germany (1940–1941). Deputy head of the Main Directorate of the Soviet Property Abroad (Germany) (1947–1949). During Beria's short rule after Stalin's death, headed the MVD in Georgia. Arrested on June 30, 1953. On December 23, 1953, condemned to death together with Beria and Merkulov and shot. Not rehabilitated (Petrov and Skorkin, *Kto rukovodil NKVD*, pp. 167–168).

Dobzhansky, Theodosius (1900–1975), Soviet-American geneticist and evolutionist. Started his career at the Genetics Department of Leningrad State University. In 1927 left the Soviet Union to work in the laboratory of Thomas H. Morgan in the United States. Did not return to the Soviet Union in 1931 and became a "defector." Wrote a series of fundamental monographs on genetics, evolution, and human behavior (*Genetics and Origin of Species* (1937), *Mankind Evolving: The Evolution of the Human Species* (1962), etc.).

Dukes, Paul (1889–1967), British musician and spy. Came to Russia in 1909 and became assistant conductor at the Mariinsky (now Kirov) Theater in St. Petersburg. In 1918 was recruited by British Intelligence (SIS) and returned to Russia under the code name ST 25. In Petrograd from November 1918 to September 1919. Knighted for his service in Soviet Russia. See Dukes, Paul, *Red Dusk and the Morrow: Adventures and Investigations in Red Russia* (Garden City: Doubleday, Page, 1922), pp. 1–224, and Dukes, Paul, *The Story of "ST 25": Adventures and Romance in the Secret Intelligence Service in Red Russia* (London: Cassell and Co., 1938), pp. 37–44.

Dzerzhinsky, Felix (1877–1926), the first chairman of the VCheKa/ OGPU. A Polish noble by origin. In 1895 joined a Social Democratic group, then the Social Democratic Party of Poland and Lithuania. Arrested in 1897, 1900, 1905, 1908, 1912. Sentenced to 3 years of hard labor and released after the February Revolution of 1917. On his suggestion, the Politburo (later Presidium) of the Central Committee of the Bolshevik Party was organized in October 1917. During the Bolshevik coup, a member of the Petrograd Military-Revolutionary Center of the Party. From December 20, 1917, and until his death in 1926, was VCheKa/OGPU chairman. Also commissar of Internal Affairs (1919–1923), commissar of Ways of Communication (1921–1924), chairman of the Supreme Council of the National Economy (VSNKh) (1924–1926).

Efroimson, Vladimir (1908–1989), geneticist, a pupil of Nikolai Koltsov and Sergei Chetverikov, and an outspoken fighter against Lysenko. Studied at Moscow University but was not allowed to graduate because of the arrest of his father. In the late 1920s, worked at the State Roentgen Institute. From 1930–1932, at the Trans-Caucasian Institute of Silkworm Breeding. Arrested in 1932 in Moscow, sentenced to three years' imprisonment after refusing to testify against Nikolai Koltsov. Released in 1936, worked at the Central Asian Research Institute of Silkworm Breeding in the city of Tashkent (Uzbekistan). In 1938, his monograph on genetics of silkworms was destroyed on the order of local officials. From 1939, at the All-Ukrainian Station of Silkworm Breeding. In 1941, volunteered for the army; served as a medical and intelligence officer. From 1945, at the Darwinism and Genetics Department in the city of Kharkov. Fired in 1948. In 1949 arrested again after sending the analysis of Lysenko's falsifications to the Party Central Committee. Released in 1955, rehabilitated in 1956. Restored his report on Lysenko's falsifications and sent it to the General Prosecutor's Office. While working as a bibliographer at the Library of Foreign Languages in Moscow, in 1964 published the monograph *Introduction to Medical Genetics*. Head of the Genetics Department at the Moscow Institute of Psychiatry under the Ministry of Health (1967–1976). Forced to retire after his protest against the incarceration of the dissident General Pyotr Grigorenko in a special MVD psychiatric prison hospital. At the Academy Institute of Developmental Biology (1976–1989). Two of his most important monographs were published after his death.

Eitingon, Naum (1899–1981) joined the CheKa in the town of Gomel (Belorussia) in 1920. From 1923, deputy head of the OGPU Eastern Department (Moscow). From 1925, in the Foreign (Intelligence) Department: in China, Turkey, France, and Belgium (1931–1933). Head of the Eighth Division of this department (1933). In China, then in Spain during the Spanish Civil War (under different alias). In 1939–1940, organized the successful assassination of Leon Trotsky in Mexico and a spy network in the United States. Deputy head of the First NKVD Directorate (1941), and from July 1941, deputy head of the NKGB Special Group. Deputy head of the Fourth NKVD/NKGB Directorate (1942–1946). In charge of the assassination attempt on German Ambassador

Franz von Pappen in Turkey (1943). Organized the anti-German partisan movement on the Nazi-occupied territories (1942–1945). Also in charge of cleansing Poland, Czechoslovakia, Bulgaria, and Romania of anti-Soviet military groups. Unsuccessfully tried to organize the escape of Trotsky's murderer Ramon Mercader from a prison in Mexico (1943–1944). After World War II, continued the NKGB/MGB cleansing in Poland and Lithuania. Major general (1945). Deputy head of the MGB Department DR (terrorism) (1946–1951). Together with Pavel Sudoplatov and Grigory Mairanovsky, took part in political assassinations. Arrested in 1951, released in 1953. In May 1953, appointed deputy head of the MVD Ninth Department. On August 20, 1953, arrested again, tried on March 6, 1957, and condemned to 12 years' imprisonment. Kept in Vladimir Prison. Released in 1964. An editor at the Foreign Literature Publishing House. Rehabilitated in 1990.

Engelhardt, Vladimir (1894–1984), biochemist and one of the founders of molecular biology in the USSR. Academician (1953). In 1959, organized and directed the Academy Institute of Radiation and Physical-Chemical Biology (in 1964 renamed the Institute of Molecular Biology). Secretary academician of the Academy Biological Branch (1955–1959). Anti-Lysenkoist.

Fedotov, Pyotr (1900–1963) joined the CheKa in 1922 at the Northern Caucasus. From 1937, in Moscow. Head of the Second Directorate of the NKVD (1938–1941), then NKGB (February 1941–July 1941), then NKVD again (July 1941–April 1943), then NKGB/MGB (1943–1946). Head of the First MGB Directorate (Foreign Intelligence) and deputy MGB minister (1946–1947). Deputy chairman of the Committee of Information (KI) under the Council of Ministers (1947–1949), deputy chairman of the KI under the Foreign Ministry (1949–1952), head of the First MVD Main Directorate (counter-espionage) (1953–1954), head of the First MVD Directorate (1953–1954), head of the Second KGB Directorate (1954–1956), and at the High KGB School (1956–1959). Dismissed from the KGB in 1959 (Petrov and Skorkin, *Kto rukovodil NKVD*, pp. 418–419).

Fefer, Isaak (1900–1952), Jewish poet and writer. Joined the Bolshevik Party in 1919. Secretary of the Jewish Anti-Fascist Committee (JAC) (1942–1948). In 1943, together with JAC Chairman Solomon Mikhoels, visited the United States, Canada, Mexico, and Great Britain; they lectured about Nazi atrocities against the Jews and about JAC activity. Also a secret NKVD/MGB informer under the alias "Zorin" (1944–1948). Tried in 1952 together with the other JAC members, condemned to death and shot. Rehabilitated (Kostyrchenko, *Out of the Red Shadows*, pp. 39–43).

Figatner, Yurii (1889–1937), Party figure, member of the Control Commission of the Central Committee (1925–1934), head of the Main Inspection of the Council of People's Commissars (Sovnarkom), and member of the Presidium of the Sovnarkom (1929–1937). Chairman of the State Commission on cleansing the staff of the Academy of Sciences of "class enemies" (1929). Arrested and shot in 1937.

Filimonov, Mikhail (1910–1958) joined the NKVD in December 1938. Head of the NKVD Fourth Special Department (1939–1941), and head of a department within the Fourth Directorate of the NKVD/NKGB/MGB (1942–1946). A supervisor of Mairanovsky's experiments on prisoners. Discharged from the central MGB in Moscow in 1947 and sent to the Ukrainian MGB, from which he was fired in 1954 because of his drinking problem (Petrov and Skorkin, *Kto rukovodil NKVD*, pp. 421–422).

Fitin, Pavel (1907–1971) joined the NKVD in 1938. Deputy head and then head of the Fifth Department (Foreign Intelligence) within the NKVD Main State Security Directorate (GUGB) (1938–1941), head of the First Directorate (Foreign Intelligence) in the NKGB/NKVD/NKGB (1941–1946), deputy MGB representative in Germany (1946–1947). From 1947, in charge of regional and republican MGB/MVD branches. On November 11, 1953, dismissed from the MVD (Petrov and Skorkin, *Kto rukovodil NKVD*, p. 423).

Frank, Gleb (1904–1976), biophysicist. Graduated from Crimean University (1925). At the Medical Faculty of Moscow University; published papers jointly with his professor Aleksandr Gurvich. At the Leningrad Physical-Technical Institute (1929–1933), head of the Biophysics Department at the All-Union Institute of Experimental Medicine (VIEM) (1933–1946), then at the Institute of Experimental Biology (under the directorship of Professor Gurvich). Head of the Academy Laboratory of Biophysics of Isotopes and Emission (in 1952, renamed the Institute of Biophysics) (1943–1952) and head of the Radiation Laboratory within the Medical Academy (1946–1948), which later became the Institute of Biophysics. Director of this institute (1948–1951). Director of the Academy Institute of Biophysics (1957–1976). Corresponding member of the Medical Academy (1945), of the USSR Academy (1960), academician (1966). In 1947, joined the Communist Party. Stalin Prize (1949 and 1951). Knew about Mairanovsky's experiments and supported him.

Frinovsky, Mikhail (1898–1940) joined the VCheKa (Moscow) in 1919. Deputy head of the NKVD (1936–1937), head of the NKVD Main State Security Directorate (GUGB) (1937–1938). After the fall of Yezhov in April 1939, commissar for the navy. Arrested on March 6, 1939, and shot on February 4, 1940. Not rehabilitated (Petrov and Skorkin, *Kto rukovodil NKVD*, pp. 425–426).

Gertsovsky, Arkady (or **Aaron**) (1904–?) joined the VCheKa in 1920. Deputy head (1938–1940 and 1941–1943), and head (1941) of the NKVD First Special Department, head of the NKGB/MGB Department "A" (Archive) (1943–1953). Arrested in 1953 and in 1955 sentenced to 10 years' imprisonment in labor camps (Kokurin and Petrov, *Lubyanka*, pp. 28–29, 107–110, 263, and Sudoplatov, A., *Tainaya zhizn'*, vol. 2, p. 485).

Gorbunov, Nikolai (1892–1938), Party figure. Joined the Party in 1917. Graduated from Petrograd Technological Institute (1917). Secretary of the Council of People's Commissars (Sovnarkom) and Lenin (1917–1919); also head of the Scientific-Technical Department of the Supreme Council of the

National Economy (VSNKh) (1918–1919). Executive secretary of the Sov-narkom (1920–1929), head of the Department of Scientific Institutions of the Sovnarkom (1923–1929), and rector of the Moscow Higher Technical College (1923–1929). Member and vice president of the Agricultural Academy (VASKhNIL) (1929–1931), director of the Karpov Institute of Chemistry (1931–1933). Academician (1935), permanent secretary academician (1935–1938). Arrested on February 19, 1938. On September 7, 1938, con-demned to death as a spy and shot. Rehabilitated in 1956.

Gorky, Maxim (1868–1936; pseudonym of **Aleksei Peshkov**; "gorky" means "bitter" in Russian), the only major Russian writer actively involved in the Social Democratic movement. Followed the Bolsheviks, but often at odds with Lenin. His involvement gave the Bolsheviks prestige and ability to raise money. Published a series of novels, plays, and poems, of which the play *The Lower Depth* (1902), staged by Konstantin Stanislavsky, became the most popu-lar. In 1902, Tsar Nicholas II did not approve his election to the academy. Two writers, Anton Chekhov and Vladimir Korolenko, left the academy in protest. Lived abroad (1906–1913). Opposed the Bolshevik seizure of power in 1917. Attacked Lenin's dictatorial methods in his newspaper *New Life* until July 1918. From 1919 onward, cooperated with Lenin's government and helped writers and scientists. Emigrated, lived in a villa in Sorrento, Italy (1921–1928). Re-turned to the Soviet Union (1928) and became a prop of Stalinist political or-thodoxy. In 1931, took part in the trip of a group of Soviet writers to the main construction projects conducted by prisoners of the NKVD labor camps. In 1934, together with the other 31 writers, published a book titled *The White Sea–Baltic Stalin Canal* (translated into English in 1935 under the title *Belomor*), which glorified the NKVD and slave labor (see details in Aleksandr Solzhenit-syn's *The Gulag Archipelago, 1918–1956*; vol. 3, pp. 81–102). President (1934–1936) of the Soviet Writers' Union, which obliged writers to follow the literary method of Socialist Realism, i.e., to be political propagandists. Died in 1936 when he was under medical treatment for tuberculosis. In 1938, during the show trial of Nikolai Bukharin and others, three doctors were accused of killing Gorky. The former NKVD commissar Genrikh Yagoda "confessed" that he had ordered Gorky's assassination.

Gorsky, Anatolii (1907–?) joined the OGPU in 1928. NKVD/NKGB deputy *rezident* and then *rezident* in London (1936–1944). Controlled Kim Philby and other English spies. Transferred to Washington (1944–1946). On October 24, 1945, met with former U.S. vice president and Secretary of Com-merce Henry A. Wallace, who proposed to invite a group of Soviet physicists to witness American achievements in the atomic project. In the Committee of In-formation (1947–1952), then at the Second MGB Directorate (Andrew and Gordievsky, *KGB*, p. 293; Weinstein and Vassiliev, *The Haunted Wood*, pp. 283–285; Andrew and Mitrokhin, *The Sword and the Shield*, pp. 83–85, 90, 113, 124, 142–143; Trubnikov, V. I., ed., *Ocherki istorii Rossiiskoi vneshnei razvedki* [Essays on the History of the Russian Foreign Intelligence], vol. 4., 1941–1945 [Moscow: Mezhdunarodnye Otnosheniya, 1999], pp. 261–263 [in Russian]).

Govorov, Leonid (1885–1941), botanist. Head of the Section of Leguminous Plants in the All-Union Plant Breeding Institute (VIR) and professor of genetics at Leningrad University. Created a worldwide collection of leguminous plants in the VIR. Arrested on February 15, 1941, and on July 9, 1941, sentenced to death. Shot on July 27, 1941. Rehabilitated in 1956.

Grashchenkov, Nikolai (1901–1965), neurologist. Joined the Bolshevik Party in 1918. Graduated from Moscow University (1926). At the Medical Faculty of Moscow University (later Moscow First Medical Institute) (1926–1933) and at the All-Union Institute of Experimental Medicine (VIEM). Deputy commissar of health (1937–1939), director of the VIEM (1939–1944). During World War II (1941–1945), consultant to the Red Army on problems of neuropathology and neurosurgery. Director of the Neurological Institute within the Medical Academy (1944–1948). Professor at the Central Institute of Final Medical Education in Moscow (1951). Corresponding member (1939), member of the Medical Academy (1944), member of the Belorussian Academy of Sciences (1947). President of the Belorussian Academy (replaced the geneticist Anton Zhebrak) (1948–1951). Supported Mairanovsky.

Gurvich, Aleksandr (1874–1954), cytologist, author of the theory of mitogenetic radiation of dividing cells. Graduated from the Medical Faculty of Munich University (Germany) (1897). At Bern University (Switzerland) (1901–1905). Chair of the Anatomy and Histology Department at the Bestuzhev Courses in St. Petersburg (1907–1914); in the army (1914–1918). At Simferopol University in the Crimea (1919–1924), chair of the Histology and Embryology Department of the Medical Faculty at Moscow University (1924–1929), head of the Laboratory (then Department) of Experimental Biology at the Institute of Experimental Medicine (IEM, then VIEM) in Leningrad (1930–1945), director of the Institute of Experimental Biology (Leningrad) within the Medical Academy (1945–1948). Retired in 1948 after Lysenko's triumph; continued to work at home. In 1949 was accused of being the mythical Jewish Masonic Lodge's "Grand Master." Stalin Prize (1940).

Ignatiev, Semyon (1904–1983), Party and MGB figure, from 1937–1950, in different Party positions. Head of the Department of the Party, Trade Unions and Komsomol [Communist Youth] Cadres of the Central Committee (CC) (1950–1952) and, simultaneously, MGB minister (1951–1953). Also a member of the Presidium (Politburo) (1952–1953) and from March–April 1953, secretary of the CC. Later in different regional Party positions. Resigned in 1960 (Naumov and Sigachev, *Lavrentii Beria*, p. 448).

Ioffe, Abram (1880–1960), physicist. After graduating from the St. Petersburg Technological Institute (1902), at the laboratory of Wilhelm Roentgen (the discoverer of X-rays) in Munich. From 1906, at the Polytechnic Institute in St. Petersburg. Corresponding member (1918), academician (1920). Director of the Physical-Technical Institute in Petrograd/Leningrad (1923–1950). Vice president of the academy (1932–1960), and secretary academician of its Physics Division (1942–1945). Took part in the Soviet atomic project. In 1942, joined the Communist Party. Hero of Socialist Labor (1955).

Kaganovich, Lazar (1893–1991), Party figure. Joined the Party in 1911. Secretary of the Central Committee (CC) (1924–1925 and 1928–1939), and a Politburo member (1926–1929 and 1930–1957). First secretary of the Ukrainian Central Committee (1925–1928 and 1947), first secretary of the Moscow Committee (1930–1935), commissar of transportation (1935–1944), member of the State Committee of Defense (1942–1945). Deputy chairman (1944–1953), and first deputy chairman (1953–1957) of the Council of Commissars/Ministers. In 1957 dismissed from the CC; director of a small local plant (1957–1961).

Kapitsa, Pyotr (1894–1984), physicist. Graduated from Petrograd Polytechnical Institute (1919). At Cavendish Laboratory (Cambridge University, England) (1921–1934). Corresponding member (1929), academician (1939). In 1934 was forced to stay in the Soviet Union. Director of the Academy Institute of Physical Problems (1935–1946 and 1955–1984). From 1946–1954, under house arrest because of his opposition to Lavrentii Beria and refusal to participate in the Soviet A-bomb project. Stalin Prize (1941 and 1943), Hero of Socialist Labor (1945). Nobel Prize for physics (1978).

Karpechenko, Georgii (1899–1941), plant geneticist and cytogeneticist, studied the role of ploidy (the increase in chromosome number by doubling) in plant speciation and evolution. Organizer and head of the Genetics Laboratory within the All-Union Plant Breeding Institute (VIR) (1925–1941). From 1929–1931, at several American laboratories, including Thomas H. Morgan's at Columbia University (New York). In 1932, organized the Plant Genetics Department at Leningrad University. Arrested on February 17, 1941, tried together with Nikolai Vavilov and Leonid Govorov on July 7, 1941, and shot on July 28, 1941. Rehabilitated in 1956.

Karpinsky, Aleksandr (1847–1936), "the father" of Russian geology. Graduated from St. Petersburg Corpus of Mining Engineers (later the Mining Institute) (1866), then professor there (until 1896). Director of the Geological Committee in St. Petersburg (1885–1903). Academician (1886). The first elected (not appointed) president of the academy (1916–1936). In 1929, tried to resign after the OGPU cleansed the academy of 781 employees allegedly connected with the "Monarchist Plot."

Kartashov, Sergei (1914–1979), colonel, head of the Fourth Department of the MGB Third Directorate (Military Counterintelligence) (1946–1948). Transferred to Budapest as an adviser to the Hungarian Security Service (AVH) (1948). Later, until his retirement in 1967, a consultant to the head of the First KGB Directorate (Intelligence).

Khariton, Yulii (1904–), physicist, graduated from St. Petersburg Polytechnical Institute, then received Ph.D. from Cambridge (1926–1928). Returned to

Leningrad, organized and headed a laboratory to study explosives at the Leningrad Institute of Chemical Physics. Important research on nuclear chain reactions (1939–1941). Scientific director of the secret institute Arzamas-16 (1946–1992). Academician (1953). In 1956 joined the Communist Party. Hero of Socialist Labor (1949, 1951, and 1954).

Khrushchev, Nikita (1894–1971), first secretary of the Communist Party (1953–1964) and premier of the Soviet Union (1958–1964). Joined the Bolshevik Party in 1918. Started his career in the Ukraine (1925), in Moscow from 1931; second secretary (1933), then first secretary of the Moscow City and Moscow Regional Committees (1935–1938). Member of the Central Committee (from 1934), Politburo member (1939–1964). First secretary of the Ukrainian Communist Party (1938–1941, 1944–1949). During World War II, a political adviser to the Red (Soviet) Army. First secretary of Moscow City Committee again (from 1949). In charge of agriculture as a Politburo member until 1951. In September 1953, replaced Malenkov (Stalin's heir) as first Party secretary. In 1954, reduced Stalin's security system to a small committee (KGB) under the USSR Council of Ministers. In 1955, removed Malenkov from premiership. In 1956, during the Twentieth Party Congress, delivered a speech about political crimes during the years of Stalin's regime; millions of political prisoners were released. On October 14, 1964, dismissed as Party first secretary and chairman of the Council of Ministers by his protégé and deputy, Leonid Brezhnev.

Kobulov, Amayak (1906–1955), at various high positions within the Georgian OGPU/NKVD (1927–1938). First deputy NKVD commissar of the Ukraine (1938–1939), then adviser at the Soviet Legation in Berlin (1938–1941), NKGB/NKVD commissar of Uzbekistan (1941–1945). First deputy head of the Main NKVD/MVD Directorate of Prisoners of War (1945–1951). First deputy head of the Gulag (1951–1953) and also deputy head of NKVD/NKGB Department S (atomic intelligence) (1946–1953). Arrested on June 27, 1953, condemned to death on October 1, 1954, and shot on February 26, 1955. Not rehabilitated (Petrov and Skorkin, *Kto rukovodil NKVD*, pp. 233–234).

Kobulov, Bogdan (1904–1953), the elder brother of Amayak, from 1922 in the Georgian CheKa. In 1938, deputy commissar of State Security of Georgia; transferred to Moscow. Head of the NKVD Investigation Department (1938–1939), head of the Main Economic Directorate (GEU) (1939–1941), deputy NKGB/NKVD commissar (1941–1945), deputy head of the Main Directorate of the Soviet Property Abroad (Germany) (1946–1953), first deputy MVD minister (March–May 1953). Arrested and tried along with Beria, Merkulov, and Dekanozov, condemned to death and shot on December 23, 1953. Not rehabilitated (Kokurin and Petrov, *Lubyanka*, p. 148; Petrov and Skorkin, *Kto rukovodil NKVD*, pp. 234–235).

Kolchak, Aleksandr (1870–1920), Russian admiral and Arctic explorer. The leader of the White movement in Siberia (1918–1920). In November 1918, pronounced supreme ruler of all Russia in the city of Omsk. In January 1920, after the defeat of his army, interrogated for nine days by Bolshevik investigators and executed by a firing squad. (Luckett, Richard, *The White Generals: An Account of the White Movement and the Russian Civil War* [New York: Viking Press, 1971], pp. 213–228, 343–347; Lincoln, W. Bruce, *Red Victory: A History of the Russian Civil War* [New York: Touchstone Book, 1989], pp. 19, 230–269).

Koltsov, Nikolai (1872–1940), prominent zoologist and geneticist, and an outspoken critic of Lysenko. Graduated from Moscow University (1894), then professor there (1895–1911). Also professor at the High Educational School for Women (1903–1918). In Germany, France, and Italy (1897–1900; 1902–1903). Corresponding member (1915), member of the Agricultural Academy (VASKhNIL) (1929). Organized (1917) and directed the Institute of Experimental Biology. In 1939, removed from all posts. Died on December 2, 1940, of a heart attack; the same day his wife committed suicide.

Komarov, Vladimir I. (1916–1954) joined the NKVD in 1938. Investigator at the Special Department (1939–1942), secretary to Head of the Special Department Viktor Abakumov (from 1942). Deputy head of the MGB Department for Investigation of Especially Important Cases (1946–1951). Was involved in the investigation of all main cases of that period. Arrested in 1951 after the fall of Abakumov and tried together with Abakumov and his men. Shot on December 19, 1954. Not rehabilitated (Stolyarov, *Palachi i zhertvy*, pp. 26–27; Petrov, "Sudy protiv chlenov NKVD-MGB," pp. 430–431).

Komarov, Vladimir L. (1869–1945), botanist. Graduated from St. Petersburg University (1894), then professor there (1898–1934). Corresponding member (1914), academician (1920). Vice president (1930–1936), president of the academy (1936–1945); also president of the All-Union Botanical Society (1940–1945) and honorary president of the Geographical Society (1940–1945). Deputy of the USSR Supreme Soviet (1938–1945). Stalin Prize (1941 and 1942), Hero of Socialist Labor (1943).

Kondratiev, Nikolai (1892–1938), economist. Assistant minster of food supply in the Provisional Government (1918). Director of the Market Institute within the USSR Commissariat of Finances (1920–1928). Arrested on June 19, 1930, and on January 26, 1932, sentenced to 8 years' imprisonment as the alleged leader of the Labor Peasant Party (TKP). Imprisoned in the town of Suzdal. On September 17, 1938, resentenced to death on charges of organizing the TKP, directing its activity, and the counterrevolutionary activity in Suzdal Prison. Shot immediately after the trial. Rehabilitated in 1963.

Kovalev, Sergei (b. 1930), biophysicist and human rights activist. Graduated from Moscow State University (1954). At the Belozersky Laboratory of Bioorganic Chemistry of Moscow University. Joined the Initiative Group for Human Rights in Moscow (May 1969). An editor of the underground magazine *Chronicle of Current Events* (1971–1974). Expelled from the university. On December 28, 1974, arrested on the charge of alleged "anti-Soviet agitation and propaganda" (Article 70 of the Soviet Criminal Code). In December 1975 tried and convicted to 7 years' imprisonment in a labor camp and 3 years of exile. Spent the term in Perm labor camps and Chistopol Prison. Later lived in the town of Kalinin (now Tver). In 1986 returned to Moscow and joined the Moscow Helsinki Group. In 1990, elected deputy of the Russian Federation Supreme Council (1990–1993) and then lower State Duma chamber of the Russian Parliament. Chaired the Committee on Human Rights of the Supreme Council (1990–1993) and Commission on Human Rights under the Russian president (1993–1996). His furious fight against human rights violations during the Chechen war (1994–1996) resulted in his dismissal. Beginning in 1990, co-chairman of Memorial. In 2001, was still a member of the Duma, representing the liberal Union of the Rightists (SPS).

Kravchenko, Valentin (1906–1956) joined the NKVD in 1937. An engineer at the NKVD Second Special Department (1938–1939), head of the NKVD Special Technical Bureau (1939–1941), head of the NKVD/MVD Fourth Special Department (1941–1947; 1949–1953) (Petrov and Skorkin, *Kto rukovodil NKVD*, p. 249).

Kruglov, Sergei (1907–1977), Communist Party and MVD figure. In the Central Committee (1931–1934), then in 1938 joined the NKVD. Deputy NKVD commissar (1939–1941), at different positions in the army and NKVD (1941–1943), first deputy NKVD commissar (1943–1945), NKVD/MVD commissar/minister (1945–53), first deputy MVD minister (March–June 1953), MVD minister (1953–1956). In 1956, demoted to deputy minister of construction of hydroelectric stations. Deputy head of a regional industry office (1957–1958). Retired in 1958. In 1945, awarded with an honorary British knighthood (Petrov and Skorkin, *Kto rukovodil NKVD*, pp. 251–252).

Krupskaya, Nadezhda (1869–1939), Lenin's wife, secretary, and coworker. The daughter of a tsarist official. Married Lenin in 1897 in order to accompany him to exile to Siberia. After Lenin's death in 1924, held nonimportant Party positions. Silenced by Stalin during the purges of the 1930s. In 1938, did not defend Bukharin, who appealed to her during his show trial. Died in 1939, possibly from poisoning.

Krylenko, Nikolai (1885–1938), prosecutor and organizer of the Soviet court system. Joined the Bolshevik Party in 1904. The Bolshevik Party's representative in the Duma (1913), and then in exile to Switzerland. Returned in 1917. A member of the Petrograd Military Revolutionary Committee, supreme commander in chief and political commissar for military affairs. Russian chief prosecutor of the Supreme Tribunal (March 1918), chairman of the Economic Department of the VCheKa (1920). The principal prosecutor in the major trials of the 1920s. The Russian Federation commissar for justice (1931–1933), the USSR commissar for justice (1936–1938). Arrested on February 1, 1938, and tried and executed on July 29, 1938. Rehabilitated in 1955.

Krzhizhanovsky, Gleb (1872–1959), Party and Soviet science figure. A Party member from 1893, a Central Committee member (1924–1939). Head of the first energy committee, Goelro (State Energy Committee) (1920–1925), and then Glavenergo (1930–1932), of the State Planning Committee, Gosplan (1925–1930), deputy commissar of education (1932–1936). Academician (1929), director of the Academy Institute of Energy (1930–1959), vice president of the academy (1929–1939).

Ksenofontov, Ivan (1884–1926), Party and VCheKa figure. Joined the Party in 1903. One of the founder-members of the VCheKa Collegium, deputy chairman of the VCheKa (1919–1921), chairman of the VCheKa and other tribunals. Head of Stalin's Private Secretariat (1921–1926) (Leggett, *The CHEKA*, p. 452).

Kuibyshev, Valerian (1883–1935), Party figure. President of the Party Control Commission (1923–1935), Politburo member (1926–1935), vice chairman of the USSR Council of Commissars, chairman of the Committee for Help to Scientists (1931–1935).

Kurchatov, Igor (1903–1960), physicist and science administrator. Graduated from Simferopol Crimean University (1923). Head of the Nuclear Physics Laboratory at the Academy Physical-Technical Institute (from 1927). From 1943, scientific director of the Soviet atomic project. Academician (1943). From 1946, head of Laboratory No. 2 (later the Academy Institute of Atomic Energy [IAE]). The Laboratory/IAE produced the first Soviet atomic bomb in 1949, and in 1953, a thermonuclear (hydrogen) bomb. In 1948, joined the Communist Party. Hero of Socialist Labor (1949, 1951, and 1954).

Landau, Lev (1908–1968), physicist. Graduated from Leningrad University (1927). Until 1932, at Leningrad Physical-Technical Institute, then at Kharkov Physical-Technical Institute. From 1937, head of the theoretical group at the Institute of Physical Problems. In 1938–1939, imprisoned. Released after the personal intervention of Pyotr Kapitsa. Academician (1946), Hero of Socialist Labor (1954), Nobel Prize for physics (1962) (Holloway, *Stalin and the Bomb*, p. 450).

Lapshin, Yevgenii (1900–1956) joined the NKVD in 1937. Acting head of the NKVD Second Special Department (September–March 1939), head of the new NKVD Second Special Department (Department of Operational Equipment) (1939–1941). For the next 5 months, head of the NKGB Fourth Department. From July 31, 1941, until April 12, 1943, head of the NKVD Second Special Department (July 1941–1943), head of NKGB/MGB Department "B" (Operational Equipment) (1943–1946). From October 1946, head of the city of Tula MGB regional branch. Later transferred back to Moscow (Petrov and Skorkin, *Kto rukovodil NKVD*, p. 265).

Lenin (pseudonym of **Ul'yanov**), **Vladimir** (1870–1924), founder of the Bolshevik Party. Joined the Marxist movement in 1888. Graduated from the Law School of Kazan University (1891). A public defender in St. Petersburg (1893–1995). Arrested in 1895 and spent the next 15 months in jail; exiled to Siberia for three years. Left Russia (1900) and lived mainly in Switzerland. In 1903 became the leader of the Bolsheviks. Returned to Russia in November 1905, after the Russian Revolution of 1905 (January 1905). Proclaimed the theory of the "hegemony" of the proletariat in the democratic revolution, with the goal of establishing a "revolutionary democratic dictatorship of the proletariat and the peasantry." Abroad from 1907–1917. Published his main works on the analysis of the capitalist economy and system. In April 1917, German authorities permitted him and his closest lieutenants to pass through Germany to neutral Sweden and then on to Russia with the hope that his presence would destabilize Russia and help Germany win the war. In November 1917, inspired the Bolshevik coup. The first chairman of the Council of Commissars (1917–1924). By spring of 1922, fell seriously ill (had syphilis). Died on January 22, 1924.

Leonov, Aleksandr (1905–1954) joined the OGPU in 1926. Head of the Sixth (Investigation) Department of the Main Directorate of the Military Counterintelligence (SMERSH) of the Defense Commissariat (1943–1946), then of the MGB Department for Investigation of Especially Important Cases (1946–1951). Arrested in 1951 along with Abakumov and his men. On December 19, 1954, condemned to death and shot after the trial.

Levitsky, Grigory (1878–1942), cytogeneticist. Head of the Cytology Department at Vavilov's All-Union Plant Breeding Institute (VIR) (1925–1941). Corresponding member (1932). Introduced the scientific term "karyotype" to describe a species-specific complex of chromosomes. Arrested in 1932, 1937, and 1941. Died in prison in 1942. In 1945, members of his family were also arrested.

Likhachev, Mikhail (1913–1954) joined the NKVD in 1937. Deputy head of the Investigation Department of the Main SMERSH Directorate (1943–1946), then of the MGB Department for Investigation of Especially Important Cases (1946–1951). In 1946, also headed a group of SMERSH officers in charge of controlling Soviet investigators and prosecutors at the Nuremberg Trial. Participated in the organization of several show trials in Moscow and abroad, including the anti-Semitic Slansky trial in Prague in 1949. Arrested on July 8, 1951, along with Abakumov, Leonov and Komarov. On December 19, 1954, shot after the trial.

Lozovsky (or **Dorizo**), **Solomon** (1878–1952), state figure. Joined the Bolshevik Party in 1901. General secretary of the Profintern (Red International of Professional Unions) (1921–1937), director of the state publishing house Goslitizdat (1937–1939), and deputy foreign commissar/minister (1939–1946), deputy head (1941–1945) and then head (1945–1948) of the Soviet information agency Sovinformburo. In 1948, chair of the Department of Foreign Affairs at the High Party School under the Central Committee. Arrested in 1949 as a member of the Jewish Anti-Fascist Committee (JAC) and shot in 1952 after the trial against the JAC.

Lunacharsky, Anatolii (1875–1933), Party figure. Joined the Party in 1898. Arrested and imprisoned during the Russian Revolution of 1905. In 1909, joined the writer Maxim Gorky in Capri, Italy. In March 1917, joined Leon Trotsky and Lenin in Russia. Soviet commissar of education (1917–1929). Saved many historic buildings and works of art from destruction. Wrote many plays (three were published in 1923 in English). Personal friend of Bernard Shaw, Bertolt Brecht, and other famous writers. Chairman of the Scientific Council of the Central Executive Committee (1929–1930). Academician (1930). Director of the Institute of Russian Literature (Pushkin's House) (1932–1933). In 1933, appointed Soviet ambassador to Spain. Died soon after.

Luppol, Ivan (1896–1943), historian and Marxist philosopher. Academician (1939), director of the Institute of World Literature. In 1942, a cell mate of Nikolai Vavilov in Saratov Prison. Died in a labor camp in Mordovia in 1943 (Tolz, *Russian Academicians*, p. 43; Vavilov and Rokityansky, "Golgotha," p. 833).

Lysenko, Trofim (1898–1976), agronomist and author of pseudotheories on the inheritance of acquired characters. Graduated from Kiev Agricultural Institute (Ukraine) (1925). Member of the Ukrainian Academy of Sciences (1934), of the Agricultural Academy (VASKhNIL) (1935), and of the USSR Academy (1939). Director of the Odessa Institute of Genetics and Breeding (1936–1938), and the Academy Institute of Genetics (1940–1965); president of VASKhNIL (1938–1956; 1961–1962), and head of the Genetics Department of the Timiryazev Agricultural Academy in Moscow (1948–1965). Editor of the journals *Vernalization* (1935–1941) and *Agrobiology* (1946–1965). Deputy head of the USSR Supreme Soviet (1938–1956). Head of the Lenin Hills Experimental Station of the Academy of Sciences (1966–1976). Stalin Prize (1941, 1943, and 1949), Hero of Socialist Labor (1945).

Mairanovsky, Grigory (1899–1964), biochemist and poison expert. Graduated from Tbilisi University (1919) and from the Second Moscow Medical Institute (1923). Head of secret laboratories in the Bach Institute of Biochemistry (1928–1935) and in the All-Union Institute of Experimental Medicine (1935–1938), head of Laboratory No. 1 within the NKVD/NKGB (1938–1946). Used prisoners condemned to death for experiments with poisons. In the late 1940s, participated in political assassinations as a member of Pavel Sudoplatov's special team. Arrested on December 12, 1951, in connection with Abakumov's arrest. Tried on February 14, 1953; condemned to 10 years' imprisonment. Kept in Vladimir Prison. In 1953, 1957, and 1958, brought to Moscow and interrogated about his experiments during investigations in the Beria, Eitingon, and Sudoplatov cases. In 1961, after release from prison, was ordered to leave Moscow for Makhachkala (near the city of Baku), where he headed a small biochemical laboratory.

Malenkov, Georgii (1902–1988), Party figure. Joined the Party in 1920, became Stalin's secretary (1928–1930). First secretary of the Moscow Regional Committee (1930–1934), head of the Personnel Department of the Orgburo in the Central Committee (1934–1939), one of five secretaries of the Central Committee (1939–1946; 1948–1953), head of the Directorate of Cadres of the Committee (1939–1946), member of the State Defense Committee (1941–1945). Member of the Politburo and deputy chair of the USSR Council of Ministers, Sovmin (1946–1955). Before Zhdanov's death in 1948, was his rival within the Politburo; viewed as Stalin's successor. After Stalin's death, chair

(1953–1955) and then deputy chair (1955–1957) of the Sovmin. In 1957, dismissed by Khrushchev and demoted to director of a hydroelectrical station in Siberia. In 1961, expelled from the Communist Party (Naumov and Sigachev, *Lavrentii Beria*, p. 462; Hahn, Weiner G., *Postwar Soviet Politics: The Fall of Zhdanov and the Defeat of Moderation, 1946–53* [Ithaca: Cornell University Press, 1982], pp. 34–51; 104–113, 156–160; Ra'anan, Gavriel D., *International Policy Formation in the USSR: Factional "Debates" During the Zhdanovshchina* [Hamden, CT: Archon, 1983], pp. 12–24).

Meister, Georgii (1873–1943), plant breeder, director of the Saratov Agricultural Experimental Station and chair of the Genetics and Selection Department at Saratov Agricultural Institute (1923–1937). Member of the Agricultural Academy (VASKhNIL) (1935). In 1937, vice president and then acting president of the VASKhNIL. The main proponent of the agreement of geneticists and agronomists with Lysenko. Arrested in 1938 and later shot.

Men'shagin, Boris (1902–1984), lawyer and the longest Soviet political prisoner kept in solitary confinement. Born in the city of Smolensk into a lawyer's family. In 1919, joined the Red Army. In 1929, refused to join the Bolshevik Party and resigned. Graduated and became a lawyer in Moscow (1931–1937). In 1937–1941, defended people arrested on political charges in Smolensk. After the conquest of Smolensk by Nazi troops in 1941, was appointed burgomaster. In April 1943, witnessed the discovery of a mass grave of Polish officers killed in 1940 by the NKVD near the village of Katyn. In late 1943, escaped with his family to Karlovy Vary (Chechoslovakia), where he was detained by mistake by the Americans for a few weeks. In search of his family, went back to the Soviets not knowing that his family had successfully escaped to the Americans. On May 28, 1945, was arrested by the Second SMERSH Directorate, transferred to Moscow and kept in Lubyanka Prison. Refused to testify at the Nuremberg Trial (1946) in favor of the Soviet version of the Katyn Massacre. On September 12, 1951, sentenced to 25 years' imprisonment. From November 30, 1951, in Vladimir Prison, where was kept under No. 29 until 1954. Spent 23 years in solitary confinement. Released on May 28, 1970, and assigned to live in remote state-supported nursing homes in northern Russia under constant KGB surveillance.

Menzhinsky, Vyacheslav (1874–1934), VCheKa/OGPU figure. Like Dzerzhinsky, was of Polish origin. Deputy commissar (1917–1919), then commissar of finances. Deputy head (1919), then head (1920–1922) of the VCheKa Special Department (OO), head of the GPU Secret-Operational Department (1922–1923), first deputy chairman (1923–1926), then chairman of the OGPU (1926–1934) (Gerson, Lennard D., *The Secret Police in Lenin's Russia* (Philadelphia: Temple University Press, 1976), p. 315; Leggett, *The CHEKA*, pp. 264–275; Kokurin and Petrov, *Lubyanka*, p. 11).

Merkulov, Vsevolod (1895–1953) joined the Georgian CheKa/OGPU (1921–1932), then a Georgian Communist Party functionary (1934–1938). Deputy head (1938), then head (from December 17, 1938) of the NKVD Main

State Security Directorate (GUGB); also head of the GUGB Third Department and first deputy NKVD commissar. NKGB commissar (February–July 1941), first deputy NKVD commissar again (July 1941–April 1943), and NKGB commissar/MGB minister (1943–May 1946), head of the Main Directorate of the Soviet Property Abroad (Germany) (1947–1950), minister of state control (1950–1953). Arrested on August 19, 1953, and tried together with Beria. Shot on December 23, 1953. Not rehabilitated (Petrov and Skorkin, *Kto rukovodil NKVD*, pp. 296–297).

Meshik, Pavel (1910–1953) joined the OGPU in 1932. Deputy head of a division within the OGPU/GUGB Economic Department (1933–1935), then in different departments. Head of the Investigation Division of the NKVD Economic Department (1939–1940), head of the NKVD Economic Directorate (1941–1943), deputy head of the SMERSH Main Directorate (1943–1945). In 1945, in Poland. Deputy head of the First Main Directorate under the Council of Commissars/Ministers (in charge of the Soviet atomic project) (1945–1953). Ukrainian MVD minister (March–June 1953). Arrested on June 30, 1953, tried together with Beria and Merkulov, condemned to death on December 23, 1953, and shot. Not rehabilitated (Petrov and Skorkin, *Kto rukovodil NKVD*, p. 297).

Michurin, Ivan (1855–1935), amateur agronomist and plant breeder. Attempted to prove the inheritance of acquired characteristics by developing varieties of fruit trees and berries. Honorary member of the Agricultural Academy (VASKhNIL) and of the Academy of Sciences (1935). Lysenko named his own pseudotheories the "Michurinist biology."

Mikhoels (Vovsi), Solomon (1890–1948), Jewish actor, theater director, and teacher; director of the Moscow State Jewish Theater (1929–1948). Chairman of the Jewish Anti-Fascist Committee (JAC) (1942–1948). In 1943, together with the JAC Secretary Isaak Fefer, visited the United States, Canada, Mexico, and Great Britain, where they lectured about Nazi atrocities and the JAC activity. On January 13, 1948, killed together with an MGB agent, Golubov-Potapov, on Stalin's personal order in the city of Minsk (Belorussia). On the order of MGB Minister Abakumov, First Deputy MGB Minister Sergei Ogol'tsov, and Head of the Belorussian MGB Lavrentii Tsanava, the assassination was staged as a truck accident. The killing of Mikhoels triggered the official anti-Semitic campaign, which ended up as a case against the JAC members and later, as the Doctors' Plot case.

Mikoyan, Anastas (1895–1978), Party and state figure. Joined the Bolsheviks in 1915. Commissar of inner and foreign trade (1926–1930), commissar of supply (1930–1934), commissar of food industry (1934–1938), and commissar/minister of foreign trade (1938–1949). Deputy chairman of the Council of Commisars/Ministers (1937–1955), member of the State Committee of Defense (1942–1945), minister of trade (1953), first deputy chair of the Council of Ministers (1955–1964), chairman of the Supreme Council (1964–1965), and member of the Presidium of the Supreme Council (1965–1974). A Polit-buro/Presidium member (1935–1966). Retired in 1974.

Mironov, Lev (1895–1938; pseudonym of **Lev Kagan**) joined the OGPU Economic Directorate in 1924. Head of this directorate (1931–1934), then head of the GUGB Economic Department (1934–1936), head of the Third (Counterintelligence) Department of the Main State Security Directorate (GUGB) (1936–1937). Arrested on June 14, 1937, and shot on August 29, 1938. Not rehabilitated (Petrov and Skorkin, *Kto rukovodil NKVD*, pp. 300–301).

Mitin, Mark (1901–1987), Marxist philosopher. Joined the Communist Party in 1919. Graduated from the Institute of Red Professors (a special Party college) (1929), director of the Marx and Engels Institute in Moscow (1939–1944). Chief editor of the Party magazine *Under the Banner of Marxism* (1930–1944), member of the Central Committee (1939–1944; 1950–1956). Academician (1939), deputy director of the Academy Institute of Philosophy, member of the Academy Presidium (1939–1946). Took part in the "discussion" on genetics in 1939 and in the events of 1948. Stalin Prize (1943).

Molotov (Skryabin), Vyacheslav (1890–1986), Party and state figure, a Politburo member (1926–1957). Secretary of the Central Committee of the Ukrainian Communist Party (1920–1921), secretary of the Central Committee (1921–1930), first secretary of the Moscow Committee (1928–1929), chairman of the Council of People's Commissars (Sovnarkom) (1930–1941), Foreign commissar/minister (1939–1949), deputy chairman of the State Committee of Defense (1941–1945), deputy chairman (1941–1942; 1946–1953) and then first deputy chairman (1942–1946; 1953–1957) of the Sovnarkom/Council of Ministers, foreign minister (1953–1956), minister of state control (1956–1957), ambassador to Mongolia (1957–1960), head of a group of Soviet representatives at the International Agency on Atomic Energy (1960–1962). In 1962, was forced to retire and was expelled from the Party. In 1984, restored as a Party member. Actively joined with Stalin, Yezhov, and Beria in drafting numerous arrest lists and signing death sentences during the years of the Great Terror (1936–1938).

Muralov, Aleksandr (1877–1937), Party and state figure. Commissar (1923–1929), then deputy commissar (1929–1937) of agriculture. In 1935 replaced Vavilov as president of the Agricultural Academy. Arrested in 1937 because of his brother, Nikolai (1887–1937), also a Party functionary and a victim of the Pyatakov Show Trial (January 23–30, 1937). Nikolai was shot on February 1, 1937, before Aleksandr. Both brothers were rehabilitated (Conquest, *The Great Terror*, pp. 147–167; Tikhanova, V., ed., *Rasstrel'nye spiski. Vypusk 1: Donskoe kladbishche, 1934–1940* [The Lists of the Executed. Issue 1: Donskoe Cemetery, 1934–1940] (Moscow: Memorial, 1993), pp. 78 and 81 (in Russian).

Muromtsev, Sergei (1898–1960), microbiologist, worked in a secret NKVD/NKGB laboratory; experimented on humans. Graduated from the Medical Faculty of the First Moscow University (1923); a veterinarian scientist. In 1931, one of the organizers of the centralized State Control System of Veterinarian Preparations. In 1938, joined the NKVD; headed a group working on bacteriological toxins as a part of Mairanovsky's laboratory. Also worked on a special method of preparation of vaccines for animals (1934–1943). In 1948, supported Lysenko and was one of the appointed academicians to the Agricultural Academy. Acting director of the Gamaleya Institute of Epidemiology and Microbiology within the Medical Academy (1956–1960). Due to the opposition at this institute and within the Medical Academy, not approved as director. Stalin Prize (1946).

Nasonov, Dmitrii (1895–1957), cytophysiologist. Corresponding member (1948) and a member of the Medical Academy (1945). Head of the Cytology Laboratory at the All-Union Institute of Experimental Medicine (VIEM) (1932–1945), head of the General Morphology Department at the VIEM (1945–1948), director of the VIEM (1948–1950), chair of the Department of Comparative Physiology at Leningrad University (1945–1948). Lost this position because of his opposition to Lysenko. Head of a small laboratory on general cell physiology at the Academy Zoological Institute (1951–1953). In 1954–1955, this laboratory became the Academy Institute of Cytology (IC) (formally established in 1957). Directed this institute until his death in 1957.

Nikolaev-Zhurid, Nikolai (1897–1940) joined the Special Department of the Red Army in 1919. Head of the Leningrad NKVD Regional Branch (1935–1936), then head of the Second (Counterintelligence) Department (1936–1937) and of the Fifth (Special) Department (1937–1938) of the NKVD Main State Security Directorate (GUGB). Arrested in 1938, tried and shot in 1940. Not rehabilitated (Petrov and Skorkin, *Kto rukovodil NKVD*, pp. 318–319).

Ogol'tsov, Sergei (1900–1977) joined the CheKa in 1919. First deputy NKGB/MGB commissar/minister (1945–1952). Responsible (the curator) for the MGB Department for Investigation of Especially Important Cases (1946–1951). After Abakumov's arrest, acting minister (July–August 1951), Uzbek MGB minister (February–December 1952), first deputy MGB minister (December 1952–March 1953). On March 11, 1953, dismissed and on April 3, 1953, arrested on the charge of organizing the assassination of Solomon Mikhoels. Released on August 8, 1953, and dismissed from the MGB (1954). In 1959 deprived of his lieutenant general rank (Petrov and Skorkin, *Kto rukovodil NKVD*, p. 323; Naymov and Sigachev, *Lavrentii Beria*, pp. 471–472).

Oldenburg, Sergei (1863–1934), orientalist. After graduating from the Oriental Languages Department of St. Petersburg University (1885), in libraries in France and England. From 1894, professor of Indian language and literature at St. Petersburg University. Helped to organize expeditions to Tibet and Chinese Turkestan. Extraordinary academician (1903). From 1904, permanent secretary of the academy (1904–1929). Minister of education in the Provisional Government (July–August 1917). In September–October 1919, arrested as a member of the Kadet Party. In 1929, dismissed as permanent secretary. Director of the new Academy Institute of Oriental Studies (1930–1934), chairman of the Commission for the Study of the History of the Academy (1932–1934) (Tolz, *Russian Academicians*, pp. 108–122).

Oparin, Aleksandr (1894–1980), biochemist and author of the theory of the origin of life. Graduated from Moscow University (1917). In 1922, introduced his concept of a primordial organism arising in a brew of already formed organic compounds at a meeting of the Russian Botanical Society. In 1924, published his theory in Russian; the English version was published in 1938 *(The Origin of Life)*. Corresponding member (1939), academician (1946). Director of the Bach Institute of Biochemistry (1946–1980), secretary academician of the Academy Division of Biological Sciences (1949–1956). From the late 1940s to early 1950s, actively supported pseudotheories of Trofim Lysenko and Olga Lepeshinskaya. Organized the first international conference on the origin of life in Moscow (1957). In 1950, was appointed a member of the Soviet Committee in Defense of Peace and a member of the International Council for Peace. Vice president of the International Federation of Scientists (1952; 1962). Awarded many Soviet decorations.

Orbeli, Leon (1878–1958), physiologist. Graduated from the Military-Medical Academy (MMA) in St. Petersburg (1904). Academician Pavlov's assistant at the Institute of Experimental Medicine (1907–1920); also, in Germany and Britain (1907–1920). Head of the Physiology Department at the Leningrad Medical Institute (1920–1931), and of the Physiological Department at the MMA (1925–1950); also director of the MMA (1943–1950). Director of the Institute of Physiology (1936–1950), the Institute of Evolutionary Physiology and Pathology of Higher Nervous Activity (1939–1950), and the Institute of Evolutionary Physiology (1956–1958) (all within the Academy of Sciences). Corresponding member (1932), academician (1935), member of the Armenian Academy of Sciences (1943) and the Medical Academy (1944). Secretary academician of the Academy Biology Division (1939–1948), and first vice president of the academy (1942–1946). Head of the All-Union Physiology Society (1937–1950). Forced to make many compromises, especially regarding Lysenko. Stalin Prize (1944), Hero of Socialist Labor (1945), four Lenin Order awards; colonel general (1944).

Ovakimyan, Gaik (1898–?) joined the OGPU in 1931 while a graduate student at the Bauman Higher Technical School in Moscow. Assigned to the Foreign Intelligence; deputy head of the OGPU Scientific Intelligence (1933). Sent to the United States under cover as an engineer for the American-Soviet Trading Corporation (Amtorg). Undertook study for a doctorate in chemistry at New York University. Arrested by the FBI in 1941 during a meeting with an agent. Allowed to return to Moscow. In December 1943, as head of the American Department of the First Directorate (under the alias "General Alexander Ossipov"), together with the head of the First NKGB Directorate, Pavel Fitin, took part in the negotiations with the head of the Office of Strategic Services (OSS), General William J. Donovan, about possible cooperation of the NKGB with the OSS. Left the MGB in 1947 for full-time scientific work (Haynes and

Klehr, *Venona*, pp. 392–393; Weinstein and Vassiliev, *The Haunted Wood*, pp. 240–248).

Ovchinnikov, Yurii (1934–1988), bioorganic chemist. The youngest academician (elected in 1970) and the youngest vice president of the academy (1971–1988). From 1971, head of the Section of Chemical-Technological and Biological Sciences of the Academy Presidium. Directed the huge Academy Institute of Bioorganic Chemistry and was a leading proponent of using molecular biology and genetics methods for creating new types of biological warfare. Also a member of the Central Committee.

Panyushkin, Aleksandr (1905–1974) joined the Far Eastern OGPU branch in 1927. From 1938, in Moscow. Ambassador to China (1939–1944), first deputy head of the International Information Department within the Central Committee (CC) (1944–1947), chief secretary of the Committee of Information (April–November 1947), ambassador to the United States (1947–1952), and again to China (1952–1953), head of the First Main MVD Directorate (July 1953–1954), head of the First Main KGB Directorate (1954–1955). Later headed the Personnel Department of the Diplomatic and CC Foreign Economy Directorate. Retired in 1973 (Petrov and Skorkin, *Kto rukovodil NKVD*, pp. 333–334).

Parin, Vasilii (1903–1971), physiologist. Graduated from the Medical Faculty of Perm University (1925); later in the Physiology Department of this faculty (1928–1932). Chair of the Normal Physiology Department at the Medical Institute in Sverdlovsk (now Yekaterinburg) (1933–1940), rector of the First Moscow Medical Institute (from 1941), and deputy commissar of health (in charge of science) and plenipotentiary of the Commissariat of Health in charge of anti-epidemic actions (from 1942). A member (1944) and secretary academician of the Medical Academy (1944–1947; 1957–1960). Wrote the statutes of this academy. Arrested in 1947 in connection with the Roskin-Klyueva "case." Sentenced on April 8, 1948 to 25 years' imprisonment as an "American spy." Kept in Vladimir Prison. Released in November 1953. Head of the Physiology Laboratory at the Institute of Therapy (1954–1956), director of the Institute of Normal and Pathologic Physiology (1960–1971) and the Institute of Medical-Biological Problems (1965–1969). Academician (1966), vice president of the Medical Academy (1967–1971). Party member from 1939.

Pavlov, Ivan (1849–1936), physiologist, Nobel Prize (1904) winner, created the theory of conditional reflex and pioneering studies relating human behavior to the nervous system. Graduated from St. Petersburg University (1875) and the Military-Medical Academy in St. Petersburg (1879). Head of the Physiology Department there (1895–1924), director of the Institute of Experimental Medicine (1891–1936), and director of the Academy Institute of Physiology (1925–1936). Full academician (1907). An outspoken critic of the Bolsheviks. Unfortunately, at the end of Pavlov's life and especially after his death in 1936, the Soviet propaganda presented him as a scientist who became a supporter of the Bolshevik regime.

Pervukhin, Mikhail (1904–1978), state figure. Joined the Party in 1919. Commissar (minister) of the Electric Power Industry (1939–1940; 1953–1954), deputy chairman of the Council of Commissars/Ministers (Sovmin) (1940–1944; 1950–1953; 1953–1955), first deputy chairman of the Sovmin (1955–1957), minister of chemical industry (1942–1950), and minister of the medium machine building (i.e., atomic industry) (April–July 1952). Chair of the State Committee on Foreign Economic Affairs of the Sovmin (1957–1958), then ambassador to East Germany (1958–1963). Head of a directorate within the People's Industrial Council (1963–1965) and head of a department within Gosplan (1965–1978) (Naumov and Sigachev, *Lavrentii Beria*, p. 474).

Peters, Yakov (1886–1938), a founder-member of the VCheKa/OGPU Collegium. Chairman of the VCheKa (July–August 1917). During the late 1920s–1930s, chairman and later a member of the Party's Central Control Commission, collegium member of the Commissariat for Workers' and Peasants' Inspection and its head for the Moscow Region, first deputy chairman of the Moscow City Soviet and of the Moscow Regional Soviet's Executive Committee. Arrested on November 26, 1937, sentenced to death on April 25, 1938, and shot the same day (Leggett, *The CHEKA*, pp. 267–268; Yeremina and Roginsky, *Rasstrel'nye spiski*, p. 318).

Pitovranov, Yevgenii (1915–?) headed the Second MGB Main Directorate (1946–1951), deputy MGB minister (1951). Arrested after the fall of Abakumov, but released soon in December of 1952. Head of the new First (Foreign Intelligence) MGB Directorate (December 1952–March 1953). Later reduced to deputy head of the Counterintelligence (Second) MVD Directorate. From 1953–1957, at high KGB positions in Germany. Head of the Fourth KGB Directorate (1957–1960), then head of the High School of the KGB (1962–1966). In 1966, transferred to the reserve (Parrish, *The Lesser Terror*, p. 311–312; Naumov and Sigachev, *Lavrentii Beria*, p. 475; Murphy et al., *Battleground Berlin*, pp. 44–45, 463).

Platonov, Sergei (1860–1933), historian. Academician (1920). Director of the Pushkin House in Leningrad, the Institute of Russian Literature, and the Academy Library. Arrested on January 12, 1930, together with two daughters. On August 8, 1931, sentenced to 5-year exile. Died on January 12, 1933, in exile in the city of Samara.

Pokrovsky, Mikhail (1868–1932), historian. Turned to political activity after the Bolshevik Revolution and became the most trusted Party leader in humanitarian sciences. Headed the Communist Academy, Institute of History, Institute of Red Professors, and Society of Marxist Historians, and was a member of the editorial boards of the journals *Marxist History* and *Class Struggle*. Died of cancer in 1932.

Polyansky, Yurii (1904–1993), protozoologist, anti-Lysenkoist. Graduated from Petersburg University. At the Leningrad Pedagogical Institute (from 1928), chair of the Invertebrate Zoology Department (from 1933). Also at the Laboratory of Invertebrate Zoology of the Petergoff Biological Institute within

Leningrad University. Later chair of the Animal Genetics Department of Leningrad University. In 1941, volunteered for the army. Deputy rector, then acting rector of Leningrad University (1945–1948). Dismissed after Lysenko's triumph in 1948. At the Murmansk Biological Station (1949–1955), chair of the Invertebrate Zoology Department at Leningrad University (1955–1982), head of the Academy Laboratory of Cytology of Unicellular Organisms in the Institute of Cytology (1982–1987). Corresponding member of the academy, president of the Society of Protozoologists and honorary member of many international societies. Two Lenin Awards, Hero of Socialist Labor.

Poskrebyshev, Aleksandr (1891–1965), Stalin's secretary. Joined the Bolshevik Party in 1917. Head of the Administration Directorate of the Central Committee (CC) (1922–1923), deputy secretary of the CC (1924–1929), head of the Secret Department of the CC (1929–1934), head of the Special Sector of the CC (i.e., Stalin's secretariat) (1934–1952), secretary of the Presidium and Bureau of the Presidium of the CC (1952–1953). According to Nikita Khrushchev, Stalin "always dictated to Poskrebyshev, and then Poskrebyshev would read it back to him." Helped Yezhov and Malenkov to draw up lists of victims in 1937–1938. Member of the CC (1939–1953). Retired in 1953 (Naumov and Sigachev, *Lavrentii Beria*, p. 477; *Khrushchev Remembers*, pp. 292–293).

Prezent, Isaak (1902–1969), philosopher and Trofim Lysenko's main theoretician. Graduated from the Faculty of Social Sciences of Leningrad University (1926). Joined Lysenko in 1928. Professor of Leningrad University (1931–1937; 1943–1952). Played the main role in staging official "disputes" and conferences against anti-Lysenkoists, the August 1948 Session of the Agricultural Academy (VASKhNIL). Appointed member of the VASKhNIL (1948). Chair of the Department of Darwinism at Moscow and Leningrad Universities and Dean of the Biology Faculty of Moscow University (1948–1952).

Prokofiev, Georgii (1895–1947), lawyer, graduated from Kiev University. Joined the Party in 1919, and the VCheKa Foreign (Intelligence) Department (INO) in 1920. Deputy head of the GPU Abroad Department of the INO (1921–1922) and of the Special Bureau of the OGPU on Deportation of Anti-Soviet Elements of the Intelligentsia (1922). Deputy head of the INO (1922–1924), head of the OGPU Information Department (1924–1926), head of the OGPU Economic Directorate of the OGPU/NKVD (1926–1931), deputy chairman/commissar of the OGPU/NKVD (1932–1936). In 1936, demoted to deputy commissar of communication. Arrested on April 11, 1937, tried and shot on August 14, 1937. Not rehabilitated (Petrov and Skorkin, *Kto rukovodil NKVD*, pp. 349–350).

Pryanishnikov, Dmitrii (1865–1948) botanist, physiologist, and agrochemist, the author of the theory of nitrogen nutrition of plants. Graduated from Moscow University (1887) and Petrovskaya Agricultural and Forest (now Timiryazev Agricultural) Academy (1889). From 1895, chairman of the Agrochemistry Department there. Founded the Scientific Research Institute of Fertilizers and Insecto-Fungicides, and All-Union Institute of Fertilizers,

Agrotechnics, and Soil Studies, now named after him. Academician (1929), and member of the Agricultural Academy (1935). Hero of Socialist Labor, Lenin Prize, two Orders of Lenin. Defended many arrested scientists.

Raikhman, Leonid (1908–1990) joined the OGPU in 1924. Before 1937, in the Leningrad NKVD Branch, then transferred to Moscow. Deputy head of the Second Main MGB (Counterintelligence) Directorate (1946–1951). Arrested in 1951, but released in 1953 on Beria's order. Head of the Control Inspection Office of Following Minister's Orders (March–June 1953). Dismissed from the MVD in 1953. In 1956, tried and found guilty only of "negligence" (Article 193-17a of the Russian Criminal Code at the time). Condemned to 5 years' imprisonment, but was released soon after the trial (Kokurin and Petrov, *Lubyanka*, p. 72; Voitolovskaya, A. L., "Sud nad sledovatelem" [vyderzhka iz knigi 'Po sledam mego pokoleniya'] [Trial against an investigator (an excerpt from the book "Tracing Steps of My Generation")], in Okhotin and Roginsky, *Zven'ya*, vol. 1, pp. 400–429 [in Russian]).

Rapoport, Iosif (1912–1990), geneticist, the discoverer of chemical mutagenesis and an outspoken fighter against Trofim Lysenko. In Koltsov's Institute of Experimental Biology until 1941; volunteered for the army. Defended his dissertation during a short leave from the front. Remained in the army after he lost one eye. In 1948, at the August session of the Agricultural Academy, openly opposed Lysenko. As a retaliation, was expelled from the Party and lost his job. In 1957, Academician Nikolai Semenov invited him to the Academy Institute of Chemical Physics to continue to work on genetics; head of the Department of Chemical Genetics (1965–1990). In 1962, promoted a candidate for Nobel Prize. Was not supported by the Science Department of the Central Committee after he refused to restore his Party membership. Died in a car accident.

Rapoport, Yakov D. (1898–1962) joined the VCheKa in 1918. At the Economic Directorate of the OGPU (1924–1930), head of different construction projects conducted by prisoners of the OGPU/NKVD/MVD labor camps (1930–1956). Retired in 1956. Deputy director of the Gidroproekt Institute (Petrov and Skorkin, *Kto rykovodil NKVD*, pp. 356–357). As a devoted Chekist was praised in Maxim Gorky's *Belomor* (pp. 108–116).

Redens, Stanislav (1892–1940), husband of Anna, sister of Nadezhda Allilueva (Stalin's wife). Joined the VCheKa in 1918, secretary of the VCheKa (1919). After appointments to regional CheKa/GPU offices, assistant to the Council of Commissars and to GPU Chairman Felix Dzerzhinsky (1924–1926). Later at different high positions in the government and the OGPU. Head of the Moscow Regional NKVD (1934–1938). On January 20, 1938, demoted to NKVD commissar of the Kazakh Republic. Arrested on November 22, 1938. On January 21, 1941, sentenced to death and shot on February 12, 1940. Rehabilitated in 1961 (Petrov and Skorkin, *Kto rukovodil NKVD*, pp. 357–358).

Reshetnikov, Stepan (1897–1941?) joined the Economic Directorate of the OGPU in 1931. Head of the Third Department of the NKVD Economic

Directorate (March–October 1940). Later transferred to the NKVD branch in the regional city of Tula. Declared missing in action during the war (Petrov and Skorkin, *Kto rukovodil NKVD*, pp. 359–360).

Rodos, Boris (1905–1956) joined the regional NKVD in the city of Odessa (the Ukraine) in 1933. An investigator and then deputy head of the NKVD/MGB Department for Investigation of Especially Important Cases (1938–1947). Demoted to deputy head of the Crimean Regional MGB (1947–1952). Arrested in 1953, tried and shot in 1956 (Sudoplatov, A., *Tainaya zhizn'*, vol. 2, p. 531).

Roedel, Willy (1897–1947), Nazi figure. During World War I served at the French and Russian fronts. In 1925 joined the NSPD (Nazi Party); Brigade-fuhrer SA. From 1936, served as diplomatic courier for Hans Schroeder, chief of the Personnel Division of the Judenreferat D III within the Abteilung Deutschland (a part of the Nazi German Foreign Ministry in charge of Jewish problems). In July 1944, joined the German legation in Bucharest (Romania) as ambassador's adjutant and head of the Information Department. In August 1944, arrested together with the other members of the legation by the Romanian army. Handed over to the Soviet military and brought to Moscow on September 7, 1944. Died from a heart attack or was murdered in 1947 (Personal Information Form from Politisches Archiv des Auswartigen Amt, Bonn, Germany).

Roskin, Grigory (1892–1964), protozoologist and cytologist. Graduated from the Moscow Commercial Institute and Shanyavsky University. Worked in France; returned to Nikolai Koltsov's laboratory in Moscow in 1913. From 1917, at Koltsov's Institute of Experimental Biology and later, also in the Histological Laboratory of the Zoological Institute within Moscow University. From 1930, chair of the Histology Department of the Biological Faculty of this university. From 1931, worked together with his wife, the microbiologist Nina Klyueva, on the anti-carcinogenous action of the substance cruzin extracted from the parasitic protozoan *Trypanosoma cruzi*. In 1947 Stalin personally named Roskin and Klyueva "anti-patriots." They were tried by a "Court of Honor." Academician Vasilii Parin, who gave a copy of their monograph on cruzin to American colleagues, was imprisoned as an "American spy."

Ryasnoi, Vasilii (1904–1995), a Party functionary, joined the NKVD Main State Security Directorate (GUGB) in 1937. Head of the Gorky Regional NKVD branch (1941–1943), commissar of the Ukrainian NKVD (1943–1946). First deputy NKVD commissar (1946), MVD deputy minister (1947–1952), MGB deputy minister (1952–1953), head of the Second Main MVD Directorate (Counterintelligence) (March–May 1953), head of the Moscow and Moscow Region MVD branch (1953–1956). In 1956, discharged from the MVD. Director of the construction of the Volga–Baltic Sea canal (1956–1958), head of a building department in a road-building company (1956–1988). Retired in 1988 (Kokurin and Petrov, *Lubyanka*, pp. 153–154; Naumov and Sigachev, *Lavrentii Beria*, p. 481).

Ryumin, Mikhail (1913–1954), deputy head of a division within a SMERSH department and then of the Third Main MGB Directorate (Military Counterintelligence) (1945–1947), then at the Department for Investigation of Especially Important Cases (1947–1951), head of this Department and deputy MGB minister (1951–1952). Fired on November 14, 1952, and arrested on March 17, 1953. Tried on June 2–7, 1954, and sentenced to death. Shot in July 1954 (Stolyarov, *Palachi i zhertvy*, pp. 41–43 and 203–204; Naumov and Sigachev, *Lavrentii Beria*, p. 481).

Safonov, Grigory (1904–1973), deputy USSR chief (general) prosecutor (1939–1947), then general prosecutor (1948–1953) (Naumov and Sigachev, *Lavrentii Beria*, p. 482).

Sakharov, Andrei (1921–1989), nuclear physicist and prominent human rights activist. Graduated from Moscow University (1942), and from 1945, at the Academy Physics Institute. Defended his doctoral thesis at age 26; academician at age 32. Recruited into the H-bomb program in 1948; at the secret institute Arzamas-16 (1950–1968). Together with academician Igor Tamm, developed the theoretical basis for controlled thermonuclear fusion. In 1961, opposed Premier Nikita Khrushchev's plan to test a 100-megaton hydrogen bomb. In 1968, published in the West the essays *Progress, Coexistence, and Intellectual Freedom*. In 1980, after his denunciation of the Soviet invasion of Afghanistan, exiled to the closed city of Gorky (now Nizhnii Novgorod) and deprived of his Hero of Socialist Labor awards. In 1984, Sakharov's wife, Elena Bonner, was convicted of anti-Soviet activities and was also confined to Gorky. In December 1986, the Soviet government under Mikhail Gorbachev released Sakharov and Bonner and they returned to Moscow. In April 1989, elected to the Congress of People's Deputies. Died on December 14, 1989, after Gorbachev, who presided the deputies' meeting, interrupted Sakharov's speech. Nobel Prize for Peace (1975).

Sanotsky, Vladimir (1890–?), toxicologist. Graduated from the Military-Medical Academy in Petrograd (1914). From 1925 onward, studied the mechanism of action of toxic substances and methods of treatment of injuries caused by such substances; worked on the pathology caused by radiation. Head of a laboratory, then deputy director, and finally director of the Institute of Pathology and Therapy of Intoxications (1934–1952). Corresponding member of the Medical Academy. Supported Mairanovsky.

Savchenko, Sergei (1904–1966), one of Khrushchev's men. The Ukrainian NKGB/MGB minister (1934–1949), head of the First Main MGB Directorate and deputy MGB minister (1951–1953), deputy head of the Second Main Directorate (March–June 1953). Later transferred to the MVD/KGB Directorate of Construction Troops. In 1955, discharged to the Soviet army reserve "as not corresponding to his position" (Petrov and Skorkin, *Kto rukovodil NKVD*, pp. 371–372).

Sazykin, Nikolai (1910–1985) joined the regional NKVD branch in the city of Stalingrad in 1937. From 1938, in Moscow. NKVD/NKGB commissar of Moldavia (1941), head of the NKVD Third Special Department (1941–1943), head of the NKGB Second Directorate (Counterintelligence) (1943–1944), NKGB plenipotentiary in Estonia (1944–1945), deputy head of Department S (atomic bomb intelligence) of the NKVD/NKGB (1945–1947), assistant to deputy chairman of the USSR Supreme Council Lavrentii Beria (1947–1953). Head of the Fourth (Secret Political) MVD Directorate (1953), head of Special Courses at the Moscow School of High Education for Leading Cadres of the MVD/KGB (1953–1954). Dismissed from the KGB in 1954 because of "the facts discrediting the name of the KGB commanding officer." Worked in the system of the Ministry of Medium Machine Building, i.e., of atomic energy (Petrov and Skorkin, *Kto rukovodil NKVD*, pp. 372–373).

Schmalhausen, Ivan (1884–1963), zoologist and evolutionist. Graduated from Kiev University (1907) and later professor at this university (1912, 1921–1941). Member of the Ukrainian Academy of Sciences (1922) and director of its Zoological Institute in Kiev (1930–1941). Academician (1933) and director of the Academy Institute of Evolutionary Morphology in Moscow (1936–1948), chair of Moscow State University Department of Darwinism (1939–1948). Fired after Lysenko's triumph in 1948. Senior researcher (1948–1955) and head (1955–1960) of the Embryology Laboratory at the Academy Institute of Zoology in Leningrad.

Schwarzman, Lev (1907–1953), journalist and then NKVD/MGB investigator. A secret informer of the OGPU/NKVD from 1930, joined the NKVD in 1937. Deputy head of the NKVD Investigation Department (from 1940). From the mid-1940s to early 1953, deputy head of the MGB Department for Investigation of Especially Important Cases. Worked as a pair with Vladimir Komarov. Arrested in 1953 after Beria's fall, tried and shot on December 23, 1953 (Stolyarov, *Palachi i zhertvy*, pp. 28–31).

Sedov, Lev (or **Leon**) (1906–1938), the son of Leon Trotsky. Actively worked in the Left Opposition headed by his father, a Communist Party faction that tried to withstand Stalin's rising power. In 1933 joined Trotsky in exile to Turkey, then followed him to Norway and Paris. Stayed in Paris after Trotsky left France for Mexico in 1937. In 1936, published a book in which he analyzed Stalin's show trials of 1935–1936 (the English translation: Sedov, Leon, *The Red Book on the Moscow Trial* (London: New Park Publications, 1980). On February 16, 1938, died in a hospital in Paris a few days after an unsuccessful surgical operation. Possibly poisoned.

Semashko, Nikolai (1874–1949), physician and state figure. Commissar of health (1918–1930), later a teacher and a researcher. A member of the All-Union Central Executive Commission.

Semenov, Nikolai (1896–1986), physicist and chemist. Graduated from Petrograd University. At Leningrad Physicotechnical Institute (1920–1931), and from 1931, director of the new Leningrad Institute of Chemical Physics. Later this institute moved to Moscow. Academician (1932). In 1947, joined the Communist Party. Nobel Prize for chemistry (1956) for work on chain reactions performed in the 1920s–1930s (Holloway, *Stalin and the Bomb*, p. 451).

Serebryansky, Yakov (1892–1956; pseudonym of **Yakov Bergman**) joined the VCheKa in 1919. Worked in different countries as an agent and head of terrorist groups (1923–1937). Arrested in 1938 and condemned to death. Pardoned in 1941. From 1941 to 1945, worked in Sudoplatov's department of the NKVD/NKGB (1941–1945), and again under Sudoplatov in the MVD (March–June 1953). Arrested in 1953 and on March 30, 1956, died during an interrogation in Butyrka Prison (Petrov and Skorkin, *Kto rukovodil NKVD*, pp. 380–381).

Serov, Ivan (1905–1990) joined the NKVD in 1939 in Moscow, then NKVD commissar of the Ukraine. First deputy NKGB commissar (1941), deputy commissar/minister of the NKVD/MVD (1941–1947), first deputy MVD minister (1947–1954), KGB chairman (1954–1958), then head of the Military Intelligence (GRU) (1958–1963). Unimportant high military positions (1963–1965) (Petrov, and Skorkin, *Kto rukovodil NKVD*, pp. 380–381).

Shalamov, Varlam (1907–1982), writer. A law student at Moscow University. Arrested in 1929, sentenced to 3 years in the infamous Solovki Camp. In 1937 arrested and sentenced again, spent 5 years in the most inhuman Kolyma camps. In 1943 received an additional 10-year term for "praising the efficiency of the German army" and describing the writer and Nobel laureate Ivan Bunin as a "classic of Russian literature."

Shcherbakov, Aleksei (1901–1945), Party figure. Head of the Department of Culture and Education of the Central Committee (CC) (1935–1937), second secretary of Leningrad Regional Party Committee (1936–1937), first secretary in some regions of Siberia and the Ukraine (1937–1938), first secretary of the Moscow and Moscow Regional Committees and a secretary of the CC (1938–1945), head of the Sovinformburo and the Main Political Directorate of the Red Army (1941–1945), head of the Department of International Information of the CC (1943–1945), a candidate to the Politburo (1941–1945). According to the MGB-created version, was killed by the Jewish "doctors-killers" (Naumov and Sigachev, *Lavrentii Beria*, p. 498).

Shepilov, Dmitrii (1905–1995), jurist, economist, and Party figure. Party member from 1926. Graduated from Moscow University (1926) and from the Institute of Red Professors (1932). Deputy head (1935–1937), then head (1937–1940) of the Section of Agricultural Science in the Central Committee (CC), professor of Economics at the Higher Party School (a college for the Party elite) (1935–1941), head of the Directorate of Agitation and Propaganda of the CC (Agitprop) (1947–1953), member of the Presidium (i.e., the Politburo) and minister of foreign affairs (1956–1957). Dismissed from all posts by Nikita Khrushchev in 1957 (Krementsov, *Stalinist Science*, pp. 304–305).

Shirshov, Pyotr (1905–1953), oceanographer and state figure. From 1929, worked at the Academy Botanical Institute, then at the Academy Arctic Institute. Became famous in 1937–1938 after participating in the expedition of the drifting station Northen Pole. Awarded a Doctor of Sciences degree and a title of a Hero of the Soviet Union. Academician (1939). First deputy head of the Main North Marine Directorate (in charge of transportation of people and goods along the Arctic coast) (1939–1942), commissar/minister of the Marine Fleet (1942–1948). Personally responsible for transportation of prisoners by ships to the worst labor camp system, Dalstroi, in the Far East. In 1946, his own wife was arrested and perished in one of the Dalstroi camps. Director of the Academy Institute of Oceanology (1946–1953). After his death, this institute was named after him. A bay on Franz Josef Land and an underwater ridge in the Bering Sea also bear his name.

Shpigelglass (or **Spigelglass**), **Sergei** (1897–1939), incorrectly named in many sources as **Mikhail** (for instance, Andrew and Gordievsky, *KGB*, p. 138), joined the VCheKa Special Department approximately in 1920. From 1935, deputy head of the NKVD Foreign (Intelligence) Department within the Main State Security Directorate (GUGB). Organized many NKVD operations abroad, including assassinations in Spain during the Spanish Civil War (1936–1939) and in France. In February 1938, succeeded Slutsky as acting head of the NKVD Foreign Department (the GUGB Seventh Department). Arrested and shot in 1939.

Shumsky, Aleksandr (1890–1946), Party figure and Stalin's victim. Joined the Ukrainian Bolshevik Party in 1920. Member of the Comintern Executive Committee, head of the Ukrainian Legation in Warsaw (Poland) (1922–1924), the Ukrainian commissar of Education (1924–1933). In January 1933, accused of Ukrainian nationalism and arrested. Exiled to Saratov, where he was killed in 1946 (Sudoplatov, A., *Tainaya zhizn'*, p. 550).

Sisakyan, Norair (1907–1966), biochemist and Lysenkoist. Corresponding member (1955), academician (1960). Secretary academician of the Academy Biology Division (1959), chief scientific secretary of the academy (1960–1966). In 1956, elected a member and vice president of the International Astronautical Academy. President of the Thirteenth UNESCO General Assembly (1964–1966).

Slutsky, Abram (1898–1938) joined the VCheKa in 1920 in Turkestan (Central Asia). At the Economic Directorate of the OGPU in Moscow in 1926. From 1929, at the Foreign (Intelligence) Department; head of this department from 1935. Was poisoned on February 17, 1938 (Petrov and Skorkin, *Kto rukovodil NKVD*, pp. 383–384).

Speransky, Aleksei (1888–1961), pathologist. Worked with Academician Pavlov (1923–1928). Head of the Experimental Department at the Institute of Surgical Neuropathy in Leningrad (1926–1928), the Department of Pathophysiology at the Leningrad Institute of Experimental Medicine (1928–1934), and the Department of General Pathology at the All-Union Institute of Experimental Medicine (VIEM) in Moscow (1934–1945). Director of the Academy Institute of General and Experimental Pathology (1945–1954), head of the Department of General Pathology of the Institute of Normal and Pathological

Physiology (1954–1961). Academician (1939), and member of the Medical Academy (1944). In 1950 was among those physiologists who were criticized by the Lysenkoists. However, supported Mairanovsky.

Stalin (pseudonym of **Dzhugashvili), Joseph** (1879–1953), secretary general of the Bolshevik Party (1922–1953), premier of the Soviet state (1941–1953), a ruthless dictator. From 1894–1899, in a theological school in Georgia. Joined the Party in 1898, and between 1902 and 1913 was arrested seven times for revolutionary activity, undergoing repeated imprisonment and exile. In 1907, participated in a robbery of a bank in Tiflis (Tbilisi) on order to "expropriate" funds for the Bolshevik Party. A Central Committee member (1912–1913, 1917–1953), and a Politburo member (1919–1953). From April 1922, general secretary of the Party, and succeeded Lenin in January 1924. Honorary academician (1939). In May 1941 appointed himself chairman of the Council of Commissars. During World War II, from June 1941 until May 1945, headed the State Defense Committee.

Steinberg, Matus (1904–?), NKVD/MGB agent. Born near Odessa (then Romanian territory) and from 1923, lived in Belgium and France. In 1924, joined the Belgian and then French Communist Parties. Served in the Red Army (1926–1927). From 1928, at the GPU, then NKVD Foreign Department. In 1957, he and his accomplice, Elsa Shukter (1904–?), were arrested in a Moscow hotel, the Balchug, in connection with the revolt in Hungary in 1956 (details are unknown). On March 14, 1958, they were sentenced to 10 and 5 years' imprisonment, respectively. Kept in Vladimir Prison. Shukter was released in January 1961, and Steinberg, in January 1966 (Steinberg's and Shukter's prisoner cards in Vladimir Prison).

Stepanov, Mikhail (1900–1940) joined the VCheKa in 1920. Head of the Secret Department (1929–1931) and of the Special Department of the Leningrad Branch of the OGPU (1931–1933). Later held different regional positions. Arrested in 1938, condemned to 12 years of labor camps in 1940 and the same year died in a camp (Petrov and Skorkin, *Kto rukovidil NKVD*, pp. 395–396).

Stern, Lina (1878–1968), physiologist. Graduated from Geneva University (1903), and became professor there (1917–1925). Moved to Moscow, professor at the Second Moscow Medical Institute (1925–1949), director of the Academy Institute of Physiology (1929–1949). Academician (1939), member of the Medical Academy (1944) (the only woman elected to both academies). In 1949 arrested as a member of the Jewish Anti-Fascist Committee. On July 18, 1952, sentenced to 3 years' imprisonment and 5 years' exile (other defendants were sentenced to death and shot). However, not expelled from the academy. In July 1953 amnestied and released. A special decision of the Academy Presidium in 1954 permitted her to set up a new laboratory for her old staff at the Institute of Biophysics. Stalin Prize (1954).

Sudoplatov, Pavel (1907–1996) joined the CheKa in 1921. In 1927 at the Secret Political Department of the Ukrainian OGPU in the city of Kharkov (then the capital of the Ukraine). From 1933, in the OGPU Foreign Department in Moscow. In Finland, Germany, Austria, Switzerland, France (1934–1938); investigated Ukrainian nationalists. Assassinated the leader of the Ukrainian nationalists, Yevhen Konovalets, in Holland (1938). Deputy head of NKVD Fifth (Intelligence) Department within the NKVD Main State Security Directorate (1939–1941); in 1940, in charge of the organization of Leon Trotsky's assassination in Mexico. Deputy head of the First (Intelligence) NKGB Directorate (1941), head of the Special Group, which became the NKVD Second Department (1941–1942), head of the Second Department, which became the NKVD/NKGB/MGB Fourth Directorate (1942–1946). In 1946, head of the DR (terrorism) MGB Department (former Fourth Directorate) (1946–1950), of Bureau No. 1 (1950–1953), of the MVD Ninth Department (1953). In the late 1940s, organized and took part in political assassinations together with Naum Eitingon and Mairanovsky. Arrested on August 21, 1953. Simulated madness. On September 12, 1958, sentenced to 15 years' imprisonment. Kept in Vladimir Prison. After the release, became a ghost writer. Rehabilitated in 1990.

Sukachev, Vladimir (1880–1967), botanist and outspoken anti-Lysenkoist in the 1950s. Graduated from the Forestry Institute in St. Petersburg (1902), became professor there (1925–1941). At the Academy Botanical Museum (1912–1918), professor at the Forestry Institute (later the Forest-Technical Academy) (1919–1941), chair of the Acclimatization Department of the Department of Geobotany (1924–1926), director of the Academy Botanical Garden (1931–1933) and the Academy Institute of Forestry in Moscow; and professor at the Moscow Forest-Technical Academy (1944–1948) and Moscow University (1948–1951). Corresponding member (1920), academician (1943). In 1916, a member-founder and from 1946 on, president of the All-Union Botanical Society. Awards by the Geographical Society in 1912, 1914, 1929, 1947. President of the Moscow Society of Naturalists (1955–1967). Despite his Party membership (from 1937), started a crusade against Trofim Lysenko and his followers. To punish him, in 1961 the Central Committee ordered the transfer of his Institute of Forestry from Moscow to the city of Krasnoyarsk in Siberia. He was too old to move to Siberia.

Suslov, Mikhail (1902–1982), Party figure. At the Central Committee (CC) from 1944. Secretary of the CC and the main Party ideologist (1947–1988). Chief editor of the main Party newspaper *Pravda* (1949–1951), a Politburo (Presidium) member (1952–1953; 1955–1982) (Naumov and Sigachev, *Lavrentii Beria*, p. 487).

Sverdlov, Yakov (1885–1919), one of the main non-émigré Party leaders. In exile to Siberia (1912–1917), the first year with Stalin. Like Stalin, an early editor of the Bolshevik newspaper *Pravda*. In 1917, an unofficial secretary general of the Bolshevik October Revolution, then secretary of the Central Committee, Politburo member, and the first president of the Soviet Republic. Played an important role during the Civil War (Doyle in Bazhanov, p. 243).

Tagantsev, Vladimir (1889–1921), geographer, son of an outstanding criminologist, academician, and former senator, Nikolai Tagantsev (1843–1923). Secretary of the Sapropelic Society within the Russian Academy in the former Tagantsev family's country estate. Arrested in 1921 (together with other representatives of intelligentsia) as an alleged member of the anti-Soviet Petrograd Armed Organization. After a closed trial, Tagantsev, his wife, and other members of this "plot" were sentenced to death and shot.

Tamm, Igor (1895–1971), physicist. After graduating from Moscow University (1918), taught physics at several institutions. From 1934, worked at the Academy Physics Institute. Academician (1953). Together with Yakov Zeldovich, Andrei Sakharov and others, was a key scientist in the creation of the Soviet H-bomb. Hero of Socialist Labor (1953). In 1956 openly confronted Lysenko at the Academy General Assembly. Nobel Prize for physics (1958) (Holloway, *Stalin and the Bomb*, pp. 294–319).

Tarle, Eugeny (1875–1955), historian, author of books on the history of Russia, France, and other European countries. Corresponding member (1921), and academician (1927). Arrested on January 28, 1930. In 1931 sentenced to 5 years' exile to the city of Alma-Ata (Kazakhstan). Released in 1932 after the intervention of Minister of Culture Anatolii Lunacharsky. Returned to Leningrad and continued his career.

Tarusov, Boris (1900–?), biophysicist. Graduated from Odessa University (1924). At the Bakh Institute of Biochemistry (1931–1940), head of a laboratory at the All-Union Institute of Experimental Medicine (from 1938). Studied the action of toxins with cells and biological action of radiation. In 1953, created the Biophysics Department at the Biological Faculty of Moscow State University, which he chaired until death. Supported Mairanovsky.

Timofeev-Ressovsky, Nikolai (1900–1981), geneticist, one of Nikolai Koltsov's pupils. In 1925, with his wife, Elena, also a geneticist, was invited to Oscar Vogt's Institute of Neurology in Berlin. Head of the Laboratory of Genetics at the Kaiser Wilhelm Institute in Berlin (1935–1945). Coauthored several papers with German atomic physicists Karl Zimmer and Max Delbrück. In 1944 his eldest son, a member of the anti-Nazi underground group that helped foreign slave workers to escape and hide, perished in the Mauthausen concentration camp. Arrested in 1945 by the NKVD and sentenced to 10 years' labor. Almost died of pellagra in the Karaganda system of labor camps. Transferred to a special secret biophysics institute within the MGB (1947–1955). In 1955 organized a biophysics laboratory at the Academy Ural Division. In 1964 organized the Department of Genetics and Radiology at a new Institute of Medical Radiology within the Medical Academy in the town of Obninsk. In 1971 this laboratory was closed by KGB order. Professor-consultant at the Institute of Medical-Biological Problems in Moscow (1972–1981). Rehabilitated after his death.

Trotsky, Leon (1879–1940, pseudonym of **Lev Bronstein**), Communist theorist and state figure. Joined underground Socialist movement in 1896 and in 1898 was arrested and exiled to Siberia. In 1902, escaped from exile with a forged passport bearing the name "Trotsky." Joined Lenin in London, but during the split of the Party in 1903, sided with the Mensheviks. Returned to Russia in 1905 and played an important role in the revolution of 1905. Arrested in 1906 and exiled again in Siberia. In 1907, escaped from exile once again and settled in Vienna, then in Switzerland, and finally in Paris. At the outbreak of World War I was expelled from France and Spain. In mid-May 1917, returned to Petrograd and was jailed by the Provisional Government. While imprisoned, was formally accepted to the Bolshevik Party and elected to the Central Committee. Released in September and elected chairman of the Petrograd Soviet of Workers' and Soldiers' Deputies. After the revolution, commissar of foreign affairs and commissar of war. During the Civil War and the period of War Communism that followed, was the number-two man next to Lenin. During Lenin's illness from 1922–1924, isolated by Stalin. In 1925, removed from the War Commissariat, then expelled from the Politburo in 1926, then from the Central Committee, and finally from the Party. In January 1928, exiled to Central Asia together with principal followers. In 1929, banished from Soviet territory. Moved to Turkey, then to France, to Norway, and finally was forced to seek asylum in Mexico. Was the object of two assassination attempts ordered by Stalin. The second, organized by Pavel Sudoplatov and Naum Eitingon, succeeded, and on August 20, 1940, Trotsky died of a stabbing wound caused by an ice pick.

Tsanava, Lavrentii (1900–1955) joined the local CheKa branch in Georgia in 1921. At the Georgian Regional OGPU in Tbilisi (1930–1933), then at different state positions in Georgia (1933–1937). NKVD commissar of Belorussia (1938–1941). Head of the NKVD Special Departments at different fronts (1941–1943), NKVD/MGB commissar/minister of Belorussia (1943–1951), head of the Second MGB Main Directorate and deputy MGB minister (1951–1952). Dismissed on February 15, 1952, and arrested on April 4, 1953, as a co-organizer of the assassination of Solomon Mikhoels. Died in prison on October 12, 1955 (Petrov and Skorkin, *Kto rukovodil NKVD*, pp. 431–432).

Tsitsin, Nikolai (1898–1980), botanist. Member of the Agricultural Academy (VASKhNIL) (1932). Director of the Siberian Institute of Cereal Industry (1934–1938), of the All-Union Agricultural Exhibition (VSKhV) in Moscow (1938–1949; 1953–1957), vice president of the VASKhNIL (1938–1948), director of the Academy Main Botanical Garden in Moscow (1945–1980). Elected academician in 1939 together with Trofim Lysenko. Did not support Trofim Lysenko in 1947–1948. As retaliation, dismissed from the VSKhV directorship and as vice president of the VASKhNIL. President of the International Association of Botanical Gardens and the Fourteenth International Genetics Congress. Joined the Party in 1938. Deputy of the USSR Supreme Soviet. Twice Hero of Socialist Labor, Stalin and Lenin Prizes, seven Lenin Orders.

Tulaikov, Nikolai (1875–1938), agronomist. Academician (1932). Director of the Saratov Institute of Grain Farming, head of the Scientific Committee of the Commissariat of Agriculture (from 1917). Lenin Prize (1929). Arrested with some of his colleagues in 1937 after Trofim Lysenko and one of his cronies, Vsevolod Stoletov, proclaimed Tulaikov "a saboteur" and a campaign of public meetings followed. Tried and shot on January 20, 1938.

Ulrich, Vasilii (1889–1951), military prosecutor. In the early 1920s, chairman of the Military Tribunal of the Internal Security (OGPU) Troops. Chairman of the Military Collegium (MC) of the USSR Supreme Court (1926–1948). The number of victims sentenced to death at the MC meetings presided by Ulrich is countless: Between October 1, 1936, and September 30, 1938, alone, 30,514 persons were condemned to death and an additional 5,000 persons were sentenced to various terms in labor camps. Dismissed in 1948 and assigned to the Military Law Academy (Parrish, *The Lesser Terror*, pp. 205–207).

Unshlikht, Iosif (1879–1938), one of the founders of the VCheKa in 1917. In 1919, participated in the short-lived Government of the Republic of Lithuania and Belorussia, and in 1920, in a similar Polish government. Deputy chairman of the VCheKa/OGPU (1921–1923), in charge of military intelligence (1923–1925), deputy commissar of defense and deputy chairman of the USSR Military Council (1925–1930), deputy chairman of the Central Executive Committee of the Soviet Council of Deputies (VSNKh) (1930–1933), then at different high positions in the Soviet government (1933–1937). A candidate to the Central Committee (1925–1937). Arrested on June 11, 1937, tried on July 28, 1938, and shot on July 29, 1938 (Leggett, *The CHEKA,* pp. 271–273; Kolpakidi, Aleksandr, and Dimitrii Prokhorov, *Imperia GRU: Ocherki istorii rossiiskoi voennoi razvedki* [The GRU Empire: Essays on the History of the Russian Military Intelligence] [Moscow: Olma-Press, 2000], vol. 2, pp. 423–424 [in Russian]; Yeremina and Roginsky, *Rastrel'nye spiski,* p. 411).

Vannikov, Boris (1897–1962), state figure. Joined the Communist Party in 1919. Deputy commissar (1937–1939), then commissar (1939–1941) of defense industry. Arrested (June–August 1941). Deputy commissar of defense industry again (1941), commissar of armaments (1942–1946), deputy chair of the Special Committee and head of the First Main Directorate under the Council of Ministers (in charge of the A- and H-bomb projects) (1945–1953), first deputy minister of medium machine building (i.e., of atomic industry) (1953–1958). Hero of Socialist Labor (1942, 1949, 1954) (Naumov and Sigachev, *Lavrentii Beria,* p. 433).

Vavilov, Nikolai (1887–1943), botanist and geneticist. Graduated from Moscow Agricultural Institute (1911). Director of the Institute of Applied Botany (1924–1929), the Plant Breeding Institute (VIR) (1930–1940), and the Academy Institute of Genetics (1933–1940). Member of the Ukrainian and the USSR Academies (1929). President (1929–1935), and then, from 1935–1938, vice president of the Agricultural Academy (VASKhNIL) (1953–1938), president of the All-Union Geographical Society (1931–1940). Member of the Central Executive Committee of the Soviet Council of Deputies (VSNKh) (1926–1935). Published more than 350 original papers and monographs in different languages. Discovered the law of homologous series in hereditary variation and centers of origin of cultivated plants. Arrested in 1940 because of his long-term stand against Trofim Lysenko. Sentenced to death on July 9, 1941; not executed. On July 26, 1941, the death penalty was commuted to 20 years' imprisonment in labor camps. Died in the city of Saratov, in Saratov Prison on January 26, 1943.

Vavilov, Sergei (1891–1951), physicist, the younger brother of Nikolai Vavilov. Graduated from Moscow University (1914), became professor there and head of the Physics Department at the Institute of Physics and Biophysics (1918–1932), director of the Academy Physics Institute (from 1932), scientific deputy director of the Academy Optical Institute. Academician (1932). President of the academy (1945–1951). According to Andrei Sakharov's memoirs (p. 77), Vavilov accepted the post of president because he had been informed that Trofim Lysenko and Andrei Vyshinsky were the other candidates for this position.

Vernadsky, Vladimir (1863–1945), the founder of geochemistry and biogeochemistry. Developed the biosphere theory (the total mass of living organisms that process and recycle the energy and nutrients available from the environment). Graduated from St. Petersburg University (1885). Professor at Moscow University (1890–1911). Ordinary academician (1912). Active member of the Constitutional Democrats Party and a minister in the Provisional Government in 1917. Escaped arrest by the Bolsheviks by moving to the Ukraine and Crimea. Back to Moscow in 1921, then abroad (1922–1926). After his return, founded several laboratories and institutes. From 1927, directed the Academy Biogeochemical Laboratory (in Leningrad).

Vinogradov, Vladimir (1882–1964), therapist. In 1937, as an expert, confirmed the indictment against his teacher, Professor Dmitrii Pletnev. In 1944, elected to the Medical Academy. In 1951, chief therapist at the Kremlin Hospital, chair of a department at the First Moscow Medical Institute, head of the Electrocardiography Department at the Institute of Therapy of the Medical Academy, and editor in chief of the journal *Terapevticheskii arkhiv* [Therapist's Archive]. In 1953, one of the main victims of the Doctors' Plot case (Naumov and Sigachev, *Lavrentii Beria*, p. 434).

Vlodzimersky, Lev (1903–1953) joined the local OGPU branch in the town of Zheleznovodsk in 1928. In Moscow from 1937. Deputy and then head of the Investigation Department of the Main Economic Directorate within the NKVD (1939–1940), first deputy of the Third Department of the NKVD Main State Security Directorate (1940–1941), head of the NKGB Investigation Department (1941) and the NKVD Department for Investigation of Especially Important Cases (OVD) (1941–1943). In 1946–1947, in the city of Gorky, and from 1947 until March 1953, in Germany under Vsevolod Merkulov. Head of the OVD Department within the new MVD (March–June 1953). Arrested on July 17, 1953, tried and shot on December 23, 1953, along with Beria and others. Not rehabilitated (Petrov and Skorkin, *Kto rukovodil NKVD*, p. 132).

Volf, Moisei (1880–1933), economist. Head of the Agricultural Section of the State Planning Committee (Gosplan) (late 1920s–1933). Arrested in March of 1933 together with the other 34 agricultural specialists. Accused of trying "to create a condition of famine in the country." Condemned to death and shot (Joravsky, *The Lysenko Affair*, p. 73).

Vovsi, Miron (or **Meyer**) (1897–1956), physician and Solomon Mikhoels's cousin. In 1937, among those doctors who denounced Dr. Dmitrii Pletnev. During World War II, the Red Army's chief physician. After World War II, professor at the Central Institute for Advanced Medicine. In 1952–1953, accused of playing the leading role in the Doctors' Plot. In April 1953, released. Died of consequences of injuries obtained during brutal interrogations.

Vyshinsky, Andrei (1883–1954), prosecutor. A Menshevik from 1903, then a Bolshevik (1920). In 1918, joined the Public Prosecutor's Office. Professor (the 1920s) and rector of Moscow University (1925–1931). The RSFSR (i.e., Russian Republic) prosecutor (1931–1935), then Soviet general prosecutor (1935–1949). Organizer of show trials of the 1930s. Academician (1939). Member of the Central Committee (1939–1954), foreign minister (1949–1953), Soviet ambassador to the United Nations (1953–1954).

Yagoda, Genrikh (or **Yenokh**) (1891–1938) joined the Social Democratic movement in 1904. From 1911 to 1912, arrested several times and in 1912 exiled to the city of Simbirsk in Siberia. Returned to Petrograd in 1913 and married a niece of Yakov Sverdlov, Ida Averbach. At the front (1914–1917). During the Bolshevik Revolution, a member of the Petrograd Bolshevik Military Organization. Joined the CheKa in 1919. NKVD commissar (1934–1936). Demoted to commissar of communication. Arrested on April 3, 1937, tried and condemned to death along with Bukharin and other defendants. Shot on March 15, 1938. Not rehabilitated (Petrov and Skorkin, *Kto rukovodil NKVD*, pp. 459–460).

Yakovlev, Yakov (1896–1938; pseudonym of **Yakov Epstein**), Party and state figure. Commissar of agriculture (1929–1934), head of the Agricultural Department of the Central Committee (1934–1937). Arrested on October 12, 1937 (together with Aleksandr Muralov). On July 29, 1938, condemned to death and shot. Rehabilitated in 1957 (Reznik, S., "Pravda i lozh' o Vavilove i Lysenko" [The truth and lies about Vavilov and Lysenko], *Voprosy Istorii Estestvoznaniya i Tekhniki* 2 (1992):62–78 (in Russian); Yeremina and Roginsky, *Rasstrel'nye spiski*, p. 465).

Yakovleva, Varvara (1884–1941?), Party figure. Joined the Bolshevik Party in 1904. In exile to Siberia in 1910 and 1913. Took part in the revolutions in Moscow in 1905 and 1917. In Moscow CheKa and a member of the VCheKa Presidium (1918), deputy chair, then chair of the Petrograd VCheKa (1918–1919), secretary of the Moscow Bureau of the Bolshevik Party (1920–1922). Thereafter, at different governmental and Party positions. Follower of Trotsky until 1926. In March 1938, a witness at the Bukharin show trial. Later arrested, tried, and died in a labor camp (Leggett, *The CHEKA*, p. 450; Conquest, *The Great Terror*, p. 134).

Yakushkin, Ivan (1885–1960), botanist. From 1932, head of the Plant Department at the Timiryazev Agricultural Academy. Member of the Agricultural

Academy (1935). A secret informer of the NKVD/MGB. Was used as a head of the NKVD commission of experts that denounced Vavilov.

Yanshin, Aleksandr (1911–), geologist and geographer. Academician (1958). Vice president of the academy responsible for the Earth Sciences Division (1982–1988), director of the Institute of Lithosphere, president of Moscow Society of Naturalists, head of the Academy Scientific Council on the Problems of Biosphere (from 1982).

Yenukidze, Avel (1877–1937), Party and state figure, a personal friend of Stalin. Secretary of the Central Executive Committee and chair of the Politburo's Commission on Assistance to the Work of the Academy of Sciences (1925–1929), a member of the Central Committee (1934–1935). Expelled from the Party in 1935 and demoted to a low-level job in the city of Kharkov. Arrested on February 11, 1937, sentenced to death on October 30, 1937, and shot the next day. Rehabilitated in 1959 (Tikhanova, *Rasstrel'nye spiski*, p. 150).

Yepishev, Aleksei (1908–1985), MGB and military figure. Deputy MGB minister for cadres (1951–1953), ambassador to Romania (1955–1960), then to Bulgaria (1960–1962), head of the Main Political Directorate of the Soviet army and navy (1962–1985) (Naumov and Sigachev, *Lavrentii Beria*, p. 442).

Zakovsky (Stubis), Leonid (or **Genrikh**) (1894–1938) joined the VCheKa in 1918, at different regional OGPU/NKVD branches. deputy NKVD commissar (January–April 1938). Arrested on April 30, 1938, tried and shot on August 29, 1938. Not rehabilitated (Petrov and Skorkin, *Kto rukovodil NKVD*, p. 199).

Zarubin, Vasilii (1894–1972) joined the VCheKa in 1921, sent to China. From the 1920s–1930s, in Germany, France, Denmark, and Switzerland. The NKVD/NKGB *rezident* in the United States under the alias "Zubilin" (1941–1944), played a key role in collecting information on the Manhattan Project. Recalled to Moscow to face a false accusation of working for the Germans. Deputy head of Foreign Intelligence (from 1944). In 1948, transferred to the reserve for health reasons (Voskresenskaya, *Pod psevdonimom Irina*, pp. 56–57, 259–266; Trubnikov, *Ocherki*, pp. 203–215; Haynes and Klehr, *Venona*, p. 394).

Zavenyagin, Avraamii (1901–1956), Party and state figure. Joined the Party in 1917. Director of a truck/car plant in the city of Dneprodzerzhinsk (1932–1933), of the Magnitogorsk Industrial Complex (1933–1937), deputy commissar of heavy industry (1937–1938), director of the Norilsk Industrial Complex and commandant of the labor camp for prisoners who built and worked at this plant (1938–1941), deputy Narkom/minister of the NKVD/MVD (1941–1951), deputy head of the First Main Directorate under the Council of Ministers, i.e., of the Soviet A-bomb project (1945–1953), deputy minister (1953–1955), and then minister of medium machine building, (i.e., of atomic energy) (1955–1956). Hero of Socialist Labor (1949, 1951) (Kokurin and Petrov, *Lubyanka*, p. 147).

Zbarsky, Boris (1885–1954), biochemist. Graduated from Geneva University and St. Petersburg University. Assisted in the organization of the Karpov

Chemical Institute (1918) and the Bach Institute of Biochemistry (1920), acting director of both institutes until 1930. Joined the Communist Party in 1930. From 1933, chaired the Biochemistry Department of the Moscow First Medical Institute, and from 1939, head of the Laboratory on the Preservation of Lenin's body. In 1937 was among those doctors who denounced Dr. Dmitri Pletnev. Arrested in February 1952 as an alleged member of the Doctors' Plot. Released in December 1953. Died in October 1954 from a heart attack in the middle of a lecture.

Zenkevich, Lev (1889–1970), invertebrate zoologist. Academician and deputy secretary academician of the Academy Division of Oceanology, Atmosphere Physics, and Geography. Also chaired the Department of Invertebrate Zoology at the Biological Faculty of Moscow State University.

Zhdanov, Andrei (1896–1948), Party figure, the leading Party ideologist of the 1940s. Different posts from 1922–1934. First secretary of the Leningrad Regional and City Committees (1934–1944), secretary of the Central Committee (1934–1946), Politburo member (1939–1948), member of Military Councils (1941–1945). Chair of the Union Council of the Supreme Soviet (1946–1947). Played an important role in Trofim Lysenko's triumph in 1948. Supposedly was killed by Jewish doctor-killers (Naumov and Sigachev, *Lavrentii Beria*, p. 444; Hahn, *Postwar Soviet Politics*, pp. 19–66, 94–113; Ra'anan, *International Policy Formation*, pp. 12–170).

Zhdanov, Yurii (1919–), Andrei Zhdanov's son and Party figure. Graduate student at the Academy Institute of Philosophy (1945–1948), head of the Department of Science within the Directorate of Propaganda and Agitation (Agitprop) of the Central Committee (1947–1948), of the Science Sector within Agitprop (1948–1950), of the Department on Science and Higher Education (1950–1952), and of the Department on Natural and Technical Sciences and Higher Education (1952–1953), rector of the Rostov-on-Don University (1957–1989). Corresponding member (1970). Played an important role during Lysenko's triumph in 1948. On Stalin's order, in 1949 married Stalin's daughter Svetlana (they divorced in 1953) (Naumov and Sigachev, *Lavrentii Beria*, p. 444; Allilueva, *Twenty Letters*, pp. 197–211).

Zhebrak, Anton (1901–1965), geneticist and anti-Lysenkoist. Graduated from Timiryazev Agricultural Academy (1925) and the Institute of Red Professors (1929). In 1930–1931, Rockefeller Fellow at Thomas H. Morgan's laboratory at Columbia University, head of the Genetics Department of the Timiryazev Agricultural Academy (1935–1948). Elected to the Belorussian Academy of Sciences (1940) and president of this academy (May–October 1947). Joined the Party in 1928 and was an official of the Central Committee Science Department (1945–1946). At the end of 1948 lost all posts because of anti-Lysenkoist position. Professor of botany at the Moscow Institute of Timber Industry (1948–1949) and then at the Moscow Pharmacological Institute (1949–1965).

Zhemchuzhina (Karpovich), Polina (1897–1970), Party figure and Molotov's wife. Head of the Main Directorate of Perfume, Cosmetic, Synthetic, and Soap Production within the Food Industry Commissariat (1936–1937), deputy commissar of Food Industry and then commissar of Fisheries (1937–1939), head of the Main Directorate of Textile Industry within the Commissariat/Ministry of Light Industry (1939–1948). Arrested in 1948 in connection with the Jewish Anti-Fascist Committee case, tried in 1949 and convicted to five-year exile. Sent to Kazakhstan. In early 1953, brought to Moscow and brutally interrogated in connection with the Doctors' Plot case. In March 1953, released after Stalin's death and rehabilitated.

Zhuk, Sergei (1892–1957), hydraulic engineer, one of the main organizers of the slave labor in the USSR. Graduated from Petrograd Institute of Railroad Engineers (1917). Directed the construction of the main large hydroelectric complexes: the White Sea–Moscow Canal, the Volga-Don Complex, etc. (the 1920s–1950s). In 1942, joined the Party and became head of the Gidroproect within the NKVD (in 1957 it was named after him). Academician (1953), major general of Engineering and Technical Services. Received a number of the highest Soviet awards.

Zhukovsky, Semen (1896–1940) joined the NKVD in 1936. Head of the Third (Counterintelligence) Department of the NKVD Main State Security Directorate (GUGB) (1937), head of the GUGB Twelfth (Operational Equipment) Department (1937–1938), deputy NKVD commissar 1938). Arrested on October 23, 1938, tried and shot on January 24, 1940. Rehabilitated in 1955 (Petrov and Skorkin, *Kto rukovodil NKVD*, pp. 192–193).

Zhupakhin, Sergei (1888–1940) joined the OGPU in 1922. From 1927–1929, head of the Secret Department of the Secret-Operational Directorate of the Leningrad Branch of the OGPU (1927–1929), deputy head of this department (1929–1931), head of the Economic Department of the branch (1931–1932). Arrested on December 14, 1938, tried on May 16, 1940, and shot. Not rehabilitated (Petrov and Skorkin, *Kto rukovidil NKVD*, p. 193).

Zilber, Lev (1894–1966), microbiologist and virologist, the author of the virus theory of cancer. Graduated from Petrograd University (1917), and from the Medical Faculty of Moscow University (1919). At the Institute of Microbiology under the Commissariat of Health (1920–1929), director of the Microbiology Institute in Baku (Azerbaijan) and chair of the Microbiology Department in the local university (1929–1931). Arrested in 1931, soon released. From 1932, at the Mechnikov Institute of Sera and Vaccines. In 1934, organized the Central Viral Laboratory. In 1937 arrested again on charge of "disseminating encephalitis." Released in 1939, but arrested for the third time in 1940. Sentenced to imprisonment in labor camps. Part of the term spent in a secret NKVD chemical laboratory, where he was in charge of production of alcohol from reindeer moss. Secretly wrote a manuscript on the virus etiology of cancer. Released in March 1944. Head of the Department of General Immunology and Oncology at the Gamaleya Institute of Epidemiology and Microbiology (1946–1966).

APPENDIX II: TRANSLATED DOCUMENTS

1. Yevgeniya Allilueva's prisoner card (Memorial's Archive [Moscow], fond 171. Prisoner cards from Vladimir Prison).

2. Anna Allilueva's prisoner card (Memorial's Archive [Moscow], fond 171. Prisoner cards from Vladimir Prison).

3. Molochnikov's prisoner card No. 1 (Memorial's Archive [Moscow], fond 171. Prisoner cards from Vladimir Prison).

4. Molochnikov's prisoner card No. 2 (Memorial's Archive [Moscow], fond 171. Prisoner cards from Vladimir Prison).

5. Moroz-Morozov's prisoner card (Memorial's Archive [Moscow], fond 171. Prisoner cards from Vladimir Prison).

6. Shatunovskaya's prisoner card (Memorial's Archive [Moscow], fond 171. Prisoner cards from Vladimir Prison).

7. Tumerman's prisoner card (a shortened version rewritten by V. Danilova in 1990).

8. Levina's prisoner card (a shortened version rewritten by V. Danilova in 1990).

9. Goldstein's prisoner card (Memorial's Archive [Moscow], fond 171. Prisoner cards from Vladimir Prison).

10. A letter to Stalin signed by V. Abakumov and S. Ogol'tsov regarding Bureaus Nos. 1 and 2, dated August 4, 1950 ("Special Files" of the Politburo, Archive of the President of the Russian Federation, F. 3. From the materials declassified in 1992 for the Communist Party case).

11. An archival record from the Medical Academy of Sciencies Archive regarding Mairanovsky's career from 1928–1940, dated January 5, 1962 (Memorial's Archive [Moscow], fond 1, op. 1, d. 2872).

12. A certificate issued by the Bach Institute of Biochemistry regarding Mairanovsky dated June 10, 1934 (Memorial's Archive [Moscow], fond 1, op. 1, d. 2872).

13. A certificate issued by the KGB confirming Mairanovsky's employment by the NKVD/MGB from 1938–1951 and his arrest in 1951, dated January 22, 1962 (Memorial's Archive [Moscow], fond 1, op. 1, d. 2872).

14. An archival excerpt from a transcript of a meeting of the Scientific Council on October 20, 1943, of the VIEM regarding the approval of Mairanovsky's title as professor, dated July 3, 1963 (Memorial's Archive [Moscow], fond 1, op. 1, d. 2872).

15. A certificate No. 82061 issued by Vladimir Prison regarding Mairanovsky's imprisonment, dated December 13, 1961 (Memorial's Archive [Moscow], fond 1, op. 1, d. 2872).

16. Mairanovsky's prisoner card No. 1 (from the file of Vladimir Prison).

17. Mairanovsky's prisoner card No. 2 (from the file of Vladimir Prison).

18. Eitingon's prisoner card (Memorial's Archive [Moscow], fond 171. Prisoner cards from Vladimir Prison).

19. Liberman's prisoner card (Memorial's Archive [Moscow], fond 171. Prisoner cards from Vladimir Prison).

20. Clauberg's prisoner card (Memorial's Archive [Moscow], fond 171. Prisoner cards from Vladimir Prison).

21. Zeiss's prisoner card (Memorial's Archive [Moscow], fond 171. Prisoner cards from Vladimir Prison).

22. Sudoplatov's prisoner card (Memorial's Archive [Moscow], fond 171. Prisoner cards from Vladimir Prison).

23. Parin's prisoner card (a shortened version rewritten by V. Danilova in 1990).

DOCUMENT 1

Yevgeniya Allilueva's Prisoner Card[1]
I. Front side
1.   Last Name: Prisoner 22
2.   Name: female
3.   Patronymic Name: —
4.   Year of birth: 1898
5.   Place of birth: —
6.   Address: —
7.   Profession (speciality): —
8.   Place of work, position: —
9.   Party membership: —
10.   Nationality: a Russian
11.   Citizenship: USSR
12.   Date of the arrest: —
13.   Type of crime: —
14.   Paragraphs of the UK [Criminal Code]: —
15.   Place of the fulfillment of the card (mention the prison, KPZ [police station], camp, colony): —
June 8, 1948   Person who filled out the card: V. Danilova
[Right column]
Organ (in charge of the arrest): —

No. of the Case: 858
[Nos. of the Corpus-Nos. of the Vladimir Prison cell, date of the transfer]
2–13
2–32; July 22, 1948
1–63; July 7, 1949
2–30; August 27, 1949
2–24; October 22, 1949
2–18
2–37; January 6, 1950
1–70; September 13, 1950
2–37; September 29, 1950
3–34; September 27, 1951
2–39; December 4, 1951

II. Back side
Convicted by: Special Council [OSO] under the MGB
Date: May 29, 1948
Paragraphs of the UK [Criminal Code]: 58–1a, 58–10 pt. 1, 58–11
Term: 10 TZ [years of imprisonment]
Beginning of the term: October 10, 1947
End of the term: October 10, 1957
Following the order of the MVD leaders from April 27, 1953, on April 29, 1953 [the prisoner] left for Inner [Lubyanka] Prison of the MVD in Moscow

DOCUMENT 2

Anna Allilueva's Prisoner Card[2]
    I. Front side
    On the top: Category 70, especially dangerous
    1. Last Name: Prisoner 23
    2. Name: —
    3. Patronymic Name: —
    4. Year of birth: 1896
    5. Place of birth: —
    6. Address: —
    7. Profession (speciality): —
    8. Place of work, position: —
    9. Party membership: —
    10. Nationality: a Russian
    11. Citizenship: USSR
    12. Date of the arrest: December 10, 1947
    13. Type of crime: —
    14. Paragraphs of the UK [Criminal Code]: —
    15. Place of the fulfillment of the card (mention the prison, KPZ [police station], camp, colony): —

June 6, 1948   Person who filled out the card: V. Danilova
[Right column]
Organ (in charge of the arrest): —
No. of the Case: 855
[Nos. of the Corpus-Nos. of the Vladimir Prison cell, date of the transfer]
2–29
2–39; June 19, 1948
2–17; June 16, 1949
1–35; July 7, 1949
2–43; August 29, 1949
2–38; January 6, 1950
1–64; September 13, 1950
2–38; September 13, 1950
3–14; September 27, 1951
2–38; December 4, 1951

II. Back side
Convicted by: Special Council [OSO] under the MGB
Date: December 27, 1952
Paragraphs of the UK [Criminal Code]: 58–10 pt. 2, 58–11
Term: 5 + 5 TZ [years of imprisonment]
The term was increased to 5 more years of imprisonment. Beginning of the term: February 4, 1953
End of the term: February 4, 1958
Following the order of the MVD leaders from April 27, 1953, on April 29, 1953 [the prisoner] left for Inner [Lubyanka] Prison of the MVD in Moscow

DOCUMENT 3

Molochnikov's Prisoner Card No. 1[3]
I. Front side
On the top: 70 hostile activity
1.   Last Name: Prisoner 21
2.   Name: —
3.   Patronymic Name: —
4.   Year of birth: 1899
5.   Place of birth: the city of Novgorod
6.   Address: Moscow, Serafimovicha Str., 2, ap. 208
7.   Profession (speciality): Candidate of Technical Sciences
8.   Place of work, position: Leningrad Institute of Technology
9.   Party membership: —
10.   Nationality: a Jew [a Russian was crossed out]
11.   Citizenship: USSR
12.   Date of the arrest: December 10, 1947
13.   Type of crime: —

14.   Paragraphs of the UK [Criminal Code]: 19–58–1a, 58–10 pt. I, 58–11

15.   Place of the fulfillment of the card (mention the prison, KPZ [police station], camp, colony): —

June 10, 1948 Person who filled out the card: V. Danilova

[Right column]

Organ (in charge of the arrest): —

No. of the Case: 866

[Nos. of the Corpus-Nos. of the Vladimir Prison cell, date of the transfer]

2–38 [crossed out]

3–53 [crossed out]; July 7, 1948

2–14; October 3, 1948

2–50; March 29, 1949

2–27; June 16, 1949

2–10; June 17, 1949

1–51; July 7, 1949

2–10; July 27, 1959

2–13; January 6, 1950

1–89; September 13, 1950

2–13; September 29, 1950

3–8; September 27, 1951

3–5; October 17, 1950

2–14; December 4, 1951

II. Back side

Convicted by: Special Council [OSO]

Date: May 29, 1948

Paragraphs of the UK [Criminal Code]: —

Term: 25 TZ [years of imprisonment]

Beginning of the term: December 10, 1947

End of the term: December 10, 1972

With confiscation of possessions

DOCUMENT 4

Molochnikov's Prisoner Card No. 2

I. Front side

On the top: M. 70

1. Last Name: Molochnikov

2. Name: Nikolai

3. Patronymic Name: Vladimirovich

4. Year of birth: 1899

5. Place of birth: the city of Novgorod

6. Address: Moscow, Serafimovicha Str., 2, ap. 208

7. Profession (speciality): Candidate of Tech.[nical] Sciences

8. Place of work, position: Leningrad Institute of Technology

9. Party membership: former member of the VKP (b) [Bolshevik] Party
10. Nationality: a Jew
11. Citizenship: USSR
12. Date of the arrest: December 10, 1947
13. Type of crime: treason of the Motherland
14. Paragraphs of the UK [Criminal Code]: 19–58–1a, 58–10 pt I, 58–11
15. Place of the fulfillment of the card (mention the prison, KPZ [police station], camp, colony): Vladimir Special Prison of the MVD
June 10, 1948 Person who filled out the card: V. Danilova
[In handwriting] this card was written on August 29, 1953
[Right column]
Organ (in charge of the arrest): Department for the Investigation of Especially Important Cases
No. of the Case: 866
[Nos. of the Corpus-Nos. of the Vladimir Prison cell, date of the transfer]
2–14; December 4, 1951

II. Back side
Convicted by: Special Council [OSO] under the MGB of the USSR
Date: May 29, 1948
Paragraphs of the UK [Criminal Code]: 19–58–1a, 58–10 pt. I, 58–11
Term: 25 TZ [years of imprisonment]
Beginning of the term: December 10, 1947
End of the term: December 10, 1972
[The prisoner] arrived from Lefortovo Prison of the MVD in Moscow on June 10, 1948.
On April 2, 1954 [the prisoner] was released.
According to the decision of the Military Collegium of the USSR Supreme Court No. 4n–02641/54 dated March 20, 1954 the case was abolished on the basis of Article 4 of the RSFSR UPK [the Russian Federation Criminal-Procedural Code]. [The prisoner] left for the destination of his living, the city of Moscow.

DOCUMENT 5

Moroz-Morozov's Prisoner Card[4]
I. Front side
On the top: 70, socially dangerous as a/S [anti-Soviet element]
1. Last Name: Moroz-Morozov
2. Name: Moroz-Morozov, Iosif
3. Patronymic Name: Grigorievich
4. Year of birth: 1886
5. Place of birth: city of Mogilev, BSSR [Belorussia]
6. Address: Moscow, Lesnaya Str., 29, ap. 12

7. Profession (speciality): medical attendant

8. Place of work, position: Deputy Director, Administrative and Household Equipment Section of the Institute of Physiology of the USSR Academy of Sciences

9. Party membership: not a member of the Party

10. Nationality: a Jew

11. Citizenship: USSR

12. Date of the arrest: February 10, 1948

13. Type of crime: anti-Soviet propaganda

14. Paragraphs of the UK [Criminal Code]: 58–10, pt. II, 58–11

15. Place of the fulfillment of the card (mention the prison, KPZ [police station], camp, colony): Special Prison No. 2 of the MVD, Vladimir Region

June 16, 1948; July 22, 1948 [two dates] Person who filled out the card: V. Danilova

[Right column]

Organ (in charge of the arrest): MGB Department for Especially Important Cases

No. of the Case: –

[Nos. of the Corpus-Nos. of the Vladimir Prison cell, date of the transfer]

2–17

2–38; July 22, 1948

3–56

2–36; October 1, 1948

1–53; July 7, 1949

2–22; August 27, 1949

2–35; January 6, 1950

1–100 [?]; September 13, 1950

1–58; September 16, 1950

2–35; September 29, 1951

3–49; April 27, 1951

2–36; December 4, 1951

II. Back side

Convicted by: Special Council [OSO] under the MGB

Date: May 29, 1948

Paragraphs of the UK [Criminal Code]: 58–10 pt. II, 58–11

Term: 15 TZ [years of imprisonment]

Beginning of the term: February 10, 1948

End of the term: February 10, 1963

On April 10, 1953 [the prisoner] left for Inner [Lubyanka] Prison of the MVD in Moscow in the disposal of the MVD [1st] Deputy Head Com.[rade] Kobulov. The reason: an oral instruction of the MVD [1st] Deputy Head [Bogdan] Kobulov on April 3, 1953.

DOCUMENT 6

Shatunovskaya's Prisoner Card[5]

I. Front side

[At the top, the left side] soc[ially] dangerous as a/S [anti-Soviet element] (70)

1. Last Name: Shatunovskaya
2. Name: Lidiya
3. Patronymic Name: Aleksandrovna
4. Year of birth: 1906
5. Place of birth: the city of Odessa
6. Address: Moscow, Serafimovicha Str., 2, ap. 145
7. Profession (speciality): none
8. Place of work, position: a housekeeper
9. Party membership: not a Party member
10. Nationality: a Jewess
11. Citizenship: USSR
12. Date of the arrest: December 17, 1947
13. Type of crime: —
14. Paragraphs of the UK [Criminal Code]: 58–1a [treason of the Motherland], 58–10 pt. II [anti-Soviet nationalistic propaganda], 58–11 [membership in an anti-Soviet organization]
15. Place of the fulfillment of the card (mention the prison, KPZ [police station], camp, colony): Prison No. 2 in the city of Vladimir

June 24, 1948   Person who filled out the card: Danilova

[Right column]

Organ (in charge of the arrest): Investigation Department for Especially Important Cases of the MGB of the USSR

No. of the Case: 911

[Nos. of the Corpus–Nos. of the Vladimir Prison cell; date of the transfer]
2–25
3–54; July 7, 1948
2–13; October 2, 1948
1–56; July 7, 1949
2–12; August 27, 1949
2–26; August 31, 1949
2–33; January 6, 1950
1–99; September 13, 1950
2–33; September 29, 1950
3–32; October 27, 1951
2–32; December 31, 1951
3–33; February 16, 1952
3–32; February 25, 1952
3–33; March 17, 1952
3–60; May 7, 1953

2–28; May 13, 1953
3–33; May 19, 1953

II. Back side
Convicted by: Special Board of the MGB (OSO)
Date: May 29, 1948
Paragraphs of the UK [Criminal Code]: 58–1a, 58–10 pt. II, 58–11
Term: 20 years of imprisonment
Beginning of the term: December 27, 1947
End of the term: December 27, 1967
On May 27, 1954 [the prisoner] was released and the case was cancelled; the decision of the Military Collegium of the USSR Supreme Court No. UN 05028/54 dated May 12, 1954. [She] went to the place of her residence in Moscow.

DOCUMENT 7

Tumerman's Prisoner Card (a shortened version)[6]
[On the top, to the right] physicist
Last Name: Tumerman
Name: Lev
Patronymic Name: Abramovich
Year of birth: 1898
Place of birth: the town of Berdichev
Address: Moscow, Serafimovicha Str., 2, ap. 145
Place of work: Institute of Physics of the AN USSR [Academy of Sciences], Senior Researcher
Nationality: a Jew
Citizenship: USSR
Convicted by: Special Board of the MGB (OSO)
Date: May 29, 1948
Paragraphs of the UK [Criminal Code]: 19–58–1a (treason of the Motherland),
16.   58–10 pt. I [anti-Soviet propaganda], 58–11 [membership in an anti-Soviet organization]
Term: 20 years of imprisonment
Date of the arrival in Vladimir Prison: June 26, 1948
On July 3, 1954 [the prisoner] was transferred to Inner [Lubyanka] Prison of the KGB under the USSR SM [Council of Ministers] in Moscow[7]
Note: socially dangerous as a/S [anti-Soviet element; the same as on the card of his wife, Lidiya Shatunovskaya, see the previous Document No. 6]

DOCUMENT 8

Levina's Prisoner Card (a shortened version)[8]
[On the top, to the right] (scientific worker)

Last Name: Levina
Name: Revekka [Rebekka]
Patronymic Name: Saulovna
Year of birth: 1899
Place of birth: the village of Zhagorie [Zagorie] of the Lithuanian SSR
Address: Moscow, Bol'shaya Kaluzhskaya Str., 13, ap. 6
Place of work: Institute of the Economy of the AN USSR [Academy of Sciences], Senior Researcher
Nationality: a Jewess
Citizenship: USSR
Convicted by: Special Board of the MGB (OSO)
Date: May 29, 1948
Paragraphs of the UK [Criminal Code]: 58–10 pt. II (anti-Soviet propaganda), 58–11 [membership in an anti-Soviet organization]
Term: 10 years of imprisonment
Date of the arrival in Vladimir Prison: June 28, 1948
On June 29, 1953 [the prisoner] was transferred to Butyrka Prison of the MVD USSR in Moscow

DOCUMENT 9

Goldstein's Prisoner Card[9]
 I. Front side
 [On the top] American spy
 1. Last Name: Goldstein
 2. Name: Isaak
 3. Patronymic Name: Iosifovich
 4. Year of birth: 1892
 5. Place of birth: Zamoscie, Poland
 6. Address: Moscow, ul. Ogareva, 3, ap. 16
 7. Profession (speciality): economist
 8. Place of work, position: USSR Academy of Sciences, researcher
 9. Party membership: none
 10. Nationality: a Jew
 11. Citizenship: USSR
 12. Date of the arrest: December 19, 1947
 13. Type of crime: espionage
 14. Paragraphs of the UK [Criminal Code]: 58–1a, 58–10 p. I
 15. Place of the fulfillment of the card (mention the prison, KPZ [police station], camp, colony): Prison No. 2, [the city of] Vlad[imir]
June 20, 1950 Person who filled out the card: Soldatov
 [Right column]
 Organ (in charge of the arrest): Department for the Especially Important Cases of the MGB of the USSR
 No. of the Case: 174

[Nos. of the Corpus-Nos. of the Vladimir Prison cell, date of the transfer]
1–102; June 19, 1950
1–80; June 19, 1950
2–92; June 20, 1950
1–78; August 21, 1950
3–46; September 12, 1950
2–2; November 9, 1950
3–3; September 27, 1951
2–2; December 4, 1951
2–20; October 17, 1953

II. Back side
Convicted by: Special Council [OSO] under the MGB of the USSR
Date: October 29, 1949
Paragraphs of the UK [Criminal Code]: espionage
Term: 25 years of t/z [imprisonment]
Beginning of the term: December 19, 1947
End of the term: December 19, 1947
Property to be confiscated
[The prisoner] died on October 30, 1953

DOCUMENT 10

A letter to Stalin signed by Abakumov and Ogol'tsov[10]
B.[ook] 3

SPECIAL FILE [a stamp]

Top Secret

Central Committee of the VKP(b) [Bolshevik Party]

To: Com.[rade] I.V. STALIN

We are presenting to you two drafts of the Decisions of the C[entral] C[om-mittee] of the VKP(b):

First: On the creation of the Bureau No. 1 for *the terrorist activity abroad*, on the approval of the structure of this Bureau and on the appointment Com.[rade] P. A. Sudoplatov its Head and Com.[rade] A. M. Korotkov its Deputy Head;

Second: On the creation of the Bureau No. 2 for *the execution of special tasks within the Soviet Union*, on the approval of the structure of this Bureau and on the appointment Com.[rade] V. A. Drozdov, currently working Deputy Minister of State Security of the Ukrainian SSR (information is provided), its Head.

We ask for your decision.

ABAKUMOV.
OGOL'TSOV.

I do not object. I. S. [Stalin's resolution in handwriting]

No. 6990/A

August 4, 1950

DOCUMENT 11

ACADEMY OF MEDICAL SCIENCES
SCIENTIFIC ARCHIVE
Moscow, Solyanka Street 14   Tel. K 7–82–13
No. 20–167   January 5, 1962
To Citizen Mairanovsky Grigory Moiseevich
Moscow G–21, Frunzenskaya Naberezhnaya, 8, ap. 17
ARCHIVAL RECORD
According to the partly preserved documents about the work of Maira-
novsky Grigory Moiseevich at the Bach Institute of Biochemistry of the
Narkomzdrav [Commissariat of Health] and the Gorky All-Union Institute of
Experimental Medicine [VIEM], it is possible to recreate the following se-
quence of citizen G. M. Mairanovsky's duties at those institutes:

1. Aspirant [post-graduate student] at the Bach Institute of Biochemistry,
   1928–1929.
2. A researcher at the Bach Institute of Biochemistry, 1929–1932.
3. Senior Researcher at the Bach Institute of Biochemistry, 1932–1933.
4. Head of the Toxicology Department at the Bach Institute of Biochemistry, 1933–1935.
5. Head of the Special Laboratory at the Gorky All-Union Institute of Experimental Medicine [VIEM], 1935–1937.
6. Senior Researcher at the Special Toxicological Laboratory of the Gorky
   All-Union Institute of Experimental Medicine [VIEM], 1937–1938.
7. Senior Researcher at the Pathology Department of the OV [Poison Sub-
   stances] Therapy at the Gorky All-Union Institute of Experimental Medicine, 1938–1940.

Citizen G. M. Mairanovsky was dismissed from the Gorky All-Union Institute of Experimental Medicine on February 16, 1940.
Head of the Scientific Archive
of the USSR MAS [Medical Academy]   S. Novikov
Senior Keeper of Archives   R. Khlebnikova

DOCUMENT 12

R S F S R
People's Comissariat of Health
A. N. Bach STATE SCIENTIFIC
INSTITUTE of BIOCHEMISTRY
June 10, 1934
No. 580
Vorontsovo pole, 9
Tel: 5–34–20
C E R T I F I C A T E

Given to Com.[rade] MAIRANOVSKY G. M. Currently he is Deputy Director of the A. N. Bach Institute of Biochemistry.

Secretary of the Institute   (Sorokina)

Signature

Seal of the A. N. Bach Institute

DOCUMENT 13

A copy from a copy

USSR

Komitet Gosudarstvennoi Bezopasnosti [KGB]

under the USSR Council of Ministers

Personnel Department

January 22, 1962

No. 14.4/M–4329

Moscow

C E R T I F I C A T E

Given to Grigory Moiseevich Mairanovsky, born 1899. He worked at the NKVD-MGB from September 15, 1938 till December 1951. He was dismissed because he had been tried [by court] and convicted.

The information is based on the archival personal file and was given for submission to the social security office.

Head of the Personnel Department of the KGB

under the USSR CM [Council of Ministers]   (Ovechkin)

Seal

DOCUMENT 14

ACADEMY OF MEDICAL SCIENCES of the USSR

ALL-UNION SCIENTIFIC-RESEARCH INSTITUTE OF MEDICAL and MEDICAL-TECHNICAL INFORMATION

Moscow, Zh–240, Ust'inskii proezd, 2/14   Tel: K 7–79–49

No._____   July 3, 1963

To citizen MAIRANOVSKY G. M.

ARCHIVAL EXCERPT

Protocol [transcript] No. 13

Of the meeting of the Scientific Council of the VIEM

on October 20, 1943

Present: 20 members of the Scientific Council (a list of names)

Chairman: Director of the VIEM Professor Grashchenkov

Agenda:

3. Approval of scientific degrees and titles.

Hearing: 3. Approval of the Professor of Pathophysiology title of C.[omrade] Mairanovsky G. M.

Decision: 3. To provide C. Mairanovsky G. M. with the scientific title Professor of Pathophysiology

Voting: "yes" 16, "no" 1, "abstentions" 2
Chairman:
Professor N. I. Grashchenkov   signature
Scientific Secretary:
Professor C. A. Kharitonov   signature
Head of the Scientific Archive:
Bagdasar'yan S. M.   signature
Seal of the Scientific Archive of the Medical Academy

DOCUMENT 15

R S F S R
Ministry of Interior   A Copy
Prison No. 2
Vladimir Region
December 13, 1961
CERTIFICATE No. 82061
Series No.VTs
Given to citizen GRIGORY MOISEEVICH MAIRANOVSKY, born in
1899 in the city of Batumi, nationality Jew. He was condemned by a Special
Council of the MGB of the USSR on February 14, 1953 to 10 years of impris-
onment according to the paragraphs 193–17a and 179 of the Criminal Code.
He served his term in the MVD prisons from December 13, 1953 until De-
cember 13, 1961 and was released after finishing his term.
Head of the Prison   signature
Head of the MVD Unit   signature
Secretary of the Prison   signature
Seal of Vladimir Prison No. 2

DOCUMENT 16

Mairanovsky's Prisoner Card No. 1[11]
  I. Front side
  1. Last Name: Mairanovsky
  2. Name: Grigory
  3. Patronymic Name: Moiseevich
  4. Year of birth: 1899
  5. Place of birth: the city of Batumi [Georgia]
  6. Address: Moscow, Frunzenskaya naberezhnaya, 10A, ap. 17
  7. Profession (speciality): medical pharmacologist
  8. Place of work, position: Senior Engineer, Laboratory No. 1 OOT MGB of
the USSR
  9. Party membership: former member of the USSR Communist Party
  10. Nationality: a Jew
  11. Citizenship: USSR
  12. Date of the arrest: December 13, 1951

13. Type of crime: —

14. Paragraphs of the UK [Criminal Code]: 193–17-a [abuse of his position], 179 [illegally keeping strong acting chemicals]

15. Place of the fulfillment of the card (mention the prison, KPZ [police station], camp, colony): the city of Vladimir, Special Prison of the MGB

March 6, 1953   Person who filled out the card: V. Danilova

[Right column]

Organ (in charge of the arrest): Department for the Especially Important Cases of the MGB of the USSR

No. of the Case: 51

[Nos. of the Corpus–Nos. of the Vladimir Prison cell, date of the transfer] 3–57; March 3, 1953

II. Back side

Convicted by: Special Council [OSO] under the MGB of the USSR

Date: February 14, 1953

Paragraphs of the UK [Criminal Code]: 193–17-a, 179

Term: 10 years of TZ [imprisonment]

Beginning of the term: December 13, 1951

End of the term: December 13, 1961

[The prisoner] arrived from Butyrka Prison of the MGB of the USSR, Moscow, on March 3, 1953.

On June 7, 1953 [the prisoner] was taken to Inner [Lubyanka] Prison of the MVD of the USSR, Moscow. The reason: a request No. 16/10/3–155783 of the 1st MVD Special Department dated June 4, 1953.

DOCUMENT 17

Mairanovsky's Prisoner Card No. 2[12]

I. Front side

1. Last Name: Mairanovsky

2. Name: Grigory

3. Patronymic Name: Moiseevich

4. Year of birth: 1899

5. Place of birth: the city of Batumi [Georgia]

6. Address: Moscow

7. Profession (speciality): a doctor

8. Place of work, position: Senior Engineer, Laboratory No. 1 OOT MGB of the USSR

9. Party membership: former member of the VKP (b) [Bolshevik] Party

10. Nationality: a Jew

11. Citizenship: USSR

12. Date of the arrest: December 13, 1951

13. Type of crime: abuse of his position and illegally keeping strong acting chemicals

14. Paragraphs of the UK [Criminal Code]: 193–17-a, 179

15. Place of the fulfillment of the card (mention the prison, KPZ [police station], camp, colony): Prison No. 2

July 6, 1956 Person who filled out the card: I. Shchelanova

[Right column]

Organ (in charge of the arrest): 2nd Main MGB Directorate

No. of the Case: 51

[Nos. of the Corpus-Nos. of the Vladimir Prison cell, date of the transfer]

3–22; July 4, 1956

3–43; September 19, 1956

2–36; October 31, 1956

2–23; December 6, 1956

1–48; January 28, 1957

4–38; March 20, 1957

1–67; March 26, 1957

2–11; April 17, 1957

2–52; August 5, 1957

2–29; July 5, 1958

2–5; August 6, 1958

2–36; August 15, 1958

2–19; September 17, 1958

3–69; March 23, 1960

II. Back side

Convicted by: Special Council [OSO] under the MGB of the USSR

Date: February 14, 1953

Paragraphs of the UK [Criminal Code]: 193–17-a, 179

Term: 10 years of TZ [imprisonment]

Beginning of the term: December 13, 1951

End of the term: December 13, 1961

[The prisoner] arrived from Butyrka Prison on July 4, 1956. According to the decision of the Commission of the Presidium of the USSR Supreme Council, the protocol [transcript] No. 135 from September 3, 1956, the term of the punishment remains unchanged.

On March 2, 1957 [the prisoner] was taken to Inner [Lubyanka] Prison of the KGB under under the USSR Council of Ministers, Moscow. The reason: a request No. 30/3/553 of the MVD Prison Department dated February 26, 1957.

On September 6, 1958 [the prisoner] was taken to Inner [Lubyanka] Prison of the KGB under under the USSR Council of Ministers, Moscow. The reason: a request No. SP–004/s7 of the Military Collegium of the USSR Supreme Court dated August 29, 1958.

On September 17, 1958 [the prisoner] arrived back from Inner [Lubyanka] Prison of the KGB under the USSR Council of Ministers, Moscow.

On June 7, 1953 [the prisoner] was released after serving his term of punishment and went to Moscow.

DOCUMENT 18

Eitingon's Prisoner Card[13]

I. Front side

[There are coded letters to the left of the last name (M "P") and in the middle of the top of the card (T/K)]

1. Last Name: Eitingon
2. Name: Naum
3. Patronymic Name: Isaakovich
4. Year of birth: 1899
5. Place of birth: the city of Mogilev [Belorussia]
6. Address: Moscow, Chkalova Str., 46/48, ap. 72
7. Profession (speciality): a military servant
8. Place of work, position: former Deputy Head of the MGB Special Bureau
9. Party membership: former member of the USSR Communist Party
10. Nationality: a Jew
11. Citizenship: USSR
12. Date of the arrest: August 20, 1953
13. Type of crime: treason of the Motherland
14. Paragraphs of the UK [Criminal Code]: 17–58–1b [treason of the Motherland]
15. Place of the fulfillment of the card (mention the prison, KPZ [police station], camp, colony): Prison No. 2 of the UMVD of the Vladimir Region

March 18, 1957   Person who filled out the card: Yurin

[Right column]

Organ [in charge of the case]: General Prosecutor of the USSR

No. of the Case: 393

[Nos. of the Corpus-Nos. of the Vladimir Prison cell; date of the transfer]

1–40; March 16, 1957
2–12; April 17, 1957
2–28; May 23, 1957
2–30; October 14, 1957
2–23; August 1, 1958
2–13; August 6, 1958
2–23; March, 1960
2–23 [?]
2–33; November 23, 1961
2–32; December 25, 1961
1–76; January 12, 1963 [together with Sudoplatov]
2–56; February 22, 1963 [Sudoplatov was put in on May 22, 1963]
2–32; June 26, 1963 [together with Sudoplatov]
2–50; September 17, 1963

2–32; November 2, 1963

II. Back side
Convicted by: Military Collegium of the USSR Supreme Court
Date: March 6, 1957
Paragraphs of the UK [Criminal Code]: 17–58–1b along with 51–9k
Term: 12 years of imprisonment, 3 years of disfranchisement of political rights and a partial confiscation of the property
Beginning of the term: August 20, 1953
End of the term: March 20, 1964
[The prisoner] arrived from Inner [Lubyanka] Prison of the KGB under the USSR Council of Ministers, Moscow, on March 16, 1957.

According to the decision of the Military Collegium of the USSR Supreme Court from November 14, 1963, 1 year 5 months [from the date of the first arrest in October 1951 till the release in March 1953] were included in the term of punishment. [To consider] March 20, 1952 [as the starting date of the term].[14]

On March 20, 1964 [the prisoner] was released after serving his term of punishment.

DOCUMENT 19

Liberman's Prisoner Card[15]
I. Front side
1. Last Name: Liberman
2. Name: Grigorii
3. Patronymic Name: Borisovich
4. Year of birth: 1900
5. Place of birth: the town of Sol'tsy, the North-West [now Novgorod] region
6. Address: Moscow, Kurbatov by-street, 3a, ap. 7
7. Profession (speciality): chemist, ingeneer-technologist
8. Place of work, position: Leningrad, the Military-Chemical Academy, professor
9. Party membership: former member of the Communist (Bolshevik) Party
10. Nationality: a Jew
11. Citizenship: USSR
12. Date of the arrest: March 31, 1935
13. Type of crime: treason of the Motherland, terrorist acts
14. Paragraphs of the UK [Criminal Code]: 58–1a, 58–7, 58–8, 58–11
15. Place of the fulfillment of the card (mention the prison, KPZ [police station], camp, colony): Special Prison No. 2 of the MVD of the Vladimir Region
October 13, 1947　　　　　　　Person who filled out the card: V. Danilova
[Right column]
Organ (in charge of the arrest): UGB of the NKVD, city of Moscow

No. of the Case: 27,940
[Nos. of the Corpus-Nos. of the Vladimir Prison cell, date of the transfer]
3–63
2–22, May 10, 1945
3–75
3–33, December 7, 1945
2–6, October 1, 1946
2–55, October 8, 1946
3–23, December 1, 1947
3–44, June 9, 1948
3–56, February 5, 1949
3–44, February 9, 1949
3–63, March 27, 1949
2–36, October 26, 1949
3–23, November 17, 1949
3–42, December 1, 1949

II. Back side
Convicted by: the Military Collegium of the USSR Supreme Court
Date: April 31 [this date is on the card], 1940
Paragraphs of the UK [Criminal Code]: 58–1b [sic!], 58–7, 58–8
Term: 15 TZ [years of imprisonment]
Beginning of the term: March 31, 1935
End of the term: March 31, 1950

On January 19, 1949 [the prisoner] was transferred to Lefortovo Prison of the MGB in Moscow. No. 20/1/675 of the MVD Prison Department. [The prisoner] arrived back [in Vladimir] on February 4, 1949.

On March 3, 1950 [the prisoner] left for the city of Krasnoyarsk (in disposal of Head of the UMGB of Krasnoyarsk Region) through the city of Gorky Prison to be transported to the location of exile. The reason: an order of the MGB Department A No. 18/30–17126 dated December 19, 1949.

DOCUMENT 20

Clauberg's Prisoner Card[16]
  I. Front side
  1. Last Name: Clauberg
  2. Name: Carl
  3. Patronymic Name: —
  4. Year of birth: 1898
  5. Place of birth: the town of Wupperhoff (Germany)
  6. Address: the village Schinkel near the city of Kiel
  7. Profession (speciality): professor-gynecologist
  8. Place of work, position: the town of Koenigschutte, director of two gynecological clinics

9. Party membership: not a member of the party

10. Nationality: a German

11. Citizenship: Germany

12. Date of the arrest: June 24, 1945

13. Type of crime: Decree from April 19, 1943

14. Paragraphs of the UK [Criminal Code]:

15. Place of the fulfillment of the card (mention the prison, KPZ [police station], camp, colony): Special Prison No. 2 of the MVD of the Vladimir Region

March 14, 1955; January 16, 1959   Person who filled out the card: V. Danilova

[Right column]

Organ (in charge of the arrest): 3rd Main Directorate of the MGB of the USSR

No. of the Case: 1035

[Nos. of the Corpus-Nos. of the Vladimir Prison cell, date of the transfer] 3–34; November 14, 1954

II. Back side

Convicted by: Special Council [OSO] under the MGB of the USSR

Date: July 3, 1948

Paragraphs of the UK [Criminal Code]: Decree from April 19, 1943

Term: 25 TZ [years of imprisonment]

Beginning of the term: June 24, 1945

End of the term: June 24, 1970

Valuables found on the arrest should be confiscated

[The prisoner] arrived from Lefortovo Prison of the MGB in Moscow on July 30, 1948

On August 13, 1955 [the prisoner] left for Inner [Lubyanka] Prison of the KGB in Moscow. The reason: Decision of the 1st Department of the KGB Investigation Directorate from August 2, 1955.

DOCUMENT 21

Zeiss's Prisoner Card[17]

I. Front side

[On the top, to the right] German spy

1. Last Name: Zeiss

2. Name: Heinrich

3. Patronymic Name: Ludwigovich[18]

4. Year of birth: 1888

5. Place of birth: the city of Frankfurt-on-Main

6. Address: Berlin, Sigmundstrasse 5

7. Profession (speciality): medical microbiologist

8. Place of work, position: former Chief of the Military-Hygiene Institute of the [German] Naval Academy in Berlin

9. Party membership: not a member of the party

10. Nationality: a German

11. Citizenship: Germany

12. Date of the arrest: September 14, 1945

13. Type of crime: —

14. Paragraphs of the UK [Criminal Code]: 58–6 pt. I [espionage], 58–9 [a wrecker], and 58–11 [membership in an anti-Soviet organization]

15. Place of the fulfillment of the card (mention the prison, KPZ [police station], camp, colony): Special Prison No. 2 of the UMVD of the Vladimir Region

July 30, 1948   Person who filled out the card: V. Danilova

[Right column]

Organ (in charge of the arrest): 2nd Main Directorate of the MGB of the USSR

No. of the Case: 1032

[Nos. of the Corpus-Nos. of the Vladimir Prison cell, date of the transfer]

3–15

2–26; July 30, 1948

II. Back side

Convicted by: Special Council [OSO] under the MGB of the USSR

Date: July 10, 1948

Paragraphs of the UK [Criminal Code]: 58–6 pt. I, 58–9, and 58–11

Term: 25 years of TZ [imprisonment]

Beginning of the term: September 14, 1945

End of the term: September 14, 1970

[The prisoner] died on March 31, 1949

DOCUMENT 22

Sudoplatov's Prisoner Card[19]

I. Front side

[There are coded letters in the middle of the top of the card: T/K]

1. Last Name: Sudoplatov

2. Name: Pavel

3. Patronymic Name: Anatolievich

4. Year of birth: 1907

5. Place of birth: the city of Melitopl, the Ukrainian SSR

6. Address: Moscow, Markhlevskogo Str., 9, ap. 3

7. Profession (speciality): a worker of the MVD organs

8. Place of work, position: Head of the 9th Department of the 2nd Main Directorate

9. Party membership: former member of the USSR Communist Party

10. Nationality: a Ukrainian

11. Citizenship: USSR

12. Date of the arrest: August 8, 1953

13. Type of crime: treason of the Motherland

14. Paragraphs of the UK [Criminal Code]: 17–58–1b

15. Place of the fulfillment of the card (mention the prison, KPZ [police station], camp, colony): Prison No. 2

September 9, 1958   Person who filled out the card:

[Right column]

Organ [in charge of the case]: General Prosecutor of the USSR

No. of the Case: 493

[Nos. of the Corpus–Nos. of the Vladimir Prison cell; date of the transfer]

2–7; September 19, 1958

2–32; August 4, 1959

2–42; March 23, 1960

2–32 [written by a pencil]

1–76; January 12, 1963 [together with Eitingon]

1–70 [written by a pencil]

2–56; May 22, 1963 [transferred to Eitingon, who had been in this cell from February 22]

2–32; June 26, 1963 [together with Eitingon; on September 17, 1963 Eitingon was taken away from this cell and put back on November 2, 1963; finally Eitingon was released on March 20, 1964]

2–43; August 26, 1965

2–22; December 17, 1965

II. Back side

Convicted by: Military Collegium of the USSR Supreme Court

Date: September 12, 1958

Paragraphs of the UK [Criminal Code]: 17–58–1b [treason of the Motherland] along with 51–9k

Term: 15 years of imprisonment and 3 years of disfranchisement of political rights

Beginning of the term: August 21, 1953

End of the term: August 21, 1968

[The prisoner] arrived from Inner [Lubyanka] Prison of the KGB under the USSR Council of Ministers, Moscow, on September 19, 1958.

On June 7, 1953 [the prisoner] was released after serving his term of punishment and went to the place of residence in the town of Pokrov, Vladimir Region (the address of his relatives is: Moscow, Koroleva Str., 9, ap. 239)

DOCUMENT 23

Parin's Prisoner Card (a shortened version)[20]

[On the top, to the right] scientific worker

Last Name: Parin

Name: Vasilii

Patronymic Name: Vasilievich
Year of birth: 1903
Place of birth: the city of Kazan
Address: Moscow, Serafimovicha Str., 2, ap. 148
Place of work: the USSR Medical Academy of Sciences, Secretary Academician
Nationality: a Russian
Citizenship: USSR
Convicted by: Special Board of the MGB (OSO)
Date: April 8, 1948
Paragraphs of the UK [Criminal Code]: 58–1a (treason of the Motherland) with confiscation of the personal property
Term: 25 years of imprisonment
Date of the arrival in Vladimir Prison: July 30, 1948
On October 29, 1953 [the prisoner] was transferred to Inner [Lubyanka] Prison of the MVD in Moscow
Note: American spy

SELECTED
READINGS

Abarinov, Vladimir. *The Murders of Katyn*, with a foreword and chronology by C. Pogonowski. New York: Hippocrene Books, 1993.

Adler, Nanci. *Victims of Soviet Terror: The Story of the Memorial Movement*. Westport, CT: Praeger, 1993.

Albats, Yevgenia. *The State Within a State: The KGB and Its Hold on Russia—Past, Present, and Future*. Translated by C. A. Fitzpatrick. New York: Farrar, 1994.

Aleksandrov, Vladimir Ya. *Trudnye Gody Sovetskoi Biologii: Vospominaniya Sovremennika* [The Hard Years of Soviet Biology: Memoirs of a Contemporary]. St. Petersburg: Nauka, 1993 (in Russian).

Alibek, Ken, with S. Handelman. *Biohazard: The Chilling True Story of the Largest Covert Biological Weapons Program in the World—Told from the Inside by the Man Who Ran It*. New York: Random House, 1999.

Andrew, Christopher, and Oleg Gordievsky. *KGB: The Inside Story*. New York: Harper Perennial, 1991.

Andrew, Christopher, and Vasilii Mitrokhin. *The Sword and the Shield: The Mitrokhin Archive and the Secret History of the KGB*. New York: Basic Books, 1999.

Annas, George J., and Michael A. Grodin, eds. *The Nazi Doctors and the Nuremberg Code: Human Rights in Human Experimentation*. New York: Oxford University Press, 1992.

Astaurov, Boris L., and Pyotr F. Rokitsky. *Nikolai Konstantinovich Koltsov*. Moscow: Nauka, 1975 (in Russian).

Bailes, Kendall E. *Science and Russian Culture in an Age of Revolutions: V. I. Vernadsky and His Scientific School, 1863–1945*. Bloomington: Indiana University Press, 1990.

———. *Technology and Society Under Lenin and Stalin: Origins of the Soviet Technical Intelligentsia, 1917–1941*. Princeton: Princeton University Press, 1978.

Bereanu, Vladimir, and Kalin Todorov. *The Umbrella Murder*. Oxford: TEL, 1994.

Belyaev, Dmitri K., and Vladimir I. Ivanov, eds. *Vydauyshchiesya sovetskie genetiki* [Outstanding Soviet Geneticists]. Moscow: Nauka, 1980 (in Russian).

Berg, Raissa L. *Acquired Traits: Memoirs of a Geneticist from the Soviet Union*. New York: Viking, 1988.

Berry, Michael J., ed., *Science and Technology in the USSR*. Burnt Mill, U.K.: Longman, 1988.

Blyum, A. V. *Sovetskaya tsenzura v epokhu total'nogo terora, 1929–1953* [Soviet Censorship During the Epoch of Total Terror, 1917–1953]. St. Petersburg: Akademicheskii Proekt, 2000 (in Russian).

Boag, J. W., P. E. Rubinin, and J. Shoenberg, eds. *Kapitza in Cambridge and Moscow: Life and Letters of a Russian Physicist*. New York: North-Holland, 1990.

Bobrenjow, Wladimir, und Waleri Rjasanzew. *Das Geheimlabor des KGB: Gespenster der Warsanowjew-Gasse*. Berlin: Edition Verlags-Gmb-H, 1993.

Bobryonev, Vladimir. *"Doktor Smert," ili Varsonofievskie prizraki* ["Doctor Death," or the Ghosts of Varsonofyevsky Lane]. Moscow: Olimp, 1997 (in Russian).

Bobryonev, Vladimir A., and Valery B. Ryazentsev. *The Ghosts of Varsonofyevsky Lane: Laboratory of Death—How the Soviet Secret Police Experimented on People and Poisoned Their Enemies*. Translated by Catherine A. Fitzpatrick (unpublished manuscript, 1996).

―――. *Palachi i zhertvy* [Executioners and Victims]. Moscow: Voenizdat, 1993 (in Russian).

Bukharin, Nikolai. *How It All Began*. Translated from Russian by George Shiver. New York: Columbia University Press, 1999.

Che-Ka. Materialy po deyatel'osti chrezvychainykh kommissii [Che-Ka: Materials on the Activity of Extraordinary Commissions]. Berlin: Orfei, 1922 (in Russian).

Chebrikov, V. M., G. F. Grigorenko, N. A. Dushin, and F. D. Bobkov, eds. *Istoriya sovetskikh organov gosudarstvennoi bezopasnosti: Uchebnik, "Sovershenno sekretno"* [History of the Soviet Security Service: A Textbook, "Top Secret"]. Moscow: Vysshaya Shkola KGB, 1977 (in Russian), available at http://www.fas.harvard.edu/~hpcws/documents.htm.

Conquest, Robert. *The Great Terror: A Reassessment*. New York: Oxford University Press, 1990.

Costello, John, and Oleg Tsarev. *Deadly Illusions*. New York, Crown, 1993.

Deriabin, Peter, and Frank Gibney. *The Secret World*. Garden City, NY: Doubleday and Co., 1959.

Dobkin, Aleksandr I., and Arsenii B. Roginsky, eds. *Zven'ya* [The Links]. *Historical Almanac*. Vol. 2. Moscow: Progress, Phoenix, Atheneum, 1992 (in Russian).

Dolgun, Alexander, and Patrick Watson. *An American in the Gulag*, New York: A. Knopf, 1975.

Domaradsky, I. V. *"Perevyortysh" (Rasskaz "neudobnogo" cheloveka)* ["Trouble-maker" (The Story of an "Inconvenient" Person)]. Moscow: N.p., 1995 (in Russian).

Dragavtsev,V. A., ed. *Soratniki Nikolaya Ivanovicha Vavilova* [Coworkers of Nikolai IvanovichVavilov]. St. Petersburg:VIR, 1994 (in Russian).

Dukes, Paul. *Red Dusk and the Morrow: Adventures and Investigations in Red Russia.* Garden City: Doubleday, Page, 1922.

_____. *The Story of "ST 25": Adventures and Romance in the Secret Intelligence Service in Red Russia.* London: Cassell and Co., 1938.

Dzhirkvelov, Ilya. *Secret Servant: My Life with the KGB and the Soviet Elite.* New York: Harper and Row, 1987.

Efroimson, Vladimir P. *Genial'nost' i genetika* [Genius and Genetics]. Moscow: Russkii Mir, 1998 (in Russian).

Felshtinsky, Yuri. *VCHK-GPU.* Benson, VT: Chalidze Publications, 1989 (in Russian).

Geissler, Erhard, and John Ellis van Courtland Moon, eds. *Biological and Toxin Weapons: Research, Development, and Use From the Middle Ages to 1945.* New York: Oxford University Press, 1999.

Gerson, Leonard D. *The Secret Police in Lenin's Russia.* Philadelphia: Temple University Press, 1976.

Getty, J. Arch, and Oleg V. Naumov. *The Road to Terror: Stalin and the Self-Destruction of the Bolsheviks, 1932–1939.* New Haven:Yale University Press, 1999.

Gillispie, C. C., ed. *Dictionary of Scientific Biography.* New York: Charles Scribner's Sons, vol. 7, 1973; vol. 15, supp. 1, 1978.

Graham, Loren R., *Science in Russia and the Soviet Union: A Short History.* Cambridge: Cambridge University Press, 1993.

_____. *Science, Philosophy, and Human Behavior in the Soviet Union.* New York: Columbia University Press, 1987.

_____. *The Soviet Academy of Sciences and the Communist Party, 1927–1932.* Princeton: Princeton University Press, 1967.

_____. *What Have We Learned About Science and Technology from the Russian Experience?* Stanford: Stanford University Press, 1998.

Graham, Loren R., ed. *Science and the Soviet Social Order.* Cambridge: Harvard University Press, 1990.

Granin, Daniil. *The Bison: A Novel About a Scientist Who Defied Stalin.* Translated by A. W. Bouis. New York: Doubleday, 1989.

Heller, Mikhail, and Aleksandr N. Nekrich. *Utopia in Power: The History of the Soviet Union from 1917 to the Present.* New York: Summit Books, 1986.

Hodos, George H. *The Show Trials: Stalinist Purges in Eastern Europe, 1948–1954.* New York: Praeger, 1987.

Holloway, David. *Stalin and the Bomb: The Soviet Union and Atomic Energy, 1939–1956.* New Haven: Yale University Press, 1994.

Huxley, Julian. *Soviet Genetics and World Science: Lysenko and the Meaning of Heredity.* London: Chatto and Windus, 1949.

Ipatieff, Vladimir N. *Life of a Chemist.* Translated by Haensel and Lusher. Stanford: Stanford University Press, 1946.

Joravsky, David. *The Lysenko Affair.* Cambridge: Harvard University Press, 1970.

Josephson, Paul R. *Totalitarian Science and Technology.* Atlantic Highlands, NJ: Humanities Press International, 1996.

Kalugin, Oleg, with F. Montaigne. *The First Directorate: My 32 Years in Intelligence Against the West.* New York: St. Martin's Press, 1994.

Kassow, Samuel D. *Students, Professors, and the State in Tsarist Russia.* Berkeley: University of California Press, 1989.

Katkov, Georgy. *The Trial of Bukharin.* New York: Stein and Day, 1969.

Khokhlov, Nikolai. *In the Name of Conscience.* Translated by E. Kingsbery. New York: David McKay, 1959.

Knight, Amy. *Beria: Stalin's First Lieutenant.* Princeton: Princeton University Press, 1993.

_____. *Spies Without Cloaks: The KGB's Successors.* Princeton: Princeton University Press, 1996.

Kokurin, A. I., and N. V. Petrov. *Lubyanka: VChK-OGPU-NKVD-MGB-MVD-KGB, 1917–1960, Spravochnik* [Lubyanka: VChK-OGPU-NKVD-MGB-MVD-KGB, 1917–1960, a Reference Book]. Moscow: MFD, 1997 (in Russian).

Kolchinsky, E. I. *V poiskakh sovetskogo "soyuza" filosofii i biologii* [In Search of the Soviet "Union" Between Philosophy and Biology]. St. Petersburg: Dmitrii Bulanin, 1999 (in Russian).

Kolpakidi, Aleksandr, and Dmitry Prokhorov. *Imperia GRU: Ocherki istorii rossiiskoi voennoi razvedki* [The GRU Empire: Essays on the History of the Russian Military Intelligence]. Vol. 2. Moscow: Olma-Press, 2000 (in Russian).

Koltsov, Anatoly V. *Sozdanie i deyatel'nost' Komissii po izucheniyu estectvennykh proizvoditel'nykh sil Rossii, 1915–1930 gg.* [The Creation and Activity of the Commission for the Study of Natural-Productive Forces of Russia, 1915–1930]. St. Petersburg: Nauka, 1999 (in Russian).

Kostyrchenko, Gennadi. *Out of the Red Shadows: Anti-Semitism in Stalin's Russia.* Amherst, NY: Prometheus Books, 1995.

Kozlov, V. A., and S. V. Mironenko, eds. *Arkhiv noveishei istorii Rossii. Tom I. "Osobaya Papka" I. V. Stalina: Iz materialov Sekretariata NKVD-MVD SSSR 1944–1953. Katalog dokumentov* [Archive of Contemporary Russian History. Vol. I. The "Special Files" for I.V. Stalin: From Materials of the NKVD-

MVD of the USSR, 1944–1953]. Moscow: State Archive of the Russian Federation, 1994 (in Russian).

_____. *Arkhiv noveishei istorii Rossii. Tom IV. "Osobaya Papka" L. P. Berii. Iz materialov Sekretariata NKVD-MVD SSSR 1946–1949. Katalog dokumentov* [Archive of Contemporary Russian History. Vol. IV. The "Special Files" for L. P. Beria: From Materials of the NKVD-MVD of the USSR, 1946–1949]. Moscow: State Archive of the Russian Federation, 1996 (in Russian).

Krasnaya kniga VCheKa [The VCheKa Red Book]. Vol. 2, 2nd ed. Moscow: Izdatel'stvo politicheskoi literatury, 1989 (in Russian).

Krementsov, Nikolai. *Stalinist Science.* Princeton: Princeton University Press, 1997.

Kudryavtsev, I. I., ed. *Arkhivy Kremlya i Staroi ploshchadi: Dokumenty po "Delu KPSS"* [Archives of the Kremlin and Old Square: Documents on the "Communist Party Case"]. Novosibirsk: Sibirskii Khronograf, 1995 (in Russian).

Levitsky, Boris. *The Uses of Terror: The Soviet Secret Police, 1917–1970.* Translated by H. A. Piehler. New York: Coward, McCann and Geoghegan, 1972.

Lubrano, Linda L., and Susan Gross Solomon, eds. *The Social Context of Soviet Science.* Boulder: Westview Press, 1980.

Lysenko, Trofim D. *Heredity and Its Variability.* Translated by T. Dobzhansky. New York: King's Crown Press, 1946.

Medvedev, Zhores A., *The Rise and Fall of T. D. Lysenko.* Translated by I. M. Lerner. New York: Columbia University Press, 1969.

Medvedev, Zhores A., and Roy A. Medvedev. *A Question of Madness.* New York: Alfred A. Knopf, 1971.

Melgunov, Sergei P. *Krasnyi terror v Rossii: 1918–1923* [The Red Terror in Russia, 1918–1923]. (Moscow: Puico, 1990) (in Russian).

Men'shagin, Boris G. *Vospominaniya: Smolensk . . . Katyn . . . Vladimirskaya Tur'ma . . .* [Memoirs: Smolensk . . . Katyn . . . Vladimir Prison . . .]. Paris: IMCA-Press, 1988 (in Russian).

Mlechin, Leonid. *Predsedateli KGB: Rassekrechennye sud'by* [The KGB Chairmen: Declassified Biographies]. Moscow: Tsentrpoligraf, 1999a (in Russian).

Müller-Hill, Benno. *Murderous Science: Elimination by Scientific Selection of Jews, Gypsies, and Others in Germany, 1933–1945.* Translated by G. R. Fraser. Cold Spring Harbor, MI: Cold Spring Harbor Laboratory Press, 1998.

Naumov, V., and Yu. Sigachev. *Lavrentii Beria, 1953* [Lavrentii Beria, 1953]. Moscow: Mezhdunarodnyi Fond "Demokratia," 1999 (in Russian).

Okhotin, Nikita G., and Arsenii B. Roginsky, eds. *Zven'ya: Historical Almanac* [The Links]. Vol. 1. Moscow: Progress; Phoenix: Atheneum, 1991 (in Russian).

Orlov, Alexander. *The Secret Story of Stalin's Crimes*. New York: Random House, 1953.

Parrish, Michael. *The Lesser Terror: Soviet State Security, 1939–1953*. Westport, CT: Praeger, 1996.

Pavlovskii, Yevgenii N., ed. *Pamyati Akademika L. S. Berga* [In Memory of Academician L. S. Berg]. Moscow: Izdatelstvo Akademii Nauk SSSR, 1955 (in Russian).

Petrov, N. V., and K. V. Skorkin. *Kto rukovodil NKVD 1934–1941: Spravochnik* [Who Directed the NKVD, 1934–1941: A Reference Book]. Moscow: Zven'ya, 1999 (in Russian).

Polyansky, Yuri I. *Gody prozhitye: Vospominaniya biologa* [The Years I Lived Through: Memoirs of a Biologist]. St. Petersburg: Nauka, 1997 (in Russian).

Popovsky, Mark. *Manipulated Science: The Crisis of Science and Scientists in the Soviet Union Today*. Translated by P. S. Falla. Garden City, NY: Doubleday, 1979.

———. *The Vavilov Affair*. Hamden, CT: Archon Books, 1984.

Povartsov, S. *Prichina smerti—rasstrel* [Execution Was the Cause of Death]. Moscow: Terra, 1996 (in Russian).

Radzinsky, Edvard. *Stalin*. Translated by H. T. Willetts. New York: Anchor Books, 1996.

Rapoport, Louis. *Stalin's War Against the Jews: The Doctors' Plot and the Soviet Solution*. New York: Free Press, 1990.

Rapoport, Yakov. *The Doctors' Plot of 1953*. Translated by N. A. Petrova and R. S. Bobrova. Cambridge: Harvard University Press, 1991.

Roberg, Jeffrey L. *Soviet Science Under Control: The Struggle for Influence*. New York: St. Martin's Press, 1998.

Rokityansky, Ya. G., Yu. N. Vavilov, and V. A. Goncharov, eds. *Sud palacha: Nikolai Vavilov v zastenkakh NKVD. Biograficheskii ocherk. Dokumenty* [The Trial of an Executioner: Nikolai Vavilov in the Torture Chamber of the NKVD. A Biographical Sketch. Documents]. Moscow: Academia, 1999 (in Russian).

Rubenstein, Joshua, and Vladimir P. Naumov, eds., with introductions. *Stalin's Secret Pogrom: The Postwar Inquisition of the Jewish Anti-Fascist Committee*. Translated by Laura Esther Wolfson. New Haven: Yale University Press, in association with United States Holocaust Memorial Museum, 2001.

Sakharov, Andrei. *Memoirs*. Translated by R. Lourie. New York: Alfred A. Knopf, 1990.

Schnol, Simon E. *Geroi i zlodei rossiiskoi nauki* [Heroes and Villains of Russian Science]. Moscow: Kron-Press, 1997 (in Russian).

Sgovio, Thomas. *Dear America! Why I Turned Against Communism*. Kenmore, NY: Partners' Press, 1979.

Shatunovskaya, Lidiya. *Zhizn' v Kremle* [Life in the Kremlin]. New York: Chalidze Publications, 1982 (in Russian).

Shentalinsky, Vitaly. *Arrested Voices: Resurrecting the Disappeared Writers of the Soviet Regime.* New York: Free Press, 1996.

Smirnov, M. B., ed. *Systema ispravitel'no-trudovykh lagerei v SSSR, 1923–1960: Spravochnik* [The System of Correction Labor Camps in the USSR, 1917–1960: A Reference Book]. (Moscow: Zven'ya, 1998 (in Russian).

Soyfer, Valery N. *Lysenko and the Tragedy of Soviet Science.* Translated by L. Gruliow and R. Gruliow. New Brunswick, NJ: Rutgers University Press, 1994.

Stetsovsky, Yurii, *Istoriya sovetskikh repressii* [History of Soviet Repressions]. Vols. 1 and 2. Moscow: Znak-SP, 1997 (in Russian).

Stolyarov, Kirill. *Palach i zhertvy* [Executioners and Victims]. Moscow: Olma-Press, 1997 (in Russian).

Sudoplatov, Andrei. *Tainaya zhizn' generala Sudoplatova* [The Secret Life of General Sudoplatov]. Vols. 1 and 2. Moscow: Sovremennik, 1998 (in Russian).

Sudoplatov, Pavel. *Spetsoperatsii: Lubyanka i Kreml, 1930–1950 Gody* [Special Operations: Lubyanka and the Kremlin, the 1930s–1950s]. Moscow: Olma-Press, 1998 (in Russian).

The Situation in Biological Science: Proceedings of the Lenin Academy of Agricultural Sciences of the USSR, July 31-August 7, 1948: Complete Stenographic Report. New York: International Publishers, 1949.

Tikhanova, V., ed. *Rasstrel'nye spiski. Vypusk 1. Donskoe kladbishche, 1934–1940* [The Lists of the Executed. Issue 1: Donskoe Cemetery, 1934–1940]. Moscow: Memorial, 1993 (in Russian).

Timofeev-Ressovsky, N. V. *Vospominaya: Istorii, napisannye im samim, s pis'mami, fotografiyami i dokumentami* [Memoirs: Stories Written by Himself with Letters, Photos, and Documents]. Moscow: Soglasie, 2000 (in Russian).

Timofeev-Ressovsky, Nikolai. *Vospominaniya* [Memoirs]. Moscow: Pangeya, 1995 (in Russian).

Tolz, Vera. *Russian Academicians and the Revolution: Combining Professionalism and Politics.* New York: St. Martin's Press, 1997.

Trubnikov, V. I., ed. *Ocherki istorii Rossiiskoi vneshnei razvedki* [Essays on the History of the Russian Foreign Intelligence]. Vol. 4, 1941–1945. Moscow: Mezhdunaodnye Otnosheniya, 1999 (in Russian).

Tucker, Robert C., and Stephen F. Cohen, eds. *The Great Purge Trial.* New York: Grosset and Dunlap, 1965.

Turkevich, John. *Soviet Men of Science: Academicians and Corresponding Members of the Academy of Sciences of the USSR.* Princeton: D. Van Nostrand, 1973.

Vaksberg, Arkady. *Stalin Against the Jews.* Translated by A. W. Bouis. New York: Alfred A. Knopf, 1994.

_____. *Stalin's Prosecutor: The Life of Andrei Vyshinsky*. Translated by Jan Butler. New York: Grove Weidenfeld, 1991.

Volkogonov, Dmitri. *Autopsy for an Empire: The Seven Leaders Who Built the Soviet Regime*. Eedited and translated by Harold Shukman. New York: Free Press, 1998.

_____. *Stalin: Triumph and Tragedy*. Translated by H. Shukman. New York: Grove Weidenfeld, 1991.

Vorontsov, Nikolai N., ed. *Nikolai Vladimirovich Timofeev-Ressovsky*. Moscow: Nauka, 1993 (in Russian).

Vucinich, Alexander. *Empire of Knowledge: The Academy of Sciences of the USSR (1917–1970)*. Berkeley: University of California Press, 1984.

_____. *Science in Russian Culture: A History to 1860*. Stanford: Stanford University Press, 1963.

Waller, J. Michael. *Secret Empire: The KGB in Russia Today*. Boulder: Westview Press, 1994.

Weiner, Douglas R. *A Little Corner of Freedom: Russian Nature Protection from Stalin to Gorbachëv*. Berkeley: University of California Press, 1999.

Weinstein, Allen, and Alexander Vassiliev. *The Haunted Wood: Soviet Espionage in America—the Stalin Era*. New York: Random House, 1999.

Yakovlev, B. *Kontsentrastionnye lageri SSSR* [Concentration Camps in the USSR]. Munchen: Institute for the Study of the History and Culture of the USSR, 1955 (in Russian).

Yaroshevskii, M. G., ed. *Repressirovannaya nauka* [Repressed Science]. Leningrad: Nauka, 1991 (in Russian).

_____. *Repressirovannaya nauka. Vypusk II* [Repressed Science, issue 2]. St. Petersburg: Nauka, 1994 (in Russian).

Yeremina, L. S., and A. B. Roginsky, eds. *Rasstrel'nye spiski: Moskva, 1937–1941, "Kommunarka," Butovo* [Lists of the Executed: Moscow, 1937–1941, Kommunarka and Butovo]. Moscow: Obshchestvo "Memorial," 2000 (in Russian).

Yesakov, V. D., ed. *Akademiya Nauk v resheniyakh Politburo TsK RKP(b)-VKP(b), 1922–1952* [The Academy of Sciences in Resolutions of the Central Committee of the Russian/All-Union Communist (Bolshevik) Party, 1922–1952]. Moscow: Rosspan, 2000 (in Russian).

Zbarsky, Ilya, and Samuel Hutchinson. *Lenin's Embalmers*. Translated by B. Bray. London: Harvill Press, 1998.

Zirkle, Conway, ed. *Death of a Science in Russia: The Fate of Genetics as Described in Pravda and Elsewhere*. Philadelphia: University of Pensylvania Press: 1949.

INDEX